Landscape between Ideology and the Aesthetic

Historical Materialism Book Series

The Historical Materialism Book Series is a major publishing initiative of the radical left. The capitalist crisis of the twenty-first century has been met by a resurgence of interest in critical Marxist theory. At the same time, the publishing institutions committed to Marxism have contracted markedly since the high point of the 1970s. The Historical Materialism Book Series is dedicated to addressing this situation by making available important works of Marxist theory. The aim of the series is to publish important theoretical contributions as the basis for vigorous intellectual debate and exchange on the left.

The peer-reviewed series publishes original monographs, translated texts, and reprints of classics across the bounds of academic disciplinary agendas and across the divisions of the left. The series is particularly concerned to encourage the internationalization of Marxist debate and aims to translate significant studies from beyond the English-speaking world.

For a full list of titles in the Historical Materialism Book Series
available in paperback from Haymarket Books, visit:
https://www.haymarketbooks.org/series_collections/1-historical-materialism

Landscape between Ideology and the Aesthetic

Marxist Essays on British Art and Art Theory, 1750–1850

Andrew Hemingway

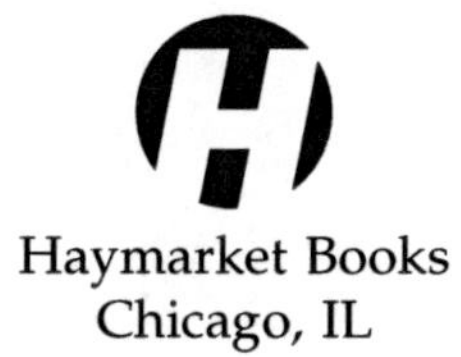

Haymarket Books
Chicago, IL

First published in 2016 by Brill Academic Publishers, The Netherlands
© 2017 Koninklijke Brill NV, Leiden, The Netherlands

Published in paperback in 2017 by
Haymarket Books
P.O. Box 180165
Chicago, IL 60618
773-583-7884
www.haymarketbooks.org

ISBN: 978-1-60846-831-7

Trade distribution:
In the US, Consortium Book Sales, www.cbsd.com
In Canada, Publishers Group Canada, www.pgcbooks.ca
In the UK, Turnaround Publisher Services, www.turnaround-uk.com
All other countries, Ingram Publisher Services International, ips_intlsales@ingramcontent.com

Cover design by Jamie Kerry of Belle Étoile Studios and Ragina Johnson.

This book was published with the generous support of Lannan Foundation and the Wallace Action Fund.

Printed in Canada by union labor.

10 9 8 7 6 5 4 3 2 1

Library of Congress Cataloging-in-Publication data is available.

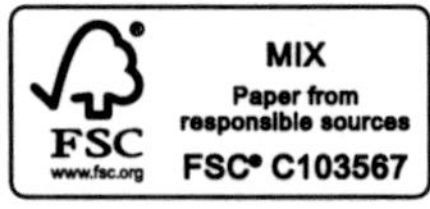

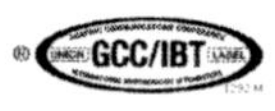

Contents

Aesthetics and Ideology

Landscape and Ideology

Acknowledgements

I remain grateful to the following individuals for their comments and useful critical suggestions in relation to the previously published material: J.R.R. Christie, Carol Duncan, the late John Gage, Tamar Garb, Harriet Guest, Barry King, Dian Kriz, Neil McWilliam, the late Ann Pullan, Peter Smith, and Trevor Fawcett. I also owe a large debt to staff at the Local Studies Library in Norwich, who were unfailingly generous in sharing their knowledge over many years. (The Library was tragically destroyed by fire in 1994). For ongoing discussion of aspects of British art or landscape painting over the years, my thanks to David Bindman, Leo Costello, Tom Gretton, Nick Grindle, Angela Miller, Alex Potts, William Vaughan, and Alan Wallach. The students in my class on 'Romantic Landscape Painting in Britain: Nature – Capitalism – Modernity' at the City University of New York Graduate Center in winter 2013 helped me to new perspectives on the theme through their curiosity and intelligent questionings. My special thanks to Dr Chin-tao Wu for inviting me to speak in Taipei and to Dan Sherman and his colleagues for the invitation to give the Bettie Alison Rand lectures at Chapel Hill. Rosanna Woensdregt at Brill answered my many queries patiently and efficiently, and Danny Hayward's careful readings of the text saved me from numerous errors and inconsistencies. Finally, I am deeply grateful to Steve Edwards for suggesting this collection and for his contributions to its realisation.

Without the love and support of my wife, Carol Duncan, and my daughter, Mary Hemingway, the book would not have been possible.

Sources and Occasions

The following essays have been published previously and are reprinted here with only cosmetic alterations and some updating of the bibliography: 'Meaning in Cotman's Norfolk Subjects', *Art History*, 7, no. 1 (March 1984): 57–77; 'Academic Theory versus Association Aesthetics: The Ideological Forms of a Conflict of Interests in the Early Nineteenth Century', *Ideas and Production*, issue 5 (1986): 18–42; 'Genius, Gender, and Progress: Benthamism and the Arts in the 1820s', *Art History*, 16, no. 4 (December 1993): 619–46; 'Regarding Art and Art History' appeared in the College Art Association's *Art Bulletin*, 94, no. 2 (June 2012): 163–5. I have not tried to moderate the somewhat waspish tone of the first two, a reminder of an earlier moment in which theoretical and political battle lines in art history were more starkly drawn than they are today.

'The Science of Taste in the Eighteenth Century: Philosophical Criticism and the Scottish Historical School' is a much shortened and revised version of an article published in the *Oxford Art Journal*, 12, no. 2 (1989): 3–35, under the title 'The Sociology of Taste in the Scottish Enlightenment'. 'Cultural Philanthropy and the Invention of the Norwich School' is a condensed version of an article that appeared in *Oxford Art Journal*, 11, no. 2 (1988): 17–39. The first section of 'John Crome's "Local Scenery": Iconography and the Ideology of the Picturesque' originally appeared as 'Subject-Matter in the Work of John Crome', in *Landscape Research*, 9, no. 3 (winter 1984): 30–40; the remainder was written for this collection.

'The Bourgeois Critique of the Monopoly of Taste' began life as a chapter of my doctoral thesis, but was omitted from that text for reasons of length. 'Sheep as a Pictorial Motif: Pastoral and Counter-Pastoral' has been developed from a paper titled 'Livestock in the Landscape: Animals and Property Relations', delivered at the History Workshop Conference on Animal Imagery, held at Queen Elizabeth House, Oxford, in 1985. 'Artisanal Worldview in the Landscapes of Crome' was first sketched for a lecture at the Western Art History Workshop 4: Faces of New Left Art History, held at the Institute of European and American Studies, Academia Sinica, Taipei, Taiwan ROC, in October 2013. 'Constable and the City: The Artist and his Audience', was originally conceived for the symposium on Constable held in July 1991 in connection with the Tate Gallery's *Constable* exhibition of that year; it was subsequently revised and expanded for a lecture at Brown University, Providence, RI, in February 1992. 'The Field of Waterloo Exposed: Turner, Byron, and the Politics of Reaction', was written for the Bettie Alison Rand Lecture series, which I delivered at the University of North Carolina, Chapel Hill, in March/April 2016.

The articles from *Art History* are reprinted by permission of the Association of Art Historians. 'Subject-Matter in the Work of John Crome' is © of the Landscape Research Group Limited, reprinted here by permission of Taylor & Francis Limited., www.tandfonline.com, on behalf of the Landscape Research Group Limited.

Theoretical Apologia

In 1992, I published *Landscape Imagery and Urban Culture in Early Nineteenth-Century Britain*, a Marxist reading of British naturalistic landscape painting of the period 1800–30.[1] The essays in this volume extend, supplement, and in some respects revise the arguments of that book. Those in Part One seek to establish the ideological terms in which painting could be thought as an art in the late eighteenth and early nineteenth centuries; those in Part Two address problems in the interpretation of specific landscape paintings.

My aim in assembling the present collection was not just to bring together a selection of previously published material; a substantial part of it was written for this occasion or has not been printed before. I have been motivated to return to the theme of British Romanticism for two main reasons. First, because I think we still await a historical writing of the visual arts in Britain in the period of Hobsbawm's 'Age of Revolution' (1789–48) that does justice to the extraordinary cultural energies released by the twin processes of rapid economic growth and political revolution.[2] Second, because one of the signal most productive strands in rethinking Marxism in recent decades has been the recovery of the romantic dimension of the Marxist tradition, evident say in the fresh attention given to figures such as William Morris, the young Lukács, and Ernst Bloch.[3] Romantic art needs reconsideration in light of this new awareness of Romanticism's anti-capitalist credentials. A book of essays written for a variety of occasions over three decades can only do so much, but I hope at least that it indicates the ways in which some of the most interesting art of the early nineteenth century was shaped by the acute class conflicts of the period, and in some instances registered a recoil from the social and cultural concomitants of capitalist modernity.

But I should be clear that this is a book of Marxist *art history*. However much history it includes, its object is aesthetic; it does not seek to illuminate

---

1 Hemingway 1992, which is a revised and shortened version of Hemingway 1989.

2 It has become clear that the term 'Industrial Revolution' will not cover the dynamic forces at work in the British economy, which centred more on trade and finance than on manufacturing. The term also leads to misleading expectations about the nature of the bourgeoisie. See Hilton 2006, pp. 2–24.

3 Löwy and Sayre 2001 makes the case for the continuing importance of Romanticism for the tradition of Marxist critique.

history through art – although that may be one of its side effects – it seeks to historicise the aesthetic, in my view the only way to do justice to art in its relative autonomy. Correspondingly, the reader should expect to encounter the traditional methods of art-historical science, style analysis and iconography. In my view these remain indispensable tools; other analytical methods such as semiology may supplement them in useful ways, as I indicate in Chapter Seven, but they do not supplant or displace them. It is their relationship with Marxist categories that remains at issue, and particularly that of ideology.

What follows is a sketch of the theoretical debates that set the terms for this work when it was begun in the 1980s together with an attempt to position it in relation to the larger academic field of British art studies since then. This is intended as more than an amble down memory lane. The fragmentation of the New Left in the 1980s may have caused debates on Marxist method in art history to falter or reach an impasse, but in my view they were not resolved. Correspondingly, there is no way to revivify the long and productive tradition of Marxist inquiry in the field without returning to the problems of that moment and seeking a resolution at a higher level. Places where I think more theoretical refinement is necessary should become evident from what follows.

Landscape and the Social History of Art

My ambition to write on landscape painting from a socio-historical perspective had a long gestation, partly shaped by experiences as a graduate student, first at the University of East Anglia, where I studied for an MA from 1972–4, and then as a part-time doctoral student at University College London over the years 1977–89. Although I wound up working on landscape pretty much by accident, it was in fact a good moment to begin a research project in this area, since in addition to the work of John Gage – which set a new intellectual standard for landscape studies in Britain[4] – the 1970s had seen a series of important exhibitions at the Tate Gallery organised by Leslie Parris and Conal Shields, including *Constable: The Art of Nature* (1971), *Landscape in Britain, 1750–1850* (1974), and the bicentennial *Constable: Paintings, Watercolours & Drawings* (1976).[5] The second of these in particular was a remarkably innovative display, which not only demonstrated that landscape painting was linked to a complex

---

4   Centrally Gage 1969 (1).

5   See also Parris and Shields 1969.

social practice of viewing landscape, but also brought to more general notice a range of paintings in which the depiction of labour was a central iconographic feature, including George Robert Lewis's 1815 *Hereford, Dynedor, and Malvern Hills, from the Haywood Lodge, Harvest Scene, Afternoon* (Tate Gallery, London), Peter De Wint's *A Cornfield* (1815; Victoria & Albert Museum), and John Linnell's, *Kensington Gravel Pits* (1813; Tate Gallery, London).

Landscape was a hot topic in art history back then in a way that is almost impossible to imagine now, its resonance greatly increased by the political realignment within British conservatism wrought by the Thatcher governments. One of the books that particularly spoke to that moment was *English Culture and the Decline of the Industrial Spirit* by the American historian Martin J. Wiener, which appeared in 1981.[6] Wiener criticised the British political elite for a long-term wariness of industry and commerce, which he traced back to the feudalisation of the industrial bourgeoisie in the nineteenth century, and complained of a persistent pastoralism in British culture that had contributed to the nation's long-term economic decline. Keith Joseph, Thatcher's ideological guru, who saw the old conservatism associated with Tory landed gentry as a brake on economic modernisation, reportedly gave a copy of the book to every cabinet minister. It helped instrumentally to define the divisions within the British right between old 'one nation Toryism' and Thatcherite neo-liberalism. So I am not exaggerating when I say the culture around landscape had more than merely academic resonance.

One register of the reactionary climate Thatcherism generated was the furore provoked by a number of innovative studies of the social significance of landscape painting and landscape gardening that appeared in the 1980s. Their titles are well-known: John Barrell's *The dark side of the landscape: The rural poor in English painting, 1730–1840* (1980); the catalogue to the Tate Gallery's 1982 exhibition *Richard Wilson: The Landscape of Reaction*, written by David Solkin; Michael Rosenthal's *Constable: The Painter and his Landscape* (1983) and Ann Bermingham's *Landscape and Ideology: The English Rustic Tradition, 1740–1860* (1986). With the exception of Barrell's book, all of these grew out of doctoral theses. And in fact, Barrell's own thesis had issued in his seminal 1972 book *The Idea of Landscape and the Sense of Place, 1730–1840: An Approach to the Poetry of John Clare*, which anticipated these later studies in some respects. I must also mention the string of important articles and essays on picturesque landscape by the geographer Stephen Daniels, culminating in

---

6 Wiener 1981. For a brilliant history of the Tory conception of a social landscape – scathing about the contemporary ideological variant – see Everett 1994.

his major monograph on Humphry Repton – although this did not appear until the end of the following decade.[7]

The shrill reactions of both conservative and liberal critics to the new scholarship was epitomised in the outrage provoked by the 1982 Wilson exhibition, a response that led the editor of the glossy art magazine *Apollo* to speculate on the potential for subtle and insidious infiltration of Marxist influence in 'art publications' now that former KGB Chairman Yuri Andropov had become General Secretary of the CPSU.[8]

It was easy to position a social history of art in contradistinction to the dominant model of scholarship on British art, represented at its best by historians such as John Hayes and Michael Kitson, which – whatever its considerable contributions to empirical knowledge – essentially operated with an 'art history as the history of artists' model,[9] combined with a style history that for all its sophistication lacked the critical historical consciousness of the German-language pioneers of the practice. The idea of some kind of social history of art enjoyed growing appeal in the 1970s, as both session themes and individual papers at the annual Association of Art Historians' conferences from 1976 onwards demonstrated. But despite the opposition they sometimes met from conservatives, most of these interventions were not Marxist. Moreover, a sophisticated alternative to the Marxist variant had already appeared in the form of Michael Baxandall's *Painting and Experience in Fifteenth-Century Italy: A Primer in the Social History of Pictorial Style*, first published in 1972. In a well-known critique of the character of British intellectual life from 1968, Perry Anderson made some shrewd criticisms of the empiricism and psychologism of establishment art history and observed that a 'historical sociology of art – the examination of its concrete mode of production – is a condition of its differential intelligibility';[10] yet the question remained as to whether this 'historical sociology' was to be Marxist.

---

7   Daniels 1999. For a listing of Daniels's earlier essays, see Bibliography.

8   Sutton 1983 (1), p. 3. In the same issue, Sutton published an extended review of the exhibition (Sutton 1983 [2]) in which he repeatedly referred to Solkin as 'Dr Solkin' or simply 'the Doctor', as if somehow a doctoral degree was an impediment to the insights that came naturally to the gentleman scholar and amateur. For the *Apollo* editorial and the critical response more generally, see McWilliam and Potts 1983.

9   For a contemporary critique of this model, see Hadjinicolaou 1978, Chapter 2.

10   Anderson 1969, p. 257.

Ideology: Althusserianism and Its Limits

The intense and sometimes sharp-tempered debate around art-historical methodology and politics of the late 1970s and 1980s essentially registered the impact on the discipline of a younger generation of historians who had either been formed within the New Left or identified with its spirit and achievements.[11] The journal *Block* – key mouthpiece of this formation – was launched in 1979, and the Association of Art Historians' journal *Art History* (which had begun publication only the year before) also accommodated contestatory positions. However, the cutting edge of left cultural theory at this time was represented by the film studies journal *Screen* and the Stencilled Occasional Papers of the University of Birmingham's Centre for Contemporary Cultural Studies (CCCS). As regards Marxism these foregrounded the innovations of Louis Althusser, whose structuralist, anti-humanist variant of Marxism was also prompting intensive debate among Marxist historians and sociologists.[12] Both *Screen* and CCCS tried at the same time to negotiate the challenge of new-wave feminism to traditional leftist politics, and did so partly by supplementing Althusserianism with a theory of the subject drawn from Lacanian psychoanalysis, a move facilitated by the fact that Althusser – unlike many more orthodox Marxists – acknowledged psychoanalysis as a 'science' and had paid tribute to Lacan's re-working of Freud in a well-known essay of 1964.[13] Also important was the fact that Althusser's variant of Marxism seemed cognate with another fashionable new branch of inquiry, namely semiology, which had been reaching a wider readership in the English speaking world since the publication of translations of Roland Barthes's *Elements of Semiology* (1964) in 1967 and *Mythologies* (1957) in 1972. Although this '*nouveau mélange*', as Jonathan Rée called it,[14] proved philosophically unsustainable – it was quickly superseded in fashionable appeal by the vogue for French post-structuralist theories – for a few years it enjoyed considerable authority.

In relation to these developments, the new social history of British landscape painting looked theoretically rather innocent. Of its exponents, the most openly engaged with theoretical questions was Ann Bermingham; but she was

---

11   I have sketched this moment in Hemingway 2006, pp. 175–95. See also Roberts 1994, pp. 1–36.

12   On Althusserianism in *Screen*, see McDonnell and Robins 1980. For a more positive appraisal, see Easthope 1983.

13   'Freud and Lacan', in Althusser 1971, pp. 181–202.

14   Rée 1985, p. 338.

a self-declared 'eclectic'[15] and did not broach the theoretical questions that her work – like that of Barrell, Solkin and Rosenthal – posed in relation to *Screen* theory. That is, all four advanced arguments about the relationship between landscape art and class conflict in the eighteenth and early nineteenth centuries that overtly proclaimed their debt to the work of the British 'culturalist' Marxists E.P. Thompson and Raymond Williams, which was directly contrary in many of its premises to Althusserianism. This disjunction was dramatically exposed in the intense debate sparked by Thompson's long intemperate critique of Althusser's Marxism, published in 1978 under the title 'The Poverty of Theory'.[16] For Bermingham there was no evident contradiction between affirming obligations to Althusser, Thompson and Williams on the same page.[17] Yet central to Thompson's critique were his rejection of Althusser's declared anti-humanism, his contrary insistence on the notion of 'experience',[18] and his resolute defence of empirical method against what he took to be Althusser's structuralist idealism. The work of Barrell, Rosenthal, and Solkin aligned them, consciously or not, with Thompson's Marxism; but the theoretical presuppositions of their work remained largely unspoken.[19]

As the presence of 'ideology' in the title of this volume flags, my own work was conceived in a more theoretically partisan spirit. At one level this is a register of when I conceived the project from which the essays derive. I am referring to the almost talismanic power the term 'ideology' had for Marxists in the 1970s and 1980s. (Terry Eagleton was on the mark when he wrote in 1991 that a perceptible decline in the term's currency indexed a 'pervasive political faltering' among the 'erstwhile revolutionary left').[20] It denoted a concept that promised to demystify not just political discourse, but also the whole gamut of intellectual life and the social functions of culture from the high arts right down to vernacular speech and the rituals of everyday life.[21] Most

---

15   Bermingham 1987, p. 5.

16   'The Poverty of Theory: or an Orrery of Errors', and 'Afternote', in Thompson 1978, pp. 193–397, 402–6. For a measured critique, see Anderson 1980. For the debate and further bibliography, see the section 'Culturalism: The Debate around *The Poverty of Theory*', in Samuel (ed.) 1981, pp. 375–408. Thompson vehemently rejected the label of 'culturalism' while acknowledging that he and Williams had become 'very close indeed ... on critical points of theory' – Thompson 1978, p. 399.

17   Bermingham 1987, pp. 4, 195–6.

18   Thompson 1978, p. 299.

19   For a statement of principle by Rosenthal, see Rosenthal 1984, which catches the embattled mood of the moment but does not address this issue.

20   Eagleton 1991, p. xii.

21   For a symptomatic example, see Blackburn (ed.) 1972.

importantly, it would do much (if not everything) to explain why the majority of the working class in advanced capitalist societies were so resistant to the appeal of revolutionary socialism when the present scheme of things was so patently contrary to their collective interests. And yet, as the author of a fine and widely read exposition of the concept observed in 1979, ideology was 'perhaps one of the most equivocal and elusive concepts one can find in the social sciences',[22] while a prominent Marxist critic had described it two years before as 'one of the least developed "regions" of Marxist theory'.[23]

The degree of contestation around the concept was formidable.[24] And the focal point was certainly Althusser's radical recasting of it in *For Marx* (1965) and the essay 'Ideology and Ideological State Apparatuses' (1969),[25] which exerted enormous influence over debate in Britain for two decades. Althusser dismissed the vernacular Marxist idea of ideology as false consciousness – in fact an equation Marx himself had never made despite his negative conception of ideology's functions.[26] Instead, he refigured it as the general principle of the formation of all social subjects, which invariably defined 'the imaginary relationship of individuals to their real conditions of existence';[27] at the same time, he drew a rigid demarcation between the realm of ideology and that of science. This conception is scarcely less normative than the 'false consciousness' thesis and made it hard to imagine how the experience of political struggle – all conducted in the realm of ideology – fed in to the development of Marxist theory, conceived as taking place in a self-contained sphere of truth production that was philosophical in character, subjectless,[28] and detached from empirical historical inquiries. Althusser dissociated ideology from 'ideas' as such and saw it rather as ideas inscribed in a whole range of social practices and institutions, gathered under the umbrella of Ideological State Apparatuses.[29] He also made

---

22   Larrain 1979, p. 13. For a recent history and survey of developments in the concept that sets a new standard in important respects, see Rehmann 2014.

23   Hall 1977, p. 28. Another register of the notion's complexity is the conference proceedings recorded in Hänninen and Paldán (eds.) 1983 – for the context of which, see Rehmann 2014, Chapter 9.

24   Eagleton 1991 identifies sixteen possible meanings of the term (pp. 1–2).

25   Althusser 2005; 'Ideology and Ideological State Apparatuses', in Althusser 1971, pp. 121–73. The latter essay, which first appeared in print in French in 1970, was extracted from a larger work, *On the Reproduction of Capitalism*, published posthumously in 1995 (Althusser 2014).

26   Larrain 1983, Chapter 1.

27   Althusser 1971, p. 153.

28   Althusser 2014, p. 188.

29   Althusser 1971, pp. 155–9.

a useful distinction between 'ideology *in general*', the ubiquitous principle of subject interpellation, and 'particular ideolog*ies*', which 'always express class positions'.[30]

There is no need to rehearse the larger criticisms of Althusser's theses here,[31] but two points need to be made to define my own position. First, Althusser emphasised that his theory of ideology was conceived to address the question of how labour power was reproduced in capitalist societies; the answer was that ideology qualified subjects for their roles in relations of production. He thus offered what appeared to be a functionalist argument that restricted all ideologies to the work of interpellating class subjects.[32] Second, beyond a useful emphasis on the multiplicity and contradictoriness of different ideologies, Althusser had little to say about the production of particular ideologies or the domain of what in other contexts would be called the sociology of knowledge.

The essays collected here were written under the sign of Göran Therborn's post-Althusserian theory of ideology, published in 1980, which, with two reservations, remains for me persuasive. For Therborn, ideology refers to 'that aspect of the human condition under which human beings live their lives as conscious actors in a world that makes sense to them to varying degrees. Ideology is the medium through which this consciousness and meaningfulness operate.'[33] But while Therborn accepts Althusser's innovation in conceiving ideology as the principle of subject formation, he corrects and adumbrates it in many important respects, endowing it with the meaningful theory of agency so signally absent from Althusser's conception.[34] Thus Therborn introduces a dialectical element into the concept of interpellation, arguing that interpellation does not only involve the *subjection* of subjects to their social role, but also their *qualification* for meaningful action.[35] He refuses the distinction between science and

---

30 Althusser 1971, p. 150.

31 Larrain 1979, pp. 154–64; Larrain 1983, pp. 91–100; Eagleton 1991, pp. 136–54; Rehmann 2014, Chapter 6, and *passim*.

32 I say 'appeared to be' because Althusser emphatically rejected the charge of functionalism in his 'Note on the ISAs', first published in a German translation in 1977, claiming that his critics had missed his emphasis on the role of class struggle in the formation of ideologies (Althusser 2014, pp. 218–20). Given the absence of any account of the proletarian class struggle in ideology in the 1969 essay I think those who like me mistook his position as functionalist can be forgiven the mistake. There is some address to the issue in the 'Note on the ISAs' but it hardly makes for an adequate solution to a crucial problem. Cf. Rehmann 2014, pp. 152–5.

33 Therborn 1980, p. 2.

34 On Althusser's theory, see Therborn 1980, pp. 8–9, 10, 16–17, 85, 104.

35 Therborn 1980, pp. 17–18.

ideology as mutually exclusive categories, and points out that the scientificity or truth of a discourse does not preclude it functioning to ideological effect. Moreover, human beings have the capacity to judge on certain truth claims, whether they are ideological or not.[36] Ideologies are multiple and protean, they 'differ, compete, and clash,' and they are not reducible to class ideologies – even if in class societies any given set of ideologies is overdetermined by class relations.[37] Thus ideologies of gender, race, religion, and philosophy, for instance, all have their place and Therborn faults Althusser in his assumption that the relationship between class groups and particular ideologies is simply transparent.[38]

My reservations are as follows. Therborn is insistent that the notion of 'interests' should be discarded as a 'utilitarian residue' in Marxism, since it implies 'normative conceptions of what is good and bad and conceptions of what is possible and impossible' as 'given in the reality of existence' and only accessible through 'true knowledge of the latter'.[39] I agree that Marxist analyses have often invoked class interests in a reductive, crassly materialist sense, which does not do justice to the complexity and historical specificity of human needs and desires. But I am not convinced that the concept can be simply jettisoned or that the notion of exploitation (which remains central to Therborn's thinking) is intelligible without it. And how else are we to explain the principle by which 'different classes *select* different forms of non-class ideologies'?[40]

In Therborn's scheme of things ideological production has 'relative autonomy'. At the same time, he argues that 'intellectuals, specialists in discursive practice, are institutionally linked to social classes', their formation as distinct groups is one 'aspect of the social division of labour'.[41] Although this is an improvement on Althusser, it does little to advance the problem of the class determination of particular ideologies, or again, to understanding the sociology of knowledge. We have at least to recognise that those qualified for the role of 'specialists in discursive practice' have either made a sincere 'accommodation' to or discovered a 'sense of representation' in the established social order – or at least accept the need to pretend to such.[42] Correspondingly, they

---

36   Therborn 1980, pp. 33–4.

37   Therborn 1980, pp. 26, 27, 38.

38   Therborn 1980, pp. 8–9.

39   Therborn 1980, p. 5. See also pp. 10, 71.

40   Therborn 1980, p. 39.

41   Therborn 1980, p. 72.

42   On 'accommodation' and 'sense of representation', see Therborn 1980, pp. 95–7.

are motivated to produce forms of discourse that promote and legitimate the interest of the ruling class or group, whether or not this entails 'false or deceptive beliefs'.[43] Eagleton is surely correct when he writes that ideology must have some 'specific connotations of power-struggle and legitimation, structural dissemblance and mystification', or the term becomes vacuous.[44]

The essays in the first part of this volume were conceived as attempts to consider as ideology the specialist belief systems that informed the production and reception of early nineteenth-century British landscape painting. My argument is that these practices were represented through distinct forms of discourse,[45] namely philosophical criticism – the nascent aesthetics generated by the empiricist philosophies that dominated systematic thinking among the hegemonic class groups and their ideologues – and the academic theory of painting, which acquired increasing authority through the professionalisation of the painter's craft in the eighteenth century. (These may be conceived in Gramsci's terms as the products of 'traditional intellectuals' and 'organic intellectuals', respectively).[46] As I argue in Chapters One and Two, these discourses were cognate but distinct, in some ways mutually supportive in other ways antagonistic, or at least in tension. Both can be considered as forms of 'science', in that both articulated the highest understanding of the phenomena of aesthetic reception and pictorial practice available in the society in question. At the same time, they represented 'the *promotion* and *legitimation*' of the interests of the social groups concerned, and in the case of philosophical criticism of the most powerful social groups.

'Cultural Philanthropy and the Invention of the Norwich School', which makes up Chapter Five, was conceived as a study of the origins and formation of an ideological figure, and the way this assumed material existence in Althusser's sense through texts, exhibitions, art collecting, and museumification. This does not, of course, make it an Ideological State Apparatus – the attribution of too many ideological structures to state power is a flaw in Althusser's theory – but it does point to its functions both in bolstering the hegemonic power of a local bourgeoisie and within a larger nationalist discourse of Englishness that served class interests.

---

43   Eagleton 1991, pp. 28–9.

44   Eagleton 1991, p. 110. See also Rehmann 2014, pp. 6–7.

45   For relations between ideology and discourse, see Eagleton 1991, Chapter 7; Rehmann 2014, pp. 180–5.

46   Gramsci 1971, pp. 3–23.

Ideology and the Work of Art

The relationship between such discourses as philosophical criticism and art theory and the category of ideology seems straightforward enough; they may both be denoted as 'aesthetic ideologies' that take a range of different material forms from the academy and artist's studio, to the exhibition room and the house, to the rituals of travel and tourism and so forth. But the relationship between artworks and the category is more complex and problematic. It raises the question of whether art should simply be subsumed under ideology – as some Marxists have argued[47] – or whether it exceeds or falls outside it. In 'Ideology and Ideological State Apparatuses' Althusser included 'Literature, the Arts, sports, etc.' under the 'cultural ISA';[48] but in an earlier published letter he had written that relations between art and ideology posed a very complicated and difficult problem: *'I do not rank real art among the ideologies*, although art does have a quite particular and specific relationship with ideology'.[49] He expanded on this claim: 'Art (I mean authentic art, not works of an average or mediocre level) does not give us knowledge in the strict sense ... but what it gives us does nevertheless maintain a certain *specific relationship* with knowledge'. Significant works of literature 'make us *see, perceive* (but not *know*) something which *alludes* to reality'.[50] Concise and undeveloped as they were, Althusser's comments on literature and art at least posited *'real art'* as a category that stood outside the negative functions of ideology as a mechanism of subjection and proposed that it had some cognitive value, even if this necessarily fell short of true knowledge as such.

The implications of Althusser's theory for the Marxist study of literature in its relative autonomy as a practice was that to achieve scientific status it would have to be purged of all empiricism and humanism, 'interpretation' would be replaced by 'explanation', and criticism superseded by the study of

---

47   Werckmeister 1973, pp. 505–6. Werckmeister has been a dogged and consistent defender of this position, which draws its authority from *The German Ideology*. There are two obvious responses: (1) should we accept a statement made in 1846 right at the emergence of historical materialism as a theoretical doctrine as holding good for the mature Marx, particularly since it was not published in Marx and Engels's lifetime? (2) even if the statement does represent a consistent position – and there are reasons to doubt that – should that set unsurpassable limits on the development of Marxist thought on aesthetic matters given that Marx left no systematic exposition of his aesthetic views?

48   Althusser 1971, p. 137.

49   Althusser, 'A Letter on Art in Reply to André Daspre' (April 1966), in Althusser 1971, p. 203.

50   Althusser 1971, p. 204.

'literary production'. Two notable texts advanced this programme – though in very different idioms – Pierre Macherey's *Theory of Literary Production* (1966) and Terry Eagleton's *Criticism and Ideology* (1976).[51]

For Macherey, writing of the novel,

> Even though ideology itself always sounds solid, copious, it begins to speak of its *own absences* because of its presence in the novel, its visible and determinate form. By means of the text it becomes possible to escape from the domain of spontaneous ideology, to escape from the false consciousness of self, of history, and of time ... Art, or at least literature, because it naturally scorns the credulous view of the world, establishes myth and illusion as visible objects.[52]

In another place, Macherey speaks of a 'real *determinate* disorder' in the literary work that relates to the disorder of ideology, 'which cannot be organized into a system', for 'the order which it [the work] professes is merely an imagined order, projected on to disorder, the fictive resolution of ideological conflicts, a resolution so precarious that it is obvious in the very letter of the text where incoherence and incompleteness burst forth'.[53] As in psychoanalysis, gaps in the text arise because of what ideology cannot mention, but in the novel ideology 'begins to speak of its *own absences*'; the unconscious of the work – which is 'the play of history beyond its edges' – is displayed 'in a kind of splitting' within it.[54]

Eagleton, who in *Criticism and Ideology* offers a very fine-grained critique of Althusser and Macherey's theory of literature, noted the vague and rhetorical character of Althusser's formulations and suggested that it was 'as though the aesthetic must still be granted mysteriously privileged status, but now in embarrassedly oblique style'.[55] Picking up on Althusser's unelaborated distinction between 'authentic art' and 'works of an average or mediocre level', Eagleton devoted the final essay of his book to the question of aesthetic value,

---

51   Macherey 1978; Eagleton 1998.

52   Macherey 1978, pp. 132–3. See also, pp. 60, 64.

53   Macherey 1978, p. 155. On the contradictoriness of ideologies, cf. Althusser 2014, pp. 194, 199–200, 219; Rehmann 2014, pp. 260, 287.

54   Macherey 1978, pp. 94, 132.

55   Eagleton 1998, p. 84. For Althusser and Macherey more generally, see pp. 82–101. Eagleton has retrospectively acknowledged the book's indebtedness to Althusserianism at the same time as stressing his reservations about Althusser's work more broadly. See Eagleton and Beaumont 2009, pp. 133–6.

arguing that this was a question Marxist criticism could not dodge and for which it had to provide a 'materialist *explanation*'.[56] Building on Macherey's formulations he suggested that the aesthetic was not 'some hierarchical division of levels within the work', but rather 'a matter of the work's irreducibility to the historic-ideological of which it is the product'. Works transcended their immediate moment of production not because they were 'universal', but because the specific circumstances of their making allowed them to make the 'depths and intricacies' of a complex ideological conjuncture 'vividly perceptible' in 'a play of textual significations'.[57] Ideology, inscribed in the very substance of the work, was paradoxically what gave it its value.

How far were these theses transferrable to the visual arts? Literary criticism, Macherey remarked, was quite different from other forms of art criticism because the medium of its objects was language: 'Neither music nor painting is a language ... among all forms of artistic expression, literature alone is related to language, even though it is not itself a language'.[58] Elsewhere he noted that the literary work, while it imitated 'the everyday language which is the language of ideology', was also an 'autonomous entity' that had to be marked off from both 'scientific propositions' and 'everyday speech'.[59] For Eagleton, literature was perhaps 'the most revealing mode of experiential access to ideology that we possess'.[60] This poses a problem for Marxist art history in that although one might speak of a kind of image vernacular – particularly with the proliferation of images in advanced capitalist societies – images, for all their subtlety and suasive power, do not provide the universal medium of self-reflection, communicable thought, or interpersonal communication in the way language does. Correspondingly, the theory of the iconic sign is far less developed than that of the linguistic sign and the connections between the two are far from straightforward.[61]

The sole attempt to theorise a scientific history of art on Althusserian principles was Nicos Hadjinicolaou's *Art History and Class Struggle*, first published

---

56   Eagleton 1998, p. 162.

57   Eagleton 1998, pp. 177–8.

58   Macherey 1978, p. 136.

59   Macherey 1978, p. 59. Althusser himself clearly thought paintings could have effects analogous to those he ascribed literature – see his essay 'Cremonini, Painter of the Abstract', in Althusser 1971, pp. 209–20. For a commentary on this text, see Sprinker 1987, pp. 284–7.

60   Eagleton 1998, p. 101.

61   But see Goodman 1981; and 'Critique of Iconism', in Eco 1979, pp. 191–217. For a recent critique of Goodman's theory of the image from a phenomenological perspective, see Wiesing 2010, pp. 21–3.

in French in 1973, which also remains the only 'how to do it' book of Marxist art history. Although the author was no less emphatic than Macherey in distinguishing the true Marxist perspective from all empiricist, humanist, and historicist deviations, the book is more in dialogue with both bourgeois models of art history and the work of earlier self-styled Marxist historians than *A Theory of Literary Production* is with their literary equivalents. This is because although Hadjinicolaou regarded the art history of Wölfflin and the Vienna School as unscientific – pre-scientific might be more accurate – he accepted its premise that the fundamental subject matter of the discipline is style. (This is not to say that Hadjinicolaou dismisses iconology – he acknowledged it as a *'technique'* in art history – but he found Panofsky's philosophical problematic 'highly questionable' and the method became 'dubious' when it pretended to cover the discipline as a whole.)[62] In this respect, Hadjinicolaou followed the line of thinking pursued by two Hungarian Marxist art historians who came out of the Budapest Sunday Circle, Frederick Antal and Arnold Hauser, namely that the way to Marxify art history was by establishing a sociology of artistic styles that linked them with the specific outlooks (that is the ideologies) of particular classes or class fractions. Hauser had already published an important essay on the value of the concept of ideology for the history of art in his 1958 book *The Philosophy of Art History*,[63] but although this anticipated several of Hadjinicolaou's theses it did so in the language of humanist and historicist Marxism and he found it unsatisfactory.[64] By contrast, he hailed Antal as having produced the 'only important studies' that 'laid the foundations for a science of art history' and affirmed the 'scientific rigor of his insights'.[65] Nonetheless, even Antal was guilty of a humanistic error in his apparent assumption 'that the ideology of a social class ... is "translated" through the medium of the artist into the realm of art', and he also tended to accord too much importance to subject matter in defining the ideology of a picture and used imprecise terms such as 'philosophy', 'outlook', and 'ideas', when what he had really meant was ideology.[66]

---

62   Hadjinicolaou 1978, pp. 44–9.

63   'The Sociological Approach: The Concept of Ideology in the History of Art' in Hauser 1963, pp. 21–40. Hauser proposed a rather tighter set of formulations in Hauser 1971.

64   Hadjinicolaou 1978, p. 19, n. 1.

65   Hadjinicolaou 1978, pp. 79, 80.

66   Hadjinicolaou 1978, pp. 92–3. Antal's theoretical statements are disappointingly bland by comparison with the sharpness of his specific historical studies – see his 'Remarks on the Method of Art History', in Antal 1966, pp. 175–89. Hadjinicolaou drew his understanding of Antal's method primarily from Antal 1948.

Hadjinicolaou's remedy for Antal's lack of precision was to introduce the term 'visual ideology' in place of style. (The original French term 'idéologie imagée' is preferable in that it suggests something more tied to the iconic sign).[67] 'The ideology of a picture', Hadjinicolaou wrote, 'is literally a visual ideology and not a political or literary ideology; it can only be found within the limits of a picture's two dimensions, even though at the same time it has specific links with other kinds of ideology which may be literary, political, philosophical, and so on'.[68] Although Hadjinicolaou did not claim (as Macherey did of true art in the novel form) that in the art work ideology inadvertently disclosed itself, he did distinguish between 'positive or affirmative' and 'critical' visual ideologies. In the case of the first, it was implied that there was no contradiction between the visual form and the other types of ideology to which the work referred, in the latter there was. Rubens's *Rape of Ganymede* (*c*. 1636–7; Prado, Madrid) was representative of the first, Rembrandt's depiction of the same theme (1635; Dresden, Gemäldegalerie) was representative of the second.[69] It should be clear that Hadjinicolaou did not accord the visual arts, or painting at least, the potentially revelatory role that Macherey, following Althusser, accorded literature.

Style and visual ideology were synonymous, but in order to give style the requisite scientific gravitas unnecessarily wordy terminology was proposed with terms such as 'early Renaissance visual ideology', 'baroque visual ideology', or even 'the visual ideology of the bourgeois portrait at the end of the eighteenth and beginning of the nineteenth century'. Once the general principle was established, nothing was gained by these cumbersome locutions. Moreover, in fact style and visual ideology were not quite synonymous in that Hadjinicolaou defined the latter as 'a specific combination of the formal and thematic elements of a picture through which people express the way they relate their lives to the conditions of their existence, a combination which constitutes a particular form of the overall ideology of a social class'.[70] Thus iconology –

---

67   The translator noted there was a problem – Hadjinicolaou 1978, p. 95 n. It becomes particularly evident if one compares the discussion of the term in relation to dictionary definitions of 'visual' in the English edition and 'image' in the French. Cf. Hadjinicolaou 1978, pp. 94–5, with Hadjinicolaou 1973, p. 106. Of course the concept of image is also unstable, referring as it does to both several varieties of sign and some notion of a distinct kind of mental event that in itself can only be construed in terms that are culturally inflected.

68   Hadjinicolaou 1978, p. 16.

69   Hadjinicolaou 1978, pp. 147–8, 163–9.

70   Hadjinicolaou 1978, pp. 95–6.

'thematic elements' – came in through the backdoor and its precise role in relation to style remained undefined.

For Hadjinicolaou, the Marxist history of art would be nothing other than the history of visual ideologies. But unlike styles in bourgeois art history, these could not be associated with individual artists, regions or nations; they applied solely to classes since 'the fundamental function of ideology is determined by class relations'.[71] Individual artistic agency was just a bourgeois delusion. Moreover, different classes could not share the same visual ideology, presumably because the 'structural principles' of each style derived from the ideology of a specific social group,[72] leaving the great challenge for art history as defining the different class fractions to which the different visual ideologies belonged.[73] Value had no place in this scheme of things. Hadjinicolaou anticipated that philosophical aesthetics would follow the philosophy of history into the trashcan of bourgeois illusions.[74] Aesthetic pleasure was simply a matter of an individual's ideological self-recognition in a work. Displeasure arose from non-recognition.[75]

Hadjinicolaou acknowledged the 'schematic character' of *Art History and Class Struggle* and its 'uncertain terminology'.[76] Indeed, for all its impressive learning and sometimes incisive judgments on earlier art-historical method, it has the feel of a book written in haste and the English version received some sharply critical reviews from the left.[77] If I have returned to it more than forty years after its first publication it is because it raises fundamental problems about the objects and methods of Marxist art history that are still pertinent. In spite of Hadjinicolaou's dismissal of the aesthetic, unlike much run of the mill social history of art he does acknowledge art production as a distinct form of practice with relative autonomy and a kind of critical purchase on the world in some instances.[78]

Yet even leaving aside the fundamental (and interrelated) problems of his rigid Althusserian stance on ideology and individual agency, there are unre-

---

71 Hadjinicolaou 1978, pp. 98, 11.

72 Hadjinicolaou 1978, pp. 102, 64 n. 14.

73 Hadjinicolaou 1978, p. 107. I have substituted the more common term 'fractions' for the translator's 'sections'. The French term was 'parties'.

74 Hadjinicolaou 1978, pp. 180–3.

75 Hadjinicolaou 1978, pp. 178–9.

76 Hadjinicolaou 1978, p. 197.

77 See Berger 1978; Tagg 1978; Wallach 1981.

78 Hadjinicolaou himself was clear about the distinction between the social history of art and the Marxist history of art – see Hadjinicolaou 1986.

solved issues that invalidate the conception of 'idéologie imagée' or at least demand its modification. First, Hadjinicolaou assumes a genetic relationship between stylistic forms and the ideology of particular classes or class fractions, but the principle by which different groups select different styles is not defined. This can only be the result of some form of homology between pictorial form and ideas – as for instance, when Hadjinicolaou, following Antal, refers to the 'objective rationalism' of David's works of 1789–95;[79] yet how the suture between the linguistic material of ideology and the iconic sign occurs remains a mystery. Homology – the idea of intuited correspondences between specific cultural forms and larger ideological structures or social practices – is an inescapable tool of Marxist cultural history, but it is obviously open to the charge of impressionism and is more associated with the organicist strand in Frankfurt School Marxism, which was antithetical to the Althusserian current.[80]

Like Therborn, I find it implausible to make genetic connections between specific ideologies and specific class groups for the most part – which is not to say that certain ideas are not especially adapted to the interests of particular classes or class fractions in particular circumstances. In any case, the essentialist correspondence Hadjinicolaou proposes between ideologies and class groups founders on his awareness of the polysemy of the visual sign: 'This investment of a positive visual ideology with multiple aesthetic ideologies, contemporary or posterior, is a characteristic of the whole history of image production. This is because the positive visual ideology of a work is of necessity "polyvocal" or "polyvalent"'.[81] Nor was this problem confined to the visual arts, since, as Macherey had acknowledged in a passage Hadjinicolaou quoted, multiplicity of potential meanings was also characteristic of the literary work, even without the iconic sign's particular slipperiness in this regard.[82] Neither Macherey nor Hadjinicolaou seem to have been aware of Vološinov's conception of the sign as an inherently mutable entity, a site of conflict in the arena of

---

79   Hadjinicolaou 1978, p. 116.

80   On homology, see Raymond Williams's critical presentation of the concept in Williams 1977, pp. 103–7. Cf. Eagleton's related critique of 'adjacentism' in Eagleton 1998, pp. 171–2.

81   Hadjinicolaou 1978, p. 162. I have corrected the translation of the first of these sentences. The second was added for the English edition. For the classic discussion of polysemy in images, see 'Rhetoric of the Image' in Barthes 1977, p. 39.

82   Macherey 1978, pp. 78–9, quoted in a different translation, in Hadjinicolaou 1978, pp. 141–2. The point is reinforced by a quotation from Louis Marin about the multiple codes of the pictorial sign that Hadinicolaou cites p. 142 n. 7.

class struggle because class and 'sign community' do not correspond and the sign is invariably 'multi-accentual'.[83]

The main alternative to Hadjinocolaou was offered by the work of T.J. Clark. If this was more appealing that may have been partly because Clark did not set out his theoretical stall in such elaborate and dogmatic terms and preferred to concentrate on concrete analyses of unparalleled brilliance.[84] The oft-cited position statement 'On the Social History of Art', which forms the first chapter of Clark's *Image of the People* (1973), is essayistic and combative rather than systematic. But although it does not announce itself as a contribution to the Marxist theory of art, it was certainly widely read as such. By contrast with Hadjinicolaou's negation of the artist-creator, Clark insisted that 'the encounter with history and its specific determinations is made by the artist himself'[85] – a principle that was demonstrated in the partly biographical presentation of both *Image of the People* and its companion volume *The Absolute Bourgeois* (1973). Rather than assuming a correspondence between style and ideology, Clark stressed the complexity of relations between the two and the need for the 'history of mediations' to be written, since 'what I want to explain are the connecting links between artistic form, the available systems of visual representation, the current theories of art, other ideologies, social classes, and more general historical structures and processes'.[86]

The very term 'mediation' put Clark at odds with Althusserianism, since for Althusser the concept was an ideological residue from eighteenth-century philosophy that had nothing to do with Marx.[87] And yet Clark's observation on the relationship between the artwork and ideology was reminiscent of Macherey's formulations: 'A work of art may have ideology (in other words, those ideas, images, and values which are generally accepted as dominant) as its material, but it works that material; it gives it a new form and at certain moments that new form is in itself a subversion of ideology'.[88] This idea was further elaborated in the lengthier reflection on ideology Clark offered in an article of the following year. While he did not embrace the principle that 'ideology in general' interpellated social subjects and claimed no specific theoretical loyalty, he insisted on the artwork's relations with the 'ideological materials' that represented the conflict of social classes:

---

83   Vološinov 1973, p. 23.

84   The best account of Clark's thought in this period is in Day 2011, pp. 40–51.

85   Clark 1973 (2), p. 13.

86   Clark 1973 (2), p. 12.

87   Althusser and Balibar 1970, pp. 62–3.

88   Clark 1973 (2), p. 13.

The work of art stands in a quite specific relation to these ideological materials. Ideology is what the picture is, and what the picture is not. (We might say that 'style' is the form of ideology: and that indicates the necessity and the limitations of a history of styles.) Ideology is the dream-content, without the dream work. And even though the work itself – the means and materials of artistic production – is determinate, fixed within ideological bounds, permeated by ideological assumptions; even so, the fact that work is done is crucial. Because the work takes a certain set of technical procedures and traditional forms, and makes them the tools with which to alter ideology – to transcribe it, to represent it. This can be anodyne, illustration: we are surrounded by duplicates of ideology: but the process of work creates the space in which, at certain moments, an ideology can be appraised. The business of 'fitting' ideological materials most tightly, most completely into the forms and codes which are appropriate to the technical materials at hand is also a process of revealing the constituents – the historical, separable constituents, normally hidden behind the veil of naturalness – of these ideological materials. It is a means of testing them, of examining their grounds.[89]

I have quoted this passage at length because it represents the most sophisticated statement of the qualitative basis on which artworks are to be distinguished in relation to ideological conflicts of their moment of production. However, like Macherey's kindred propositions it seems more apposite in relation to art of the modern period, in which artists have often assumed a self-consciously critical stance in relation to society, than it does to art of earlier epochs. This was confirmed by the important article Clark published on Manet's *Olympia* in *Screen* in 1980, which reveals both the depth of engagement with *Screen* theory among many Marxist art historians at that moment – Clark's argument about the meaning of the painting is constructed in semiotic terms – and that the author's primary concern was with questions of modernism and avant-garde in relation to the contemporary situation of critical art practice.[90] Although Clark had instanced the work of Vermeer to illustrate how art could exploit 'the fact that any ideology is by its nature incoherent',[91] it was unclear

---

89   Clark 1995, pp. 251–2. The very term 'artistic creation' – with its intimations of the unique humanist subject – reads like a slap at Macherey and Hadjinicolaou.

90   Clark 1980 (1). Pushed on the argument of the work by a critical response from Peter Wollen (Wollen 1980), Clark sought to clarify his criterion of value with reference to an ill-defined quality of 'vividness' in works that were successful – see Clark 1980 (2), p. 98.

91   Clark 1995, p. 252.

how useful his criterion of value would be in relation to the art of pre-capitalist social formations, given that in some accounts the spread of capitalist relations and the penetration of the commodity form into more and more aspects of life had altered the character of ideology in profound ways.

Ideology and the Aesthetic: Adorno

Macherey and Hadjinicolaou's aversion to aesthetics was superficially paradoxical in that Althusser's major achievement was generally understood as a reawakened concern with the philosophical presuppositions of Marxism. But Althusser's reconceptualisation of Marx was so rationalist and scientistic, so epistemology-centred, that it could only accommodate art as a kind of special appendage to the domains of theory and ideology in which the normal rules were partially suspended, but not enough to qualify science's predominance. His insistence that there was an 'epistemological break' (a concept borrowed from Gaston Bachelard) between Marxist science and earlier 'prescientific theoretical practice' did not permit a sense of Marxism as itself the outcome of a dialectical process; in any case Althusser claimed that the rupture between the Marxian and Hegelian dialectics was no less absolute than the break in other areas. By contrast, the most imposing Marxist contribution to aesthetics – Adorno's *Aesthetic Theory*, which appeared in its first English translation in 1984 – assumed precisely the dialectical relationship between earlier bourgeois achievements in the field and its Marxist development that Althusser's epistemological break precluded. *Aesthetic Theory* is, amongst other things, an extended meditation on the aesthetics of Kant and Hegel and an attempt to go beyond the opposition of their respective stances.

The category of ideology stalks the pages of *Aesthetic Theory* – logically so since art and ideology are no less related in Adorno's system than they are in Althusser's. But if for him the phenomenon is just as pervasive, Adorno's conceptualisation of it is very different. Althusser, it will be recalled, emphasised the role of Ideological State Apparatuses in the reproduction of ideology, among them being the churches, schools, the family, the law, the political system, the trade unions, the arts and sports, and what he called 'the communications ISA (press, radio and television, etc.)'.[92] By contrast, it is the last of these, denominated as the Culture Industry, that for Adorno does the primary work of ideological inculcation, and he makes no reference to the state, polit-

---

92   Althusser 1971, pp. 136–7.

ical interests, or active class power in the direction or circumscription of their work. Moreover, ideology is not a principle of subject formation in all societies, it is specific to modern urban market economies, for 'where purely immediate relations of power predominate' as in slave or feudal economies 'there are really no ideologies'.[93] Without recognition of the problem of socially constituted sources of cognitive error and of the role of ideas in maintaining injustice and preventing the realisation of a rational society – which only emerges in the modern period in the thought of philosophers such as Bacon and Helvetius – there would be no conception of ideology; its very existence depends on a society that knows it is in need of justification and defence. For Adorno, the ideologies of totalitarian societies are not 'ideology in the proper sense' because they do not depend on 'content and coherence' and claim no autonomy or consistency, they are simply 'approved views decreed from above' which maintain their sway through force. True ideology entails relationships of power that are not understood by power itself.[94] For Adorno it is not the state machinery but the multiple techniques of dissemination at the disposal of the culture industry, particularly film and television, which are the real threat to critical thought; these comprise 'a closed system' under centralised control that exerts 'indescribable power'.[95] The media teach 'models of a behaviour which submits to the overwhelming power of the existing conditions'; 'individuals experience themselves as chess pieces' and can envision no alternative.[96]

In this world of reification dominated by standardised cultural products that appeal to atavistic instincts and affirm incessantly that there is no alternative to things as they are, the modern artwork is one of the few things that can unsettle ideology's pervasive spell. But this does not mean that in art truth and ideology can be neatly separated from one another; they are inextricably linked.[97] Even so, 'in artworks that are to their very core ideological, truth content can assert itself. Ideology, socially necessary semblance, is by this same necessity also the distorted image of the true. A threshold that divides the social consciousness

---

93 Adorno 1972, pp. 189, 190. This text is attributed to Adorno, with acknowledgment of Horkheimer's role in its formulation, as 'Beitrag zur Ideologienlehre', in Adorno's *Gesammelte Schriften*, ed. Rolf Tiedemann, Frankfurt a M: Suhrkamp, 20 vols., 1997, vol. 8, p. 457 n. 1. For elucidations of Adorno's theory of ideology, see Eagleton 1991, pp. 126–8; Jarvis 1998, pp. 64–7.

94 Adorno 1972, pp. 90–91.

95 Adorno 1972, pp. 200, 201.

96 Adorno 1972, p. 202. For a critique of Adorno and Horkheimer's position, see Rehmann 2014, pp. 90–98.

97 Adorno 1972, p. 234.

of aesthetics from the philistine is that aesthetics reflects the social critique of the ideological in artworks, rather than mechanically reiterating it'.[98]

The meaning of artworks for Adorno is their 'truth content' – where 'all aesthetic questions terminate' – and this can only be apprehended philosophically.[99] Simon Jarvis has remarked on the gulf separating art history from aesthetics in Adorno's thought, yet at the same time his aesthetics contains far more art history than most aesthetic systems.[100] General theories of the aesthetic necessarily miss what is interesting in the artwork, and aesthetics had come to seem obsolete because 'it scarcely ever confronted itself with its object'.[101] Philosophical interpretation of artworks, separate from history and from immanent engagement with the works, leads only to circularity.[102] On the other hand, 'contemplation that limits itself to the artwork fails it', since every artwork is the 'nexus of a problem'.[103] It is the enigmatic character of the artwork's truth content that makes philosophy the necessary medium of interpretation, and this grasping of truth necessarily entails critique.[104] But the truth of philosophy itself cannot be understood separately from the 'misfortune of history' and the truth content of artworks, on which any assessment of their value depends, is historical through and through.[105] Thus in Adorno's aesthetics, art, philosophy and history are locked in an inextricable embrace.

In the draft introduction to *Aesthetic Theory* Adorno writes that the explanation of art 'is achieved methodically through the confrontation of historical categories and elements of aesthetic theory with artistic experience, which correct one another reciprocally'.[106] However, despite his admiration for Hauser's *Social History of Art*, for him a 'noncontradictory theory of the history of art' was inconceivable.[107] I take it that part of this contradiction is that in the end there will always be something about the artwork that eludes art history's explanations and that this something is crucial to its truth. Indeed, systematic art

---

98   Adorno 1997, p. 233.

99   Adorno 1997, pp. 131, 335, 341.

100   Jarvis 1998, p. 91. I owe a great deal to the discussion of Adorno's aesthetic thought in chapters 3–4 of this book. For Adorno, the task of the individual sciences such as art history is research, whereas that of philosophy is interpretation. See Adorno 1977, pp. 125–6.

101   Adorno 1997, p. 333.

102   Adorno 1997, p. 180.

103   Adorno 1997, p. 348. See also pp. 6, 358.

104   Adorno 1997, p. 128.

105   Adorno 1997, pp. 352, 192.

106   Adorno 1997, p. 353.

107   Adorno 1997, p. 210.

history will betray the artwork precisely because of its systematic ambitions, which are inimical to the inherent heterogeneity of its object.

Adorno is emphatic that the understanding of artworks is not distinct from their 'genetic explanation', but at the same time he insists understanding and explanation are not the same because understanding misses 'the nonexplanatory level of the spontaneous fulfillment of the work'.[108] Art scholarship's tendency to confound artworks with their genesis makes it alien to art, although its familiar notions of art's causation are still granted some explanatory function.[109] Adorno does not write out the agency of the artist in the way Macherey and Hadjinicolaou do, but even so he places little weight on artists' intentions, on their 'often apocryphal and helpless theories', on 'biographical accidentalness', or Diltheyan notions of 'lived experience'.[110] Artworks are produced through the development of the idea, to which the individual life circumstances of artists are generally of little moment. They are 'coconstructed by the opposition of the artistic material, by their own postulates, by historically contemporary models and procedures that are elemental to a spirit that may be called ... objective'.[111] Thus an artist's intentions are hardly ever decisive for the artwork because the impersonal resources of technique have primacy and a work's truth content is not coincident with the consciousness or intention of its author.[112]

Neither is meaning to be discovered through that favourite of the positivistic social history of art, reception history, since the work of art's primary relation to society is through production – although reception should not be completely neglected either.[113] Similarly, artworks cannot be 'described or explained in terms of the categories of communication', since it is as labour that 'the subject in art comes into its own'.[114] Moreover, in the present situation it is not the messages of artworks that need to be comprehended but their 'incomprehensibility'.[115] Those who consider art only from the perspective of comprehension turn it into something 'straightforward' that is 'furthest from what it is'.[116]

---

108   Adorno 1997, p. 350.
109   Adorno 1997, p. 179.
110   Adorno 1997, pp. 347, 346.
111   Adorno 1997, p. 345.
112   Adorno 1997, pp. 60, 128, 151.
113   Adorno 1997, pp. 228, 193.
114   Adorno 1997, pp. 109, 166.
115   Adorno 1997, p. 118.
116   Adorno 1997, p. 122.

Art's value for Adorno lies in the fact that it 'remains something mimetic in a world of administered rationality' – 'mimetic' implying an attempt to know the object by being like it, a mode of cognition that is characteristic of cultures that have not yet succumbed to the overwhelming tendency to rationality and abstraction that accompanies the dominance of the commodity economy.[117] Successful artworks – and in Adorno's eyes there is no other kind, the unsuccessful simply fail to be art – are inherently critical, inherently in opposition to society.[118] This is what makes the autonomy of art so central to Adorno's aesthetics. Although for him, characteristically, 'art is autonomous and is not', which is to say that art's autonomy is socially constituted.[119] It is form that is the basis of this autonomy and form is correspondingly the central concept of aesthetics.[120] But nothing could be further from Adorno's project than formalism or aestheticism. Indeed, form for him is 'sedimented content' and represents 'the social relation in the artwork'.[121]

In his essay on 'Art and the Arts', Adorno acknowledged that he was 'accustomed to relating aesthetic experiences to the realm of art with which [he] was most familiar', namely music, and it would be worth considering how far his consistent emphasis on the cognitive import of form – which led him to claim that the 'tour de force' of Beethoven's great works is 'literally Hegelian'[122] – does not partly derive from the centrality of music to his thought. Which is also to say that like many aesthetic systems, Adorno's matches better with some arts than others, and that he does not seem to have been particularly well-informed on the visual arts. But leaving this issue aside, for him modernism's 'emancipation of form' held good for all the arts and had led to the 'elimination of the principle of representation in painting and sculpture'.[123]

For Adorno, painting and music are both languages, but they became more language like the less they tried to imitate the linguistic arts or to communicate specific things: 'Painting and music speak by virtue of the way they are constructed, not by the act of representing themselves; they speak all the more clearly, the more profoundly and thoroughly they are composed in themselves, and the figures of this essential form are their writing ... The similarity

---

117   Adorno 1997, p. 53.

118   Adorno 1997, pp. 118, 225.

119   Adorno 1997, p. 6.

120   This is so because 'art needs something heterogeneous in order to become art.' – see Adorno 1967, p. 375.

121   Adorno 1997, pp. 5, 255.

122   Adorno 1997, p. 185.

123   Adorno 1997, pp. 145, 90.

to language increases with the decrease in communication'.[124] This matches with Adorno's claim elsewhere that 'the more ruthlessly artworks draw the consequences from the contemporary condition of consciousness, the more closely they themselves approximate meaninglessness'.[125] The truths of art are non-propositional – 'no message is to be squeezed out of *Hamlet*'[126] – they constitute simply the intimation that things could be different. Thus when Adorno refers to the 'social critique of the ideological in artworks'[127] he does not mean the exposure of a particular class interest or the incoherence of ideology that Macherey or Clark propose authentic works of art may effect, but rather a gesture that illuminates the crushing pressure of reification and instrumental reason advanced capitalist societies generate.

Philosophically speaking, Althusser and Adorno seem at the antipodes of Western Marxism; the rigours of French rationalism as opposed to the subtle dialectic of the Hegelian tradition; unrepentant Leninism set against a refusal of party-political entanglements – though not of political speech, it should be noted. Whereas Althusser's emphasis was all on the profound rupture with bourgeois thought required for the birthing of Marxist science, with Adorno it is only through immanent critique of the bourgeois philosophical tradition that one can hope to approach the truth of things and the over-privileging of scientistic thinking is itself an aspect of reification. Whereas in Althusser's system art enjoys a privileged place, it is a marginal one in relation to the great questions of epistemology and knowledge production; for Adorno art is central to his philosophical project and to the very possibility of thinking critically in current conditions. For Adorno art is 'not an arbitrary cultural complement to science but, rather, stands in critical tension to it'; it is 'rationality that criticizes rationality without withdrawing from it'.[128]

No happy medium between these positions is possible or desirable; I acknowledge that my own sympathies are more with Adorno. And yet although the truth content of Adorno and Horkheimer's theses on the culture industry is borne out all around us as never before, the notion of subject formation they offer is clearly inadequate.[129] Here post-Althusserian theories of ideology such

---

124   Adorno 1995, p. 71. For the language character of artworks in Adorno, see also Jarvis 1998, pp. 102–4.

125   Adorno 1997, p. 340.

126   Adorno 1997, p. 128.

127   Adorno 1997, p. 233.

128   Adorno 1997, pp. 231, 55.

129   See Adorno and Horkheimer 1979, pp. 120–67. Obviously Horkheimer's role in the development of these ideas must be acknowledged.

as those of Therborn and Jan Rehmann have far more to offer in explaining individual agency and the manifold sources of resistance to the status quo as well as providing ways of conceptualising subject formation in pre-modern societies. Further, Adorno's conception of the artwork is too oriented to the defence of modernist practices to be serviceable for the art of earlier periods or indeed many epochs of non-European cultures. For him the gap between tradition and modern art is unbridgeable because of the centrality of 'the new' to the latter; style in art is a thing of the past.[130] Adorno's point that artworks are 'perishable', that while they 'constantly divulge new layers' they also 'age, grow old, and die', is well taken. His statement, 'many artworks of the past and among them the most renowned are no longer to be experienced in any immediate fashion',[131] should be inscribed over every museum portal. But if the philosopher can only point to the deceptive character of aesthetic experience offered by such works, the art historian must still explain them.[132] And here the formulations of Macherey, Eagleton, and Clark on relations of art and ideology, while certainly in need of further development, remain suggestive. The arguments in Part Two of this book try to put these formulations to the test. Further, if the ideological regime is more contradictory and less total than the one Adorno projects, then works of art may play a less singular and desperate role, may produce more varied critical experiences in the receptive subject.

Why Naturalistic Landscape Painting?

Thanks in part to the largesse of the Yale Center for British Art and Paul Mellon Centre for Studies in British Art, together with the support of Yale University Press, historical research on British art has been a growth industry since I conceived or wrote most of the essays that make up this book. The field has also changed almost beyond recognition. A major factor in this regard, at least to begin with, was the influence of a new interpretative paradigm in eighteenth-century studies that was established by John Barrell's *The Political Theory of Painting from Reynolds to Hazlitt* (1986) and David Solkin's *Painting for Money: The Visual Arts and the Public Sphere in Eighteenth-Century England* (1993). Both books involved a creative adaptation of J.G.A. Pocock's concept of the

---

130   Adorno 1997, pp. 19, 206–7.

131   Adorno 1997, pp. 4, 348–9.

132   This is not to deny that fruitful methodological insights can be gleaned from Adorno's
       works of historical criticism such as Adorno 1981.

civic humanist tradition in political thought, which defined the citizen as one rendered independent by possession of inheritable freehold in land and the right to bear arms in the public cause. Only such independent citizens could attain political virtue and republics were prone to corruption if they became dependent on powerful partial interests. Barrell argued that civic humanism provided the political armature of the dominant theory of painting in Britain from Shaftesbury's *Judgment of Hercules* (1712) to the writings and lectures of Benjamin Robert Haydon of the 1830s and 1840s; that there was in effect a civic humanist theory of painting.[133] Less interested than Barrell in the mismatch between the civic humanist conception of the polity and the actuality of capitalist society, Solkin argued that in early Hanoverian Britain the civic humanist discourse mutated into an ideology of 'commercial humanism' that sustained the consolidation of bourgeois class power in the newly emergent public sphere – Habermas being introduced to provide sociological bolster to the argument. *Painting for Money* claims to show how artistic production matched the requirements of art in eighteenth-century public life up to the foundation of the Royal Academy in 1768.

Solkin described *Painting for Money* as 'an account of ideology made visible'.[134] However, ideology is not a specifically Marxist concept, either in its origins or subsequent development. I say this because whatever else Solkin's argument may be, it is not self-declaredly a Marxist one and given the dearth of Marxist historiography in the book's bibliography perhaps he did not intend it as such. This inference is supported by the fact that class struggle barely figures in his eighteenth century. Solkin quite rightly assumes a symbiosis between the gentry and commercial and financial fractions of the bourgeoisie, which produced a common class culture that was both bourgeois and plutocratic, cemented by shared norms of 'politeness'.[135] But this happy alliance seems to enjoy its hegemony virtually uncontested since although *Painting for Money* acknowledges tensions between 'patricians and plebs', to borrow E.P. Thompson's resonant terminology – and notably in the fine chapter on Vauxhall Gardens – the political complaints from the growing ranks of the manufacturing and profes-

---

133   I laid out my objections to this hypothesis in my review of Barrell's book – see Hemingway 1987. In retrospect I regret the ungenerous tone I adopted – partly the result of an impatience with the Foucault vogue – but I still think my basic criticisms are correct. Chapters 1 and 2 in this volume propose a different model for understanding eighteenth-century discourses on art.

134   Solkin 1993, p. 276. For Solkin on method – and the utility of the concept of ideology – see Solkin 1985.

135   For a fine sketch of this process, see Rogers 1979.

sional middle class among whom norms of deference were already beginning to break down don't get a look in until the Wilkes Affair in the 1760s. The 'vaunted cultural consensus'[136] Solkin attributes to eighteenth-century England thus has a very brief lifespan and can only be maintained by ignoring the levels of unrest among 'the middling sort' before it acquired a distinct class voice.[137]

For Solkin, ideology is neatly functional so that texts by thinkers such as Hutcheson, Hume, Kames, Millar, and Smith can all be raided for quotations to sustain the proposition of a dominant ideology of 'politeness' that codified bourgeois virtues in the public sphere. How ideology gets produced or by whom and the means by which it gets transmitted are not, it seems, necessary questions.[138] For instance, the fact that many of the texts Solkin cites were produced in *Scotland*, not England, receives no comment and Solkin has not observed that the general tenor of Scottish social thought was not apologetic for commercial societies, but frequently sceptical of them despite the perceived benefits they brought. In this vision a single ideology operates like a Foucauldian discourse with no outside so that the profound religious differences of the period with all their class concomitants – which certainly bear on questions of education and taste – pass unremarked.[139] The actual contingencies and contradictions of ideological production and the complex mediations that link artworks and ideologies are also largely unaddressed. While Solkin certainly gave a holistic account that references both social division and political concerns and one can only applaud his ambition, his adaptation of Pocock's theory of civic humanism has arguably contributed to de-Marxify the social history of eighteenth-century British art. Given Pocock's professed opposition to Marxist interpretations of the period this is only consistent.[140]

---

136   Solkin 1993, p. 276.

137   'The Patricians and the Plebs', in Thompson 1991, pp. 16–96. For dissentient voices among the middling sort before 1760, see Rogers 1984; Rogers 1989; and Brewer 1980. For a very different conception of the public sphere in this period, see Eley 1981, pp. 431–2, 434.

138   An exception is Solkin's useful discussion of the beginnings of art criticism – Solkin 1993, pp. 247–59.

139   For instance, what is one to make of the following assertion: 'By the mid-eighteenth century it was widely agreed that the study of art could play a role in the socialization process' (Solkin 1993, p. 220)? How far down the social scale did this Whiggish proposition apply? Did it extend equally to non-jurors, recusants, to both high church and low church, and to the wide array of dissenting sects? After all, the last-named tended to prefer 'useful knowledge' as an educational principle over the classical curriculum of Church of England schools.

140   Obviously these sketchy comments are not intended as comprehensive appraisal of *Paint-*

In a useful literature review, Douglas Fordham has argued that the hegemony of the civic humanism/commercial humanism model has been challenged or qualified by three other developments, namely growing bodies of scholarship that address questions of the spatial dimension of cultural practices, of gender, and of imperialism.[141] One could supplement this by noting both the absence of work on the period that makes explicit reference to Marxist historical categories and the diffusion of the Visual Culture paradigm in this as in other areas of art history – that is of scholarship that treats the category art and province of aesthetics as simply one dimension of oppressive power relations and reduces questions of artistic value to matters of sociology or identity. Thus whatever contribution this large mass of scholarship makes to cultural history – and in some instances it is a very large one – in important respects it is at odds with the tradition of Western Marxism and the thought of Marx himself, for whom both art and the aesthetic were essential constituents of the history and possible destiny of the human species.

Fordham has noted that if in the early 1990s the fiercest confrontations in British art scholarship concerned the interpretation of eighteenth-century art and culture, since then much of the most innovative work has been done in the nineteenth- and twentieth-century fields. By this he does not mean all aspects of the art of those centuries, but that rather nebulous category Victorian Art and British modernism.[142] One area notably marginal to the spurt of scholarly production over the last twenty years has been the moment of Romanticism, something really rather extraordinary given that Romantic landscape painting is one of the few aspects of British visual art that enjoys a secure status in the larger scheme of Western artistic culture. This is not to say that there has not been the usual string of exhibition catalogues and cata-

---

ing for Money, which merits far more extended consideration than I can offer here. My complaint is not that an embourgeoisement of culture of the kind Solkin maps did not take place, it is that it did not take place on the terms he proposes or by such a seamlessly smooth process.

141 Fordham 2008. As Fordham acknowledges, for developments up to 1994 his review is heavily indebted to Michael Kitson's fine historiographical essay – Kitson 1994. In a later article (Fordham 2012), he argues that the 1980s social history of British art was generally negligent of issues of nation state and politics, and proposes that a 'political turn' has taken place since 2001, particularly evident in important new scholarship on British art's role in providing ideological bolster to imperialism. Unfortunately, he has nothing to say on the theories of the state and imperialism that underpin this work.

142 Fordham 2008, p. 907.

logue raisonnés, many of them very useful in their way. But there has been no significant development of the conceptual paradigm for understanding the art of the period circa 1790–1830 comparable to that Barrell and Solkin's work brought about for the eighteenth century. This is perhaps partly because Romanticism is a style category as well as a period category,[143] and the large period style categories are no longer the object of critique and refinement in art history in the way they were in the past. (Solkin's eighteenth century is not defined in period style terms, to which he seems relatively indifferent). But in actuality this is a loss as much as a gain, since Romanticism is a political term as well as a category of cultural history – something literary historians seem to understand rather better than art historians. In this regard, the work of Michael Löwy and Robert Sayre on the concept of romantic anti-capitalism has been especially fruitful in foregrounding the critical dimension of romanticism and its continuing contribution to the Marxist tradition.[144]

This brings me back to the raison d'être of the current volume. Since I began thinking about late eighteenth- and early nineteenth-century British art more than forty years ago it has struck me as extraordinary that all those phenomena that made the period such an epochal phase in British economic, social, political, and intellectual history and brought it close to a second revolutionary change of regime seemed of so little interest to art historians.[145] The work of Barrell, Bermingham, and Rosenthal, which showed that landscape painting of ordinary British scenes was not to be understood in separation from the brute realities of enclosure and the agricultural riots of 1816, 1822, and 1830, did something to redress the situation and felt like a rending of that veil of noisesome mythology of gracious Georgian country life to which so many historians and art historians have paid tribute. But this only partially addressed the problem, because the representation of agricultural practices and the rural poor was considered for the most part as a specific question of iconography and its ideological concomitants; problems in the depiction of rural labour and exploitation did not lead to considerations of the larger shifts in the field of art

---

143   It is famously the case that there was no single romantic style – rather there were many, a phenomenon that is related to the diversity of romanticism itself and its relationship with emergent nationalisms. For a discussion of this issue, see Hemingway and Wallach 2015, pp. 8–9, 13.

144   Löwy and Sayre 2001.

145   Richard Johnson has written, I think correctly, of 'a prolonged crisis in hegemony' in the period between the 1790s and 1840s – Johnson 1976, p. 50. For perhaps the most acute revolutionary moment, see Chase 2013.

production and the relationship of class forces as a whole. It was something of that kind that I attempted in my 1992 book and in the essays collected here.

The focus on enclosure and its consequences also led to a neglect of Turner, far and away the greatest landscape painter of the period, but one for whom Georgic themes were only one small aspect of a vast and various output. Although empirical studies of Turner flourished in the 1980s, they operated almost as a discrete specialism in the field and were very little touched by the new social history of landscape painting.[146]

A fundamental proviso of my work has been that Britain experienced a successful bourgeois revolution in the seventeenth century, even though it was one whose goals were conceptualised in terms of religious rather than Enlightenment ideology; but the establishment and maintenance of bourgeois hegemony none the less required a prolonged process of struggle and adaptation.[147] With regard to the seminal 1960s debate over British exceptionalism that pitted Perry Anderson and Tom Nairn against E.P. Thompson, I am most persuaded by Thompson's case – although things can certainly be learnt from both sides.[148] In the face of Anderson's judgment that the English bourgeoisie was the victim of its priority and suffered from a revolution that was incomplete, which left it 'supine', and consistently subordinate to an aristocratic political establishment, Thompson's riposte that the eighteenth-century gentry were themselves 'a superbly successful and self-confident capitalist class', an agrarian bourgeoisie with a partly urban lifestyle, seems apposite.[149] Neither, *pace* Nairn, is it the case that Britain had only a 'limited, parochial Enlightenment', constrained by a national tradition of 'blind empiricism' stemming from Bacon and Locke.[150] As Thompson pointed out, the British contribution to the Scientific Revolution and Smithian political economy can hardly be dismissed as merely provincial intellectual achievements.[151]

---

146 The journal *Turner Studies* (1980–91) published much important work but is symptomatic of this inward-looking character. The year before it folded it printed two important statements of self-reflection in the shape of Parker 1990 and Venning 1990 (1).

147 For a monumental defence of the validity of bourgeois revolution as a concept, see Davidson 2012.

148 For a bibliography of the debate, see Anderson 1992, p. 121, n. 1, which also reprints the key texts 'Origins of the Present Crisis' (1964) and 'Components of the National Culture' (1968), pp. 15–47 and 48–104.

149 Anderson 1992, p. 35; Thompson 1978, p. 43.

150 Tom Nairn, 'The English Working Class', in Blackburn (ed.) 1972, pp. 190, 196, 200. Cf. Anderson 1992, p. 32.

151 Thompson 1978, pp. 60, 62–3.

We still await a Thompsonian history of the making of the English middle class.[152] But that subordination was maintained in the eighteenth-century through relations of clientage and deference that were sustained partly through an ideology of paternalism is clear.[153] Despite the palpable tensions we can identify retrospectively as differences between class cultures, the 'middling sort' did not begin to acquire a corporate class identity until the 1760s: from that point on tensions between the industrial and professional middle class and those elements from the ruling oligarchy that effectively managed the state (in Thompson's words that 'secondary complex of predatory interests' known colloquially as 'Old Corruption') increased until, with the additional stimulus of the Revolution in France and the reactionary turn of the oligarchy at home, in the 1790s there was an ideological breach with paternalism and a new kind of class politics emerged.[154] For Thompson, while the agricultural and industrial capitalists were distinct classes,[155] it was not they who did battle in the years leading up to the 1832 Parliamentary Reform Act. Those who campaigned for reform were not opposed to aristocracy as such for the most part, and they included a substantial number of the gentry, a portion of whom had been supporters of reform since the 1770s. The bill was passed by a parliament in which one faction of the gentry and great magnates was ranged against the other. For Thompson, the result may not have given manufacturing capital much in the way of direct representation, but the result was functional enough for its interests.[156] Yet as Anderson has pointed out, the distribution of the franchise not only favoured county and small borough seats, it limited 'potential urban representation below the threshold at which an autonomous bourgeois party, with a popular following, could enter the parliamentary arena on its own terms'.[157] Given the realities of the two-party system, middle-class reformers were forced to join one of the parties of landowners, in reality usually the Whigs. On the other hand, the Reform Act finally ended any hope of political alliance between the liberal bourgeoisie and the emergent working-class movement.

---

152   Geoff Eley has drawn attention to the limitations of Thompson's account of the eighteenth century in this respect. See Eley 1981, pp. 435–6; Eley 1990, pp. 18–19. Boyd Hilton's illuminating analysis suggests something of what such a 'making' might be like. See Hilton 2006, Part 3.

153   For a particularly brilliant treatment of this theme, see Hay and Rogers 1997.

154   Thompson 1991, pp. 42, 86. For Thompson on 'Old Corruption', see Thompson 1991, pp. 29–30 and Thompson 1978, pp. 48–50.

155   Thompson 1978, p. 45.

156   Thompson 1978, p. 51.

157   Anderson 1992, p. 145.

These remarks are partly intended to set the scene for Chapter Three and Four. In the first of these I show that the struggle to articulate a middle-class perspective on the arts was a significant component in art criticism and pamphlet writing in the years leading up to the Reform Act and its aftermath. The limitations on bourgeois radicalism that Anderson identifies – and the marginalisation of Radicals in Parliament – are one of my themes here. In Chapter Four I show how critics with Benthamite sympathies, in their struggles to evaluate the popular romanticism of the 1820s, revealed some of the tensions at the heart of Enlightenment rationalism when faced with the play of imagination and desire that was one of the tendencies in art that commercial societies encouraged. Benthamism in the broad sense in which the term is used here reveals a rather more interesting and nuanced perspective on the arts than that usually associated with the philosopher's name.

The other reason for the brief historical sketch above is that I think the larger historical trends of the period are directly germane to the phenomenon of naturalism in landscape and genre painting. By naturalism I mean a style concept that embraces types of painting and print-making that were understood as accurate representations of real places in their contemporary appearance, as if seen at particular times of day, in specific seasonal moments and specific atmospheric conditions. It is a trend directly associated with that dramatic shift to more actualised depictions of rural labour Barrell et. al. did so much to bring to light. The production of such images was tied to a new concern with sketching in oil or water-colour on the spot and in some cases painting finished work outdoors, procedures that contributed to recognisable innovations in technique and colour. As I have written elsewhere, it seems that in early nineteenth-century Britain 'landscape painters became increasingly restive with academic categorisation of their genre and increasingly interested in adapting the topographical mode and Dutch models as a vehicle for serious expression. Linked with this was a more critical attitude to earlier pictorial conventions, and a commitment to improvisation and experiment *sur le motif*, which may have some connection with the authority of the natural sciences'.[158] This new approach was fundamentally at odds with the restrictive landscape aesthetic of the eighteenth-century picturesque and established norms of taste. Evidence for this claim lies primarily in a body of works from between roughly 1805 and 1825 by Constable, Crome, and Turner, as well as a

---

158   Hemingway 1992, p. 23. This quotation is excerpted from a far longer definition of naturalism, pp. 15–28. I should also acknowledge the work of Michael Kitson and John Gage in recognising and defining this phenomenon. See Kitson 1957; Gage 1969.

host of artists of lesser reputation such as David Cox, Peter De Wint, Harriot Gouldsmith,[159] George Robert Lewis, John Linnell, William Mulready, and Cornelius Varley. (Although it was also supported by some voices in the periodical press.) Not all works by these artists from the time frame belong to the category of naturalism and one of the key questions is why this style of landscape painting came to an end; the answer likely being that there was not enough of a market to sustain it for reasons I have written about elsewhere.[160]

What I now want to suggest – something that was not clear to me before – is that this new style had definite class concomitants that made it something like 'une idéologie imagée' in Hadjinicolaou's sense. I say this because I think it is inconceivable that a practice that manifested such indifference towards academic and connoisseurial norms of style and disdained gentry norms of picturesque viewing and depiction would have been possible without the collapse of deference – that 'desire for independence from the client economy' – which accompanied the upheavals of the 1790s.[161] I am well aware that this is a cause and effect relationship that is not open to disproof; in any case it is a singular event and I am not suggesting any law can be derived from it. It is essentially an intuition of the relationship between part and whole.[162] That is, I think a larger class viewpoint or ideology penetrated not only day-to-day social relations and political discourse but also extended to the arts. This embracing ideology of middle class subjectivity – which is common to both enlightenment and romanticism – could encompass artists as politically antagonistic as John Constable and John Linnell. However, that its tendency was in some respects egalitarian I have tried to demonstrate in the chapters on John Crome. I am not suggesting that the ideology of naturalism was self-consciously demotic, although it could be, as the following passage from one of its most extreme exponents illustrates: 'The result to which all these observations [concerning the depiction of natural light in paintings] tend, and which I am desirous to express plainly and openly, is this: That the Arts, in order to prosper, must once more address themselves, not to the learned antiquary, not to the curious amateur, nor to the technical admiration of mere professors, but to the general sense, to the feelings and understanding of THE COMMON PEOPLE'.[163] What I

---

159   Kathryn Moore Heleniak has performed a valuable work of recovery on this artist, see Heleniak 2005.

160   Hemingway 1992, pp. 292–8.

161   Thompson 1991, pp. 32–3, 95–6. The quotation is from Brewer 1980, p. 360.

162   For the theoretical background to this position, see Hemingway and Wallach 2015, pp. 3–6.

163   Richter 1817, p. 57. For Richter, see Hemingway 1992, pp. 24–6, 102–3, 305n55, n57; and Solkin 2008, pp. 115–19.

am suggesting is that the form of the works themselves, wittingly or unwittingly spoke of such aspirations. I think that is partly why Constable abandoned naturalism for a more old-masterish style in the early 1820s.

I return to the ideological business of the artwork. The genres and iconographical motifs from which the artist must choose to produce an intelligible work – selected either by a patron or in hopes of finding a purchaser in the marketplace – are already ideologically saturated. The same applies to the forms and techniques artists deploy to realise their object. In the differences between the historically acquired meanings that attach to these different semantic systems gaps between and contradictions within diverse ideologies can become apparent. Oftentimes the artistic agent through patronage pressure or lack of understanding performs in ways that are repetitive and unimaginative, producing works that may be skilled but prompt no unsettling of conventional patterns and expectations or mark only minor and insignificant deviations from established norms. The bulk of artistic production is of this type. But artists of greater ambition and intelligence will undertake the process of matching the ideological content with style and technique in ways that unsettle normal expectations and may give the sensibilities of the spectator a kind of cognitive jolt. These novelties sometimes come about because of the ideological needs of patron groups at odds with the dominant value system. In modern societies the field of patronage is itself socially diverse and calls on artists to choose between making works that fulfil a variety of social needs. At other times novelties occur because of the ways artists adapt, consciously or unconsciously, to social and political changes. Despite the pressure of livelihood, there is no necessary synchrony between art production and demand. With the rise of the market economy for art in the early modern period artists become more entrepreneurs in ideas and forms; this is part of the romantic ethos. Sometimes artists fail to produce art that corresponds with the ideological needs of patrons through incompetence or misunderstandings of the artistic materials with which they work. In any case, the relationship between aesthetic novelties and established norms of taste is complexly mediated.

Early nineteenth-century naturalistic landscape painting came about, we may assume, because of a burgeoning market for topography across a whole range of painting, drawing, and print media. As a result, artists were stimulated to make paintings of everyday scenes incorporating recognisable motifs of contemporary social life. Novel departures in iconography and style resulted in part out of attempts to attract patronage, in part because of artist's ambitions to give paintings of ordinary scenery an aesthetic status above the lowly rank conventional academic theory accorded them. Both topographical requirements and the painting of modern experience pushed artists to the practices of drawing, painting and even etching on the spot. But the reason this led to formal and iconographic innovations was not straightforward. We cannot explain it merely through a Gombrichian process of making and matching, although this surely played a role.[164] Sensory experience does not come in some raw unmediated form to which we can have access through suspension of the will and that we compare with pictorial conventions. Rather, it seems, there was a conscious attempt to change form and style, to rework established conventions, because they could not contain the new understandings of the age. This is most obviously the case in relation to the depiction of atmospheric observations.[165] But it was a striving for change that extended across natural and social phenomena. As the watercolour painter Henry Richter, from whom I quoted earlier, put it in an imaginary dialogue of 1817, the 'recent discovery' of 'daylight in the art of painting' 'may open the eyes of those who exert themselves to promote the Arts, to the necessity of a bold and direct appeal to Nature itself, if anything really great is to be effected. It is possible, that when the IN-DOOR gloom of our OLD PICTURES comes to be explained, the world will begin to commiserate the Arts under their long and dark imprisonment, and set free the genius of the age from the restraints of AFFECTATION and PREJUDICE; these two ponderous bars, which the Connoisseurs, the turnkeys of the dungeon, will, it is to be hoped, some day or other quietly suffer to be removed'.[166] An analogy between artistic innovation and political liberation is clearly implicit here. The formal and iconographic novelties of naturalism did not reveal the world as it was but they shook up the established codes of picture-making in ways that hinted at contradictions and fissures in contemporary ideologies of rural life. Or, at least, so I will argue in Part Two of this book.

One final note. It is necessary to say something of the regional focus of some of the essays in Part Two. As I show in Chapter Five, although the notion that the efflorescence of landscape painting in early nineteenth-century Norwich was caused by specific characteristics of the region's geography or its proximity to Holland is hardly credible, the fact remains that the city had the largest and most cohesive body of landscape painters of any British provincial city in the period. I suspect the reasons for this were partly that two singular talents (John Crome and John Sell Cotman) were born and largely made their careers there,

---

164   Gombrich 1972, pp. 157–61 and *passim*. For the later refinement of the theory, see 'Image and Code: Scope and Limits of Conventionalism in Pictorial Representation', in Gombrich 1982, pp. 278–97.

165   See Morris (ed.) 2000.

166   Richter 1817, p. 10.

and that the city had a particularly vital intellectual and cultural life. But I realise this formulation brings me perilously close to circularity and I do not find it
particularly fruitful to speculate on this question. In fact, I began work on this
project in the 1970s at a time when new scholarship by historians such as Trevor Fawcett and Francis Greenacre was demonstrating that artistic production
outside London was a far more complex and productive field than had hitherto
been supposed.[167] Focus on the conditions of display and patronage in the metropolis remain of central importance – and a quite disproportionate number
of artists lived there relative to the general artistic population[168] – but my own
work on Norwich suggests to me that micro histories of provincial artists sometimes provide insights into class interactions with patrons and the significance
of iconography that are more intimate than those we trace from the metropolitan exhibition reviews and related sources. Moreover, William Vaughan has
argued persuasively that the Romantic artist based in the provinces could in
some instances find a latitude for personal expression that would have been
denied him if his career was wholly circumscribed by residence in London.[169]
I believe this to be true of John Crome, to whom I give so much attention in
Chapters Seven and Eight.

---

167   See especially Fawcett 1973 and Greenacre 1973.
168   Vaughan 2015, pp. 37–8.
169   Vaughan 2015, pp. 42–7.

Aesthetics and Ideology

The Science of Taste in the Eighteenth Century: Philosophical Criticism and the Scottish Historical School

Philosophical Criticism and the Beginnings of Aesthetics

Prior to the eighteenth century most art writings were treatises on the individual arts that primarily concerned technical precepts and gave little address to philosophical issues. Paul Kristeller voiced a commonly accepted view in a famous essay of 1951 when he described the German philosopher Alexander Gottlieb Baumgarten as the 'founder of aesthetics', in that he was the first thinker to conceive 'a general theory of the arts as a separate philosophical discipline with a distinctive and well-defined place in the system of philosophy'.[1] Baumgarten coined the neologism 'aesthetics', but for Kristeller, Kant was the first major thinker to make aesthetics into an integral part of his overall philosophical system.

Yet if it was German thinkers who made definition of the aesthetic an integral concern of philosophy, consideration of the arts within a philosophical framework was a well-established species of inquiry in France and Britain in this period. The status of eighteenth-century British aestheticians has risen considerably since Croce dismissed them all as 'scribblers on Aesthetic or rather on things in general which sometimes accidentally include aesthetic facts';[2] in particular, since the 1930s American historians of philosophy and literary criticism have produced an extensive literature on what was known in the eighteenth century as 'philosophical criticism'.[3] Perhaps the largest claims for this discourse were made by Jerome Stolnitz in a series of articles that set out to contest the judgment of the main English language histories of aesthetics that British thinkers had only provided raw materials for Baumgarten and Kant, arguing that 'the British were the first to envision the possibility of a philosophical discipline, embracing the study of all of the arts, one which

---

1 Kristeller 1965, p. 215.
2 Croce 1978, p. 258. Cf. p. 261.
3 Major studies include: Monk 1960; McKenzie 1949; Hipple 1957; and Kallich 1970. The most comprehensive account of aesthetics and art theory in Britain is Dobai 1974–7.

would be, moreover, autonomous, because its subject-matter is not explicable by any one of the other disciplines'.[4]

According to Stolnitz, in earlier periods the values of art were always seen as 'iconic or otherwise cognitive, or moral, or social, with nothing left over that art can call its own'. The beginnings of modern aesthetics are marked by the appearance of the concept of aesthetic disinterestedness, because it gives works of art a value independent of any moral or intellectual values they embody, and implies that they should be evaluated in terms of their structure and intrinsic significance, on which alone their aesthetic stature depends. Stolnitz tracked the origins of the concept to debates over ethics and religion in the late seventeenth and early eighteenth centuries, and located its beginnings in the writings of Shaftesbury. The evolution of the concept could be traced through texts by Addison, Hutcheson, Hume, Gerard, and Burke, but amongst British eighteenth-century writers it received its most sophisticated articulation in Archibald Alison's *Essays on Taste* (1790).[5] It should be noted that Stolnitz's argument bypasses the larger meaning that aesthetics had for Baumgarten and Kant as a science of the senses and restricts it to the philosophy of the fine arts.

Whether or not Shaftesbury was the discoverer of aesthetic disinterestedness – and it is open to question whether he distinguished the moral from the aesthetic as firmly as Stolnitz claimed – it is at least clear that subsequent British thinkers conceived of a distinct aesthetic mode of experience, defined by a particular exercise of the imagination denominated as taste. By the early nineteenth century philosophical criticism was a century-long tradition of theorising on the arts that encompassed writers such as Lord Kames and Richard Payne Knight in addition to those already mentioned. It was a discourse that provided the common currency of literary criticism, and also offered principles of interpretation that could be applied to the visual arts, as they were in debates around the Picturesque in the 1790s. Moreover, it was still a vital tradition, which was continued by Francis Jeffrey (the influential editor of the *Edinburgh Review*), Dugald Stewart, and others. Jeffrey's article on 'Beauty' for the Supplement to the *Encyclopaedia Britannica* of 1824 is largely a confident review of earlier theories, which shows how authoritative this discourse had become: that for sections of the intelligentsia and their readership it had achieved the status of a science, a status that several of its main exponents had claimed

---

4   Stolnitz 1961 (1), pp. 131–2. The main earlier histories of aesthetics he had in mind were those of Bernard Bosanquet (1892) and Katherine Gilbert and Helmut Kuhn (1956).

5   An argument developed in Stolnitz 1961 (2); Stolnitz 1963 (1); Stolnitz 1978.

for it. For Romantic writers such as Coleridge, Hazlitt, and Wordsworth, philosophical criticism represented the current orthodoxy: to some extent they were critical of it, but it also left a profound influence on their conceptions.[6]

Kristeller argued that the 'familiar system of the five fine arts' was not only a concept that does not appear until the eighteenth century, but also that it 'reflects' the social and cultural conditions of that period.[7] The social factor that produced this new system was the growth of the art public, and the increasing range of concerts, operatic and theatrical performances, and art exhibitions that accompanied it. Together, these phenomena stimulated new types of comparative writing on the arts. As is well known, the growth of the urban bourgeoisie and the increasing wealth of landed society in eighteenth-century Britain contributed to the development of entertainment facilities in urban centres through which these groups could occupy their leisure time and engage in the various social rituals by which they partly defined their identities. J.H. Plumb has emphasised the huge differences between the cultural climate of late seventeenth-century Britain, in which there were 'no newspapers, no public libraries, no theatres outside London, no concerts anywhere, no picture galleries of any kind, no museums, almost no botanical gardens, and no organized sports', and the vastly changed situation one hundred years later, by which time leisure and culture had become profitable fields for capital investment. In this context there is no need to do more than simply note the expansion of the reading public, the growth of the press, and the burgeoning of new types of literature including newspapers, periodicals, and novels; the increasing popularity of public concerts, operas, musical societies, and provincial festivals, and the growth of art exhibitions in both number and content.

For Kristeller, the expansion of the art public was particularly significant because 'amateurs' were largely responsible for the early development aesthetics. Those who were unconcerned with the practicalities of producing art were more likely to see affinities between the arts, and aesthetics have usually been written from the spectator's point of view: 'The basic questions and conceptions underlying modern aesthetics seem to have originated quite apart from the traditions of systematic philosophy or from the writings of important original authors. They had their inconspicuous beginnings in secondary authors, now almost forgotten though influential in their own time, and perhaps in the discussions and conversations of educated laymen reflected in their writings'.[8]

---

6   Abrams 1953, Chapter 3, Part III; Shearer 1937.
7   Kristeller 1965, p. 226.
8   Kristeller 1965, pp. 225–6.

Only after notions developed in these 'inconspicuous beginnings' had been refined by almost a century of 'informal and non-philosophical growth' were they absorbed into a programme of systematic philosophy by Kant.

It is incorrect to suggest that eighteenth-century empiricist aesthetics lacked originality even if most of its authors, Hume and Smith excepted, were 'secondary'. And despite the qualitative advance represented by Kant's *Critique of Judgment* (1790), it is simply untrue that earlier eighteenth-century writings on taste developed 'quite apart from the traditions of systematic philosophy'. Notable contributions to philosophical criticism were produced by 'amateurs' such as Burke, Kames, and Payne Knight – that is to say by individuals from outside the academy – but university professors such as Hutcheson, Smith, Gerard, and Reid also played a key role in the discourse's development and institutionalisation. There is nothing to distinguish the contributions of holders of university chairs from those of the more talented amateurs in terms of theoretical cogency. Like other types of philosophising, philosophical criticism was not produced for a specialist academic audience, it was directed at 'gentlemen' in general and was geared to their norms of education and experience. It was widely reviewed in the periodical press, and the more successful treatises went through several editions.

But Kristeller was percipient in recognising that the nascent aesthetics was written from the point of view of the audience for art works, rather than from that of their makers. Textual evidence can be found in many texts of philosophical criticism which show that its authors were perfectly well aware of the novelty of their project, and of the new kind of authority they were conferring on the critic. Thus Addison, whose essays 'On the Pleasures of the Imagination' (published in *The Spectator* in 1712) have been claimed as the first modern aesthetic treatise,[9] wrote in a slightly earlier paper: 'It is likewise necessary for a Man who would form to himself a finished Taste of good Writing, to be well versed in the Works of the best Cricks both Ancient and Modern. I must confess that I could wish there were Authors of this Kind, who beside the Mechanical Rules which a Man of very little Taste may discourse upon, would enter into the very Spirit and Soul of fine Writing, and show us the several Sources of that Pleasure which rises in the Mind upon the Perusal of a noble Work'.[10] This conception of explaining the experience of aesthetic pleasure in terms of principles discovered by the 'science' of human nature, defines the central project of philosophical criticism. It was conceived as an inquiry that would induce

---

9   Tuveson 1960, pp. 92, 117; Kallich 1970, p. 45.

10   Addison and Steele 1945, vol. 3, p. 272.

general principles from observed regularities in human behaviour, and subject received authorities to critical scrutiny on that basis.

The idea that they were putting the analysis of the arts on a scientific footing led many writers to assert the value of criticism, and to claim in some cases that critics could produce more balanced and judicious judgements than artists themselves. In his 'Soliloquy: or Advice to an Author' (1710), Shaftesbury claimed that the critic too was a species of genius, 'for to all Musick there must be an Ear proportionable'.[11] Fortified with the new philosophy of the mind that had been developed in conjunction with seventeenth-century paradigm shifts in the natural sciences, later theorists of taste attended to the systematisation of the arts with a zeal for extending the progress of knowledge into new fields. Alexander Gerard described the aim of his *Essay on Taste* (1759) as 'to shew that principles of science form the most accurate standard of excellence in the fine arts', and claimed that such 'philosophical enquiries' were not mere 'amusements of the idle' but had 'real and extensive utility', since 'they are both a stimulus to genius, and a corrective to taste'. Further, 'the principles established by means of them, admit as indubitable certainty, and as great precision, as those of any science'.[12]

The logic of this project is revealed in Alison's *Essays on Taste*, in which the author lamented the cyclical decline of the arts in earlier cultures, and blamed it partly on the lack of philosophy among artists.[13] Their class allegiances and the relative dignity of their own social status, predisposed such thinkers to assume the authority to legislate on the arts. They represented a group that saw itself as the 'natural' leaders of society in cultural as well as political matters and were not predisposed to acknowledge the autonomy that artists increasingly claimed for themselves.[14]

While the education of the eighteenth-century gentleman (in any of his various definitions) might encourage a high level of literary culture, it was unlikely to furnish much knowledge of the plastic arts, except for those who undertook the Grand Tour. It is thus hardly surprising that critics gave little attention to painting until the Picturesque controversy of the 1790s. The principles of painting for gentlemen were set out in a series of treatises, written sometimes by artists and sometimes by amateurs, but uniform in deriving their materials from academic theory and the well-known histories of the art. None of these treatises were aesthetics in the sense we have been using the term; that is, they

---

11   Cooper 1714, vol. 1, pp. 234–40, 264.

12   Gerard 1963, p. 274.

13   Alison 1815, vol. 2, pp. 116–17. Cf. Home 1785, vol. 1, p. 358.

14   On which see 'The Romantic Artist', in Williams 1961, Chapter 2.

were not general theories of the arts. None the less, they have a relevance to the present discussion in that generally they state plainly that they were directed at gentlemen, and frequently assert the authority of the informed amateur over artists in judgements of taste. Count Algarotti's *Essay on Painting* (1764) was typical in this respect since while it addressed artists, it urged them to submit their works to public judgement, as 'there are no better judges of his art than men of true taste and the public'.[15] If philosophical criticism claimed to speak from a position that licensed it to legislate on artistic practice, artists were quick to resent this assumption, which seemed contrary to their interests. As I show in the essay 'Academic Theory versus Association Aesthetics', in the early nineteenth century a number of painters produced texts that expressly contradicted the value of statements on the arts by non-professional persons.

Philosophical criticism has been well charted by historians of philosophy and literature, and in recent years it has been used to support historical arguments around painting and art theory of the eighteenth and early nineteenth centuries. However, there has been no attempt to give a systematic account of the distinctive features of philosophical criticism as a mode of discourse, and it seems widely assumed that it was equivalent to other forms of writings about the arts, and particularly to academic theory. By contrast, I make a demarcation between academic theory and philosophical criticism not only in terms of their methodologies and objects of inquiry, but also in terms of the subject positions they assume in their readerships and the interests they represent.[16] Like any discourse considered as an ideology, philosophical criticism needs to be analysed in terms of the body of intellectual materials from which it was made up, and also situated in relation to the context of its production and the interests which it served.

The epistemology and method of philosophical criticism have been addressed comprehensively by others and I shall deal with them summarily here. My main concern is rather with the context of its production. While it has been noted on occasion that most original thinking on the arts in eighteenth-century Britain was done in Scotland, the connection between this phenomenon and the Scottish Enlightenment has received scant attention.[17] Yet for all the major Scottish thinkers, their system of criticism was integrated with a lar-

---

15   Algarotti 1764, p. 143.

16   Hipple 1957 precisely ignores this distinction. It is respected in the chapter organisation of Dobai 1974–7. I developed this point at length in my review of John Barrell 1986 – see Hemingway 1987.

17   This point is at least implicit in Dobai's chapter 'Die ästhetischen Theorien der schottischen Denker', in Dobai 1974–7, vol. 2, Pt. 1, Sect. 3.

ger social theory that comprised both a natural history of the human mind and a natural history of society, the two being seen as interconnected. Theorists of the arts who did not write on other matters rested their projects on general propositions about the mind and society established in the Scottish context. It is the connections between philosophical criticism and the larger project of Scottish social thought that I sketch in the main body of what follows. To begin with, however, I explain the discourse's epistemological presuppositions and set it in relation to other modes of philosophical inquiry current in the period.

Epistemological Foundations of Philosophical Criticism

A contemporary review of Alison's *Essays on Taste* observed that 'all our knowledge is derived by experience; and as it has been from the patient method of experiment and observation that the greatest discoveries in physical science have been made, it is reasonable to suppose that the same method of research will be equally successful in the philosophy of the human mind'.[18] Such statements about the 'science' of criticism were made by other eighteenth-century commentators and are a logical corollary of the model of philosophy dominant in the period, that is to say, of the philosophy that had emerged in the previous century which assumed that epistemology was the basis of inquiry, and that this would be established psychologically through the mind's reflection on its own operations according to the principles of observation and experiment that 'natural philosophers' applied in the physical sciences.[19] The single most influential text of this new philosophy was John Locke's *Essay Concerning Human Understanding* (1690) and in the early eighteenth century it provided the model of the mind at the basis of new thinking about the arts.

The epistemology of Locke's *Essay* was partly a response to the practices of seventeenth-century science, although other contemporary developments also determined its arguments. The *Essay* met an ideological need for a model of the mind that would bring intellectual processes into nature, without making them wholly material phenomena as Hobbes's system had done. Despite the heterodoxy of some of Locke's opinions, the success of the work was enormous, partly because its system was linked with that of Newtonian science, and like that discourse, it was assimilated into the dominant orthodoxy of Anglican

---

18   *Monthly Review*, new series, 3 (1790), p. 361.

19   For a key statement of this project, see 'Introduction' in Hume 1978, pp. xiii–xix. On the reorientation of philosophy in the seventeenth century, see Rorty 1980, Chapters 1 and 3.

natural theology.[20] Central to Locke's *Essay* was the rejection of the doctrine of innate ideas. Instead, Locke argued that 'the materials of all our knowledge' are 'simple ideas', which are derived from either sense impressions or the reflection of the mind on its own operations. The mind is wholly passive in its reception of 'simple ideas', but by the activity of the understanding, it is able to produce 'complex ideas' from these basic materials.[21] Thus a fundamental premise of Locke's epistemology is that human beings know reality only through sense impressions and the self-reflection of the mind; both the essence of things and their final causes are unknowable. While Locke was not a sceptic, and the *Essay* presupposes a philosophical realism, he defines truth solely in terms of the 'right joining or separating of signs', signs being 'ideas or words'.[22] The locus of reality is thus shifted to the perceiving mind with important implications for aesthetics.[23]

Locke himself produced no writings on the arts and his influence in the field of aesthetics is somewhat paradoxical, for his *Essay* seems to devalue the experiences that fall in its domain. Although Locke recognised the irrational aspects of the mind and tried to account for them in the chapter 'Of the association of ideas' added to the fourth edition of the *Essay* (1700), he made understanding, which he limited to cognition and opinion, the sole active principle in thought. However, while his 'understanding' is an efficient instrument for the production of knowledge from sensory experience, Locke does not account for any immediate apprehensions of value. There are no innate principles of morality, and we come to the understanding of moral law by the 'light of nature, i.e. without the help of positive revelation'. The mind has no contact with higher truths except through the senses and Locke makes even the comprehension of God essentially rational.

While Locke claimed humanity had the power to discover good and evil through the senses he left it morally neutral. Since our knowledge in such matters derives from experience, which might differ in many respects from individual to individual, it was hardly surprising that history displayed such a variety of moral attitudes among different peoples at different times. Indeed, this variety was part of Locke's argument, for conscience can hardly be a proof of innate principles if 'some men, with the same bent of conscience, prosecute

---

20   In relation to these points, see Osler 1970; Yolton 1956; and Yolton 1970.

21   Locke 1829, Book 4; Chapter 1: 1.

22   Locke 1829, Book. 4; Chapter 5: 2.

23   For Locke's thought generally I draw on Aaron 1955. On its implications for aesthetics, see: Tuveson 1960 and Stolnitz 1963 (2).

what others avoid'.[24] Thus Shaftesbury was led to complain that Locke had thrown all 'order and virtue' out of the world, and made the idea of them 'unnatural'. In his *Inquiry Concerning Virtue*, Shaftesbury accounted for moral judgments by postulating an 'inner sense' that responded to the mind's self-reflection.[25] Shaftesbury's follower, Francis Hutcheson, subsequently described this as a 'moral sense', and also postulated a separate 'internal sense', to account for 'our power of perceiving the beauty of regularity, order, harmony'.[26] Thus the view of the understanding presented in Locke's *Essay* was so inimical to aesthetic judgment that some thinkers felt obliged to postulate an independent faculty to account for it. This certainly contributed to the emergence of a view of the aesthetic as a distinct form of knowledge.[27]

Locke's new science of the mind implied a completely new approach to the theory of the arts, which should logically be analysed in relation to their psychological effects. Just as the new science took a critical attitude to ancient authorities and rejected scholastic logic, so too did Locke's inquiry into mental processes; the implication for writers on the arts was that they should discover their principles from the dispassionate observation of mental phenomena, rather than by appealing to the rules and practices of the ancients. This change is signalled by Addison, who observed that 'Musick, Architecture and Painting, as well as Poetry and Oratory, are to deduce their Laws and Rules from the general Sense and Taste of Mankind, and not from the Principles of those Arts themselves; or in other words, the Taste is not to conform to the Art, but the Art to the Taste'.[28] Generally speaking, philosophical criticism took its mode of inquiry from Locke and Hume; that is, experience was dissected into its basic elements, which were then pieced together into complex wholes. Although most thinkers made some reference to final causes, they were extraneous to the operation of the mental mechanism. The aim of inquiry was to resolve aesthetic 'complex ideas' into 'simple ideas' and emotions, and establish the causation of these.[29]

---

24 Locke 1829, Book. 1; Chapter 3: 8.

25 Cooper 1714, vol. 2, pp. 414–15. See also Tuveson 1960, Chapter 2.

26 Hutcheson 1973, pp. 24–5. Cf. p. 36: 'This superior power of perception is justly called a sense because of its affinity to the other senses in this, that the pleasure does not arise from any knowledge of principles, proportions, causes, or the usefulness of the object, but strikes us at first with the idea of beauty.'

27 This point is well developed in Tuveson 1960.

28 Quoted in Hipple 1957, p. 7. Cf. Home 1785, vol. 1, pp. 12–13.

29 For a useful account of the general approach, see Hipple's introduction to Gerard 1963, pp. xi–xvii.

Although the principle had been enunciated earlier by Shaftesbury and Addison, Hutcheson's *Inquiry Concerning Beauty, Order, Harmony, Design* (1725) was the first text to take as the starting point for systematic inquiry the Lockean proposition that 'beauty is taken for the idea raised in us, and a sense of beauty for our power or receiving this idea'.[30] Thus instead of fixing beauty as an essential quality in external objects as traditional theories had done, Hutcheson made beauty an idea in the perceiving mind. Although Hutcheson maintained that this idea was aroused only and always by a combination of uniformity with variety in external objects, this cannot disguise the shift from an objectivist to a phenomenalist viewpoint. Subsequently all the major British aestheticians accepted this phenomenal account of the nature of beauty, which was an inescapable consequence of sensationalist epistemology.

Associationist Theories

Lord Kames wrote of Locke's contribution to the science of logic that to him 'the world is greatly indebted, for removing a mountain of rubbish, and moulding the subject into a rational and correct form'.[31] But in one essential respect Kames departed from Locke's model, in that the association of ideas was a key explanatory principle in his psychology, whereas it had been a minor aspect of Locke's. In this regard Kames's *Elements of Criticism* (1762) set the pattern for the major texts of philosophical criticism right into the nineteenth century in that association was central to the systems of Alison, Payne Knight, Jeffrey and Stewart.

Use of association to explain the psychological mechanisms of taste was a result of the larger currency of the concept. Although the principles of connection between thoughts had been given some attention by Aristotle, association did not become the subject of any extended inquiry until it was investigated by Hobbes and Locke in the seventeenth century. Having denied a priori ideas, and reduced the basis of epistemology to sense impressions and the mind's reflections on itself, the new philosophy had still to account for the complex experiences of memory, imagination, and ratiocination. The mechanical model of the mind provided by association psychology was the solution to this problem.[32]

Despite Hobbes's earlier usage of the association principle, in the eighteenth century the concept was generally accredited to Locke, who gave it its name. Yet

---

30   On the significance of this see Stolnitz 1961, p. 201.

31   Home 1785, vol. 1, p. 443.

32   See Warren 1921; McKenzie 1949; Kallich 1970.

Locke actually had little to say on how ideas are connected. Although association in some sense must account for his complex ideas and for the 'natural correspondence' of ideas, Locke's only use of the term was in the supplemental chapter 'Of the association of ideas', where it primarily designated a cause of error, explaining those things which seemed 'odd' and 'extravagant' in the 'opinions, reasonings and actions of other men'. It was this conception of association that Hutcheson made use of in his *Inquiry*. While Hutcheson allowed that association could be a powerful source of pleasure, its main function in his system is as a cause of individual vagaries of taste, which must be rooted out by the processes of reason. For Hutcheson, the real idea of beauty only arises from the apprehension of uniformity with variety, it cannot arise from association.[33]

In the second quarter of the eighteenth century a number of thinkers rejected this negative evaluation of association, of whom Hume and Hartley are the most important for my concerns. Like Locke, Hume made sense impressions the basis of knowledge, but he differed from him in using association as the essential 'uniting principle' of the mind; he compared its importance in human nature with that of gravity in physical nature and attributed vast consequences to the three principles of association he identified, viz. resemblance, contiguity, and cause and effect. For Hume, these principles were 'the only links that bind the parts of the universe together, or connect us with any person or object exterior to ourselves'.[34] Association is thus fundamental to Hume's accounts of both causation and reasoning. In Hume's epistemology, as in Locke's, the immediate objects of knowledge are perceptions, and the world of things is ultimately unknowable. Thus beauty and deformity are not qualities in objects themselves, but qualities of sentiment aroused by our perception of them. In 'Of the Standard of Taste', from the *Four Dissertations* of 1757, Hume describes the sceptical position as being, 'to seek the real beauty, or real deformity, is as fruitless an inquiry, as to pretend to ascertain the real sweet or real bitter'.[35] But as in the *Treatise of Human Nature*, Hume rejects scepticism.[36] Habit and custom may be the only foundations of what we assume to be established verities, but they are necessary to both the coherence of individual identity and social organisation.

---

33   Hutcheson 1973, especially Sections VI and VII.

34   Hume 1978, pp. 10–13, 662.

35   Hume 1963, pp. 235, 240. On Hume's aesthetics, see: Brunius 1952; Cohen 1958; Mossner 1967.

36   Raymond Williams gives a finely balanced account of Hume's scepticism in his 'David Hume: Reasoning and Experience', in Williams 1983.

In various statements across Hume's writings association appears as the 'natural' principle that orders imagination and taste, and although it can cause individual deviations from proper norms, it is not just a source of misconnections and disorder as it had been for Hutcheson.[37] However, while association is a key principle in Hume's system, he did not work through its implications for the theory of the arts. The essay on criticism he promised in the 'Advertisement' to the *Treatise of Human Nature* was never written, and his fragmentary essays on criticism and the arts are suggestive, but not systematic. Nonetheless, Alexander Gerard's *Essay on Taste* (1759) and Kames's *Elements of Criticism* both display the influence of Hume's ideas, and Payne Knight openly acknowledged his admiration of Hume in his *Analytical Inquiry*. However, it was David Hartley's use of association in his *Observations on Man* (1749) that probably provided the psychology for most major theories of taste produced around 1800.[38] For Hartley, association is not just the 'uniting principle' of the mind, all intellectual pleasures and pains derive from it and it is the basis of that 'invention' which produces 'new beauties in works of imagination and new truths in matters of science'.[39]

Hartley's *Observations* contains a substantial section on the 'Pleasures and Pains of Imagination', which offers explanations of the experiences of beauty and grandeur, and includes considerations on architecture, music, painting, and poetry among other causes of pleasure. As a Christian moralist, representative of the widespread tendency to coordinate theology with modern science and philosophy, Hartley's principle concern was to demonstrate the moral functions of association. He argued that it was through association that objects acquired an emotional and spiritual significance they did not have in themselves: 'Some degree of spirituality is the necessary consequence of passing through life. The sensible pleasures and pains must be transferred by association more and more every day, upon things that afford neither sensible pleasure nor sensible pain in themselves, and so beget the intellectual pleasures and pains'.[40]

Although the variety of impressions and associations that individuals experience in the course of their lives are unique, there are also many similarities among them. This has important implications for Hartley's moral theory, and also for the standard of taste. Hartley claimed that sensations such as those of colour could produce a basic aesthetic pleasure, but such pleasures are

---

37   See Kallich 1970, pp. 76–7. See also Kallich 1946.

38   For Hartley's influence, see Kallich 1970, pp. 129–30.

39   Hartley 1791 and 1801, Part 1, p. 434.

40   Hartley 1791 and 1801, Part 1, p. 82.

strongest in youth and as the individual progresses to adulthood they become increasingly overlaid by associations. Like other devotees of natural theology, he claimed that through nature the mind could be led to the 'exalted pleasures of devotion', at least for those who already apprehended the 'power, knowledge, and goodness' of its creator.[41]

In Hartley's system beauty is a complex idea with a multiplicity of causes, as it was for all the major exponents of philosophical criticism who followed him with the exception of Burke, who rejected the association principle.[42] However, if, for eighteenth-century British thinkers, beauty was no longer an intrinsic property of objects, the qualities they identified as producing the *idea* of beauty had inevitably to be discovered in objects hitherto seen as beautiful in themselves. Further, although the idea that custom and habit were crucial determinants of both morality and reasoning was a central theme of the most original thought of the period, nearly all writers on taste sought to justify universal values in the terms of their own systems, and the 'standard of taste' remained a consistent preoccupation.

If the reputation of the great works of European culture was secure, when the term beauty was applied to them it had different connotations. Indeed, as philosophical criticism came to base itself on increasingly sophisticated systems of association psychology, its exponents felt obliged to assert that traditional models of beauty did not represent a set of fixed norms, but rather exemplified types of object with a common signifying function. Given the changeability of human cultures that history displayed, it was possible that quite different types of object could have that same function in the future. In his *Essays on Taste*, Alison argues that no forms are originally beautiful: forms only produce the idea of beauty from their function as signs expressive of fitness, or expressive of emotion. This means that there is potentially no limit to the objects of taste. Payne Knight, who was more fiercely critical of traditional rules in the arts even than Alison, claimed that: 'The pleasures of imagination ... have been varied and augmented in every succeeding age of civilised society; and we know not how much further they may yet be varied and augmented'.[43]

But not only had it become increasingly difficult to set limits to beauty, it had also ceased to be the sole aesthetic category. Although the idea of beauty received little analysis as such, it pervaded treatises on the arts in Antiquity and the Renaissance. The new inquiry into the psychological principles of aesthetic

---

41   Hartley 1791 and 1801, Part 1, p. 421. Cf. his rapturous account of the order of the universe, Part 2, pp. 247–8.

42   Kallich 1954.

43   Knight 1808, p. 235.

pleasure forced recognition of a variety of emotions that no single category could plausibly contain. Eighteenth-century thinkers generally divided these emotions into two types, the beautiful and the sublime. Although some, such as Gerard, sought to define more, the development of the concept of the sublime was the single most important factor in ending the primacy of beauty. The new connotations of the word gradually became apparent in texts by Addison, John Dennis, and Shaftesbury, but a firm demarcation between them was first made by Gerard in his *Essay on Taste*, before Burke made them mutually exclusive emotions excited by opposite types of object in his *Philosophical Inquiry into the Origin of Our Ideas of the Sublime and Beautiful* (1757). Burke's importance as an aesthetician consists mainly in his recognition that the kinds of experience that his contemporaries denominated sublime were incompatible with traditional notions of beauty and in making the sublime a more powerful emotion.

The question of why a stylistic conception from classical rhetoric should have undergone such a radical transformation demands a more complex answer than I can give here. In this context it is only necessary to make a few basic points. Firstly, since the thinkers I am concerned with conceived their inquiry as grounded in basic psychological principles, and treated art primarily as the imitation of nature, they discovered the causes of aesthetic emotions in both nature and art. Indeed, they began their analyses with responses to nature, which for them could produce more powerful aesthetic responses than any product of human artifice. In her famous study *Mountain Gloom and Mountain Glory: The Development of the Aesthetics of the Infinite*, Marjorie Hope Nicolson argued that the emergence of the category of the sublime was directly linked with new theories of the cosmos developed in the seventeenth century. The discoveries and hypotheses of the new astronomy broke traditional notions of an animate circumscribed universe and of a hierarchy of celestial spheres, and substituted for them the conception of an infinity of worlds in absolute space. Traditional notions of beauty paralleled those of cosmology in that the concept of a harmonious universe, ordered and moving by divine plan, matched aesthetic values of order and harmony. By contrast, traditional aesthetic norms could not accommodate vastness and irregularity. Nicolson gave particular importance to changing attitudes to mountains in breaking the supremacy of order and harmony, and validating an 'aesthetic of the infinite'.[44]

The aesthetics of the sublime was intimately linked with the efforts of advocates of the new natural philosophy, such as some of the Boyle Lecturers, to demonstrate that the latter was not incompatible with the truths of revelation

---

44   Nicolson 1959.

as manifested in the scriptures. The idea that the cosmos provided evidence of divine handiwork was ancient; the problem was to match the new conceptions of it with computations of the age of the earth, the creation of the species, and the Flood as these were understood from the Biblical account. In the late seventeenth and early eighteenth centuries, the truths of natural philosophy were fought over by free-thinkers and the different factions of the orthodox, and forms of natural theology were advanced by each in support of their moral, social, and political views. The main difference was over the weight to be given to the evidence of nature and unassisted reason against that to be attributed to revelation; conservatives, being committed to the latter, attacked Latitudinarians for depending too much on the former and thereby playing into the hands of Deists and other free-thinkers. However, the argument for the existence of God from the design of the cosmos became increasingly commonplace.[45]

The idea that the cosmos displayed a 'design' that was also the model of the aesthetic was given a completely new emphasis from the writings of Shaftesbury onwards. Frequent references to the argument from design in philosophical criticism, and the truism that the highest experience of taste lay in contemplation of the order of the natural world, suggest that natural religion, mediated through theological orthodoxy, functioned with philosophical criticism as mutually reinforcing discourses with the same kinds of integrative ideological effects. Natural theology justified the inequalities of the social order by asserting that they, like the differences between species in the natural order, were divinely ordained according to the 'Government' of the deity.[46] The connection between the argument from design and broadly conservative interests, indicates that the sublime aestheticised a hierarchical patriarchal cosmos, a cosmos that presented a model of government precisely analogous to that which prevailed in eighteenth-century society, as this appeared from the perspective of the dominant class and its ideologues.

The Social Theory of the Scottish Enlightenment

In comparison with the seventeenth, the eighteenth century was not a particularly creative period in English thought; it did, however, witness a remarkable intellectual efflorescence in Scotland. Just as the stimulus for seventeenth-

---

45   The literature on this area is extensive, but see: Jacob 1977; Jacob 1976; Jacob and Jacob 1980; Redwood 1976; Wilde 1980; Wilde 1982.

46   For a classic statement of the creed, see Butler 1736, p. 65.

century intellectual advances in Britain came from the process of bourgeois revolution, so those of the Scottish Enlightenment were the fruit of the revolutionary transition from feudalism to capitalism in 'North Britain'.[47] Central to this achievement was the development of a secular and totalising theory of society, a natural history of social relations that worked through the implications of Locke's environmentalism for the understanding of historical development and anticipated some aspects of Marxism's science of society.[48] It was the Scottish intelligentsia – deeply concerned with polite culture – who initiated philosophical criticism as a form of systematic inquiry. Of the main exponents of the new genre, Hutcheson, Hume, Gerard, Kames, and Alison were all products of the Scottish social and political environment, although Hutcheson was born in Ireland and taught in Dublin before becoming Professor of Moral Philosophy at Glasgow. Payne Knight, an English squire, based his *Analytical Inquiry* on Scottish models.

Scottish social theory was the product of an intelligentsia closely interwoven with the fraction of less well-off aristocracy that made Edinburgh the focus of its social life after the Union of 1707. This aristocratic oligarchy was a progressive, modern-minded elite that in the absence of a local legislative institution distinguished itself as the heir to the old governing class by a commitment to agricultural improvement and capitalist development. The fraction of literati that emerged in Edinburgh by the 1720s was partly comprised of the professoriate of the reformed university, but the leading literary clubs were actually dominated by gentry and lawyers. (By contrast, in Glasgow the professoriate controlled intellectual life).[49] Nicholas Phillipson has described the literati and provincial oligarchy of mid-eighteenth-century Edinburgh as a complex social unit in which the 'collective will to understand was a substitute for the sort of political action from which an earlier generation had derived its identity'.[50]

Because the intelligentsia was so closely involved with the transformation of Scotland into a capitalist society the theory it produced was centrally concerned with the effects of the new order of things on manners, morals, and

---

47   Neil Davidson makes the case for understanding the main developments of eighteenth-century Scottish history in these terms in Davidson 2003 and addresses the relationship between the Scottish Historical School and the revolutionary process in Davidson 2012, Chapter 3.

48   Important literature on this topic includes: Phillipson 1973; Phillipson 1981; Meek 1976; Hont and Ignatieff 1983.

49   Emerson 1973. On the importance of lawyers in the opposition to feudal remnants, see Davidson 2003, pp. 47–9.

50   Phillipson 1975, p. 448.

traditional norms of citizenship. This concern issued in a new type of moral theory, exemplified by Smith's *Theory of Moral Sentiments*, which offered a more private conception of virtue in place of the civic humanist model of active citizenship, derived from the warrior ethic of aristocratic societies.[51] While they tended to argue that commercial societies had some unfortunate effects on morals and collective psychology, the Scottish School generally regarded them as preferable to earlier stages of human development. In Smith's words, 'The progressive state is in reality the cheerful and the hearty state to all the different orders of the society'.[52] The Scots' appraisal of feudal society was a negative one in nearly all respects, and they did not conceive landed society as the locus of political virtues. In contrast to the civic humanist model Smith and Hume were concerned with the justification of inequality, and with the security of property rights in different kinds of society, concerns that derive from the Natural Law tradition.[53]

Despite the closeness of the intellectual circles that produced it, Scottish social theory was not linked with any single political position; but it was predominantly progressive and Whiggish. This may be illustrated through Millar's statement, 'there is thus, in human society, a natural progress from ignorance to knowledge, and from rude, to civilised manners, the several stages of which are usually accompanied with peculiar laws and customs'.[54] However, Duncan Forbes and other commentators have stressed that the Scots' conception of the progress needs to be distinguished from the naive optimism of Hartley, Priestley, and Godwin.[55] While Smith certainly represented commercial societies as preferable to earlier types, he did not believe in human perfectibility and saw unmistakable disadvantages in progress. Kames, although he was a strong Whig and advocate of Scottish economic development with an essentially optimistic view of humanity's moral character, also argued a cyclical model of the progress and decline of societies. The persistent tension in the Scottish inquiry is seen most acutely in Adam Ferguson's *An Essay on the History of Civil Society* (1767), which articulates eloquently the anxiety that specialisation and commercialisation threaten essential qualities of human nature, while excessive refinement has extinguished classical ideals of citizenship. Even John Millar, the most politically radical of the Scottish thinkers, was only a Foxite Whig, who

---

51   See Phillipson 1983.

52   Smith 1976 (1), vol. 1, p. 99.

53   Pocock 1983.

54   Citations are from the text of the 1779 edition of Millar's *Origin of the Distinction of Ranks*, reprinted in Lehmann 1960, p. 176.

55   See Forbes 1975 (1), chapter 5, and Forbes 1975 (2).

advocated a mixed constitution and did not favour universal suffrage. While they were relatively sympathetic to bourgeois interests, the Scottish school did not conceive of the bourgeoisie as a class, and were not the apologists of those eighteenth-century groups conventionally associated with that term. Their conception of progress, unlike that of nineteenth-century liberalism, was neither propagandistic nor blasé.

The new naturalistic approach to historical studies that assumed the primacy of economic and cultural variables in the formation of human consciousness emerged in a succession of works by Smith, Kames, Ferguson, and Millar published in the 1760s and 1770s. It was quite directly inspired by the example of seventeenth-century developments in the natural sciences, and sought to apply scientific methods in the study of 'man'; for epistemology and psychology it took the sensationalist theories of Locke and Hume. Scottish thought socialised and historicised the study of human behaviour. It represented the individual as a social being determined as much by the division of property and organisation of labour as by political forms. History was conceived as a stadial progress – usually divided into four modes of subsistence: hunting, pasturage, agriculture, and commerce – to which corresponded different institutions and manners. Its study became a synthesising approach to human societies, in which the development of changing forms of social life was explained in terms of changing property relations and power struggles between social groups with different places in these property relations, as nations passed from barbarism to commerce, luxury, and refinement. The law of unintended consequences was a fundamental assumption. Human beings made their own institutions, but were as individuals fundamentally determined by their circumstances. The importance of Scottish theory as a precedent for Marx's thought should be self-evident – although 'modes of subsistence' do not designate different forms of exploitative relationship and should not be equated with 'modes of production'.[56]

In general, Scottish social thought placed refinement and the arts among the main advantages of commercial societies, and this helps to explain the connections between it and inquiries into the nature of taste. I suggested earlier that philosophical criticism encouraged some questioning of traditional artistic values, both because it rejected a priori principles and established authorities in favour of principles 'discovered' by empirical investigation, and because it dealt with responses of the mind, which were notoriously various both within com-

---

56   Important early characterisations of the Scottish School from a Marxist perspective
       include: Pascal 1938; and Meek, 'The Scottish Contribution to Marxist Sociology', in Meek
       1967. For a more critical appraisal of the relationship, see Ignatieff 1981.

mon cultural contexts and across diverse ones. The Scots' science of society was characterised by the introduction of a new kind of argument from historical and anthropological evidence in the analysis of morals and political institutions, most clearly exemplified in general theories of social development such as Ferguson's *Essay on the History of Civil Society* (1767) and Millar's *Origin of the Distinction of Ranks* (1771). The environmentalist approach this entailed is well-illustrated by Millar's assertion, 'That the dispositions and behaviour of man are liable to be influenced by the circumstances in which he is placed, and by his peculiar education and habits of life, is a proposition that few persons will be inclined to controvert'.[57]

A central task of philosophical criticism was to reconcile this 'scientific' premise with the need to justify the authority of the dominant social groups in taste, as it was justified in politics and other spheres of belief. By 1800, Scottish thinkers had produced a substantial body of sophisticated reflections on the social basis of aesthetic norms. These really begin with Hume's 'Of the Rise and Progress of the Arts and Sciences' and 'Of Refinement in the Arts' in his *Essays Moral and Political* (1742), which relate the arts to his more general theses on the connections between modes of subsistence, political institutions, and manners. Although 'Of the Standard of Taste' in the *Four Dissertations* (1757) was not original in theme, it marked a new level of sophistication in thinking on the problem. A crucial unpublished text was Smith's Lectures on Rhetoric and Belles Lettres, which he gave at Glasgow from 1752 onwards as a private class in addition to his functions as Professor of Moral Philosophy. The lecture notes were destroyed at Smith's request shortly before his death, but are known today through student notes made in 1762–3. While the lectures are not a treatise on taste as such, they contain numerous comments on the different arts and ground beauty of expression in psychological principles, making extensive use of association. More importantly here, Smith makes a number of connections between developments in style and the different stages of social development.[58] Hugh Blair and Millar were among the students who attended Smith's rhetoric course, and Blair was lent Smith's notes, which influenced both his own lecture course at Edinburgh and his published *Lectures on Rhetoric and Belles Lettres* (1783).[59] The currency of the view that taste was to a large extent a matter of custom, and therefore socially relative,

---

57   Millar 1803, vol. 4, p. 174.

58   Smith 1983, pp. 111–12, 135–8.

59   On the immense success of Blair's work, which was essentially an exercise in popularisation, see Hipple 1957, p. 122.

must also have been increased by Smith's persuasive comments on the issue in his *Theory of Moral Sentiments*.[60]

Reflections on the social bases of taste did not appear only within specialised texts on criticism, they also appeared in works of 'conjectural history' such as Kames's *Sketches* and Ferguson's *Essay*, and in narrative histories such as Hume's *History of England* (1754–61, first complete edition 1763). Indeed, some of the most profound and coherent reflections on the culture of commercial societies appear in the fourth volume of Millar's *Historical View of the English Government* (1803). In what follows I shall be concerned with two aspects of Scottish thought as it bore on the arts: firstly, with how it naturalised the functions of taste as those of a class-specific social group; and, secondly, with how it conceived the effects of commercial societies on the formation of taste.

It is symptomatic that none of the conjectural histories or treatises on taste I have consulted address the capacity for taste in women. The only taste that demanded definition was the taste of the gentleman. This may be an index of more than just the assumed readership of such texts or gendered preconceptions as to who should exercise authority in the arts. Most of their authors assumed that women possessed neither the power of judgment nor the moral range to comprehend the most sublime objects. But the Fine Arts were held to call into play those feelings of 'humanity' and 'exquisite fellow-feeling' said to be particularly characteristic of women,[61] and perhaps for this reason there seemed a dangerously feminine aspect to their cultivation. It is notable that Smith alleged that it was weak men who are drawn to the Fine Arts, exemplifying the point through the person of Shaftesbury.[62] In his essay 'Of the Delicacy of Taste and Passion', Hume recommends the exercise of taste as a way of both developing the capacity for judgment, and as a 'cure' for excessive 'delicacy of passion'; but when he describes the effects of study of the beauties of 'poetry, eloquence, music, or painting', it is in terms of distinctively private virtues.[63]

When Hume directly addresses the issue of female taste in 'Of Essay Writing', it is because of the role it plays in sociability. The argument here is that the separation of 'the learned' from the 'conversable world' – the realm of polite conversation dominated by the 'fair sex' – has unfortunate results for both; men of letters need to be engaged with society, and polite culture needs to

---

60   See 'Of the Influence of Custom and Fashion upon our Notions of Beauty and Deformity', in Adam Smith 1976 (2), pp. 194–200.

61   Smith 1976 (2), p. 190.

62   Smith 1983, p. 57.

63   Hume 1963, pp. 5–6.

be provided with serious materials for discussion. Hume claims that 'women of sense and education' are 'much better judges of all polite writing than men of the same degree of understanding', and that 'all men of sense, who know the world', respect the judgment of women in relation to such books 'as lie within the compass of their knowledge', even though their 'delicacy of taste' is 'unguided by rules'. Women's judgment is only unreliable when it bears on books of devotion and gallantry, in relation to which it is perverted by their 'greater share of the tender and amorous disposition'. Women thus tend to a highly sensitive taste, but have an innate propensity that distorts their judgment and which they must struggle to control, a propensity that does not distort the judgment of men. But Hume does not envisage a category of 'women of letters', and when it comes to discussing the 'Standard of Taste', the ideal critic he describes is a writer and a man. Thus while women in the 'conversable world' may advise men in judgments of taste, it is not their function to take on the public office of the critic.[64]

In the long and fascinating chapter 'Of the rank and condition of women in different ages' that begins *On the Origin of the Distinction of Ranks*, Millar effectively makes the position of women an index of the level of societies in the scale of progress: 'Their condition is naturally improved by every circumstance which tends to create more attention to the pleasures of sex, and to increase the value of those occupations that are suited to the female character; by the cultivation of the arts of life; by the advancement of opulence; and by the gradual refinement of taste and manners'.[65] Millar seems to slip between attributing the 'peculiar delicacy and sensibility' that comprises the character of women to their 'original constitution' or to their education and 'way of life'.[66] However, in the early stages of the improvement of arts and manufactures, women obtain 'that rank and station' that is best suited to their 'character and talents' within the home. In ages of opulence, they 'are encouraged to quit that retirement which was formerly esteemed so suitable to their character ... to appear in mixed company, and in public meetings of pleasure'. As they enter more into public life, they seek to distinguish themselves by 'polite accomplishments that tend to heighten their personal attractions'.[67] This is the apex of progress for women of the higher ranks of society, and it brings with it

---

64   See Hume 1963, pp. 568–72. Mary Wollstonecraft uses Hume to exemplify the degradation of the character of women in Wollstonecraft 1982, p. 145.

65   Lehmann 1960, p. 203. Kames takes a similar position in the chapter 'Progress of the Female Sex', in Home 1788.

66   Lehmann 1960, pp. 219–20.

67   Lehmann 1960, p. 224. Cf. Home 1788, vol. 2, pp. 41–2.

the danger of licentious and dissolute manners. For Millar women are 'naturally excluded' from the 'pursuits of ambition' in public affairs, and the 'polite accomplishments' to which he refers are only such as will generate the passions appropriate to the female character. These do not include the serious refinement of taste, which is congruous only to men, like other 'public affairs'.

Scottish Social Theory and the Theory of Taste

The justification of a standard of taste presented no problems for thinkers who based judgement on the notion of an internal sense or senses. The theory had been developed in the first place to ward against relativism in moral judgements and was equally fitted to deny relativism in matters of taste. Thus Shaftesbury found it self-evident that the 'Foundation of a right and wrong taste' in both aesthetic and moral matters must lie in 'the very nature of things'. No more than later thinkers could he deny the plurality of observable tastes, but he simply attributed them to ignorance, self-interest, and passion.[68] While both morality and taste derive from innate senses, these faculties need to be refined and cultivated. The rules of art, like those of behaviour, can be learnt. Obviously the refinement of taste is possible only for those with wealth and leisure, but unlike some of his successors, Shaftesbury did not elaborate on this issue. However, his consideration of the political and social conditions in which taste is likely to develop in the public in the 'Letter Concerning the Art, or Science of Design' does anticipate some themes of Scottish thought.[69]

For Hutcheson, who took up Shaftesbury's 'inner sense' concept, there was also a relatively simple justification of aesthetic norms, and even in Gerard's *Essay on Taste*, in which the notion of a single sense has proliferated into seven operative senses, supplemented by extensive use of association, the author still maintains an uncompromising absolutism on the existence of the standard – deviations are simply the result of 'weakness or disorder' in the individual concerned.[70] In Gerard's account, 'great sensibility of taste' is to be expected only among the 'polite' ranks of 'polite' nations, and quite simply, the 'bulk of mankind', 'engrossed by attention to the necessaries of life', have no opportunity to develop the 'elements of taste which nature implanted in their souls', and which therefore become 'corrupted and lost'.[71]

---

68   Cooper 1714, vol. 1, pp. 336, 340; vol. 2, p. 416.

69   Cooper 1714, vol. 3, pp. 393 ff.

70   Gerard 1963, p. 72.

71   Gerard 1963, pp. 188, 205.

However, the increasing authority of associationist models in the psychology of philosophical criticism made taste necessarily more relative, and justification of a standard more complex. Although Hume refers to a sense that operates in moral and aesthetic judgements in both the *Treatise of Human Nature* and the *Enquiry Concerning ... Morals*,[72] this sense is integrated with the larger emotional and sentimental capacities of human nature in a way it is not in the writings of Shaftesbury and Hutcheson. For Hume there are types of beauty that immediately 'command our affection and approbation', but particularly with regard to the fine arts and sciences, 'a fine taste is, in some measure, the same with strong sense, or at least depends so much upon it that they are inseparable'.[73]

Hume and Kames

Hume is emphatic that the inspiration of the poet is not of supernatural origin, but owes much to judgement and learning. Equally, he asserts the importance of 'argument and reflection' in the fine arts, and of reasoning and comparison in the cultivation of taste, in order for them to have a 'suitable influence on the human mind'.[74] However, in the second *Enquiry* Hume is particularly firm on the differences between reason and taste, and claims that while Shaftesbury had first noted the distinction, he had yet sometimes confused the two. The standards of reason are 'eternal and inflexible', founded in the 'nature of things', but the standard of taste depends upon the 'internal frame and constitution of animals', and derives from that Supreme Will which gave each order of existence its peculiar nature, 'Truth is disputable, not taste'.[75]

The criterion of judgement in matters of taste is not truth but pleasure, and what gives pleasure cannot be wrong. For Hume, reason 'discovers objects as they really stand in nature, without addition or diminution', while taste is a 'productive faculty', 'gilding or staining all natural objects with the colours borrowed from internal sentiment'. But this assertion of the primacy of sentiment did not lead Hume to relativism. While acknowledging the variety of individual tastes, he sought to identify general principles in the common features of human nature. In 'Of the Standard of Taste' he maintains that 'some

---

72   Hume 1978, p. 612; Hume 1975, pp. 173, 294.

73   Hume 1963, p. 5. An indication of the irrational and feminine connotations of the term taste is provided by Wollstonecraft's repeated insistence in the *Vindication* that taste without judgement is merely emotion – Wollstonecraft 1982, pp. 160, 166, 183, 223, 277, 284–5.

74   Hume 1975, pp. 173.

75   Hume 1975, pp. 170–3, 294.

particular form or qualities, from the original structure of the internal fabric are calculated to please and others to displease'.[76] When the 'natural' effect does not occur this is due to an 'imperfection' in the sense of the individual concerned, a defect akin to physical deformity or disease.

Consistent with his critical attitude to traditional authorities more generally, Hume did not accept a priori rules in the arts.[77] The only rules worth acknowledging are those derived from the regularities observed in experience. Although Hume was conservative in his artistic preferences – he accepted the dramatic unities, and thought Sophocles and Racine preferable to Shakespeare – he put the old rules on a new foundation by replacing the authority of the classics with principles derived from 'human nature'. The rules that he affirmed were based on the similar reactions of individuals in similar circumstances. Even though there is 'something approaching to principle in mental taste', disagreements continue, and 'education, custom, prejudice, caprice, and humour, frequently vary our taste of this kind'.[78] Critics should divest themselves of the prejudices of their own age and nature. In assessing works from other times and places they should try to imagine themselves in the situation of the audience for which they were first intended: 'We may observe, that every work of art, in order to produce its due effect on the mind, must be surveyed in a certain point of view, and cannot be fully relished by persons, whose situation, real or imaginary, is not conformable to that which is required by the performance'.[79]

Such awareness of cultural positioning points the way to a more relativistic criticism. For Hume, religious errors are the most permissible in works of art, providing they do not extend to 'bigotry or superstition'; but we need not go against our moral sentiments in the interests of taste. Thus, Hume finds that even Homer and the Greek tragedians at times display an inexcusable lack of humanity and decency. Notwithstanding all our efforts, some degree of diversity in judgements of taste will remain as a result of historical and personal factors and should be tolerated.[80]

If Hume made a distinction between moral and aesthetic judgements, he clearly saw them as analogous mental functions and frequently discussed them together. He was thus in a good position to assert that the cultivation of the arts

---

76   Hume 1963, p. 238. For Hume's views on the uniformity of human nature, see Forbes 1975 (1), Chapter 4.

77   Hume 1963, pp. 235–6.

78   Hume 1963, p. 165.

79   Hume 1963, p. 244.

80   Hume 1963, pp. 249–54.

contributes to the refinement of manners. Predictably, this refinement is the prerogative of the propertied classes, and the Fine Arts are easily lost because 'they are always relished by a few only, whose leisure, fortune and genius, fit them for such amusements'.[81] Like other forms of learning and refinement, the arts will thrive only in a particular type of social context, and in 'Of the Rise and Progress of the Arts and Sciences', Hume claims 'freedom' as a necessary precondition of their development. It is a contradiction to expect them to rise in a monarchy, for while republics necessarily create laws monarchies do not and a climate of security is necessary to intellectual progress. Once the arts and sciences have appeared they will continue under any government, although monarchies tend to favour the arts and republics the sciences.[82] A certain degree of luxury is necessary to the progress of either; therefore, both are stimulated by the coming together of people in towns, both depend upon the growth of commerce and manufactures. Over-refinement is the defect of modern cultures, and is always more dangerous than simplicity, the defect of the ancients. For Hume, this danger threatened contemporary English and French culture alike.[83]

While he held a cyclical view of the history of cultures, Hume's position was generally a progressive one. Unable to recognise the achievements of non-European cultures, he saw Europe as the perennial source of civilization. He equated the modern nation states of his time with the city states of ancient Greece, and maintained that competing independent states, 'connected together by commerce and policy' were the best environment for the advancement of learning and the arts.[84] Yet although the English are already superior to the Greeks in refinement and knowledge, they are inferior in literature, and refined manners are not conducive to the development of language.[85] For Hume, as for Smith, decline in the beauty of language is one of the costs of progress.[86]

Hume's claim that the increasing consumption of commodities that 'serve to the ornament and pleasure of life' is advantageous to society is congruent with the general orientation of Scottish social thought. Industry and the arts satisfy natural appetites, stimulate the mind, and are conducive to happiness and virtue. A characteristic of individuals in commercial societies is their 'soci-

---

81   Hume 1963, p. 125.

82   Hume 1963, pp. 116–19.

83   Hume 1963, p. 131. Cf. p. 201.

84   Hume 1963, p. 120.

85   A comment that appears in 'Of National Characters', Hume 1963, p. 214.

86   Smith 1983, pp. 12–13.

ability', the fruit of an urban lifestyle. Commerce and manufactures promote the growth of knowledge, which by encouraging wiser laws is in turn advantageous to industry. For Hume, 'tradesmen and merchants', 'that middling rank of men', are the best and firmest basis of public liberty, for they will not submit to slavery, and seek equal laws to protect them from the tyrannies of monarchy and aristocracy: 'Thus industry, knowledge, and humanity, are linked together, by an indissoluble chain, and are found, from experience as well as reason, to be peculiar to the more polished, and, what are commonly denominated the more luxurious ages'.[87]

Hume was emphatic about the advantages of commercial societies, but he was not an apologist for the one in which he lived. He saw both merits and weaknesses in English political institutions. Equally, he was critical of English art and literature, which he tended to compare unfavourably with the arts of France. These reservations were developed in the *History of England*, where the account of each reign or period is followed by an appendix on 'Government and Manners', or in the volumes dealing with later periods, on 'Manners', 'Finances', 'Commerce', 'Manufactures', 'Learning and the Arts' in various combinations. E.C. Mossner has observed that Hume's practical criticism did not live up to the project he had advocated in 'Of the Standard of Taste'.[88] His theory of knowledge was so strongly normative in itself that he could only see cultural forms that were contrary to what he understood as common sense and reason as nonprogressive. Nonetheless, Hume's *History* is important in initiating a mode of argument that seeks to insert the history of the arts in a larger framework of historical developments.

Kames's *Elements of Criticism* is related to Hume's writings both in its use of association, and in its account of the standard of taste. Indeed, it has been suggested that Kames intended the text as the systematic treatise Hume had promised in his 1739 advertisement to the *Treatise of Human Nature*, but failed to produce.[89] Still, it should be noted that Kames, a less sceptical thinker than Hume, was far more complacent about the ordering of the world by divine plan. Thus Kames claims it is an intrinsic capacity of human nature to find pleasure in the sensations of eye and ear, akin to the moral sense. This leads him to define an intrinsic beauty associated with the sense of sight, which includes pleasures deriving from regularity, uniformity, proportion, order, and simplicity. Thus although beauty is one type of emotion, it can have a multiplicity of causes and

---

87   'Of the Refinement of the Arts and Sciences', in Hume 1963, p. 278.
88   Mossner 1967, p. 246.
89   Ross 1972, p. 261.

is complex in nature. Grandeur is produced by large objects, and like beauty is an agreeable sensation, but serious, rather than sweet and gay. Sublimity originally denotes the effect of height, but is applied transitively to that which elevates the mind. But there are also ideas of relative beauty that depend on reflection and understanding.[90]

For Kames, as for Hume, the association of ideas is the fundamental cohesive principle of the mind, and he accepted the latter's three principles of connection, but added to them a fourth, the principle of order. According to Kames, the mind is so designed that we have a divinely implanted propensity to relish associations connected by principles of unity and order; that which violates the natural tendency of the mind causes displeasure; a work of art is like 'an organic system' in this regard.[91] Relative beauty is derived from understanding how means are related to some good end or purpose, and in its highest form it is experienced from contemplating the design of the works of nature.[92]

Having identified this innate relish for connection and order, Kames can fix the standard of taste, like that of morals, in a common human nature that is invariable and universal, the same in all ages and all nations.[93] A part of this nature is an original attachment to every object that elevates the mind; even those persons who prefer 'low and trifling amusements' acknowledge its existence.[94] Justice too is naturally ordained, for it is natural for the individual to adapt his behaviour to the 'station allotted him by providence'.[95]

Kames consistently discusses the 'discipline' of taste in terms that emphasise its connections with morality. Thus, 'no discipline is more suitable to man, nor more congruous to the dignity of his nature, than that which refines his taste, and leads him to distinguish in every subject, what is regular, what is orderly, what is suitable, and what is fit and proper'.[96]

Presumably, this discipline is not congruous to women, whose 'character' and 'rank' do not require them to make such discriminations. Just as uniformity of morals is necessary to society, so too is uniformity of taste. Progressive that he

---

90   Home 1785, vol. 1, Chapters 3–4.

91   Home 1785, vol. 1, p. 27. Cf. on language, vol. 2, p. 80. On the aesthetic state of mind, see vol. 1, p. 315.

92   Home 1785, vol. 1, pp. 330–2.

93   Home 1785, vol. 2, pp. 491–2.

94   Home 1785, vol. 1, p. 231.

95   Home 1785, vol. 1, pp. 191, 347–8. For Kames, 'The form of government ... that is the most consonant to nature, is that which allots to each their proper station'. Democracy and despotism are both equally 'contradictory to nature' – Home 1785, vol. 2, p. 247.

96   Home 1785, vol. 1, p. 333.

is, Kames concludes that as 'we' would not derive the rules of morality from 'the common sense of savages', so 'we' should not derive from them the rules 'that ought to govern the fine arts'. Instead these must be discovered from those rules 'most general' and 'most lasting' in 'polite nations'.[97] While all human beings have the potential to experience the emotions of taste, only a decisive minority do so. Those who rely for their food on bodily labour are totally lacking in the higher forms of taste, and thus the majority of mankind are excluded from its exercise; while of the remainder, many are disqualified by a corruption of the faculty: 'The common sense of mankind must then be confined to the few that fall not under those exceptions'.[98]

It is in the nature of human societies that 'many hands must be employed to procure ... the conveniences of life', and fortunately the majority 'fall in readily with the occupations, pleasure, food, and company' proper to their station; if a fine taste were universally developed, they would resent their humble occupations. Yet without the underlying uniformity of taste, 'there could not be any suitable reward, either of profit or honour, to encourage men of genius to labour'. Moreover, this uniformity helps soften the inequalities between social ranks, for since taste is a source of pleasure that 'all ranks' may to some degree enjoy at public spectacles and amusements, it is 'no slight support to the social affections'.[99]

Situated midway between the pleasures of the senses and those of the intellect, the pleasures of taste prepare the mind for higher things. They promote benevolence, and by 'cherishing love of order enforce submission to government' and strengthen the 'bond of society'.[100] Further, they have a more specific function in commercial societies, where they can prevent the fruits of commerce being wasted in vice and wanton pleasures. In the Dedication of the *Elements of Criticism*, addressed to George III, Kames asserts that the Fine Arts are necessary to establish Britain's greatness:

> A flourishing commerce begets opulence; and opulence inflaming our appetite for pleasures, is commonly vented on luxury, and on every sensual gratification: Selfishness rears its head; becomes fashionable; and infecting all ranks, extinguishes the *amor patriae*, and every spark of public spirit. To prevent or retard such fatal corruption, the genius of an Alfred cannot devise any means more efficacious, than the venting opulence

---

97   Home 1785, vol. 2, p. 498.
98   Home 1785, vol. 2, p. 500.
99   Hume 1785, vol. 2, pp. 489, 495–500.
100   Hume 1785, vol. 1, p. v. Cf. pp. 11, 100.

> upon the Fine Arts: riches so employed, instead of encouraging vice, will excite both public and private virtue.[101]

Kames's warning about the dangers of luxury derives from the discourse of civic humanism, but consonant with his progressivism he offers an antidote to the selfishness and corruption commerce threatens: private and public virtues alike will be safe if the nation's rulers operate an enlightened policy of the arts.

The larger historical framework of Kames's system is set out in his *Sketches of the History of Man* (1774), in which he attempted to popularise ideas from both the *Elements of Criticism* and his *Essays on the Principles of Morality and Natural Religion* (1751). In the section titled the 'Origin and Progress of the Arts' Kames follows Hume in asserting that competing nation states provide the most fertile environment for progress, citing those of Greece and Renaissance Italy as evidence. Taste flourishes in urban societies and not in feudal ones, and Britain is still backward in the arts because it was the last polite nation to take to town life.[102] For Kames, the arts are progressive, but he conceived the history of both the arts and sciences on a cyclical model, claiming that the thirst for novelty, while productive in early stages of development, tends to produce retrogression when the arts are in perfection. This conception of 'novelty' as a cause of both progress and retrogression in the arts is a recurrent motif in Scottish social thought. It may be connected, at least by analogy, with the equally recurrent idea that progress in agriculture and manufactures is driven on by the endless urgings of human desire, which can never be satisfied.[103] Kames seems to assert an almost dialectical relationship between a cyclical tendency in the arts, the development of societies from barbarism to opulence, and the rise and fall of political liberty; but this is not clearly worked out.[104]

In his sketches of the 'Progress and Effects of Luxury' and 'Rise and Fall of Patriotism', Kames offers a far gloomier prognosis of Britain's cultural prospects than he had suggested in the dedication to *Elements of Criticism*. On the one hand, commerce is necessary to support patriotism, while on the other, 'a continual influx of wealth into the capital' generates luxury and selfishness that destroy it. 'Indulgence in corporeal pleasure' has diminished the military spirit of the English nobility, and their minds have been rendered effeminate by indolence. Indeed, nobleman, merchant, and manufacturer all suffer from the 'gradual decay of manhood'. Although the Fine Arts humanise the mind, too

---

101   Hume 1785, vol. 1, p. vii.

102   Home 1788, vol. 1, pp. 210–11.

103   On this, see for example Smith 1976 (1), vol. 1, p. 181.

104   Home 1788, vol. 1, p. 282.

great indulgence in them consumes time which the nobility should spend in more important duties. Kames finds the prospect a melancholy one, 'It grieves me, that the epidemic distempers of luxury and selfishness are spreading wide in Britain'. Given the contradictory tendencies generated by commerce, as Kames defines them, it seems the nation is bound for 'indolence, sensuality, corruption, prostitution, perdition'.[105]

Ferguson and Millar

Written at a far higher level than Kames's works, Adam Ferguson's *Essay on the History of Civil Society* (1767) and John Millar's *View of the English Government* (1803) may stand as opposite poles of the Scottish inquiry in relation to the affirmation of modernity.

Ferguson's *Essay* articulates a well-defined conception of human nature grounded in the discourse of civic humanism as the basis for an equally clear public morality. Ferguson stresses the active and creative character of human beings and argues that happiness derives from pursuit rather than attainment; possession does not produce pleasure.[106] The tendency of individuals to define themselves through property leads to the obsessive pursuit of wealth, which is a corruption of their nature since it distracts them from their 'happier and more respectable qualities'.[107] In contrast to his more sanguine contemporaries, Ferguson asserts that urban life is not conducive to happiness, for the best parts of the human character are not encouraged by those 'nurseries of affectation, pertness, and vanity, from which fashion is propagated, and the genteel is announced ... in great and opulent cities, where men vie with one another in equipage, dress, and the reputation of fortune'.[108]

A quite different kind of culture, and one characteristic of an earlier stage in social development, is required to foster virtue and happiness. Modern commercial culture is corrupted by its pervasive individualism. In contrast to the societies of Ancient Greece and Rome, in which the public was all important and the individual nothing, in modern societies 'the state is merely a combination of departments, in which consideration, wealth, eminence,

---

105   Home 1788, vol. 2, pp. 330, 334, 135–53, 339. Similar ideas on the relationship between the arts and society to those of Hume and Kames were stated in a more systematic and perhaps glibber way in the first volume of the *History of the Reign of the Emperor Charles V* (1777), by William Robertson, Principal of Edinburgh University from 1762–93.

106   Ferguson 1966, pp. 41, 216, 225. On Ferguson, see Forbes's Introduction to Ferguson 1966 and Kettler 1977.

107   Ferguson 1966, pp. 12–13.

108   Ferguson 1966, pp. 39–40.

or power, are offered as the reward of service'.[109] Ferguson finds it painful that in conversation the 'interests of trade' have come to 'give the ton to our reasonings'.[110]

The connection between economic advance, security, and peace was hardly open to debate; but for Ferguson the downside was also inescapable. While he acknowledged the general logic of stadial theory, that 'a people can make no great progress in cultivating the arts of life' without specialisation of skills and the division of labour, he found this separation of skills inimical to national spirit, since each craft tends to engross 'the whole of a man's attention' and distract him from concern with the good of the commonwealth. For him, as for Smith, the division of labour tended to contract the abilities of the individual workman and limit his mental capacity. Modern societies produce a complex diversity of social types, which contrasts sharply with the relative homogeneity of earlier stages.[111] The more individuals consider themselves as practitioners of a particular profession or craft, the less they think of themselves as citizens; and once matters of state and war become the 'objects of separate professions' they are worse administered. Further, the growth of wealth tends to issue in corruption, which enervates democratic and monarchical states alike.[112]

In Ferguson's scheme, the literary arts flourish most in the early stages of society. In such periods, language is simple, free, and varied, and allows liberties to the poet denied in later times. When men are not separated by 'distinctions of rank or profession', they live and speak in the same way, and thus the poet does not have to adapt his language to the 'singular accents of different conditions', his use of language is not bound by established rules, and he has more freedom to innovate in expression.[113]

While Ferguson gave artists a high standing in modern societies because they are 'bound to no task', his view of the functions of the arts is not optimistic, and is consonant with his strictures on materialism, self-interest, and the pursuit of private pleasures. At one point he comments ironically how even in states 'where different orders of men are summoned to partake in the government of their country' and where the active vigilance of the citizens is necessary for the preservation of liberty, 'they, who, in the vulgar phrase, have not their fortunes to make, are supposed to be at a loss for occupation, and betake themselves to solitary pastimes, or cultivate what they are pleased to call a taste

---

109   Ferguson 1966, p. 56.
110   Ferguson 1966, p. 145.
111   Ferguson 1966, pp. 189–90. Smith 1976 (1), vol. 1, pp. 143–4.
112   Ferguson 1966, pp. 218, 251, 254–5.
113   Ferguson 1966, p. 174.

for gardening, building, drawing, or music. With this aid, they endeavour to fill up the blanks of a listless life, and avoid the necessity of curing their langours by any positive service to their country, or to mankind'.[114] In fact, for those with a happy disposition, capacity, and vigour, such service would produce a more genuine happiness. The refinements of 'a polished age' are dangerous, because they enervate the military spirit of a nation, and Ferguson is ultimately contemptuous of such periods and of that which goes under the name of 'politeness', when, 'men, being relieved from the pressure of great occasions, bestow their attention on trifles'.[115] Refinement encourages effeminacy; a truly vigorous mind is produced by contending with difficulties, not by leisure and retirement.

Ferguson's low opinion of the 'commercial arts', which 'seem to require no foundation in the minds of men, but the regard to interest', and his frequent references to the examples of public virtue of Ancient Greece and Rome, seems to link his statements with those among his contemporaries who were critical of the alliance of mercantile wealth and a faction of the landed oligarchy that ran eighteenth-century Britain, and looked to an oppositional and public-spirited gentry as the best safeguard of the nation's political health.[116] There is no suggestion in the *Essay* that the middling ranks are a safeguard of liberty, and the measures of national culture it invokes are too military and political in character to give much weight to literature and the arts.

John Millar's writings offer a radically different political vision, one that implies a considerably more sanguine vision of the role of the arts. His *Historical View of the English Government* (1803) integrates many of the conclusions he had reached in the *Origin of the Distinction of Ranks* (1771) with an analysis of a specific historical instance driven by immediate political concerns. Millar was well-known as a political radical, and a 'zealous member' of the Society of Friends of the People, although, in fact, he was only a Foxite Whig who envisaged a restricted franchise based on the 'union of wealth and talent'. He advocated limited monarchy and asserted that the constitution established in Britain in the reign of William III was a 'mixed form of government', 'remarkable for its beautiful simplicity', 'in which the powers committed to different orders of men were so modelled and adjusted as to become subservient to one great purpose, the preservation of the rights and liberties of the people'.[117] However, there is no

---

114   Ferguson 1966, pp. 56–7.

115   Ferguson 1966, pp. 256. Cf. 231–2.

116   That the book satisfied the ideological needs of quite a wide readership is suggested by the fact that it went through seven editions between 1767 and 1814.

117   Millar 1803, vol. 4, p. 76. Earlier Millar wrote that 'the interest of those who are governed

perfection in human contrivance, and a government devised for one age cannot continue to be equally suitable to a changing nation. Because of the increasing wealth of Britain, the constitution of the early eighteenth century had come to require revision.

Deeply interested by the French Revolution, Millar was shaken by the British White Terror of the 1790s, which convinced him of the need for major reforms.[118] His reflections on eighteenth-century history indicate his concern with the climate of repression and the *Historical View* utilises elements from the discourse of civic humanism to criticise developments of the period – although it takes positions unlike those of Ferguson. Thus Millar's second chapter, 'Political Consequences of the Revolution' (of 1688–9), concerns the growth of royal influence as a result of increasing revenues from taxation and the expansion of the civil and military establishments, both effects of the nation's growing opulence. The increasing patronage of the Crown has become a threat to liberty, and an insidious corrupting force throughout the social order.[119] The National Debt and increase of taxation were characteristic concerns of those with reservations about commercialisation. These developments affected the pervasive ethos of society that Millar saw as 'a mercantile people: a people engrossed by lucrative trades; and professions, whose great object is gain, and whose ruling principle is avarice'.[120]

However, the pervasive thrust of Millar's text is thoroughly progressive. For him, as for Smith, the economy has a natural tendency to improvement, which can only be hindered by attempts at state regulation.[121] Further, economic growth promoted social well-being: 'The tendency of improvement in all the arts of life, and in every trade or profession, has been uniformly the same; to enable mankind to gain a livelihood by the exercise of their talents, without being subject to the caprice, or caring for the displeasure of others; that is,

----

is the chief circumstance which ought to regulate the powers committed to a father, as well as those committed to a civil magistrate; and whenever the prerogative of either is further extended than is requisite for this great end, it immediately degenerates into usurpation, and is to be regarded as a violation of the natural rights of mankind' (Lehmann 1960, p. 243). Millar's biographer, John Craig, claimed that he 'treated with the utmost contempt all assertion of metaphysical Rights, inconsistent with practical utility', and was 'ever decidedly hostile to the system of universal suffrage'; but consideration should be given to the context of this statement. See Craig 1806, pp. cxiv.

118   See Lehmann 1960, p. 56, and Chapter 7; Meek 1967, pp. 46–7.

119   Millar 1803, vol. 4, pp. 78–99.

120   Millar 1803, vol. 4, p. 94.

121   Millar 1803, vol. 4, pp. 116, 128.

to render the lower classes of the people less dependent upon their superiors'.[122] The influence of superior wealth had been diminished by the frequent alienation of landed estates since the abolition of entail in England; and the 'mercantile interest' had acquired an increasing (and appropriate) influence on government.

Given the benefits of commercial progress, it seems almost paradoxical that the British political system is in such an unsatisfactory state. For the factor that may counterbalance the corrupting tendencies commerce has unleashed is the spirit of liberty that it has also generated: 'The rapid improvements of arts and manufactures, and the correspondent extension of commerce, which followed the clear and accurate limitations of the prerogative, produces a degree of wealth and affluence, which diffused a feeling of independence, and a high spirit of liberty, through the great body of the people; while the advancement of science and literature dissipated the narrow political prejudices which had prevailed, and introduced such principles as were more favourable to the equal rights of mankind'.[123] While the English people have become politically timid, this timidity has limits. Should the oppression of government extend to the 'fundamental rights' of property, the mercantile interest would be likely to resist with a 'desperate valour'.[124] Unlike Smith in the *Wealth of Nations*, Millar does not represent mercantile interests in general as a partial and corrupting influence in the political sphere. For him, the problem seems rather that the ministry uses its patronage to divide the mercantile interest and prevent it from speaking with one voice.[125]

Yet like Smith and Ferguson, Millar was concerned about the destructive effects of the division of labour on the individual. Contrasting the urban pin-maker with the 'peasant', he found that the former would be better-dressed, less coarse, and have more 'book-learning' but would be 'greatly inferior in real intelligence and acuteness'.[126] Conversely, the rest of the community 'advance in knowledge and literature' as the mechanics descend into 'a thicker cloud of ignorance and prejudice'. In this respect, the effect of commercial progress is to widen the gap between rich and poor. Millar hoped that the wealthy would understand it was in their interests to 'cultivate the minds of the common

---

122   Millar 1803, vol. 4, p. 128. Smith had earlier observed that commercial societies brought to an end extensive relations of personal dependence. See Smith 1976 (2), vol. 2, pp. 711–13.

123   Millar 1803, vol. 4, p. 100.

124   Millar 1803, vol. 4, pp. 198–201.

125   Millar 1803, vol. 4, p. 137.

126   Millar 1803, vol. 4, pp. 144–56. Smith famously used the instance of pin-making to characterise the division of labor in the *Wealth of Nations*.

people' as a way of promoting virtue and reducing crime.[127] Anticipating the Utilitarians and English liberal reformers of the 1820s and 1830s, he argued that an expansion and reform of education was needed to promote virtue and reduce vice. But like them, Millar saw inequality as both inevitable and beneficial, and followed the general pattern of Scottish moral philosophy in regarding the assumption of authority and respect for authority alike as natural propensities.[128] This clearly has implications for his position on the distribution and enjoyment of taste.

In his chapter on 'The Effects of Commerce and Manufactures and of Opulence and Civilization upon the Morals of a People', Millar seeks to define how the 'dispositions and behaviour of man' are determined by the circumstances of commercial society. Whereas pasturage societies produce a disposition to martial exploits and courage, commercial societies promote sociability and demonstrative manners. The military virtues go into decline (which is not a disadvantage), but the increase of wealth tends to produce 'dissipation and voluptuousness, a tendency that may be observed in all countries where the people have made great advances in the accumulation of wealth, and in which the arts administer to luxury and extravagance'.[129] It is a tendency reinforced by the relentlessly competitive character of life, which erodes generosity and private familial virtues. Although Millar's judgment on the manners of commercial societies is ultimately favourable, it is hardly unequivocally affirmative, since they tend invariably to corrupt behaviour and erode benevolence.

For Millar, unlike Ferguson, the martial virtues are connected with actions of killing, which while they can be vindicated by necessity, are 'barely reconcilable to strict justice' and repugnant to humanity. While he too sees the Fine Arts as a distraction for the idle, he is less dismissive of their value. As a result of the unequal division of the increasing wealth produced by commerce and manufactures, there is a growing class of persons who have the leisure to indulge in 'what is called pleasure'. Such persons need to occupy their minds to prevent themselves sinking into apathy, and consequently they 'seek amusement by artificial modes of occupying the imagination', in sports and diversions: 'Hence the introduction and improvement of the elegant and fine arts, which entertain us by the exhibition of what is grand, new or beautiful, and which afford a delightful exercise to our taste, or a pleasing agitation of our passions'.[130]

---

127   Millar 1803, vol. 4, p. 158.
128   Millar 1803, vol. 4, pp. 129, 309.
129   Millar 1803, vol. 4, p. 230.
130   Millar 1803, vol. 4, pp. 139–40.

Millar's *Historical View* articulates the cyclical model of the history of the Fine Arts that appears in several of the texts I have discussed. Poetry is 'naturally progressive', but when it and the other arts have reached a certain point they go into decline characterised by over-refinement, excessive ornament, and lack of simplicity. In such phases, 'The grand and sublime are deserted in the pursuit of mere novelty and variety; and a corrupted taste becomes more habituated to factitious and sophisticated embellishments'. It is a 'natural improvement' when this has occurred to abandon verse, and 'in more natural and easy expression, to exhibit such pictures of life and manners as are calculated to please the understanding, and to interest the passions'. Such 'compositions' can be 'extended and diversified without end', and are 'peculiarly adapted' to the combined exercise of the imagination and judgment 'agreeable to a refined and philosophical age'. This explains why the state of society in England and France is inimical to epic poetry, which 'demands from the reader an alertness, and intensity of application, which few persons are capable of maintaining'. Thus the novel (the form to which Millar is referring above) has almost entirely superseded it and become the 'chief amusement' of the leisured.[131]

From the preceding paragraphs it will be evident that Millar linked the emergence of the novel form directly to the character of the contemporary social order. He explains the forms of modern drama in a similar way. Theatrical productions involve a degree of expense that means they can only appear in opulent cultures. Further, since comedy feeds off 'instances of impropriety and absurdity', and these are more likely to be felt in the diversified societies characteristic of commercial and manufacturing countries, due to the 'separation and multiplication' of trades and professions. These diversities include differences of education, habit, and opinion, but extend to bodily forms and psychology, for 'the standard of dignity and propriety is different according to the character of the man who holds it, and is therefore contrasted with different improprieties and foibles. Every person, though he may not be so conceited as to consider himself in the light of a perfect model is yet apt to be diverted with the apparent oddity of that behaviour which is very different from his own'.[132] Hence humour is particularly important in England (the country most advanced in commerce and manufactures), where it is also encouraged by the climate of political freedom. However, Millar detects a recent falling-off in English comic talent, which may have arisen due to permanent changes; perhaps the division of labour has now advanced to such a degree, that skills are 'so minutely sep-

---

131   Millar 1803, vol. 4, pp. 319–34.
132   Millar 1803, vol. 4, pp. 361–2.

arated from each other' as to form very little 'peculiarity' in those who practice them, thereby diminishing humour's field. Further, the application of the English to business is such, that they are unlikely to acquire that quickness and flexibility of the imagination that would lead them from humour to wit.[133]

Scottish social theory, whether applied in 'conjectural history' or in specific historical narratives, inserted the arts into the progress of societies as a 'reflection' of the manners and psychology generated by economic and political institutions. For, Ferguson, Millar and others, they were an integral feature of a succession of social totalities. Logically, the arts were in turn an influence on manners and psychology; but while statements to this effect were common in essays on taste and morals, they did not lead to extended inquiries within histories. Conversely, the delimited domain of philosophical criticism meant that it did not generally prompt direct considerations of the relationships between the stadial progress of societies, and the changing character of cultural forms. While an historical framework was assumed, authors focused principally on contemporary culture and their predominant concern was to establish a universal psychology of the aesthetic. The issues of evaluation and prescription, which were fairly peripheral to history, were quite basic to essays on taste. This point is exemplified in the last major text I consider here, Alison's *Essays on the Nature and Principles of Taste*, the most thorough-going and consistent application of the association principle to the theory of taste.[134]

Archibald Alison

Unlike Kames, Alison made no use of the concept of internal senses, and his model of the mind does not compartmentalise it into discreet faculties. In his Introduction, he tells us that the imagination should not be considered as a separate and peculiar faculty and the effects attributed are to be explained in terms of the mind's general principles. For Alison, there is no single emotion of taste, which is always a complex emotion, comprising the production of a simple emotion and a particular 'exercise of the imagination'. The trains

---

133   Millar 1803, vol. 4, pp. 374–5.

134   Alison's *Essays on Taste* were first published in Edinburgh in 1790, but seem to have attracted little notice initially. There was no second edition until 1811, but this was quickly followed by four more over the years 1812–25. The success of the second edition was probably due to Francis Jeffrey's very favorable review in the *Edinburgh Review* 18, 36 (May 1811), but it may also have benefited from the success of Payne Knight's impressive use of association theory in his *Analytical Inquiry into the Principles of Taste*, which went through four editions between 1805 and 1808. The fullest account of Alison seems to be that in the *Dictionary of National Biography*.

of association that arouse emotions of taste are distinguished by an over-riding principle of connection, a single pervading emotion, and the intensity of our aesthetic response depends upon unity of effect, which derives from resemblance. Ordinary trains of thought lack this general relation.[135]

Reason and judgement play no role in the free play of the imagination that characterises taste, and the mind must be detached from personal concerns and interests for it to be susceptible to aesthetic experience: 'In such trains of imagery, no labour of thought, or habits of attention, are required; they rise spontaneously in the mind, upon the prospect of any object to which they bear the slightest resemblance, and they lead it almost insensibly along, in a kind of bewitching reverie, through all its store of pleasing or interesting conceptions'.[136] The pleasures produced by an object are thus cumulative: the more extensive the associations connected with it, the stronger is the emotion of beauty of sublimity it produces.

Alison consistently emphasises that matter is neither beautiful nor sublime in itself. As we have seen, this was a fundamental premise for post-Lockean aesthetic theory, and one that had been asserted equally by Kames. Where Alison differs from his predecessors is in his belief that not only are forms and colours not intrinsically beautiful, but that matter in itself is incapable of prompting aesthetic emotion. The external senses through which matter is known to us can only produce sensations, not emotions. Material phenomena only produce emotions by acting as signs for qualities that do produce them: 'the qualities of matter are not to be considered as sublime or beautiful in themselves, but as being the SIGNS or EXPRESSIONS of such qualities, as, by the constitution of our nature, are fitted to produce pleasing or interesting emotion'. Confusion has arisen because of a phenomenon akin to what Barthes describes as the naturalisation of second order discourse: 'In such cases, the constant connection we discover between the sign and the thing signified, between the material quality and the quality productive of Emotion, renders at last the one expressive to us of the other, and very often disposes us to attribute to the sign, the effect which is produced only by the quality signified'.[137]

---

135   Alison 1815, vol. 1, pp. 4–15, 70–7, 120.

136   Alison 1815, vol. 1, p. 21.

137   Alison 1815, vol. 2, p. 416; vol. 1, p. 179. 'Myth Today' in Barthes 1973, pp. 109–59. Alison himself acknowledged that his doctrine of signs was partly modelled on that of Thomas Reid (with whom he corresponded) and the conception must have had considerable currency both through Reid's lectures at Aberdeen and Glasgow, and through the essay 'Of Taste', in Reid 1785, pp. 733, 735–6, 749. See also Reid 1973, pp. 41–2.

Although Alison's insistence that all emotions of taste depend upon association introduces a measure of relativism into his system, he was as committed to the standard of taste as any of his predecessors. The *Essays* restate the conventional cyclical model of artistic change, but recast it in associationist terms. The Fine Arts, having reached the apogee of their development, have always degenerated because the 'nature of these Arts themselves' afford 'no permanent principles of judging'. Artists tend to place undue weight on skill and the 'display of Design', which are relative to the period in which a work is produced; they give insufficient attention to character and expression, which 'arise from certain invariable principles of our Nature'. The pleasures associated with the former are inferior to those associated with the latter, which do not depend upon familiarity with the arts. This over-concern with design is fuelled by the public's desire for novelties. It is because both artists and public alike generally lack the sensitivity and science to understand the permanent principle of art that Alison hopes to see the diffusion of 'more just and philosophical principles', and the arts rescued from the 'sole dominion of the Artists'.[138]

Alison only *hoped* that there were 'circumstances in the modern state of Europe' that might check the cyclical decline of the arts; none the less, he offers an essentially progressive model. The simplicity (that is, uniformity and regularity) characteristic of the early stages of art was due to the associations these qualities have with design and skill. Imitation of nature and rivalry between artists make those qualities less a sign of skill in later stages and as the arts improve towards refinement they are distinguished by variety. However, to earn the admiration of all ages, art must have qualities that appeal to the 'uniform constitution of Man and of Nature'. In all the arts that involve the beauty of form, the artist must disengage his mind from 'the accidental Associations of his age, as well as the common prejudices of his Art; to labour to distinguish his productions by that pure and permanent expression, which may be felt in every age'.[139]

For Alison, while judgement plays no part in aesthetic pleasure it is central to criticism, which now functions to distinguish true taste from mere fashion. Yet if art must be measured against the permanent principles of human nature, there are no fixed forms that will produce the relevant effect. The beauty of all forms depends on their functions as signs expressive of fitness to purpose, or expressive of emotion, and this means there is potentially no limit to the objects of taste: 'Instead of a few forms which the superstition of early taste

---

138   Alison 1815, vol. 2, pp. 108–17.
139   Alison 1815, vol. 2, pp. 199–200.

had canonised, every variety, and every possible combination of form, is thus brought within the pale of cultivated taste; the mind of the spectator follows with joy the invention of the artist; wherever greater usefulness is produced, or greater fitness exhibited, he sees, in the same forms, new Beauty awakening'.[140] If there was an original and primitive beauty there could be no progress, whereas a benevolent creator has organised nature for human improvement.

Alison's system thus provided criteria by which traditional achievements in the arts and new developments alike could be justified in common terms. Further, it acknowledged that history itself legitimised the great works of the past because of the cultural values associated with them. For Alison, the appeal of Greek art does not depend on its intrinsic principles, since, for him, 'Beauty of Design' is historically relative, whereas beauty of expression is felt more universally. There is a beauty of proportion in his system, but this depends upon an expression of fitness, a calm and rational pleasure inferior to the expression of emotion. Alison's explanation is thus surprisingly modern-sounding: Greek art's emotional appeal derives from the wealth of connotations it has for the educated classes, 'an enthusiasm which is founded upon so many, and so interesting Associations'.[141]

Just as Alison recognised historical variation but asserted a supra-historical standard, so too he reconciled a diversity of individual tastes with a uniformly distributed capacity. This he achieved by making normative a class-structured society that enables a few persons to develop their faculties, but disqualifies the majority from doing so, for 'the generality of mankind live in the world, without receiving any kind of delight from the various scenes of beauty which its order displays'.[142] Alison's explanation of variations in taste follows the pattern we have seen in other essays: they arise from the intrinsic differences between individuals, from the differences between youth and age, and from the diverse habits of thought produced by different occupations. To an important extent, the capacity for taste seems to depend upon education.[143] Alison asserts the common humanity of the 'lower orders', but claims that their 'vulgar and degrading occupations' disfigure their minds and bodies alike.[144] The state of mind most favourable to the emotions of taste, when the imagination is 'free and unembarrassed', is generally limited to those who do not labour, and who are not pre-occupied with commerce, learning, or personal advancement.

---

140   Alison 1815, vol. 2, p. 433.
141   Alison 1815, vol. 1, pp. 97, 155, 166–7. Cf. p. 400.
142   Alison 1815, vol. 1, p. 63.
143   Alison 1815, vol. 2, p. 160.
144   Alison 1815, vol. 2, p. 274 – although note the qualification to this pp. 275–6.

Consequently, 'It is only in the higher stations ... or in the liberal professions of life, that we expect to find men either of delicate or comprehensive taste. The inferior situations of life, by contracting the knowledge of men within very narrow limits, produce insensibly a similar contraction in their notions of the beautiful and sublime'.[145] Moreover, Alison's norm is antithetical to the emergent capitalist metropolis. Those who are doomed to spend their early years in 'populous and commercial cities', where 'narrow and selfish pursuits' prevail, will have their sensibilities blunted, particularly since they will lack contact with nature. The 'vulgar pursuits of life' have a 'melancholy tendency' to 'diminish, if not altogether destroy', our sensibility to the 'scene of moral discipline' offered by the 'Material Universe around us'.[146] In line with the strand in Scottish thought that articulated criticisms of some aspects of commercial societies, Alison's text restricts the full exercise of taste to a leisured rural class and a few in the liberal professions.

Some Conclusions

Scottish social theory did not offer any single view on the character and prospects of contemporary culture. There was a general consensus that taste was formed through habit, custom, and the influence of an individual's social environment; at the same time there was a concern to define universal values, while allowing for innovation and change, in short, for progress. However, there were substantial differences in the evaluation of modern commercial societies, and quite marked distinctions between the unequivocal progressivism of early Kames, the more nuanced positions of Smith and Millar, and the pessimism of Ferguson. There was, however, no clear-cut divide between critique and affirmation, and the works of thinkers such as Smith and Millar mix both elements. Neither was there a simple development from one to the other. Equally, in relation to taste and the arts, while there was an increasing tendency to look favourably on modern artistic forms, taste remained a faculty ever prone to degeneration in commercial societies, which philosophers must work hard to preserve from moral corruption and fashion. What Duncan Forbes described as the 'sceptical Whiggism' of the Scottish School extended to their view of culture.

The Scots' natural history of society should certainly be understood as a phase of bourgeois ideology, but in the context the term 'bourgeois' needs

---

145   Alison 1815, vol. 1, p. 89.
146   Alison 1815, vol. 2, p. 444.

some qualification. While the development of the English ruling class since the mid-sixteenth century is conceived most usefully as a process of embourgeoise-ment,[147] it is a truism that eighteenth-century landed capital retained many of the interests and trappings of an aristocratic class. The elements in the Scottish landed class that formed 'society' in Edinburgh, however enthusiastic their commitment to modernisation, retained some of the cultural assumptions of a patrician elite. It is thus not surprising that the intelligentsia that grew out of that formation, and which to an important extent represented its interests, would produce a species of social theory that articulated doubts about the effects of progress on the morals and manners of society, including the Fine Arts. It is equally consistent that while rejecting the principle of aristocracy it questioned the political virtues of the urban bourgeoisie – or at least some fractions of it – and tended to represent the gentry as the social group best able to rise above narrow self-interest. As we have seen, Scottish social thought tended to give landed society a kind of authority in matters of taste that it denied to other fractions of capital.

In short, if the term 'bourgeoisie' is to be applied to the eighteenth-century Scottish and English gentry, then it is necessary to identify them as a specific type of bourgeoisie, distinct from the urban-based manufacturing and mercantile bourgeoisie that became a vocal force in politics in the early nineteenth century. For not only are those bourgeoisies distinguishable in terms of the spheres of the economy from which they extracted their wealth (if imperfectly so), they are distinguishable, more importantly, in terms of their distinctive political and religious cultures. After all, the intra-class struggles of the post-Waterloo period surely involved more than just a conflict of interests, they also involved a conflict between a model of political authority founded in custom, and one founded in a secular and rationalistic conception of the modern state as one in which all forms of property would rule in the interests of all citizens. While the thought of the Scottish School contributed to that latter conception, it had to be remade to do so, and the elements of custom filtered out of it.

Equally, in relation to the social constituency of the arts, before the 'natural' hierarchy of merit in taste and practice could be free to emerge unencumbered by the restrictive growths of aristocratic privilege, progress would have to be turned into an unqualified good, and the potential equality of all citizens within the nation state would need to be asserted. I address these ideological shifts in Chapters Three and Four.

---

147   See especially Corrigan and Sayer 1985.

Anand Chitnis has exemplified the changing character of Scottish thought in the early nineteenth century through an analysis of the *Edinburgh Review*, founded in 1802. Particularly significant in this respect is a debate between Dugald Stewart and Francis Jeffrey occasioned by Jeffrey's reviews of Stewart's life of Thomas Reid and his *Philosophical Essays* of 1804 and 1810. In these, Jeffrey questioned the value of the philosophy of the mind, which he argued was inherently conjectural and incapable of increasing human power, and demoted it relative to the natural sciences. Chitnis suggests that this is symptomatic of a significant shift, whereby, 'utility in the shape of the practical sciences and education, was seen by the younger generation as having a more important place in society than the mental philosophy that had been all consuming in the heyday of Hume and Reid'.[148]

This reorientation is linked with attacks on the English universities that appeared in the *Edinburgh* in 1808–10, and the extensive support it gave to the University of London and to the formation of the Mechanics' Institutions in the mid-1820s. The *Edinburgh* recommended the education of workmen and employers alike in the principles of political economy, because it claimed that science would demonstrate to the former that they had as much interest in the maintenance of the social order as the latter. In a departure from the generally more complex positions of the eighteenth-century thinkers, the middle class was represented by the magazine as the guarantor of progress and the social group that would prevent a tyranny of either the aristocracy or the lower orders.

The *Edinburgh Review* can be seen as exemplifying not only a shift in Scottish thought, but also a larger ideological shift, whereby the complex social philosophy of Smith, Millar, and Ferguson, with its profound moral concerns, was replaced by the dismal science of classical economics, based in J.G.A. Pocock's words on a 'restrictive and reductionist theory of the human personality'.[149] In the process, a theorist of the calibre of John Millar simply fell from view and British culture effectively lost the only discourse that involved a truly synthesising approach to the study of society; hence partly its extraordinary failure to make any significant lasting contribution to the development of sociology in the nineteenth century.[150] In its most profound aspects, the spirit of the Scottish inquiry was taken up not by the nineteenth-century political economists but by Marx.

---

148   Chitnis 1976, p. 217. See also Fontana 1985, especially Chapter 3.
149   Pocock 1983, p. 251.
150   On which see Anderson 1992, pp. 51–6.

Postscript (2014)

This essay was originally conceived as a supplement to Ronald L. Meek's classic article 'The Scottish Contribution to Marxist Sociology', first published in 1954 and then reprinted in an amended version in 1967. Meek intended to show that the thinkers of the Scottish School had not only in some regards anticipated and probably influenced the materialist theory of history associated with Marx and Engels in their emphasis on the primacy of the 'mode of subsistence' in defining property relations, and their determining effect, in turn, on the system of laws and government; they also recognised that these were always linked with developments in a society's 'taste and sentiments' and 'general system of behaviour', in Millar's words.[151] Meek thus acknowledged, but did not explore, the way in which Scottish social theory indexed the progress of social forms to changes in 'manners, morals, literature, art and science'.[152] In part I wanted to make up that gap.

I now see the issue as more complex than I then realised. Meek acknowledged the distance that separated the Scots' materialist conception of history from that of Marx and Engels.[153] Millar, for instance, saw societies as being divided into something like classes ('ranks'), but he did not see class relations as exploitative and antagonistic, let alone as contradictory. Correspondingly, he could not conceive class conflict as motoring historical change. However, thinking within the parameters of scientific Marxism, Meek saw Marx's achievement as lying in a recombination of 'Classical sociology' and 'Classical political economy' – which as we have seen became sundered in the early nineteenth century – and the linking of them to a theory of history and an ethics.[154] He was silent about the profound *philosophical* distance that separates Marx from the Scottish School, the vast difference in epistemology and method. The fact that Marx had to pass through Hegel to produce the Marxian dialectic falls quite outside the picture – perhaps unintentionally but certainly symptomatically given Meek's social scientific mind set.

With their essentially bourgeois notions of historical progress and Lockean conception of the understanding, neither Millar nor any of his contemporaries could imagine a *self-critical* emancipatory rationality as an actor in the historical process. A reason grounded in induction will always tend to accept the parameters of what is. The other side to this is that the Scottish School had no

---

151   Meek 1967, pp. 37–8; 41.

152   Meek 1967, p. 42.

153   Meek 1967, pp. 43–5.

154   Meek 1967, pp. 49–50.

conception of ideology, of socially interested distortions of reality in the realm of ideas and belief. Class differentials in judgments of taste are simply due to the limitations of experience imposed by lack of education, cultivation, and leisure. It was easy and logical to make this argument partly because Locke's system did not separate epistemology from psychology but made the former dependent on the latter.

Discussions of the aesthetic attitude grounded in inductive procedures could never achieve the clarity and rational consequence that Kant's epistemology brought to definition of the aesthetic domain. If taste is only conceived on the basis of generalisations from observed phenomenon, to be justified as an ameliorator of manners or at best a handmaid to natural religion, its potential as a special mode of cognition linked with the promise of human freedom cannot be envisioned. Artistic forms are only reflexes of the particular character of the societies in which they appear; an important insight, but one that in itself would point no further than to an empirical sociology of art and literature. The very social groundedness of Scottish social theory as a self-conscious aid to the progressive forces in commercial society defines its limitations. All of which is to say that for all its impressive insights, the Historical School's thinking on taste remained largely confined within the domain of ideology. Inequalities in the aesthetic domain could be acknowledged, but they were the result of the inequalities in property and status without which progress was inconceivable. No vision of an emancipated aesthetic order was possible on this basis.

Academic Theory versus Association Aesthetics: The Ideological Forms of a Conflict of Interests in the Early Nineteenth Century

This essay is concerned primarily with a few articles from British periodicals and newspapers of the early nineteenth century, a lecture by the painter Benjamin Haydon, written in 1837, and some observations made by Royal Academicians in lectures and other publications. Taken together, these materials represent the main published response of artists to the concept of the association of ideas as it was used in treatises on taste, the British contribution to the emergent discourse of aesthetics in this period. In general, their response was hostile, and even when artists recognised the explanatory value of association theory they were largely unable to integrate it with their own accounts of painting. Only a few landscape painters adopted the theory with any enthusiasm.

My justification for considering this obscure region of ideology is that I believe that early-nineteenth-century painting and its social functions cannot be effectively explained without a systematic analysis of the discourses and institutions that in part determined them. The term 'ideology' is not used in this essay to demarcate a distinction between 'false consciousness' and science. Following Göran Therborn, I take ideology to refer to 'that aspect of the human condition under which human beings live their lives as conscious actors in a world that makes sense to them in varying degrees'.[1] It includes both 'everyday notions' and 'institutionalized thought-systems and discourses'. I take as presuppositions that (a) the functioning of ideologies is not most usefully discussed in terms of their misrecognition of the real character of social relations, and (b) ideologies are not simply reducible to class ideologies, and that non-class ideologies have a 'historicity and materiality' that involves specific forms of social organisation, and cannot simply be read as effects of the dominant mode of production, and (c) relations and conflicts between ideologies are not *usually* directly determined by class relations, although ideologies are always linked with classes, and always imbricated in the overall pattern of power relations between class groups.

---

1 Therborn 1980, p. 2.

I depart from Therborn in regarding 'motivation by interest' (in a wide sense of that term) as a necessary concept in explaining human agency.[2] In this essay 'ideology' is not regarded simply as the discourses *with* which human subjects represent and advance their material interests, but also as the medium *within* which their understanding of themselves as 'conscious actors' is constituted and that partly *defines* their interests. Following Pierre Bourdieu, I regard the sphere of artistic practice as a sub-field of a larger cultural field of 'symbolic production', in which social groups struggle to achieve a kind of 'cultural capital'. This 'cultural capital' often has some economic value, it confers prestige and even authority on its possessors, and it is used to confirm the prevailing hierarchy of social differences.[3]

The dominant social fractions (in this case the British landed oligarchy) sought to legitimise their domination either through their own ideological production or by employing ideologues as intermediaries. Association aesthetics was a kind of discourse that, I shall show, transparently legitimated the power and influence of the landed gentry in the cultural field. However, most ideologues only serve the dominant class groups incidentally, and the dominated fraction of professional producers always tends to make forms of cultural capital pre-eminent in its hierarchy of distinction. Thus artists, who with few exceptions saw themselves as maintaining the values of the contemporary social order, at the same time struggled to maximise their influence in the cultural field by referring to themselves a special status through the professional discourse of art theory. Their success or failure in advancing their claims was seen by them as having both symbolic and material repercussions.

To begin with, it is necessary to set out the general character of the contending discourses with which I am dealing. It is indisputable that the eighteenth century saw the beginnings of a new type of literature, in which 'the various arts were compared with each other and discussed on the basis of common principles'. This new science of aesthetics was generally known in Britain as philosophical criticism. It was a type of discourse concerned with the spectator's experience of works of art and the 'disinterested' contemplation of nature, and differed markedly from the specialised treatises on individual arts, concerned mainly with technical precepts, that had formed the predominant art literature hitherto. Paul Kristeller, in a well-known essay, argued that this development occurred due to the rapid expansion of cultural production in the eighteenth

---

2   Therborn 1980, p. 5. On agency, see Bhaskar 1979, Chapter 3.
3   Bourdieu 1992; Bourdieu 1993, Chapter 1.

century, brought about by the growth of a new type of public.[4] Although this thesis is not in itself sufficient explanation, neither the vast proliferation of this literature, nor the specific character it assumed, will be effectively explained until historians of aesthetics pay more attention to the social functions of the discourses they describe.

According to Kristeller, the new literature developed outside the 'traditions of systematic philosophy', and was produced by 'secondary authors, now almost forgotten ... and perhaps in the discussion and conversations of educated laymen reflected in their writings'.[5] While Kristeller was right in claiming that most authors of philosophical criticism (with the exception of Hume) were not major thinkers, he was incorrect in his suggestion that they stood outside 'the traditions of systematic philosophy', unless this term is interpreted in some exclusive Germanic sense. British eighteenth-century aesthetics developed primarily on the heritage of Locke. In its most interesting and distinctive form, so-called psychological criticism, it sought to extend the empirical investigation of mental functions that Hobbes and Locke had primarily initiated to the responses of the mind to nature and works of art categorised by the term 'taste'. Its exponents thus tried to create systems that elaborated on the prevailing model of the mind, and worked within the main stream of British philosophical speculation.

The most important texts of philosophical criticism, with the exception of those of Burke and Payne Knight, were all products of the Scottish School. They could be listed as Frances Hutcheson's *An Inquiry Concerning Beauty, Order, Harmony, Design* (1725), Hume's essay 'Of the Standard of Taste' (1757) and other sporadic forays into the field, Alexander Gerard's *An Essay on Taste* (1759), Lord Kame's *Elements of Criticism* (1762), and Archibald Alison's *Essays on Taste* (1790), together with the rather lesser efforts of Thomas Reid and Hugh Blair.[6] Of the exceptions I have listed, I would argue that Burke, as an ambitious Irish 'gentleman' was in a somewhat similar social position to some of the Scottish writers, while Knight's *Analytical Inquiry into the Principles of Taste* (1805) is a later work that follows a pattern set largely by the Scots.

The Scots' contribution to philosophical criticism was part of the major development of social theory by the Scottish School in this period, and as such belongs to the broader phenomenon known as the Scottish Enlightenment.

---

4   Kristeller 1965, p. 225.

5   Kristeller 1965, p. 226.

6   An invaluable but uneven guide to this literature is provided by Dobai 1974–7. In my view, Shaftesbury's contribution to philosophical criticism has been overstated, most notably by Cassirer 1951, pp. 312, 332.

The causes of this complex phenomenon are clearly beyond my scope here, but it seems probable that given the *relative* economic backwardness of Scotland and the political marginalisation of the dominant fractions of Scottish society after the Union, ambitious lesser gentry/professionals like Hume and Kames, and aspiring academics like Gerard and Blair, would have been particularly motivated to advance themselves in the cultural field, by forms of symbolic production that proved their superiority to their materially advanced southern neighbours. Certainly there is evidence to suggest that these factors contributed to the importance of the legal, academic, and clerical professions in eighteenth-century Scotland. These highly specific socio-economic and political circumstances, together with the institutions of the Scottish University system and a flourishing publishing industry, provided conditions that fostered Scottish philosophical criticism.[7]

By the early nineteenth century the dominant theory in British aesthetic speculation was a form of associationism derived partly from Hume, but to a much greater extent from David Hartley's *Observations on Man* (1749). Although the work of Lord Karnes was still widely read, the most influential, consistent, and sophisticated expositions of the theory were Alison's *Essays on Taste* (republished in 1811, 1812, 1815, 1817, and 1825), and Richard Payne Knight's *Analytical Inquiry into the Principles of Taste* (in its fourth edition in 1808).

The theory of association depended on the presuppositions that the human mind could be studied by the same kind of empirical procedures that seventeenth-century scientists such as Boyle had developed to study the natural world, and that this study would reveal regular principles in its workings, akin to natural laws. These principles were preordained by the creator of the universe (usually conceived as the god of Christianity), and thus had a teleological significance; in most cases they were interlinked with the preordained order of the natural world through natural theology. Working on the basis of Locke's account of cognition, these theorists regarded the nature of matter as unknowable, and insisted that beauty or sublimity were not qualities inherent in material things but the responses of the mind (emotions) produced by certain types of external stimuli. Although all these thinkers remained committed to the idea of a standard of taste, the idea was defended with less and less conviction (or at least dogmatism), until in Knight's *An Analytical Inquiry* it has become thoroughly etiolated in what he described as a 'sceptical view' of the subject. Awareness of the cultural relativity of taste really begins with Hume's celebrated essay on the theme, and its develop-

---

7   See Chitnis 1976 and the references in Chapter One.

ment is connected with the larger contribution made to historical studies by the Scottish School.

Association theory offered an explanation of aesthetic pleasure as a particular function of the imagination, a kind of disinterested pleasure produced by certain types of trains of associated ideas, which are stimulated by objects in the real world or by their representation in works of art that act as signs for these ideas. No object has any intrinsic aesthetic quality. They only become productive of such qualities through human experience in particular cultural contexts. This theory was, of course, used to sustain eighteenth-century norms of taste, but that it licensed new types of art production was evident to its exponents, who welcomed some such developments while maintaining the value of generally accepted achievements.

Despite its limitations, association aesthetics offered the nearest thing to 'science' in the explanation of the experience of works of art then available, providing a kind of proto-semiology, infused with teleological and universalist assumptions about human nature, which in themselves could be marshalled to serve the ideological interests of the class for which it was produced. The mode of address of association aesthetics and the range of literary culture it assumed in its readers, presupposed that they belong to a particular class, and tended to exclude those who did not. Further, it was a discourse that explicitly hailed its readers as leisured gentlemen. Characteristically, association aesthetics did not treat the 'lower orders' as genetically inferior and incapable of aesthetic experience (this would have contradicted its universalist assumptions), it simply argued that they were placed at a level in the social scheme that made it impossible for them to achieve the necessary competences. Alison, for example, alleges that 'the man of business' and the 'philosopher' will have acquired habits of thought that unfit them for this 'indulgence of the imagination' while 'the common people, undoubtedly, feel a very inferior Emotion of Beauty from such objects, to that which is felt by men of liberal education, because they have none of those Associations which modern education so clearly connects with them'.[8] Only those whose social rank guarantees them the necessary education and freedom from worldly concerns can fully enjoy this pleasure. Payne Knight was equally clear about who he was addressing.[9]

The other contending discourse with which I am concerned, academic theory, set out from identical social assumptions, predictably so, since it was pro-

---

8   Alison 1815, vol. 1, p. 20; vol. 2, p. 160.

9   Knight 1808, pp. 293–4. Knight's elitism is even clearer in his review of Northcote's *Life of Reynolds* see Knight 1814, pp. 263, 272, 276.

duced by professional artists, a group that had a strong stake in the prevailing structure of social relations and also operated as the ideologues of the dominant social fractions in some degree. Thus Reynolds, like the philosophical critics, maintained that the norms of taste were fixed in the universal characteristics of human nature, but also regarded the 'lower orders' as unfitted by their place in the social hierarchy to enjoy 'intellectual entertainments'.[10] The 'refined taste' for the higher arts is 'the consequence of education and habit: we are born only with a capacity of entertaining this refinement, as we are born with a disposition to receive and obey all the rules and regulations of society; and so far it may be said to be natural to us, and no further'.[11]

In eighteenth-century aesthetic theory, as in social theory of the period, the inequalities of the contemporary social order are turned into an inevitable feature of advanced societies and found to be 'natural', turned into 'an ideal expression of the dominant material relationships' as Marx and Engels put it.[12] Like his friend Burke, Reynolds was a conservative defender of an 'entailed inheritance' of received wisdom, who saw an inequitable distribution of economic and cultural capital alike as inescapable. In reality, the Royal Academy contributed to ensure that the 'lower orders' had no opportunity to acquire the distinction it marketed by physically excluding them from its exhibitions through an entrance fee introduced expressly for that purpose.

However, in other respects the theory of painting was a very different type of discourse from philosophical criticism, and most of it took the form of lectures. It was produced by professional artists mainly as an ideology to maintain academic authority and teaching practices, and was explicitly directed at professional artists and students, although it also found a readership among the dominant class fractions, for whom knowledge of painting was one kind of cultural capital, if a kind less important than, say, some knowledge of ancient literature. (It was probably of more value in this respect to aspiring members of the professional and commercial bourgeoisie like J.J. Angerstein or Samuel Rogers, and particularly to those moving into the ranks of landed society such as the Hoare family at Stourhead).[13] As with philosophical criticism, the mode of address of academic theory explicitly assumed a particular type of reader (an aspiring artist), and contributed to form a particular kind of subjectivity.

---

10   Reynolds 1975, Discourse 11, l. 26–30.

11   Reynolds 1975, Discourse 13, l. 136–41.

12   Marx and Engels 1977, p. 64.

13   Woodbridge 1970. See especially the letter from Henry Hoare to Richard Colt Hoare, December 1755, quoted pp. 22–3.

The antecedents of academic theory went back to the fifteenth century, but its immediate models were late seventeenth-century continental texts by André Félibien, Charles Alphonse du Fresnoy, and Roger de Piles, together with the influential writings of the early eighteenth-century English painter Jonathan Richardson. In format, the lectures of the Royal Academy's Professors of Painting – Barry, Opie, Fuseli, Phillips, and Howard – are all essentially similar. (Although organised around the same assumptions, Reynolds's *Discourses* were produced as presidential addresses for the annual prize-giving to students and have a somewhat different format.) Their basic problematic was like that of Jonathan Richardson's *Theory of Painting* in that it assumed the practice of painting could be comprehended as a number of parts, which were discussed separately in different lectures. Invention, Expression, Composition, Design, Colour, and Chiaroscuro provided the basic categories that governed what could be said in the discourse. The academicians generally gave some attention to the history of painting, although the extent to which they did so varied.

Academic theory was not concerned with psychological principles or the emotional responses of the spectator; it was oriented around the practice of production, not that of response. Indeed, it was not based around a model of the mind, except in the most schematic sense; it was based upon a set of received principles derived from earlier artistic practice and discourse. It followed the other major strand in Enlightenment aesthetics beside the empiricist tradition, that of Cartesian rationalism, and rested on the belief that the arts have certain *a priori* principles that are founded in 'Nature' and 'Reason'. Following in a long tradition, Reynolds asserted in his first *Discourse*, 'It must of necessity, be that even works of Genius, like every other effect, as they must have their cause, must likewise have their rules'.[14]

In fact, Reynolds's approach to rules is notoriously ambiguous. Both he and the Professors of Painting always emphasised that ultimately Genius is above rules, a widely accepted precept in the later eighteenth century, partly due to the influence of Edward Young's *Conjectures on Original Composition* (1759). Reynolds referred to Young's book in his eleventh *Discourse*. But to have abandoned belief in a priori principles in painting would have required a complete rethinking of academic discourse, and would have threatened the authority of the academic edifice. Its continuing hold is indicated by Lawrence's statement in his presidential address at the 1823 prize-giving: 'There may be new combinations, new excellencies, new paths, new powers ... there can be no new

---

14   Reynolds 1975, Discourse 1, l. 92–7.

PRINCIPLES in art; and the verdict of ages ... is not now to be disturbed'.[15] The fact that Lawrence made this statement at all suggests he may have felt that the old principles were under some threat, probably as a result of the increasing pre-eminence of landscape and genre painting and a growing challenge to academic shibboleths connected with that development.

At the core of academic theory was the idea that the highest achievements in painting and sculpture depended on a perfected vision of the human form: the ideal. According to Reynolds, 'Ideal Beauty, is the great leading principle by which works of genius are conducted'.[16] The artist achieves this form by re-iterated analysis and comparison of objects in nature, which leads him to the 'central form' of each species that is nature without blemishes or imperfections. It is 'natural' for the mind to find pleasure in such forms; although, contradictory as it may seem, Reynolds recognised that the mind had to be educated to do so. Whilst Reynolds's particular formulation of the ideal was to meet strong criticism from Hazlitt, Haydon, and others in the early nineteenth century, essentially similar notions of it were advanced in the lectures of the Professors of Painting up to those of Henry Howard, delivered between 1833 and 1847.

Academic theorists could hardly ignore the vast output of speculation on taste in the eighteenth century, which not only appeared as dense scholarly treatises, but was also popularised through articles and reviews in the periodical press. Reynolds's departures from some of the traditional positions of art theory were probably prompted in part by his awareness of these developments. His familiarity with the association doctrine is evident at a number of points in his writings, and particularly in his third *Idler* paper of 1759, in which he suggested that species are all equally beautiful, and only come to be preferred through the association of ideas – although within each species the beautiful is to be found in a central form.[17] Opie, Phillips and Howard all referred to the association of ideas in their lectures, Opie even describing it as 'that wonderful and powerful principle';[18] but their awareness of the doctrine did not induce them to any reformulation of academic discourse, despite the fact that the writings of Alison and Knight clearly contradicted the idea that there could be any immutable principles of beauty fixed in particular forms.

The fact that no reconciliation or integration between these two discourses was possible is particularly clear from the writings of Fuseli, who reviewed

---

15   Lawrence 1824, p. 19.

16   Reynolds 1975, Discourse 2, l. 122–3.

17   Joshua Reynolds, 'The True Idea of Beauty', *The Idler*, no. 82 (10 November 1759).

18   Wornum (ed.) 1848, p. 245.

Alison's *Essays on Taste* for the *Analytical Review* in 1790. Fuseli clearly understood the basic issue for he began his review by stating, 'Whether the source of beauty and sublimity is in mind or in matter, is a question which has divided past, and will probably divide future philosophers'.[19] While he was reasonably favourable to Alison's work as a source of 'much entertainment', Fuseli suggested that he had pursued a favourite theory to ridiculous extremes. He gave an account of a number of Alison's positions without comment, but clearly felt unhappy with the proposition that natural phenomena are in themselves incapable of producing emotions and only arouse them by acting as signs for emotions to which they are connected by convention and habit.[20] Fuseli seems prepared to acknowledge that *some* sounds and colours acquire meanings through association, but clung to the conviction that others have an intrinsic capacity to produce particular effects. Predictably, he objected most strongly to Alison's rejection of the idea of an innate beauty of forms. Fuseli reviewed only the first volume of Alison's work, and it was in the second that Alison's ideas on form were fully developed, but his basic response would only have been confirmed if he read them: Alison's arguments were over-theoretical and ultimately specious.

In his lectures as Professor of Painting, delivered initially in 1801–4, Fuseli virtually ignored the association principle. He defined the nature that the painter represents as 'the general and permanent principles of visible objects, not disfigured by accident, or distempered by disease, not modified by fashion or local habits', while beauty is 'that harmonious whole of the human frame, that unison of parts to an end which enchants us'.[21] This is the only beauty he acknowledges, and it is experienced through a kind of perception produced by an 'inward sense' available only to those with the 'highest degree of education'. Despite some slight variations, all of the Professors of Painting took a similar position.

Finally, it must be stressed that artists used academic theory as a symbolic weapon to assert their dignity and claims to a special social status, which in turn would bring them tangible material rewards. With the exception of Fuseli, the Academy's professors consistently emphasised the moral utility of painting; art contributed to the refinement of manners.[22] They also claimed that achievement in the Fine Arts was the gauge by which the culture of

---

19   Henry Fuseli, review of Archibald Alison's *Essays on Taste, Analytical Review*, series 1, 7
      (May 1790), p. 26.

20   Ibid., p. 28.

21   Fuseli 1831, vol. 2, pp. 21–2.

22   E.g., Reynolds 1975, l. 80–6.

a nation would be judged by future generations.[23] It was only the highest achievements in painting, monumental history paintings, which could bring a nation a high status, and equally, only the most intellectual aspects of artistic practice could raise the painter to the level of 'a man of Genius'. Reynolds's view was a commonplace: 'The value and rank of every art is in proportion to the mental labour employed in it, or the mental pleasure produced by it … In the hands of one man, it [i.e. painting] makes the highest pretensions, as it is addressed to the noblest faculties: in those of another, it is reduced to a mere matter of ornament; and the painter has but the humble province of furnishing our apartments with elegance'.[24] The corollary of this position was that the imitation of nature could not be the sole aim of painting. Together these ideas served to legitimise and indeed produce a hierarchy within the artistic profession.

The idea that 'genius' could raise artists far above their normal class origins and make them equal, if not superior, to the wealthy and powerful had obvious attraction. The Academy sought to foster these pretensions through its ceremonies and titles, and through its Annual Dinners, where artists rubbed shoulders with people of the highest rank. Artists were highly conscious of the status that had allegedly been achieved by painters in the Ancient World and in Renaissance Italy, and writers from William Aglionby in the late seventeenth century onwards trotted out the examples of favours bestowed by monarchs and popes on great artists with monotonous regularity. Flaxman made the point particularly boldly in his memorial address on the death of Thomas Banks (1805), in which he quoted from the French historian Charles Rollin to the effect that as rulers of society have been assigned their rank by divine providence, so there is also a divine ranking of intellects: 'It forms, from the assemblage of the learned of all kinds, a new species of empire, infinitely more extensive than all others, which takes in all times and nations, without regard to age, sex, condition, or climate; here the plebeian finds himself on a level with the nobleman, the subject with the prince, nay, often his superior'.[25]

Among the relatively conservative and establishment membership of the Royal Academy, such claims were advanced discretely and with restraint, but outsiders could be more extreme. Thus Hazlitt, whose political position was far more radical than that of the generality of academicians, not only claimed that genius was much higher than mere aristocratic title, but also that self-

---

23   Fuseli 1831, vol. 3, pp. 41–2.
24   Reynolds 1975, Discourse 4, l. 1–8.
25   Flaxman 1892, pp. 277–8.

love and pride made it impossible for 'the great' to have any real feelings for the highest forms of art.[26] Academicians, ideologues of the dominant social fractions, generally did not make such subversive claims, but they did use academic discourse, which also formed them, as a symbolic system to advance their interests in the cultural field.

Academic lectures were clearly not the appropriate place for artists to confront the challenge of association aesthetics, and their responses were largely presented within the framework of specialist art magazines and the periodical press. As we have seen, philosophical criticism represented an essentially spectator-oriented approach to the arts, which in some cases emphasised their pleasure effects more than their didactic functions. Further, the key texts of association aesthetics, those of Alison and Payne Knight, were quite explicit that artists themselves did not have the proper qualifications to make balanced judgments on the arts.[27] It is therefore not surprising that artists' responses to association aesthetics were interwoven with arguments alleging the lack of qualifications of non-professionals to judge on the arts, criticisms of the perceived deficiencies of contemporary patronage, and calls for a regular system of state support for High Art. Thus although neither of these discourses can be derived directly from the interests of their exponents, the inquiry concerning the forms of spectator experience and the systematisation of craft skills and forms of earlier expression do clearly relate in their different ways to the social positioning, roles, and experience of their exponents, and the usage of these discourses could serve real symbolic and material interests.

For artists strongly committed to high art and the shibboleths of academic theory, opposition to philosophical criticism hinged on the fact that it rejected the notion that certain forms had a transcendent aesthetic status. For such artists, philosophical criticism pursued that which was inscrutable in essence: it was abstract hypotheses, the inconsequence of which betrayed the *practical* ignorance and incompetence of its authors. Hostility to the pretensions of criticism, in the more general sense of the term, is clearly evident from the first significant art magazine published in Britain, *The Artist*, which ran from 14 March 1807 to 1 August 1807, and then for twenty numbers in 1809, being republished in two volumes in 1810. It was edited by the artist Prince Hoare, and the majority of the articles were by him and other artists and architects, including James Northcote, John Hoppner, John Opie, John Flaxman, J.F. Rigaud, John Soane, and

------

26   Hazlitt 1873, pp. 162, 453.

27   Alison 1815, vol. 2, pp. 116–17. Payne Knight's condescension towards artists was evident in his writings and also made explicit in conversation. See Messmann 1974, p. 119, and Potts 1982, p. 72.

James Elmes. Other contributors included George Cumberland, Isaac D'Israeli, and Thomas Hope. From the beginning, the magazine was belligerently assertive about the qualifications of artists to adjudicate on the arts, and the lack of qualifications of non-professionals. In the preface to volume I, its aim is described as being to provide 'a more easy channel' than that 'provided by regular treatises', through which artists themselves could familiarise the public with artistic principles. The introduction to the first number opens with a diatribe against the influence of 'dilettantes' and 'dabblers': 'There are many elegant writers in the present day, possessed of every requisite for discoursing on the Arts, except a practical acquaintance with them'.[28]

'Criticism' is the butt of several articles, of which the most revealing is an anonymous essay entitled 'Metaphysical Criticism on Works of Invention', which appeared in the eighth number in 1809. In this the principle central to academic theory, that criticism should draw its precepts from tradition, from the example of earlier art, rather than trying to uncover the general principles by which the mind responds to art works, is clearly articulated: 'It appears to me that criticism, as applicable to subjects of taste, is a safe guide only while she draws her conclusions, by direct analogies, from existing and established models. For, whenever she presumes to promulgate doctrines, founded on deductions from *assumed* first principles, is not the basis for such criticism, however ingenious a *mere hypothesis*? and can any hypothesis be resorted to as a safe and unerring rule?'[29] Departures from this empirical principle are branded as scholasticism, and the article goes on to insist that aesthetic quality can only be recognised through feeling; although analysis may tell us something of how feeling comes about, it is inevitably posterior to it. The objects of taste are defined in the nature of things. Taste is a sense designed to recognise such objects, an original capacity of human nature that is cultivated through practice. The art of the ancients provides the soundest basis for rules and theory because it has been the source of pleasure for so long.

It is significant in relation to this re-iterated accusation that critics, mere literary men, lacked the necessary qualifications to judge on painting and the plastic arts, that *The Artist* also carried a number of critiques of the doctrine of 'ut pictura poesis', the most substantial of which is James Northcote's essay 'On the Independency of Painting on Poetry'. All of these emphasised that painting was a distinct and independent art with its own specific means of

---

28   *The Artist*, 1, 1 (14 March 1807), pp. 9–10. Reprinted in Hoare 1810.

29   Anon., 'Metaphysical Criticism on Works of Invention', *The Artist*, 2, 8 (1809), p. 110.

producing pleasure and communicating ideas, and which was not dependent on connections with or imitation of literature for its effects.[30]

It was in the context of this publication that John Hoppner, a prominent portraitist and academician, published a savage review of Payne Knight's *Analytical Inquiry* in May 1807, the first of a number of attacks on Knight's critical writings by artists. The hostility that Knight aroused was not based on a single cause, and it might not have been so violent had it been so. It was because he came to represent both a type of discourse that contradicted academic theory in some respects and the influence of a social clique which it seemed could really influence the livelihood of artists, and also because he was already notorious for the publication of moral and political views deeply offensive to some shades of conservative opinion, that he became such a prime target for artistic hostility.[31]

As a member of the Committee of Taste, set up by the government in 1802 to organise the national war monuments in St. Paul's, and as a founder member of the British Institution established by a group of patrons in 1805 to foster the Fine Arts, Knight was no more likely to attract criticism as a meddling and ill-informed connoisseur than any other member of those bodies with a similar background. What made Knight so conspicuous, was that, first, he publicly rejected the pretensions of artists as moralists, and criticised both the credo of High Art itself, and one of its leading British exponents, James Barry, regarded by many artists as a martyr to the High Art cause;[32] and secondly, he combined personal arrogance with professed disdain for the judgments of artists and had the temerity to doubt the high estimation that many of them set on the recently imported Elgin Marbles.

Knight's unjustified reputation for Jacobinism, his open religious scepticism and contempt for contemporary sexual mores made him an easy target. Hoppner seized on his scepticism and claimed that it made Knight a menace to public morality. Misrepresenting Knight's position, he claimed that he was of the type who deny any innate principles of morality, thus making everyone

---

30   James Northcote, 'On the Independency of Painting from Poetry', *The Artist*, 1, 9 (9 May 1807), pp. 1–16. Cf. 'Letter from A. Speculator on the Connection Generally Supposed to Exist between Poetry and Painting', ibid., 1, no. 15 (20 June 1807); 'Strictures on the Late School of France', ibid., no. 20 (25 July 1807); and Henry Fuseli, review of Uvedale Price, *An Essay on the Picturesque*, in *Analytical Review*, series 1, 20 (1794), p. 259. On the history and significance of 'ut pictura poesis', see Lee 1967.

31   On Knight's moral and political views, see Messmann 1970, pp. 83–97; Potts 1982, and Clarke and Penny (ed.) 1982, pp. 5–6, 10–11.

32   Knight 1808, pp. 457–60; Knight 1810; Knight 1814, p. 291.

free 'to constitute himself the creator of good and evil'. This scepticism in matters of morality is presented as analogous to Knight's scepticism in matters of taste: 'Of all dogmatizers, however, none seem to have committed greater outrage upon nature than those who deny the existence of beauty; or who refer the measure of it, at least, to every man's rude or inunatured (sic) opinion'.[33]

Again this was a misrepresentation of Knight, who maintained that aesthetic pleasures (like moral values) are culturally and historically relative, but also claimed the faculty of taste was part of the design of a supreme being, implanted for the benefit of humanity, and functioning according to stable principles. Hoppner accused Knight of confusing taste with fashion, and like academic theorists in general appealed to an innate aesthetic sense to justify transcendent norms. Given Knight's reputation, Hoppner predictably pointed to his 'grossness' in linking the sexual appetites of the different races (and even of animals) with their diverse norms of physical beauty. Sceptical philosophers such as Knight, Hoppner concludes, 'would take from nature the direction of our senses, and deliver them over to the guidance of fashion or habit', furnishing 'argument for the indulgence of vicious taste, and the most depraved appetites, while he hardens the mind against virtue'.[34] This is really more of a denunciation than an argument, and Hoppner was clearly harking back to the criticism directed at Knight from the far right of the political spectrum in the 1790s. However, lurking within this diatribe is some rudimentary perception that Knight's sophisticated treatise contradicted the simplistic and dogmatic account of aesthetic pleasure offered by academic theory, and the model of the artist as a specially gifted category of subject it implied.

Hostility to critics and aestheticians comparable to that manifested in *The Artist* also figures in the writings of one of the most respected of early nineteenth-century artist writers, Martin Archer Shee, whose *Rhymes on Art* (1805) and *Elements of Art* (1809), whatever their value as poetry, provide one of the most interesting commentaries on contemporary culture by an artist of the period. Shee had been made an academician in 1800, and was to succeed to the presidency of the Academy in 1830. He was to distinguish himself by his bland rejection of all criticisms of that institution when he appeared before the 1835–6 Parliamentary Select Committee on Arts and Manufactures, a committee packed with reformers and 'liberals', predisposed to be hostile to the Academy as an 'aristocratic' corporation.

---

33   John Hoppner, 'On the Supposed Influence of Fashion on our Opinions of Beauty', *The Artist*, 1, 9 (23 May 1807), p. 2.

34   Ibid., p. 11.

However, Shee's main writings on art appeared before he came to identify so closely with the artistic and social establishment, and they were seen on their appearance as one of the main statements of artistic discontents. In both the *Rhymes* and the *Elements*, Shee complained vigorously of the lack of patronage for High Art in Britain, and blamed it, in no uncertain terms, on the dominant commercialism of British society. Not that Shee was hostile to commerce as such, but he argued that the rich and powerful were failing to 'set an example of liberal policy and enlightened wisdom to the world', as befitted 'this great empire'. Shee was in no sense a political radical, but he blamed successive British governments for failing to grant any state support to the arts on the false grounds of 'public economy', and attacked 'the cold tribe of subservients, desk-drudges and deputies', the placemen who infected 'the higher reaches of authority' and degraded its 'noblest functions'.[35]

Those familiar with political discourse of the period will recognise this as a criticism of the Pittite faction among the Tories, who dominated the administration. (Not that the Whigs had a different approach to government when in office). It is significant, I suspect, that Shee expressed these views in the *Elements* (1809) rather than in the *Rhymes* (1805), because in 1808 Major Hogan had published charges of corruption in the army directly implicating the Duke of York, which led to a major row in Parliament in January 1809, the setting up of a Committee of Inquiry, and finally the resignation of the Duke as Commander in Chief in March. In connecting state neglect of the arts with political corruption, Shee was taking precisely the same line as that established in Leigh Hunt's *Examiner*, that outspoken organ of middle class reform, in 1808. However, while the *Examiner* denounced the Academy as yet another corrupt body, of a type with Parliament, Shee attributed the improvement of the arts in Britain to the exertions of the academicians. He astutely took elements from the prevailing political discourse that could be used to argue for the artists' interest.[36]

Whatever the precise nature of Shee's political sympathies (and they were probably Whig at this time), he wrote primarily as a professional artist contributing to the more general effort to raise the status of painters in English society. Some of his assertions in *Rhymes on Art* became a by-word for the highest estimation of artistic status. He claimed of the painter that 'his ideas

---

35   Shee 1809 (1), pp. 372–82, 226–8.

36   See, for example, R.H. [Robert Hunt], 'State of the Arts in Great Britain', *Examiner*, no. 2, 10 January 1808; and R.H., 'Royal Academy', *Examiner*, no. 43, 23 October 1808. For an outstanding characterisation and contextualisation of the *Examiner*, see Roe 2005. See also Stout 1949.

are exalted, his feelings are refined beyond the comprehension of common minds, or the attainment of ordinary occupations' and even went so far as to assert that the painter was superior in his necessary attainments to the poet.[37] It is not surprising that someone prepared to distinguish the worth of artists as a category of individual in these terms placed little value on the opinions of public or critics. The neglect of artists by the public was presumably due to the failure of society's leaders to provide a proper example, and in *Rhymes on Art* Shee appears mainly concerned with the presumptions of connoisseurs, the traditional bogey-men of English artists: 'Lookers-on, we are gravely told, know more of the game than those who play it; and strange to say! the best judges of art are not to be found amongst those who devote to it their lives, but those who bestow upon it their leisure!'[38] The heavy and indignant irony of this passage makes it an important precedent for Haydon's celebrated assault on Payne Knight published in the *Examiner* and the *Champion*, another liberal reform paper, in March 1816. In the *Elements of Art*, Shee's attacks were direc-ted more against the growing tribe of newspaper and periodical critics, who, he claimed, misled public taste, puffed the 'reptiles' who were prepared to flatter them, libelled merit, and were, all in all, 'the nightmare of Genius'. Unlike the poet, historian, or philosopher, the painter was not judged by his peers.[39]

Holding such positions in common with *The Artist*, one might have expected Shee to be strongly antipathetic to the presumptions of philosophical criti-cism, and indeed, he remarked archly in the *Elements of Art*, 'If the influence of Taste upon the British public were indeed, in any reasonable degree, pro-portionate to the discussions which it has produced, we should certainly rank high in the scale of national refinement'.[40] Further, Shee reassured his readers of his attachment to the prevailing organisation of society by his marked hos-tility to the 'visionary speculations of modern philosophy', by which he meant any attempt to realise the ideals of the Enlightenment through a fundamental restructuring of the social order. In *Rhymes on Art* he refers approvingly to Burke, observing that 'it never can be safe to trifle with doctrines, which incul-cate contempt for the gathered wisdom of ages'.[41] It was precisely the aesthetic variant of the 'gathered wisdom of age' that provided the bedrock of academic theory.

---

37   Shee 1805, pp. 105–7, 112.

38   Shee 1805, p. 71.

39   Shee 1809 (1), pp. 333–4, 338.

40   Shee 1809 (1), p. 2.

41   Shee 1805, pp. 50–4.

Considering his attachment to these positions, it seems almost inconsistent that Shee should express approval of Payne Knight's *Analytical Inquiry*. But in *Elements of Art* he acknowledged that while he could not 'coincide in all the opinions' of its author, he applauded him for maintaining 'the cause of intellectual liberty' against the 'advocates of regular system and dogmatic criticism' with 'manly sense' and 'acute argument'. This was a clear reference to the violent hostility to critics that Knight had voiced in the *Analytical Inquiry* and his insistence that rules and respect for precedent tended to hamper the workings of genius.[42] (Shee quoted from a passage in the *Inquiry* relating to this latter point). However, while Shee could clearly find positions in Knight's work that broadly coincided with statements about rules in Reynolds's writings, and more generally in academic discourse, nothing suggests that he had engaged with the full implications of association aesthetics. Further, on the key issue of the moral end of painting they represented contrary views, with Shee consistently insisting on the moral importance of the arts.

By 1809 the scandal over Knight's *Discourse on the Worship of Priapus* (1786) was more than twenty years old, and the *Progress of Civil Society*, which had provoked charges of Jacobinism against him, had been published thirteen years before. Knight had recently reiterated his conservative Whiggism in *A Monody on the Death of the Right Honourable Charles James Fox* (1806–7), and Shee, who probably held comparable political views, no doubt felt he could approve the *Analytical Inquiry* without appearing sympathetic to Knights's notorious scepticism and unconventional views on sexuality. The treatise was a highly successful publication and Shee realised it deserved serious consideration. He may also have wished to ingratiate himself with a Director of the British Institution, since in 1809 he also published a letter addressed to that body calling on them to support a plan for the encouragement of history painting.[43] However, taken as a whole, Shee's writings show the same concern with the status of artists as a professional group and the related antipathy to criticism and philosophical treatises on the arts that are characteristic of artists' discourse in the early nineteenth century. His relatively favourable response to Knight's *Analytical Inquiry* was a somewhat maverick view that coincided with both personal interests and political concerns.

Animosity to Knight was not confined to the short-lived art magazines of the early nineteenth century, it was also expressed in the newspaper and non-specialist periodical press. It is not surprising that the reactionary *Quarterly*

---

42   Knight 1808, pp. 234–5, 253–4, 274–9.

43   Shee 1809 (2).

Review should look for an opportunity to savage Knight, since his outspoken Whiggism and hostility to Christianity had made him a target for the Tory press before.[44] However, Knight was also subjected to criticism from the other side of the political spectrum, some of the most telling attacks on him appearing in the *Examiner* and the *Champion*. It is impossible to tell how far the publication of these attacks was the result of the personal connections between Haydon, who wrote most of them, and their respective editors, Leigh Hunt and John Scott. Although he was to associate himself with some of the major liberal causes of his day, Haydon was basically Tory in his political sympathies and despite all his blustering and posturing about 'principle' generally had his eye on the main chance. He wrote from the viewpoint of a professional artist, disaffected with the main institution of his profession, but attached to its professional creed in a way that bordered on fanaticism.

The discourse of High Art was central to Haydon's self-conception as a subject, and provided the justification for his reckless borrowings and sometimes unconventional behaviour. However, in the context of these papers his criticism of the academy and of connoisseurs, and his passionate exposition of the value of High Art and equally passionate pleas for state support (principally for himself), did not simply represent an expression of personal and professional interests. In the *Examiner*, and to a lesser extent in the *Champion*, the alleged shortcomings of the Royal Academy and the degraded state of contemporary British art were repeatedly criticised, and treated as evidence of the corrupt condition of the dominant social elite. For both papers Haydon was a hero, a champion of true and great art and of Britain's national honour in the field of culture at a time when the artists of the Academy were too self-interested to do their duty, and Britain's governors were too corrupt, and had too narrow a view of their obligations, to provide artists with the proper kind of encouragement. In both these papers then, political and cultural criticism were tightly interwoven.

Haydon published his first broadside against Knight in the *Examiner* in early 1812, in the form of a ten-page riposte to Knight's review of the *Works of Barry*, which continued over three numbers.[45] It is indicative of either the strength of Haydon's friendship with Leigh Hunt, or the importance Hunt accorded his

---

44　'Lord Elgin's Collection of Sculptured Marbles', *Quarterly Review*, 14 (June 1816), pp. 534–5. For a sketch of the periodical press of the 1810s and 1820s, see Bauer 1953, Chapter 2.

45　Benjamin Robert Haydon, 'To the Critic on Barry's Works in the *Edinburgh Review*, Aug. 1810', in *Examiner*, no. 213, 26 January 1812; no. 214, 2 February 1812; and no. 215, 9 February 1812. A useful introduction to Haydon is George 1967. Roe 2005 is insightful on Haydon's relationship with Hunt.

views, that Haydon was allowed to hold forth at such length. Looked at dispassionately, Knight's review contained some positions similar to Haydon's own, and Haydon conceded 'the soundness of advice' in some parts of it. He agreed with Knight over the shoddy execution of many academicians' paintings, and shared his views on the undue reverence for damaged 'old masters' among the cognoscenti and his distrust of academic institutions; indeed, much of Haydon's article was less a criticism of Knight than of the Academy, which had become 'a *vast organ* of *bad taste* and corruption'. (In relation to the impact of Knight's critique of academies, from which the Royal Academy was excluded, it is worth noting that in 1810 the *Reflector*, a short-lived quarterly magazine edited by Hunt, published an article defending academies and Barry's character against Knight's aspersions. But this article was not vituperative in tone, and referred to Knight as 'our friend').[46] Haydon, however, could not accommodate Knight's high estimation of Dutch and Flemish art, his dislike of monumental painting, his criticism of public patronage, and perhaps most of all his disdain for claims that painting had a moral influence. Making the familiar analogy between painting and poetry, Haydon asked rhetorically if painting was 'merely an imitative Art?' And answered inevitably in the negative, 'You mistake the means for the end: the imitative part of Painting is only the means of exciting poetical and intellectual associations'.[47]

It is interesting that at this stage Haydon should be prepared to concede points of agreement with Knight, and that he should make use of the key principle in Knight's aesthetic in defending the moral value of painting against him. That he recognised something in the association argument could be recuperated is confirmed by a comment he made on Raphael's cartoon of the *Sacrifice at Lystra* in a series of articles on the cartoons published in both the *Examiner* and the *Annals of the Fine Arts* in 1819. In this he describes painting as, 'An Art, whose modes of conveying intellectual associations are the imitation of natural objects'.[48] But he had already defined style in art (in opposition to manner) in terms of the ideal, of discovering the '*essential*' in natural objects and discarding 'the aberrations produced by time, accident, disease, or other causes', and he claimed that the 'mere imitation' of such objects, 'independently of any idea', was a source of pleasure. Thus Haydon mixed a basically academic viewpoint

---

46   'On the Responsibility of Members of Academies of Arts', *The Reflector*, 2 vols., (1812) no. 2, Art. 13, pp. 388–408.

47   Haydon, 'To the Critic ...', in *Examiner*, no. 213, 26 January 1812.

48   Benjamin Robert Haydon, 'On the Cartoon of the Sacrifice at Lystra', *Annals of the Fine Arts*, 4, 13 (1819), p. 238; also printed in *Examiner*, no. 592, 2 May 1819, and no. 593, 9 May 1819.

on ideal form as a source of aesthetic pleasure with references to association theory, as a way of arguing for the intellectual and moral element in the effect of painting. He would continue to maintain this position when he gave more direct consideration to philosophical criticism in the public lectures of his later years.

The *Examiner* strongly supported Haydon in his attack on Knight, and in June 1812 Leigh Hunt criticised the British Institution for not awarding a prize to Haydon's *Macbeth*, and accused Knight of influencing the other directors against the artist.[49] The campaign against Knight was to be resumed in 1816, when it became known that this connoisseur who had a seat on the Parliamentary Select Committee on the Elgin Marbles had expressed reservations about their merits.

The reasons why artists and some writers took up the cause of the Elgin Marbles in this period cannot simply be explained by their transcendent merits. It is certainly true that they contributed to a reassessment of the nature of the ideal in Greek art, and provided ammunition to those like Hazlitt and Haydon who were critical of some of the formal conventions of eighteenth-century High Art; but equally important was their symbolic function as objects of national pride. They had, so the story ran, arrived just at the most auspicious moment, when the British School had the potential to match British achievements in arms, only being held back by the underdeveloped taste of the public and the lack of proper examples. Britain now stood a chance to rival the great age of Pericles. No other country had this advantage, or indeed was in a position to make use of it. At one fell swoop the nation had acquired a treasure comparable to the purloined riches of the Musée Napoléon.

In the midst of this heady mix of nationalist passion and professional aspiration, Knight's scholarly and measured, if largely unsound, reservations could only come as confirmation of one of the reiterated idées fixes of artistic groups: here was another meddling and opinionated connoisseur attempting to foist false judgments on a gullible public, and now unfortunately in a position to do real harm by influencing the Parliamentary Committee against the purchase of the Marbles. The *Examiner* gave Haydon's long article 'On the Judgement of Connoisseurs being preferred to that of Professional Men, – Elgin Marbles, etc.' a prominent place in the main body of the paper in March 1816. Haydon wrote warmly on the deficiencies of taste among the nobility and higher classes,

---

49 'Royal Academy', *Examiner*, no. 233, 14 June 1812; no. 234, 21 June 1812. Haydon himself believed that Payne Knight 'has pursued me with the malignity of a Demon' – see entry for 19 November 1814 in Haydon 1960–3, vol. 1, p. 398.

deficiencies he blamed on the defects of university education. Echoing Shee, he argued that in no other profession was the opinion of amateurs preferred to that of professionals. He now latched on to Knight's reputation for scepticism and irreligion, and linked this with his scepticism over the Marbles.[50] Knight's 'portion of capacity', which he acknowledged, was particularly regrettable because misapplied. However, the *Examiner* was not unmitigatedly hostile to Knight; it allowed occasional approving references to his probity and talents to appear, and it also published his reply to the assault on his reputation in the *Quarterly Review* in 1816.[51]

Knight got much less of a fair deal from the other main organ open to Haydon, John Scott's *Champion*.[52] Scott was never as critical of the British political establishment as Hunt and he was almost obsessively hostile to France, in April 1816 even accusing the *Examiner* of having become 'a grossly anti-English publication'. Already in his period with *Drakard's Paper*, Scott had maintained the position that the low state of British painting was due to the *'perversion of Public Taste'*, which was led by 'half a dozen fashionable Cognoscenti'.[53] He continued to voice this view as editor of the *Champion* from 1814–17, as well as making regular denunciations of the Royal Academy. To Scott, who was no great enthusiast for the British Institution either, Knight clearly appeared as the kind of fashionable connoisseur he abominated. It is very likely that his front page article, 'Parliamentary Purchase of the Elgin Marbles', published three weeks before Haydon's 'On the Judgement of Connoisseurs', had a formative influence on that piece, just as the tone of Haydon's criticisms of the Academy was probably modelled on that of earlier articles in the *Examiner* by Leigh and Robert Hunt.[54] Haydon was not in reality quite the lone heroic voice in the wilderness crying out against academic iniquities that he made himself out to be.

In his article on the Marbles, Scott deplored the fact that 'base criticism' had sought to 'undervalue these precious works', and repeated his view that hitherto a poorly informed public had been 'left at the mercy of one or two oracles' whose first object had been the promotion of their own 'personal consequence', a charge also levelled by Hunt and Haydon in the *Examiner*. By a number of

---

50   Benjamin Robert Haydon, 'On the Judgement of Connoisseurs being preferred to that of Professional Men, – Elgin Marbles, etc.', *Examiner*, no. 429, 17 March 1816.

51   'Mr. Payne Knight's Answer to the *Quarterly Review*', *Examiner*, no. 441, 9 June 1816. For responses contra and pro Haydon's article, see J.W., 'Letter to the Editor', *Examiner*, no. 432, 7 April 1816; Mariette, 'Letter to the Editor', *Examiner*, no. 434, 21 April 1816.

52   For Scott, see Hayden 1969, pp. 68–70. For a conspectus of Scott's opinions, see Scott 1815.

53   'The Fine Arts', *Drakard's Paper*, no. 11, 21 March 1813.

54   'Parliamentary Purchase of the Elgin Marbles', *Champion*, no. 164, 25 February 1816.

allusions Scott left no doubt that he was referring to Knight. In the following month the *Champion* published Haydon's article on the same day as it appeared in the *Examiner*, and the paper's implacable hostility to Knight was reaffirmed in June, when it printed an anonymous letter, virtually hysterical in tone, which contemptuously dismissed Knight's refutation of the charges made against him in the *Quarterly Review*.[55]

It is indicative of the importance of context in establishing the significance of ideological interventions that in the *Examiner* and the *Champion* Haydon's attacks on Knight seem part of a more general cultural critique, linked with a reformist politics – although it is noteworthy that Haydon did not connect the deficiencies of the Academy with the corruption of political institutions, as Robert Hunt consistently did in his exhibition reviews. However, transferred to the *Annals of the Fine Arts*, a quarterly magazine that ran from 1816–20 and was edited by Haydon's friend the architect James Elmes, they lose all connotations of reformism, and simply blend in with a larger discourse around professional interests. Indeed, although it printed several of Hazlitt's art essays, the political position of the *Annals*, in so far as it is ascertainable, was reactionary.[56] While regretting the lack of state encouragement for art in Britain, the magazine did not attribute this to political corruption, and some statements in its pages were sympathetic to contemporary patronage.[57] (Obviously the text of its five volumes does not present a straightforward unity). Like Haydon, the *Annals* turned academic discourse against the Academy, largely blaming the preponderance of careerists and portrait painters within the institution for the failings of contemporary British art. Haydon was the magazine's darling, who, according to Elmes, stood the 'most prominent in the art'.[58]

The first number was dedicated to the Select Committee on the Purchase of the Elgin Marbles, and contained a highly favourable review of 'On the Judgement of Connoisseurs'.[59] Haydon's critique of Knight's review of the *Works of*

---

55 A.S., 'Mr. Paine Knight', [sic] *Champion*, no. 180, 16 June 1816.

56 This is particularly clear in the review of Henry Sass's *A Journey to Rome and Naples, Performed in 1817* (1818), which attacked the author in personal terms for his democratic politics – see *Annals of the Fine Arts*, 3, 9 (1818), pp. 311–12.

57 J.E.S., 'General Observations on the Culture of the Fine Arts in Britain', *Annals of the Fine Arts*, 2, 6 (1817): pp. 306–12; Review of Italian, Spanish, Flemish, Dutch and French Pictures at the British Institution in 1818, *Annals of the Fine Arts*, 3, 9 (1818), p. 279.

58 Editor, 'To Correspondents', *Annals of the Fine Arts*, 3, 9 (1818), p. 332. Cf. Review of W.P. Carey's *Critical Description and Analytical Review of Death on the Pale Horse*, *Annals of the Fine Arts*, 3, 8 (1818), pp. 88–9.

59 'Review of New Books on Art', *Annals of the Fine Arts*, 1, 1 (1816), pp. 97–101.

Barry was reprinted in the second and third numbers, and a string of further articles by him followed. The *Annals* reasserted the position that *The Artist* had taken on the value of artists' statements with particular reference to Haydon's writings, namely that 'we are quite convinced, that one line written by an artist does more good to public taste than huge volumes written by technical amateurs'. Indeed, it was probably referring to that magazine when it claimed that Haydon had 'settled for ever the question, as to the capability of painters to write their thoughts, which everyone must recollect was so prevalent eight or nine years ago'.[60] As a magazine that proclaimed itself primarily an organ of professional artists, the *Annals* belonged to the same category as *The Artist*, and it relied partly on the same kinds of discourse, and advanced similar positions to champion the judgment and interests of artists as a professional class fraction.

Although the *Magazine of the Fine Arts* was edited by the publicist and antiquarian John Britton, who allegedly wrote much of it himself, the character of the text suggests a close identification with artists' interests. Britton was in this and other publications a warm friend to the British School, who tended to emphasise what he saw as its positive qualities, rather than lamenting its failure to produce a substantial body of High Art. The articles in the *Magazine* sometimes found good in the Academy, were judiciously critical of Haydon, and generally took a line distinctively different from that of the *Annals*. Britton's attitude towards the landed classes was that of a sycophant, not surprisingly considering that they provided a large part of the market for his publications and dominated the Society of Antiquaries.[61] This, together with his close involvement with topographical artists and interest in landscape painting, helps to explain why the *Magazine*'s criticism of contemporary patronage was considerably less strident than that of the *Champion* and *Examiner*. Nonetheless, the *Magazine* still described the final aim of artistic production as 'moral effect', and found a 'decisive proof of a want of taste for the essence of the arts' in the fact that no modern artist had found sufficient patronage to devote himself to 'ideal art' with 'great and striking success'.[62]

---

60   Review of W.P. Carey's *Critical Description*, p. 88.

61   On the obsequiousness of Britton, see Review of John Britton's *Architectural Antiquities of Great Britain*, in *Review of Publications of Art*, 1, 4 (1808), pp. 321, 337–43. Dobai 1970–4, vol. 3, p. 300, is wrong in saying the *Magazine of Fine Arts* was edited by Elmes and he exaggerates its similarity with the *Annals*. For Britton's authorship, see Jones 1849.

62   'Jupiter nursed in the Isle of Crete by the Nymphs and Corybantes. Painted by Mr. Cristall with outline engraving by G. Cooke', *Magazine of Fine Arts*, 1, 6 (1821), pp. 455–6. Cf. the interesting discussion of Quatremère de Quincy's *Considérations morales sur la destina-*

While moderate in its handling of the contemporary public, the *Magazine* carried one of the longest and most thorough critiques of philosophical criticism to appear at the time, which mainly comprised an attack on the association aesthetic of Alison, with particular reference to his account of the sensations of beauty produced by the contemplation of forms. I have been unable to discover the author of this, but it was written either by an artist, or by someone sympathetic to the claims of artists, and who accepted the inherited wisdom of academic theory.

The article begins with an assertion of a type that should now be familiar: 'It is generally agreed that the reader who has perused all the dissertations of the learned critics who have written on the principles of taste in the Fine Arts, often remains as ignorant and as destitute of such principles as he could have been previously to entering on such a course of study'.[63] Indeed, it is 'certain' that artists will often deduce principles from their own observation of nature and its effects, which although they cannot explain their cause are of more practical use than principles learnt from books. The practice of artists in itself shows that theories that attribute the effect of beauty to particular lines or colours must be erroneous. The author thus rejects Hogarth's line of beauty and grace, Burke's definitions of the beautiful and sublime, Price's picturesque, and Knight's sense aesthetic of light and colour – although in fact this plays a subsidiary if important role in Knight's system, which depends mainly on association as an explanatory principle. The 'puerile arbitrary classification' of the sources of pleasure as beautiful or sublime marks the insufficiency of these theories, and 'no powers of oratory' can 'protect them from contempt'.[64] At the present time (1821), the association of ideas is generally regarded as 'the only source of our perception of beauty', but the theory has been carried to absurd extremes. Alison, its most popular exponent, has forced the doctrine 'far beyond its legitimate extent', and has given insufficient weight to 'beauties of fitness and utility'.

The text betrays the standpoint of artists not only because it defends principles allegedly deduced from practical experience, but also in its focus on the issue of form, so central to academic theory. As I pointed out earlier, Alison, following Reid, maintained that objects are only beautiful insofar as they act as signs for certain emotions, and consequently, 'The fact is ... that in no class of objects is there any such permanent Form of Beauty'. To every supposed

---

      tion des ouvrages de l'art (1815) in C., 'On the Application of the Imitative Arts', *Magazine of Fine Arts*, 1, 6, (1821), pp. 419–26.

63   Anon., 'On the Principles of Taste', *Magazine of Fine Arts*, 1, 5 and 6 (1821), p. 321.

64   Ibid., pp. 322–3.

norm there are exceptions, and regarding the human form, 'it is very easy to see ... that the most different Forms of Feature are actually beautiful: and that their Beauty uniformly arises from the Expressions of which they are significant to us'.[65] Beauty of proportion, according to Alison, arises from a more general beauty of fitness to purpose, but this in itself does not account for the profound delight we experience from the human form. Although certain proportions are necessary for human forms to produce ideas of beauty or sublimity, they are not their main cause. It is from being expressive of various natural qualities or from 'the expression of pleasing or interesting qualities or dispositions of mind that the Human Form derives all its positive Beauty'.[66]

It was this position that the critic of the *Magazine of Fine Arts* found particularly objectionable. Having accused Alison of giving insufficient attention to fitness, design, or utility in his treatment of forms, and argued that there are numerous contradictions to his categorisation of the expressive qualities of natural forms, he proceeded to tackle him on proportion and the idea of a central form of beauty. While he concedes Alison's point that there is no single form which alone is beautiful, he argues that the effort to create such a central form tends to improve taste and that a kind of original form can be separated out and distinguished from the particularities that arise from accidental circumstances such as the effects of labour. He is also adamant that the European races, and particularly the Greeks, set the norm for human proportion; other races being degraded 'by the effects of their wretched climates and Habits'.[67]

According to the *Magazine's* critic, Alison had confused character with form, and he asserts, in contradiction, that all beauty of the human form depends upon proportion and fitness, although he acknowledges that works of art can scarcely avoid combining some character of expression with form. (Some academic theorists, notably Barry and Fuseli, had seen beauty of form as a rather bland beauty, and emphasised expression instead). The expertise of artists is clearly at stake here, for the critic claims: 'The most ignorant of mankind are judges of character and expression', while the rules that govern 'the inherent beauty of form' may never be ascertained, and 'can only be felt by those who have observed, compared, and studied'. Despite the arguments of association theory, 'we shall continue to think that positive beauty resides in form, independently of any mental qualities and passions, and capable of expressing them all'. Considering the 'futility' of Alison's premises, their

---

65   Alison 1815, vol. 1, p. 359; vol. 2, p. 254.

66   Alison 1815, vol. 2, pp. 321–30.

67   Anon., 'On the Principles of Taste', pp. 401–4.

'extensive circulation and adoption' is extraordinary, and demonstrates how eager people are to be 'spared the trouble of thinking for themselves'.[68]

The concern of this critic with the account of beauty of form in association aesthetics was not coincidental. He had seized on the argument in Alison's work that was potentially most damaging to the authority of academic discourse and the practice of High Art. That this is the case is, I believe, confirmed by the position Haydon had taken in his commentary on Raphael's *Sacrifice at Lystra*, and even more so by that of his fourteenth lecture, written many years later, in 1837.[69] In the lecture 'On Beauty, whether caused by Association', Haydon poses the question of whether the emotion of beauty is caused by associations, or by 'immediate impression through the eye, on the brain' and comes down resoundingly in favour of the latter hypothesis, with some qualifications.

Haydon's basic point is an elaboration of the straightforward view he had advanced in 1819. The emotion of beauty cannot be reduced to one single principle: sometimes it is a simple sensation excited at once by sight, sometimes it is a complex one depending on association. But before associations productive of beauty can occur, there must be something in form and colour to arouse that emotion.[70] In direct contradiction of Jeffrey,[71] the leading exponent of associationism after Alison, Haydon claimed that there is a natural capacity for perceiving beauty akin to the organs of sense, and differing in strength from individual to individual. The idea of internal senses that guided aesthetic and moral judgments had been developed by Shaftesbury, Hutcheson, and Gerard in the eighteenth century. Although taste was still widely referred to as a sense in a casual way in the early nineteenth century, by then inner sense theory had been entirely superseded in philosophical criticism. Haydon could not accept the general definition of beauty given by Alison, Jeffrey, et. al., and he criticised their 'inexact' use of the term. 'Common sense' would not permit Haydon to see beauty is such objects as a pug-dog. While he conceded a role to association, it could not be the sole cause of the emotion of beauty: 'I maintain there is something in the construction of every object named beautiful which excites the emotion independently of all association, and that subsequent reminiscences but confirm the first impression'.[72] Alison and Jeffrey confused beauty with expression.

---

68 Ibid., 418–19, 414.

69 Entry for 3 September 1837, in Haydon 1960–3, vol. 4, p. 431.

70 Haydon 1844–6, vol. 2, p. 255.

71 Haydon 1844–6, vol. 2, pp. 259, 263, 266–7.

72 Haydon 1844–6, vol. 2, p. 264.

As in so many of his arguments, Haydon appealed to his putative creator in support of his case. Beauty cannot be just a human convention it must have a final cause – a position that leads him to contradict Reynolds's view that the ideal of Beauty must vary from race to race. According to Haydon, his god cannot have made black people in *his* own image. His god has given human beings certain capacities of inherent sensibility, and this sensibility is particularly responsive to a type of form found in perfection among Europeans.

Haydon's ultimate nostrum is that beauty is a female principle, for 'there is nothing in the world beautiful, but the perfect face and figure of woman, and ... there is nothing dignified with that appellation which has not either by association, or form, or colour, some relation to that creature'.[73] Everything beautiful, physically or intellectually, has a 'feminine tendency' and the male form has nothing essentially beautiful in it – a position probably influenced by Burke's gendering of the beautiful and sublime, but one that departed from a basic premise of academic theory.

Making due allowance for Haydon's desire to appeal to the audience of public lectures with some striking and simple idea, this position, for all its absurdity, is related to his consistent concern with the human figure as the core of great art and the proper vehicle for expression. To concede that beauty of form was not fixed in the nature of things but was culturally relative would have cut away from the prestige of the fetishes of academic theory – Greek Sculpture, Italian art of the sixteenth century, and so on, the status of which rested to an important extent on their alleged perfection of form. It would also have undermined the authority of academic discourse and the traditional hierarchy within the artistic profession, and therefore seemed to threaten the claim to a special cultural capital that artists sought to advance in the wider social arena.

Haydon articulated the logic of the artists' position within the prevailing ideologies that bore directly on their practice. Faced with the increasing authority of a new species of discourse that contradicted the discourse through which they thought their own practice, and explicitly denied their qualifications as arbiters of that practice, artists responded by questioning the grounding assumptions of the new discourse and the qualifications of its exponents. This did not lead to any significant developments in art theory, and despite some attempts to rethink the academic hierarchy (most notably in the lectures of Charles Robert Leslie),[74] the academic theory of painting continued to be organised around similar principles throughout the century. Artists continued

---

73   Haydon 1844–6, vol. 2, pp. 237, 288.
74   Published as Leslie 1855.

to guard their stake in the cultural field through a kind of discourse that claimed that the mysteries of artistic practice can only be fully apprehended intuitively by the professional practitioner, and to resist the claims of ideologues outside the profession such as Ruskin to legislate on their competences. Although association theory continued to have some influence, the kind of leisured patrician culture assumed by the aesthetics of Alison and Knight became increasingly marginalised, challenged by a new bourgeois culture unconducive to elaborate aesthetic speculations, and such treatises on taste ceased to be produced.

As should be evident from the above, if the particular character of association aesthetics and academic theory cannot be derived directly from the class relations of the period, both these ideologies played an active role in shaping, and indeed producing a conflict of interests between artists and elements within the dominant social groups. In bourgeois art history, aesthetic discourse and art theory are treated as if they were removed from material social concerns, or affected by them only superficially. The aim of this study has been to begin to situate them back within the struggles for power and influence of which they were a part.

Bourgeois Critiques of the Monopoly of Taste

The 'Middle Class' Interest in Politics: From Anti-War Liberalism to the Philosophic Radicals

The period of the Anglo-French Wars saw the consolidation of an identifiable middle class interest in the political sphere, together with forms of discourse that proclaimed that class as the essential source of moral and political virtues, in contradistinction to the landed and unpropertied classes.[1] The formation of this interest can be traced back to the Wilkes affair and the American Revolution, but it gained new cohesion though the campaign for the repeal of the Test and Corporation Acts in 1787–90, the economical and administrative reform movements of the 1780s, and the wave of provincial associations and societies of various sorts that began to appear in these years; the economic, political, and ideological repercussions of the wars with France gave it a new militancy.[2] By the 1810s the sense of competing interests – that also stood for different ways of life, different ethics, and different political ideals – had entered the press in liberal newspapers such as *The Champion* and *The Examiner*,[3] where one of its forms was a critique of corruption in cultural matters that centred on the Royal Academy and attacks on the irresponsibility and lack of virtue of the nation's rulers, manifested in their opposition to any state provision for the Fine Arts. This discourse gained new intellectual muscle in the 1820s in magazines influenced by the Utilitarians such as the *London Magazine* and *Westminster Review*, and also issued in several polemical pamphlets and books. Its main political manifestation was the Parliamentary Select Committee on the Arts and their Connection with Manufactures of 1835–6. These ideological forms of the class struggle in culture are the theme of this chapter.

In discussing this phenomenon, we encounter the familiar problem that English usage does not generally distinguish in the way that French and German do between 'middle class' and 'bourgeoisie'. For the purpose of this study it is important to discriminate between the former, who may be described as persons generally of moderate wealth, neither exploited nor exploiters, who

---

1   For the dissent of the middling sort prior to this period, see Rogers 1984; Rogers 1989; and Brewer 1980.

2   Briggs 1956; Ditchfield 1974; Torrance 1978; Tolley 1969; Cookson 1982.

3   See Chapter 4 for further references.

are petty-bourgeois, self-employed, state or public service workers, professional persons, and so on; and the latter, owners of capital and the means of production, whose wealth derives from surplus value extracted from propertyless wage labourers.[4] In the early nineteenth century English usage of the term 'middle class' could encompass both. However, although there seems to have been no sense of conflict or tension between the two groups, their different positions in relations of production meant their interests were not identical. The ideologues who enunciated the viewpoint of bourgeois interests generally spoke from the position of intellectuals or professional persons; their vision of human progress in which the arts and sciences would advance in accompaniment with capitalist trade and industry once the constraints of feudal privilege had been shucked off endowed those interests with a kind of cultural gravitas. This was part of the ideological armoury commercial and industrial fractions of the bourgeoisie could deploy in its struggles with the landed bourgeoisie, which includes the aristocracy in this case. But in fact the cultural capital – to draw on Bourdieu's terminology – that accrued to artists and intellectuals as members of the middle class was a relatively weak currency in the social power it bought compared with the real capital of the bourgeoisie. All the more reason for middle class ideologues to emphasise its value by contrast with mere wealth, however illusory this stance was.

The liberal non-conformist intellectuals that formed the backbone of the anti-war movement developed arguments that represented the coalescence of the longstanding grievances of Dissenters and an established concern with parliamentary reform, together with 'principled' opposition to the government's economic policies (particularly its tax legislation and attempts to regulate internal trade), moral outrage over what was seen as an interventionist war with a sovereign state that represented progressive ideals (at least in the 1790s), and fierce criticism of the corruption and inefficiency of the dominant oligarchy. These arguments rested on forms of rational Christianity and on a progressivism derived from Hartley, Priestley, and Scottish eighteenth-century thought. The movement's extensive provincial base was partly fuelled by the grievances of middle-class groups with little or no political representation, who were bitterly opposed to the dominance of Tory and High Church interests at a local level. The resolution of these groups was hardened by loyalist persecution of Dissenters and reformers in the 1790s as a threat to the national interest.[5]

---

4 Although it deals with a very different historical moment, my thinking on this matter is indebted to Wright 1985, pp. 37–43, 86–92.

5 Cookson 1982, Chapter 1 and *passim*.

Disunited in its attitude towards government policies, the bourgeoisie had no class-based organisation in the political forum. But while it was fragmented and lacked a political forum, it had fostered forms of discourse that clearly and overtly represented its interests as a class, and which are to be found extensively in the newspaper, and more especially, the periodical press, in the latter of which liberal influence predominated. Liberal intellectuals of the type who gathered around the Unitarian dissenter Dr John Aikin – one of the most prominent magazine editors of the period – used journalistic outlets and pamphlets to voice the resentments of new types of bourgeois wealth against the undue influence of the landed oligarchy and City interests within the body politic. They identified a 'war faction' that enforced an inequitable tax system, ignored key interests within the state, and depressed the middle class. War was seen as providing economic opportunities for a few wealthy men to exploit, while forcing unnecessary burdens and suffering on the rest of society. The evils of war were as much political, social, and moral, as they were economic; the general progressivism of the opposition movement led them to represent it as a kind of social disease or malaise. This tied in with attacks on the laxity and indulgence of the aristocracy, which were part of the strategy by which a middle class identity was established.

The anti-war liberals took from Scottish social theory the idea that the middle class was the backbone of liberty, the main bulwark against aristocratic oppression and corruption. Their ideology was essentially meritocratic and directly critical of aristocratic privilege.[6] It was a liberalism that was also overtly capitalist, taking its principles from Smithian economics and making little use of arguments about the condition of the poor to advance its cause. This stance was precisely matched by the distance it took from artisan radicalism and popular agitation. In the postwar period bourgeois interests found a political focus in opposition to the Corn Laws, as a transparent expression of the interests of the landed classes, and in an increasing tendency to regard parliamentary reform as the fundamental strategy for bringing the state's economic policy more into line with the needs of the commercial and industrial sectors. The sense of a distinct bourgeois interest was reinforced by increasing working-class unrest and the emergence of distinctly proletarian forms of political organisation.[7]

In the 1820s representation of the bourgeois outlook took its most pungent form in the output of intellectuals who took Bentham's Utilitarianism as their

---

6 Cookson 1982, pp. 27–8.
7 E.g. see the examples of working-class resistance discussed in Foster 1974, pp. 34–43, 49–61.

basic creed, the Philosophic Radicals.[8] The group's chief organ was the *Westminster Review*, founded in 1824, and edited by John Bowring, a merchant, linguist and intimate of Bentham's. (In fact, Bowring was disliked by James Mill and the contributors were divided into two camps, with James Mill, Francis Place, and the younger Philosophic Radicals ranged against Bowring and his allies).[9] The first number of the magazine contained an attack on the *Edinburgh Review* and reviews in general by Mill, and William Thomas has described the *Westminster* as a kind of 'anti-review'.[10] The *Edinburgh* was a notably Whiggish and liberal publication that had expressed approval of Bentham and carried articles by Mill, but the *Westminster* was critical of Whigs and Tories alike. It attacked the clergy and the law, and was implacable in its hostility to the hereditary nobility. Correspondingly, it was ardent in its identification of the middle class as 'the strength of the community', containing 'beyond all comparison, the greatest proportion of the intelligence, industry and wealth of the state'.[11]

Culture and the Arts in the *Westminster Review*

The *Westminster*'s general approach to culture in its early years is directly related to this position and to its understandable tendency to identify the dominant culture as a culture of the landed classes. The idea of the patrician 'man of taste' was treated with contempt as a direct manifestation of snobbism and hollow claims to social distinction based on wealth and privilege. While it was not opposed to literature and art per se, at times it came close to sounding so and certainly downgraded literature in the hierarchy of knowledge, evaluating far above it those that its authors could more readily regard as 'useful'. In a critique of Washington Irving's *Tales of a Traveller* of 1825, the *Westminster* described the hereditary nobility as 'a gang of about a hundred and eighty families converting all the functions of government into means of a provision for themselves and their dependents, and for that purpose steadily upholding and promoting every species of abuse, and steadily opposing every

---

8   Marxist historiography has generally not been complimentary about Utilitarianism. For Anderson and Nairn it was symptomatic of the British failure to generate what they saw as a proper Enlightenment; Benthamism was only 'a crippled parody' of a 'general theory of society' or 'philosophical synthesis' – Anderson 1992, p. 57.

9   Nesbitt 1934, Chapter 2.

10   Thomas 1979, p. 159.

11   Quoted in Nesbitt 1934, p. 79.

attempt at political improvement'.[12] They were 'feeble, profligate and extravagant' persons, whose lack of proper employment and idleness drove them to find release from 'ennui' in 'war, gaming, or drunkenness', and whose profligacy led many of them into debt.[13] On a number of occasions in 1824–5 the *Westminster* accused poets generally of an unfortunate propensity for sentimental sympathy toward this class because of the appeal of the Age of Chivalry to the imagination.

For the *Westminster*, the hereditary nobility was simply a parasitic class fattening off the productive classes of society. Its view of the use of culture by this class was equally stark: 'There is a small class of readers in this country who are Somebody, and there is a very large class who are Nobody'. This class of somebodies depended for their wealth on an unjust system of taxation, and further, 'Besides this substantial privilege, and perhaps as a result of it, the Somebodys have also assumed that of having a circle and taste exclusively their own; of keeping at a distance any Nobody who dares approach; and at the expense of the excluded class, indulging in all the pleasure of arrogance and malignity: trampling with as much contempt on the necks, as it were, of their pursuits, opinions, and wishes, as the Sovereign of Ashantee does on the nape of his sable attendants'.[14] These privileges were partly reproduced by what the *Westminster* called elsewhere the 'monastic system' of education in the Universities, an education that primarily inculcated habits of indolence and vice.[15] It was unfashionable to develop the mind in the universities, and even Greek and Latin, the main stuff of aristocratic education, were not pursued 'to any extent'. Literature was studied as a substitute for 'useful inquiry'. '*Polite* Literature, and what are called the fine arts', dependent on 'powers of the imagination', were cultivated 'at the expense and almost to the destruction of the powers of judgment'. Such literature, which avoided all serious matters, provided no basis for the education of the nation's leaders and its value was overrated. The 'man of taste' 'will assert that the reading of poetry is the highest of human pleasures; and gravely maintain that twenty lines of Virgil will assuage grief and alleviate the pangs of disappointment; he will lament the slow progress of the fine arts in this country; will promote them by his patronage; become life-director of some painting institution, and vote away by thousands, money extorted from the indigent and laborious many, in order that

---

12   'Tales of a Traveler. By Geoffrey Crayon, Gent.', *Westminster Review*, 2, 4 (April 1824), p. 339.

13   Ibid., p. 343.

14   Ibid., p. 335.

15   'Outlines of a Philosophical Education ... By George Jardine', *Westminster Review*, 4, 7 (July 1825), pp. 152, 166.

the opulent and idle few may visit gratuitously some thirty or forty pictures, about which the mass of contributors are perfectly indifferent'.[16] Statements of this type effectively accepted the sociology of taste of eighteenth-century criticism and social thought, but by denying that polite culture led to virtue and enlightenment and refusing the hierarchical order of landed society as either natural or desirable, the Philosophic Radicals turned its normative claims on their head.

From the *Westminster*'s perspective, the preoccupation with polite literature was the 'disease of the age' – a judgment that becomes more understandable in relation to the contemporary proliferation of reviews and magazines – and distracted from consideration of its serious problems: 'Literature is a seducer; we had almost said a harlot'. Commerce and progress were not built on literature, but on the natural sciences, and the sciences of politics, law, and political economy.[17] William Thomas has written of the *Westminster*'s 'arrogant condescension' towards writers and the attitude of 'literary puritanism' that arose from its insistence on judging literature by the principle of utility.[18] However, these qualities were the concomitants of its social insights and pungent effect. The *Westminster*'s cultural criticism should be seen not merely as a self-display of the Philosophic Radicals' Philistinism, but as an embryonic ideology critique that had real political purchase in the context of 1820s Britain. In charging that literature and art had an instrumental value as manifestations of symbolic power it anticipated Bourdieu's insight.[19] It should also be noted that the magazine was not totally dismissive of the values of literature and praised some poets such as Thomas Moore very highly, while stressing that the principles of imagination were inimical to those of reasoning and science.

The Philosophic Radicals' onslaught on polite culture was directly linked with their concern with education as a means of fostering social harmony by teaching all orders of society where their rational interests lay. It was certainly driven first and foremost by what Richard Johnson (following E.P. Thompson) has called an impulse to 'class cultural-control' directed particularly at the better off and more literate sectors of the working class, one part of which was a concern to extirpate 'indigenous working-class educational practices'.[20] But

---

16   'Tales of Traveler. By Geoffrey Crayon, Gent.', p. 337.

17   'Outlines of Philosophical Education ... By George Jardine', p. 166.

18   Thomas 1979, p. 162.

19   'On Symbolic Power', in Bourdieu 1992, pp. 163–70.

20   Johnson 1976, pp. 49–50, 44. In a succession of important essays, Johnson has demonstrated that the object of working-class education for reformers was primarily to inculcate norms of subservience and to replace working-class cultures of resistance with

it was also directed against what was perceived as the obsolete polite culture of the landed classes, which diverted them from more useful pursuits: 'The real happiness of men, of the mass, not of the few, depends on the knowledge of things, not on that of words'.[21] However, Bentham's followers did see some value in the arts, and in 1827 the *Westminster* took up and developed an idea that had been expressed before and which was to be used in the 1830s by the parliamentary radicals active in the Select Committee on the Arts and Manufactures, namely that a better taste needed to be inculcated among the labouring population so that handicraft goods would be improved in quality and compete more effectively with those of France. The *Westminster* argued that all arts and crafts, indeed all labour skills, had an intellectual element, and therefore working people needed a sound general education to achieve the best results. If French workpeople surpassed those of Britain in producing pottery, carpets, printed cottons and metalwork, this was because their taste was more refined; they had received an 'insensible education' through the 'abundance and cheapness of prints, a public exposure of statues, and an universal reading of their own best writers'. This education also made them more honest and law-abiding because it diverted them from 'those brutal and coarse amusements which are the acknowledged disgrace of our populace';[22] a strikingly anti-nationalist position in the context of the British newspaper and periodical press of the period, which was always prone to see the French people as bloodthirsty Jacobins.

The demands of trade and social order required state action. The state should provide art education, as component of general education, and this outlay would be more than repaid by increasing competitiveness and a decline in the cost of skilled labour. Thus the interests of the bourgeoisie were seen to demand an extension of artistic education to the lower orders, a thing regarded as unnecessary and undesirable in eighteenth-century philosophical criticism, which frequently remarked that because the lower orders did not have the opportunity to develop their taste, they remained contented with the aesthetically deprived condition that nature and god had foreordained. The

---

middle-class morals and patterns of behavior. See Johnson 1970; Johnson 1976; Johnson 1979.

21   'Outlines of Philosophical Education ... By George Jardine', p. 166. For the ideological implications of this emphasis on facticity in the thinking of bourgeois educational reformers in the early nineteenth century, see Shapin and Barnes 1976.

22   'Library of Useful Knowledge', *Westminster Review*, 7, 4 (April 1827), pp. 284–5. The Library of Useful Knowledge, the object of this review, was the pet child of Henry Brougham – see Aspinall 1927, pp. 231–3.

Westminster specifically refuted the idea that the nurturing of taste among the labouring classes would make them discontented with their lot; rather, it would make them more biddable and respectable.[23]

George Nesbitt, in his study of the *Westminster Review*, noted a distinct change in the magazine's position on literature signalled particularly by Bowring's review of Tennyson's *Poems, Chiefly Lyrical* of January 1831. Bowring argued that the 'law of progression' should operate in poetry as in the sciences and that progress in 'the real science of mind' could lead to new advances in poetry; 'the machinery of a poem is not less susceptible of improvement than the machinery of a cotton-mill', for 'the great principle of human improvement is at work in poetry as everywhere else'. Poetry's value as a disseminator of patriotism, national feeling and character was now extolled on the basis of the mechanistic conception of mental functions that the Utilitarians took from association psychology. There was 'nothing mysterious, or anomalous, in the power of producing poetry, or in that of its enjoyment; neither the one nor the other is a supernatural gift bestowed capriciously'. The great increase in the 'ease, power, and utility' with which states of mind could be analysed as a result of progress in 'metaphysical science' provided the poet with tools whereby he could now achieve 'greater truth and effect' in his representation of human action than his predecessors.[24]

Such a position ran counter to Coleridge's philosophy and conception of poetry in almost every respect, yet in 1830 the *Westminster* had already retracted its earlier position that poets are not reasoners and had published a very favourable article on Coleridge, despite his reactionary politics.[25] By this date the coherence of the group around the *Westminster* had sharply declined as result of internal squabbles, the scandal over the Greek loan in 1826, and the ineffectual defence of its position in response to Macaulay's critique in his three *Edinburgh Review* articles of 1829.[26] Perhaps because of a growing uncertainty of direction, the *Westminster* showed an increasing readiness to co-opt progress in the arts to the general argument on the progressive character of the age; but this also matches with the tendency of bourgeois texts on culture in the 1830s, which suggests that larger factors were at work.

---

23   'Library of Useful Knowledge', pp. 278–9, 284, 285–6.

24   Nesbitt 1934, pp. 151–60.

25   'The Poetical Works of S.T. Coleridge', *Westminster Review*, 12, 23 (January 1830), pp. 1–31.

26   Nesbitt 1934, pp. 130 ff. On the Greek Loan, see also Thomas 1979, pp. 163–7.

Two Middle Class Tracts on the Arts from the Early 1830s

Given the downgrading of literary and artistic culture in Utilitarian thought it is not surprising that the bourgeois intelligentsia of the early nineteenth century did not generate systematic treatises on the arts comparable with those of philosophical criticism. Such production could have been considered superfluous since the aesthetics of Alison and Knight relied on essentially the same psychology and epistemology as Utilitarianism and already provided consistent explanations of aesthetic functions, whatever their implicit or explicit acceptance of a social hierarchy dominated by the landed classes. The publication of such treatises seems to have come to an end with the contributions of Jeffrey and Stewart, and speculation now took the form of review articles in periodical literature, which with the advent of the *Edinburgh Review* in 1802 began to offer more space for extended reflections; Jeffrey's essays are symptomatic in this respect.[27] Reflecting both the increased leisure time and affluence of bourgeois groups in an expanding urban capitalist society, periodical literature developed into one of the most important literary forms of the early nineteenth century.

Outside of the periodical press the position of bourgeois class interest in the cultural field was advanced through the pamphlets and books of an assorted collection of littérateurs, artists, and parliamentary radicals in the 1830s and 1840s. In relation to the visual arts, bourgeois interests were given political focus in the Parliamentary Select Committee on the Arts and Manufactures of 1835–6,[28] attacks on the Royal Academy, a campaign to get art galleries and monuments opened to the public free of charge, and moves that led to the setting up of the Normal School of Design.

Consistent with the increasing autonomy of the cultural field, there seems to have been a kind of two-way traffic between the political representatives of the bourgeoisie and elements in the intelligentsia anxious to identify their interests with those of a rising class. In the early 1830s two liberal intellectuals published texts that linked the well-being of the arts and sciences with the advancement of the bourgeoisie in the largest terms, James Millingen's *Some Remarks on the State of Learning and the Fine Arts in Great Britain* (1831) and Richard Henry Horne's *Exposition of the False Medium and Barriers Excluding Men of Genius from the Public* (1833). The fact that these were published in the years around the Parliamentary Reform Act can hardly be coincidental. Although the bases

---

27   For the *Edinburgh Review*, see Clive 1975; Fontana 1985.
28   On which, see Gretton 1998.

of their critique and the solutions they proposed were somewhat different, both texts argued that aristocratic government was directly hostile to science, learning, and the arts,

Millingen (1774–1845), the son of a Dutch merchant, grew up in England and was educated at Westminster School, before his family immigrated to France in 1790. After some employment in banking, he settled in Italy, becoming a prominent antiquarian through his work on coins, medals, and Etruscan vases. A member of learned societies in Britain, France, and elsewhere, his interest in public policy on the arts in Britain seems directly related to his own situation: 'When Science does not constitute a distinct profession, it can never attain any great degree of eminence'.[29] *Some Remarks* begins by critiquing the idea, said to have been gaining ground in Britain, that the state had no duty towards or interest in encouragement of the arts and sciences, which should be treated like other commodities and left to find their 'natural' price in the market. On the contrary, Millingen argued, many objects of public utility can only be achieved through political actions in the common interest. Every other state in Europe had established literary and scientific institutions; the decline of science and literature in the United Kingdom was down to the misconceived and deliberate policy of a corrupt aristocratic regime that 'seems to have been influenced by the principle that the bulk of mankind can only be governed by the suppression and debasement of their intellectual faculties, and that the institutions of civil life rest for their support on the ignorance of the greatest part of those who live under them'.[30] These were the principles of the party that had run the state for the previous half century. We might expect a laissez-faire attitude to cultural production to be the dream child of bourgeois Philistinism; but Millingen associated it with an aristocratic faction.

Using the language of liberal critiques of aristocratic corruption developed during the Anglo-French Wars, Millingen argued that 'in modern Aristocracies, this contempt of Learning is encreased (*sic*) by the prejudice of the Feudal times, which considered every profession, except the sword, as derogatory to the rank or dignity of that class'. In Britain, where an 'Aristocratic faction' had undermined the constitution and acquired 'supreme power' in the state, 'a man whose profession is learning, is esteemed by the great in no other light than as a helot or serf'.[31] In other European nations men of learning are honoured and rewarded; in Britain only the military is.

---

29   Millingen 1831, p. 12. Information on Millingen's life is from 'Millingen, James', *Dictionary of National Biography*, London: Smith, Elder, and Co., 1885–1900.

30   Millingen 1831, p. 2. Cf. p. 72.

31   Millingen 1831, p. 4.

Millingen proceeded to criticise the inadequacies of the universities, the provision of museums and libraries, and the constitution of British learned societies. The only learned body for which he had any respect was the Royal Academy, which owed nothing to the British government, a government that refused encouragement to the Fine Arts, and actually impeded them through its fiscal policies. The parsimony of the British state contrasted with the generosity of the French.[32] The refusal of Pitt and Greville to finance Lord Elgin's expedition to Greece in 1799 was symptomatic of their 'systematic hostility against intellectual improvement'. Under the Tory administrations of the war years, the 'system of corruption' developed to such an extent that it destroyed 'the love of liberty and every generous sentiment', replacing them with 'extremes of either servility or licentiousness' – in effect a return to the culture of clientage that John Brewer has argued was so oppressive to the middling sort in the eighteenth century.[33] The spirit of the age in British society was a pervasive selfishness combined with 'general skepticism' and the sacrifice of principle to expediency, tendencies that had infected the church and corrupted the press.[34] The remedy lay in the spread of learning, which would promote religion and help refine the 'lower orders', who educational reformers of the period regarded as alarmingly irreligious. As evidence Millingen claimed that crime was less in France than in Britain and did not require such sanguinary laws to enforce it because French learned institutions had inculcated a greater respect for property.[35] The contemporary movement to reform the British constitution led him to hope for kindred reforms in the cultural sphere through the establishment of proper institutions of learning.

While advocating a similar remedy to Millingen's *Some Thoughts*, Horne's *Exposition* is very different in tone and style from that text; its style might be described as an exuberant Hazlittism. The son of an army quartermaster, educated at Dr John Clark's School in Enfield, Horne was the pattern of a romantic adventurer, serving in the Mexican Navy in 1825 and traveling in the United States and Canada before settling in London in 1828–9. He became a devotee of Hazlitt – although he never met him – and with Charles Wells put up the writer's tombstone. His London circle of acquaintances included writers, philosophers, economists, politicians, and scientists; among whom were the ardent Benthamite Dr Southwood Smith, the Reverend Dionysius Larcher, and Dr Leonhard Schmitz (all members of the Society for the Diffusion of Useful

---

32   Millingen 1831, pp. 13, 48 ff.
33   Millingen 1831, pp. 72–3. Brewer 1980, pp. 345–8.
34   Millingen 1831, p. 78.
35   Millingen 1831, p. 70.

Knowledge) and radicals such as the Unitarian Minister and Anti-Corn Law League spokesman, W.J. Fox, and the republican engraver, W.J. Linton.[36] Horne published a long poem in the *Athenaeum* in 1828, but his first book was the *Exposition*, which spoke enough to the mood of the times as to go through two editions. Confirmation of the radicalism of Horne's politics is provided by his second book, *Spirit of the Peers and People: A National Tragi-Comedy* (1834), a burlesque in prose and blank verse, which represents the oppression of the English people by the crown, nobility, and church, with the Duke of Wellington playing chief villain and William IV as his puppet.[37]

The *Exposition* is a wide-ranging work in which the argument extends to poets, philosophers, 'authors in general', dramatists, composers, performers, actors, singers, novelists, painters and sculptors, and men of science. Under the heading 'Statement of Facts', the first part of the text deals with the circumstances of 'men of genius' of these different types. Drawing on Hazlitt's writings and a broader vein of Romantic theory, Horne affirms a category of true genius that is quite different from ordinary persons and difficult for the latter to understand.[38] For this reason, genius inevitably meets with disappointment and suffering, indeed, a 'common stone meets with more ready patronage than a man of genius', whose fate is to be 'driven through the inhospitable desert of mortality, or tossed upon its bleak and stormy seas', finding a haven only in posterity.[39]

Such has been the lot of genius since the times of Homer, and it might seem that its situation is therefore pretty hopeless. However, in the second part of the book, 'Exposition of Causes', Horne identifies a number of barriers that keep men of genius from the public, such as publishers' readers, theatre managers, Royal Academicians, and so on. The problem is that 'it requires genius to discover genius: there must be, in some respects, an equality in kind, though not in degree, fully or even rightly to appreciate original works of truth and power'. Average professional critics are influenced in their judgments by 'the verbal mould, style, and mannerisms, rather than the only true evidence, which is the spiritual'.[40] Hence Napoleon was the greatest patron of genius and art ever, because his genius matched that of those he supported.[41] The remedy that Horne offers in the final part of the book hardly seems to meet the demands of

---

36   Pearl 1960, pp. 20–4.

37   Pearl 1960, pp. 20, 27–9.

38   Horne 1833, p. 252.

39   Horne 1833, p. 1.

40   Horne 1833, pp. 105, 107–8.

41   Horne 1833, pp. 111–12.

the situation; it was the setting up of a Society of English Literature and Art for the encouragement and support of men of superior ability, 'a regular final college'. It was hardly surprising no such society had been established under the last reign, when government had squandered its resources on enormous salaries, sinecures, and pensions 'to individuals of no capability or merit'; but under the new regime inaugurated by the Parliamentary Reform Act, such a plan should be favoured by both Houses and receive support from government funds.[42]

The unalloyed progressivism that Horne shared with the decidedly ascetic proponents of Philosophic Radicalism, sits a little uncomfortably with his ardent veneration for intellectual and artistic genius. At the end of a chapter on 'Private and Public Judgment', in which he called for enlightened and comprehensible criticism, Horne wrote: 'We shall here conclude by pointing to the advancing March of Intellect, whose advent is hailed with admiration, with gladness, and with sun-ward hope! By all who love to know that mankind are bursting the last links of the earth-grinding chain of wide-spread despotism, and to behold ignorance propelled like a retiring sea, before a prophetic voice; – bearing upon its surface far away, the tossing wrecks of the countless rich insignia and cabalistic charters of slavery and intolerant selfishness'.[43] In this vision of the irresistible advance of Enlightenment and democracy, the flourishing of the arts and sciences is linked with a radical house-cleaning of the aristocratic political order (which the 1832 Parliamentary Reform Act did not bring) but the relationship between this progress and the socio-economic scheme of things remains unspoken. This is a transformation at the level of the ideal, the fantasy of the middle-class professional in their uncomfortable relation to the economic and social power of bourgeoisie.

Horne's critique of contemporary painting built on criticisms developed in the liberal press in the early nineteenth century. As exemplified by the Royal Academy's exhibitions, the English School had attained a level of mechanical excellence but displayed no imagination; a condition exemplified by the success of the 'all-admired' Sir Thomas Lawrence and his followers. The 'elegance of style' characteristic of this 'polite taste' had rendered the public 'too effeminate' to endure the higher works of art, attempts to produce which – Horne was presumably thinking of Barry and Haydon – only lead to penury for their practitioners. The 'facsimiles' of 'bloated personal vanity', 'destitute of all real beauty, energy, expression, or fine character' that comprise the bulk of the dis-

---

42   Horne 1833, p. 297.
43   Horne 1833, p. 273.

play at Somerset House are 'the signs of the times!' The Academy's exhibitions have justly been surpassed in popularity by those of the Society of Painters in Water-Colours. Considering the insistently male character of genius in Horne's book this is an unexpected conclusion, since watercolour was widely viewed as a less manly medium than oil painting.[44]

Picking up an argument that the painter George Foggo had recently made in an article in the *New Monthly Magazine*, whose precedence he acknowledged, Horne denounced the Royal Academy as a monopoly run by a private interest.[45] The Academy's type of education destroyed the energy of rising genius; but the march of progress would sweep the body away: 'The Royal Academy is a pompous body of pretensions that confute themselves. The public can no longer be deceived, and will not be fooled; the measure of monopoly is full, and indignation must at last speak out'.[46] As an institution the Academy was of no value to the nation; and it was of no value either to the Academicians, or at least, to those worthy of that rank. Horne's stance was very much in tune with that of a group of Parliamentary radicals that had emerged in the early 1830s, led by the M.P. for Liverpool, William Ewart,[47] which had a keen concern with art education as an instrument for improving the design of British manufactures to make them more competitive with those of France. As we have seen, design education had been one of the concerns of the *Westminster Review* in the mid-1820s, and the London Mechanics' Institute, founded in 1824, had held various drawing classes, as did some of those set up in the industrial regions.[48] The Parliamentary group, which also included Henry Brougham and Joseph Hume, was inevitably predisposed to be critical of the Royal Academy, as a body that manifestly failed to provide any education in the sphere of the decorative arts, and that under the cover of royal patronage made specious claims to be a public institution. The self-elected nature of the Academy, the invidious distinction of academic rank, the notorious secretiveness of its proceedings, its reputation

---

44   Horne 1833, pp. 75–80.

45   Accusations of this type against the Academy went back to its beginnings, which, as David Solkin has shown, sparked a controversy that was inextricably enmeshed with the Wilkes affair. See Solkin 1993, pp. 259–68. More recently Holger Hoock has argued for the role of the Academy as an instrumentality of the late Hanoverian state – see Hoock 2003.

46   Horne 1833, p. 224.

47   The coherence of this grouping should not be overestimated. W.A. Munford – Ewart's biographer – has written of them that they were not a party, 'not even a tolerably organized group. They had no common policy and no common meeting place outside the House'. They also had no recognised leader. See Munford 1960, pp. 72–3.

48   Bell 1963, pp. 48–9, 64–5.

for infighting, the shortcomings of its exhibitions and complaints of partiality and injustice levelled against them, all made it easy for the institution to be represented as a corrupt, monopolistic, aristocratic body.

The House of Commons Select Committee on the Arts and Their Connection with Manufactures and Its Aftermath

The movement to establish an academy in the mid-eighteenth century had generated schemes that projected an institution to offer training in the decorative arts; there was also the example of J.J. Bachelier's industrial school, established in Paris in 1762. In Britain it was clearly deliberate policy on the part of the fledgling academicians to exclude the decorative arts from the Academy's membership and curriculum as too menial, hence the demeaning status allotted to engravers as Associates only.[49] Reynolds's statement in his first *Discourse* that a taste in manufactures could not be formed by an academy founded on mercantile principles, but that progress in the higher arts would foster taste in the lesser arts, seems highly pointed. The strategy of exclusion was presumably related to the goal of professionalisation, the determination to establish painting as a liberal as opposed to a manual art, and the increasing autonomy of the intellectual field.[50] The idea that commerce and manufactures would benefit from progress in the Fine Arts was used by the founders of the British Institution in 1805, who claimed the body had as its 'primary object' 'to encourage and reward the talents of the Artists of the United Kingdom; so as to improve and extend our manufactures, by that degree of taste and excellence of design, which are to be exclusively derived from the cultivation of the Fine Arts; and thereby to increase the general prosperity and resources of the Empire'.[51] In 1809, the short-lived journal *The Artist* printed a statement by the Directors of the British Institution soliciting governmental support for annual prizes, and affirming their conviction 'that not only the civilization and refinement of a people, but also their manufactures and resources, in a great degree, depend on the progress of the Fine Arts'; this was because the skill of those 'inferior artists' employed in industry must depend on the excellence of the example provided by artists working in the 'higher departments'.[52] However ungrounded the 'conviction' of the Governors may have been in concrete evidence, it

---

49   On these exclusions, see Solkin 1993, p. 266.

50   Bell 1963, pp. 21–7; Reynolds 1975, p. 3.

51   Quoted in Fullerton 1982, p. 61.

52   'The Second Series Concluded', *The Artist*, 2 (1809), pp. 417–22. In the presentation of

continued to have considerable influence and helped determine the early form taken by education in the decorative arts in Britain, which centred round drawing skills.

It is probable that at least two considerations influenced the gentry and aristocrats who dominated the British Institution in formulating this view, both of which may be seen as ways of maintaining patrician hegemony in the arts. The first was the need to justify patronage of a type and standard of art that they believed was necessary to dignify the nation's culture in the face of a rising tide of commercialism that seemed to threaten traditional standards in the fine and decorative arts alike. The second was the hope that the calibre of national taste in manufactures could be raised through example and education. In this connection, Payne Knight's disdain for modern mass-produced goods needs to be remembered, as does Thomas Hope's advocacy of a national system of drawing instruction for all youths of 'ingenuous birth'.[53] Hope was on the original committee of the British Institution, and Knight quickly joined it. For both, the model of taste in the arts and of the social diffusion of that taste was provided by Ancient Greece.

The idea that the design of manufactures could be improved by reflections form the 'higher departments' was sedulously propagated by some proponents of high art, most notably by the journalist William Paulet Carey. Trevor Fawcett has shown that the idea had some take up in the provinces and was one motivation in the setting up of art schools in major urban centres outside the metropolis.[54] It also provided a central theme of the Report of the House of Commons Select Committee on the Arts and their Connection with Manufactures, set up at Ewart's instigation, which sat in 1835–6; although some witnesses explicitly refuted it in their evidence.[55] The Report's 'Introduction' begins by lamenting the lack of encouragement given to the arts of design in Britain, and drew an

---

its mission, the British Institution moved between claiming for the Fine Arts the noble purpose of raising 'the standard of morality and patriotism' and asserting their value to commerce. For the former, see the untitled remarks in the body's exhibition catalogue for 1811; for the latter, see the 'Draft of proposed application to the King for a fund for triennial premiums' in the Minute Books of the British Institution, entries for 19 and 26 January 1810 (Victoria and Albert Museum) – which provide the basis of the statement in *The Artist*.

53   Knight 1795, pp. 55–6; Thomas Hope, 'On Instruction in design, and the Requisite Qualifications for judging Works of Art', *The Artist*, 1, no. 8 (2 May 1807), p. 5.

54   Fawcett 1973, pp. 39–52.

55   For Ewart and the Select Committee, see Munford 1960, pp. 76–84. Although Ewart came from a Liverpool merchant family, he had attended Eton and Oxford, was a gifted Latinist, and enjoyed an extensive Grand Tour in 1821–3.

unfavourable comparison between the nation and some 'despotic countries', by which its authors presumably meant some of the German states: 'To us, a peculiarly manufacturing nation, the connexion between art and manufactures is most important; – and for this merely economical reason (were there no higher motive), it equally imports us to encourage art in its loftier attributes: since it is admitted that the cultivation of the more exalted branches of design tends to advance the humblest pursuits of industry, while the connexion of art with manufacture has often developed the genius of the greatest masters in design'.[56] The developments of the arts and manufactures thus coexist in a happy and mutually beneficial relationship, at least if we accept the universal consensus implied by 'since it is admitted', which brooks no disagreement.

Considering that the Committee had been established at the instigation of bourgeois radicals and that its line of inquiry was clearly dominated by them, this conclusion is not surprising. Neither is the hostility that several witnesses expressed towards the Royal Academy, which the line of questioning was calculated to draw out. (Ewart regarded the Academy as an offensive monopoly, an opposition that was sharpened by the fact that it was to be given space in the new National Gallery building rent free).[57] Such witnesses clearly recognised that they could gain the Committee's ear by appeals to political economy and democratic principles. The Neo-Classical sculptor and politician George Rennie – who had suggested the idea of the Committee to Ewart in the first place – pointed out that the French economist Jean Baptiste Say had doubted the utility of academies in his *Cours complete d'économie politique*.[58] The landscape painter T.C. Hofland – a founder member of the Society of British Artists, set up in 1823 as a rival exhibition site – also attacked the Academy and called for free trade in art.[59] While the history painter and print-maker George Foggo, after referring to Adam Smith, suggested that artists' grievances would be met if the arts were to have 'the same system of free trade that every other department of industry is allowed to follow'.[60] Haydon sought to appeal more to the Committee's political predilections, at least by analogy: 'In fact, the academy is the House of Lords without King or Commons for appeal. The artists are at the mercy of a despotism whose unlimited power tends to destroy all feel-

---

56   House of Commons 1836, Part 1, p. iii.

57   Munford 1960, p. 76.

58   House of Commons 1836, Part 2, p. 56. For Rennie, see 'Rennie, George (1802–1860)', *Dictionary of National Biography* (London: Smith, Elder & Co. 1885–1900).

59   House of Commons 1836, Part 2, pp. 105–7.

60   House of Commons 1836, Part 2, p. 122.

ing for right or justice'.[61] While the architect C.R. Cockerell found the taint of aristocracy in the handling of architectural commissions in which the 'aristocratical principle of our government has been especially illustrated', with the consequence that 'patronage and the opinions of persons in authority' have prevailed 'in a great measure over public opinion and merit'.[62]

The representatives of the Academy, and particularly its President, Martin Archer Shee, played into the Committee's hands by an unabashed display of arrogance. When asked about the relevance of political economy for the arts, Shee flatly denied that art and trade were to be in any way equated. Further, the public was ignorant and incompetent to judge art to an extraordinary degree. Even those from the 'enlightened class of society' were incompetent; artists alone were fitted to decide who should or should not receive academic honours.[63] The Committee remained convinced of the beneficence of Smith's 'invisible hand' in the arts as elsewhere in the economy, for 'it seems probable that the principle of free competition in art (as in commerce) will eventually triumph over all artificial institutions'.[64] But laissez faire in matters of production and exchange needed to be backed up by the provision of public galleries, wider art educations, and some forms of state encouragement.

I have already mentioned the historical painter and lithographer George Foggo (1793–1869) as a witness before the Select Committee; he was also one of the most inveterate campaigners against the Academy in this period. His father, a Fifeshire watchmaker, was an ardent republican and extremely active in the campaign against African slavery, who immigrated to France in 1799 hoping to find there a more sympathetic political climate. George and his brother James Foggo (1789–1860) studied in Paris with the Neo-Classical republican painter Jean-Baptiste Regnault. After the brothers returned to Britain in the late 1810s, they set up a studio together in London and worked to advance the cause of public history painting on the French model with a massive painting sixteen feet by twenty-six on the theme of the *Destruction of Parga*.[65]

---

61   House of Commons 1836, Part 2, p. 89.

62   House of Commons 1836, Part 2, p. 188.

63   House of Commons 1836, Part 2, pp. 162, 164–5.

64   House of Commons 1836, Part 1, p. viii.

65   'Foggo, George' and 'Foggo, James', in *Dictionary of National Biography* (London: Smith, Elder & Co., 1885–1900). For the *Destruction of Parga*, see 'Exhibition of Messrs. J. & G. Foggo's Historical Painting of the Destruction of Parga, 23 New Bond Street', *Weekly Literary Register and Review of the Arts*, vol. 1, no. 3 (20 July 1822). The painting does not seem to have survived but a lithograph of it, dated to 1819, is in the British Museum Print Room (1842, 0319.14). Four thousand Greeks of the free city of Parga evacuated to Corfu in

In 1833 George Foggo published a long letter, 'The Royal Academy Exposed, From Authentic Documents and Undoubted Facts', in the *New Monthly Magazine*, which argued that the current Parliamentary Committee on corporate bodies seemed to aim at 'the very root of monopoly – the great engine of injustice', but unfortunately did not extend its inquiries to some of the more injurious institutions based on invidious distinctions. The Royal Academy was one such, since 'it is manifest that the Prince, his Ministers, nay, the Parliament itself have lent their power to a body of men who have no legally corporate existence, though through the supineness of others of equal talent with themselves, and countenanced by authority, they exercise unlimited control over the fine arts of this country'.[66] In fact, the Academy had done little to promote and much to hinder the arts, since its members tried to create a 'universal subserviency to their dictation and interest'. Foggo particularly lamented the inadequacies of academic education, the mismanagement of the annual exhibitions, the privileges of Varnishing Days, prejudices against historical painting, the Academicians' role in Customs inspections of imported works of art, and their sorry record in promoting public monuments. The Academy had no better claims to consideration as a public body than the Society of British Artists or the Society of Painters in Water-Colours; thus it was outrageous that it should be rehoused in the new National Gallery. Foggo recast the longstanding grievances of excluded artists in the language of liberal politics, and complained rhetorically, 'Surely this is not to continue; the first building ever erected out of the funds of a free people will not be made a disgrace to the administration that procured us the Reform Bill – a lasting monument of vanity and degraded art; nor will an uncontrolled self-elected body of men be longer permitted to usurp our rights'.[67]

Over the next few years Foggo became active in the campaign to extend and reform art education, publishing two six-penny pamphlets on the theme and acting as Secretary to the Committee to promote free public access to national monuments, museums, and art galleries. His *Letter to Lord Brougham, On the History and Character of the Royal Academy* (1835) was ostensibly occasioned by the report that Brougham had described the Academy as an excellent institution at the annual dinner of the Artists' General Benevolent Institution. The pamphlet rehearsed the same complaints as the *New Monthly Magazine* article,

---

       1819 as a consequence of the cession of Parga to the Ottoman Empire in 1817 by treaty with Britain, which ruled it briefly after 1815.

66   Foggo 1833, p. 74.

67   Foggo 1833, p. 82.

and claimed that the Academy reduced artists to a state of dependency incompatible with the vocation of High Art. Clearly appealing to the prejudices of the commercial and industrial interests with which Brougham was associated, he asked, 'Why should not the country be left to apply its own talent, free from the interference of a monopoly? Then the manufactures would again profit by the exertions of genius, as they once did in the days of Wedgewood and Helicot, of Boydell and of Rundel; they would find their natural course; nor would it be longer considered derogatory for artists to employ their talent in the improvement of the mechanical production, or in the communication of that talent'. Foggo specifically connected the Academy with the corrupt state of the country in the pre-Reform era, and, since the nation had now been 'much improved and liberated', he called on Brougham, in the name of Reform and freedom, to assist in 'rending the fetters of genius', and bring the arts to the same level of progress.[68] The basis of this stance was articulated more directly in Foggo's 1837 pamphlet, *Results of the Parliamentary Inquiry Relative to Arts and Manufactures*, occasioned by the influence of the Royal Academy on the setting up of the Normal School of Design. In this he referred to the examples of Ancient Athens and Renaissance Florence as proof that freedom was the 'parent' of commerce, virtue, and the arts: 'In either case a few years of commercial freedom gave life and spirit to the arts, and in both the fall of genius followed close upon the extinction of commerce and independence'.[69]

Like George Rennie and Frederick Hurlstone, Foggo was one of the artist members of the committee formed to campaign for free admission to monuments, museums, and galleries, which in 1837 also included Joseph Hume (the chairman), William Ewart, Francis Place, Dr George Birkbeck,[70] and Dr John Bowring, and forty-three M.P.s. In the *Report* of the public meeting of this body, held at Freemason's Hall in May 1837, the most interesting speech is that of Thomas Wyse, M.P. (1791–1862), a deeply cosmopolitan figure who came from an Anglo-Irish landed family, supported a string of liberal causes, and was a major player in the Catholic Association; he was also a tireless advocate of

---

68   Foggo 1835, p. 15. Brougham – a quintessentially careerist and opportunist politician – had
      a reputation for radicalism that far exceeded his actual views. In fact, he played a small role
      in the passage of the Reform Bill and described himself in 1831 as by disposition 'a very
      moderate and very gradual reformer'. See Aspinall 1927, pp. 184, 190. This matches with
      his highly instrumentalist conception of mass education as an 'insurance against social
      convulsion' and his aversion to unions – Aspinall 1927, pp. 239, 250.

69   George Foggo, *Results of the Parliamentary Inquiry Relative to Arts and Manufactures*
      (London: 1837), p. 14.

70   For whom see Kelly 1957.

popular education who influenced Lord John Russell's 1839 Education Act.[71] Wyse had a profound interest in art and classical scholarship, nurtured by extensive travels in Italy, Greece, and the Near East. His expertise made him an obvious candidate to sit on the Select Committee on the Arts and Manufactures in 1834 and he chaired the Parliamentary Select Committee on Art Unions in 1844–6.[72] At the May 1837 meeting Wyse complained that national monuments and the exhibitions of the Royal Academy were not truly national because they had been reserved for a class. He dismissed the imputation that the English people were unfit to enjoy their monuments, and, like the *Westminster Review* in 1827, referred to the respectful behaviour of the French populace. In fact, it was not the English people but the English *nobility* that had a reputation abroad for vandalism of works of art. Wyse emphasised the cognitive insights offered by the works of Rembrandt, Raphael, and Michelangelo, describing the artist as a public educator who should direct his works to the whole nation: 'I would not have the artist a mere trader or mechanic. I would have him a creator, – an originator of ideas, a man who corrects as well as a man who pleases. I conceive that he of all others ought to be anxious for the awards of so mighty a judge as a whole nation'.[73] Like the *Westminster Review*'s appraisal of Brougham's Library of Useful Knowledge, Wyse argued that progress in the arts was part of a larger process of education that would have great benefits for morality and public order. Invoking the authority of Bentham, he claimed that the anxiety of 'the people for improvement in their moral and mental condition' was the distinguishing feature of the age.[74]

Wyse's conception of history and of the relationship of art and society are set out clearly in a speech he gave to a gathering of artists at the Freemasons' Tavern in December 1842. Here he insisted that art could not be left solely in the hands of the great and wealthy, or at least not 'without risk of perversion and degradation'; this applies equally to an aristocracy as to a monarchy, since 'the arts that flourish are those which rise out of the feelings and taste of the great body of the people; which reflect them, which appeal to them; which, in fact, are no other than a more perfect exemplification of their intellectual and moral

---

71   Wyse is a fascinating and symptomatic individual, who deserves a modern biography. For his work as an education reformer, see Auchmuty 1939, Chapter 10.

72   King 1964, pp. 116–19; King 1985, pp. 97–116.

73   *Report of the Proceedings at a Public Meeting, Held at the Freemasons' Hall, On the 29th of May, to Promote the Admission of the Public without Charge ...* (London, 1837), p. 22.

74   *Report of the Proceedings at a Public Meeting*, p. 24.

being'.[75] History confirmed this judgment. For it was not individual patrons such as Lorenzo de Medici who were responsible for the revival of letters, but the institutions of church and state, and particularly the town councils of the Italian city states; it was emphatically not the princes or the nobility. Echoing a commonplace of Philosophic Radicalism, Wyse claimed that 'the education of the middle class renders inevitable the education of all above and below them'.[76] Their example would help to raise the lower orders and force the upper class onwards, even against their will.[77]

There were grounds for optimism, Wyse averred, in the Government Schools of Design, the Art Unions, the Mechanics' Institutions, and particularly the Houses of Parliament decorations.[78] He looked forward to more decorations to public buildings in future. However, there were still deficiencies in the present state of aesthetic consciousness due to the lack of educational provision in the schools and universities. By ignoring the plastic arts, the classical education of which men of rank and fortune boasted left out one half of the classical mind.

British education compared unfavourably with that on mainland Europe, and Wyse expressed the hope that other colleges and universities would follow the example of London's King's College, which had established a chair of aesthetics in emulation of German universities.[79] The nation was rich and powerful, but until it would contribute to the progress of the arts and literature its civilisation was incomplete. Only by following the example of Germany in the decoration of public buildings could art be got into 'the eyes and hearts of a people'. 'I trust the time is fast approaching', Wyse wrote, 'when, instead of being a luxury, it will be considered a necessary, the enjoyment of which will be as natural to man as his breathing; as essential to the full sustainment of his intellectual and moral health as wholesome bodily food to his physical'.[80]

This was not an egalitarian stance. Wyse's biographer has written of him that 'he had no real conception or anticipation of democracy as it is understood in a

---

75   'Speech by T. Wyse, Esq., M.P., to a meeting of artists at the Freemasons' Tavern, 17 December 1842', printed in Pye 1845, p. 180.

76   Pye 1845, p. 181.

77   For Wyse's concern with the degradation of the labourer, see Johnson 1976, p. 49.

78   Pye 1845, p. 183. For the struggle between working-class members and middle-class reformers in the Mechanics' Institutions, see Prothero 1981, pp. 191–203; Thompson 1983, pp. 743–5, 777–8; Kelly 1952; Kelly 1957, Chapters 5 and 6.

79   Pye 1845, p. 180.

80   Pye 1845, p. 184. On the significance of the German example in art and aesthetics for British art reformers in the early nineteenth century, see Vaughan 1979, Chapters 1 and 2. For Ewart on Germany, see Munford 1960, pp. 40–1.

twentieth-century sense'.[81] Rather, he typifies the embourgeoisement of a fraction of the landed class. A highly intellectual politician, he adopted progressive ideas because he believed their development was inevitable and unstoppable. His elitism is particularly clear from his 1836 text *Education Reform: or, the Necessity of a National System of Education*, which conceded the right of the aristocracy to lead the nation, but maintained it was a right it had to earn by attaining superior knowledge.[82] Widely read, Wyse knew the writings of Schiller as well as those of the Scottish School. In line with the latter tradition, he conceded that the progress of civilisation inevitably brought with it 'vices and abuses': 'The very arts which seem most to raise and embellish life, introduce, also, in their train habits of effeminacy and self-indulgence. They create new wants, which become, in turn, from servants, masters. They concentrate the entire being within self, they render self-sacrifice, an absurdity, – duty, a difficulty; they fix all enjoyments in the material world; they add to riches a fictitious value, measured by the lowest passions of our nature'.[83] This 'sensualism' finds a counterpart in the character of political economy, much moral philosophy, and the narrowly utilitarian estimation of values. Further, the division and subdivision of labour, physical and mental, tends to restrict the range of experience. These tendencies can only be checked by a good general education that embraces the intellectual, moral, and physical being of the individual. Wyse particularly emphasised the importance of 'Aesthetic' education in promoting the growth of the spiritual faculties.[84]

But there was also a more instrumental aspect to Wyse's argument for the education of all classes. If labourers are instructed they will cease to be 'presumptuous' and 'discontented' and learn to understand the necessity of their station being as it is. Education will meliorate the rub of social inequality, 'continue to raise the other classes in proportion as you raise his, and you will keep all society in its original relative position. The whole shell will swell out simultaneously. There will be no jagged prominences. No one body will be elevated into an unjust pre-eminence over others; but the entire mind, character, resources, of the country will be enlarged'.[85] More pointedly, universal education is the great remedy against the horrors of unionism – those 'dissocial doctrines' that strike at 'the very framework of all society' – and which arise

---

81   Auchmuty 1939, p. 77.

82   Wyse 1836, p. 354. The book was intended to have comprised two volumes, but only one
       appeared.

83   Wyse 1836, p. 52.

84   Wyse 1836, pp. 89–91, 195–202. On education in drawing, see pp. 133–8.

85   Wyse 1836, p. 385.

because education is unevenly spread: 'We see a crowd of squalid artisans press round an inflammatory proclamation or a delusive placard in the street, and we rail against Reading and Writing. We should rather regret, that when they had been taught to *read* a placard, they had not also been taught the truths which would have enabled them to detect a fallacy, and to laugh at an imposter!'[86] Universal education and access to a sacral realm of culture and edifying monuments to national greatness will teach the working class that their true interests are served by joyfully and patriotically accepting their lot in life. Wyse's spluttering and splenetic denunciation of unionism, was the other face of bourgeois liberalism. It shows that the concern to promote social harmony through education and the arts was grounded as much in fear and class hatred as it was in values of enlightenment. Art Galleries would be weapons against Owenism and, to anticipate slightly, Chartism.

Positions similar to those of Wyse were advanced in Edward Edwards's substantial book, *The Fine Arts in England; their State and Prospects Considered relatively to National Education* (1840). The author, a prominent figure in the public library movement, emerged in the 1830s as a pamphleteer addressing a number of current liberal concerns: university education, the management of museums, and reform of the Royal Academy. Born in 1812, the son of a London builder and raised as a Dissenter, he has been characterised as representative of a type of rising young man who had not been educated at university but at the Mechanics' Institutes.[87] This may be so, but along the way he also acquired a wide acquaintance with German and French literature and was sufficiently erudite to compile a catalogue of French medals in 1837.[88] It was out of the literary and intellectual circle in which Edwards moved that the idea of the London Art Union emerged in 1837, and he was its Honorary Secretary until a financial scandal forced his resignation in the following year. He was a close friend of Joseph Hume and was involved with him in the Committee that led to the meeting at the Freemasons' Hall in 1837 to promote free access to monuments, museums and galleries.[89] In 1839 Edwards published privately a pamphlet titled *A Letter to Sir Martin Archer Shee ... on the Reform of the Royal Academy*, which drew strongly on evidence brought before the 1835–6 Parliamentary Select Committee. Superficially moderate in tone, Edwards was conciliatory towards Shee and

---

86   Wyse 1836, pp. 419–20.

87   Munford 1960, p. 90.

88   Greenwood 1902, pp. 7–9.

89   Greenwood 1902, pp. 9–13; King 1964, pp. 102–3, 106; King 1985, pp. 35–46. Ewart was particularly close to Edwards, partly because of their shared interest in the municipal library movement – see Munford 1960, pp. 89–90, 127–33, 150.

declared he had no sympathy with those who wanted to abolish the Academy, denying that the concept of trade was applicable to art. But the reforms he proposed were radical. The Academy's problem was that it united disparate functions. To turn it into a truly national institution, it should become a strictly honorary body and a school. Membership should be unlimited, the class of associate abolished, and engravers admitted to full honours. To end the academicians' undue influence in the display and marketing of art, the Academy should be divested of its exhibition functions, which should be taken over by an elected and renewable management body chosen by the artists.[90] These recommendations were reiterated and developed in *The Fine Arts in England* of the following year.

Edwards opened his book by asserting that the 'rank' of a nation is determined by its showing in the Fine Arts. However, his differs from earlier statements of this kind in claiming that this does not just mean 'the possession of distinguished professors in one or more of their branches', rather, it means the extent to which 'the humanising influence of the arts' is to be found in the population as a whole.[91] History shows that this is the general aim to which the arts are to be applied. But to attain this end in the present age the government must make certain interventions. Edwards argues eloquently that the great artistic achievements of the past arose out of a collective idea motivated by a single guiding principle. Thus the cathedrals of the Middle Ages 'were exponents of a new element in the onward march of civilization, and their builders went forth in all the strength of men, whose lives were devoted to one great object, and whose minds could grasp everything that tended to its attainment. Everywhere the same ideas are impressed upon the visible forms of Art, – religious feeling, – resistance to the oppressions of decaying feudalism, have their types and emblems in the simple habitation of the citizen, as well as in the cathedral and the public hall'.[92] The idea that the guiding spirit of artistic achievement must not be isolated among artists or an elite but must pervade society is also explicit. Thus, in fourteenth-century Italy too 'the product and progress of art were felt to be of universal interest, greater or less in degree, indeed, but without distinction of rank or class'. The arts can never attain the first rank of achievement if they minster only to luxury.[93]

While Edwards's predictable attachment to laissez-faire economics leads him to insist that he had 'no love for the forcing system, either in knowledge

---

90   Edwards 1839.
91   Edwards 1840, p. 12.
92   Edwards 1840, pp. 30–1.
93   Edwards 1840, pp. 32–3.

or commerce', he argued nonetheless that the state had a 'natural office' to intervene in the preparatory training of artists.[94] In modern Britain the predominant impulse of art was to connect itself with commerce, and here the government should take as its 'primary duty' to 'clear away obstructions, and watch that artists and men of letters, no less than merchant, have a clear field of competition'.[95] But while laissez faire remained the guiding principle, the state should provide direct encouragement by offering opportunities for useful and necessary public works. It should also provide direct encouragement by funding a sufficient number of museums and art galleries and making a 'truly qualitative education within the reach of all'. However, there are limits to state interventionism in this model. Although Edwards thought existing educational provision compared unfavourably with that in some other European nations, he did not envisage compulsory state education; rather the desire for education should be encouraged by making rights and franchises dependent on it. The gaps in provision by existing voluntary agencies would be plugged by state provision and standards maintained by a national inspectorate.[96] The specific needs of the arts would be met through the foundation of Schools of Design and a reformed Royal Academy with a state subsidy.

Edwards reiterated the commonplace that continued support for the 'higher branches' of the arts was partly justified by their commercial benefits; indeed the 'highest commercial interest of England ... demands the liberal employment of the arts for public and national purposes' since an improved taste in design is necessary if the nation's goods are to compete in the international market.[97] However, he gave far more weight to the claim that the arts contribute to the 'worthiest objects of good government', namely: 'RELIGION – CIVILIZATION – SOCIAL ORDER'.[98] Experience showed that nothing was more dangerous to a community than excessive individual magnificence among the upper classes, unaccompanied by any melioration of the lot of the poor. This position is reminiscent of that of Payne Knight and the Foxite Whigs in the 1790s, alarmed at the threat to property rights conjured up by the French Revolu-

---

94   Edwards 1840, p. 28.

95   Edwards 1840, pp. 34–5.

96   Edwards 1840, pp. 35, 291, 305. This was effectively the pattern of educational provision established in the 1830s and 1840s, namely a decentralised voluntary provision with a weak state authority that provided an inspectorate and regulated teacher training in order to foster professionalisation (Johnson 1976, p. 46). The Committee of the Privy Council on Education was established in 1839.

97   Edwards 1840, p. 186. Cf. p. 325.

98   Edwards 1840, p. 193.

tion. For Edwards, dread of unionism superseded that of Jacobinism. But as a patrician Knight simply could not envisage that the bourgeoisie – let alone the labouring classes – would ever develop any significant aesthetic sensibility except in rare isolated instances. Such a possibility did not lie in the natural order of things. By contrast, Edwards, a middle-class democrat, could ask rhetorically how 'we' should judge a government like that of the present that manifestly failed in its duties in a time of crisis, when the means were to hand that offered themselves as 'the readiest and most powerful to enable *all* to gratify, in some degree, that love of the Beautiful and Magnificent, which is natural to all men', and that were at the same time 'the means most powerful to dispel that very ignorance of the many, which, when opposed to the isolated splendour of the few, has heretofore given to envy and discontent all their destructive strength'.[99] The answer was self-evident.

Although Edwards's plea for the dissemination of aesthetic culture reads in part as a statement of class interest, there was also a moment of romantic anxiety in thinking – as there was in Wyse's – that the unrestrained pursuit of individual self-interest and the dominance of calculative reason that were concomitants of capitalist development were impoverishing social life. State intervention was necessary to ensure the continued exercise of the whole range of human faculties, since 'Everywhere we see triumphant the faculty of means to ends which are themselves menial. Everywhere man's dominion over brute matter is rapidly extending itself, but often at a cost, which, for the time, is indeed fearful. As the struggle of daily existence becomes keener, and occupies thought and action more and more engrossingly, it surely becomes of gravest importance to make every possible provision for those highest faculties – the Sovran REASON – the IMAGINATION – the SOUL'.[100] It comes as no surprise to find that in 1848 Edwards refused to be sworn in as a special constable in case of an attack on the British Museum, where he then worked. He was outraged by the 'disgraceful proclamations' against the Chartists and determined to sign the petition for the Charter.[101]

We have obviously moved a long way from the patrician conception of the arts as functioning to preserve the elite from the corruption and licentiousness concomitant with idleness and to inculcate the virtues of rulers. Radical intellectuals such as Bowring saw that polite culture needed to be refashioned to

---

99   Edwards 1840, pp. 186–7.

100   Edwards 1840, p. 346.

101   Greenwood 1902, p. 63. See also the remark on Chartism in Edward Edwards to Charlotte
        Edwards, 30 April 1848, in Munford 1960, p. 175. In later life Edwards became a conservative
        and converted to Anglicanism.

give it a democratic face and re-functioned to advance bourgeois standing, to represent the bourgeois interest 'as the common interest of all the members of society', to give bourgeois ideas 'the form of universality, and represent them as the only rational, universally valid ones'.[102] Art would now have a far larger public and educative function: to teach national values, national history, civic virtue, and morality to all classes of society, while giving pleasure to all. However, this remains a vision that restricts production of art to a special caste of makers who are 'direct and efficient co-agents',[103] in Edwards's words, in preserving the bourgeois social order. It remains a vision in which the mass of the population will not decide their own aesthetic fare but will eat that ordained for them by a paternalistic state. Despite political differences, Wyse and Edwards shared an essentially hierarchical conception of culture as an implement in a larger strategy to civilise subaltern groups; the arts would effectively function as implements of class-cultural control. At the same time as they were formulating this vision, much blunter means of managing the working class were being set in place through police legislation and the Poor Law Amendment Acts of the 1830s and 1840s. But the campaign to claim high culture for the bourgeoisie was double edged. At the same time as it sought to prescribe culture to the working class, it sought to seize it from the aristocracy in the name of the nation. Behind all the rhetoric of ending the cultural monopoly claimed by one form of property, was the ambition to erect another in which it would appear as if property played no role.

Coda: Towards a Proletarian Critique

Class politics entails class consciousness. In the early nineteenth century a substantial element within the British bourgeoisie began to act as a class politically because they had the ideological resources to think as a class; they had a bourgeois ideology.[104] The researches of E.P. Thompson, John Foster, and others have demonstrated that in the same period elements within the work-

---

102   Marx and Engels 1974, pp. 65–6.

103   Edwards 1840, p. 193.

104   This essay was written at the time of a profound rethinking of British working-class history, in which Jones 1983 played a major role. Jones's project of treating class as more a discursive than an ontological reality (p. 8), correspondingly granting politics a new level of autonomy, was a salutary corrective but failed to register the idealism of Saussurean linguisics and its detachment of language from social practice (p. 20). For an important critique, see Foster 1985.

ing class began to practice a class politics, because they too had begun to acquire a class ideology, albeit a less well-formed one than that of the bourgeoisie.[105] (Not surprisingly since the means of intellectual production were largely denied them). This raises the question as to whether or not there was a proletarian critique of the hegemonic culture as well as a bourgeois one. Such a critique, while it might draw on some leitmotivs of radical bourgeois discourse – and particularly its insistent accusations of corruption – would be essentially different in its conception of art's functions in the social totality.

The moment in the mid-1820s when radical bourgeois thought had recognised polite culture as an instrument of class power quickly passed. It had rested on both resentment at invidious distinctions and a moral critique of waste and idleness. But a far more subversive critique could be offered: that the possibility of enjoying such distinctions depended on the extraction of surplus value through the oppression and impoverishment of the labouring classes. The Philosophic Radicals offered a cultural critique at an essentially political level because they had no complaint against the economic system as such – although in their eyes it needed purging of some unnecessary and inefficient interferences – and were amongst the leading exponents of political economy, the science that explained and naturalised it. Only from a position that dissected the economic system through the critique of political economy could the economic basis of high culture be attacked. This required some degree of identification with the interests of the labouring and unpropertied class groups.

In the early years of the century, the emergent theory of working-class radicalism was dominated by the ideas of Paine and Cobbett, although in London the agrarian socialism of Thomas Spence's followers also attracted a significant body of adherents.[106] In the latter part of the second decade, working-class radicals such as Richard Carlile (although he might be better described as petty bourgeois in origins and attitude),[107] and John Wade and Francis Place in the *Gorgon*, were beginning to disseminate Utilitarian doctrine to a working-class readership. The *Gorgon* purveyed the banal dicta of political economy to trade unionists at the same time as insisting on the Ricardian principle that labour was the source of all value. However, the marriage of working-class radicalism and a political economy that relied on the labour

---

105 Partly in the light of Jones's researches, it became evident that Thompson's thesis needed some qualification – see Eley 1990, 22–35.

106 Thompson 1963, pp. 672–73; Thompson 1984, Chapter 1.

107 Thompson 1963, p. 841.

theory of value involved too much self-abnegation to last. From the early 1820s some of the radicals associated with the weekly *Trades Newspaper*, notably John Gast and Thomas Hodgskin, rejected the idea of a natural self-adjusting economic order that, if left to itself, served the best interests of labour and capital alike. Hodgskin's *Labour Defended Against the Claims of Capital* (1825) was one of the first essays to develop the critique of political economy from a radical perspective and marks the beginning of a new kind of socialist theory.[108] As Noel Thompson has shown, Hodgskin's text belonged to a brief flowering of socialist theory in the rapidly expanding working-class press of the late 1820s, which instead of simply denouncing political economy as an instrument of capitalist interests, sought to refashion it into an anti-capitalist theory. This productive wave of radical thinking had petered out by the middle of the following decade.[109]

The only writings from this period I have discovered that come near to offering a critique of high culture from the standpoint of the proletariat are the two publications of that mysterious figure who wrote under the pseudonym of Piercy Ravenstone, *A Few Doubts as to the Correctness of Some Opinions Generally Entertained on the Subjects of Population and Political Economy* (1821) and *Thoughts on the Funding System and its Effects* (1824). These do not belong to the discourse of emergent socialism but rather to the more backward-looking phase of critique that preceded it, which imagined some form of return to an earlier, simpler way of life was yet possible. This does not mean that Ravenstone's critique lacked purchase. Marx described *Thoughts on the Funding System* as 'a most remarkable work', while for the Marxist historian Max Beer its author was 'one of the seminal minds of the period'.[110] Although there has been some debate about Ravenstone's identity, it seems very likely that he was Richard Puller (1789–1831), the scion of a merchant family and a director of the South Sea Company.[111] Beer described Ravenstone quite astutely as 'essentially a Tory democrat', a kind of 'Cobbett *édition de luxe*'.[112] Most recently Noel Thompson has characterised his position as 'physiocratic, Tory anti-capitalism',

---

108   Thompson 1963, pp. 838–87; Prothero 1981, pp. 225–31.

109   For the reasons why this phase of theorising ended when it did, see 'Conclusion' in Thompson 1984, pp. 219–28.

110   Beer 1929, vol. I, p. 251. For a consideration of Marx's references to Ravenstone, see King 1983, pp. 366–9.

111   Thompson 2010, pp. 304–7, lays out the evidence for Ravenstone's identity with Puller. There remains some question as to whether the author may have been Puller's son, also Richard.

112   Beer, 1929, vol. I, pp. 251, 252.

and stressed the radicalism of his analysis.[113] But although he was a radical democrat, Ravenstone was no socialist. He did not favour the abolition of private property and accepted social hierarchy as inevitable; at the same time property rights held no absolute status for him and were only lawful insofar as they were used justly.[114] Although the tendency of historians to categorise Ravenstone as one of the 'Ricardian Socialists' has been misleading, his theory, like theirs, anticipated Marx's thought in more ways than is often acknowledged and Marx himself had a more generous and complex response to it than Engels and his immediate successors.[115]

Ravenstone accepted the negative features of commercial societies that Smith, Millar, and Ferguson had identified on the basis of the civic humanist model of the polis, but his critique differed fundamentally from theirs in that he added to their disadvantages that of the increasing impoverishment of the labouring classes. His critique thus diverges from the predominant Whiggism of the Scottish School (Ferguson excepted), and opens up the path to far more politically radical conclusions. His adaptation of the Scots' socio-historical theory is clearly marked by the differences between Enlightenment Scotland and the England of the 1820s in that Ravenstone's writings are polemical interventions with no pretence to academic distance that draw on the language of liberal politics developed by the wartime opposition press. Ravenstone was writing in the aftermath of the twenty-year period of warfare that followed the French Revolution and after the political violence and repression of the post-Waterloo years, at a time of widespread social unrest when distinctly working-class forms of political organisation were appearing. However, although Ravenstone was an advocate of universal suffrage – or at least male suffrage – he did not directly identify with the beginnings of the working-class movement. Beer described his social ideal as 'a nation consisting in the main of peasant proprietors, handicraftsmen, and other useful labourers, with a minimum of government and taxation under the control of those who serve the community by hand and head'.[116] Although the significance of the gesture is not unambiguous, it needs to be noted that Ravenstone sent a copy of *A Few Doubts* to Brougham.

Ravenstone's essentially dynamic conception of history and his ideas on the relationship between labour, capital, and class anticipate Marx's in import-

---

113   For the physiocratic dimension of Ravenstone's thought in context, see Thompson 1988, Chapter 1.

114   Thompson 2010, pp. 318–19.

115   King 1983, pp. 369–70.

116   Beer 1929, vol. 1, p. 251.

ant respects. Convinced of the variety of human societies and the plasticity of human nature, he regarded change as inescapable and despite the pessimistic and cyclical elements in his thought he saw the species as progressive, refusing to accept Malthusian conceptions of natural scarcity.[117] The growth of productivity is related to the growth of population. Correspondingly, technological innovations do not arise simply because of the genius of individuals such as Arkwright and Watt, but as a result of the 'spirit of the age', that is in response to social needs. The principle of the steam engine was known long before it was applied.[118] Ravenstone took up the Scottish idea that laws and political forms are intrinsically linked to property relations and argued that 'tranquillity' is impossible if laws and the constitution are not sympathetic to the 'manners' of a people – by which he seems to mean the 'arrangement of property'. For 'if property confer power, the political condition of a people cannot but be mainly influenced by the manner in which it is distributed'.[119]

Seeing labour as the source of all wealth, Ravenstone was scathing about the idea that capital in itself was wealth-producing: 'property is in reality but a rent charge on productive industry'.[120] He seems to have accepted the Scots' stadial theory of social development and saw that as human society became more productive it was not necessary for all labour to be devoted to producing the means of existence, that some could be released to be 'advantageously occupied in adding to the comfort, in contributing to the ornament of society'.[121] The 'ornament of society' may refer to learning and the arts, but it can also refer to a leisured minority devoted to gracious living that does not labour. In *A Few Doubts* Ravenstone suggests that if the social minority occupied with such things becomes too numerous it imposes a burden on the industrious: 'When their interests clash with those of the other classes of society; when the useful is sacrificed to the ornamental; when the main arch of the building is cast away to make room for triumphal arches, and all their accomplishments of festoons and garlands'.[122] Although Decimus Burton's Wellington Arch – which might seem to precisely match Ravenstone's notion – was not built until 1826–30, there was much public discussion of a victory monument in the years after 1815. In that year a Parliamentary committee was set up to invite designs for

---

117   Ravenstone 1824, pp. 49, 57–9, 12.
118   Ravenstone 1824, pp. 1–43.
119   Ravenstone 1821, p. 427.
120   Ravenstone 1824, p. 14.
121   Ravenstone 1821, p. 431. Cf. on stadial theory, Ravenstone 1824, pp. 10–11.
122   Ravenstone 1821, p. 431.

one, the issue was discussed in the House of Commons, and in 1817 John Soane, official architect to the Office of Works, exhibited a drawing for one at the Royal Academy.[123]

The presence in a society of too large a class of idle persons, who are by definition a burden on the productive, is incompatible with the freedom and happiness of the people and leads to poverty and increasing crime. Ravenstone accused the nation's legislators of operating a system of class justice. *Thoughts on the Funding System* contains scathing attacks on the Corn Laws, the practices of Irish landlords, and landlords' exactions from farmers: 'It is to property alone that systematic injustice can be profitable'.[124] Industry (in the sense of productive labour) is the sole source of wealth; trade adds nothing to value and capital, rent, and taxes are all equally unproductive. Although in themselves they are 'not necessarily evils, they become so when carried to excess', because 'all equally represent the share of the idle in the earnings of industry'.[125]

Ravenstone described the aim of *A Few Doubts* as to show the real cause of the 'increase of wretchedness in this country'. Like Marx's *Capital* it is essentially a critique of political economy from the perspective of an intellectual who identified, at least in some degree, with the proletariat – one of those bourgeois ideologists who, in the words of Marx and Engels, 'have raised themselves to the level of comprehending theoretically the historical movement as a whole'.[126] In *Thoughts on the Funding System*, Ravenstone attacked 'Science' as obscurantist, corrupt, and interested, in effect offering a kind of ideology critique. As Marx and Engels famously observed in *The German Ideology*, in one of its forms ideology naturalises the status quo in the interests of the dominant class.[127] So too for Ravenstone, 'Because a thing was, they thought it could not be otherwise. The anomalies which in every country are created by the artificial regulations of men, they confounded with the great principles which govern and uphold this world. The abuses of society were to them as sacred as its primary and fundamental institutions'.[128] The most oppressive governments have consistently promoted political economy, which is the most 'injurious' doctrine to society ever 'broached'; it makes 'industry ancillary to riches' and 'men subordinate to property'.

---

123   Brindle 2001, pp. 59–65.

124   Ravenstone 1821, pp. 450–71; Ravenstone 1824, pp. 69–70.

125   Ravenstone 1821, p. 430. Cf. Ravesntone 1824, p. 38 – for Ravenstone the Jews are a people whose wealth depends on capital rather than industry (p. 79).

126   Marx and Engels 1998, p. 47.

127   Marx and Engels 1974, pp. 65–6.

128   Ravenstone 1824, pp. 4, 7, 72, 6.

In such societies the people are doomed to toil for the benefit of their masters alone: 'All rights will belong to the rich, all duties will be left to the poor. The people will be made to bow their necks beneath the yoke of the harshest of all rulers, the aristocracy of wealth'.[129] Political economy falsely represents consumption rather than industry as the source of wealth, and the constant object of social institutions was to elevate the idle at the expense of the productive classes.[130] Since the luxuries of life are consumed by the idle, trade and manufactures grow fastest when the condition of the people is at its most wretched.[131] In these circumstances the wealthy imagine artificial wants and even hire others to consume what is superfluous. This logic is illustrated by the Corn Laws, which at the same time as enriching the already wealthy have reduced the labourers to bare subsistence wages and the condition of slaves: 'it is impossible to extract more from the wretchedness of the people'.[132] Following the normal pattern of radical political discourse in this period, Ravenstone also attributes current problems to the fiscal policies of the war-time governments. The real expenses of the war had been met through taxation, while the stock created had only swelled the profits of a small number of contractors with the result that a tiny portion of the nation enjoyed great luxury while the 'middling and lower classes were robbed of almost every comfort'. Drawing on a well-rehearsed rhetoric against corruption, Ravenstone argued that the National Debt was not incurred from the 'hard earnings of industry', but was composed of 'a bloated and putrid mass of corruption wholly made up of fraud, peculation, and of jobs'.[133] The Debt had created a 'new set of patricians' that had robbed the 'ancient gentry' – whose families had given the nation its reputation in 'arts and arms' – of 'a large portion of their property'.[134]

It is such statements that justify the description of Ravenstone as Tory, and in *A Few Doubts* he refers back to a better time when the only property had been land, when in periods of war the gentry had comprised a militia, and when there was no public debt. He also called for a restoration of the ancient constitution.[135] But, as I have indicated, Ravenstone was not simply backward looking, a restitutionist romantic anti-capitalist.[136] Although he regarded the

---

129   Ravenstone 1824., p. 7.

130   Ravenstone 1824, p. 11.

131   Ravenstone 1824, p. 13.

132   Ravenstone 1824, pp. 23, 70.

133   Ravenstone 1824, pp. 27–30.

134   Ravenstone 1824, pp. 34, 51.

135   Ravenstone 1821, pp. 430, 466.

136   On which category, see Löwy and Sayre 2001, pp. 59–63.

'Funding System' as morally repugnant, substituting usury for real trade, he also saw it as eroding prejudices of birth and rank by making money the only basis of distinction. By breaking up large masses of property, it gave power to the law and increased the security of the state; by destroying the perpetuity of property it stimulated activity and offered new opportunities. The Funding System emerges as a necessary evil that counteracts the greater evil arising from the entrenched system of primogeniture.[137] However, nations like Britain that depend too much on capital and in which the unproductive class becomes excessively large are prone to decline into 'exhaustion and decrepitude'.[138] Ravenstone thought the country was heading for a revolution on the French model, one that could only be averted through a greater diffusion of wealth, an end to unjust laws and governmental corruption, and the shifting of taxes from articles of consumption onto property.

In light of the positions I have outlined it will come as no surprise that Ravenstone's comments on modern culture are uniformly negative. The simple age before the advent of commercial society had 'raised the stupendous piles for the worship of God, which towering beyond the daring of modern genius, still look with derision on the puny and paltry buildings with which capital trafficking in religion had studded our streets, as if to mark the poverty of our conceptions and the littleness of our means'.[139] This remarkable passage anticipates that whole tradition of romantic anti-capitalism that stretches through Carlyle, Pugin, and Ruskin to Morris. But it leaves unanswered the question of what resources contemporary artists and architects might draw on to build a healthier culture. Ravenstone leaves no doubt that the present age is not favourable to the arts, because wealth is so unevenly distributed. He cites the history of France, Spain and Italy, 'before their regeneration', to support his view that an increase in property, if it is concentrated only among the wealthiest, is harmful to the arts and sciences. In all three cases:

> A miserable and degraded people every where produced a vicious and contemptible gentry; idleness corrupted the rich; the distress of the poor increased the temptation to vice; the arts and sciences were almost extinct, for the funds for the maintenance of the idle were barely sufficient for the support of the hereditary rich. Whilst Italy had citizens, every town was filled with artists and poets, – with men who immortalized the

---

137   Ravenstone 1821, pp. 52–6.
138   Ravenstone 1821, pp. 77–8.
139   Ravenstone 1821, p. 75.

age in which they lived. She could boast a Dante, a Raffaelle, and Ariosto. When she had only gentry, her glory was limited to fiddlers and singers.[140]

For all the Tory motifs in his thought, Ravenstone is consistent in maintaining that the highest cultural achievements come in early capitalist society. At points in *Thoughts on the Funding System* he almost seems hostile to the material manifestations of culture as such, referring to the 'useless accumulation which now takes place in the hands of individuals in the shape of buckles and buttons, of pictures and statues'.[141] But as his admiring reference to the great communal buildings of the Medieval Period makes plain, it is the wasteful and individualistic culture of modern capitalism that rouses his disgust, not the arts per se.

Ravenstone's comments on culture are mere asides in a social and political critique, but their implications are clear enough. Only in a society where labour is properly rewarded for its product, where the unproductive are reduced to their proper roles and influence, and the whole population – or at least its male part – enjoys equal rights, can great cultural achievements be expected. His stance was far to the left of the Philosophic Radicals' critique both because it was neither blandly optimistic nor progressive and did not identify itself with the bourgeoisie, and, more significantly, because it took a critical stance on the fact that high culture was the product of exploitative property relations; while they recognised the structural nature of social inequality in commercial societies, the eighteenth-century Scottish School did not register unequal property relations as exploitative. Such ideas did not receive immediate development, presumably because they seemed of little direct relevance to working-class radicals. After all, the mode of social distinction high culture offered rubbed against the bourgeoisie not against them. It was the bourgeoisie that needed to appropriate it to establish their hegemony, to provide the appropriate decorative embellishments of bourgeois state formation, to demonstrate their superiority to Old Corruption's *ancien régime*.

---

140   Ravenstone 1821, p. 472.
141   Ravenstone 1824, p. 20.

Genius, Gender, and Progress: Benthamism and the Arts in the 1820s

'They hate all grace, ornament, elegance. They are addicted to abstruse science, but sworn enemies of the fine arts'. Thus Hazlitt described Jeremy Bentham and his followers in *The Plain Speaker* in 1826.[1] However, while Hazlitt captures the tenor of Bentham's own writings, many of those who accepted the Benthamite critique of aristocratic culture[2] were not prepared to subject the Fine Arts to the same reductive and philistine measure as the philosopher himself. The aim of this essay is to explore the terms in which the Utilitarians and their allies negotiated the category of the aesthetic, as this was manifested in some forms of Romantic art, and to show how conflicts of value were bound up not only with differences in class cultures, but with complex and contradictory attitudes towards gender and the social role of women.

Bentham's followers, the Philosophic Radicals,[3] were something like the vanguard of bourgeois ideology in early nineteenth-century Britain. They articulated a sweeping critique of aristocratic lifestyles, political institutions, and law based upon the secular and rationalist strands in Enlightenment social thought, and did so in the name of the middle class – a class that they looked to as the standard-bearer of human progress. The philosophy of Utilitarianism was thus one of the key intellectual resources of progressive politics, and liberals had almost necessarily to define their position in relation to it. As the work of Davidoff and Hall has shown, the outlook of the bulk of the provincial middle class was generally far less secular and critical of established institutions than that of their self-styled representatives in the metropolis.[4] But what they lacked in terms of representativeness, the Benthamites made up for in prominence in the public sphere. Moreover, the demand that the running of the state be made visible to the public, and answerable to it, was central to their ideology.[5]

---

1 'Of People of Sense', in Hazlitt 1930–4, vol. 12, p. 248.

2 I use the term 'aristocratic' here in the sense it was used by contemporaries to describe the culture of the landed classes.

3 On this group, which includes thinkers, writers for the periodical press, and politicians, see Thomas 1979.

4 Davidoff and Hall 1987.

5 Habermas 1991, pp. 99–101.

They contributed to the growing periodical press, which was fundamental to the concept of open public debate, both through their own journal the *Westminster Review*, and through their influence on sympathetic writers in other publications such as the *London Magazine*.

Utilitarian suspicion of the aesthetic worked at two levels, functional and ideological. In relation to the first, the Benthamites associated the arts with the leisure-time pursuits of an enervated and corrupt landed class, which ran the machinery of state exclusively in its own interests, and used knowledge of classical literature and the practice of picture collecting to distinguish itself from those it regarded as its social inferiors. They thus objected to the way the arts functioned invidiously as marks of social status. Secondly, they distrusted their ideological effects, because they associated the arts with forms of representation that were not subject to the normal rules of cognition, and thus potentially stood in the path of Enlightenment, the process they saw as the basis for the creation of a more rational and hence a more just and happier social order.

It was the Benthamites' commitment to rational dissection of traditional culture that also made it possible for some of them to arrive at a relatively modern view of the oppression of women, for the 'critique of unearned privilege', which Sabina Lovibond has described as central to feminism, was fundamental to their project.[6] In what follows, I show how the critique of aristocracy, distrust of the aesthetic, and radical views on gender inequality were correlated in liberal periodicals of the 1820s in which Benthamite influence was strong. As in Benthamite discourse itself, my main focus will be on the critique of aristocracy, but considerations of gender will emerge as a persistent and recurrent theme. This is because in questioning Romantic notions of artistic power (which seemed to them groundless), the Benthamites produced a less masculinised model of the artist than that generally current, and allowed more space for a woman of genius to appear. However, it will be shown that the language in which both aesthetic effect and intellectual achievement were valorised was pervaded by a macho rhetoric that made it hard to conceive a public type who was not in some sense heroic. In attempting to envision the role of the artist in a more enlightened social order, Bentham's followers departed in important ways from the stark assessment of the arts Bentham himself gave but, nonetheless, his pronouncements were a catalyst to theirs, and it is to them I now turn.

---

6   Lovibond 1989, p. 12.

Bentham and the Aesthetic

In Bentham's social theory, the fundamental measure of laws and institutions is the principle of utility, that is, whether they contribute to 'the greatest happiness of the greatest number'. Any course of action should be assessed solely in terms of the relative quantities of pleasure and pain it produces. Pleasure is good and pain is bad, and this is the foundation of morality. However, despite Bentham's attempt to ground his system in these simple verities, at the heart of it lay a contradiction between the principle of an interventionist state, which was necessary to regulate the competing claims of individual interests, and the principle of *laissez faire*, derived from Smithian economics, which assumed that the economy was a naturally self-regulating sphere in which the competition of interests ultimately worked to the benefit of all. This contradiction never became acute for the Benthamites because of their assumption that the interests of the middle class (who stood to profit most from their proposed legal and political reforms) were the common interest, and indeed were synonymous with progress. For this reason, they perceived no inconsistency in their attachment to the principle of democracy and their elitist concept of government. Government properly belonged to the propertied classes, and its role was to educate all to understand their true interests: 'the magistrate operating in the character of a tutor upon all the members of the state'.[7]

Like Locke, who he regarded as 'the Father or intellectual science', Bentham saw no cognitive value in art. In *The Rationale of Reward*, he describes the fine arts as arts of *amusement* only, whose sole utility lies in the pleasure they give 'to those who take pleasure in them'.[8] One of the obstacles in the path of his project to subject political and legal institutions to the cleansing light of reason was what he called 'the poverty and unsettled state of language', and Bentham wished to develop a morally neutral language, purged of all sentimental associations, which would be a truly scientific vehicle for social analysis. Imagination and concern with linguistic harmony hampered the proper workings of reason.[9] Worse yet, poetry is the 'natural' enemy of truth, for 'truth, exactitude of every kind, is fatal to poetry'. The poet's business 'consists in stimulating our passions, and exciting our prejudices', he must 'see everything through col-

---

7   Bentham 1988 (2), p. 63. In his first published work Bentham describes the defining characteristic of political society as obedience – see Bentham 1988 (1), p. 43. On the central tensions of Bentham's thought, see Coates 1950. On its larger political implications, see Corrigan and Sayer 1989, pp. 144–9.

8   Bentham 1825, p. 205.

9   See, for example, Bentham 1988 (2), pp. 13–16, n. 1.

oured media, and strive to make everyone else do the same'. This reasoning justified Bentham in his notorious pronouncement that, all in all, the child's game of push-pin was more valuable than music and poetry, because it was enjoyed by more people, and its pleasures were (from his perspective) always innocent. The main reason to value the fine arts was that they distracted individuals the 'most difficult to be pleased' from giving over their leisure to the more vicious pursuits of drunkenness, slander and gaming, and absorbed the energies of 'idlers', who in earlier times had found their amusement in warfare.[10] Just as Bentham's demand for a new rational and unadorned language was a bourgeois critique of the obscurities of aristocratic power, so was his philistine attitude towards the arts a class critique of the mysteries and privileges of aristocratic culture, a fact which was not lost on his followers in the *Westminster Review*.

Bentham's system (again like that of Locke) can valorise no kind of judgement other than that of reason in the narrowest sense. His determination to ground morality solely in the magic principle of utility corresponds with his insistence that sentiment, sympathy, and understanding provided no secure basis for agreement.[11] Entirely consonant with this rejection of moral judgement was the assertion that judgements of taste are groundless. One taste is as good as another, and the only basis for choosing between them is the pleasure associated with each for the individual.[12] Not surprisingly, the Fine Arts and Belles Lettres had no place in the educational programme Bentham devised for his proposed Chrestomathic School, a school of 'useful learning'.[13]

The connection between Bentham's reductive moral theory and his hostility to the fine arts was well understood by Hazlitt, who pointed out that his concept of psychology was facile and mechanistic, and that he was unable to distinguish either between different types of pleasure or between pleasures and goods. Hazlitt also saw the political dangers in progressives characterising the cognitive effects of the aesthetic as reactionary obfuscation, and significantly cited the Benthamites' dismissive response to Burke's *Reflections on the Revolution in France* (1790) as exemplifying their limitations: 'That work is to them a very flimsy and superficial performance, because it is rhetorical and figurative, and they judge of solidity by barrenness, of depth by dryness. Till

---

10   Bentham 1988 (2), pp. 206–8.
11   Bentham 1988 (2), pp. 17–20, n. 1. For a critique of Utilitarian morality, see McIntyre 1984, Chapter 6.
12   Bentham 1825, p. 208.
13   Bentham 1983.

they see a little farther into it, they will not be able to answer it, or counteract its influence; and yet that were a task of some importance'.[14] As we shall
see, other liberal intellectuals, attracted by the iconoclasm of the Benthamite
critique of traditional institutions, were equally unwilling to hand over art to
reaction. But Bentham's thought was not only conceptually inadequate with
regard to the aesthetic, it could not encompass important aspects of the lifestyle and ideology of the class with which he identified. Art was too central to
bourgeois culture, and its status functions too important, for it to be relegated
to the province of mere pleasure.

Benthamism in the *Examiner*

The word that focused Bentham's aversion to art was 'poetry', and for many
of his contemporaries 'poetry' stood for something like the general principle of
the aesthetic, a term that as Bentham himself noted was still associated primarily with German philosophy.[15] In British art criticism of the 1820s, the adjective
'poetic' had quite a wide currency to denote a particular type of imaginative
landscape painting produced by the painters John Martin and Francis Danby,
although it was also applied to some aspects of Turner's work. This usage is
well exemplified in Robert Hunt's reviews in the *Examiner*. In what follows, I
use critical responses to the works of Martin and Danby to provide a focus for
exploring the ways in which bourgeois intellectuals tried to negotiate between
Benthamite progressivism and their commitment to the aesthetic. This focus
is justified both because such art seemed to epitomise the poetic principle in
painting to contemporaries, and also because it was highly successful with a
broad middle-class public and attracted considerable attention in the press.
The main periodicals I draw upon are the *Examiner* and the *London Magazine*,
but reference will be made to some others to illustrate the currency of significant attitudes. The periodical press was a field in which different discourses
came together, where phenomena usually considered in discrete texts were
discussed adjacently, and where new developments in politics, society and cultural production all had to be made sense of. My analysis assumes that despite
the evident disparities the periodical texts display, there are some principles

---

14   Hazlitt 1930–4, vol. 12, p. 247. Apart from 'On People of Sense', Hazlitt's main critique of
      Utilitarianism is in the character sketch of Bentham in *The Spirit of the Age* – see Hazlitt
      1930–4, vol. 11, pp. 5–16. For an outstanding analysis of this issue, see Park 1971, Chapter 2.
15   Bentham 1983, pp. 188–9 n., 193 n. The broader connotations of 'poetry' are well exempli-
      fied in Mill 1981.

of coherence within them and that editorial policy would probably ensure common sympathies among the contributors. At the least we may suppose that opinions readers encountered in one section of a magazine would have been seen as not incongruous with those they encountered in other parts of it.[16]

From its establishment in 1808 into the 1820s, the *Examiner* was one of the foremost organs of the opposition press, as well as an important review of art, literature and the theatre. A sixteen-page Sunday paper, it was edited by Leigh Hunt until 1820, and then by his nephew Henry Leigh Hunt in the ensuing decade.[17] The *Examiner* of the 1820s was consistently sympathetic to the writings of Bentham and, like the Philosophic Radicals, it claimed to stand for the principles of reason and intellect.[18] While not 'Utopian', it looked forward to a future democratic state founded on universal suffrage, within which property would command the degree of influence appropriate to it.[19] Social distinctions would not be erased, but there would cease to be what the paper regarded as the artificial distinctions of title. All religions would be equally tolerated and there would be no political exclusion on the principle of race.[20]

---

16   Klancher 1987, pp. 48, 51. On art criticism more generally, see Hemingway 1992, Chapter 7.

17   For the history of the *Examiner*, see Hayden 1969, pp. 66–7; Stout 1949. For Hunt, see also Roe (ed.) 2003 and Roe 2005.

18   'our venerable and patriotic countryman BENTHAM, – a man who has spent his whole life in exercising his great mental powers with a continual yearning for the good of mankind', from 'State of Spain', *Examiner*, no. 655 (16 July 1820). For reviews of Bentham's works, see, for example: 'Bentham's Radical Reform Bill', *Examiner*, no. 627 (2 January 1820); 'Mr. Bentham's New Political Work', *Examiner*, no. 860 (25 July 1824). The *Examiner* was also favourable towards the Benthamite *Westminster Review* – see 'Literary Notices', *Examiner*, no. 887 (30 January 1825).

19   'We assert, that with the widest possible extension of the suffrage, the House of Commons would always be filled by men of wealth, rank and education.' – 'Reform of Parliament-Representation of Edinburgh', *Examiner*, no. 950 (16 April 1826). The 'universal suffrage' referred to in this text may only be male suffrage, but William Thompson's *Appeal of One-Half the Human Race, Women, against the Pretensions of the other Half, Men*, which the *Examiner* approved in the same year, was a critique of James Mill's arguments against the enfranchisement of women.

20   In 1819 the *Examiner* stated that more atrocities had been performed in the name of Christianity than in that of the pagan religions, and it objected to the unity of church and state. See 'A Specimen or Two of the Intellectual Faculties of My Lord Liverpool', *Examiner*, no. 625 (19 December 1819). The *Examiner* warmly supported toleration for Jews, but expected them to assimilate with gentile society and to participate in what it understood as the universal march of social progress. See 'Jews Free School', *Examiner*, no. 888 (6 Feb-

The main obstacle to this 'grand march of social circumstance' was what the *Examiner* described as 'aristocracy' or 'oligarchy', and the principle of 'legitimacy' on which it rested. This principle was unreasonable and hence unjust, and led to the abuse of power and vice. The landed classes were unfit to govern because they were lazy and ill-educated, the public schools breeding only 'elegant retainers of stupidity', 'ready-made tyrants and courtiers'.[21] The arguments of reaction were feeble and illogical, and its spokesmen intellectual nonentities. 'Intellect' was on the side of democracy, while 'Legitimacy' was the principle of 'the Few', and was opposed to the 'fixed and guarded rights' which were the principle of 'the Many'. 'The conflict', it was claimed, 'remains plainly, and almost avowedly, between Intellect and Power, the Pen and the Sword'.[22] What this emphasis on the power of mind partly signifies is that the *Examiner* presented itself as the voice of an intellectual fraction of the middle class; while it found the middle class at large the most virtuous and intelligent class, it asserted that intelligence and merit, rather than property or rank, were the ultimate basis of social distinction.[23] Indeed, the *Examiner* regarded some of the characteristics of commercial society, as it then existed, as incompatible with its principles. For instance, it supported Robert Owen's protests at the condition of children in manufacturing towns, and refused to accept that a 'natural law' of the economy tended to depress wages to the 'lowest wretchedness'. Its claim that a 'starving people' had a 'right' to be fed through taxes on the rich,[24] sug-

<hr>

ruary 1925); 'Literary Notices. Hebrew Literature', *Examiner*, no. 938 (29 January 1826). On the rights of coloured people, see 'Free People of Colour', *Examiner*, no. 857 (4 July 1824); 'Free People of Colour – West Indian Proceedings', *Examiner*, no. 911 (17 July 1825). Roe 2005 is informative on Hunt's West Indian heritage.

21   See, for example, 'On the Intellectual Inferiority of Parliament to the Demands of the Age', *Examiner*, no. 528 (8 February 1818); 'Cause of the Inferiority of Parliament to the Demands of the Present Age', *Examiner*, no. 531 (1 March 1818); 'Desperation of the Corrupt', *Examiner*, no. 678 (24 December 1820). On the public schools, see 'Death at Eton – Public Schools', *Examiner*, no. 893 (13 March 1825).

22   'State of Public Affairs', *Examiner*, no. 729 (23 December 1821).

23   For an acute analysis of this process of audience formation, see Klancher 1987, pp. 61–8. Klancher's analysis of *Blackwood's Magazine* (pp. 52–61) shows that this strategy was not confined to liberal journals, but it would seem that the paradigmatic reader 'interpellated' by the *Examiner* and *London Magazine* has different powers from his *Blackwood's* counterpart, that 'progress' united readers of the former in the onrush of widening understanding, while for the latter the 'advancement of knowledge' is a more mysterious and less pervasive phenomenon in which the reader is less certain of his role.

24   'On the Employment of Children in Manufactories', *Examiner*, no. 536 (5 April 1818). See also the article under this title *Examiner*, no. 535 (29 March 1818). 'Alarming State of the

gests that the *Examiner* did not go along with the Philosophic Radicals in their wholesale embrace of the *laissez-faire* principle.

The only issue on which the *Examiner* was in open disagreement with Bentham was that of the value of poetry. Reviewing *The Rationale of Reward* in 1825, the paper concluded that 'the very contracted nature of Mr BENTHAM's exclusive line of study' had prevented him from giving proper attention to the arts, and directly contradicted his assertion that poetry, by its very nature, gave a false representation of reality. By contrast, the reviewer likened the images of poetry to the effect of a microscope, claiming that they magnified rather than distorted, so as to describe 'affections we intensely feel': 'Poetry, speaking of course of what really deserves the name, is rather abstractive than false – it abstracts all shadow from its light, and all light from its shade at pleasure – not to demonstrate but to impress; not to convey facts, but images and associations. Of all men, we deem genuine poets the least of *liars*'.[25]

This was consistent with views expressed in other numbers of the paper. For instance, an essay on 'Fiction and Matter-of-Fact', printed earlier in the year, also insisted that the measurable truths of logic and science and the truths 'we feel with our hearts and imaginations' were not incompatible, and that 'mathematical truth is not the only truth in the world'. It went on to ask how it was that an age remarkable for the growth of science should also be one in which literary taste should be so attracted to 'fictions of the East', 'solitary and fanciful reveries', 'the wild taste of the Germans', and 'a new and more primitive use of the old Pagan Mythology'. And found the answer in the stimulus that politics and the development of science itself had given the imagination. The discovery of new secondary causes brought the mind up against the same realm of the vast and incomprehensible as had preoccupied philosophers in the past: 'The imagination recognizes its ancient field, and begins ranging again at will, doubly bent upon liberty, because of the trammels with which it has been threatened'.[26] The paintings of John Martin and Francis Danby might have served as illustrations of this hypothesis.

People', *Examiner*, no. 971 (10 September 1826); 'Hints on Political Economy', *Examiner*, no. 986 (24 December 1826).

25   'Political Examiner' (review of Bentham's *Rationale of Reward*), *Examiner*, no. 904 (29 May 1825).

26   'The Wishing Cap, No. 22 – Fiction and Matter-of-Fact', *Examiner*, no. 883 (2 June 1825). For a comparable statement on the promise of the 'new generation', see 'Cause of the Inferiority of Parliament to the Demands of the Present Age', *Examiner*, no. 531 (1 March 1818).

While Bentham associated the arts with reaction, the *Examiner* saw them as natural allies of progress. For just as the principle of Legitimacy was incompatible with Intellect, it was equally incompatible with Literature, and, we may assume, the other fine arts too. The 'inevitable progress of knowledge' must call into question the 'pretensions' of kings, who were, by the nature of their authority, 'ready-made haters of knowledge'. This was so because the 'pretensions' of kings did not rest on merit, while Literature could recognize no other basis for distinction, and thus its pretensions were 'essentially levelling and jacobinical'.[27]

The *Examiner* on Poetry, Genius, and Women

A similar veneration of intellect informed the *Examiner*'s art criticism. The paper supported what it called the British School, and gave high praise to some contemporary artists such as West, Fuseli, Flaxman and Haydon. However, it was severely critical of the record of the dominant elite as patrons, and accused the aristocracy generally of failing in its duty to foster British art. The *Examiner* regularly called for a reform of the Royal Academy and state support of the arts, and criticised successive governments for not enacting a policy of public patronage like that of France. This failing was a by-product of the larger corruption of the political establishment, but was also attributed to the commercial character of the nation.[28] According to the *Examiner*, a reform of Parliament would be directly beneficial to art.[29]

Although the *Examiner*'s position on the arts was intrinsically bound up with its critique of British culture in the larger sense of the term, the criteria by which it evaluated art were not directly political ones. They were criteria drawn principally from the discourse of academic theory, but modified in response to the more philosophical theories of the arts developed in the eighteenth century. Robert Hunt accepted the conventional hierarchies of the academic creed and regarded depiction of the human figure as the core of pictorial art, because it showed the 'intellectual part of man'. Landscape painting was made more significant and intellectual by the introduction of figures, and ideal landscape was superior to 'common landscape' because it took a rarer kind of mental vision to separate the 'beautiful, noble, and pure', from the 'ordinary

---

27   'Proposed Royal Academy of Literature', *Examiner*, no. 709 (5 August 1821).

28   'Efficient Patronage of Art', *Examiner*, no. 681 (21 January 1821); 'A Brief Sketch of the State of the Fine Arts in Great Britain', *Examiner*, no. 934 (1 January 1826).

29   'Want of a Public Gallery of Paintings', *Examiner*, no. 728 (7 January 1822).

and obvious'. Thinking within the framework of association psychology, Hunt argued that painters should select scenes which would awaken those 'moral analogies and feelings' that are the most pleasing of the impressions of nature. This selection required special mental powers from artists, whose minds 'must be imbued with the properties of the subjects they represent, immersed in their very essence, feeling the passions and thinking the thoughts of mankind'.[30]

Great art being the expression of a quality of individual genius, which was innate, it followed that excellence was to be recognised by originality.[31] For Hunt, paintings such as Danby's *The Delivery of Israel out of Egypt* (1825, *fig. 1*) seemed to depart from any of the established models of the landscape genre: he could see them neither as 'familiar' nor as conventional 'historical' landscapes, and he distinguished them as 'poetic' to stress their emotional effect.[32] For him this species of art was the most difficult and hence also the most valuable. In 1819 he gave Martin's first major success, *The Fall of Babylon* (private collection),[33] a long and laudatory review, which emphasised both the intellectual capacity needed for such a work and the painting's power over the spectators. After itemising the range of knowledge and skill the picture involved, the review asserted that it required 'a mind nobly daring and confident in its resources', and 'a lively and poetical imagination' that could 'convey to the spectator a consciousness of something supernatural, at least of the sublime, and warm and expand his fancy, set his mind thinking and his heart feeling with a deep and delightful intensity'. To support this claim for the work's power, Hunt referred to spectators crowding around the picture at the British Institution, exclaiming with admiration, studying it from close to and from a distance, going away and then returning to study it again. The adjectives 'strong' and 'nobly daring', which are used to characterise Martin's mind, suggest a concept

---

30   'Exhibition of Paintings in Water Colours', *Examiner*, no. 747 (20 May 1822); 'Royal Academy', *Examiner*, no. 751 (17 June 1822).

31   'Royal Academy', *Examiner*, no. 751, 26 May 1822. This valorisation of originality (commonplace in the period) finds a parallel in Bentham's distinction between 'Expositors' and 'Censors' in *A Fragment on Government*. The Expositor concerns himself only with the law as it is, while the Censor shows it as it ought to be; the former relies primarily on apprehension and memory, while the latter is the truly creative thinker. See Bentham 1988 (1), pp. 7–8.

32   See the notice on Danby's *Delivery of Israel out of Egypt* in 'Royal Academy', *Examiner*, no. 902 (15 May 1825). Hunt applies essentially the same criteria to distinguish 'poetry' from other forms of artistic representation as the younger Mill, for whom poetry was characterised by the unselfconscious presentation of individual emotion. In Mill's argument, this distinction intersected 'the whole domain of art'. See Mill 1981, pp. 348–50.

33   For this work, see Myrone (ed.) 2011, pp. 97–8.

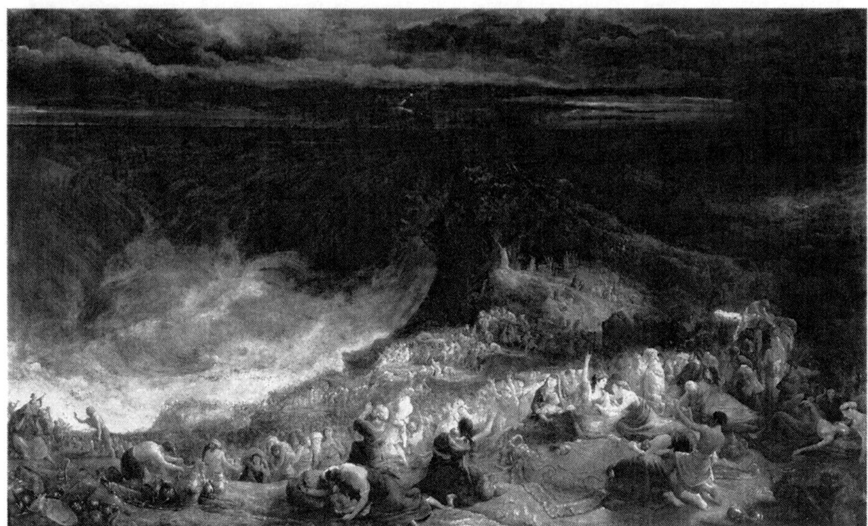

FIGURE 1   *Francis Danby,* The Delivery of Israel out of Egypt, *1825, oil on canvas, 58¾ × 94 ½ in (149.5 × 240 cm)*
©HARRIS MUSEUM AND ART GALLERY, PRESTON, LANCASHIRE, UK/BRIDGEMAN IMAGES.

of intellect which is masculinised. But the effect of the work on the spectator is likened to that of a woman on her lover. After leaving the work, 'thrilling' with its 'strange and felicitous impression', the spectator views 'most other pictures' absent-mindedly, 'like a lover who is but half attentive to other women, in a delicious reverie on the superior charms of her who has the keeping of his heart'. While the critic himself is 'in love with genius', he would not wish to be seen as 'like amorous lovers, blind to defect', and Hunt found Martin's brushwork and outlines 'somewhat hard', and 'a theatrical look' about some of his figures.[34]

In the narrative of this criticism, the artist communicated his feelings spontaneously to the spectator, and overwhelmed his imagination. The ideal spectator was necessarily masculine, but he had to succumb to the power of the work over him, not through reason but through yielding emotionally. In 1821, *Belshazzar's Feast* (*fig. 2*) was described as 'a scene so various, so magnificent, portentous, and pathetic, as to gratify all the serious faculties of the mind, and to fill them with wonder and delight'. Martin was among the few 'whose works

---

34   'British Institution', *Examiner*, no. 580 (7 February 1819). Hunt again likened the critic to a 'happy intense lover' in his review of Martin's *Belshazzar's Feast* two years later. See 'British Institution', *Examiner*, no. 683 (4 February 1821). On Martin's pursuit of difficult subjects,

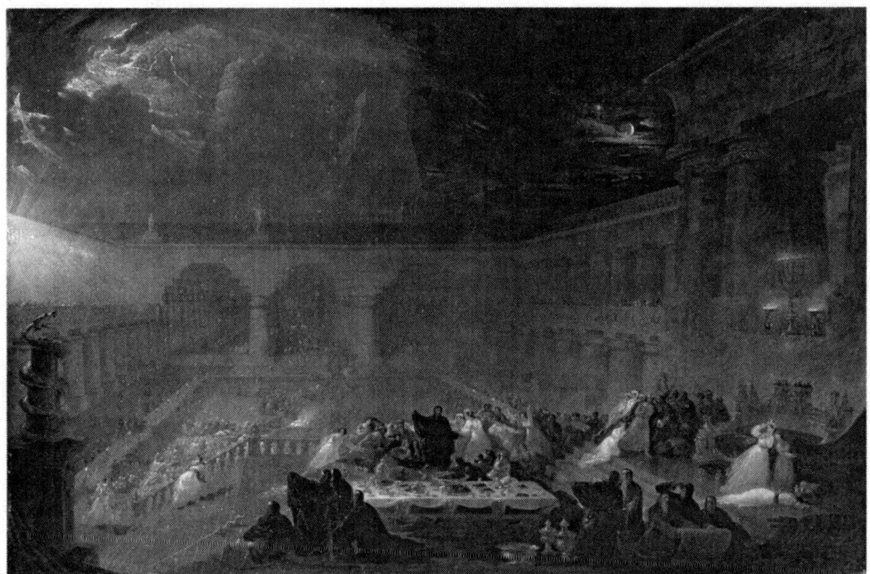

FIGURE 2   *John Martin, 1789–1854, British, Belshazzar's Feast, 1820, oil on canvas, 31½ × 47½ in (80 × 120.7 cm). This is a smaller version of the picture exhibited in 1821, which is in a private collection.*
YALE CENTER FOR BRITISH ART, NEW HAVEN, PAUL MELLON COLLECTION

delight by striking upon all those strings of feeling by which the mind is vehemently moved', and, like Michelangelo and Raphael, he could 'lay claim to an extraordinary character for originality and sublimity'.[35] The mind of genius and the mind of the receptive spectator are both conceived as masculine, but the

---

see the discussion of his *Macbeth* (National Gallery of Scotland, Edinburgh) in 'British Institution', *Examiner*, no. 635 (5 March 1820).

35   'British Institution', *Examiner*, no. 683 (4 February 1821). Such metaphors of artistic power were not singular to the *Examiner*. The *Morning Herald*, one of the papers most consistently favourable to Martin and Danby in the 1820s, claimed that *Belshazzar's Feast* 'electrified the spectator by a tremendous flash of genius'. Its effect was *irresistible*. It was not like that 'celestial power which uniting its efforts with nature and probability, entrances us by our own consent', rather it was that 'relative of eccentricity, which notwithstanding its incongruities, compels our acknowledgment of its superiority'. The idea of power could hardly be more emphatic. See 'British Institution, Pall Mall', *Morning Herald*, 29 January 1821. Cf. the review of the *Fall of Babylon* in 'British Gallery', *New Monthly Magazine*, no. 61 (1 March 1819). However, it is important to note that Martin's work did not signify the power of imagination to everyone. Hazlitt found his literal-minded attempts to represent the sublime in vast perspectives 'an instance of total want of imagination' – see Hazlitt 1930–4, vol. 11, p. 252, and vol. 18, pp. 155–6. For *Belshazzar's Feast* see Myrone (ed.) 2011, pp. 99–108.

work itself is both seductively feminine and powerfully masculine at the same time. In the discourses of eighteenth-century philosophy within which criticism was conceived reason was an active and sternly male principle, associated with the roles of public men; while imagination, associated with the moral sympathies of daily life and the individual experiences of aesthetic pleasure, was more ambiguously gendered. Not surprisingly, therefore, attempts to describe the exercise of taste produced a tangle of gender contradictions in the metaphors used to evoke the aesthetic effect and critics seeking to establish artists and intellectuals as a new kind of heroic figure were almost forced to describe the power of the artist and of his art in metaphors that shift between violation and seduction of the spectator.

The effects of Danby's work, which achieved critical prominence a few years later, were described somewhat differently. The distinction was summed up in a review of the British Institution exhibition of 1826: 'Mr MARTIN's picture, *The Deluge*, is a forcible appeal to the imagination, which "it seizes", as it were, "by storm". – Mr DANBY's picture represents *Solitude; the moment of Sun-set, with the Moon rising over a ruined City*. Mr DANBY appeals to the imagination through the medium of a select choice of Nature, the best way in which it can effectively be awakened'.[36] Danby's talent was defined as a capacity to give 'natural' representations of scenes appropriate to the 'moral sentiment and feeling' suggested by his subjects. On these grounds, the *Examiner* gave highly enthusiastic responses to the exhibition of *Sunset at Sea after a Storm* (Bristol Museum and Art Gallery) in 1824, and to that of *Christ Walking on the Sea* (Forbes Collection, London) in 1826.[37] It praised *An Enchanted Island* (*fig. 3*) of 1825 for achieving that combination of naturalistic effect with imaginative power it had found lacking in Martin's work.[38]

To summarise then, the *Examiner* explained the status it gave to 'poetic landscape' paintings partly through the alleged powers of mind involved in their production, and partly through their power over the spectator's emotions. This latter claim precisely valorised an effect that Bentham saw as inimical to the proper order of reason, and implied that it was far more than a species of

---

36   'British Institution', *Examiner*, no. 940 (12 February 1826). Both pictures are now lost, although Martin's is known through a mezzotint – see Myrone (ed.) 2011, pp. 130–1.

37   'Royal Academy', *Examiner*, no. 854 (14 June 1824); Royal Academy, *Examiner*, no. 955 (21 May 1826). Greenacre 1988, no. 20 and fig. 17.

38   'British Institution', *Examiner*, no. 889 (13 February 1825). Other papers made a similar distinction. Thus, when the *Morning Herald* reviewed *An Enchanted Island*, it described its effect as like a 'most delightful daydream', the 'spell' of which 'fascinates the sense and forcibly detains the attention of all around'. – 'British Gallery, Pall Mall', *Morning Herald*, 28 January 1825.

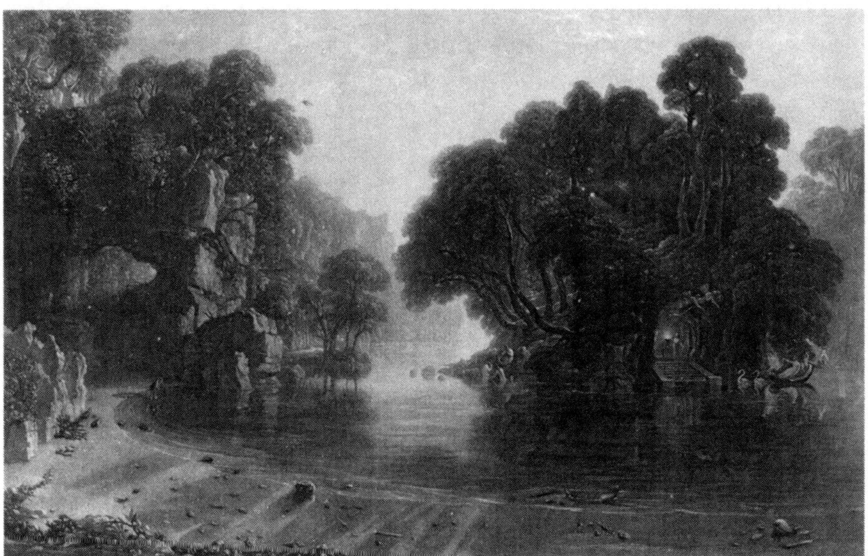

FIGURE 3   *G.H. Phillips after Francis Danby,* An Enchanted Island, *1825, mezzotint engraving.*
             The painting is in a private collection.
             © THE TRUSTEES OF THE BRITISH MUSEUM

individual pleasure akin to that of eating a good pudding. To understand the
concern of the *Examiner* and other papers with the potency of contemporary
art, we need to see their criticism in the larger context of middle-class English
nationalism. It needs to be understood in relation to a larger pattern of critical
discourse in which nations were pictured like manly individuals in competition
with one another, and it was imperative to assert the 'vigour' of the national
school. Incapacity in High Art was equivalent to a deficiency in the nation's collective virility. To have failed to produce High Art was evidence of the debilitat-
ing effects of luxury (a term with markedly feminine connotations), and of the
absence of manly public spirit among those responsible for the nation's destiny.

In the course of a commentary on the limitations of the Royal Academicians
from 1817 Hunt observed, 'It is one of the main propensities of genius to triumph
over difficulties in its unquenchable ardour for eminence: and the want of
resolution to confront and combat them argues a dwarfishness of mind, a
puerility of spirit, disowned and disdained by true genius'.[39] If the patron class
did not care enough for High Art to support it, then the leaders of the artistic
community must propagate and raise such an art by their own energy and force

---

39   'Royal Academy', *Examiner*, no. 490 (18 May 1817).

of will. The main exponents of High Art described themselves, and were in turn described, as the martyred heroes of the British School. A key figure in this martyrology was James Barry, who characterised his aims, in letters published posthumously in 1809, as a Quixotic endeavour to establish 'a solid *manly taste* for real art in the place of our trifling, contemptible passion for the daubing of little inconsequential things, portraits of dogs, landscapes, &c' – a type of picture that had served only to 'disgrace' Britain to the rest of Europe.[40] The campaign for High Art was thus represented as a struggle on the part of lone artist-heroes to save the nation's honour from the slur of aesthetic effeminacy; Benjamin Robert Haydon's career can partly be understood as an acting out of this ideology of patriotic combat with brush and palette.[41] The type of individual genius who could labour in such a contest was only conceivable as masculine. It is thus not surprising that Hunt, one of Haydon's staunchest supporters, should assert in his obituary of Angelica Kauffman in 1808 that 'the grandeur of epic painting has never been conceived by female hand. In poetry, painting and musical composition, its best strength has been adequate only to the gentler feelings of the human heart'.[42]

While the *Examiner*'s art criticism did not incorporate the category of 'woman of genius' its literary reviews did – although it probably regarded her province as distinct (and ultimately inferior) from that of male genius. Thus, it applauded the sentimental, and highly successful, romantic poetry of 'L.E.L.' (Letitia Elizabeth Landon), which some other periodicals criticised as being not only repetitive, but also as trivial and even pernicious. While acknowledging the limited range of L.E.L.'s talents, the *Examiner* praised her 'general powers', and said it would be as 'ungrateful' to criticise her for being great in 'one branch of composition only', as it would be to criticise Claude for not being Raphael.[43] If there was rather more ideological space for a woman

---

40   James Barry to the Duke of Richmond, 29 August 1773, in Barry 1809, vol. 1, p. 241.

41   For Haydon on the nation's need for great art, see 'On the Cartoon of Raphael', *Annals of the Fine Arts*, 4 (1819), pp. 559–62. For changing conceptions of artistic genius in this period, see Kriz 1997.

42.   'Angelica Kaufman', *Examiner*, no. 3 (17 January 1808).

43   The phrase 'woman of genius' occurs in a review of Hannah More's *Moral Sketches of Prevailing Opinions and Manners*, in *Examiner*, no. 625 (19 December 1819). (The paper did not regard More as one and objected strongly to her theology). Review of *The Troubadour and Other Poems* by L.E.L., *Examiner*, no. 915 (14 August 1825). For Landon's tragic career, see Blanchard 1841.

       As a measure of the *Examiner*'s relative enlightenment it may be noted that almost contemporaneously the *London Magazine*, in the years before it passed into Bentham-

writer of genius, as the *Examiner*'s position suggests, this is likely to have been both because painting was a professionalised trade, difficult of access to women, because the representation of the naked body was central to its highest achievements, and because those genres in which women did make substantial contributions – such as portraiture and still-life – were devalued. Further, the artist had to move in the public realm in ways the writer did not.

To some extent Hunt's heavy masculinisation of pictorial practice looks a little out of place juxtaposed with the rather more liberal positions that the *Examiner* adopted on the role of women more generally. For instance, at the time of the Queen Caroline trial in 1820, the paper published a sequence of articles attacking the behaviour of George IV and his supporters through a scathing critique of the double standard. The monarch should not expect a standard from Caroline different from that which applied to himself, for 'adultery is either a crime in everybody, or it is not'. Prevailing social mores made virtue a sham, and indeed had morally deleterious effects, for they were contrary to natural sympathies and caused extensive unhappiness, infidelity, and prostitution. The laws of society had been made by men in a barbaric period; they were selfish and unjust, and represented an abuse of power.[44] This position was consonant with that of Bentham who, while he argued that man should be the master in the domestic sphere and function as the guardian of his wife, also insisted that the offences relating to the duties of both partners were entirely reciprocal.[45]

---

ite hands, regularly published reviews and articles that asserted roundly that there had been no great women writers not just because of the limitations of women's education, but because the inherent character of their sex suited them to 'inactive, peaceful and domestic offices', and barred them from the 'external duties of life'. Women are great in 'conversational qualities', but can never attain 'extremes of intellect', 'profundity of thought and sublimity of imagination'. See 'Differences between the Mental Powers of the Sexes – Letters from the Country, no. 11', *London Magazine*, series 1, 11 (March 1824), pp. 293–9. Cf. 'The Drama', *London Magazine*, series 1, 7 (April 1823); 'The Drama', *London Magazine*, series 1, 1 (January 1824); 'Notes from the Pocket-Book of a Late Opium-Eater, no. IV, False Distinctions', *London Magazine*, series 1, 9 (June 1824).

44   This account of the *Examiner*'s position is based on: 'Question between the King and Queen', *Examiner*, no. 650 (11 June 1820); 'Meeting of the House of Lords and the Queen', *Examiner*, no. 660 (20 August 1820); 'Brief Summary of the Various Points of Cruelty and Injustice, in the late Persecution of the Queen – and its General Results', *Examiner*, no. 675 (3 December 1820). For the significance of the case, see Laqueur 1982. Support for Caroline transcended normal political loyalties – see Davidoff and Hall 1987, pp. 149–55.

45   Bentham 1988 (2), pp. 258–60, 280–3.

The *Examiner*'s critique of what it described elsewhere as the 'wrongs of woman' needs to be understood in relation to its larger critique of aristocratic manners. A recurrent image in the paper was that of the lower-class woman seduced, or threatened by the upper-class male.[46] In 1825 it attacked the morals of the aristocracy by citing a court case in which the son of a 'Right Honourable' had married the daughter of his father's huntsman, separated from her shortly after, and then sued for damages nine years later because she had lived with another man and had children with him. Such cases showed that the British aristocracy was 'frivolous, heartless, insolent, and sensual', a 'class in which the extreme of what is contemptible and pernicious is oftener found than in any other'.[47] Predictably, the *Examiner* also attacked aristocratic marriage practices, in which, it charged, the interests of 'wealth and birth' took precedence over 'affection and moral propriety'.[48] Implicit in this critique is a conception of human nature that represents the viewpoint of the liberal middle class. The *Examiner* characterised relations between the sexes as a natural function that should be governed by a natural morality, by reason and affection.[49] This conception included an image of woman as predisposed to specific character traits and concomitant norms of behaviour. Men were the 'natural guardians of the female sex', while women had a 'natural desire' to experience 'nuptial bliss'.[50] However, women were capable of acts of public virtue, at least in so far as they involved support of a husband or a brother. In 1821 the paper took exception to an article in *The Times*, which asserted that the behaviour of Mary Ann Carlile, sister of the radical publisher Richard Carlile, was immodest and unfeminine. It was, the *Examiner* claimed, fully consistent with 'the nature and habits' of their

---

46   See the remarkable account of the pursuit of a young woman by a 'young man of fashion' in 'The Wishing Cap, No. v, "On Seeing a Pigeon Make Love"', *Examiner*, no. 848 (2 May 1824). The author's capacity to see things from the woman's position is notable: 'What is sport to the man in these cases, is very often death to the lady'. See also the letter 'Seduction', *Examiner*, no. 980 (12 November 1826).

47   'High Life Morality', *Examiner*, no. 919 (11 September 1825).

48   'Marriage Laws', *Examiner*, no. 845 (11 April 1824). The paper also called for an ending of the Church of England's monopoly on the marriage rite and the institution of a civil marriage contract.

49   As in other respects, it offered the example of the United States as a more natural order. See the review of *View of Society and Manners in America, by an Englishwoman*, in 'Literary Notices', *Examiner*, no. 712 (26 August 1821).

50   These phrases come from 'Fine Arts', *Examiner*, no. 669 (22 October 1820), and a review of Lucy Aiken's *Memoirs of the Court of Queen Elizabeth*, *Examiner*, no. 719 (14 October 1821).

sex for women to support their male relatives against the misuse of power, indeed to do so demonstrated 'the finest impulse of affection and moral courage'.[51]

This sensitivity to some of the injustices perpetrated against women and hints that they should play a role in the public sphere (albeit a subordinate one) suggests that some of the *Examiner*'s writers may have been aware of Bentham's support for female enfranchisement, and his critique of prevailing laws as they bore on relations between the sexes.[52] The paper also gave signs of being sympathetic to the most advanced feminism of the period, that of elements in the Owenite Movement. While it consistently described Owen's theory as Utopian, the *Examiner* also praised his efforts as an 'unmixed good', and hailed the establishment of Owenite communities, because they would show the more equitable distribution of wealth possible in a less 'artificial' and 'immoral state of society'.[53] In a very favourable review of the first numbers of the *Co-operative Magazine* in 1826, it described the Owenites as 'distinguished by amiable and virtuous dispositions' and referred to what has been described as the founding text of socialist feminism, William Thompson's *Appeal of One-Half the Human Race, Women, against the Pretensions of the other half, Men, to retain them in political and thence in civil and domestic slavery* (1825), as 'just and convincing'.[54] Nonetheless, it would be inappropriate to discover in the *Examiner* a kind of proto-feminism. Its position would probably be better defined as a philanthropy towards women, consonant with middle-class norms of domesticity and gentility. Considering the role or religion in the self-effacement of middle-class women, it may be significant that it was a paper with a secular tone, in which discussions of religion had a small place except where they bore on liberal politics.

---

51   'Persecution – the Carliles', *Examiner*, no. 722 (25 November 1821). A prosecution of Mary Carlile for 'impious and blasphemous libel' was instigated by the Society for the Suppression of Vice in July 1821. On Richard Carlile, see Thompson 1963, Chapter 16.

52   Boralevi 1987, pp. 166–70, 172. Boralevi, however, certainly goes too far in describing Bentham as 'the father of historical feminism' (p. 165). See also Williford 1975. It is worth noting in this connection that Bentham also had an exceptionally enlightened attitude towards male-male sexual practices, arguing that they were a 'natural' form of behaviour and should be decriminalised. See Dellamora 1990, pp. 12–14, 244 n. 68.

53   'Mr. Owen's Plan – Establishment at Harmony', *Examiner*, no. 922 (2 October 1825).

54   'Literary Notices', *Examiner*, no. 938 (29 January 1826). On Thompson's *Appeal*, and on Owenism and feminism more generally, see Taylor 1983, esp. pp. 17, 22–4. Although, following Taylor, I attribute the *Appeal* to Thompson, the role of Anna Wheeler in its making should be noted.

Seen in relation to the ideas on politics, social progress, literature, and art that cluster in the *Examiner*, the appraisals of Martin and Danby I discussed earlier seem informed by much larger concerns. Literature and art are clearly connected with the 'march of social circumstance', with the progress of intellect and the forces that would ultimately defeat 'Legitimacy'. In a review of the Royal Academy exhibition of 1821 Hunt asserted that the pleasures of taste were next in value to those of domestic morality and patriotism. Those who had 'so far risen above the common capacities and pursuits of their race' as to contribute to the nation's stock of these 'invaluable pleasures' deserved its gratitude. Martin was listed among those who were currently 'running the race of moral and intellectual glory', together with Bentham, Cartwright, Bennet, Byron, Campbell, Scott, Davy, Haydon and Hilton. All these had given 'the best possible direction to their natural powers for the advantage of their species'.[55] The value that the *Examiner* placed on intellectual power, whether it be in political theory, legislation, philosophy, literature, or art, meant that its criticism was predisposed to valorise the works of Martin and Danby as a manifestation of progress. But its emphasis on the *power* of intellect meant that it effectively masculinised the new type of public benefactor, with which it replaced the heroic public man of civic humanist discourse. Martial virtues ceased to be qualifications for the public sphere, but it remained an essentially masculine realm.

Hunt's ideal of a virile genius was grounded in the very high value he accorded the poetic and the immense power he claimed for it. But from a philosophical perspective which questioned that the effects of such power were either beneficial or useful, the artist could be a less heroic type, and maybe even a woman. For a brief moment in the mid-1820s, the Philosophic Radicals shed the cold light of the Utilitarian principle on aristocratic culture, and sought to demystify art by showing that it functioned as a vehicle of reactionary social interests. At the same time, they came close to neutering genius. In the pages of the *Westminster Review* they expressed a disdain for mere 'literature' and 'what are called the fine arts' that echoed the value system of Bentham's *Rationale of Reward*, and clearly articulated the class outlook underlying this critique: 'There is a small class of readers in this country who are Somebody, and there is a very large class who are Nobody'. This class of Somebodies ('a gang of about a hundred and eighty families') depended for their wealth on an unjust system

---

55   'Royal Academy', *Examiner*, no. 697 (13 May 1821). Figures in this list lesser known today
      include the lawyer and progressive politician Henry Grey Bennet, who advocated Catholic
      Emancipation and defended Queen Caroline at her trial; Major John Cartwright, the
      suffrage reformer; Thomas Campbell, the poet; and the history painter William Hilton.

of taxation, and ran government as 'a means of provision' for themselves and their dependants. And 'besides this substantial privilege', 'the Somebodys have also assumed that of having a circle of taste exclusively their own; of keeping at a distance any Nobody who dares approach; and at the expense of the excluded class, indulging in all the pleasure of arrogance and malignity'.[56] These privileges were partly reproduced by the universities where the study of ancient languages was pursued as a 'substitute' for 'useful inquiry'. The *Westminster Review* damned the preoccupation with 'polite literature' as 'the disease of the age', and on a number of occasions accused poets generally of an unfortunate tendency to aristocratic sympathies because of the appeal of feudalism to the literary imagination.

In the *London Magazine* the critique of the aesthetic was not so extreme, but the poetic principle was not accorded the status it enjoyed in the *Examiner*, where Utilitarian influence was less marked. The emasculation of art that accompanied this critique was strikingly consonant with the Radicals' advanced views on the capacities of women; for them, the mysteries of art and received views of the inferiority of female capacities were alike barbaric remnants of an earlier stage of social development.[57]

Benthamism in the *London Magazine*

The *London Magazine* is well known to historians of literature, but its reputation rests mainly on the first series from January 1820 to December 1824, when writers such as Carlyle, Clare, De Quincey, Hazlitt, Lamb, and Stendhal were among the contributors. However, it is the third series of 1828–9 that interests me here. Editorship of the magazine was taken over by the Philosophic Radical Henry Southern at the end of 1824, and he became its proprietor in September 1825. In April 1828 it was bought by Charles Knight, and run by him and Barry St Leger until its demise in the following year. From early 1821 onwards the *London Magazine* consistently took a liberal position, and it became a committed advocate of parliamentary reform and repeal of the Corn Laws.[58] Unlike the

---

56 Review of Washington Irving's *Tales of a Traveler*, *Westminster Review*, 2 (October 1824). This phase of the magazine's history is discussed in Nesbitt 1934, Chapter 5. See also Thomas 1979, pp. 157–67.

57 On the stadial theory of social development that the Benthamites took from the Scottish School and the condition of women as an index of progress within it, see Chapter One.

58 Bauer 1953, pp. 89–91. Bauer underestimates the interest of the second and third series

Examiner, it was primarily a literary and artistic review, and its coverage of current politics was less direct than that of a Sunday paper, while its coverage of contemporary literature was broader. This means that the *London Magazine*'s art criticism was framed somewhat differently from that of the *Examiner*.

In its third series, the *London Magazine* began to celebrate the decline of a militaristic mentality it associated with aristocracy, and proclaimed the advancement of knowledge and virtues of peace. Britain being a country in which five-sixths of power, two-thirds of wealth, and nine-tenths of intelligence came from the 'commercial classes', it was improper that government continued to be dominated by the 'aristocracy and landed interest' and headed by a general who ran it for their benefit.[59] The *London Magazine* objected to '*real* property' being defined only in terms of land, and, concomitantly, it attacked the 'narrow, selfish, aristocratical, and *territorial* spirit of the mass of country gentlemen', and their abuse of power in the magistracy.[60]

While the magazine was not oblivious to the dehumanising effects of commercial civilization, it maintained that all its 'barter and brokerage' was at least superior to the 'armed legions of olden time'. Viewing the commercial centre of London and the port, one writer noted the contrast between 'the incessant toil for the support of individual respectability and luxury', and the 'many' who are 'naked, starving, and utterly forsaken of men', But any hope of relieving these unfortunates was deemed 'probably utopian', and such concerns were lost among the magazine's incessant paeans to progress. Britain's destiny was to 'subdue the earth' through commerce, which would carry the 'seeds of knowledge and truth into the most distant regions'. The 'cranes and wagons' and the noise of workshops were not 'vulgar things', for they were 'accomplishing the purposes of Providence'.[61]

From the *London Magazine*'s perspective, the great problem for the nation was not the cultural effects of capitalism, but the aristocracy, which was standing still 'in the midst of improvement'. While 'every other class' was 'advancing in knowledge, liberality and sound principle', the aristocracy was 'as firmly attached to bygone policy and obsolete prejudices' as their ancestors were to

---

and her assertion (p. 328) that the Fine Arts were not covered in the magazine after 1825 is incorrect. Art reviews ceased in 1826–7, but were resumed in 1828–9. I have discussed the art criticism of the second series in Hemingway 1992, pp. 125–34.

59   'The New Ministry', *London Magazine*, series 3, 1 (July 1828).

60   'Reforms in the Law, No. IV – The Magistracy Bill', *London Magazine*, series 3, 1 (July 1828).

61   'The Colosseum', *London Magazine*, series 3, 3 (February 1829). See also the celebration of the spectacle of commerce and industry in the Pool of London, in 'Private Bills of the Session 1828', *London Magazine*, series 3, 2 (September 1828).

feudalism.[62] Like the *Examiner*, the *London Magazine* pilloried the intellectual limitations of the landed classes and attacked the public school system.[63] It condemned the personal display and ritualised manners of high life and the world of fashion.[64] Religion had been spoilt in the 'gilded drawing room', while love and 'the endearments of courtship' were reduced there to a 'mere dead and unaffecting show'. Fashion corrupted all it touched, including the arts.[65]

As we have seen, the *Examiner*'s heroic model of artistic genius was partly premised on a notion of British cultural virility that was rooted in the larger middle-class nationalism of the period. By contrast, an article simply titled 'Notes on Art', which appeared in the *London Magazine* in April 1828, took the strikingly anti-national position that there neither was, nor had been, a British School, and asserted that the nation's art was inferior to that of France. This position may be related to the Philosophic Radicals' objection to the current francophobia of much of the periodical press.[66] According to the *London Magazine*'s critic, great art had to be infused with a sense of vitality throughout, which showed that the artist was truly enamoured with his subject, that he painted natural objects '*con amore*'. Their lack of concern with details and their tendency to over-generalise showed that British artists generally did not have 'sufficient spirit of sympathy with external nature' to animate the objects they painted. Moreover, the times were unpropitious to great painting, because they were full of momentous events and issues of public concern that tempted artists into the delusive realm of historical painting, distracting them from what should be their real preoccupation – humble subjects of visual interest. The progress of knowledge also tended to mislead artists, who felt they ought to keep up with the developments of abstract reason: 'Works of art and fancy, painting and poetry ... flourish most in the early stages of civilization, before philosophy and science have too much generalised or multiplied the ordinary

---

62   'A Comparative View of the State of Trade in the Years 1826, 7, & 8', *London Magazine*, series 3, 2 (October 1828).

63   See, for instance, 'The Duke of Newcastle's Opinions upon Toleration and Liberality', *London Magazine*, series 3, 2 (October 1828), p. 356. On the public schools, see 'Diary for the Month of April', *London Magazine*, series 3, 3 (May 1829).

64   For a brilliant critique of fashion as a principle of social ontology, see 'On Fashion' and 'More Fashions', *London Magazine*, series 2, 2 (August 1825), pp. 585–92, (September 1825), pp. 88–95.

65   'The Religious World Displayed in a Series of Sketches Chiefly from the Life of the Rev. Edward Irving', *London Magazine*, series 3, 2 (August 1828), pp. 46–7.

66   See, for example, 'Periodical Literature, The Edinburgh Review', *Westminster Review*, 1, 1 (April 1924), pp. 521–5.

topics of reflection ... Art is the growth of individual genius, and of individual observation; it is making much out of a little; whereas general reasoning and knowledge consist in reducing a great deal in to a small compass'. The imagination could not keep up with the understanding, and with the progress of knowledge art tended to be measured by a false standard, for it could not give 'a concrete representation of all that the other suggests in the abstract'. In what I take to be a jibe at Martin, the critic complains that everything has to be conceived on a huge scale.[67] For him, art was not intertwined with progress as other liberal critics were claiming;[68] rather its greatest utility was in an earlier stage of social development – a position comparable to that taken by the *Westminster Review* in 1824–5 and which also arrives at the same judgment as Hegel, if by rather a different route.

Applied to the 1828 Academy show, these criteria led the *London Magazine*'s reviewer to liken the effect of Turner's *Dido Directing the Equipment of the Fleet, or the Morning of the Carthaginian Empire* (Tate Gallery, London) to the perceptions of an epileptic. The response to Danby's *An Attempt to Illustrate the Opening of the Sixth Seal* (*fig. 4*) is yet more revealing:

> On the whole, we think his performance the triumph of this sort of apocalyptic painting, which is founded on faith, rather than reason; and which, instead of imitating, reverses all we know of nature. The antithesis, is, however, marked and intelligible. The sun is black, the moon red, the earth blue, the flesh green, &c. We know what we have to expect; there is a sufficient unity and keeping in contradiction and absurdity, and not a mere aggregate of littleness and confusion. It is like Mr Shelley's poetry, fanatical and self-willed, but better articulated and made out. We do not applaud the class; we cannot deny the merit of the execution.

Earlier in the review, the critic had observed that it was useless for Protestant monarchs to patronise art, for only the Catholic religion blended 'sensible objects and lofty imagination together in an indissoluble union', and proceeded to claim (absurdly) that to have eminent painters, Britain would have to part with its constitutional monarchy: 'We prefer to all the glories of art, the light of freedom, and the sober gifts of its dry nurse, reason'. Contemporary art, tended mainly to the 'prosaic and commonplace', but when it did not, 'It only flies out in to excess and violence, soars beyond the 'visible diurnal sphere', becomes as

---

67   'Notes on Art', *London Magazine*, series 3, 1, 1 (April 1928).
68   For instance, the *London Magazine*'s own art critic in the second series.

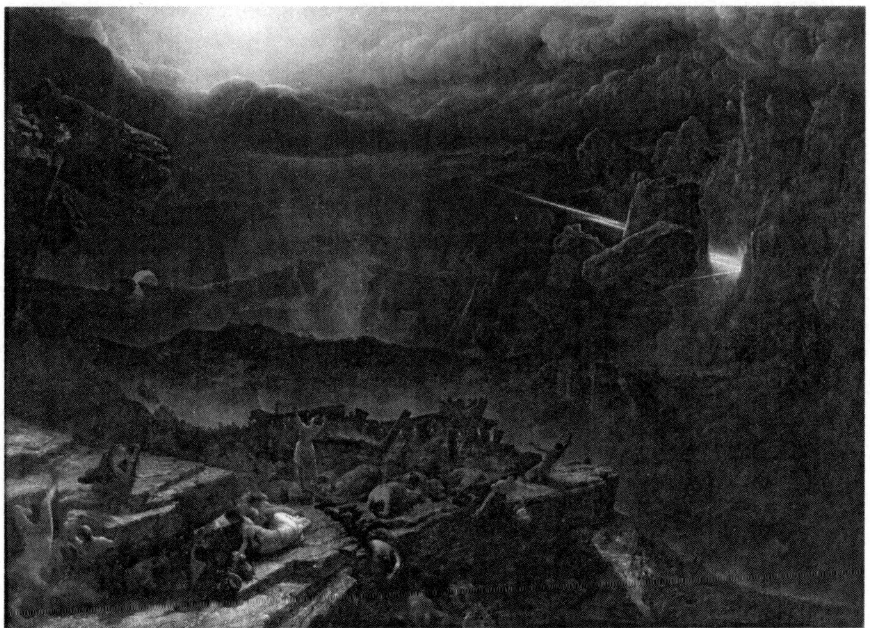

FIGURE 4   *Francis Danby,* An Attempt to Illustrate the Opening of the Sixth Seal, *1828, oil on canvas, 73×101⅝ in (1854×2580 cm) National Gallery of Ireland, Dublin*
PHOTO: © NATIONAL GALLERY OF IRELAND

wild as the dreams of Swedenborgianism, turns the world upside down, and produces only prodigies and distortion'.[69]

This critique connects poetry, irrationalism and political reaction in a way that again parallels the *Westminster Review*'s response to contemporary literature, and is more than a merely philistine response. The most successful works of Martin and Danby (whatever their differences) depended on a kind of spectacular display of apocalyptic fantasies designed to appeal to the lowest common denominator of popular middle-class taste at a time when such fantasies were much in vogue.[70] They were hardly the elevated exercise of the imagination Hunt made them out to be, and partisans of Enlightenment might well question their value.

69   'Notes on Art, The Exhibition of the Royal Academy', *London Magazine*, series 3, 1, 3 (June 1828).

70   For the class base of Martin's art, see my 'The Politics of Style: Allston's and Martin's *Belshazzars* Compared', in Hemingway and Alan Wallach (eds.) 2015, pp. 122–43. Martin Myrone argues for a different view in his 'John Martin: Art, Taste and the Spectacle of Culture', in Myrone (ed.) 2011, pp. 11–21.

Growing Benthamite influence in the *London Magazine* was signalled by a long article on the Lancastrian System and other attempts to provide elementary education that opened the third series. This stated emphatically that there was a *'new power'* in society, 'the power of working people to read, *and, therefore, to think'*; a power that made 'the ultimate amelioration of the human race quite certain'.[71] Equally Benthamite were statements in the literary reviews to the effect that the laws of property were unjust to women, and that they should have 'equal rights' in the 'republic of letters'. The magazine's reviewers avoided the condescending gallantry of much criticism of the period (including that of the *London Magazine* itself in 1826–7), and the editor opined that, 'We are inclined to think a mere compliment to the sex of a writer, a perfect insult to her intellectual equality'.[72]The magazine's new orientation was signalled by a repeated insistence that art and literature should effectively contribute to the process of human 'amelioration' by offering a significant moral message in a clear and popular form. Its rather mixed response to the work of Danby and Martin can be explained in relation to what appears a general commitment to this criterion among contributors, and a corresponding aversion to what it described as 'mysticism' in literature. Thus the *London Magazine* conceded the merit of Wordsworth and Coleridge, but claimed their theories had led them into 'the most outrageous absurdities'. They had 'failed to seize upon the practical point of sympathy with the age in which they live', whereas the popularity of Byron and Scott was 'unbounded', because they wrote for the 'great family of mankind'. The *London Magazine* set itself against those men of genius who always sought the mysterious and devalued the 'intelligible' and 'popular'. 'We, on the contrary, are inclined to maintain that nothing ever really permanent and excellent was not popular, in the most extended sense of the word'.[73] This echoes the position taken in an extended critique of modem German literature, which had appeared in May 1828, where it was argued that 'unnecessary involvement and gratuitous obscurity', of which some German writers were

---

71   'Education of the People', *London Magazine*, series 3, 1 (April 1828), pp. 12–13. Cf. 'Popular Education', *London Magazine*, series 3, 3 (May 1829).

72   'The Editor's Room', *London Magazine*, series 3, 1 (June 1828). However, the limitations of the editor's egalitarian vision are indicated by the ideal woman he describes in 'A Few Dogmas on Women', *London Magazine*, series 3, 1, 2 (May 1828). She is a woman whose mind is brilliant, and who 'shines in and enjoys the world', but finds 'her heart's happiness at home' (p. 308). For an example of the new reviewing style, see 'Miss Mitford's Tragedy of Rienzi', *London Magazine*, series 3, 2 (November 1828), pp. 525–35.

73   'The Editor's Room', *London Magazine*, series 3, 2 (October 1828), p. 428.

guilty, were not characteristic of the great writers of the past.[74] The aversion to 'mysticism' that the *London Magazine* displayed in relation to German Romanticism was extended to its French counterpart in a review of Victor Hugo's *Les Orientales* in 1829, which advised the author to look for subjects other than the 'ghastly and disgusting', and pleaded for the 'romantic' to be 'somewhat more soberly indulged in – kept a little within the bounds of reason and probability, and restrained from encroaching on the regions of frenzy'.[75]

The ideal of wholesome and intelligible art was also propagated in the *London Magazine*'s drama criticism, where it verged on the prudish. On several occasions the magazine complained of the 'profligacy' of recent theatre, and argued that many plays (including Shakespeare's *Measure for Measure*) were unfit for the stage because of the 'direct naming and representing' of 'indecent acts', unacceptable both by women actors and before female audiences. It rejected the view that 'purity' was 'allied to dullness', and claimed that the 'noblest' intellects had 'always' realised their greatest successes through a combination of 'loftiness of principle and the exquisite beauty of delicacy'.[76] Consonant with this stress on the didactic function of the arts, when the *London Magazine*'s art critic praised Benjamin Robert Haydon's Hogarthian picture *The Chairing of the Member* (*fig. 5*), it was because it was a non-heroic subject with a useful *moral*. This illustrated the general thesis: 'In painting, as in poetry, an heroic subject is not essentially necessary to the development of the very highest imaginative powers; and the scenes of familiar life are certainly *more difficult* to represent, not only with perfect truth, but with truth lighted up by the brilliant hues which only genius can bestow' (my emphasis). Haydon's picture vividly depicted the evils arising from the system of imprisonment for small debts, and for this reason it was valuable.[77] Such narrowly didactic criteria, based in an essentially secular morality, were not congruent with the spectacular effects and supernatural subjects of Martin and Danby.

As we have seen, the work of these artists was directly linked with Romantic poetry in the *London Magazine*'s review of the 1828 Academy exhibition. In the

---

74   'The Mystic School', *London Magazine*, series 3, 1 (May 1828). In its first series the *London Magazine* had given a lot of attention to German literature. On the reception of German Romanticism, see Stokoe 1926 and Vaughan 1979.

75   'Modern French Poetry', *London Magazine*, series 3, 3 (March 1929), p. 242.

76   'The Present Proceedings of the Theatres', *London Magazine*, series 3, 3 (May 1829), p. 432. Cf. 'Diary for the Month of November', *London Magazine*, series 3, 3, 10 (January 1829), pp. 66–7.

77   'Mr. Haydon's Picture of Chairing the Members' (*sic*), *London Magazine*, series 3, 2 (November 1828).

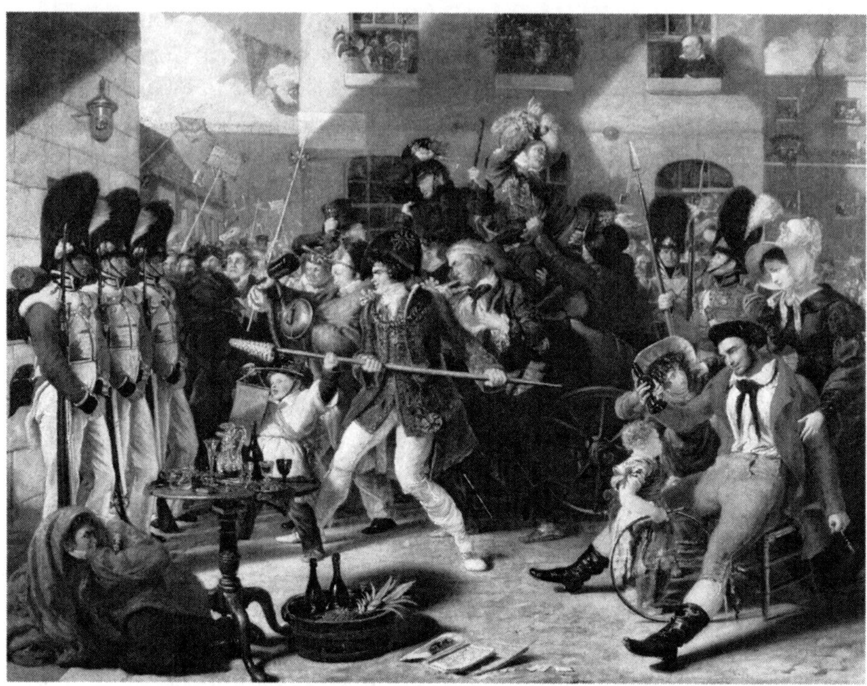

FIGURE 5   *Benjamin Robert Haydon,* The Chairing of the Member, *1828, oil on canvas,*
             60 × 75½ in (152.4 × 191.8 cm) Tate Britain
             © TATE, LONDON, 2015

following year, when the magazine reported the burning of York Minster by Jonathan Martin, the brother of the artist, as a protest against the profligacy of the clergy, it connected the dreams that had inspired the incendiarism with 'the recent literary fashion of talking of dreams and omens as things to be attended to'. While it disclaimed the idea that Jonathan Martin's mind had been shaken by such literature, 'We do think that such things being frequently brought before the minds of weak and slightly-educated people may have an effect little thought of indeed by the writers to whom we allude'.[78] Seeing education as the primary means of spreading enlightenment, and regarding much of the population as standing in need of their own paternalistic guidance, the Benthamites viewed the vogue for supernatural effects in the arts (as in

---

78   'Diary for the Month of February', *London Magazine*, series 3, 3 (March 1829). No mention
       is made of Jonathan Martin's connection with the artist, but this is not surprising given
       that the latter was not mentioned during the trial. For Jonathan Martin, see Feaver 1975,
       pp. 58–9, 223 n. 66.

Danby's *An Attempt to Illustrate the Opening of the Sixth Seal*) as obscurantist and potentially dangerous.

I do not wish to present the text of the *London Magazine* as a seamless unity; it would be surprising if it were. And I must acknowledge that the very same number contained a review of the British Institution exhibition which praised Danby's *The Moon Rising over a Wild and Mountainous Country* (whereabouts unknown), and *Sunset* (Graves Art Gallery, Sheffield) – although neither of these were apocalyptic works.[79] However, I do want to suggest that given the nature of the Benthamites' social vision,[80] it is entirely consistent that a magazine like the *London Magazine*, in which their influence was pronounced, should contain criticism that was averse to poetic landscape and some types of romantic literature.

Genius, Gender, and Progress

The *London Magazine* gave its own judgment on the organ of extreme Benthamism in its final number in 1829. Although the *Westminster Review's* critique of church, state, and society was 'possibly a very meritorious one', it was too negative and too abstract ever to become 'very popular'; the author concluded: 'Our passion for the *utile* as opposed to the *dulce* is not quite so violent as that of the scribes in the Westminster'.[81] Nonetheless, if the *London Magazine* was more favourable to the poetic principle than the *Westminster Review*, like that magazine it had recast artistic genius in a less heroic and more philosophical mould. In contrast to the hero/martyr described by Barry and Haydon, who gave his great works to an uncomprehending public out of a selfless patriotism, the *London Magazine* offered an image of the artist who responded to the

---

79   'Notes on Art', *London Magazine*, series 3, 3, 12 (March 1829). For these pictures, see
      Greenacre 1988, pp. 104–5. Later in the year the *London Magazine* printed a long and
      enthusiastic review of Turner's *Ulysses Deriding Polyphemus* (Tate Gallery, London), which
      asserted that although the effect was 'unnatural', it was so 'poetical' as to force on the
      spectator the belief that however Mount Gibel now appeared, it must have looked as
      Turner had depicted it in 'olden time': 'Turner is romantic, but he romances with taste
      and the poet's spirit'. See 'The Exhibition of the Royal Academy', *London Magazine*, series
      3, 3, 15 (June 1829).

80   For example, see 'Fables of the Holy Alliance, Rhymes on the Road, etc. etc.', *Westminster
      Review*, 1, 1 (January 1824); 'Tales of a Traveller, By Geoffrey Crayon Gent.', *Westminster
      Review*, 2, 4 (June 1824).

81   'The Reviews of the Quarter', *London Magazine*, series 3, 3, 15 (June 1829), pp. 589–90.

'enthusiasm' of a whole people, 'Genius is but a particle caught up and exalted by the general flame: no man is great or excellent but by sympathy with the spirit of the age or country in which he lives'. Patronage in itself was ineffectual to bring forth great art, and the magazine criticised British patrons for acting solely from a mixture of 'jealousy and pride'. They (the '*Somebodys*' that the *Westminster Review* had identified in 1824) had no real enthusiasm for art, but gave only so as to be confirmed in the superiority of their 'rank and fortune'.[82] Underlying these statements was a recognition that patronage implied subservience, a position made yet more explicit in a review of Martin Archer Shee's works in the *Westminster Review* in 1820. Like a number of texts by bourgeois radicals that appeared in the following decades, this insisted that artistic achievement was inextricably connected with 'liberty' and that the aristocratic principle of patronage was antithetical to it.[83]

Neither the *London Magazine* nor the *Examiner* were as consistent in their radicalism as the *Westminster Review* which, while it represented the 'middle class' as the 'strength of the community',[84] also found it politically timid, and called on it to 'vindicate' its 'rank in the Commonwealth'.[85] Like those journals, it described the landed classes as operating a form of conspiracy against other forms of property through the agency of the state. It was emphatic in its anti-clericalism, its support for complete religious toleration, and its anti-slavery stance.[86] It was also consistent in its statements on the talents of women. The second number of the magazine contained an attack on the pervasive idea of 'female character' by the young J.S. Mill, and later articles by different authors took similar positions. A critique of chivalry, attributed to William Stevenson, asserted, 'When women are regarded and treated as they ought to be, then will manners be what they ought to be; and what is of much greater moment, both sexes will co-operate, though by different means, towards the

---

82 'Notes on Art', *London Magazine*, series 3, 1, 1 (April 1828). Cf. Shee's description of 'men of genius' as 'luminous points on the great disc of society', in Shee 1805, p. 31 n.

83 'Patronage of Art', *Westminster Review*, vol. 12, no. 25 (July 1830). See the discussion of the positions of Thomas Wyse and Edward Edwards in Chapter Three.

84 Review of Bentham's *Chrestomathia* and *Public Education*, *Westminster Review*, 1, 1 (January 1824).

85 Review of William Godwin's *History of the Commonwealth of England*, *Westminster Review*, 8, 16 (October 1827). Cf. 'Radical Reform', *Westminster Review*, 12, 23 (January 1830).

86 'Corporations and Test Acts', *Westminster Review*, 9, no. 17 (January 1828); 'Disabilities of the Jews', *Westminster Review*, 19, 20 (April 1829) – 'The Jews are as true-born Englishmen as one half of the nobility' (p. 438); 'Slavery in the West Indies', *Westminster Review*, 11, 22 (October 1829).

advancement of society in knowledge and happiness'. Women should therefore 'discountenance' any behaviour not based on the premise that they were equal to men in 'their capacity for knowledge and usefulness'.[87]

The implication of this was that when the *Westminster* reviewed L.E.L.'s poems, it criticised the author for colluding with stereotypes of women by her concentration on the theme of love, and described her romantic male heroes as barbaric types because of their martial attributes.[88] Conversely, it rebutted use of the term 'masculine' in criticism of Lady Morgan's writings, because of her 'disdain for many of the sentiments and prejudices of her own sex' and her 'spirited adoption of opinions of her own upon many points, with regard to which, the orthodox have decreed, that no female upon any pretence should hold any opinion underived from authority'.[89] What such criticism suggests is that the Benthamites wished to end the 'effeminacy' of women and recast them in the mould of a masculine type, that they had no way of giving a positive value to what were seen as characteristically female attributes of sympathy and imagination.[90]

For the *Westminster*, the progress of literature was intimately bound up with the progress of science, and science advanced through the efforts of men who had 'silently, and almost imperceptibly, changed the whole face of some great department of human knowledge'. Such individuals might be 'comparatively unknown' in their day, and others might 'attract more notice from the crowd', for the philosopher, 'though he may produce incalculable good, can only do so by degrees almost impalpable to common observation'. Nonetheless, philosophers were the 'real fountain of blessings' to humanity, and those who it ought 'principally to honour'.[91] This model of the philosopher as benefactor is considerably removed from the heavily masculinised heroic intellects that artists such as Haydon pictured themselves, who are closer to the martial ideal of public man associated with aristocratic culture. Its presence in the *Westminster Review* goes some way to explaining why the magazine could insist on the equality of women thinkers, and why the heroic artist does not figure in the *London Magazine* in its Benthamite phase. The mundane themes

---

87   'The History of Chivalry, or Knighthood and its Times', *Westminster Review*, 5, 9 (January 1826).

88   'Poetry of L.E.L.', *Westminster Review*, 7, 13 (January 1827). The magazine also attacked the prevalent view that for a woman to attempt to support herself was degrading.

89   'National Tales of Ireland', *Westminster Review*, 9, 18 (April 1828).

90   It is significant in this respect that Bentham's moral theory excluded the principle of sympathy – see Bentham 1988 (2), pp. 13–16.

91   'Rationale of Judicial Evidence. J. Bentham', *Westminster Review*, 9, 17 (January 1828).

recommended in the *London Magazine*'s review of Haydon's *Chairing of the Member* seem to demand a correspondingly less heroic artist type. However, nothing on show in the exhibitions he covered prompted the critic of the third series to address the possibility of the female genius in painting, so this can only stand as a hypothesis. As I noted earlier, it was probably easier for the category of writer to accommodate female genius than for the category of painter to do so, but the omission likely registers more the relatively small number of exhibits by women artists, especially in the genres with most status. By contrast the work of women writers such as L.E.L., Mary Mitford and Lady Morgan was too successful to be ignored.

I hope it is clear from the above that I am not trying to claim that there was some simple necessary correspondence between Benthamite progressivism, the demystification of the aesthetic and a critique of the current status of women. But rather that there was a tendency for these positions to be aligned, and that this was not accidental. Generally speaking, Benthamism does not have a good press these days. We tend to associate it with the inhumanities of the 1834 Poor Law Amendment Act, with the grossly materialistic Victorianism of Dickens's 'Mr Gradgrind', or, worse yet, with the modern principle of self-surveillance that Michel Foucault described as 'Panopticism' after Bentham's model prison. However, it is important to remember that, whatever its limitations, early nineteenth-century Benthamism was an instrument of radical critique, and that its paternalistic model of the state was balanced by a vision of individual hedonism (if a rather cramped one), and a commitment to freedom of opinion and equality of opportunity – although this did not necessarily lead individual Benthamites to radical conclusions with regard to either gender or class power. That it was capable of producing important insights the *Westminster Review*'s analysis of the social functions of aristocratic culture (Bourdieu *avant la letter*) clearly shows. And neither should we simply dismiss its critique of the aesthetic as Hazlitt did. Setting aside Bentham's own aversion to poetry as a pollution of the pure processes of reason, his followers were correct to argue that the play of unrestrained fantasy was likely to produce an art of no cognitive value and could lead to a sentimental attraction to reactionary politics. In this postmodern moment, when once again it has become *chic* to see pleasure itself as an unquestionable good (but without any corresponding commitment to Enlightenment), their concerns have a certain resonance.

CHAPTER 5

Cultural Philanthropy and the Invention of the Norwich School

This essay has two aims. First, I want to consider the evolution of the category of the Norwich School of Painting as a discursive construct. In other words, I want to suspend the assumption that there was something there in the past possessing an inherent unity that demands the appellation 'Norwich School' and sketch how the category was expanded from a relatively modest label to a nebulous historical entity with all the characteristics of a myth. I want to consider its value as a hermeneutic tool in relation to the objects it customarily encompasses – to indicate what it produces, but also to suggest something of what it serves to conceal. Secondly, I want to offer some hypotheses as to why this concept took the form it did in terms of its usefulness to important interest groups. This entails considering the nineteenth-century bourgeoisie's usage of the visual arts to augment their social status, at the same time as demonstrating their responsible stewardship of wealth by improving the 'lower orders' in the interests of social control.[1] It is thus concerned with what American sociologists and historians have termed 'cultural philanthropy', and I shall argue that the institutionalisation of the Norwich School exemplifies some general features of culture's functions in bourgeois society, given a particular inflection by local conditions in Norfolk.

'Norwich School' is customarily taken to refer to a group of artists who lived and worked in Norwich for all or part of their careers in the years c. 1800–80. The leading figures of this group were John Crome, John Berney Crome, James Stark, George Vincent, Robert Ladbrooke, Joseph Stannard, Alfred Stannard, Robert Dixon, John Thirtle, John Sell Cotman and his sons Miles Edmund and John Joseph Cotman. In addition, more than twenty other artists, professional and amateur, have been associated with the group. Supporters of the school idea have claimed that they were linked by their common geographical base, by the fact that they often exhibited together, by various kinds of professional and personal relationships, by relatively slight formal affinities between some of their works, and by their concern with the representation of distinctive local scenery.

---

1   I agree with the critique of the 'social control' concept in Jones 1983, pp. 76–89, but the term has a pertinence for some of the phenomena I am describing.

The key institution in establishing their association is the Norwich Society of Artists, which held meetings from 1803 until the mid-1830s, and ran exhibitions from 1805–33, with a two-year break in 1826–7.[2] Despite the stylistic and formal diversity of art produced by Norwich artists, their association and shared experience of the Norfolk region has been said to endow their works with common aesthetic traits. Such an assumption of shared identity underlies the conception of the Norwich School elaborated in my short book on the subject of 1979.[3] It was not a conception that I had invented; it was an established ideological motif, about which I was somewhat sceptical, but which I had not subjected to rigorous critique. I now believe that the critique and abandonment of the concept would lead to more effective and historically coherent interpretations of the art concerned.

Firstly, it should be noted that the Norwich School concept in its modern form did not exist in the early nineteenth century, although the term itself was used as early as 1816 in a letter by John Crome.[4] In relation to my argument, it is important to distinguish between the connotations of the term at the regional and at the national level. I begin with the former.

The Norwich School in the Norwich Press up to *c.* 1860

The discursive field in which 'Norwich School' first acquired currency was the local press, that is, the two Norwich papers the *Norwich Mercury* and *Norfolk Chronicle*. The *Mercury* referred to 'the founders and supporters of this school' in its review of the second Norwich Society exhibition of 1806. In 1814, Norwich was said to have the first 'school of design' on the model of the Royal Academy to be established in Britain outside London, and in 1816 it referred to 'our academy'. In 1817, during the period from 1816–18 when Norwich briefly had two artists' societies and two exhibitions, it referred to there being 'two academies of pictures', although in the following year it said that both exhibitions were 'pupils of the same school'. In this review, the *Mercury* commented that 'while Norwich proceeds with equal steps in supporting those more popular and universal amusements, music, and the drama – there has been originated and preserved amongst us A SCHOOL OF DESIGN that is become perhaps more fertile and more rich in production than even its warmest supporters could

---

2   Rajnai 1976.
3   Hemingway 1979.
4   Clifford and Clifford 1968, p. 90.

have anticipated in the time'. Such usage of the terms 'school' and 'academy' continues in later years.[5] The meaning of 'school' in such contexts seems fairly clearly the sense defined in the 1814 edition of Johnson's *Dictionary* as 'a state of instruction', rather than the alternative sense of 'a system of doctrine as delivered by particular teachers'.

There were solid reasons for talking about Norwich as an art centre in this way. According to its articles, the Norwich Society of Artists had been founded in 1803 'for the purpose of an enquiry into the Rise, Progress, and Present State of Painting, Architecture, and Sculpture, with a view to discover and point out the best methods of study, to attain greater perfection in these arts'.[6] The articles refer to the Society as the 'Academy' at several points, and although in retrospect its exhibitions have seemed the Society's most important function (partly because they are the only aspect of its activities of which we have a record), to its members the fortnightly discussion meetings throughout the year may have been as important. In fact, there was no real academy in Norwich, in the sense of a drawing school, until the 1830s, but there were some important master-apprentice relations, such as those between Crome and Stark and Vincent, and between Robert Ladbrooke and Joseph Stannard.

However, in 1820 another kind of construction began to emerge when the *Mercury* referred to John Crome as one who 'may almost be said to be the father of the art in Norwich'. In the review of the Society's exhibition in 1821, which followed Crome's death in April, it described his pupils Stark and Vincent as 'foremost in the ranks of talent' and his son J.B. Crome as 'an able supporter of his father's school'. Thus began a dual usage of the term 'school' to refer to the Society and its exhibitions, and to refer to the relationship between Crome and his main pupils. In 1822 Crome was described as 'the founder of the Norwich School of Painting', and the landscapes of Stark, Vincent, and J.B. Crome were said to be 'of the same school'. The currency of this second usage is confirmed by the *Mercury*'s comment in 1831 that a Stark painting was 'a specimen of the true Norwich School – that founded by the deceased Mr. Crome', and by its remark in 1839, that the work of Samuel Colkett 'retains much of the manner which has been designated as that of the Norwich School, and which has descended through Mr. CROME to his followers'. Such statements simply could not apply to the works of the Ladbrookes, Stannards, or Cotmans.[7]

---

5   *Norwich Mercury*, exhibition reviews of 16 August 1806; 13 August 1814; 17 August 1816; 1 August 1817; 1 August 1818. See also 11 August 1821; 2 August 1823; and 'The Artists' Society', 16 January 1830.

6   Rajnai 1976, p. 7.

7   *Norwich Mercury*, exhibition reviews of 29 July 1820; 18 August 1821; 3 August 1822; 30 July

It is important to consider at this point that the *Norwich Mercury* was one paper in a city that had two, and that its reviews only certainly represent the opinions of one person – its proprietor Richard Mackenzie Bacon, who had been taught drawing by Crome and was a 'schoolfellow and friend' of his eldest son. At one level, the construction of the Norwich School it offered can be understood as the interested view of an amateur member of the Norwich Society, who seems to have sided with the Crome faction in the Secession dispute of 1816. (This appears to have occurred because Ladbrooke, Thirtle, and James Sillett wanted to amend the rules to reduce the influence of amateurs in the running of the Society).[8] The construction of Norwich art in the *Norfolk Chronicle* – which was edited by sometime artist and drawing master William Stevenson up until his death in 1821, and thereafter by his son Seth William Stevenson – was generally more lowkey. Significantly, perhaps, neither of the Stevensons were members of the Norwich Society.[9] Although the *Chronicle* consistently expressed pride in the Norwich exhibitions as a manifestation of the talents of Norfolk, and it too described Crome as the 'founder' of the Norwich Society in 1821 and referred casually to a 'Norwich School' in 1825,[10] the terms 'school', 'academy', and 'Norwich School' simply did not have the same currency in its reviews.

That the idea of a Norwich School in the sense of a distinctive common art was by no means generally accepted is clear from two statements from the 1830s. In 1830, the textile merchant Colonel John Harvey made a speech as President of the Artists' Conversazione in which he expressed the hope that 'hereafter some particular graces of design and colouring may become the characteristics of the Norfolk and Suffolk Institution of Artists, and raise its fame to a height that its present members may scarcely indulge in even in imagination'.[11] This clearly implies that Harvey could not yet discern any such 'particular graces'. Crome's patron, Dawson Turner, was even clearer on this point in his memoir of the artist published to accompany the second edition of Crome's etchings in 1838 where he maintained that a Norwich School had not materialised due to Crome's untimely death.[12] Dawson Turner's closeness to Cotman (who wrote to him in a letter of 1834 that his 'often told DREAM' was

---

1831. See also 'The Artists' Conversazione', 15 January 1831; and 'Norwich Art', 25 January 1834.

8   Correspondence in the *Norwich Mercury*, 16 and 23 August 1823.

9   For Bacon and Stevenson, see Chambers 1829, pp. 1092–4, 1284.

10   *Norfolk Chronicle*, exhibition reviews of 9 August 1818; 18 August 1821; and 6 August 1825.

11   'The First Conversazione', *Norwich Mercury*, 23 January 1830.

12   Wodderspoon 1876, p. 7.

the 'downfall' of 'the family of Crome')[13] must have made him well aware that the community of Norwich artists was not one big happy family with Crome as *pater familias*, but was actually divided by sometimes rancorous professional rivalries, with perhaps Crome, Ladbrooke, and Cotman factions.

A few further points need to be made here about early constructions of Norwich art, and particularly those of the *Norwich Mercury*. Foremost, the *Mercury* was consistently disposed to treat the presence of a talented body of artists in Norwich as evidence of the progress of British civilisation, in terms that meshed in with the discourse of bourgeois progressivism in the 1820s and 1830s, for which I take the *Westminster Review* to be paradigmatic. (In connection with this, it should be noted that Bacon was on the committee of the Society for the Diffusion of Useful Knowledge, and also on that of the Norwich Mechanics' Institute, set up in 1825).[14] However, this conflicted with its frequent complaints over the general lack of patronage and art interest in the city, a stance that may partly reflect Bacon's closeness to the artistic community.

In 1816 the *Mercury* had observed sanguinely that 'if the cultivation of the Fine Arts be a proof of civilization, we know not any place in the king's realm that manifests a more buoyant spirit of improvement than our native city'. The Norwich Society of Artists was cited along with the literary and musical entertainments of Assize Week and the Norwich Philosophical Society as evidence of this. In 1817 it claimed that 'a character of increasing elegance pervades all our places of resort', and discerned a 'sure advance towards refinement' in the pursuit of the arts. Such comments were couched in the language of eighteenth-century philosophical criticism and in 1830 the *Mercury* quoted Lord Kames on the softening effects of the arts in a report of the city's First Conversazione.[15]

Some exhibition reports of the late 1830s and early 1840s after the collapse of the Norfolk and Suffolk Institution for the Promotion of the Fine Arts (the Norwich Society of Artists as reconstituted in 1827) are different in tone. The exhibition of the Norfolk and Norwich Art Union (1839), the Norwich Polytechnic Exhibition (1840), and the exhibitions of the East of England Art Union (1842–4) were organised by elements in the city's bourgeoisie and local amateurs, and their function was thus different. Although they claimed to serve the interests of local artists, they were not a market display controlled by profes-

---

13   Cliffords 1968, p. 72. See also Turner 1840, p. 17.

14   For Bacon and the SDUK, see Allthorpe-Guyton with John Stevens 1982, p. 39. For the Benthamite position on art education, see review of the Library of Useful Knowledge, *Westminster Review*, 7: 283–93.

15   *Norwich Mercury*, exhibition reviews of 17 August 1816; 2 August 1817; 'The Artists' Society', 16 January 1830. See also exhibition reviews of 1 August 1818 and 3 August 1822.

sionals. Reporting the Conversazione that accompanied the 1839 exhibition the *Mercury* observed that 'the noble mansions of English Gentlemen' frequently contained rich collections, but these were only accessible to friends of the owners. By contrast, 'collections made for inspection', like those of the Norwich Art Union, 'diffused throughout the middle classes' 'gratifications' that only the affluent could afford to buy. Further, the presence of women at the Conversazione ensured refinement of manners and was in itself a civilising force: 'While the conversations in the saloons of the great runs generally upon politics or diversions, and rarely leave behind very improving impressions, the intercourse in such a party as we have described cannot fail to convey to a hundred minds new ideas and exalted feelings to diversify the present and gild the future hours of existence'.[16] An unflattering contrast between the culture of the landed classes and that of the bourgeoisie is clearly implied here. The campaigns of bourgeois radicals in the 1830s to get museums and art galleries opened free of charge and extend art education and make it more relevant to industry were based upon the Utilitarian strategy of education as a weapon of progress, which would reveal the chimerical basis of the distinctions that supposedly justified aristocratic power and privileges, raise the level of British civilisation, and reconcile the proletariat to the inevitability of their condition. The Norwich Polytechnic Exhibition was put on under the auspices of the Norwich Mechanics' Institution, representative of a class of institution designed to put the latter aspect of this policy into effect.[17] Such thinking clearly influenced the statement that the *Norwich Mercury* produced on the functions of art in connection with the East of England Art Union exhibition of 1843: 'The highest province of art is indeed, not to minister only to the calls of luxury, but to spread its exalting influence over the people; this is why painters should choose noble, moral, and beautiful subjects – why exhibitions should be thrown open equally to the high and humble, and why ... Art Unions should be liberally encouraged and supported'.[18]

Yet despite the *Mercury*'s optimistic comments on the progress of Norwich art and its refining influence in the city, it was also frequently obliged to acknowledge the lack of patronage there. As early as 1808 it observed: 'It is a curious fact, that scarcely in any place in the kingdom the arts have met with less pecuniary encouragement than in Norwich'. Thus the efforts of the artists were particularly praiseworthy. Such comments became more frequent in the

---

16   'The Conversazione', *Norwich Mercury*, 28 September 1839.

17   For Mechanics' Institutions, see Chapter Three, p. 135 n. 78.

18   'East of England Art Union', *Norwich Mercury*, 19 August 1843. For Art Unions, see King
      1985.

1820s. For example, in 1823 it claimed that 'the meaning of the word PATRONAGE, the foster-mother of genius, is totally and entirely unknown in Norwich. The late Mr. CROME once said at the close of one of his most successful exhibitions, that he had not been applied to even for the price of a picture. Even the door-money during the three public weeks is insufficient, we understand, to defray the expenses and the artists themselves actually incur an annual charge'. This situation was compared unfavourably with that in Leeds and Newcastle. The Mayor and Corporation had visited the exhibition as a body as early as 1810 and during the Secession period visited both displays, but in 1825 the *Mercury* complained that the Corporation had done nothing for Norwich art despite being feted at the artists' annual dinners.[19]

The tone of such complaints intensified after the Society reformed in 1827 and invested in a new exhibition room. A circular letter sent out in 1827 soliciting support pointedly compared the receipts of the Norwich exhibitions with those of other cities and asserted that 'scarcely a single Picture has been bought in the Norwich room', while door receipts had never covered expenses.[20] The Conversaziones of 1830–2 were a last desperate attempt to promote public interest. A report of the second series in December 1830 commented that Norwich was a city where taste was 'at so low an ebb that a public concert cannot find adequate support – a ball can with difficulty and only at long intervals be held – where a Theatre cannot keep open a few months in a year without great loss to the Patentee'.[21] In 1833 the probable dissolution of the Norfolk and Suffolk Institution was reported in the press, and the following year a letter printed in the *Mercury* announced the discontinuance of the exhibitions on the grounds of inadequate galleries and insufficient returns.[22] Ever hopeful, the *Mercury* hailed the renewal of exhibitions in 1839–44 as marking a new dawn, but public response to them was disappointing.[23]

The laments occasioned by the end of the exhibitions need to be seen in relation to a pattern of statements referring to the city's decline, which are probably

---

19   *Norwich Mercury*, exhibition reviews of 20 August 1808; 2 August 1823; 6 August 1825. Although a remark in a review in the *Norfolk Chronicle* of 25 August 1810 should also be noted: 'We must conclude these remarks with observing, that the monosyllable SOLD, upon so many of the performances, speaks more on behalf of them than we have done'.

20   Norfolk and Suffolk Institution for the Promotion of the Fine Arts, *Circular Letter to the Public* (1827), signed David Hodgson, Secretary.

21   'The Artists' First Conversazione', *Norwich Mercury*, 18 December 1830.

22   'Norwich Exhibition', *Norwich Mercury*, 26 July 1834. See also the editorial comment in this issue.

23   E.g, see 'EAST OF ENGLAND ART UNION', *Norwich Mercury*, 8 October 1842.

connected with the depressed state of its textile industry in the 1830s.[24] That the amusements of Assize Week simply did not draw in the local population any more was the subject of an article of 1835: 'THE ASSIZE WEEK: Which in our remembrance used to be the season when the county population was concentrated in Norwich, partially for business but generally for the pleasures of public enjoyment provided for all classes, is now scarcely to be distinguished by any access of company beyond the ordinary course and current of time ... What were formerly attractive diversions are no longer sought'.[25] In 1843 this decline was attributed to the greater easiness of travel to London: 'Now the access to the Metropolis is so constant, and daily becoming so much more rapid by the assistance of rail-roads, that the demands of business, formerly requiring but few visits to London, now enforcing them more frequently, enable both the higher and middle classes to avail themselves of those highest amusements which were formerly enjoyed but rarely'.[26] An article of 1841 concerning plans to establish a school of design in Norwich even described the city as 'a town which was once the seat of flourishing manufactures, which still emulates the character of a manufacturing town'.[27]

Perhaps the currency of this attitude prompted a letter from the worsted manufacturer J.W. Robberds printed in the *Mercury* in 1845, which contradicted a remark in the Report of the Commission on the Health of Towns that the city had seen its best days as a commercial centre, and 'would appear to be in the painful state of transition from a once flourishing manufacturing prosperity to its entire decline'.[28] In fact Robberds was right, inasmuch as Norwich was to acquire new industries in food processing, brewing, and shoe-making, which would replace its textiles manufactures. But this was far from obvious in the early 1840s.

It should be evident from the above that the Norwich press, and particularly the *Mercury*, was from the beginning eager to discover in the city evidence of a flourishing artistic community, and that this was described fairly frequently as a 'school'. In addition to the usage of the term I outlined earlier, the following points need to be noted. First, the dominant presence in the first fifteen or so exhibitions of views of local scenery caught attention. Thus in 1816 the *Mercury* welcomed the presence of exhibits sent from outside Norwich on the grounds that 'although our "native Burghers" would perpetuate local scenes, and fix

---

24   For the economic history of Norwich in this period, see Edwards 1963 and Edwards 1964.

25   'ASSIZE WEEK', *Norwich Mercury*, 8 August 1835.

26   'THE BALL', *Norwich Mercury*, 8 April 1843.

27   'A SCHOOL OF DESIGN', *Norwich Mercury*, 6 November 1841.

28   *Norwich Mercury*, 2 August 1845.

attention to their pictures by all the force of local attachment', comparison and competition were necessary for improvement.[29] In relation to this, it is interesting that a letter from 'A Friend and Lover of the Fine Arts' concerning the Secession published in the *Mercury* in 1823 observed that the introduction of 'works of London Artists, or any other except natives or residents, into an Exhibition avowedly intended to be Norfolk only, would not have occurred if the artists alone had been consulted'.[30] This concern with the local character of the exhibitions is confirmed by a remark in Bacon's editorial comment on the letter that 'the appearance of the pictures of able artists (which by the way must have some relation to Norfolk in order to gain admission) in our estimation benefit our local school of painting'. Presumably artists were wary of any competition in a limited market, particularly when they bore the cost of the display. In the exhibitions of the Society thereafter, the number of works sent in from outside Norwich remained very low, although the number of pictures of non-Norfolk subjects increased in the 1820s.

Secondly, of the three comments on the stylistic range of the exhibitions I have discovered, two emphasised their diversity. In 1810 the *Mercury* noted the 'various styles' of the exhibits, and in 1829 it observed that the works of J.B. Crome, George Clint, Edwin Cooper, Cotman, David Hodgson, Joseph Stannard, and Stark 'present us with as many distinct styles'.[31] The only suggestion of uniformity is a comment of 1825 which complained of the 'almost pervading manner' in the exhibition, and found a 'uniformity in the majority of the subjects and their treatment'.[32] I suspect that Bacon was simply imitating a current type of statement in the London art press rather than developing a consistent critique, or so his 1829 comment suggests. But whatever his reason, the comment was clearly inappropriate in relation to the actual variety of Norwich painting. In short, then, the 'Norwich School' had only a sketchy identity in the local press in the early nineteenth century, and insofar as it implied any kind of significant commonalities among the artists, it did so only to refer to a common place of study, practice, and exhibition, or to refer to the relations between Crome and his pupils. Further, with the ending of the Norfolk and Suffolk Institution exhibitions, and the departure of J.B. Crome and Cotman from the city in 1834 (Stark had left in 1830), it seems to have been felt that an era in the city's art life had come to an end.

---

29   'The Amusements of Assize Week', *Norwich Mercury*, 17 August 1816.
30   *Norwich Mercury*, exhibition review, 16 August 1823.
31   *Norwich Mercury*, exhibition review, 25 July 1829.
32   *Norwich Mercury*, exhibition review, 6 August 1825.

The Norwich School in the National Press

I now turn to the categorisation of Norwich painting at the national level. At the time of his death in April 1821, Crome was beginning to establish a reputation outside Norfolk and his standing locally was already high. The Norwich Society held a memorial exhibition of 111 of his works, and demand for them quickly outstripped supply – by the 1840s, forgeries were becoming a major problem to collectors.[33] An obituary notice in the *Magazine of Fine Arts* commented on his abilities as a teacher: 'His mind was too acute to exact from them [i.e. his pupils] a servile imitation of their master's style. On the contrary, he contented himself with instilling the most solid and useful principles of art and giving freedom and spirit to their pencils'.[34] Evidence of this was provided by the works of J.B. Crome, Stark, and Vincent, the two latter having 'attracted metropolitan attention to the growing talents and promise of the Norwich school of artists'.

That this group should provide the basis for the reputation of Norwich art was inevitable. Crome had exhibited occasionally in London in the years 1816–21 (and had done so earlier in 1806–12), but although his exhibits attracted a few favourable comments, they were probably too small and too local in their subject-matter to make much impact.[35] However, Stark had lived in London from *c.* 1814–19 and had joined the Academy Schools in 1817; Vincent had moved there around 1817–18. Both exhibited frequently at the British Institution and Society of British Artists (from 1824), and rather less frequently at the Academy. In the years around 1820 they had shown a number of large and ambitious pictures that had attracted highly flattering reviews, including Vincent's *On the River Yare, Afternoon* (Private Collection; British Institution, 1819) and *A Dutch Fair on Yarmouth Beach* (Yarmouth Museum; British Institution, 1821), and Stark's *Sailing Match at Wroxham near Norwich* (Private Collection; British Institution, 1819). As early as 1818, the *Literary Chronicle* described them as 'the two Norfolk heroes' in a punning reference to Lord Nelson, the Norfolk

---

33   See the letter from Charles Curtis to Joseph Sherrington, 20 March 1848 (Sherrington Papers, Norwich Castle Museum): 'I tried to get all Cromes but was forced to give it up finding it so difficult to obtain <u>originals</u>'. The word 'originals' is underlined four times in the manuscript.

34   'Memoir of the late Mr. John Crome of Norwich', *Magazine of Fine Arts*, 1821, 1: 381–2.

35   This is suggested by a comment in the *Sun* newspaper on Crome's exhibits at the British Institution in 1821: 'this artist's style is calculated to produce very powerful effects on a larger scale than we have yet seen him attempt'. – 'British Institution IV', *Sun*, 31 January 1821.

hero.[36] With the exception of Cotman in the early years of his career, no other Norwich artists had made anything like the same impact in the national scene. And Cotman had almost disappeared from view, ceasing to exhibit with the London institutions between 1811 and 1822.

A notice on the Norwich Society exhibition of 1819 in the *Annals of the Fine Arts* observed: 'The Norwich school of artists has furnished many able supporters to the metropolitan circle: Sharp, Vincent and Stark, among those who have come among us – and the Cromes, among those who stay behind, are living illustrations of this fact'.[37] Stark and Vincent were certainly seen as among the most important young landscape painters at this time, but their connection with Norwich was noted only intermittently, they were often discussed separately from each other, and no specific Norvicensian character was ever discerned in their art. Neither were they connected with other Norwich artists who exhibited less frequently in London, except with J.B. Crome in a small number of instances. Thus the usage of 'Norwich School' in the metropolitan press paralleled that in the local papers: it referred primarily to Norwich as a teaching centre, as is confirmed by the linking of the portrait and genre painter Michael Sharp with Stark and Vincent in the above statement. The only significant new idea to appear in the 1820s was articulated by W.H. Pyne in a commentary on the Norwich school in his *Somerset House Gazette* prompted by the showing of J.B. Crome's *Boats at Utrecht* (whereabouts unknown) at the British Institution in 1824, which Pyne assumed was by the artist's father:

> The excellence of the landscape and river scenery, which is so universally admired in the old masters, depended materially … upon those celebrated painters living amidst the scenes which they imitated with so much truth, and which enabled them to diffuse that charm over their compositions, which is only felt in proportion as they are facsimiles of nature. Mr. Crome is one, or rather was one of those ingenious provincial artists, whose pencil pourtrayed [sic] what he saw with unaffected simplicity, and may be regarded as the founder of a school of landscape in his neighbourhood, which promises to do credit to its ingenious preceptor, and to identify the county of Norfolk with the arts. Suffolk, we know, has been indebted

---

36   'Exhibition of Society of Painters in Oil and Water-Colours', *Literary Chronicle*, no. 12, 15 June 1818.

37   *Annals of the Fine Arts*, 1819, 4: 452. For other references to Crome and his pupils, see *Annals of the Fine Arts*, 1819, 4: 487; *Annals of the Fine Arts*, 1820, 5: 153; and 'British Institution', *Examiner*, no. 689, 18 March 1821.

to her native painter, Gainsborough. Constable, too, will help to spread the fame of the pictorial scenery of this county: and his birth place, too, by the truly English pastorals, which his admirable pencil has chosen, to perpetuate to those times to come, when future connoisseurs shall talk of him and Gainsborough, and Crome, and Vincent, and Starke [sic] as the old English masters.[38]

Pyne thus linked the Norwich group with Gainsborough and Constable as part of an East Anglian landscape school distinguished by the 'fidelity' of its works to regional scenery. This was a prophetic construction, but it did not yet match with the pressing ideological needs of an extensive or powerful social group.

After the mid-1820s, the exhibits of Stark and Vincent occasionally received favourable comments in the London press, but no notices of the same length and enthusiasm as some that their earlier showings had prompted. The Norwich School idea seems to have receded and by the 1850s it was a commonplace that Crome's work was hardly known outside Norfolk. His reputation seems to have been sustained mainly through the efforts of local bourgeois collectors, and particularly those of his patron, the Yarmouth banker Dawson Turner, who owned eleven of his paintings.[39] It was Turner who supplied Allan Cunningham with information for his account of Crome in *The Cabinet Gallery of British Pictures* (1836), and he produced his own memoir to accompany the second edition of Crome's etchings in 1838. It was probably through Turner's offices that Crome received a favourable notice in Dr Waagen's *Treasures of Art in Great Britain* (1854), and he also tried, apparently unsuccessfully, to interest Ruskin in the artist.[40] In the late 1850s, Crome's works were still fetching modest prices,[41] and the turning point in his reputation seems to have been the showing of seven of his pictures at the London International Exhibition of 1862. Several reviews of this exhibition remarked that his work was hitherto little known and had made a considerable impact. For example, *London Society* observed that Crome's pictures 'have come upon a large portion of the public with all the

---

38 'Exhibition – British Gallery', *Somerset House Gazette*, no. 25, 27 March 1824.

39 For Turner's picture collection see Turner 1840. See also the transcription of a list of 'Dawson Turner's Pictures', in Warren R. Dawson Manuscripts, vol. XXXVII (40), British Museum Add. MS 56294, pp. 166r–1168v, 171v–172r.

40 Waagen 1854, Volume 3, p. 438; John Ruskin to Dawson Turner, 10 September 1846, Dawson Turner Correspondence, Trinity College Library, Cambridge.

41 Only two of Crome's works are listed as passing through the sales rooms prior to 1862 in Graves's *Art Sales* (Graves 1970).

charm of novelty at this Exhibition'.[42] Amongst their admirers were the French naturalist critic Théophile Thoré who praised them in the highest terms in two articles published in France.[43] Of the seven Cromes shown, *Mousehold Heath* (*fig. 48*) probably attracted the most praise and in the same year the National Gallery bought it for £400. In 1878, a year in which the Royal Academy's Winter Exhibition had an important Norwich School section, it bought *Slate Quarries*, and in 1879 the Victoria and Albert Museum bought *Skirts of the Forest*. The predominant value invoked to justify the new status accorded Crome's work was its 'truth'.[44]

The growth of Crome's reputation inevitably served to confirm his centrality in Norwich art. In 1866 that seminal text, Richard and Samuel Redgrave's *A Century of British Painters*, appeared, which, along with W.T. Sandby's *History of the Royal Academy* (1862), contributed to form a dominant new definition of the British School idea, in which landscape and genre painting were given far more centrality.[45] The Redgraves treated Crome, Stark, Vincent, and Cotman as the Norwich school, and said nothing of the work of any other artist. They drew early nineteenth-century Norfolk as a picturesque and unmodernised region, apparently oblivious to its progressive agriculture and major industry, and completely overlooked the modern elements in the iconography of the artists they considered. Significantly, the Redgraves observed that after the return of Stark and Cotman to London, the Norwich exhibitions ceased to be supported mainly by local artists, and 'the Norwich School as a peculiar provincial confraternity ceased to exist'.[46]

If Crome's standing had risen considerably as a result of the 1862 International Exhibition, that of the other Norwich artists had not – although a Vincent *View of Greenwich Hospital* was shown there and apparently made some impression.[47] The 'School' only began to regain its early nineteenth-century status as a result of the section devoted to it in the Royal Academy's Winter Exhibition of 1878, which was selected by the painter J.C. Horsley. This included works by Crome, Stark, Vincent, Cotman, and Joseph Stannard, so its represent-

---

42   'Another Day at the Exhibition', *London Society*, August 1862, p. 190. For other comments, see notices on the exhibition in *Illustrated London News*, 12 July 1862, 41: 46; *Times*, 1 May 1862. I am grateful to Penelope Gurland for these references and that in n. 44.

43   Thoré 1863, Introduction, p. 15 and Appendices, p. 15; Thoré 1870, pp. 263–5.

44   For example: 'Notes on Art', *Sunday Times*, 20 July 1862.

45   A shift that had begun with Allan Cunningham's *Lives of the Most Eminent British Painters and Sculptors* (1829), as William Vaughan has shown in Vaughan 1990, pp. 15–17.

46   Redgrave and Redgrave 1947, p. 357.

47   Perhaps the picture illustrated in Dickes 1905, p. 518.

ation of Norwich art still excluded several artists who would later seem important.[48] Many reviewers made the customary references to Crome as the 'founder and fountain-head' of a Norwich School, the most extreme of whom was the landscape painter and etcher Edwin Edwards. Edwards rejected the idea that there had been a dearth of patronage in Norwich, and claimed that Crome's 'school was an outgrowth of that larger East Anglian school which is England's strongest title to be regarded as a nation capable of the highest artistic achievement'.[49] However, amongst the chorus of praise, there was a dissenting voice in the review of *The Builder*, which described the 'point' of the Norwich School section as 'somewhat of an illusion', and continued: 'In the first place, there is no "Norwich School". What is so called consists simply of Crome, and some inferior artists who imitated him, and of Cotman, who was quite above imitating Crome or any one else, and whose whole style and manner is so distinct from that of Crome and the Cromites as to preclude all idea of classing him with them'.[50] But this percipient view was not to prevail.

On the basis of the 1878 exhibition and the response it produced, it is hard to see how the larger concept of the Norwich School – which was finally set out in W.F. Dickes's monumental *Norwich School of Painting* (published by the Norwich house of Jarrolds in 1905) – could have come about at a national level. It seems clear that this larger concept was developed locally, and we can attribute it to two factors: first, the efforts of interested individuals among the Norwich artists, and second, the ideological needs of elements in the Norwich bourgeoisie.

Institutionalisation of the Norwich School in Norwich

In 1858, the *Norwich Mercury* published a series of four articles on Crome by its sub-editor, John Wodderspoon – himself an amateur artist. These were subsequently printed as a pamphlet, which appeared in two editions, in 1858 and 1876. Wodderspoon gave a sketchy account of the Norwich Society of Artists and made only brief comments on some of its members. But his essay

---

48　Among interesting reviews are those in 'Old Masters at the Academy', *The Graphic*, 17, 12 February 1878; 'Old Masters at Burlington House', *Illustrated London News*, 12 January 1878; 'Old Masters at the Academy', *Daily Telegraph*, 5 January 1878.

49　Edwin Edwards, 'Old Crome', *Norwich Mercury*, 19 January 1878.

50　'The Old Masters Exhibition', *The Builder*, 17 (12 January 1878). Crome's growing reputation is illustrated by: Mary M. Heaton, 'John Crome', *The Portfolio* (1879), pp. 33–6, 48–51; 'Old Crome', *The Graphic*, 24 (13 August 1881); and Paget 1882.

is interesting partly because it emphasised how the picturesque qualities of Crome's pictorial Norfolk were being destroyed by the modernisation of the countryside, and described the scenery of the Yare and the Broads as the distinctive elements in the Norfolk landscape. Crome was again represented as a painter of simple truth, and linked with Gainsborough and Constable as a type of artist produced organically by the East Anglian landscape. Wodderspoon followed Dawson Turner in representing Crome as a model of virtue and industry, and as a charismatic character who had galvanised Norwich painting. He had been the 'rising sun of the painter's art in East Anglia' and had gradually imparted 'principles which eventually gathered to themselves an academical importance, and formed that style and treatment of nature on canvass, called the Norwich School'.[51] Quite what the role of the Ladbrookes, Cotmans, and Stannards might have been in Norwich art was left unexplained, but there could be no historical reason for saying that they took their principles from Crome.

Two years later the centrality of Crome was finally qualified by David Hodgson's pamphlet *A Reverie, or Thoughts Suggested by a Visit to the Gallery of the work of Deceased Norfolk and Norwich Artists*. This is a poetic outpouring by an artist who had contributed a substantial number of works to all the Norwich Society exhibitions 1813–33, and whose father had been one of its founders. His text was the first to associate the Cotmans, Ladbrookes, and Stannards with Crome and his followers at a more equal level, thus suggesting a new conception. Hodgson particularly acknowledged the role of Robert Ladbrooke and of Ladbrooke's sons, who were both embittered by hagiographic accounts of Crome in the Norwich press at a time when their father's work was all but forgotten.[52] The Ladbrookes seem to have made some effort to disseminate a different picture, for by 1873 John Berney Ladbrooke was in correspondence with a French writer, Henri Perrier, who published what seems to be the first French account of the Norwich School in the *Gazette des Beaux-Arts* in that year. Perrier's article praised highly the work of both Henry and Robert Ladbrooke and its effect may be guessed from the fact that Ernest Chesneau praised Robert Ladbrooke equally with Crome in his *La Peinture anglaise* of 1882.[53]

---

51   Wodderspoon 1876, pp. 12–13.

52   Hodgson 1860. The Ladbrooke's view is set out in a letter from Henry Ladbrooke to John Berney Ladbrooke of 1858 in 'Norfolk and Norwich Artists deceased to 1898', bound volume of material collected by James Reeve (British Museum Print Room), and Henry Ladbrooke, 'Dottings', *Eastern Daily Press*, 22, 25, and 27 April 1921.

53   Henri Perrier, 'De Hugo van der Goes à John Constable', *Gazette des Beaux-Arts*, 7 (1873), pp. 253–66.

In actuality, although Robert Ladbrooke's work has a kind of earthy vitality, he was far from Crome's equal and the work of his son Henry was less than mediocre.

The Ladbrooke view of things was also perpetuated through James Reeve, Curator of the Norwich Museum 1851–1910, who had been taught painting by J.B. Ladbrooke. Reeve's notes show that he learned a less heroic view of Crome from the Ladbrookes and his enthusiasm for Cotman's work probably helped to give Cotman a new importance in the construction of the School.[54] Although Reeve never published a book on Norwich painting, he amassed a vast collection of documentation, and supplied Dickes with the information for his *Norwich School of Painting*.[55] Dickes's book remains the only comprehensive study of Norwich artists and it was the first historical account to bring together the whole range of amateur and professional artists working up until the 1880s and denominate them as a 'school'.

But the emergence of a broader concept of the Norwich School, a concept that made far more profound claims for the relationship between Norfolk's geography and Norwich painting, cannot be attributed simply to the efforts of interested individuals like the Ladbrookes. The concept clearly had an ideological function for a wider social grouping. The Norwich School was effectively redefined and institutionalised mainly through a series of exhibitions organised in the city by a variety of local institutions over the years from 1860 to 1902. Some of these institutions had a philanthropic orientation, while others were directly concerned to promote Norwich art. Another key agency was an immensely powerful and wealthy Norwich family that was an institution in its own right, namely the Colman dynasty.

The exhibition of 'Deceased Local Artists' organised in 1860 by the Norfolk and Norwich Fine Arts Association was the first of these exhibitions and a turning point in establishing a new importance for the Norwich School in the city's culture. The Association put on its first exhibition in 1848 and arranged further displays of contemporary art in 1849, 1852, 1853, 1855, 1856 and 1860, which included works by a wide range of local and non-local art-

---

54   See the notes on Crome by James Reeve in 'Norfolk & Norwich Artists. Biographical Sketches, Notices of Works, &c.', manuscript volume in Local Studies Library, Norwich.

55   Reeve's collected materials comprise seven bound volumes in the British Museum, divided between the Print Room and the Manuscript Room, and two more were in the Local Studies Library, Norwich. Reeve sold part of his collection of Norwich School drawings to the British Museum in 1902. Many of his Cotman drawings ended up in the collection of R.J. Colman.

ists.[56] While it included a mix of Norfolk gentry and Norwich bourgeois among its vice-presidents, the Association's council was made up exclusively of Norwich bourgeois and amateur artists, with the former predominating by 1855. In 1860 the committee of the Living Artists' exhibition was headed by the liberal M.P. J.H. Tillett, later J.J. Colman's running mate, and Colman himself had been on the council in 1856. I have not discovered who was on the committee of the Deceased Artists' exhibition, but it described its aim as that of 'obtaining as complete a view of what is termed the NORWICH SCHOOL OF PAINTING as possible'.[57]

'Deceased Local Artists' contained 318 paintings and drawings by a diverse body of artists, both amateur and professional, who had worked in Norwich in the eighteenth and nineteenth centuries, and grouped them as a school for the first time. Among them, Crome, who was represented by 44 works and some of his etchings, was clearly intended to stand pre-eminent. The *Norwich Mercury* again hailed Crome's paternity in the procreation of Norwich art: 'Here stands the worthily honoured bust of "The father of the Norwich School", surrounded by children whose works bear witness to their origin, and whose celebrity has well supported their parent's power, and to whom may the quotation be truly applied – "By their fruits shall ye know them"'.[58] The loaded metaphors of this passage indicate precisely how patriarchal was the mythology of artistic power. It also raises the question of why Cotman, who had two talented artist sons, and Robert Ladbrooke, who also had two artist sons and taught Joseph Stannard, were not attributed any comparable potency. Crome's centrality was partly established by according Cotman a secondary status. Represented by 30 works, sixteen of which were in the relatively feminised medium of water-colour, Cotman was described as 'another giant' but one 'of a totally different school'. Further, while his work was often 'meretricious', Crome's never was – he simply 'soared above' all other Norwich artists. The *Mercury*'s reports discussed a range of other Norwich artists but ignored Robert Ladbrooke, eleven of whose pictures were on show – an omission that seems distinctly invidious.

---

56   Catalogues to these exhibitions were collected in a series of bound volumes in the Norwich Local Studies Library at the time I wrote this essay.

57   Norfolk and Norwich Fine Arts Association, *Exhibition of the Works of Modern Artists at the Government School of Art, Free Library, Norwich* (1860).

58   'THE EXHIBITION', *Norwich Mercury*, 29 August 1860. For further reports of the exhibition, see *Norwich Mercury*, 1, 12, 15, and 19 September and 17 October 1860. The bust, now in the National Portrait Gallery, was by Pellegrino Mazzotti. It was exhibited at the NSA exhibition in 1821.

The *Mercury* was fairly dismissive about the Living Artists' exhibition of 1860 and opined that the committee would have done better to concentrate all its energies on the other. This suggests that the growing concern with promoting early nineteenth-century Norwich art in the later years of the century was partly a result of the city's inability to sustain much contemporary artistic production of significant quality, a circumstance confirmed by the declining numbers of local artists showing in the exhibitions of the local Art Unions and the Norfolk and Norwich Association for the Promotion of the Fine Arts (1848–60). After the early death of the talented John Middleton in 1856, no significant landscape painter was based in the region. Attempts to support contemporary local art by a continuing provision of exhibitions organised and funded by the local bourgeoisie continued in 1868–72, but met a lukewarm response from local artists and 'scanty patronage' from the 'wealthier classes' of the region.[59]

The diminishing vitality of local art, together with the relative decline in Norwich's importance as a manufacturing city, may be understood as contributing to the urge among the city's bourgeoisie to find some major cultural distinction in its past. The more grandiose definition of the Norwich School that emerged with the Deceased Artists' Exhibition of 1860 was continued through a sequence of loan exhibitions in the later years of the century. These were the Loan Collection of the Works of Norfolk and Suffolk Artists exhibited at a 'Soirée' in August 1874, which was arranged in connection with the Annual Meeting of the British Medical Association held in Norwich in that year; the Norwich Art Loan Exhibitions of 1878 and 1885 in aid of the restoration of the Church of St. Peter Mancroft; the Fine Art Exhibition in aid of the New Norfolk and Norwich Hospital of 1883; and the Art Loan Exhibition in aid of the St. George's Club for Working Girls of 1902. The 1874 exhibition was essentially the accompaniment to a fashionable social occasion, although in its aftermath it was opened to the public for two days at a small fee. It included 83 oils and 85 water-colours by deceased Norwich artists, and 79 works by living artists.[60] The 1878 exhibition, which was shown over three weeks, included 581 works and juxtaposed Norwich art with that of earlier periods and schools. The catalogue had a special section, 'Pictures of the Norwich School', which contained 112 oils, but further pictures by Norwich artists were scattered throughout different parts of the exhibition, and featured prominently in the Water-colour

---

59   'THE EXHIBITION', *Norwich Mercury*, 22 August 1868.

60   'Loan Collection of Works of Art at St. Andrew's Hall', *Norwich Mercury*, 15 August 1874.

Drawings section. Jeremiah James Colman, who had lent nothing to the 1874 exhibition, loaned a few significant works to that of 1878.[61]

The growing importance of his collection was still more evident in 1883, when a separate room was hung with 47 works belonging to him, almost all of which were by Norwich artists. The 1883 exhibition was part of a Bazaar intended to raise money to clear off the debts incurred by the building of the new Norfolk and Norwich Hospital. It was again a major social occasion, since the hospital was opened by the Duke and Duchess of Connaught – that is, Prince Arthur, Queen Victora's third son, and his wife.[62] The pattern of the 1878 St. Peter Mancroft Restoration exhibition was repeated in that of 1885, which brought together a very diverse selection of works by earlier artists of different schools, contemporary British painters (local and non-local), and 89 oils and a sizable number of watercolours by artists of the 'Norfolk and Norwich School'. J.J. Colman was one of the patrons of the exhibition and lent 41 works, far more than any other lender.[63] This whole sequence of events suggests that exhibitions of works of art had come to seem an appropriate accompaniment to some of the major public rituals of the Norwich bourgeoisie in this period.

Finally, the 1902 exhibition can symbolise the interweaving of bourgeois interests in cultural leadership and philanthropy that I explore in what follows.[64] The St. George's Club and Home for Working Girls had been started by the Congregationalist pastor, the Revd. R. Hobson, around 1888, and then taken up by Mrs. Gurney, later Lady Talbot de Malahide. Its aim had been 'to teach the working girls in the city, and to keep them from the many dangers to which they are exposed'. This involved providing 'a home for girls employed in the factories and workshops of the city with classes and social evenings for their instruction and amusement'.[65] Colman was one of the two biggest contributors to the Pictures section of the exhibition, lending 16 of the collection of 174 miscellaneous works on show, among which the 'Norwich School' predominated.

---

61   'Norwich Art Loan Exhibition', *Norfolk News*, 23 November 1878; 'The St. Peter Mancroft Fine Art Exhibition', *Norwich Mercury*, 20 November and 7 December 1878.

62   'Opening of the New Hospital', *Eastern Daily Press*, 21 August 1883; 'The HOSPITAL BAZAAR', *Eastern Daily Press*, 23 August 1883; 'The New Norfolk & Norwich Hospital', *Norwich Mercury*, 22 August 1883.

63   *Catalogue of the Norwich Art Loan Exhibition in Aid of the Fund for the Restoration of St. Peter Mancroft Church* (1885).

64   *Catalogue of the Art Loan Exhibition in Aid of St. George's Club for Working Girls in St. Andrew's Hall, Norwich* (1902).

65   See the reports on the Club and Exhibition in *Eastern Daily Press*, 3 February, 1 March, 10 April, and 26 May 1902.

The 1902 exhibition was primarily a philanthropic affair and the pictures were surrounded by a vast array of miscellaneous objets d'art and curios, including mementos of Lord Nelson, war relics, and a waxwork display. That the philanthropic aspects of the scheme should have been so central to its inception is almost certainly symptomatic of the level of social unrest in a city that was to return a socialist M.P. four years later.

One final set of exhibitions needs to be noted. These were the series of major loan exhibitions of works by Thirtle (1886), Stark (1887), J.S. Cotman (1888), and E.T. Daniell (1891), which were put on by the Norwich Art Circle. James Reeve was particularly instrumental in organising these, while J.J. Colman, who was a member of the Circle, was a major lender. The exhibitions had informative scholarly catalogues, that on Cotman being the first significant account of the artist. The Cotman exhibition was shown later in the year in a slightly reduced form at the Burlington Fine Arts Club.[66]

This succession of temporary exhibitions, important as they were, could not give the Norwich School the kind of institutional permanency that its supporters wanted. To provide this a gallery of local art was needed, and it was to establish such an institution that the East Anglian Art Society was founded. In 1872 its president, the brewer J.B. Morgan, together with 'some few other gentlemen', began collecting money on an annual basis to buy works of the 'Norwich School', which as a result of their growing market value were 'gradually disappearing from the County where they were produced'.[67] The Society was formally set up in 1876, when it applied to the Norfolk and Norwich Museum for permission to place two screens in one of its rooms to show 'a small collection of Pictures by Local Artists'. The Society issued annual reports from 1880–93 from which it is clear that J.B. Morgan and J.J. Colman were the leading lights, being president and vice-president respectively throughout its existence. John Gurney and Samuel Gurney also played important roles, and J.H. Tillett was on the Committee. Nearly all the Society members were from Norwich and its suburbs, which again demonstrates that it was the city's bourgeoisie rather than the local gentry who had discovered an interest in the School idea. The society's objective was to establish a 'permanent Picture Gallery in Norwich worthy of its artistic reputation', but with annual subscriptions ranging from 10 shillings to £2 from about 50 members, it never commanded the funds to build a significant collection. In several years it proved impossible to make acquisitions, and

---

66 Norfolk & Norwich Art Circle 1985, pp. 12–13.

67 *First Annual Report of the East Anglian Art Society, with a List of the Members, Pictures, &c.* (Norwich 1880). The EAAS published 14 annual reports, 1880–93, which provide a record of its members and acquisitions.

the 88 paintings, drawings, and etchings that the Society gave to the Norwich Museum in 1894 included no major works. The sole picture by Crome, *A View on the Wensum* (*fig. 46*), was a much damaged early work, and the examples of Vincent's and Stark's output were minor.

Founded in 1824, the Norfolk and Norwich Museum was primarily devoted to natural history and antiquities. It had continual financial problems due to the costs incurred in putting up its building in 1837–8, and, like many similar institutions, it depended for its survival on municipal government. As with the Norfolk and Norwich Art Union and its successor bodies, the ostensible aim of the Museum was public enlightenment; it was therefore logical that it should welcome the proposal to display the East Anglian Art Society collection.[68] The Museum finally passed to the city in 1894 under the provisions of the Public Libraries Act of two years earlier and was housed in Norwich Castle, which had been bought for the purpose, and converted partly through funds raised by public subscription. The gift of the East Anglian Art Society enabled the Museum to open with a collection of 'Norwich School' pictures, and J.J. Colman gave Joseph Stannard's major painting *Thorpe Water Frolic* (*fig. 6*) – a most appropriate picturing of class harmony in early nineteenth-century Norwich – to coincide with the opening.[69] In 1896 the Museum received a bequest of 351 oils and water-colours from the artist and teacher J.W. Walker, which was made up largely of works by minor late nineteenth-century British painters. Thus the Norwich School element in its holdings was completely swamped by a mass of non-local work, most of it mediocre or worse. This made J.J. Colman's bequest of twenty Norwich School paintings in 1898 particularly important. As the Museum's report commented: 'By its means, the best artists of the Norwich School of Painters, will at once, and for the first time, be worthily represented on the walls of the Picture Gallery; for which their works, owing to the prices they now command, could not have been acquired by purchase; and a very large advance will have been made towards the end the Committee have ever had in view, viz., the adequate representation of this famous local School in the public Gallery of the City'.[70]

---

68   Norfolk and Norwich Museum, *Report of the Proceedings of the Fifty-Second Annual General Meeting* (1877), p. 13. In addition to the museum's Annual Reports, see Southwell 1904.

69   See Norwich Castle Museum, *Report of the Castle Museum Committee to the Town Council for the year ending 31 December 1894*, p. 6. On the meanings of Stannard's work, see Hemingway 1992, pp. 284–90.

70   Norwich Castle Museum, *Report of the Castle Museum Committee to the Town Council for the year ending 31 December 1898*, p. 4. That the Museum did not cater equally for all classes of Norwich society was evident to the *Norfolk Socialist Review*, organ of the Nor-

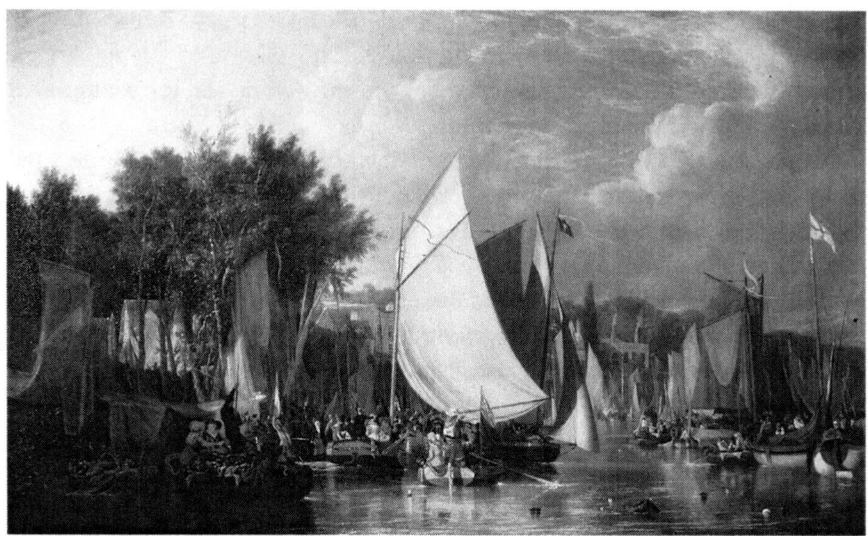

FIGURE 6   *Joseph Stannard,* Thorpe Water Frolic, *1825, oil on canvas, 42½ × 68 in*
              (108 × 172.7 cm)
              NORFOLK MUSEUMS SERVICE (NORWICH CASTLE MUSEUM AND ART
              GALLERY)

In 1903 a new extension to the Gallery was opened to house the growing
collection. The Museum seems to have made little effort to develop knowledge
of the Norwich School through its educational programme, but it did publish
a catalogue of the pictures, which went through four editions over 1897–1904.
The catalogue – which seems to have been written in the first place by James
Reeve – specifically addressed the problem of how to include Cotman as part
of the Norwich School. While admitting that his work was 'quite unlike' that of
Crome, it emphasised that Cotman was 'closely connected with Norwich and
its Artists'. While 'in the strictest sense' Norwich school 'generally meant Crome
and his pupils', it was applied in the catalogue in a wider sense to 'the whole
group of painters' who had lived in Norwich in the early nineteenth century, or
who were connected with it.[71]

---

wich branch of the Social Democratic Federation, which observed that the institution's
4.30 p.m. closing time effectively excluded the working population and called for evening
openings – 'Current Topics', *Norfolk Socialist Review*, no. 5 (May 1901).

71   *Catalogue of the Pictures, Drawings, Etchings, and Bronzes in the Picture Gallery of the
     Norwich Castle Museum* (Norwich, 1897), p. 7. See also p. 11.

Cultural Philanthropy and the Colman Family

In establishing this wider usage of 'Norwich School' the Colman Collection played an instrumental role, and it is to the significance of Norwich art for the Colmans I now turn. This requires some account of the history of the Colman firm and of the family's place in the city. The beginnings of what the *Daily Mirror* described in 1905 as 'a veritable romance in commercial enterprise' can be traced to 1804,[72] when J.J. Colman's uncle, also Jeremiah Colman, bought a flour mill in Norwich. In 1810 he moved to Stoke Holy Cross, three miles outside the city, taking over a mustard and flour business there. Colman's father was taken into partnership in the firm in 1823 and Colman himself, who was born in 1830, became a partner in 1851. The first Colman mill at Carrow in Norwich was opened in 1856, the move back to the city being partly motivated by its communications advantages and, more importantly, by its abundant supply of cheap labour. The literature published by the firm in the late nineteenth and early twentieth centuries and the accounts of it in the press have a twin aspect. On the one hand they emphasised the scale and modernity of the Carrow plant – what we might see as its proto-Fordism in some respects[73] – on the other they emphasised the 'old-fashioned' patriarchal character of Colman as an employer. In relation to the first aspect of the firm's image, the Centenary *Souvenir* of 1905 pointed out that the works had 1,000,000 square feet of flooring and 10,000,000 cubic feet of building, and stood on 32 acres of land (*fig. 7*). The Colmans employed more than 3,000 staff if those at offices outside Norwich were included. The *Souvenir* referred to the site as 'Colmanopolis' and the *Daily Mirror* described it as a 'Town within a Town'. Indeed, the plant aspired to be self-sufficient, making its own electricity and most of its own packing materials. The *Souvenir* conceded the incessant character of labour at Carrow, but sought to justify this in terms of the benevolent character of the organisation: 'As a hive of industry, with its incessant roar and rattle of machinery, Carrow is wonderful enough. But what is still pleasanter to contemplate is the philanthropy and humanity by which its atmosphere is interfused'.[74]

---

72   'Mustard Kings. Centenary of Messrs. Colman's Famous Business in Norwich', *Daily Mirror*, 4 August 1905.

73   The Colmans were hardly unaware of the latest forms of capitalist development elsewhere – in 1885, R.J. Colman visited the Pullman Factory and Village in Chicago. See Colman 1886, pp. 24–6.

74   Norfolk News Company Ltd. 1905, p. 14. Cf. Burgess and Burgess 1904, pp. 8–11, which also celebrates the speed of the work and refers to the 'magical processes' by which the products were made and packaged.

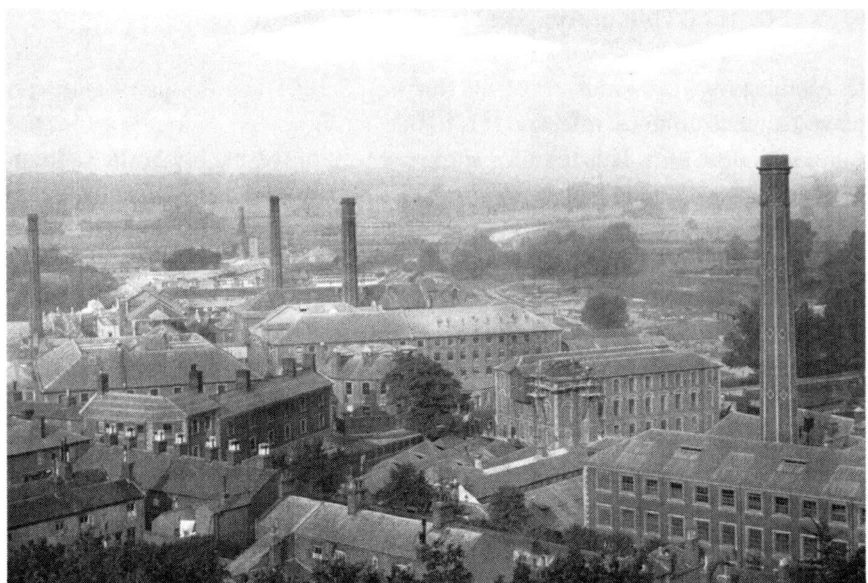

FIGURE 7   *J. and J. Colman and Sons' Carrow Works in 1900, hand-tinted glass plate*
PHOTO: UNILEVER/BNPS

The 'paternal' attitude of the Colman firm seems to have gone back to the Stoke phase – or at least, such was the image the family propagated. The *Souvenir* emphasised that the Colman line had roots deep in the agricultural, industrial, and ecclesiastical life of Norfolk.[75] It emphasised the 'rural quality' of the mill at Stoke and claimed that J.J. Colman's experience with the smaller workforce there had determined his later attitude. He was said to have looked on them as 'his cherished friends': 'Let them grow ever so vastly, he never could bring himself to regard them as mere cogs in a dividend-earning machine. He might no longer know them all by their Christian names; but he still nourished the consciousness that he was something more to them than the purchaser of their labour'.[76] Already at Stoke the Colmans built a school room and set up a clothing club. In 1857 they started a school at Carrow and a purpose-built school-house was opened in 1864.[77] J.J. Colman's philanthropic activities were conducted in concert with his wife, Caroline Cozens-Hardy, who he married in 1856 in the British School Room at Holt. She was already active in the

---

75   See also Colman 1905.

76   Norfolk and Norwich News Company Ltd. 1905, p. 17.

77   S.H. Edgar, 'Notes on the History of Colman Foods', bound typescript, formerly Local Studies Library, Norwich, pp. 234–9.

Wesleyan Reform movement before her marriage and had strong convictions on the value of education. They settled in Carrow House directly adjacent to the works. Shortly before their marriage, J.J. Colman wrote to his fiancée: 'Influence, position and wealth are not given for nothing, and we must try and use them as we should wish at the last we had done'. This stern sense of the responsibilities of his social position was matched by an equally clear view of those appropriate to the less well-placed in the social hierarchy. In a speech to his workforce at a dinner after the couple's return from their honeymoon he asserted: 'The bond between us should be mutual respect ... All classes must work somehow or other in this country if she is to maintain her high position'.[78]

Politically, Colman followed his father, a committed liberal. In 1851 he read a paper to the Norwich Young Mens' Mutual Improvement Society on the theme of 'The Nineteenth Century', which offered a vision of limitless progress. He rejoiced that the century had seen 'a vast breaking up amongst the old forms of prejudice, caste, and privilege', which were beginning to give way before 'the new and only true nobility which declares that "the mind's the standard of the man"'.[79] The paper concluded by calling young men to philanthropy. In 1871 when his friend J.H. Tillett was unseated as M.P. due to accusations of corrupt practices, Colman stood as Liberal candidate and was elected with a large majority, thus beginning a parliamentary career of nearly twenty-five years. The pamphlet through which Colman and Tillett appealed to the Norwich electorate in 1880 emphasised the former's commitment to 'every great measure calculated to advance and broaden the liberties of the people, and to promote peace and a wise management of finance'. It also emphasised the services of the firm to the local community, claiming that 'it is impossible to calculate what Norwich owes, first to the business of the firm, and next to the generosity of the gentleman who is at its head'.[80] On the one hand Colman was 'a merchant prince of the best type, a born captain of industry'; on the other he was the 'father' of his workforce and a great philanthropist. In the 1905 Souvenir the family was described as follows: 'They have been model employers ... and they have never absolved themselves from those civic and philanthropic duties which wealth imposes'.[81]

The meaning of the Colmans' interest in the Norwich School should now be beginning to emerge. At one level, at least, it was an aspect of their responsible stewardship of their wealth, their service to Norwich, and a sign of their

---

78   Colman 1905, pp. 134, 124. See also p. 112.

79   Colman 1905, p. 161.

80   Anon. 1880, p. 13.

81   Norfolk and Norwich News Company Ltd. 1905, p. 21.

commitment to the values of civilisation and progress. It showed they were not only wealth-producers but true leaders of society. When the Colman couple moved to Carrow House in 1856, Colman's enthusiasm for painting was already evident. (He began collecting the Norwich School in 1863.) He visited the Manchester Art Treasures Exhibition of 1857 and published a letter on it in the *Norfolk News* – the liberal paper in which his friend Tillett was involved – in which he compared the display with the Great Exhibition of 1851, to the disadvantage of the latter: 'Just six years back – on 1st May 1851 – the world saw Royalty and the aristocracy of birth assembled to do homage to the triumphs of industry – to-day, the aristocracy of commerce worthily represented by Manchester as its metropolis, has assembled to gaze on the triumphs which the aristocracy of mind has, at various times, created'.[82] In an unpublished manuscript, Colman stressed that while the contents of the Crystal Palace were replaceable and could perhaps be improved, the art treasures could not. Of the effects of pictures he wrote: 'A good painting tells its own tale, no matter what it be. You see at once the idea that was in the Artist's mind when he painted it, and be it joy or grief, calmness or excitement, pleasure or pain, or whatever the emotion be, it comes from the canvas to the mind of the observer'.[83] Colman's statements illustrate graphically the gloss of 'culture' that the appreciation of art was believed to confer on the sensitive observer, a gloss that was necessary to establish both individual distinction, and to advance the larger claim of the bourgeoisie to social leadership, over and above the aristocracy of rank. The Colmans' appropriation of the Norwich School may be understood in relation to such a strategy. In this respect they may stand as regional counterparts to William Hesketh Lever (1st Viscount Leverhulme) and Sir Henry Tate in their patriotic advancement of the British School.

At this point, I want to counter-pose the cultural activities of the Colmans with their practices as employers. In his sociological study of Norwich of 1910, C.B. Hawkins noted that the development of Norwich's nineteenth-century industries had depended on the large influx of unemployed agricultural workers in the early part of the century and observed how appalling their conditions must have been in that period. It was they who had provided the overstocked labour market that made possible the expansion of the laundry blue, starch, mustard, and chocolate industries.[84] By 1900 boot and shoe manufactures were the city's largest employers, with food manufactures second. The Colman fact-

---

82   J.J. Colman, 'The Manchester Exhibition', letter, *Norfolk News*, 9 May 1857.

83   Colman 1905, p. 121.

84   Hawkins 1910, Chapter 1. My thanks to Jane Beckett for discussing the Colmans with me.

ory at Carrow was the largest single employer, with a workforce of over 2,600. The firm did not use casual labour and paid the highest wages in Norwich after the city itself. But the negative side of this was that the labour was predominantly unskilled and a high proportion of it was provided by women and children. Observing the way in which the dominant character of labour imprinted itself on the workforce of a region, Hawkins referred to that of the Colmans as an example:

> This is well illustrated in the case of the great factories in Norwich which produce washing requisites, mustard, vinegar, confectionary, and a widely advertised patent wine. These are all things which have to be packed in small quantities ... The great bulk of this work is done by women, girls, and boys who make boxes, fill boxes, and wrap boxes from one year's end to another. To these simple operations the principle of subdivision is applied with scientific thoroughness, so that the task performed by individual workers becomes a purely mechanical movement of a single set of muscles. They are literally the living parts of a machine as finely and delicately adjusted as the mechanism of a watch. And it is a machine which works at appalling speed.[85]

Hawkins conceded that the parts of this machine were kept in good repair by the firm's welfare programmes, but his description remains like a paradigm of alienated labour.

Trade Unionism was relatively weak in Norwich, and there was no unionism in the food and drink trades. However, the city had a strong socialist movement and the Labour Institute provided the largest working man's club. That there were no labour troubles at Carrow may be partly explained by the fact that the Colmans provided employees with a school, a dispensary, a benefit society, a clothing club, cheap housing, a club house and sports fields. Of this pervasive paternalism Hawkins commented:

> Very little, however, seems to be expected of the employees themselves in the responsible management of these advantages. In this matter the firm plays the part of a benevolent despot. It is very hard to say, therefore, how far the various clubs – they include an Adult School – have a real life of their own.

---

85   Hawkins 1910, p. p. 42.

Such evidence suggests a kind of continuum between the Colmans' provisions for their workforce and their association with high culture. The benevolent despotism of their experiments in welfare provision (and social control) were founded on the same principle of hierarchy as their cultural philanthropy.[86]

The Colmans' project in respect of the Norwich School was brought to its conclusion by J.J. Colman's son, Russell Colman (1861–1946), whose huge collection passed to the city in 1951, on an occasion that was timed to coincide with the Festival of Britain. Comprising 228 oils and 985 watercolours, housed in purpose-built galleries emblazoned with the donor's name (*fig. 8*), it is the largest collection of Norwich art anywhere, and a monument to a particular conception of the Norwich School forever cemented with the Colman name. J. & J. Colman Ltd. modernised and expanded in the twentieth century, becoming a public company in 1935 and amalgamating with Reckitt and Sons Ltd. in 1938. Like his father, Russell Colman had a prominent public career, but it was one more oriented to the city and the county. His obituary observed that he 'disliked all political controversy' and his most important public office was as H.M. Lieutenant of Norfolk from 1929–44. His amusements were also not those of the nineteenth-century non-conformist bourgeoisie, being chiefly shooting and yachting, and in 1905 he moved the family residence from Carrow House to Crown Point, an estate on the edge of the city. If R.J. Colman's career and lifestyle has some features resembling that of the modern squirearchy, this seems to match with the old-world rustic view of Norfolk that Norwich painting had come to represent.[87]

In the early nineteenth century the best-known Norwich landscape painting was understood as an advanced and modem type of painting, the product of a major manufacturing city set in the midst of one of the most progressive agricultural regions. But, as we have seen, by the 1850s it was viewed nostalgically as the mirror of a bygone and simpler era. Some aspects of the output of Crome, Vincent, and Stark lent themselves to such an interpretation, since they had generally represented rural life in a picturesque mode, and had not

---

86   Hawkins 1910, p. 305. J.J. Colman believed firmly in Free Trade and the 'inexorable laws of the economy'. However, in 1891 he claimed that his 'desire and intention' was that union and non-union 'men' should be treated impartially at Carrow. When the TUC held its Congress at Norwich in 1894, he entertained the delegates at Carrow House. In a letter of 1893 he wrote: 'I am thankful never to have had any serious difficulty with my own Workmen, and hope always to avoid it'. See Colman 1905, pp. 369, 366.

87   *RUSSELL JAMES COLMAN September 5, 1861 – March 22, 1946*, reprinted from the *Eastern Daily Press*, 23–29 March 1946. See also Kitson 1936.

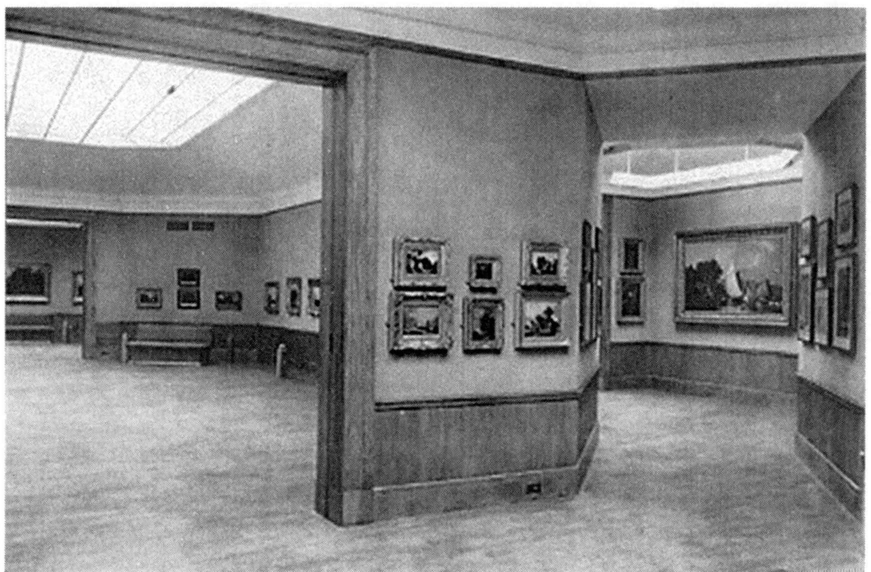

FIGURE 8   *The Colman Galleries in Norwich Castle Museum in 1951*
NORFOLK MUSEUMS SERVICE (NORWICH CASTLE MUSEUM AND ART
GALLERY)

provided an imagery of Norfolk's improved agriculture comparable with that
which Constable had produced of Suffolk. However, there were unequivocally modern elements in some of their representations of Great Yarmouth and
the local river system, and other Norwich artists had also experimented with
modern imagery, as Stannard's *Thorpe Water Frolic* illustrates. That the local
bourgeoisie and its cousins outside the region embraced this backward-looking
reading of the Norwich School was facilitated by the currency of a larger mythology of rural Englishness in the late nineteenth and early twentieth centuries,
when a diverse body of writers and artists – Rider Haggard, Kipling, P.H. Emerson and Alfred Munnings among them – pictured the rural population as the
essence of a disappearing national stock, to be contrasted with the degeneracy
of the urban proletariat. It is striking that the Broads (which had little attraction for the major Norwich artists) should have been one of the main regions
where this essential Englishness was said to be still discernible, although ultimately it was to be located more in the Home Counties.[88] In the context of the
depressed rural economy of late nineteenth-century Norfolk, in a small city

---

88   Howkins 1986; Knight 1986.

dependent on second order industries, the bourgeoisie needed to find some basis for municipal and regional pride. Beyond its wealth of medieval architecture, the Norwich School was one of the city's few marks of cultural distinction.

The Norwich School Concept in the Twentieth Century

The concept of the Norwich school was at its height in the early twentieth century, when large claims were made for its stature and influence. But the weightiness of the claims made for it did not prompt any new rigour in its definition. Dickes, who asserted that the 'teaching' of the Norwich School had become 'a distinguishing feature' of 'all British Art', explained its distinctive quality only in terms of the impact of local scenery on the natural artistic aptitudes of

> that remarkable group of artists who, owing to the then comparative remoteness of Norwich from the Metropolis, and to their own poverty, were compelled to teach themselves and their pupils Art in the beautiful academy of nature that was opened to them. Uninfluenced by prescription of tradition, but surrounded by scenery of a special sort, with the delightful features of which they could not help being in love, they boldly declared NATURE THEIR ONLY GUIDE ... it soon became evident to the world that their Art was distinguished by a speciality. Love of their native heath and rivers, hills, and woods had kept them so continually repeating the same views under every change of sunshine and shadow – their palettes were so constantly set with the same rich and mellow colours – that even when they went to other scenes their colouring and touch declared them still 'of Norwich'.[89]

However, Dickes – who was no art historian – did not define what those distinguishing features of 'colouring and touch' were; his book is essentially a sequence of individual biographies, devoid of formal analyses or comparisons.

Later commentators were equally vague. In a *Studio* Special Number of 1920, H.M. Cundall – who was at least a prolific author of books on British art – made the much-repeated claim that Norwich was the first city in England to have its own school of art, and continued: 'The word "school" is here used not in the

---

89   Dickes 1905, p. 11.

ordinary scholastic term, but to denote a body of persons who are disciples of the same master, or who are united by a general similarity of principles and methods; it also means those whose training was obtained in the same locality, and implies more or less community of doctrine and styles'.[90] Laurence Binyon was yet more mystical in an exhibition catalogue of 1927, in which he claimed that although 'the Norwich artists formulated no theory and accepted no war-cry ... there is a deep unconscious bond between them, so that many a painting, though we may be at a loss to attribute it to a particular artist, is unmistakably recognised as belonging to the Norwich School'.[91] Neither offered any justification for these claims.

No significant text on the Norwich School as such was published between 1920 and 1965, but the concept continued in currency through the exhibitions of commercial and public galleries. It was restated and somewhat modified in Derek Clifford's *Water-Colours of the Norwich School* (1965), which suggested that while the School stood for no 'special type of landscape painting', it did refer to a community of artists who had a shadowy 'corporate sense', and who worked in two traditions, one stemming from Crome and the other from Cotman. Norman L. Goldberg's catalogue to an American exhibition of 1967, *Landscapes of the Norwich School*, reverted to making assertions on the importance of Norwich art that are as grandiose, vague, and unsubstantiated as those of Dickes.[92] More recent scholarship has thankfully been more circumspect in its characterisations.[93]

The idea that the Norfolk landscape imprinted on the works of the Norwich painters a distinctive character should probably be understood as a fusion between the well-established ideological trope of the romantic genius, who discovers new truths in nature through the particular temper of his sensibility, and the conservative mythology of rural Englishness mentioned earlier. That natural phenomena can in themselves produce a particular style of representation runs quite contrary to contemporary theories of visual representation, if not to common sense. However, that a certain pattern of representation could be seen as appropriate to particular types of scenery is worth considering, in relation to the well-rehearsed idea that Norwich artists drew particularly heavily on

---

90   Cundall 1920, p. 1.

91   Norwich Castle Museum, *Catalogue of a Loan Collection of Oil Paintings, Water-Colour Drawings, etc Illustrative of the Works of Artists of the Norwich School of Painting* (Norwich 1920), p. 9.

92   Clifford 1965, pp. 39, 78–9; Goldberg 1967.

93   Moore 1985; David Blayney Brown, 'Nationalizing Norwich: the "School" in a Wider Context', in Brown, Hemingway, and Lyles 2000.

the formal models of Dutch seventeenth-century painting. Yet while Crome's enthusiasm for the works of Hobbema is legendary, and he was sometimes referred to as 'the Norfolk Hobbema' in the nineteenth century, it hardly seems more significant than Constable's enthusiasm for Ruisdael.[94] While there are three securely-attributed Crome paintings that develop on the type of Hobbema glade scene, it is really hard to see that his *The Beaters* (*fig. 44*) or the Norwich Museum's *Grove Scene* are any closer to Hobbema (*fig. 57*) than Augustus Wall Callcott's *Return from the Market* (*fig. 58*). Crome's interpretation of this and other Dutch prototypes was no less innovative than that of Turner, Constable, Mulready, and others. Such comparisons in themselves indicate that the interest of Norwich artists in Dutch art cannot be understood as a local phenomenon. Further, the usage of Dutch models was extremely various. Although the parameters of Crome's output have proved notoriously difficult to define and there has certainly been confusion between the student works of his pupils and his own, the development of J.B. Crome, Stark, and Vincent led them all to produce distinctive types of painting that have no significant style traits that would permit them to be distinguished as his followers.

Insofar as it is worth considering Norwich as a separate art centre, it is in relation to the particular conditions of patronage there and the interest in particular motifs in the local landscape. Artists who worked primarily for a local clientele, such as Crome, Thirtle, and Joseph Stannard, may have been induced to choose certain themes with local resonance, and were almost certainly obliged to work on a modest scale. It is significant that Vincent, after his move to London, painted a wide range of non-local subjects as well as Norfolk themes and often exhibited large canvases until financial problems crippled his ambitions in the mid-1820s. J.B. Crome, who remained based in Norfolk but exhibited regularly outside the county, equally showed a range of Norfolk and continental subjects, although he probably sent in sketches and smaller work to the local exhibitions that he would not have bothered to send elsewhere. It has never been possible to see Cotman's move back to Norfolk as anything but a disaster in career terms, and when he returned to painting in 1823 after his ten-year stint as an etcher and antiquarian draftsman, he concentrated primarily on continental subjects and worked in a mode explicitly designed to make an impact in the London exhibitions. This means that only the Norfolk water-colours of circa 1807–10 have a specifically local reference and these were

---

94   For Crome and Hobbema, see Chapter Seven. Constable's friend John Fisher referred to
       the artist's house in Keppel Street as 'Ruisdael House' – see Constable 1962–8, vol. 2,
       p. 232.

only a part of his output at the time. There are undoubtedly elements in the iconography of Norfolk imagery that can only be explained in relation to the associations of local history and local social occasions such as water frolics and regattas. But the aesthetic and other types of ideology which made it seem appropriate to represent such subjects were not specifically local at all. There does seem to have been an attempt to develop an imagery of the Norfolk river system, but this needs to be understood in relation to the symbology of Turner's Thames and Constable's Stour pictures.[95] Equally, the extremely interesting body of images of the Norfolk seaside resorts of Yarmouth and Cromer draw their meanings more from the larger body of representations of such places and from the general patterns of discourse about them then they do from specific features of the places themselves.

In sum, it is absurd to imagine that in the most capitalistic and urbanised society in Europe, a city that is a mere 120 miles from the capital, connected to it by excellent communications, would produce an art in any way isolated from trends elsewhere. To consider the work of Norwich-based artists as inherently distinctive in significance or style is to perpetuate an obfuscation.

---

95   See Hemingway 1992, Chapters 8 and 9.

Landscape and Ideology

Meaning in Cotman's Norfolk Subjects

It is certainly right to condemn formalism, but it is ordinarily forgotten
that its error is not that it esteems form too much, but that it esteems it
so little that it detaches it from meaning.[1]

On the bicentenary of Cotman's birth in 1982, an exhibition of his works, selected by Miklos Rajnai and Stephen Somerville, was shown at the Victoria and
Albert Museum. Responses to this exhibition among the critics of the national
press were fairly predictable.[2] The public was inevitably told that Cotman was
'a moody man', even a manic depressive, as if this information in some way held
the key to understanding his art. The only part of his output really worth bothering with, it seemed, was his early watercolours; the remainder merely testified
to personal neuroses, the adverse influence of patrons, and the dangers of provincial isolation. Another frustrated artist-hero rolls off the stocks. To some
extent, the exhibition itself logically produced these conventional responses,
since the catalogue essays by Rajnai and David Thompson, together with a
selection of works in which Cotman's later output and his achievements as an
etcher were considerably under-represented, were calculated to reinforce prevailing interpretations of the artist as a blighted genius. Rajnai has achieved
great advances in the dating and classification of Cotman's oeuvre, and he
deserves the gratitude of any historian working on British landscape painting
for the immense labour of documentation and attribution which he directed
during his years as Keeper of Pictures at the Norwich Museum. However, the
interpretation of Cotman which he has put forward follows in a long tradition
which needs to be questioned.

Rajnai has written elsewhere that the 'summit' of Cotman's artistic achievement had been reached before he returned to Norwich in 1806, although in the

---

1 Merleau-Ponty 1964, p. 77.

2 Rajnai (ed.) 1982. See, for example, the reviews in the *Sunday Times* and the *Observer*, 22 August 1982. For a more balanced and critical appraisal, see Wilton 1982.

bicentenary catalogue his greatest period is extended to 1805–12.[3] This view is a reiteration of well-established and familiar conclusions, for it was undoubtedly on the basis of his early drawings that Cotman became something of a cult figure in the interwar years, and received the accolade of a *Burlington Magazine* Special Number in 1942. The opinions of earlier authorities such as Laurence Binyon, Sydney Kitson, Paul Oppé and Martin Hardie, are consistently echoed in the present catalogue – or sometimes just directly quoted. The catalogue tells us that Cotman's style is 'extraordinarily forward-looking', but then Binyon had observed in 1904 that Cotman was born at the wrong time, and Kitson, writing in the 1930s, found some of his work was of 'an almost prophetic nature'.[4] The justification for this assessment is, of course, those unprecedented and extraordinary 'inclinations' to 'abstraction' which first manifested themselves in the Greta drawings. Of Cotman's watercolours of his first Norwich period Rajnai writes that the abstraction has become 'more obviously assertive' and that: 'All things accidental were banished, and what remains appears to be there because of the inner logic ... of the composition, rather than because of the artist's interest in representation'.[5] By these and similar remarks, Cotman is recommended to us both as singularly original, an artist of 'more marked individuality than any of his contemporaries', and as one whose achievement lay in that his work foretold an aspect of 'Post-Impressionist and Cubist art', to use Martin Hardie's words.[6] (David Thompson, echoing Adele Holcomb's 1978 essay, refers to the *cloisonné* effect of Cotman's drawings, despite the fact that the artist did not put marked bounding lines round depicted objects in his drawings of 1805–12.)[7] Indeed, what emerges is that Cotman is being assessed by the values of the type of formalist aesthetic popularised by Roger Fry and Clive Bell in the early twentieth century, the values which still, often unwittingly, dominate so much writing on art in the English-speaking countries.

In fact, neither Bell nor Fry saw in Cotman any exceptional premonition of the Cézannesque Revolution. The rather flat patterned effects of Cotman's early drawings were unlikely to hold a strong appeal for critics who placed so much emphasis on the interplay of volumes and space in an almost architectural sense. Fry apparently regarded Cotman merely as the 'perfect drawing master', and Bell, whose enthusiasm for English art was never great, made occasional moderately approving references to him but was far more positive about John

---

3   Rajnai (ed.) 1982, p. 17. Cf. Rajnai 1978, p. 13.
4   Binyon 1897, p. 100, and Binyon 1904, p. 53; Kitson 1937, p. 373.
5   Rajnai (ed.) 1982, p. 16.
6   Hardie, 1966–8, vol. 3, p. 95.
7   Rajnai (ed.) 1982, p. 18. Holcomb 1978, p. 10.

Crome. However, if Fry and Bell failed to notice any exceptional formal qualities in Cotman's work, this did not inhibit Hardie and his contemporaries from proclaiming them. Rajnai and Thompson follow in their footsteps.[8]

Fundamental to Clive Bell's concept of significant form is the fragmenting of the experience of the art object, so that all associated ideas are expunged in the moment of aesthetic intuition. In Bell's theory the subject of a work of art is of no consequence whatsoever to aesthetic experience. The cognitive or representational aspects of art have no aesthetic significance.[9] The reason why some forms move us aesthetically, and others do not, is that some have been so purified that we feel them aesthetically and that others are so clogged with unaesthetic matter (e.g., associations) that only the sensibility of an artist can perceive their formal significance.[10] The artist sees the world as 'pure forms'. Art is divorced from the concerns of life, and in the world of art the emotions of life have no place. Aesthetic emotion is distinct from all others, and it is experienced strongly only by a small minority of specially endowed individuals.

Partly influenced by his discussions with Bell, Roger Fry also came to stress that associations from life are a hindrance to true aesthetic experience, particularly in his writings of *c*. 1910–30. However, as is well known, Fry was a rather more sophisticated thinker than Bell and felt that Bell had gone a little too far in denying representation any aesthetic significance.[11] Fry tussled with the problem of evaluating the representation of emotionally charged situations and objects in *Transformations* (1927), although in this work he continued to see such aspects of painting as essentially literary and, at best, 'applied art'. It was only in the lecture 'The Double Nature of Painting' (1933), that he finally accepted there were two valid approaches to painting: one oriented towards psychological effects, and the other towards more purely formal ones. Nonetheless, as Fry admitted, there had been a time when he was the 'mouth-piece' of those who enthusiastically maintained that 'the only value of painting is inherent in plastic, spatial and chromatic harmonies'.[12] Indeed, there were passages in *Vision and Design*, *The Artist and Psycho-Analysis*, and *Transformations*, in which he asserted the irrelevance of subject-matter and its associations in terms as extreme as those of Clive Bell. Thus, 'the form of a work of art has a meaning of its own and the contemplation of the form in and for itself gives rise in some

---

8   Martin Hardie reports Fry's attitude to Cotman in Hardie 1942. For Bell on Cotman see Bell 1915, p. 174, and Bell 1922, p. 110.

9   Bell 1915, pp. 68, 225.

10   Bell 1915, p. 55. See also p. 52.

11   Fry 1928, p. 295.

12   Fry 1969, p. 367.

people to a special emotion which does not depend upon the association of the form with anything else whatever', and 'now I venture to say that no one who has a real understanding of the art of painting attaches any importance to what we call the subject of a picture – what is represented'.[13] Although recent commentators on Fry have argued rightly that he should not be remembered only as the exponent of a crude formalism, it seems precisely this aspect of his work that has been most influential.[14]

This is not the place to give a full critique of formalist aesthetics, and I will restrict myself to pointing out that, first, neither the positions of Fry nor Bell are logically consistent, and there is no sound argument for excluding the 'non-formal' aspects of art objects from aesthetic experience; and, second, Fry's essentially empirical method of generalisation from personal responses is epistemologically unsound, whatever insights it permitted him as a practical critic. Fry aspired to what he saw as the objectivity of the natural sciences, but, as we all know, empirical judgments are far from value-free. His thought was fundamentally ideological in his almost total inability to recognise the socio-historical factors that conditioned his own aesthetic sensibility, a sensibility which he saw, mistakenly, as naturally given.[15]

Commentators on Cotman have not in general referred overtly to the doctrine of 'significant form', but they have either consistently ignored the associations of his subject-matter, or simply stressed its insignificance. If this interpretation is compared with the overwhelming tendency of British aesthetics in the early nineteenth century one cannot but notice a glaring contradiction: it was precisely the associations that Bell and Fry saw as a distraction, and which Cotman scholars have treated as an irrelevance, that were regarded as the basic substance of aesthetic experience in Cotman's period. When Cotman produced his drawings of 1805–12, the most widely read aesthetic treatises, those of Lord Kames, Alison, and Payne Knight, were based primarily on concepts of association psychology, borrowed partly from Hume in the case of Kames, and directly from Hartley in that of Alison and Payne Knight. By the late eighteenth century, the association of ideas had become one of the most influential concepts in psychology and philosophy, being widely applied in moral and political

---

13   Fry 1924, pp. 8, 16.

14   On Fry, I find particularly useful Lang 1962. The interpretation of Taylor 1977 seems to me highly questionable. Frances Spalding's biography (Spalding 1980) does useful work in relating Fry's criticism to his practice as an artist, but is as naive about the socio-historical determinants of Fry's aesthetic as Fry himself was.

15   On Bell, see especially Osborne 1965 and Dickie 1965. For further pertinent criticisms of formalism see Baldwin, Harrison, and Ramsden 1981.

theories as well as in philosophical criticism. Hobbes, Locke, Berkeley, Hume and many lesser thinkers used the concept in their systems, although the first attempt at a consistent and exhaustive application of it to all aspects of human experience did not come until David Hartley's *Observations of Man* of 1749, which was subsequently popularised through Priestley's abridged edition of 1775. For thinkers like these, who tried to explain knowledge largely on the basis of sense sensations, association was an invaluable instrument in accounting for the formation of complex ideas, memory and imagination, etc. Although association was controversial, and provoked charges of materialism and atheism, its usefulness attracted such major thinkers as Smith, Bentham and Godwin. It provided a form of explanation that accorded with the essentially naturalistic account of mental activity that had become prevalent in the eighteenth century and which seemed congruent with the rational scientific modes of thought that capital and industry increasingly required, while at the same time it could be used to sustain prevailing religious ideology as the works of Hartley and Alison clearly demonstrate.[16]

Alison, who was the most extreme exponent of association aesthetics, maintained a doctrine of signs, partly derived from his friend Thomas Reid.[17] In contrast to Bell and Fry, Alison asserted that there is no single, special aesthetic emotion. The qualities of matter are not aesthetic in themselves, but only as signs or expressions of our feelings. Aesthetic experience occurs through a certain exercise of the imagination, from certain sequences of association, that is, from trains of ideas which excite our emotions. For Alison, in direct opposition to Bell and Fry, the more associations the art object (or indeed any natural object considered from the perspective of taste) stimulates the better: 'the more that our ideas are increased, or our conceptions are extended upon any subject, the greater the number of associations we connect with it, the stronger is the emotion of sublimity or beauty we receive from it'.[18] The associations of ideas which give rise to this aesthetic pleasure are characterised by emotion and by an overriding principle of unity. Both Alison and Knight particularly stressed the importance of association in the aesthetic experience of landscape. For Alison, such superiority as the landscape-painter possessed over the gardener and over nature itself, depended on his or her capacity to achieve greater unity

---

16   On the general history of association theory see Warren 1921; on association aesthetics, see McKenzie 1949. Trevor Fawcett also emphasised the important of association theory for understanding the landscape painting of the period in his excellent article, Fawcett 1982 (1).

17   Alison 1815, vol. 2, p. 416.

18   Alison 1815, vol. 1, p. 37.

of effect, and thereby greater intensity of emotion: 'The momentary effects of light or shade, the fortunate incidents which chance sometimes throws in, to improve the expressions of real scenery, and which can never again be recalled, he has it in his power to perpetuate ... Above all, the occupations of men, so important in determining, or in heightening the characters of nature ... fall easily within the reach of his imitation, and afford him the means of producing both greater strength, and greater unity of expression'.[19]

There is plenty of evidence that association aesthetics was widely discussed in Cotman's Norwich. William Taylor, the city's foremost intellectual, referred to the importance of association in a lecture on landscape painting which he gave to the Norwich Philosophical Society in 1814, a society of which both John Crome and his eldest son were members.[20] Taylor's friend Dr Frank Sayers had published a 'Disquisition on Beauty' in 1793, in which he cited Hartley and Alison to support the contention that the emotion of beauty is distinguished from the pleasures of the senses by its dependence on association. Sayers particularly emphasised that the beauty of landscapes derives from the various associated ideas the mind connects with them. Although I cannot prove that Cotman was familiar with this work in 1806–12, a copy of it did appear in his 1834 sale, and it was a 1793 edition rather than either of the collected editions of Sayers' works of 1808 and 1823.[21]

The significance of association theory for the theory of painting had been acknowledged as early as Reynolds' third *Idler* paper of 1759. However, neither Reynolds nor any of the Professors of Painting at the Royal Academy made any attempt to work out its implications for conventional academic theory, with certain aspects of which it ill-accorded. John Opie, in his Academy lectures, referred to that 'wonderful and powerful principle; the association of ideas' (without elaborating on its significance), and Sayers mentioned in his 'Disquisition' that he had discussed the principle with Opie and received confirmation of his own theory from him. Opie was well-known in Norwich through his periods of residence in the city, and through his marriage to Amelia Alderson. He was a friend and mentor to John Crome, and, according to legend, knew Cotman too.[22] That Cotman discussed association aesthetics in Norwich circles is

---

19   Alison 1815, vol. 1, pp. 125–6.

20   Taylor 1814, p. 500.

21   Sayers 1808.

22   The only extensive theoretical statement by either of the Cromes to survive is John Berney Crome's 'Essay on Painting and Poetry' (manuscript, Norwich Castle Museum). This makes little direct reference to association theory, but parts of the argument clearly depend upon it.

very probable; that he knew of the theory anyway is beyond doubt. Topographical watercolour painters had reason to be more receptive to the new concepts of eighteenth-century aesthetics than were academic theorists, since the picturesque and association theories tended to confer far more status on their practice than academic theory allowed it. Thus we find Cotman's friend John Varley writing in a drawing treatise of 1816–17: 'A Painter must rest his pretensions to fame on an early and natural perception of the beauty of classification, and in *the unity of subject* ... this faculty, so rare, and so difficult of acquirement ... owes its power to its concealment, *under the garb of simple and faithful imitation of nature*, each object and its accompaniments answering to the ideas instantly raised by the mention of such scenes as those in which they occur; but surpassing them by the greater perfection of those associations which rendered those ideas estimable'.[23] Varley's phrase 'under the garb of simple and faithful imitation of nature' should serve as a salutary reminder to those who are given to see early nineteenth-century watercolours as primarily a kind of value-free record of particular locations, or as an arena for formal experiment. Considering the emphasis on association and unity of effect in this passage, it is inconceivable that Varley was unfamiliar with Alison's writings; but this is no surprise for the language of association was commonplace.

Not only were artists imbued with the ideas of association theory; since it was such a widely acknowledged principle of contemporary philosophy and moral and political speculation, it affected the evaluation of many aspects of experience. References to associations infest guidebooks and local histories and even private writings. For example, in 1788 William Windham complained in his diary of the landscape between Costessey and his estate at Felbrigg: 'There is such a dearth of objects, and poverty of ideas, in the ride from Cossey hither, as makes me always think of it with dissatisfaction'. Only thoughts of what he was going to or coming from 'protected me from the mean associations which pightels and gorse commons, Stratton and Felthorpe, naturally draw with them'.[24] That the Norfolk landscape had little to recommend it to the picturesque tourist was a commonplace of contemporary guidebooks. Indeed, it was only the associations occasioned by the prosperity of its agriculture and the antiquity of its churches that were said to redeem it for the traveller. This widespread opinion is not without relevance for Norwich art.

The purpose of this brief excursion into aesthetics has been to suggest that while for most twentieth-century commentators the significance of Cot-

---

23   Varley 1816–17, my emphases. Cf. Alison 1815, vol. 2, pp. 199–200.

24   Windham 1866, p. 141. A pightel was a small area of land enclosed by a hedge.

man's early drawings may seem to lie primarily in their purely formal qualities, neither Cotman's public, nor Cotman himself, can have viewed them in this way. Cotman's drawings may be a wonderful achievement, but they are not a wonderful achievement because they anticipate an aspect of modernist painting (which they do not), but because of the skill and inventiveness with which Cotman manipulated early nineteenth-century concepts and techniques.

In the remainder of this essay I will suggest some of the meanings that a few major drawings of Cotman's first Norwich period, the drawings in which 'abstract tendencies' are said to be most pronounced, are likely to have had for him and his contemporaries. It seems appropriate to begin with one of the drawings which Rajnai finds most irreducibly 'abstract': *The Marl Pit* (*fig. 9*). In this, he tells us, 'the tenuous balance of observed fact and abstract pattern' inevitably fascinate 'the connoisseur'. The location is of little consequence because the composition 'is such a powerful interplay of diagonal planes, of flat areas of intensive colour and of light and shade with transitions of reflected light, that the physical reality of the motif becomes of secondary importance'.[25] Rajnai has referred to the marl pits at Whitlingham in connection with this drawing, and it is possible that what he describes as the 'square shape' in the upper left is in fact the round tower of Whitlingham Church, and that the grey shapes near it are the ruins of the nave. While the church does look rather different in other renditions by Norwich artists, Cotman was not inhibited by topographical accuracy in drawings of this type. He might have removed the crockets from the top of the tower to achieve a simpler outline, or doctored the scene in other ways. Any topographical identification must be tentative, but it does at least look like a marl pit and a ruined round tower church.[26] The location may be of 'little consequence' from the point of view of an exegesis of Cotman's work in terms of anachronistic modernist categories, but if one's aim is to establish the probable meaning of the drawing for its original audience, it is essential to examine the likely associations of its subject and their place in the ideologies of the period.

Far from the subject of this drawing being insignificant, it was highly meaningful to the Norfolk bourgeoisie and gentry, the groups who visited the Norwich exhibitions in the early nineteenth century and patronised the Norwich Society of Artists. This audience was not unified in its social composition, but for many amongst it *The Marl Pit* would likely have been redolent with pleasing

---

25   Rajnai (ed.) 1982, p. 171. The statement repeats the evaluation in Rajnai and Allthorpe-Guyton 1979, p. 101.

26   For reproductions of other treatments of this subject see Hemingway 1979, plate 35; and Allthorpe-Guyton 1977, plate 6.

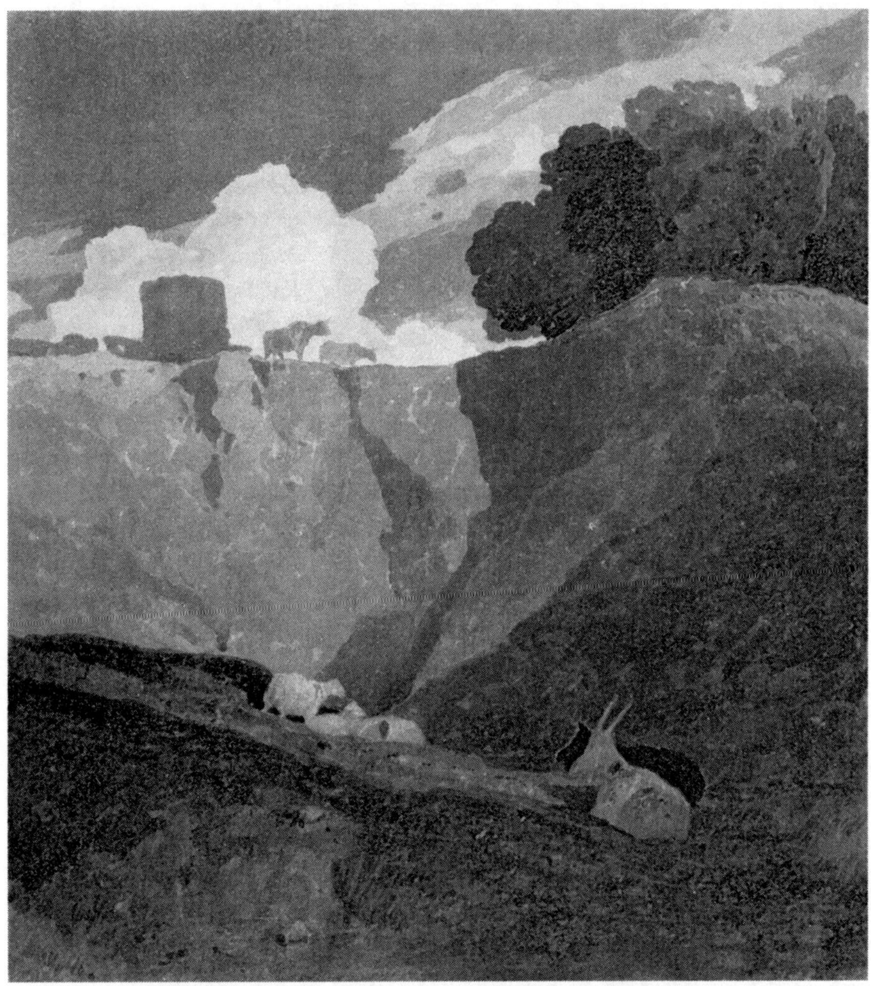

FIGURE 9   *John Sell Cotman,* The Marl Pit, *c. 1809–10, pencil and watercolour, 11⅝ × 10⅛ in (29.5 × 25.8 cm)*
NORFOLK MUSEUMS SERVICE (NORWICH CASTLE MUSEUM AND ART GALLERY)

associations. Marl was a principal foundation of Norfolk's progressive agriculture, the pride of the county. According to Arthur Young, who should have known, manuring was the 'most important branch' of Norfolk farming, and he began his account of manures with marl, as did other writers on the subject.[27]

---

27   Young 1804, p. 402. Cf. Bacon 1844, p. 267.

Rather earlier, in 1794, Nathaniel Kent had claimed that the availability of marl was one of the three natural advantages of the county, and described it as an advantage 'of inestimable value'.[28] The expense of marling discouraged fallowing and encouraged crop rotation, another important feature of the Norfolk system.

Marl is a mixture of clay and lime, which when spread on the land greatly increases its fertility. It was dug from pits, sometimes about twenty feet deep, and carried away by cart or by water. There were four main areas in which marl was found in quantity, one of which was Whitlingham. Deposits there seem to have been particularly rich, and marl from Whitlingham was carried by water to many other places in the local Norfolk craft, the wherry. Marl could be carried 50 miles by water more cheaply than it could be taken six or seven by land, and it often provided a return freight for the wherries that carried a large part of the goods imported to Norwich up river from the port of Yarmouth. It is quite probable that the wherries which appear in Cotman's superb drawing known as *Trowse Hythe* (*fig. 10*) of c. 1808–10 were being used for marl carrying. As Rajnai has observed, if the traditional title of the drawing is correct, then the wherries are certainly close to Whitlingham, a hamlet on the River Yare just outside Norwich.[29]

Whether or not the boats in Trowse Hythe carried marl, they are unmistakeably wherries. This type of boat appears in paintings by all the major Norwich artists, and again, it is a more significant subject than it might appear at first sight. River traffic to the coast was vital to the economy of Norwich in the early nineteenth century, and it is no accident that the title of James Stark's important topographical work is *Scenery of the Rivers of Norfolk* (1834). The carrying trade was conducted entirely by keels and wherries. By 1800 the keel was on the way out, and wherries, which were peculiar to Norfolk, had become increasingly large and sophisticated in design.[30] Local histories and guidebooks show them to have been a source of considerable local pride, as they remained right into the twentieth century. The following account, which comes from Richard Beatniffe's *Norfolk Tour* of 1795, is typical: 'The KEELS and WHERRIES which navigate between Norwich and Yarmouth, are acknowledged to be superior to the small craft on any other stream in England, for carrying a larger burden and being worked at a smaller expense'.[31] It is

---

28   Kent 1794, p. 8.

29   Marshall 1787, vol. 2, p. 99. Marshall particularly emphasised that marl was carried from Whitlingham by wherries.

30   Clark 1961. On the wider issue of the river system, see Edwards 1965.

31   Beamiffe 1795, pp. 114–15.

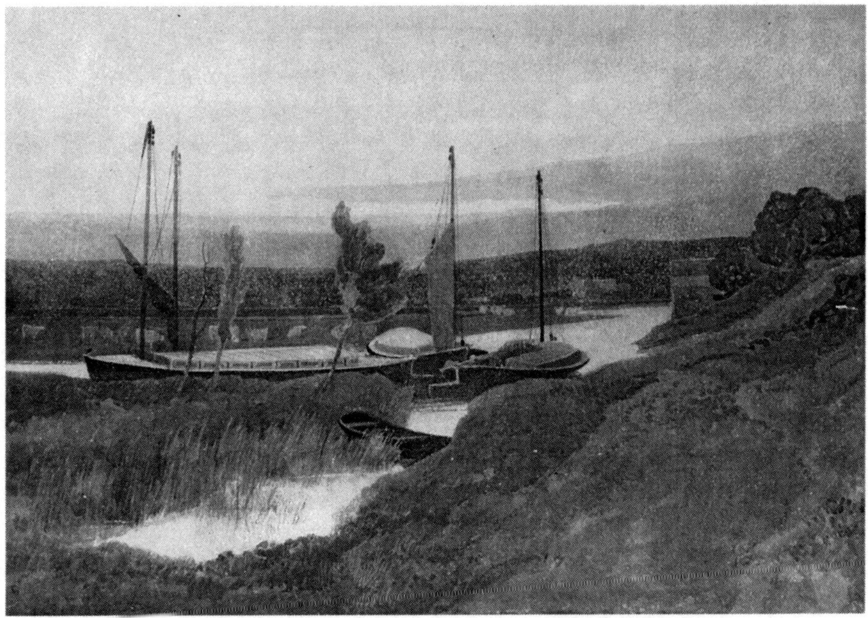

FIGURE 10   *John Sell Cotman,* Trowse Hythe, *c. 1808–10, watercolour, 12½ × 17⅜ in (31.6×44.2 cm)*
NORFOLK MUSEUMS SERVICE (NORWICH CASTLE MUSEUM AND ART GALLERY)

tempting to identify *Trowse Hythe* with Cotman's 1808 exhibit at the Norwich Society of Artists entitled *Norfolk Craft.*

To continue with the associations of agriculture, Norfolk farming was, as I have said, the pride of the local bourgeoisie and gentry. I am not, of course, suggesting that the Norwich bourgeoisie and the Norfolk gentry had identical interests and outlooks. The violence of Norwich politics in the late eighteenth and early nineteenth centuries partly signifies the conflict of interests between the city's bourgeoisie, many of whom were 'Jacobins' or reformers, and who ardently desired peace and a resumption of uninterrupted trade, and the county gentry, many of whom opposed reform at home and were also determined to defeat revolutionary France. Not that one can make simplistic equations between social groups and political outlooks, for, while there were large landowners such as Thomas Coke who were convinced reformers, so too there were ardent Tories among the Norwich manufacturers such as John Harvey.

In 1802, radical support in Norwich was still sufficiently strong to return William Smith, a notable dissenter and reformer, and the Whig Robert Fellowes in the July election, defeating William Windham and the Tory Frere by a clear if not overwhelming majority. However, when war broke out again in 1803, the widespread fear of invasion, together with a propaganda drive among the working classes, whipped up a new level of patriotic sentiment. Many former Norwich 'Jacobins' now backed the government's defence policies, which were even supported by *The Iris*, the radical Whig newspaper, edited by William Taylor. An ardent enthusiast for the French Revolution, who had visited Paris in 1790 to see for himself, Taylor now subscribed £25 to the local Volunteer Regiment and even considered enlisting in it.[32] Unanimity of support decreased in the years 1806–9, especially in the north of England where there was considerable agitation for peace, a minimum wage and constitutional reform. There were barricades in the London streets around the house of the Westminster Radical M.P. Sir Francis Burdett in 1810 and 1811–13 saw the fierce Luddite riots in Lancashire, Nottingham and Yorkshire. There were also divisions among the propertied classes between what has been called the 'old' and 'new' England, but the agitation of the new style capitalists, who with working-class support opposed the Orders of Council and the monopoly of the East India Company, and who were for peace in 1812, was successfully contained through timely concessions.[33] It was another stage in that process of compromise and adaptation between the bourgeoisie and landed interests which is such a notable characteristic of British history. On a general level it has been effectively argued that the wars with France deferred the crisis of oligarchic rule in Britain for a number of years and brought many in both gentry and bourgeoisie round to temporary support of the dominant elite. Improving landlord and manufacturing capitalist shared a fundamental ideology in political economy, and in this time of acute social unrest recognised a common interest in repressing dissent among the labouring classes. It is not, therefore, surprising that the Norfolk bourgeoisie could find much to admire in the capitalistic activities of the gentry.[34]

That a county which as recently as the seventeenth century had been noted for the poverty of its soil should become a model of progress and prosperity was, in the view of Cotman's contemporaries, 'a lesson in rural economy'.

---

32   For Norwich radicalism see Jewson 1975. For Taylor's initial response to the French Revolution, see Robberds 1843, vol. 1, pp. 68–9. By 1798 he had become increasingly 'antigallican' (vol. 1, p. 229), and his editorials in *The Iris* were strongly anti-French. [Since I published this, valuable additions to the history of Norwich politics have appeared in the form of the fine chapter on the subject in Rogers 1989, pp. 304–43, and Mark Knights essay 'Politics, 1660–1835', in Rawcliff and Wilson (eds.) 2004, pp. 167–92.].

33   See Emsley 1979, Chapters 6–8.

34   My interpretation of the relationship between the gentry and bourgeoisie derives from the debates between Perry Anderson, Tom Nairn, and Edward Thompson in the 1960s. See Introduction.

Charles II was reputed to have said that Norfolk should be cut up and used as roads for the rest of the kingdom. By contrast, George III called one of his two model farms 'The Norfolk Farm'. Eloquent tributes to Norfolk farming by Kent and Young appeared in the reports of the Board of Agriculture, and in 1829 one local historian observed that it had contributed more than any other single factor to the county's increasing population, its opulence, and the general 'elevation of its character'.[35] These improvements were said to have taken place in a remarkably short space of time. According to Nathaniel Kent, within a century the greater part of the county had been 'a wild, bleak, unproductive country, comparatively with what it now is; a full half of it was rabbit warrens and sheep-walks'.[36] In the early nineteenth century this improvement was particularly attributed to the exertions of Thomas Coke of Holkham, who received enthusiastic tributes from Norwich bourgeois like Dr Edward Rigby and Richard Bacon, editor of the *Norwich Mercury*. (John Crome was an errand boy for Rigby before he turned painter, and Rigby was Cotman's physician in 1812. Rigby was also a member of the Norwich Society of Artists from 1810 to 1817, and a patron of the Society from 1818 until his death in 1821.) Prior to Coke, it was said, scarcely 'an ear could be made to grow' in north-east Norfolk, but now 'the most abundant crops of wheat and barley wave over the entire district'.[37] Coke's reformist politics, as well as his practices as a landlord, endeared him to these local bourgeois, who strenuously recommended the improved agriculture, whatever its immediate social effects. Not that bourgeois opinion of improvement was uniformly favourable, and indeed Rigby's essay on Holkham, which was read at the Norwich Philosophical Society in December 1816, was intended to contradict charges made against Coke in the recent county elections that his system of farming had deprived the poor of employment and made corn dear (Coke was one of the main targets of anti-Corn Law demonstrators in Norwich in 1815–16). There were clearly differences of opinion amongst the local bourgeoisie as to whether the benefits of improvement outweighed the suffering it caused, but those such as Rigby, Bacon and Joseph Chambers who thought that it did, certainly had the authority of political economy on their side.[38] It was their view which accorded best with the predominant bourgeois outlook.

---

35   John Chambers, *A General History of the County of Norfolk* (Norwich and London, 1829), p. 21.

36   Kent, *General View*, vol. 1, 32.

37   Chambers 1829, pp. vi–vii.

38   Rigby 1817. Cf. Bacon 1844, pp. 1–5, and Chambers 1829, pp. xi and xxvii–xxviii. These texts are all somewhat later than Cotman's drawing, but comments in favour of improvement in

Given this background, the apparently non-committal view of agricultural landscape in Cotman's *Ploughed Field* (*fig. 11*) may not be as empty of meaning as it seems. Although the view cannot be identified, the drawing undoubtedly dates from *c.* 1808–10, and is almost certainly a view of Norfolk. At this time, the enclosure of wastes and commons and the turning of new land to the plough had strong local significance, and indeed, considering the role British agriculture was playing in the war effort, a patriotic significance too. It should be noted that several lines of hedges enclosing fields can be seen in this drawing, while the figure is one of those industrious local inhabitants whom the guidebooks praised as yeomen of 'truly English appearance'.[39] Thus what the view lacks in conventional picturesque features, it made up for in pleasing local associations, the cultivated expanse of the view being itself significant. The high prices of the war years had stimulated the pace of agricultural improvement, leading to new enclosures and the enclosure of wastes. From 1808 to 1812, the sequence of bad harvests took the price of grain to astronomical heights, causing considerable suffering amongst the poor and exacerbating social unrest. Thus Cotman's vista of improvement might signify profit and pride, but also a rather anxious hope. Cotman's sensitivity to Norfolk's improved agriculture is indicated by the well-known etching of a Norfolk plough in his *Liber Studiorum*, a plough which had already appeared in the watercolour *East Barsham Hall*, which is roughly contemporary with *A Ploughed Field*.[40]

In contrast to the clearly 'improved' landscape of *A Ploughed Field*, Cotman's three surviving views of Mousehold Heath depict apparently unenclosed wastes and sheep-walks, except in the British Museum's drawing (*fig. 12*), where a small piece of enclosure encroaches in the lower right.[41] Mousehold Heath on the north-east edge of Norwich was a popular subject with local artists. John Crome's painting in the Tate Gallery, which dates from *c.* 1815 (*fig. 48*), is probably the best known treatment of it, but Cotman also exhibited four views of the heath with the Norwich Society in 1809–10. The cause of Mousehold's popularity was certainly that it was a place of recreation for the townsfolk of

---

Beatniffe 1795 suggest that throughout this period the argument was frequently rehearsed in travel literature aimed largely at a middle-class readership. For a modern view of Coke, see Parker 1966. Amongst the middle-class radicals of Norwich in the 1790s, opinions varied as to whether or not enclosure was beneficial to society: See *The Cabinet. By a Society of Gentlemen*, 3 vols. (Norwich, 1795), vol. 1, pp. 45–58, and vol. 2, pp. 215–21.

39   Chambers 1829, p. cii.

40   Reproduced in Rajnai and Allthorpe-Guyton 1979, plate 43.

41   The other two versions are reproduced in Rajnai and Allthorp-Guyton 1979, plates 73 and 74.

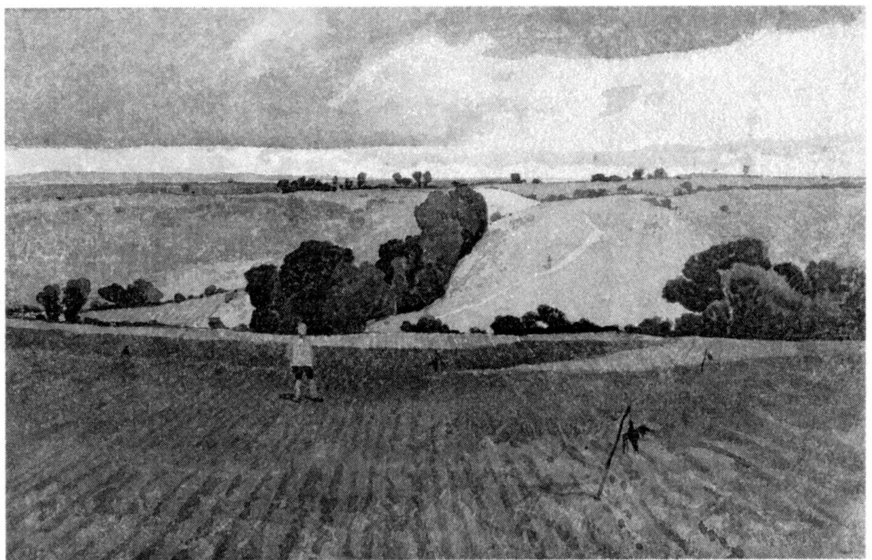

FIGURE 11   *John Sell Cotman,* The Ploughed Field, *c. 1808–10, pencil and watercolour, 9 × 13¾ in*
(*22.8 × 35 cm*)
© LEEDS MUSEUMS AND GALLERIES (LEEDS ART GALLERY) UK/BRIDGEMAN
IMAGES

Norwich. However, at the beginning of the nineteenth century this pleasure
ground was rapidly being enclosed, and thus closed to the inhabitants of the
city. This process inspired both a poem and a letter of protest, which were published in *The Iris* in April 1803. The author of the letter, who declared himself
a friend to enclosure in general, claimed that the heath had been a favourite
resort for 'many hundreds', who could be seen on a 'fine summer's evening',
engaged in sports and games: 'In short, it was the only place in the vicinity of
the city where it was possible to retire "from the busy hum of men", without
being choked with the dust of roads, and deafened with the succession of carriages'.[42] But now this free roaming over the heath was prevented by hedges. It
thus seems likely that the Norwich artists were intent on preserving for their
contemporaries a recollection of the heath as it had been, to record disappearing features of the landscape being, according to contemporary thinking, one
of the painter's functions.

---

42   The poem appeared in *The Iris*, 10, 9 April 1803. It mourned the loss of the heath, but at the
      same time welcomed 'the hand of Culture' and expanded on the pleasures derived from
      'the labours of the cheerful Swain'. The letter appeared in *The Iris*, 11, 16 April 1803.

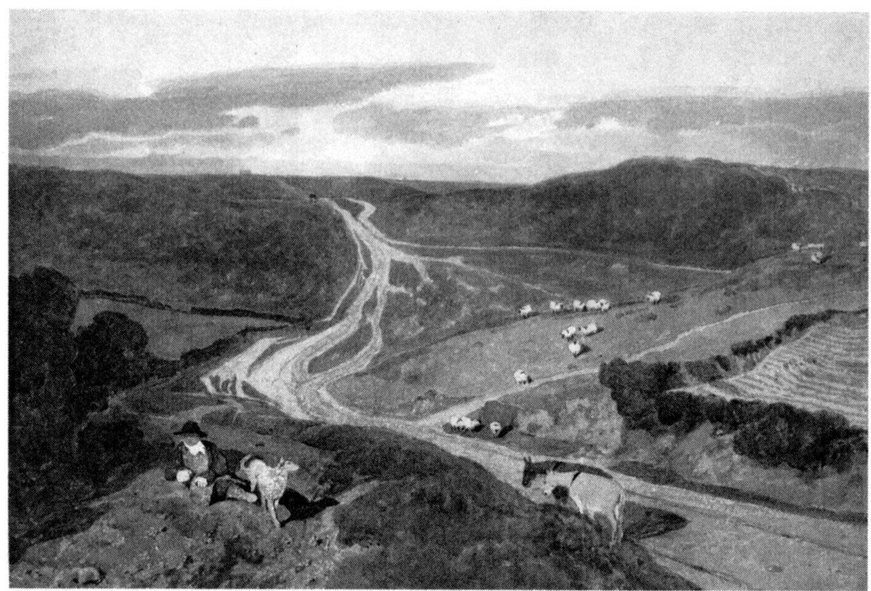

FIGURE 12   *John Sell Cotman,* Mousehold Heath, *c. 1809–10, pencil and watercolour, 11¾ × 17¼ in (29.9 × 43.6 cm)*
© THE TRUSTEES OF THE BRITISH MUSEUM

In the text to James Stark's *Rivers of Norfolk,* the local manufacturer and author J.W. Robberds complained that the theories of the political economist were misapplied when they were used to justify the sacrifice of an area necessary to the health of the city, and rich in pleasing associations, to yield such scant productivity. Robberds referred to the heath as the haunt of the Norwich schoolboys, of whom Cotman had been one, and there are other testimonies to its association with childhood. For the adult it provided more serious historical reminders: 'though other portions of our island may occupy more conspicuous stations in its public annals, or legends of romance, yet few there are which have combined in themselves a greater variety of interesting and memorable incidents'.[43] Inevitably the feature of the heath that stimulated the most emotive associations was Kett's Castle, the subject of a rather feeble vignette in Stark's work. So important was this landmark that a second poem had been inserted in *The Iris* on 23 April 1803, because the poem printed on 9 April had failed to mention it. The ruin had recently been

---

43   Robberds 1834 (not paginated). The association of the heath with childhood is confirmed by the poem in *The Iris,* no. 12, 23 April 1803: 'For ev'ry schoolboy well Kett's Castle knows'.

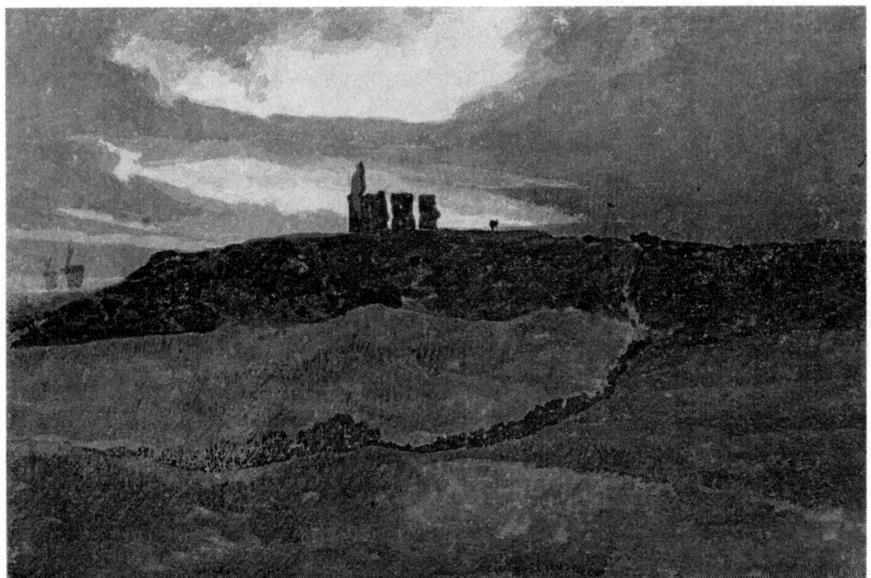

FIGURE 13   *John Sell Cotman,* Kett's Castle, Norwich, *c. 1808–10, watercolour, 8¾×12⅞ in* (22.1×32.5 cm)
NORFOLK MUSEUMS SERVICE (NORWICH CASTLE MUSEUM AND ART GALLERY)

rendered inaccessible by enclosure, and the second poem pleaded that it should not be razed as other ruins had been.

Kett's Castle so-called (in actuality the ruins of St. Michael's chapel) had been used by the Norfolk rebels led by Robert Kett in 1549. It was the subject of an impressive Cotman drawing of 1808–10 (*fig. 13*), which is probably that exhibited in 1810. Descending across the drawing from right to left is a hedge, which marks the line of an enclosure, while the patches of ochre and a reddish brown colour below the brow of the hill on the left suggest freshly cultivated ground, in contrast to the scrub and bushes immediately around the ruin. Kett's Castle is markedly different in mood from Cotman's other views of the heath. Rajnai has remarked on the 'heavy, brooding sky', which gives the 'weird silhouette' a 'special significance': 'Cotman has seldom, if ever, done a more abstract watercolor'.[44] However, the ominous dramatic effect was certainly intended to have a more than formal significance, since for the majority of the Norfolk gentry and bourgeoisie the name of Kett inspired fear, contempt and hatred. Not a guidebook or local history failed to condemn him and the rebellion he

---

44   Rajnai and Allthorpe-Guyton 1979, p. 82.

had led, although John Stacy did mention in his 1819 guide that arguments for the rebels had been aired.[45] The most complete eighteenth-century account of Kett's Rebellion is given in the third volume of Francis Blomefield's *History of Norfolk*, and it is unmitigatedly abusive about the rebels. Kett was a 'man hardy and fit for any desperate attempt' while his followers were 'scum' and a 'rascally crew'. Despite well-known testimony to their desperate bravery, the rebels were described as cowards, and worst of all they had had the temerity to ill-treat gentlemen. Their grievances, it was said, were an excuse for vandalism. Their religiosity was a sham: 'They openly declared great hatred against all *gentlemen*, whom they maliciously accused of covetousness, pride, extortion, and oppression, practiced against their tenants and the common people, and having thoroughly imbibed the wicked notions of the ancient *levellers*, they begin to put into execution their vile designs'.[46]

It is easy to see the causes of this opprobrium. Kett's Rebellion had been a well-conducted and initially peaceful protest against the erosion of customary rights, particularly by the abuse of commonage and to a lesser extent enclosure, led by men of substantial means who believed they were acting lawfully. Its aims were, in a sense, conservative, but the rebels did want to make the relationship between tenant and landlord more favourable to the former, and the 'Rebel's Complaint' has been described as 'A radical programme indeed, which would have clipped the wings of rural capitalism'.[47] Although twentieth-century historians have generally agreed that enclosure itself was not the main cause of complaint, it was said to be so in Blomefield's *History of Norfolk*, and also in the authoritative sixteenth-century account by Alexander Neville, which was well known in the eighteenth century. The intensely hostile reactions that Kett's name provoked were surely due to the obvious parallels between the Rebellion of 1549 and contemporary agrarian unrest, also in part occasioned by enclosure, which was to erupt into violence in East Anglia in 1816.[48] In this period of acute social unrest, when Norwich was a notorious centre of radical opinion, any resistance to so-called lawful authority was

---

45   Stacy 1832, p. 10.

46   Blomefield 1805–10, vol. 3, p. 223.

47   Bindoff 1949. This is the best modern account of the Rebellion, but still useful are Hammond 1933 and Tawney, 1912, part III. [When I wrote this, I was unaware of some more recent literature on the Rebellion, and particularly of MacCulloch 1979, which represents a fundamental rethinking of some aspects of the event based on hitherto unused archival sources.].

48   For the 1816 revolts see Peacock 1965 and more generally, of course, Thompson 1963, Chapter 7.

anathema to the majority of the county's propertied classes. Richard Beatniffe expressed the general view of Kett's Rebellion when he wrote: 'Popular tumult is the dangerous engine of malignant faction! and the pleasure arising from the hope of levelling all distinctions in society, one of the highest gratifications to a vulgar mind'.[49] According to Beatniffe, Kett and his cohorts had deserved their fate. Indeed, they had been treated leniently – despite the fact that 3,500 of their number had reputedly been slaughtered in the final battle. Not until 1859 was a sympathetic account of Kett written. It is testimony to the potent associations that the ruin on Mousehold Heath could conjure up that the author, Frederic Russell, observed in his preface: 'In the first place, then, I may confess to my readers, that the old ruin, overlooking Norwich, called to this day KETT'S CASTLE, now covered with ivy, has from childhood been to me an object of the deepest interest'.[50] For him Kett had been a childhood hero, and he became a symbol of the people's struggle against the injustices of feudalism.

There is little doubt, on the other hand, that Cotman and most Norwich artists were wholeheartedly patriotic in the period 1803–15, and identified with the outlook of the majority of the propertied. Although Cotman's father is known to have been a Whig voter, as was John Crome, we have seen that many one-time radicals and Whigs supported the government after the breakdown of the Amiens Peace. His fellow artists Robert Dixon and Joseph Clover both subscribed to the local volunteer regiment, and Dixon, together with the engraver Edward Bell, published a mezzotint of the uniform of the Norwich Rifle Corps, dedicated to its officers and volunteers.[51] There is abundant evidence in Cotman's correspondence of an acute self-consciousness about his own class status, not surprising in one who in his capacity as a drawing master was apt to be treated as a domestic servant. He showed a marked concern with 'respectability', and in his letters from France to his patron, the Yarmouth banker Dawson Turner, made comments both on the horrors of revolution and his distrust of liberals.[52] The counterpart to the sombre symbolism of *Kett's Castle* is Cotman's illustrations to the Reverend Robert Cory's *Narrative of the*

---

49   Beatniffe 1795, p. p. 118. See also Chambers 1829, p. 1009.

50   Russell 1859, p. vii.

51   Political differences among Norwich artists are suggested by the fact that the new rules of the Norwich Society of Artists, introduced in 1818, forbade political and theological discussions at the fortnightly meetings. The original rules of 1803 contained no such proviso. The Society's 'Articles' of 1803 and 1818 are reproduced in Rajnai 1976, pp. 6–12. The contribution of Norwich artists to another patriotic manifestation is discussed in Fawcett 1969.

52   For Cotman's comments on French politics see Kay 1926–7, part 2, pp. 116–17, 123.

Grand Festival at Yarmouth, published in 1814, a record of the victory fete organised by Yarmouth's burghers to promote social cohesion, and his etching of the Nelson Column (1817), a tribute to the local war hero. As late as 1823–4, Cotman exhibited a picture of clear patriotic significance, the *Dutch Boats off Yarmouth, Prizes during the War*, now in Norwich Castle Museum. By his treatment of the featureless masonry of Kett's Castle, Cotman made a compelling image that signified bourgeois dread of popular revolution. The contrast between this drawing and his other placid views of the heath indicates clearly his concern with precisely that unity of associations and effect, '*under the garb of simple and faithful imitation of nature*', recommended by Alison and Varley.

Cotman's increasing concern with medieval antiquities, which led him to produce a series of important etched publications between 1810 and 1822, was a direct result of the mania for antiquarianism and topography among the gentry and bourgeoisie. Indeed, Joseph Chambers, in the introduction to his *History of Norfolk*, explicitly linked the publications of Stark and Cotman with that 'laudable curiosity for county investigation'. In his letterpress to Stark's *Rivers of Norfolk*, Robberds referred to the artist's role as 'to snatch from utter oblivion those fleeting traits, on which depend some of the pleasures of the passing minute; and it is while he thus prolongs the vivid remembrance of our earlier enjoyments, that he helps to quicken in our bosoms the flow of generous feelings, and ministers to the kindliest impulses of our nature'. Stark and Cotman were both influenced by this patriotic ideology of antiquarianism, as well as by a general anxiety over the changes to the face of the countryside being brought about by modern agriculture, improvements in communications, and the 'almost daily multiplication of buildings' around Norwich.[53]

The city of Norwich was an object of considerable pride amongst the wealthier classes. It had changed drastically in the eighteenth century, but several guides still described it as 'a city in an orchard', and it was famous for its abundance of gardens.[54] Cotman's clearest celebrations of modern Norwich are the drawings of the Market Place which he exhibited in 1807 and 1809 (*fig. 14*). The

---

53   Robberds's remark should be compared with the following sentence from J.B. Crome's 'Essay on Painting and Poetry' (see note 22): 'Painting not only finds grace & decorations for the present hour, but a pleasure & solace for the future by preserving amidst the constant decay of Nature those frail & Perishable lineaments, on which in distant days the eye of affection long may fondly dwell, while the heart associates with them the soothing remembrance of its earliest feelings & its purest joys'. This may refer to both portrait and topography.

54   On the appearance of the city, see Christopher Barringer, 'The Changing Face of Norwich', in Rawcliffe and Wilson (ed.) 2004, Chapter 1.

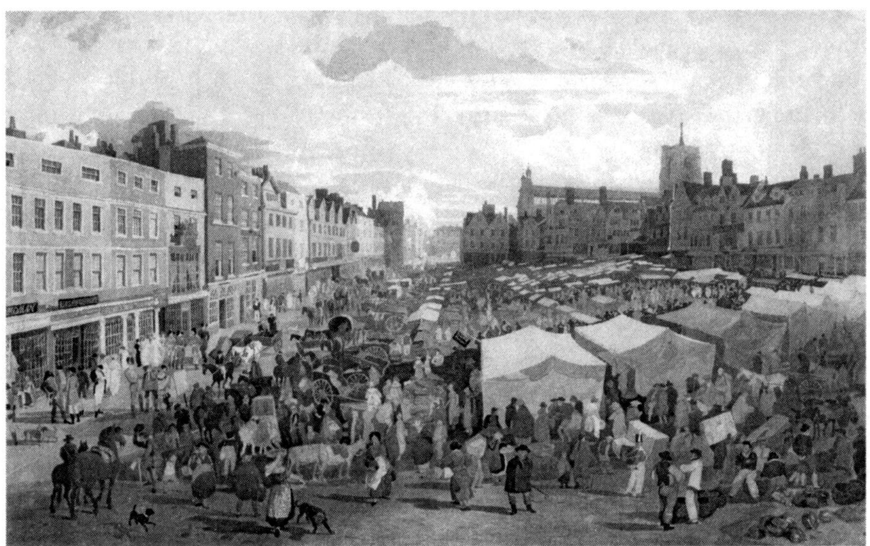

FIGURE 14   *John Sell Cotman,* Norwich Market Place, c. *1808–9, pencil watercolour,*
40.6 × 64.8 cm, Tate Britain
© TATE, LONDON, 2015

well-known drawing in Abbot Hall Art Gallery is likely to be the first of these, since the Norwich Society catalogue described the 1807 exhibit as a sketch, while the Tate Gallery's drawing is probably that of 1809.[55] An obvious symbol of economic vitality and progressive urban government, the Market Place had been paved in Scottish granite in 1731, while Gentlemen's Walk, which runs along the lower side of the market, had been paved in 1792. Cotman drew precisely the most fashionable part of Norwich, showing shops that were described as 'handsome and well-supplied' in 1829, and which by that date included news and billiard rooms. It is perhaps significant that the slightly larger finished drawing shows more of this side of the Market Place, while in the Kendal sketch the focus is more on the church of St. Peter Mancroft and the earlier houses on the west side of the market, Gentlemen's Walk being seen in shadow. In both drawings soldiers, sailors, farmers, labourers, and townspeople mingle together to make a virtual carnival atmosphere in a setting of which

---

55   Rajnai (ed.) 1982, p. 88. I disagree with Rajnai's view that the description of this drawing as a 'sketch' in the 1807 Norwich Society catalogue is 'difficult to understand'. Rajnai has accepted Marlin Hardie's argument that Cotman did not work in watercolour outdoors (p. 13). It seems to me that the evidence is against this conclusion. [For further discussion of this issue, see Hemingway 1997, pp. 196–9].

Chambers wrote: 'It is much doubted, whether any city in England has an open square of equal dimensions appropriated to a market, and the provisions sold are certainly nowhere excelled in the goodness of their quality, or the neatness of their display'.[56] According to one contemporary, writing in 1800, on market day, the 'parade-like' space 'emphatically called the Gentlemen's Walk', was thronged 'with a collection of very interesting characters; the merchant, the manufacturer, the magistrate, the provincial yeoman, the militia officer, the affluent, the thrifty and thriving tenant, the independent farmer, the officer, the clergy, faculty, barristers and all the various characters of polished and professional society'.[57] We may be sure that the half-starved textile workers, on whom so much of the city's prosperity depended, did not stroll there.

Apart from these two fine drawings of the Market Place, Cotman was mainly attracted to the antiquities of the city – not surprisingly, since they offered an even richer vein of associations than its modern features. Once again, Robberds supplies testimony for this point: 'In the view of an ancient city, like Norwich, the most prominent places are filled by objects which naturally direct the mind to those considerations [i.e. of the gallantry, heroism, and independence of our ancestors] and which are hence regarded with a warmth of feeling never excited by the tame regularity and cold elegance of modern terraces, crescents and squares'. Gothic antiquities, he tells us, can kindle a laudable feeling of national pride. This passage occurs in the text accompanying Stark's engraving of fourteenth-century Bishopsgate Bridge, a subject painted several times by Cotman.[58] In describing the view from this point, Robberds particularly emphasised the interesting ideas connected with the Castle, the city's most prominent antiquity. Cotman also drew this, exhibiting a sketch of the Castle in 1807, which is probably the drawing now in the Norwich Museum.[59] According to Robberds, the British are 'essentially a Gothic people', whose institutions, habits, tastes and spirit are all Gothic, and with whose character the Gothic style alone accorded. The venerable aspect of the Castle told of England's past glory; such decaying monuments were symbols of the decay of feudalism, which had paved the way for the nation's present commercial and industrial greatness. (Of course, in modern terms Norwich Castle is a Romanesque rather than a Gothic building, but although contemporary antiquarians clearly recognised a distinction between Saxon or Norman architecture in 'a barbarous imitation of the Roman manner' and Gothic, which they particularly associated

---

56　　Chambers 1829, p. 1102.

57　　The Reverend Joshua Larwood, quoted in Jewson 1975, p. 7.

58　　Examples are reproduced in Rajnai and Allthorpe-Guyton 1979, plates 2 and 41.

59　　Rajnai and Allthorpe-Guyton 1979, plate 46.

with the thirteenth century and after, it was easy for a non-antiquarian writer to refer loosely to any medieval building as Gothic.) Like so many nineteenth-century bourgeois, Robberds admired what he saw as feudal valour, but condemned the warrior squabbles of the Middle Ages as disruptive to trade.

Robberds was also stimulated to these reflections by the remains of the city's medieval fortifications, and particularly by the Devil's Tower, which was the subject of another of Stark's illustrations. Cotman had drawn this fourteenth-century structure in 1800, and later drawings of it are known, although none of them date from 1806–12. However, about 1807 he did make a watercolour of the better-preserved Cow Tower, which is now in a private collection.[60] Rajnai has suggested that in this and some other contemporary drawings, such as the *Interior of the Eastern Ambulatory of the Apse of Norwich Cathedral* (Ashmolean Museum), Cotman deliberately chose unprepossessing subjects to demonstrate his power of treatment of things in themselves unattractive.[61] Once again, a twentieth-century formalist outlook is being foisted on Cotman, which he cannot possibly have held, and which fundamentally misrepresents the character of artistic thinking in the early nineteenth century. For Cotman, not only was the tower redolent with meaningful associations, but its simple hulking form needed to be emphasised to draw them out. Robberds specifically recommended Cow Tower for the poetic effect of its massive outline in 1834, his description of the scene being strikingly close to Cotman's image, except in that he envisaged an evening effect while Cotman painted a broad daylight view.

The Castle apart, Norwich's most conspicuous medieval monument was the cathedral. Cotman made a series of watercolours of parts of the cathedral in c. 1807–8, one of the most notable being the *St Luke's Chapel* of 1808, now in the Norwich Museum (*fig. 15*). Rajnai has drawn attention to the alterations which Cotman made to the cathedral's structure in this drawing, notably the omission of the tower, the spire and some other features, and the aggrandisement of the chapel at the expense of the rest of the east end.[62] For him, this confirms Cotman's distinctive artistic personality; but, once more, I believe there is more to Cotman's approach than innate sensibilities can account for. If Cotman had an innate proclivity to simplification, it would be difficult to explain the late Gothic intricacies of the Abbatial House of Saint Ouen at Rouen and the many similar subjects he drew in the 1820s and 1830s, and which his letters suggest he undertook with no reluctance whatsoever.[63]

---

60   Rajnai (ed.) 1982, cat. no. 59, illustrated p. 106.

61   Rajnai (ed.) 1982, pp. 89, 100.

62   Rajnai and Allthorpe-Guyton 1979, p. 66.

63   For Cotman and the Gothic, see now also Wilcox 2012.

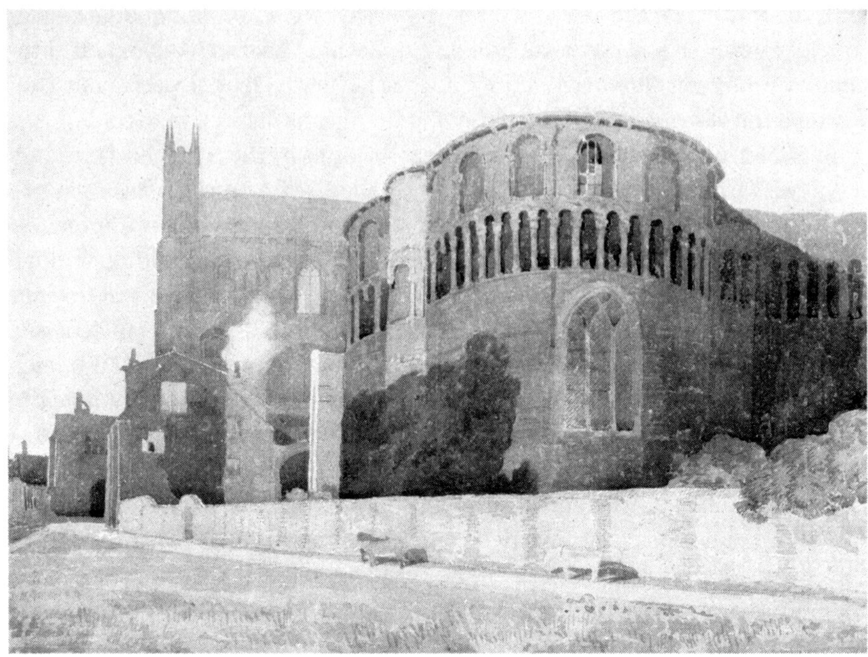

FIGURE 15   *John Sell Cotman,* St. Luke's Chapel, Norwich Cathedral, East, *1808, pencil and watercolour, 16 × 25½ in (35.2 × 46.1 cm)*
NORFOLK MUSEUMS SERVICE (NORWICH CASTLE MUSEUM AND ART GALLERY)

It seems likely that Cotman's simplification of the cathedral was conditioned by two interrelated factors: first, by the injunction to unity of effect and effacement of extraneous detail recommended by association aesthetics, and second, by a desire to concentrate on the earliest and most Norman part of the church. Norwich Cathedral, as Cotman would have known, was not very highly thought of by some contemporary antiquaries. 'Compared with many other cathedrals it is ... small in size and meagre in embellishment', wrote his friend the antiquarian publicist John Britton in 1816.[64] Britton particularly stressed the structure's dilapidation, and noted the raggedness and ruinous surface of the east end. He complained of the houses and other appendages attached to the east side of the south transept, which in Cotman's drawing are dwarfed by the bulk of the chapel so that the building's former splendour is contrasted with its present decay. However, Britton did strongly recommend the church as a particularly

---

64   Britton 1816, pp. 42–3.

fine example of Norman architecture, as did several contemporary guidebooks. Two of the major guides specifically singled out St Luke's Chapel as part of the original Norman foundation, begun by the bishop, Herbert de Losinga, in 1096.[65]

For at least one of Cotman's contemporaries, the architect William Wilkins, later Gothic additions to the church were a cause for regret. Wilkins wrote of fifteenth-century arches in the choir that while their execution and beauty might be admired, 'yet in the adoption of a taste so essentially different from the original work of the founder, we cannot but find cause to lament the loss of that simplicity and uniformity which constitutes taste chasteness & greatness of design, whatever the style of building may be'.[66] For many architectural writers in the early nineteenth century, Norman architecture was a symbol of a virile civilisation, which had overthrown the degenerate Saxons, and provided the ancestors of the nobility. Debates about the national origins of Gothic made the relationship between the ancient architecture of Norfolk and the architecture of Normandy a deeply interesting issue to contemporary antiquarians, and it was to fuel a great deal of Cotman's own antiquarian work. Thus Cotman's aggrandisement of St Luke's Chapel in this drawing may well have more than formal significance, for by this treatment he emphasised that simple massive quality which was felt to express the sobriety and virility of Norman culture, and which, for some of his contemporaries, also constituted 'taste chasteness & greatness of design'. Contemporary architectural writings suggest that Romanesque architecture was generally regarded as inferior to Gothic, but there was considerable interest in the origins of Gothic, and also, of course, a concern with uniformity of style, which Wilkins's note clearly illustrates.[67]

---

65   Chambers 1829, p. 1039; Stacy 1832, p. 132.

66   Repton 1965, text to plate 5.

67   The term 'Romanesque' was first applied to architecture in the English language in *An Inquiry into the Origins and Influence of Gothic Architecture* (1819) by the Reverend William Gunn, a Norfolk clergyman whose family were to be important patrons to Cotman. However, Gunn stood out against 'the tide of popular persuasion' in favour of Gothic – his use of the term Romanesque was correspondingly derogatory and it does not seem to have been immediately influential. A tendency to restrict the term Gothic to pointed architecture was noted as early as 1771 by the Reverend James Bentham in his *History of the Cathedral Church of Ely*, published in that year. Bentham himself disapproved of this use of the term, which he said was more appropriate to 'the old Roman way of building with round arches', as it had been practised by the Saxons and the early Normans (Bentham, reprinted in Thomas Warton et al., *Essays on Gothic Architecture*, 3rd ed., London 1808, pp. 74–6). Some years later, Francis Grose described the terminological situation thus: 'Most of the writers who mention our ancient buildings, particularly the religious ones,

I am not suggesting that once the probable associations of Cotman's subjects have been identified the meaning of his works is thereby established. To do so would be to mistake the image for the thing itself, to see the subject rather than the representation as the sign, and to reduce art to the level of ideology pure and simple. It would be as wrong to regard the subject in itself as the meaning of the work as it is to regard arrangements of colour and shape as the meaning. At any rate, with regard to Cotman, neither can be advantageously or necessarily separated from the other, or from the social discourses through which they are interpreted. Recent studies of Wilson and Monet confirm the enormous gains in aesthetic and historical understanding that can be made through rigorous investigation into the iconography and meanings of form in landscape painting.[68]

Obviously there must remain a unique and irreducible element in Cotman's art that resists historical explanation, but far more can be explained than formalist interpretations would lead one to think. This applies to his impulse towards simplification, or what is so misleadingly referred to as abstraction, in the drawings under discussion. As I have noted, this has been interpreted hitherto as some remarkable intuitive foresight, an anachronistic prophecy of tendencies in modernist painting. In fact, Cotman was only responding to the emphasis on simplification and unity of effect which he would have found in

---

notwithstanding the striking difference in styles of their construction, class them all under the common denomination of Gothic: a general appellation by them applied to all buildings not exactly conformable to some one of the five orders of architecture. Our modern antiquaries, more accurately, divide them in to Saxon, Norman, and Saracenic; or that species vulgarly, though improperly called Gothic'. (Francis Grose, *The Antiquities of England and Wales*, London, 1783–97, reprinted in *Essays on Gothic Architecture*, p. 75). Grose is particularly clear on the distinctions between what would be today described as Romanesque and the Gothic (pp. 100, 119–20). For both him and Bentham, the changeover from Norman to Gothic really takes place in the thirteenth century, Salisbury Cathedral being the key example of the new style (pp. 77–8 and 116). Similarly, G.D. Whittington, whose important and controversial *Ecclesiastical Antiquities of France* was published in 1809, distinguishes clearly between the Gothic and an earlier architecture in 'a barbarous imitation of the Roman manner', the former not achieving the 'utmost point of excellence' in France until the thirteenth century. Cotman took a copy of Whittington's book to France on his 1818 tour, and found it 'decidedly the best written book' he had read on the subject. It should then be clear that although the term Romanesque was not in use when Cotman made his drawing of St. Luke's Chapel, the differences between the Romanesque and Gothic styles had been firmly categorised, and this classification underlay Britton's recommendation of Norwich Cathedral as a fine example of 'Norman' architecture.

68   See Solkin 1982 and Tucker 1982.

both association aesthetics and contemporary academic theory. In the latter, the relevant concept was not association but *breadth*, a concept also important to John Crome.[69] According to academic theory, only through *breadth*, that is the simplification of light and shade into a meaningful compositional structure, could ordinary scenery be raised to aesthetic significance. James Barry was simply reiterating an accepted dictum when he wrote in his academic lectures with regard to the manipulation of chiaroscuro in everyday scenes: 'If ... selection be so necessary respecting objects intrinsically beautiful, how much more strenuously ought it to be endeavoured at, when we are obliged to take up with matters of less consequence?'[70] The simplification that we find in Cotman's watercolours of *c.* 1805–12, and in landscape paintings by a host of his contemporaries including Crome, Peter De Wint, Thomas Girtin, J.M.W. Turner, and John Varley, must be seen as part of an attempt to give importance to an inferior class of subject, and not just as a stylistic development which happened to occur. Cotman may have given these simplifications a personal twist, but the meaning they impart to his works, like the associations of his subjects, is only comprehensible in relation to the ideologies of his day.

Cotman's Norfolk drawings are not carriers of transcendent meaning directed at a timeless humanity, they were commodities produced for specific class groups, the Norfolk bourgeoisie and gentry of the early nineteenth century. For these groups, the drawings would serve not just as wall decorations or treasures for the portfolio, but also as records of a changing landscape and as complex works of art. In these latter two capacities they embodied various kinds of ideological matter. As I believe I have shown, the subjects of local agriculture and antiquities, far from being simply the accidentally chosen raw material for formal innovation, were selected because of their ideological resonance. However, Cotman's approach to his work, that is to the craft articles he made, was also informed by contemporary aesthetics and art theory. Like many contemporary watercolour painters, Cotman was struggling to give topography the status of serious art, for it was only by achieving this status that his social position as an artist could be secured. By his simplifications, by his subtle atmospheric effects, and by his calculated use of perspective, Cotman sought to signify to his public that his drawings were 'art' and not mere topography. The meanings of works do not therefore derive from the peculiar workings of an innate sensibility, which in some mysterious way transcends time, place, asso-

---

69   Crome's well-known reference to the concept of breadth occurs in a letter to James Stark of 1816. Clifford and Clifford 1968, pp. 90–1.

70   Wornum (ed.) 1848, p. 178.

ciation, and worldly concern; it derives from the complex of physical and social relations between these things. Cotman's innate sensibility, if such a thing can be conceived, did not give his works their status as aesthetic objects, nor even, in itself, their relative level of aesthetic value. These too are only given by particular historical circumstances.

In formalist criticism the meaning of works of art is discussed as if it were immanent in the material objects themselves. Art is treated as a natural rather than an historical phenomenon. Indeed, according to formalist aesthetics, history has no bearing on aesthetic value for great art is eternal: 'The essential quality in art is permanent'.[71] This arbitrary notion of a unitary aesthetic substance in art and its usual corollary, the idea of a single aesthetic state of mind, can only be justified by some form of idealism, and it is not surprising that Bell and Fry ultimately claimed for art a 'spiritual' or even a pseudo-religious status; indeed Bell even claimed that the perception of 'significant form' enables us to 'catch a sense of ultimate reality', of the Kantian noumena.[72] In fact, formalism is an ideological conjuring trick that spirits away the real historical meanings of works of art, and, by giving them a phony transcendental status, turns them into the religion of a few. For Bell and Fry alike, the majority of individuals 'will never be capable of making delicate aesthetic judgments'.[73] They regarded aesthetic sensibility as an innate characteristic, with which individuals are endowed in varying degrees, and that is socially mediated only in the sense that this natural proclivity is sometimes distorted by the demands of individual or collective patrons. Fry did hope for a reduction in social inequalities, since he believed that this would reduce the distortions of aesthetic judgment that arise from the function of art as a status symbol, but both Fry and Bell were distrustful of socialism, which they envisaged only as a species of statism that would reduce or destroy aesthetic liberty. Formalism thus posited a freedom from community through an asocial individualism, which has some affinities with the political individualism of bourgeois democratic theory, in that it depends on a notion of abstract individuals, who must be conceived as equals without reference to the social and historical structures that determine their consciousness and the extent of their power and influence. Thus the non-participation of the masses in aesthetic concerns is sanctified and indeed demanded. Few of them are capable of making 'delicate aesthetic judgments'; they are not so fortunately endowed.

---

71   Bell 1915, pp. 98, 102, 104.
72   Bell 1915, p. 54.
73   Bell 1915, p. 261.

In this respect bourgeois concepts of art and of aesthetic appreciation have not advanced a jot since the eighteenth century, since at least the interminable discussions of the standard of taste in that period openly accepted that the development of aesthetic sensibility, or taste, was only possible for those with wealth and leisure, and that this wealth and leisure derived from the labour of many others, who, though endowed with the same natural potentialities, would never have the opportunity to develop theirs. The introduction of universal suffrage in the bourgeois democracies has altered the system by which the hegemony of the dominant class groups is maintained, without fundamentally affecting the subordination of the masses. Just as bourgeois parliamentarianism poses as the ultimate in political liberty, so too formalism poses as a doctrine of aesthetic liberty, but both in reality effectively disqualify the masses from any real decision-making.[74] In the eighteenth century inequality was far more openly avowed in all aspects of life as a 'natural fact'. Cotman knew who he was painting for, and if we wish to understand his art, instead of merely genuflecting in front of it, we must learn to know his public and the ideologies which possessed it.

---

74 In Perry Anderson's words: 'The bourgeois state ... by definition represents the totality of the population, abstracted from its distribution into social classes, as individual and equal citizens ... Parliament, elected every four or five years as the sovereign expression of popular will, reflects the fictive unity of the nation back to the masses as if it were their own self-government. The economic divisions within the "citizenry" are masked by the juridical parity between exploiters and exploited, and with them the complete separation and non-participation of the masses in the work of parliament. This separation is then constantly presented and represented to the masses as the ultimate incarnation of liberty'. Anderson 1976, p. 26. Cf. Miliband 1969, pp. 265–7. For a commentary on some of the particular contradictions and limitations of the British parliamentary system see 'Democracy and Parliament' (1982), in Williams 1989, pp. 256–80.

Sheep as a Pictorial Motif: Pastoral and Counter-Pastoral

Like human figures, animals often featured in landscape paintings as so-called 'staffage'. But although this noun – derived from the German verb 'staffieren', meaning to decorate – implies a subordinate role, in fact animals often had a vital function in the larger meanings of works. Art objects are material artefacts with a distinctive effectivity that cannot be analysed adequately through an approach that treats them simply as 'reflections' of ideologies; but they are invariably interpreted in relation to the word, written or spoken, and it is from the complex interplay between the physical characteristics of the pictorial sign and the various discourses and experiences to which they are referred by different kinds of spectator that meanings arise.[1] In line with the work of John Barrell, Michael Rosenthal and others,[2] I assume that British nature poetry of the eighteenth and early nineteenth centuries articulates a complex mythology of rural life that offers crucial insights into the landscape painting of the period; indeed, that the forms and iconography of such painting were in some degree shaped by this literature. In what follows I argue that the imagery of domesticated animals in landscape paintings and prints referred the spectator to images and ideas in nature poetry that served to confirm prevailing ideas on the right order of property and the beneficence of the nation's political arrangements, but that this ideological ensemble came under pressure in the early nineteenth century due to social change and artists' shifting stylistic and formal objectives.

As my research on this theme developed, it became evident that my inquiries would focus on depictions of sheep and shepherds, partly for reasons of space and partly because in the poetry of rural life the shepherd was the prototypical rustic and played a correspondingly prominent role in landscape paintings. (The male focus is significant here in that the shepherdess simply does not figure in British romantic landscape art as she does in the paintings of rural life

---

1   When I conceived this essay in 1985, the principle semiological reference points were Barthes's 'Myth Today', in Barthes 1973, pp. 109–59, and 'Rhetoric of the Image', in Barthes 1977, pp. 32–51. I leave to one side here the difference between sign and image.

2   Barrell's discussion of Gainsborough's work in terms of pastoral and georgic modes of poetry was a major conceptual breakthrough. See Barrell 1980, pp. 6–16 and Chapter 1.

associated with Millet and other nineteenth-century French painters of rural life,[3] presumably because in reality young women did not perform the same function in Britain's proletarianised agriculture as they did in the French rural economy, where in many regions peasant structures still prevailed and labour was organised on a familial basis). As I will show, changing farming practices and social relations in the British countryside made such usage of the shepherd carry increasingly anachronistic connotations.[4] Because the significance of animals is given by their place in the totality of the art work, I hope that the reader will bear with me in what may seem some long digressions to establish the character of those larger wholes.

Sheep and Shepherds in British Nature Poetry

Given Pope's standing within the national literary tradition, we can assume that educated visitors to the Royal Academy summer exhibitions would have been familiar with his *Pastorals* (1709) and his *Discourse of Pastoral* (1717). Some idea of the continuing currency of the former is suggested by the fact that Robert Bloomfield's poem *The Farmer's Boy* (1800) could carry as a motto on its title page the unattributed line 'A Shepherd's Boy ... he seeks no better Name!', which opens Pope's 'Summer'. Yet if this illustrates an ideology of continuity in the literary tradition – as well as implying an outlook of contented subordination – it should also indicate how insubstantial that chain of associations was, for Bloomfield's 'Giles' is very different from 'Hylas' and 'Ægon' (shepherd's names taken from the *Idylls* of Theocritus) and the other shepherds of Pope.

In the *Discourse on Pastoral*, Pope describes keeping flocks as 'the first employment of mankind' and suggests that poetry originated from the songs of those first shepherds: 'And since the life of shepherds was attended with more tranquillity than any other rural employment, the Poets chose to introduce their Persons from whom it received the name of Pastoral'.[5] Of course, Pope emphasised that it was only the shepherds of 'what they call the Golden age' who had enjoyed this felicity and only in that remote time had the 'best of men'

---

3   I am thinking here particularly of Millet's *Shepherdess and her flock; la grand bergère* (1862–4; Musée du Louvre), a work widely seen as marking a turning point in his work towards a more idyllic view of peasant life. See Herbert 1976, pp. 131–49.

4   Two important catalogues devoted to images of rural labour that appeared since the first version of this essay was written are Spargo 1989 and Payne 1993.

5   Alexander Pope, 'A Discourse on Pastoral Poetry', in Pope 1969, pp. 3, 4.

followed the occupation. (Presumably such men were proprietors of their own flocks and not hirelings of others like contemporary English shepherds for the most part). The contemporary poet must not describe shepherds as they really are in his own day, although he should include some details of rural affairs to make his composition seem 'natural'. Moreover, only the 'best side' of the shepherd's lot should be pictured; its miseries must be concealed, as such poems were concerned not so much with the 'business' as with the 'tranquillity of a country life'.[6]

As Raymond Williams has shown,[7] Pope's view of the pastoral needs to be situated in a continuing debate over the character of pastoral poetry in the seventeenth and eighteenth centuries and it is much closer to the aristocratic courtly version than it is to that of some of the later eighteenth-century poets, who in response to the new interests of agricultural capitalism and its accompanying political forms sought to identify their idealised vision with a contemporary British reality.[8] But in the single most revered monument of the eighteenth-century nature poetry tradition, James Thomson's *The Seasons* (1726–46), Pope's prescriptions still prevail in important ways. It seems that whenever Thomson thinks of what he calls the 'swain', it is a shepherd who first comes to mind, and agriculture in the poem tends to centre more on flocks and herds than on tillage.[9] In the 'Hymn' that ends the poem, Thomson refers to the deity symptomatically as the 'GREAT SHEPHERD', and when he describes those who should make the hymn in 'rural shade' (as opposed to 'swarming cities vast') it is the shepherd who stands for the countryman.[10] Sheep and shepherds were central to a tradition of pastoral poetry going back to Theocritus and Virgil, but as this reminds us they were also central to Christian symbolism.

---

6   Pope 1969, p. 4.

7   Williams 1975, pp. 30–3 and *passim*.

8   One measure of this is the fierce critique of Pope's *Pastorals* by the radical democrat John Thelwall, who described them as the worst pastorals of modern times, only redeemed in some degree by the beauty of their versification: 'The scenery and the sentiments, the characters and the manners, the age and the superstitions, are such as no stretch of the most compliant and credulous imagination can associate together for an instant'. Thelwall particularly objected to the idea that there was any poetic character to 'hedge-cockney shepherds' of the type that could be found at Windsor given its proximity to the metropolis. See 'On Pastoral Poetry', in Thelwall 1822, pp. 56–61.

9   'The Seasons', in Thomson 1908: 'Summer', l. 63, l. 220, l. 284. Cf. 'Winter', l. 208.

10   Thomson 1908: 'A Hymn', l. 74 and l. 91.

Thomson repeatedly associates sheep with the idea of rural peace.[11] Sheep are innocent and harmless, referred to as 'soft flocks', 'ye peaceful people', a 'harmless race', and 'soft, fearful people'.[12] They also tend to be associated with mountains or desolate regions like the Scottish Isles.[13] (Turner's water-colour of *Hind Head Hill* of circa 1808 [*fig. 16*], a view in Surrey engraved for the *Liber Studorium*, seems to capture precisely this poetic topography.) Thus Thomson refers to 'bleating mountains' in contrast to the 'lowing vale',[14] and one part of the joyful vision of natural and social harmony in the well-known prospect of 'Happy Britannia' in 'Summer' is the mountains where 'flocks bleat numberless'. In this 'prospect', the valleys and meadows are the site of the harvest, while 'blackening herds in lusty droves' 'rove bellowing on the mountain side!'[15] Cattle and sheep ('herds and flocks') do mingle around brooks and rivers in the hottest days of summer when:

> ... on the grassy bank
> Some ruminating lie; while others stand
> Half in the flood, and often bending sip
> The circling surface.

But here the rustic is a contented cowherd:

> Amid his subjects safe,
> Slumbers the monarch swain; his careless arm
> Thrown round his head, on drowsy moss sustain'd;
> Here laid his scrip, with wholesome viands fill'd;
> There, listening every noise, his watchful dog.[16]

In this image not only is the 'swain' well-fed and so lightly employed that he can sleep in the noonday shade, but he rules over the animal kingdom just as his social superiors rule over him, in a telling instance of natural theology.[17]

---

11   Thomson 1908, 'Spring', l. 918; 'Summer', ll. 233–8.

12   Thomson 1908, 'Summer', l. 1153; 'Spring', l. 359; 'Summer', l. 388, l. 378.

13   Thomson 1908, 'Autumn', ll. 862–74; 'Winter', ll. 757–9.

14   Thomson 1908, 'Autumn', ll. 1266–7.

15   Thomson 1908, 'Summer', ll. 1450–1.

16   Thomson 1908, 'Summer', ll. 486–9, ll. 493–7.

17   Bloomfield provides a similar image of Giles taking a nap while bird nesting in *The Farmer's Boy* ('Summer', l. 71–4). In his massively successful *Analogy of Religion*, Bishop Butler stressed that the social and natural orders appeared by analogy 'to be a Scheme,

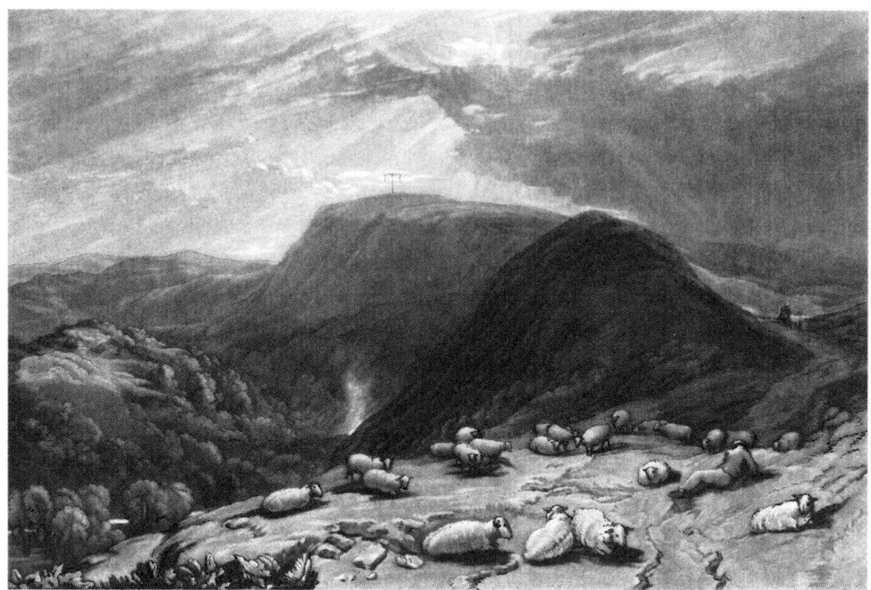

FIGURE 16   *Robert Dunkarton after J.M.W. Turner,* Hind Head Hill *for the* Liber Studorium, *etching, mezzotint and drypoint on paper, 7 × 10¼ in (17.8 × 26.0 cm) Tate Britain, London*
© TATE, LONDON, 2015

The kind of genteel image that seemed appropriate to accompany Thomson's poetic vision in the 1820s is indicated by Westall's design from 1825 (*fig. 17*). The difference between this and the far more convincing labourer in the wood engraving by John Anderson on the opening page of 'Spring' in the fourteenth edition of Bloomfield's *Farmer's Boy* from 1820 (*fig. 18*) indicates something of how the differences between the poems were understood at this juncture.[18]

System, or Constitution, whose Parts correspond to each other, and to a Whole; as neatly as any Work of Art, or as any particular Model of a civil Constitution and Government. In this great Scheme of the natural World, individuals have various peculiar Relations to other individuals of their own Species. And whole Species are, we find, variously related to other Species, upon this earth'. Butler 1736, p. 65.

18   For the complex history of illustrations to Bloomfield's poem, see Bruce Graver, 'Illustrating *The Farmer's Boy*', in White, Goodridge, and Keegan (eds.) 2006, pp. 49–69. Graver proposes that while Anderson's wood engravings for the first edition were primitivist in style and matched the georgic tone of the poem, the publishers inserted additional or replacement illustrations by other engravers in later editions that softened the georgic effect and implied the poem had a more pastoral tenor (pp. 55–62).

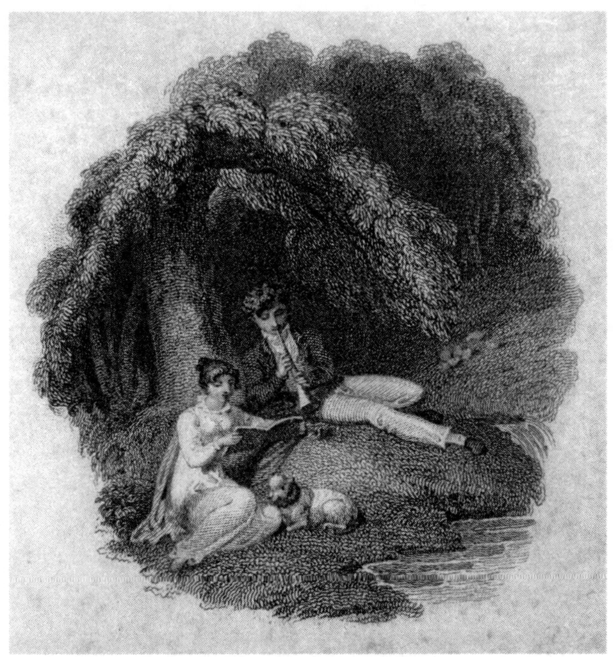

FIGURE 17
*Charles Rolls after
Richard Westall, 'Hymn',
engraving from James
Thomson,* The Seasons,
1825 edition
PHOTO: AUTHOR

However, it should be noted that the frontispiece does not depict Giles, but an unnamed ploughman, and the ploughman may be considered the georgic antonym of the pastoral shepherd in the same way as in Barthes's *Mythologies* wine is the opposite of milk.[19] In the poem, it is Giles, worn out from harrowing, who sits down on a 'green headland' and enjoys a moment's rest from toil on 'the friendly Bank's refreshing seat'.[20] The ploughman is granted no such respite.

Generally speaking, later poets too tried to relate the contemporary rural scene to ideas of peace, virtue, and social harmony, which were presented as permanent characteristics of rural life, to be contrasted with the vices and depravity of the city. Thus Cowper in *The Task* (1785) writes,

> So manifold, all pleasing in their kind,
> All healthful, are th' employs of rural life,

---

19   Barthes 1973, pp. 58–61.

20   Bloomfield 1998, p. 25, 'Spring', ll. 83–4. I have used the first edition of this selection rather than the second of 2007, because it reprints the text of the poem as it appeared in *Poems of Robert Bloomfield* (1809), which would have been the text as Bloomfield's contemporaries knew it.

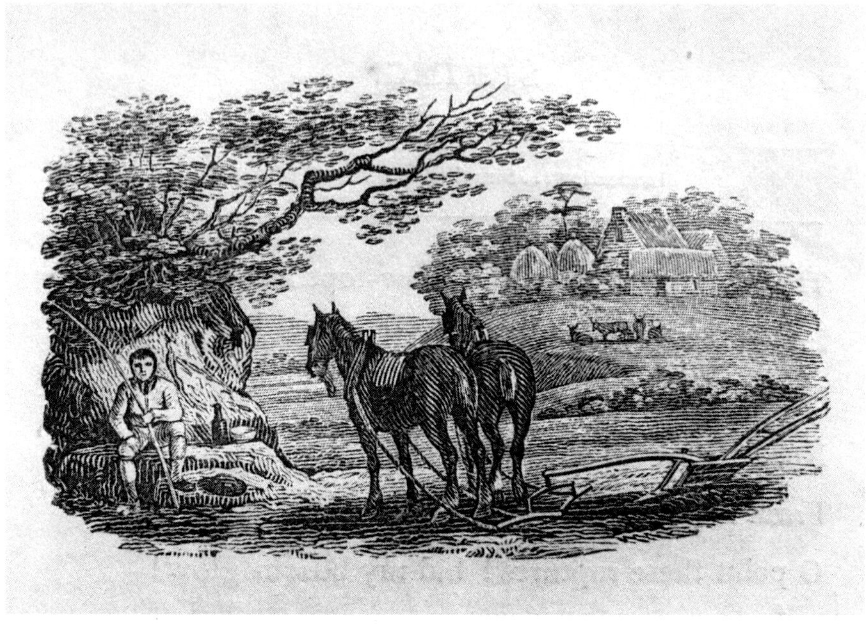

FIGURE 18   *John Anderson, 'Spring', wood engraving, from Robert Bloomfield,* The Farmer's Boy;
a Rural Poem, *14th edition, 1820*
PHOTO: AUTHOR

> Reiterated as the wheel of time
> Runs round; still ending and beginning still.[21]

And, of course:

> God made the country, and man made the town.[22]

Such views were closely linked with an ambiguous and contradictory attitude
to the contemporary political social order, as poets and other commentators
invoked the virtues of an earlier time and place to point up problems endemic
to the capitalistic social forms that were penetrating more and more aspects of
life. With increasing emphasis on the rigors or even harshness of the labourer's
lot, the shepherd, so intrinsically connected with the pastoral, became a less rel-

---

21   *The Task*, in Cowper 1926, Book 3, ll. 624–7.

22   Cowper 1926, Book 1, l. 749. For Cowper's political and social vision, see Everett 1994, pp. 71,
73.

evant figure and other kinds of agricultural occupation assumed a new importance in verse increasingly georgic in character. Indeed, by 1750, John Barrell has
suggested, georgic was 'the dominant mode of the poetry of rural life'.[23] But this
was a question of degree, not a total shift, and the shepherd remained a key
symbol, as the poetry of Bloomfield, Clare, and Wordsworth testifies. Moreover,
in the landscape art of Gainsborough – arguably the most important formulation of a distinctive British rural iconography in the eighteenth century –
the pastoral remained a recurrent theme, even if one increasingly translated
to seemingly remote mountainous regions (*fig. 19*). That remoteness is surely
the sign of a retreat not just from the world of urban modernity, but from
the modernity of the improved agriculture as well; it is the counterpart to the
intimations of poverty and social disharmony Barrell traced so persuasively in
Gainsborough's rustic genre scenes.

Poetic Captions: Thomson and Bloomfield

Early nineteenth-century exhibition catalogues are peppered with entries for
landscapes or rustic genre scenes that insert quotations from nature poetry to
accompany the picture titles:

283. J. Clover. Haymakers – Vide Thomson's 'Seasons'. (Royal Academy, 1806)
10. J. Clover. Harvest – Vide Bloomfield's Farmer's Boy. (Royal Academy, 1807)
34. J. Crome. Grove-Scene, with sheep
 'Nor undelightful is the ceaseless hum
 To him who muses thro' the woods at noon,
 Or drowsy shepherd as he lies reclined,' Thomson. (Norwich Society of
 Artists, 1806)

Constable, Turner, Crome and many others made occasional use of this practice, the significance of which varied. In some cases the poetic idea seems to
have had a determinate influence on the choice of subject and even on the way
it was represented, as in Turner's *England: Richmond Hill on the Prince Regent's
Birthday* (1819; *fig. 108*).[24] In others the poetry seems more probably an afterthought, tagged on to point to relevant associations in the discourse of poetic
rusticity, or simply to emphasise that landscape painting had the same capacity

---

23   Barrell 1983, p. 108.
24   I analyse this work at length in Hemingway 1992, pp. 241–4. But see also Chapter 11.

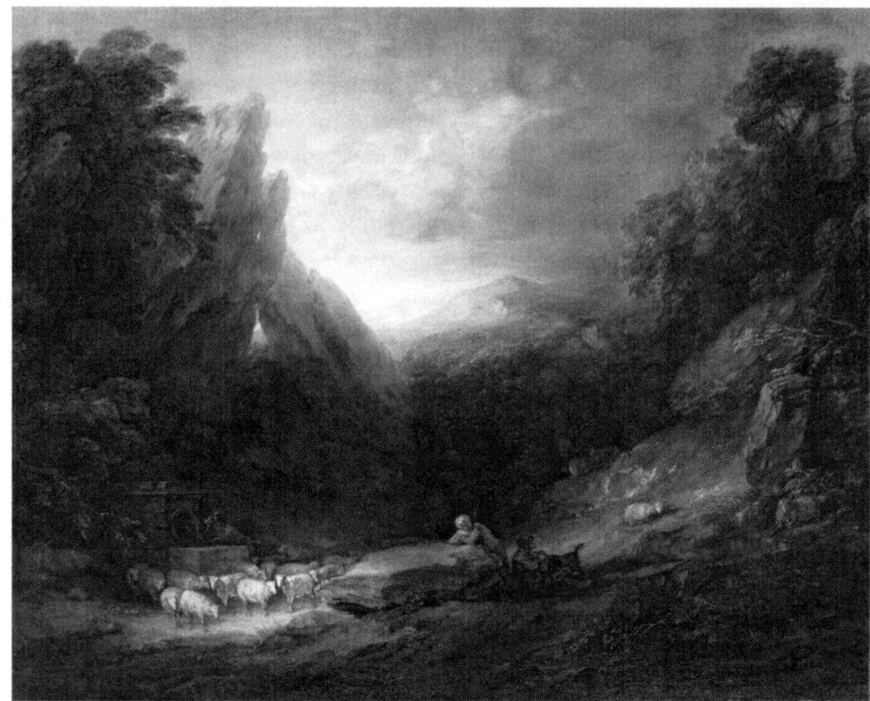

FIGURE 19   *Thomas Gainsborough, R.A. (1727–1788)*, Romantic Landscape with Sheep at a
Spring, *ca. 1783, Given by Miss Margaret Gainsborough, 1799, oil on canvas, 60½ ×
73½ (153.7 × 186.7 cm)*
PHOTO: © ROYAL ACADEMY OF ARTS, LONDON; PHOTOGRAPHER: PRUDENCE
CUMING ASSOCIATES LIMITED

as poetry to trigger complex chains of ideas and deserved comparable cultural
dignity. I suspect Constable's motivation for citing the lines from Bloomfield's
The Farmer's Boy that accompanied the catalogue entry for *Landscape. Ploughing Scene in Suffolk* (1814; *fig. 20*) was of the latter type.

> But unassisted through each toilsome day,
> With smiling brow the ploughman cleaves his way.[25]

---

25   Bloomfield, *The Farmer's Boy*, 'Spring', ll. 71–2. For analyses of this motif, see Barrell 1980,
      pp. 149–55; Rosenthal 1983, pp. 68–78. The *Farmer's Boy* was extraordinarily successful,
      selling 26,000 copies between 1800 and 1806 and going through fourteen editions before
      Bloomfield's death in 1823. Moreover, despite the fact that in his preface the Whig lawyer
      and writer Capel Lofft – who helped get the poem published – advertised the poet's
      contacts with artisanal radical circles, it had no overt political stance and appealed to

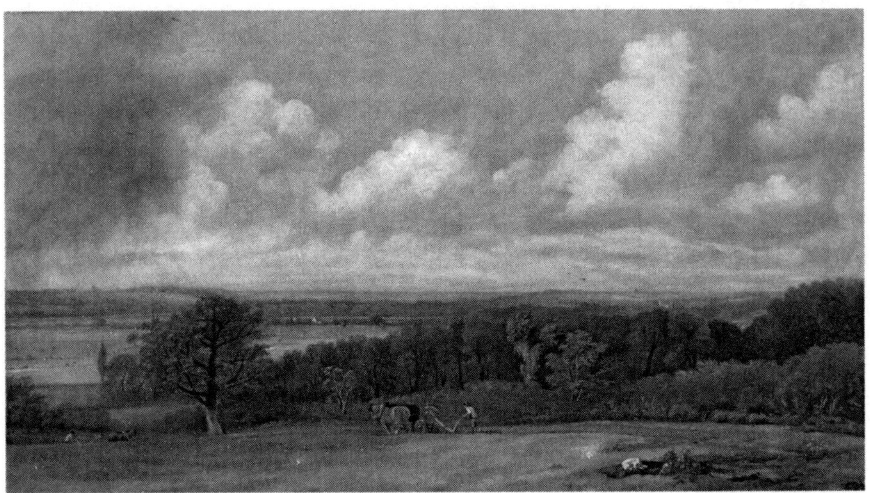

FIGURE 20   *John Constable (1776–1837)*, Ploughing Scene in Suffolk, *1824 to 1825, oil on canvas, Yale Center for British Art, Paul Mellon Collection. This is a copy of the painting exhibited in 1814.*

Constable was coat-tailing on Bloomfield's popular success. But we can assume that one of the intended effects of such quotations was to anchor the images concerned in relation to particular associations of different aspects of rural life, although obviously the meanings of the paintings were not confined to such references and could be informed by other discourses (such as those of the agricultural reports of the period)[26] and individual experiences (whether the viewing subject had direct knowledge of rural life, and if so of what kind).

Thomson was still much revered and widely read in the early nineteenth century, when *The Seasons* was published in numerous editions. However, while that poem's generalised imagery of rural life seems well-suited to complement the more overtly mythical imagery of rural England that Constable concocted in such pictures of the 1820s as *The Cornfield* (1826; *fig. 27*) or *Hadleigh Castle* (1829; Yale Center for British Art),[27] it matches less well with the specific naturalism of many of his landscapes of the years circa 1805–20, such as the *Landscape. Ploughing Scene in Suffolk.* As Constable evidently understood, Bloomfield's poem – which was also set in Suffolk, although the poet's

---

reviewers across the political spectrum. See William J. Christmas, 'The Farmer's Boy and Contemporary Politics', in White, Goodrich, and Keegan (ed.), pp. 2006, pp. 27–30.

26   Barrell 1972, Chapter 2.

27   Rosenthal 1983, pp. 174–80, 214–18.

birthplace Honington, in the northwest of the county, was far away from the Vale of Dedham – corresponded better with his more precise and seemingly mundane depictions of agricultural labour. Divided into books of each season, *The Farmer's Boy* is obviously modelled on Thomson's poem, but one register of its different class voice is the fact that it was written in rhyme rather than blank verse. Its account of rural life is also couched in far more specific and detailed terms, presenting an account of an individualised rustic living in a specific place and not a generalised panorama of the phases of the year that shifts between national and global. All in all, *The Farmer's Boy* evokes very different ideas of rural England from Thomson's 'Happy Britannia'.

Although Giles's master is 'generous', no tyrant, he never 'lack'd a job for *Giles* to do' and Bloomfield consistently emphasises the cares and toils of rustic existence: 'His life was constant, cheerful servitude'.[28] When in 'Winter' his master explains to Giles how relatively well-off he is, it is only by comparison with the sufferings and dangers of a ship's boy.[29] Just as 'Dobbin', the hardworked, patient farm horse is only relatively better off than the post horse.[30] Yet even if his lot is hard, Giles does have moments of rest (on Sunday) and contemplation, and he has a benevolent master – the poem is relentlessly paternalistic and significantly describes Giles as 'meek' and 'fatherless'.[31] But Bloomfield also emphasises how old customs and traditions are dying out, as fashion and 'refinement' break up the social cement that had once bound the rural world into a cohesive, healthy whole. In some passages in the poem he strains to fit the ideas he knows to be proper to the poetry of rural life with his first-hand knowledge of its modern day realities and at one point the poet's vision of rural contentment is explicitly contrasted with the presentday experience.[32]

Consonant with the prevailing natural theology, *The Farmer's Boy* ends with a hymn of praise to the divine order in which Bloomfield leads on from an image of Giles caring for his flock, with its 'fourscore ewes',[33] to the affirmation

---

28   Bloomfield 1998, p. 3, l. 6.

29   Bloomfield 1998, p. 36, ll. 111–26.

30   Bloomfield 1998, pp. 37–8, ll. 159–98.

31   Bloomfield's own father died young and his mother remarried. Something of this paternalistic tenor arose from the preface and editorial interventions of Capel Lofft – see White 2007, p. 11.

32   Bloomfield 1998, pp. 20–22; ll. 333–400. As White shows, Bloomfield offered a critique of contemporary society that was partly premised on recollections of an earlier organic social order that was essentially hierarchical (White 2007, pp. 21–30).

33   Bloomfield 1998, p. 3, 'Spring', l. 53.

of the deity as the 'MIGHTY SHEPHERD'. The idea of a divine and benevolent plan of nature sits even more uncomfortably with the representation of a social order that has certain depraved aspects than it does in Thomson's *The Seasons*. For while in the earlier poem corruption and vice are centred in the cities – which act as a foil to the virtuous country – in *The Farmer's Boy* refinement and fashion have begun to pollute the countryside itself.[34] Yet despite his awareness of social change and his emphasis on the harshness of Giles's lot, the rural world remains for Bloomfield the realm of moral and physical health and of the proper order of social relations. His far more down-to-earth and precise descriptions, together with his emphasis on contemporaneity, made his verses a more appropriate reference point for the specific topographical imagery and naturalistic style of Constable's 1814 ploughing scene than anything the artist could have found in Thomson's works. When we consider the larger complexion of Bloomfield's worldview, Constable's overcast sky and his rustic drudge alone behind the plough seem at one level to find their poetic counterpart very nicely in his text, implying a world of compliant submission, if not great happiness. However, at a deeper level there is a rub between the two in that Bloomfield is clear that the social order he is describing is a thing of the past – a fact reinforced by indications that the farm where Giles works is, unlike that in Constable's painting, unenclosed.[35]

The Pastoral and the Historical Past

While Bloomfield might seem a more relevant source for early nineteenth-century artists, Thomson's poem remained an armoury of ideological tropes in which animal husbandry was central. Two passages in *The Seasons* that involve sheep stand out as images that offer parallels with pictorial motifs. In 'Spring' Thomson describes a shepherd 'on a mountain brow' 'inhaling the descending sun', who feeds his numerous flock while lambs frisk around. The site of their gambols is a 'mossy mound' that was once the rampart of 'iron war' in 'ancient barbarous times':

---

34   This was not a new idea. Goldsmith lamented the evaporation of social cohesion that accompanied the spread of luxury in *The Deserted Village* (1770), while Cowper laments the decline of rural virtue in *The Task* (1785), Book 2, ll. 744–810; Book 4, 429–612. Cowper's prolonged complaint is that 'the town has ting'd the country' (Book 4, l. 553).

35   See White 2007, p. 12. Although Bloomfield opposed enclosure (p. 17), this attitude does not find expression in *The Farmer's Boy*.

When disunited Britain ever bled,
Lost in eternal broil: ere yet she grew
To this deep laid indissoluble state,
Where wealth and commerce lift their golden heads;
And o'er our labours Liberty and Law,
Impartial, watch; the wonder of a world.[36]

Thus Thomson contrasts the pastoral peace and rural innocence of the present, of which shepherd and flock are emblems, with a remote and troubled past in which the social order was far from its present state of perfection. What is occluded at this point by the rustic scene is any idea of the contemporary rural economy of which the shepherd is a part, or any notion of the city where wealth, commerce, and power really centre. The city does figure elsewhere in the poem and sometimes Thomson seems enamoured of its spectacle, but mainly he presents it as the site of vice and political corruption.[37] The perfection of the present is thus denoted paradoxically by the idea of what was seen as one of the oldest human occupations, and by the pastoral peace of a class to which neither the author nor his readership belonged.

Thomson's passage was cited directly by Constable in the unpublished letterpress for the series of mezzotint prints engraved after his works by David Lucas that was to have been titled *Landscape, Characteristic of English Scenery*, written between 1832 and 1834. The quotation appears in the text accompanying the plate of Old Sarum (*fig. 21*), which was based on an oil sketch of 1829 and is also related to a watercolour shown at the Royal Academy exhibition in 1834 as *The Mound of the City of Old Sarum, from the south* (both oil sketch and watercolour are in the Victoria and Albert Museum).[38] According to Constable, Thomson 'happily contrasts the playfulness of peaceful innocence with the horrors of war and bloodshed'.[39] As in a number of his later paintings, and notably *Hadleigh Castle*, Constable was concerned to suggest the idea of the transience of human works, and he emphasises in the letterpress that of this 'once proud and populous city' nothing remains but the site.[40]

---

36   Thomson 1908, 'Spring', ll. 853–8.

37   Thomson 1908, 'Spring', ll. 939–40; 'Autumn', l. 963–9, ll. 1235–49; 'Winter', l. 630–45. On the contradictions in the poem, see Barrell 1983, pp. 54–79.

38   For oil sketch and mezzotint, see Parris and Fleming-Williams 1991, pp. 345–7. For the watercolour, see Parris, Fleming-Williams, and Shields 1976, pp. 177–8; Reynolds 1984, p. 257.

39   Constable 1970, p. 25.

40   *Hadleigh Castle* was also shown with a quotation from Thomson's *Seasons*, which is

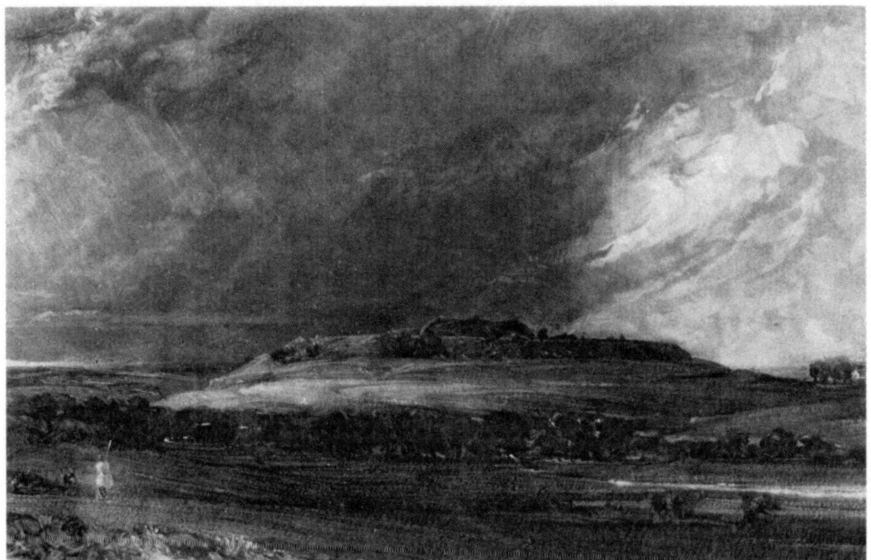

FIGURE 21   *David Lucas after John Constable,* Old Sarum, *published 1833, mezzotint, 5¼ × 8¼ (15.0 × 22.4 cm), Tate Britain*
© TATE, LONDON, 2015

However, the ideas complex that Constable wanted to evoke departs some-what from that of Thomson in that he stressed Old Sarum had also seen 'our earliest parliaments' and claimed it as the site where William the Conqueror had established the feudal system. The emphasis on parliament was given top-icality by the fact that Old Sarum was one of the most notorious rotten bor-oughs abolished by the 1832 Reform Act, a measure of which the conservative Constable was deeply apprehensive.[41] While the storm clouds in both water-colour and print seems to portend dangerous times, this is countered by the lightening sky to the left and the break in the clouds on the right. (The promise of hope is amplified in the watercolour by a rainbow – conventional symbol of resurrection – on the right edge; since this is painted largely on an attached strip of paper, it may have been added as an afterthought to the exhibition piece.) We might see this conjunction of symbols and sentiments as matching with the larger plan of Thomson's poem. *The Seasons* contains passages that

---

discussed in Rosenthal 1983, pp. 215–17. In this instance a herdsman and cows replaces the shepherd and flock as an emblem for pastoral labour.

41   On the relationship between these anxieties and the symbolism of Constable's *Salisbury Cathedral from the Meadows* (1831; Tate Gallery, on loan to National Museum of Wales, Cardiff), see Rosenthal 1983, pp. 227–34 and Rosenthal 1987, pp. 184–94.

suggest the social order of Britain is one of unrivalled beneficence and others that imply contradictory ideas of vice and corruption centred in the city. But at the end of the poem we are reassured of the divine order of things; the credo of natural theology and national election is reaffirmed. For Constable, too, the social scheme contained disturbing and unsettling features, but the overall plan of nature in which humanity played the key part was ultimately a benevolent one. Constable's shepherd and his flock dwarfed by the natural order, like the featureless earthworks that are all that remains of the once great city, declare the insignificance of human works and emphasise, by contrast, the power and majesty of the creator.[42]

Constable's image is representative of a commonplace iconographic motif in eighteenth- and early nineteenth-century painting and print imagery in which sheep and/or other pasture animals were used to conjure up the pastoral idea as a contrast, a state of otherness, to grandiose and decaying architectural remains, thus implying the transience and ultimate futility of worldly ambitions. The ingredients may be somewhat variable – an abbey may be substituted for a castle or goats may replace sheep – but the fundamental idea of the decay of human works remains the same. In time, everything human passes away and nature re-establishes itself. Trees and bushes flourish among the ruins; the most ancient forms of agriculture resume in a cyclical pattern. The attraction of such motifs was reinforced by the association of medieval castles and ecclesiastical buildings with ideas of feudal strife and monkish superstition that were acquiring new currency through the Gothic romances of authors such as Mrs. Radcliffe and the novels and poetry of Scott, and which, as Constable's text illustrates, were also part of a narrative of national state formation. The motif was still being recycled in rural poetry of the 1820s, as is shown by the following passage from John Clare's *The Shepherd's Calendar* (1827), in which the fortunate shepherd enjoys 'his summer dreams at will', bent over his hook or lying in the shade of a willow:

> Or lolling in a musing mood
> On mounds where saxon castles stood,
> Upon whose deeply buried walls
> The ivyed oak's dark shadow falls

---

42   The motif invites comparison with the hyperbolic sublime of Turner's watercolour *Stonehenge, Wiltshire* (c. 1827; Salisbury and South Wiltshire Museum), designed for Charles Heath's *Picturesque Views in England and Wales* (1824–38), in which the shepherd has been struck down by a thunderbolt.

He off picks up with wondering gaze
Some little thing of other days,
Saved from the wrecks of time ...[43]

Sheep-Breeding and the Picturesque

The pastoral tenor of such images seems completely dissociated from the ideology and practice of contemporary agriculture, with its emphasis on the scientific breeding of livestock and hard-nosed attitude towards the land as a field for capital investment and the application of agricultural science. The utilitarian view of the countryside was bolstered by the discourse of contemporary patriotism as in the Board of Agriculture's *General View of Agriculture in the County of Middlesex* (1797, reprinted 1807): 'It will readily be admitted, on a moment's reflection, that the more highly any country is cultivated, and the nearer it approaches to perfection in its rural concerns, the greater will be its increase of population ... its strength and consequence in the scale of nations'.[44] Farming for profit turned out to be patriotic. There was a pictorial imagery that corresponded to such practices in the form of livestock portraits such as Thomas Weaver's depiction of a prize sheep (1817; *fig. 22*), which often exaggerated the desirable characteristics of animals from the stockbreeder's perspective.[45] Some of the most prominent improvers had their status as such recorded in the form of portraits such as Weaver's *Thomas William Coke (1752–1842), 1st Earl of Leicester, and His Southdown Sheep* (c. 1807; *fig. 23*) or George Garrard's group portrait of 88 agriculturalists in the *Woburn Sheepshearing in 1804.*[46]

But, on the other hand, pastoral imagery was linked with the eighteenth-century discourse of the picturesque, a category had always been at odds with utility. It may well be that the pressures promoting agricultural productivity

---

43 Clare 1996–2003, vol. 1, pp. 110–11. This is from the version of 'July' published in 1827, as opposed to the much longer original (pp. 84–102) that was rejected by Clare's publisher, John Taylor, and in which this conventional motif does not appear. Clare's use of the adjective 'Saxon' is interesting given the currency of the idea in radical circles that Saxon freedoms had been suppressed by the Conquest and the imposition of the 'Norman Yoke'; it illustrates the politically variable meanings of such motifs. See Hill 1954.

44 Middleton 1807, p. vii.

45 On this phenomenon, see William Vaughan, 'Leisure and Toil: Differing Views of Rural Life, c. 1750–1850', in Spargo (ed.) 1989, p. 11.

46 On this work, see Spargo (ed.) 1989, pp. 54–5.

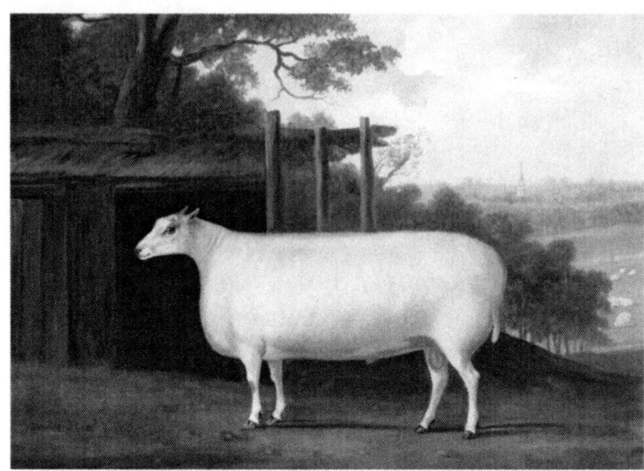

FIGURE 22
*Thomas Weaver, A Prize
Sheep by a Shelter, 1817,
oil on canvas, 17¾ × 22¼
in (45.0×58.0 cm),
National Trust, Calke
Abbey, Derby*
© NATIONAL TRUST
IMAGES

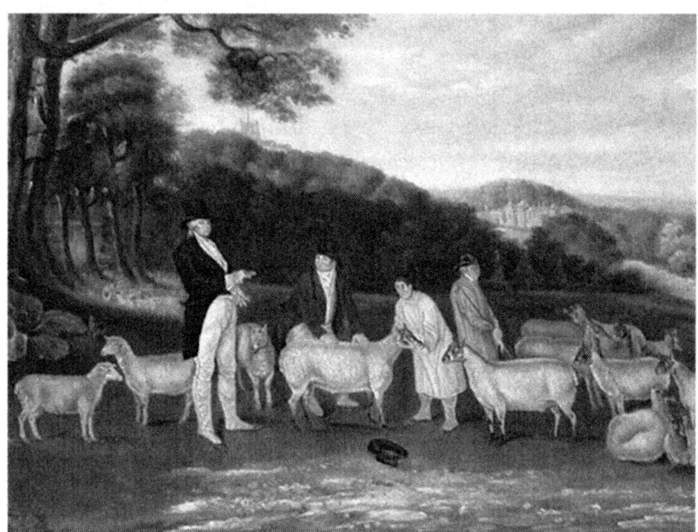

FIGURE 23   *C. Weaver after Thomas Weaver,* Thomas William Coke (1752–
1842), 1st Earl of Leicester, and His Southdown Sheep, c. *1807,
21¼ × 27¾ in (55.0×71.0 cm), National Trust, Anglesey Abbey,
Cambridgeshire*
©NATIONAL TRUST IMAGES/SUE JAMES

during the more than twenty years of war with France 1793–1815 contributed to the reformation and repudiation of the picturesque that took place in the phase of English landscape naturalism in the early nineteenth century.[47] This shift in the valuation of the visible signs of utility worked to keep the picturesque ruin with its pastoral accompaniment confined primarily to watercolour and amateur practice, against which a work such as Cotman's remarkable *Ploughed Field* (*fig. 11*) stands out in its bald presentation of improvement.

In his defence of the picturesque garden from 1794, Uvedale Price already submitted to the logic of the economic imperative: 'Where indeed men of property, either from false taste, or from a sordid desire of gain, disfigure such scenes or buildings as painters admire, our indignation is very justly excited: not so when agriculture, in its general progress, as is often unfortunately the case, interferes with picturesqueness or beauty. The painter may indeed lament; but that science, which of all other most benefits mankind, has a right to more than his forgiveness, when wild thickets are converted into scenes of plenty and industry, and when gypsies give way to the less picturesque figures of husbandmen and their attendants'.[48] Price's friend and theoretical sparring partner Richard Payne Knight would go even further in a text of the same year, asserting that the picturesque and utility could be reconciled – although he thought improvement should be a feature of the 'middle grounds and distances' in both the gentleman's estate and in landscape painting: 'Pastures with cattle, horses, or sheep grazing in them, and enriched with good trees, will always afford picturesque compositions; and inclosures of arable land are never completely ugly, unless when lying in fallow, which, I believe, is very generally disused in the present state of improved husbandry'. Against Gilpin, who had regretted that there were few scenes in nature capable of being depicted 'without considerable license and alteration', Knight replied that landscape painters made this complaint in inverse proportion to their talent.[49] For Knight the landscape of the picturesque is a real one, and, correspondingly, the pastoral is simply silly:

---

47   Hemingway 1992, pp. 19–26. Michael Rosenthal has suggested a causal relationship between the patriotic climate of the French Wars and the increasing presence of modern-day agricultural landscapes in Royal Academy exhibitions, claiming that the circumstances of the period invested 'georgic iconography' of agricultural abundance with 'profound significance'. See Rosenthal 1982, p. 112 and also pp. 96 and 108.

48   Price 1810, vol. 1, pp. 293–4. For the specific geographical and agricultural context in which Price and Knight's views on gardening were formed, see Daniels and Watkins 1994.

49   Knight 1795, pp. 42n, 45n, 46n. See also pp. 41–2: 'Still let utility improvement guide/ And just congruity in all preside.'

> Hail! Happy scenes of meditative ease,
> Where pleasure's sense and wisdom is to please:--
> Not such as, in the pastoral poet's strains,
> Fancy spreads o'er imaginary plains;
> Where love-sick shepherds, sillier than their sheep,
> In love-sick numbers, full as silly, weep;
> But such as nature's common charms produce
> For social man's delight and common use ...[50]

However, given that Knight saw Claude's work as epitomising truth of nature in the depiction of landscape particulars, the stylistic corollary of his ideas was less than straightforward.[51]

The archaism of the pastoral aside, modern day sheep – the kind that supplied the nation's wool or ended up as plates of steaming mutton – could be accommodated to the picturesque aesthetic, as Uvedale Price explained in a somewhat contorted passage in his *Essays on the Picturesque* of 1794: 'No animal indeed is so constantly introduced in landscape as the sheep, but that ... does not prove superior picturesqueness; and I imagine, that besides the innocent character, so suited to pastoral scenes of which they are the natural inhabitants, it arises from their being of a tint at once brilliant and mellow, which united happily with all objects; and also from their producing when in groups, however slightly the detail may be expressed, broader masses of light and shadow than any other animal'.[52] Thus sheep have pleasing associations but are not intrinsically picturesque; they become so because *en masse* they lend themselves to pictorial effects of breadth. Even so the picturesque and improvement do not match in conceptions of ovine form. In discussing standards of shape as a criterion of beauty, Price acknowledged the stock breeder Robert Bakewell had defined an ideal form for sheep but described it as 'a very grazier-like and material idea of beauty' that was premised on sheep's 'disposition to produce fat on their most profitable parts'.[53] The painter's or poet's idea of the beautiful was thus not the same as the farmer's, as we might expect from Weaver's painting despite the artist's clumsy attempts at picturesque accompaniments.

---

50   Knight 1795, p. 29.

51   Knight 1795, p. 47n. Knight lamented Wilson's example had so few emulators in 'the higher style of landscape', while claiming that in 'the humbler style' Morland and Ibbetson had 'arrived at great excellence' (pp. 78–9n.).

52   Price 1810, vol. 1, p. 59.

53   Price 1810, vol. 1, p. 94.

Price's concept of picturesqueness centred round the models of seven-teenth-century Dutch landscape painting, which offered relatively little in the way of pastoral imagery. This was certainly not because the classical pastoral had no appeal in the United Provinces; key texts by Horace and Virgil were translated into Dutch by the early seventeenth century and Dutch writers produced their own localised imagery of shepherds and shepherdesses in what was presented as a native landscape.[54] Sheep appear frequently in the Italianate scenes of Nicholaes Berchem and there are several images of shepherds with flocks by Cuyp, among which the *Landscape with Shepherds and Shepherdesses* (private collection, Belgium)[55] is particularly notable in suggesting the amorous connotations of the classical pastoral. But in Berchem's work sheep usually appeared in company with cattle or goats in a landscape suggestive of the Roman Campagna, not northern landscapes, while in Cuyp's the perspective structure leads the eye to a distant view of a town. With notable exceptions such as Ruisdael's *Landscape with Ruined Castle and a Church* (1665–70; National Gallery, London), the landscapes of Ruisdael and Hobbema seldom include imagery of sheep and shepherds, and even in this instance the motif is a detail painted by another artist.[56] This may have been partly because Holland was not a major wool producing country, depending on imports from Britain for its thriving cloth manufactures. Conversely, the fact that the dairy industry was such an important part of the Dutch economy may help explain why cows, rather than sheep, play such a prominent role in Cuyp's confections of the Dutch Arcadia.

The pastoral was, of course, a common motif in works of the contemporary Franco-Italian School of Claude Lorrain, Nicolas Poussin, and Gaspar Dughet; but in this iconography shepherds and flocks were associated with the Roman Campagna and motifs from Greek mythology, Ancient history, and the bible.[57] In so far as the history of landscape painting offered a powerful exemplar of pastoral imagery in a modern northern setting it was in works by Rubens, who in the last decade of his life produced a small group of paintings that follow conventions of pastoral landscape established in Venetian painting and seek to

---

54   Arthur K. Wheelock, Jr., with contributions by Jacob M. de Groot, 'Aelbert Cuyp and the Depiction of the Dutch Arcadia', in Wheelock, (ed.) 2001, pp. 18–19, 30 n. 18, n. 24, 30–31 n. 25, 31 n. 26.

55   Wheelock (ed.) 2001, catalogue no. 13,.

56   The figures are attributed to Adriaen van de Velde.

57   Despite his admiration for Claude, Payne Knight was quite clear that the formulation of the picturesque for British scenery involved a shift of artistic models from the Franco-Italian to the Dutch School – see Knight 1795, p. 45.

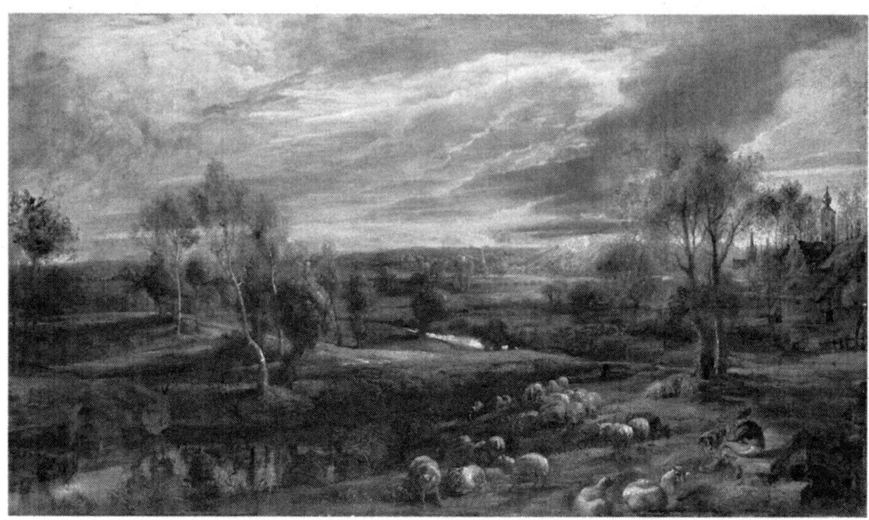

FIGURE 24   *Rubens, Peter Paul (1577–1640)*, A Landscape with a Shepherd and his Flock, *c. 1638,*
oil on oak (49.4 × 83.5 cm). Bequest of Lord Farnborough, 1839 (NG 157)
© NATIONAL GALLERY, LONDON/ART RESOURCE, NY

evoke the poetic idylls of Virgil's *Eclogues*. Particularly relevant among works
of this type is the *Landscape with a Shepherd and his Flock* (*c.* 1638; *fig. 24*),
in which the archetypal pastoral motif of the shepherd piping in solitude at
sunset is translated to the landscape of contemporary Brabant. By 1810 this
painting was in the collection of Lord Farnborough, who lent it for exhibition
at the British Institution in 1815.[58] For Uvedale Price, Rubens's work included
some of the most striking examples of the picturesque in both the disposition
of his figures and in the arrangement of light and shade; *Landscape with a*
Shepherd and his Flock could serve as a paradigm for the effect of breadth
produced by twilight that Price and so many of his contemporaries particularly
valued.[59]

---

58   For relevant landscapes by Rubens, see Brown 1996, pp. 52–6, 79–82. Lisa Vergara offers a
      rich account of Rubens's landscape iconography in Vergara 1982, but makes only passing
      reference to *Landscape with a Shepherd and his Flock* (p. 145).

59   See Price 1810, vol. 1, pp. 128–31; vol. 1, pp. 51–3.

Sheep-Shearing and Sheep-Washing

The efflorescence of landscape paintings that suggest the processes of agricultural improvement from the decade 1810–20 is in stark contrast with the evident backwardness of the pastoral motif as it appears in the iconography of the Shoreham circle around Samuel Palmer, or even in paintings by Turner such as *Bonneville Savoie with Mont Blanc* (1803; Dallas Museum of Art) and *Windsor Castle from the Thames* (1805; Tate Gallery). In the former, although the motif is a contemporary scene in the French Alps, it is represented through a pictorial structure that takes its cue from Poussin's classical road scenes, a derivation even clearer in the related watercolour in the British Museum from the year before.[60] Despite the workaday details of barge traffic, *Windsor Castle from the Thames* is also classical in structure and the two statuesque women amongst the foreground sheep wear off-the-shoulder dresses that are little removed from drapery, reinforcing the artificiality of the conception. By contrast, the interest in sheep washing and sheep shearing as motifs – as opposed to the lone shepherd with his flock – can be seen as symptomatic of the shift to a more georgic conception of the poetry of agriculture. Given the importance of industry in Thomson's *Seasons*, it is not surprising that the poem also licensed this other kind of imagery.

In addition to their pastoral role, *The Seasons* acknowledge the vital role sheep play in the national economy. In 'Summer' a relatively brief account of the harvest is followed by a much longer one of sheep-washing and sheep-shearing.[61] On this 'simple scene', Thomson argues, the 'solid grandeur' of the nation rests:

> ... hence she commands
> The exhalted shores of every brighter clime,
> The treasures of the Sun without his rage:
> Hence, fervent all, with culture, toil, and arts,
> Wide glows her land: her dreadful thunder hence
> Rides o'er the waves sublime, and now, e'en now,
> Impending hangs o'er Gallia's humbled coast;
> Hence rules the circling deep, and awes the world.[62]

---

60   Accession number TW0388.

61   Thomson 1908, 'Summer', ll. 352–422.

62   Thomson 1908, 'Summer', ll. 427–31.

Thus already in Thomson the idea of agricultural productivity came linked with ideas of the nation's political might, particularly in relation to its superiority over its main economic and colonial rival in the eighteenth century.

Poetic use of the idea of wool as the foundation of British economic preeminence was not confined to Thomson; it had been developed at much greater length in John Dyer's *The Fleece* (1757). As John Barrell has observed, although Dyer explicitly acknowledged the divisions within the contemporary social order, the poem sets out to show the harmony of interests among different occupations and ranks.[63] Following Pope's advice, Dyer displays practical awareness of sheep husbandry in the first part of the poem, but the overall drift of his text is to make the life of the shepherd sound positively Arcadian. An incessant nationalist rhetoric emphasises how well off are both sheep and shepherds in Britain, as compared with their less fortunate counterparts in other nations, while livestock as a whole become emblems of the beauty, fecundity, and general superiority of Britain:

> Such noble warlike steeds, such herds of kine,
> So sleek, so vast; such spacious flocks of sheep,
> Like flakes of gold illumining the green,
> What other paradise adorn but thine,
> Britannia?[64]

Like Thomson, Dyer gives an account of sheep-washing and sheep-shearing that is succeeded by a rustic festival in which he includes peasant songs that he claims (improbably) he had heard in Shropshire.[65]

The authority of these poetic representations of sheep-washing and sheep-shearing helps to explain the number of paintings incorporating both motifs shown in the London exhibitions in the years around 1800. For instance, Benjamin West exhibited a *Washing of Sheep* at the Royal Academy in 1796 (Rutgers University Art Gallery, New Brunswick, NJ);[66] Turner's *Walton Bridges* (c. 1806; National Gallery of Victoria, Melbourne), probably shown at his own gallery in 1807, included a sheep-washing scene in the foreground; and in 1812, Thomas Barker exhibited four pictures of shearing and washing at the British Institu-

---

63   Barrell 1983, pp. 90–109.

64   *The Fleece* in Dyer 1989, p. 52.

65   Dyer 1989, pp. 63–4.

66   Helmut von Erffa, has suggested this and a lost painting of *Harvest Home* were conceived

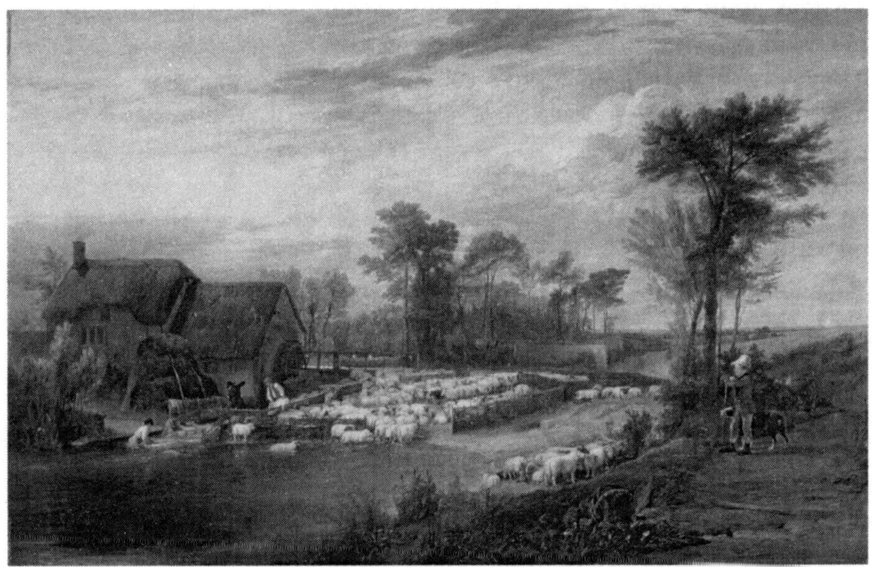

FIGURE 25   *David Wilkie,* Sheepwashing, *before 1817, oil on panel, 35½ × 68⅛ in (90.0 × 173.0 cm)*
NATIONAL GALLERIES OF SCOTLAND, SCOTTISH NATIONAL GALLERY

tion.[67] When in 1817 David Wilkie exhibited his *Sheepwashing* (*fig. 25*) at the British Institution, the catalogue entry was accompanied with twelve lines from the relevant passage in *The Seasons.* Wilkie's image was based on sketches he had made on the river Wylye at the small village of Fisheton Delamere in Wiltshire in 1814 or 1815, but the overall disposition of the motif and the striking cloud effects suggest to me that it was in part prompted by seeing Rubens's *Landscape with a Shepherd and his Flock* at the British Institution Old Masters show that same year. If I am correct, Rubens's piping shepherd becomes Wilkie's contemplative shepherd boy leaning on his staff.

Wilkie's picture does not match with the ideas of bustle and energy evoked by the lines from 'Summer' he quoted, and his pool does not have the 'bank abrupt and high' they describe; neither is Thomson's stream a mill stream. All of which suggests that the quotation from *The Seasons* was inserted as a

---

as illustrations to Thomson's *Seasons* – see Erffa 1952. Allen Staley is more sceptical in Erffa and Staley, pp. 421–2.

67   Circa 1818, Turner also produced a watercolour of *Windsor Castle from Salt Hill* ('*Sheep-Washing, Windsor*') (Tate Gallery, D08171), which was engraved for the *Liber Studorium,* but not published. Presumably one of Barker's exhibits was the 1807 *Sheep Washing* in the Victoria & Albert Museum. The Holburne Museum in Bath has a *Sheep Shearing* dated to *c.* 1810–12, but might not this be from a few years earlier?

piece of cultural validation and had not provided the motif for the scene. I suspect that by 1817 the idea of wool as the foundation of national greatness seemed less relevant than it had in 1727 when Thomson first published 'Summer', or 1757 when Dyer's poem came from the press, and that the image was mainly intended to produce connotations of a peaceful, abundant rural existence in which all takes its proper course. Interpreted in this way, the shepherd boy will one day follow the path round to the other side of the pool and take the place of his elders.[68] While praising the grouping, attitude, and expression of the sheep, a review of the painting in the *Examiner* newspaper found the landscape to be particularly laudable on account of its imitative truth. The reviewer – presumably Robert Hunt – found that the artist had 'entirely excluded the unnatural flush of colour seen in the greater part of our modern landscapes', and continued, 'we seem to look out into pure, undisguised, open daylight. We see a duplicate of nature; her twin-sister to the eye'.[69]

By contrast, the reviewer in the conservative *Morning Post* found too much Thomson in the picture because there was so much vivid detail it did not form an organic whole:

The individuality of the Poet, the minuteness of his touches, and the glowing distinctness of his parts, are not the best recommendations to the Painter. The one may, the other cannot bring his images too vividly under our eyes. May we not say that there is here too much of THOMSON in WILKIE? Nothing indeed can be more simple, natural, and correct than this effort in a new branch of the Art. The tone of the sky is exquisite, the shepherd boy full of repose and sweetness, and there is scarcely a separate point which we could help praising as admirable; yet it is evident that

---

68   In his very fine study of Wilkie, Nicholas Tromans points out that Wilkie was visiting Robert Gourlay, an acquaintance from Fyfe, but also a 'radical agricultural reformer', and indicates ways in which the motif was particularly resonant with Gourlay's concerns. However, he concludes: 'if there is an echo of a political agenda in *Sheepwashing*, it is thoroughly buried under the ostensible naturalism, which was its chief attraction to reviewers' (Tromans 2007, pp. 37–9). I agree.

69   'British Institution', *Examiner*, no. 477 (16 February 1817). The overall effect of the work did not please the reviewer of the *Repository of Arts*, who was more attuned to experimental naturalism and complained of the picture's 'monotony of colour' – 'Exhibition of the British Institution', *Repository of Arts*, 3, 15 (March 1817), p. 163. The 'Announcement of Works in Hand', *Annals of Fine Arts*, 1, 3 (1816), p. 409, also commented on the work's naturalism.

there is not that freedom of handling and masterly unison of the whole which requires great practice as well as true feeling to give.[70]

In effect this review registers the way in which the new naturalism of the 1810s – which was manifested in landscape and genre painting alike – conflicted with the notion of breadth, which was really an aspect of the picturesque derived from the Venetian, Dutch, and Flemish Schools. Breadth softened the depiction of contemporary social realities and withdrew them into a more ideal realm; without breadth they could seem to have a jarring proximity.

We can register the distinction by looking at representations of the same theme by a contemporary who treated the sheep washing theme in a number of variants, the Norwich-trained painter James Stark. Like Wilkie, Stark set his sheep washings within pictorial formats derived from Hobbema, although in Wilkie's case it is the example of Hobbema's mill scenes that is drawn on, while in Stark's the model is that of his grove compositions. The earlier of two Stark pictures titled *Sheep Washing* in Norwich Castle Museum is probably a painting exhibited at the Norwich Society of Artists in 1822,[71] which would match with its small scale; while the larger and more dramatic painting *Sheep Washing, Morning* in the Ipswich Museum (*fig. 26*) is likely to be that shown at the British Institution two years later.[72] The former picture has much the same composition as the engraving titled 'Postwick Grove' in the series of prints after pictures by Stark published over the years 1828–34 as *Rivers of Norfolk*.[73]

Stark's particular fusion of Dutch compositional formats with naturalistic light effects prompted one reviewer to perceive in his work a convincing mimesis, akin to the response that Wilkie's picture had produced: 'We can conceive nothing beyond the truth of this Artist's delineation of common nature, par-

---

70   'British Institution', No. v, *Morning Post*, 6 March 1817.

71   Accession number 1951.235.1301.

72   A second picture of sheep washing in the Norwich Castle Museum (1957.169) may relate to one of the exhibits on the theme Stark showed at the British Institution in 1848 and 1858. *Sheep Washing in Postwick Grove* (Yale Center for British Art) is a study for the painting I am tentatively dating to 1822.

73   Robberds 1834. The frontispiece page carries the title *Scenery of the Rivers of Norfolk, from Pictures Painted by James Stark*, the title by which the work is usually known. But there is also a title page that carries more information and has no frontispiece, which gives the title as *Picturesque Views on and near the Eastern Coast of England, Comprising the Romantic Scenery of the Yare, the Waveney, and the Bure, from Pictures Painted by James Stark*.

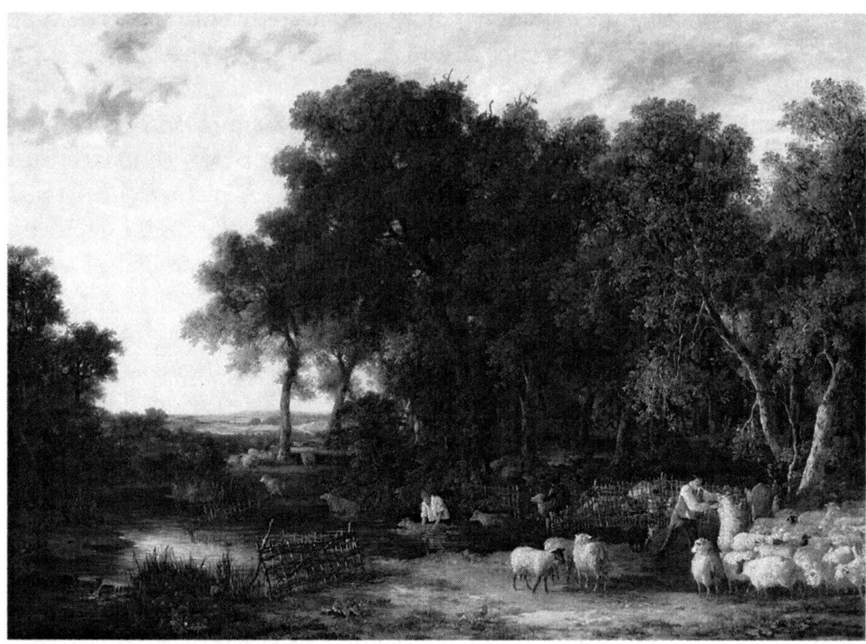

FIGURE 26   *James Stark*, Sheep Washing, Morning, *1824, oil on canvas, 32 ½ × 44 ⅛ in* (*82.6 × 113 cm*)
COLCHESTER AND IPSWICH MUSEUM SERVICES

ticularly in his Forest Scene'.[74] However, in 1824 the reviewer in the same paper observed of *Sheep Washing, Morning*: 'Mr. Stark appears to have witnessed sheep washing upon a very small scale. His picture, we apprehend, would excite a smile in any of our sheep counties. It possesses none of the requisite energy and activity; everything is too much in repose'.[75] Stark's work was thus found wanting in relation to contemporary agricultural practice. What may partly have been at stake here was the harmony of the compositional format, which was certainly linked with the idea of the non-utilitarian and picturesque. But we may also find again confirmation that the idea of wool as the basis of the nation's wealth and might was by this point obsolete, although Stark, as the child of a dyer in a city whose prosperity depended to a great extent on its weaving industry was well placed to understand the economic significance of sheep washing.

---

74   'The British Institution', *Guardian*, 11 February 1821, with reference to Stark's *Landscape*, no. 69 in the catalogue.

75   'The Fine Arts', *British Guardian and Protestant Advocate*, 3 March 1824.

Fissures in the Pastoral

The meaning of sheep in paintings and prints, like signs in any language, is affected by the combinations in which they appear. The associative or paradigmatic relations between different signs license more or less appropriately the syntagmatic relations in which they may be combined.[76] For instance, in addition to the variations in their breeds and specific appearance, sheep may appear in connection with a range of landscape types such as mountains, moors, heaths, valleys, and meadows. They may appear in combination with other animals or not. They may appear in flocks or wandering singly; being driven, grazing, being washed, being sheared; with human attendants, male or female; in different seasons, weathers, and times of day. These variations – and I could go on – are multifarious and complicated still further by the numerous stylistic idiolects within which representations are presented, whether it be idiolects that signify the style of a particular individual artist or idiolects that signify choices within the highly codified style system available to early nineteenth-century artists.[77] In the end, the aesthetic viewpoint demands that the artwork be treated as a whole and not simply as the sum of its signifying parts. Moreover, analogical signs such as painted images are resistant to the digital models of analysis developed in structural linguistics. Having said this, the digital model has its value in drawing attention to the quasi-linguistic structures that underpin aspects of the artist's 'speech', if only to register the inherently social character it shares with all other meaningful utterances. Thus the modification in pictorial codes that constituted landscape naturalism in the early nineteenth century was both a question of changes in types of explicit or implicit narrative utterances about rural life and modifications to the established idiolects of depiction, not just the result of a Gombrichian process of making and matching as a result of outdoor procedures – though this should not be denied some role. In these stylistic shifts, sheep signs played a role; given the prominence of the animal within mythologies of rural life this is only to be expected.

That modern notion of art as social critique, which would eventually acquire the label 'realism', was still only embryonic in this period, despite the lessons that might be drawn from the work of Hogarth and the more naturalistic forms being developed within contemporary genre painting by artists such as Thomas Heaphy, William Mulready, Edward Villiers Rippingille, and Wilkie.[78] However,

---

76   Barthes 1968, pp. 58–61.

77   For idiolect, Barthes 1968, pp. 21–2, 27–8.

78   Hemingway 1992, pp. 149–54. In recent years, several books have appeared that have

that the style and iconography of Wilkie's art marked a rupture with what Hazlitt described as 'an ideal of common life, of which we have had a surfeit in poetry and romance' – epitomised in painting by Gainsborough's so-called 'fancy pictures' – was well understood.[79] That there was a perceived continuity between the new genre-painting style and the new naturalistic landscape painting is illustrated in the career of William Collins, who practised with equal facility, if not great profundity, in both genres. Conscious self-criticism of the ideologies around landscape that were incarnated in the pastoral scarcely intrudes into painting, or at least has left little trace in the written record of the period.[80] Yet we can understand some paintings as standing for a less mythological and more sceptical vision on account of their formal and iconographic differences from others.

The importance of form in the presentation of an iconographic motif can be registered through a comparison of the treatment of the pastoral by Constable set against its presentation by his contemporaries George Robert Lewis and John Crome. Michael Rosenthal has argued that Constable's *The Cornfield* (*fig. 27*) – a major set-piece composition that he exhibited on five occasions in the period 1826–35 but failed to sell – is characteristic of the increasingly abstract character of the artist's vision of the Suffolk countryside in the late 1820s, stressing its departures from topography and the realities of agricultural life, its 'more conventional picturesque', and reversion from the georgic to the pastoral mode.[81] (Discrepant details include the boy and dog seemingly inattentive to the flock, the field gate off its hinges, and the untethered donkeys browsing in the hedgerow). Long before, Graham Reynolds had noted the picture's indebtedness to the type of Claudean upright composition represented by Claude's *Landscape with Hagar and the Angel* (1646; National Gallery, London; *fig. 28*), then in the collection of the artist's friend Sir George Beaumont, and the similarity of motif with Gaspard Dughet's *Landscape with a Shepherd and his Flock* (c. 1670; *fig. 29*).[82] The fact that the church tower in the distance

---

taken the interpretation of early nineteenth-century genre painting to a new level of sophistication and historical depth, notably: Tromans, et. al. 2002; Tromans 2007; and Solkin 2008.

79   'On Gainsborough's Pictures', *The Champion*, no. 82 (31 July 1814). Reprinted in Hazlitt 1930–34, vol. 8, pp. 34–7.

80   John Clare's unfinished 'Essay on Landscape' is disappointing in this regard, although its claims for the particular veracity of Peter de Wint's naturalistic effects are interesting. See Clare 1970, pp. 211–15.

81   Rosenthal 1983, pp. 179, 178. For the earlier outdoor painting (datable to c. 1817) on which the picture is based, see Lyles (ed.) 2006, pp. 116–17.

82   Reynolds, 1965, pp. 106–7. In 1823 Constable had copied Claude's *Landscape with Goatherd*

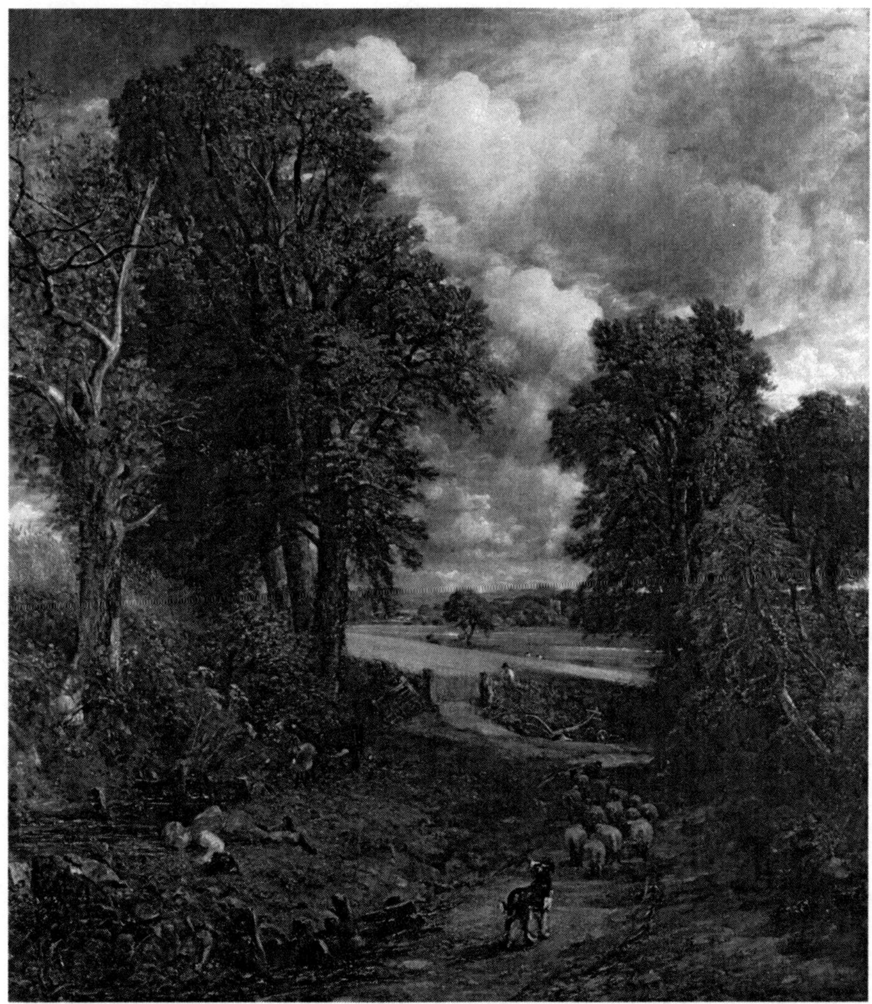

FIGURE 27   *Constable, John (1776–1837),* The Cornfield, *1826, oil on canvas (143.0×122.0cm),*
Presented by subscribers including Wordsworth, Faraday, and Sir William Beechey,
1837 (NG130)
© NATIONAL GALLERY, LONDON/ART RESOURCE, NY

departs from the topography of the Vale of Dedham as seen from the spot
where Constable located his viewpoint is certain – no such church was visible

____

and *Goats* (National Gallery, London), which has a similar compositional format. The copy
is in the Sydney, Art Gallery of New South Wales. Dughet's *Landscape with a Shepherd and
Flock,* with its pendant *Imaginary Landscape with Buildings in Tivoli,* passed through the
London sale rooms in 1801 and 1818. On Dughet's influence, see French 1980.

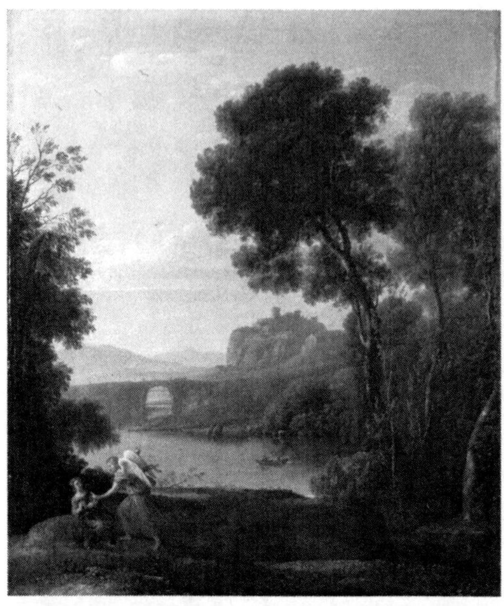

FIGURE 28
Lorrain, Claude (Gellée) (1600–1682),
Landscape with Hagar and the Angel,
*1646, oil on canvas mounted on wood
(52.2 × 42.3 cm), presented by Sir George
Beaumont, 1828 (NG61)*
© NATIONAL GALLERY,
LONDON/ART RESOURCE, NY

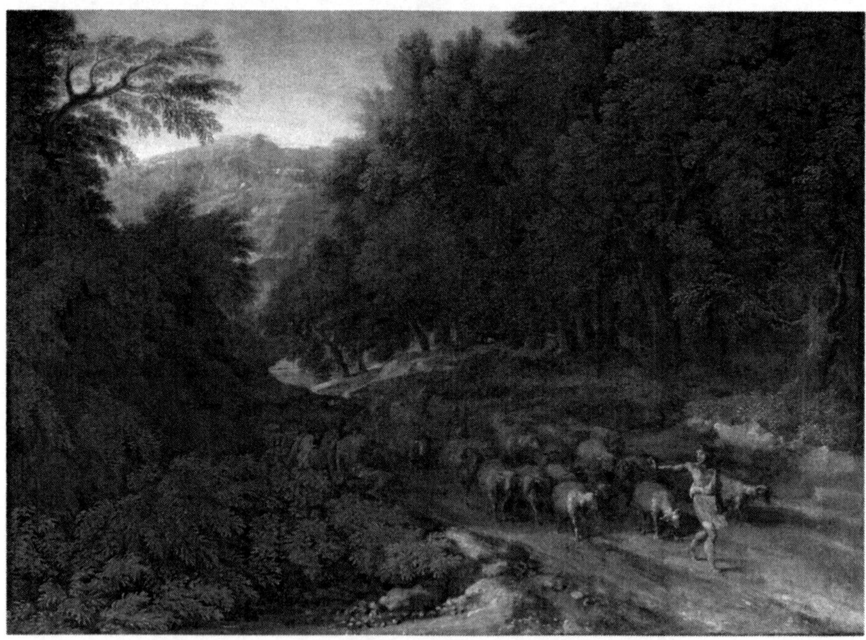

FIGURE 29   *Dughet, Gaspar (1615–1675),* Landscape with a Shepherd and his Flock, *about 1670,
oil on canvas (48.6 × 65.3 cm), Holwell Carr Bequest, 1831 (NG68)*
© NATIONAL GALLERY, LONDON/ART RESOURCE, NY

from there; but Leslie Parris and Ian Fleming-Williams have questioned whether the depiction of agricultural practices is as discrepant as Rosenthal claimed.[83] Which interpretation is more correct as to these particulars is immaterial to my argument here. With or without them Rosenthal's larger point about the shift in Constable's style of the later 1820s towards a more conventional picturesque and his turn away from the georgic mode is incontestable. *The Cornfield* is an updated pastoral in a blatantly old-masterish compositional structure. Claude and Gaspar Dughet are translated into the idiom of the English national landscape. One sees the same enclosed mythic world in William Havell's *Driving Home the Flock (fig. 30)* of 1806, which confirms the fit between theme and formal motif. Rosenthal has also pointed out the difference between the relatively precise correlation of pictorial motif and the passage from Bloomfield's *Farmer's Boy* that Constable inserted in the catalogue entry for *Landscape, Ploughing Scene in Suffolk* when he showed it at the Royal Academy in 1814, and the imprecise match between *The Cornfield* and the quotation from *The Seasons* concerning wind, trees, and fields with which he accompanied the entry for that picture in the British Institution catalogue of 1827. This difference, too, corresponds to the shift from georgic to pastoral mode.[84]

Writing on Constable's *The Cornfield* in 1826, the *Examiner's* reviewer, Robert Hunt, captures the work's seductive fusion of the actual and ideological. That is, he praised the work for both its seeming naturalism – 'he is one of the most natural Painters of his time' – and for its artificial content, 'the pure pastoral it contains'. The former quality was constituted by 'its sapphire sky and silver clouds, its emerald tress and golden grain, its glittering effect of sunlight among the vegetation'; the latter was embodied in 'the flock of sheep, the shepherd boy stretched on the ground to drink, the ploughed corn-field, the village church, &c ...'[85] However, Hunt himself seems to acknowledge the artifice of Constable's 'nature' with his string of adjectives drawn from precious stones and metals. One wonders if he recognised the specific source of the painting's Claudean compositional scheme, which reinforced the picture's standing as a 'pastoral'. Or perhaps that effect was subliminal.

When we turn to a more apparently naturalistic image such as Crome's *View on Mousehold Heath, near Norwich (fig. 31)* we do not escape references to the typology of landscape forms that had been codified from the practices of different schools and individual artists of the seventeenth century. Crome's

83   Parris and Fleming-Williams 1991, pp. 304–5.

84   Rosenthal 1987, pp. 174–5.

85   'Royal Academy', *Examiner*, no. 961 (2 July 1826).

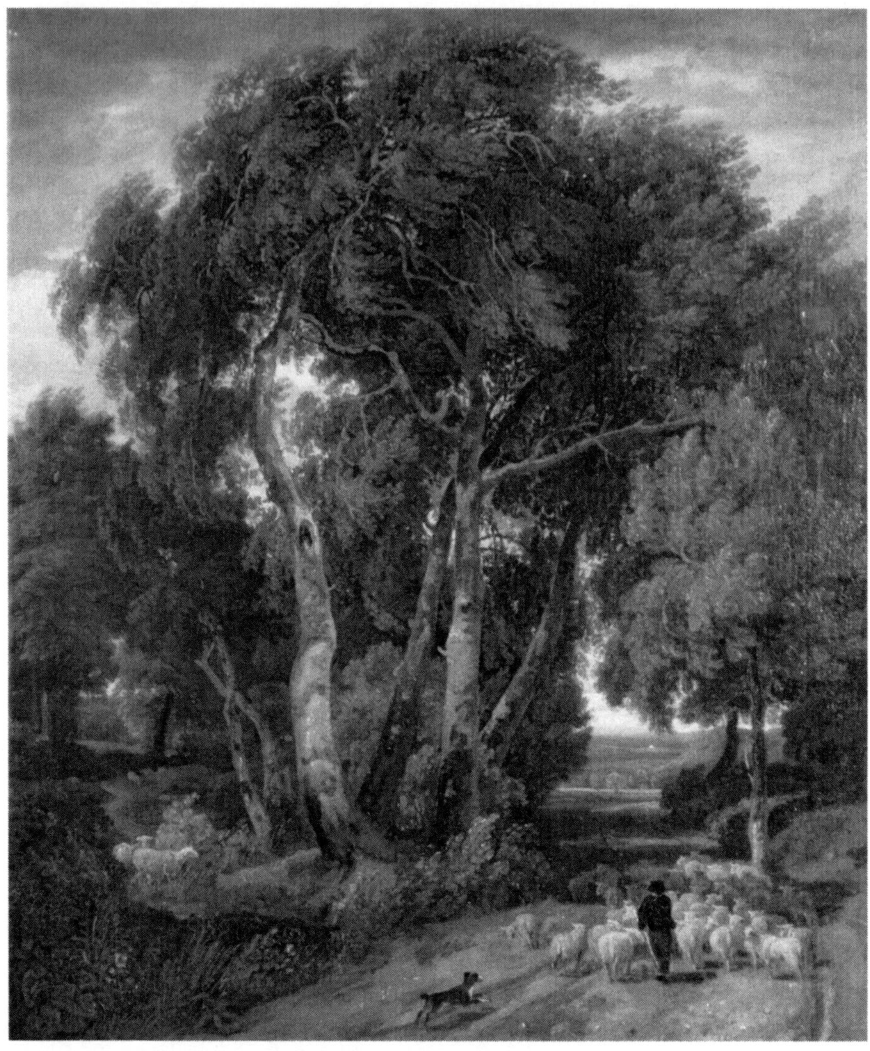

FIGURE 30   *William Havell,* Driving Home the Flock, *1806*
             BIRMINGHAM CITY MUSEUM AND ART GALLERY

picture can reasonably be identified with the *Boy Keeping Sheep – Morning,* exhibited at the Norwich Society of Artists exhibition of 1812, and with the *Boy and Sheep – Morning* lent by John Bracey to the Crome memorial exhibition in 1821.[86] With its low viewpoint and sense of being down in the terrain, the

---

86   The picture exhibited in 1821 was dated to 1815 in the catalogue, but this was presumably

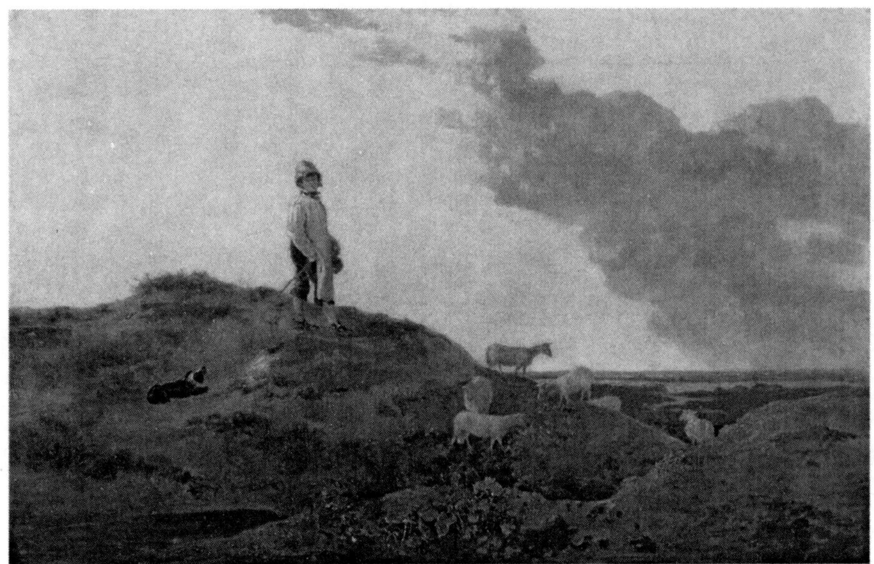

FIGURE 31   *John Crome,* View on Mousehold Heath, near Norwich, *1812?, oil on canvas, 21½ ×*
32 in (54.6 × 81.2 cm)
VICTORIAN & ALBERT MUSEUM

composition of *View on Mousehold Heath* references both the type of Ruisdael
dune landscape,[87] but also the familiar Cuyp motif of farm animals, most
usually cattle, occupying foreground space and silhouetted against a refulgent
light-filled distance. Crome's trailing asymmetrical cloud shapes also follows
a characteristic Cuypian pattern, as can be seen from comparison with that
artist's *An Evening Ride near a River* (c. 1640s; *fig. 32*), which Crome certainly
knew from John Major's engraving of 1769 and may have seen when it passed
through Christie's sale room in 1799 or perhaps when it was in Sir Francis
Bourgeois's collection.[88]

---

an error. John Bracey was a rope-maker of Great Yarmouth who in 1825 was appointed
the town's Pier Master. It is likely that the painting known today as *The Way through the
Wood* (Birmingham City Art Gallery and Museums) is the *Landscape with Sheep – Evening,*
shown at the Norwich Society in 1813.

87   Slive 2001, cat. nos. 592–626.

88   Major's print, which was titled *Contented Peasants,* was lot 409 in Crome's 1812 sale in
Norwich. A painting attributed to Cuyp simply described as *Camp Scene* appeared as
lot 85 on the first day of Crome's posthumous sale in 1821. Crome's interest in Cuyp is
most transparently evident in the picture of *Yarmouth Water Frolic* (1821; English Heritage,

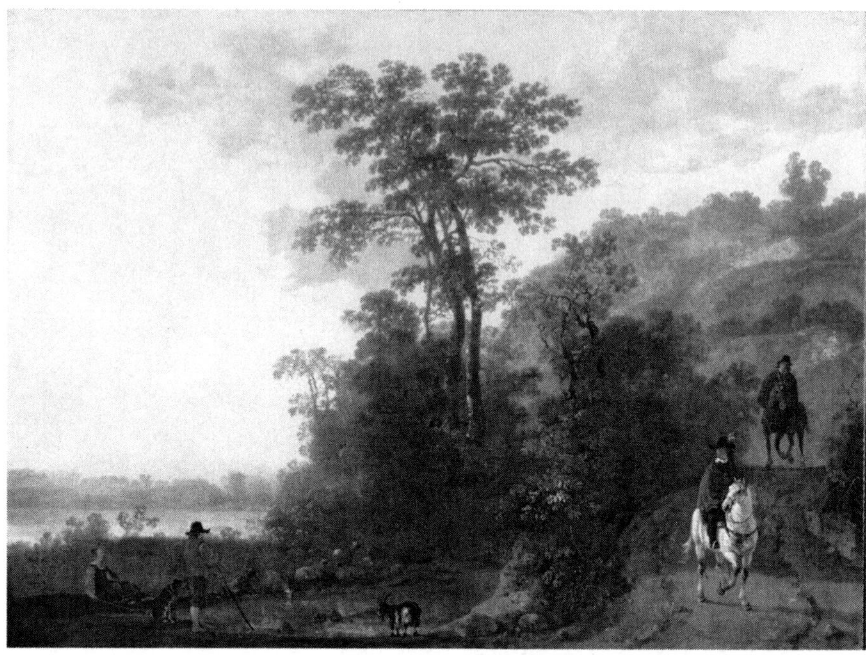

FIGURE 32 *Aelbrecht Cuyp,* An Evening Ride near a River, *c. 1640s–50s, oil on panel, 48.9 x 64.1,*
DPG96.
BY PERMISSION OF THE DULWICH PICTURE GALLERY, LONDON

Crome's composition has the feel of a sketch, a moment observed by a
wanderer over the heath who comes across a shepherd boy silhouetted against
the sky. We might associate him with Blomefield's Giles except that the terrain
depicted is quite the opposite of that in which Giles, a sometime shepherd,
guards his flock:

Kenwood House, London) that he was working on at his death, and which was finished
by his son John Berney Crome. Formally speaking, this was probably prompted in part
by seeing Cuyp's *The Maas at Dordrecht* (c. 1650; National Gallery of Art, Washington,
DC) and *View of Dordrecht (from the Maas)* (1650s; Ascott Estate, Bucks.) at the British
Institution Exhibition of Dutch and Flemish Masters in 1815. *Turner's Dort, or Dordrecht,
The Dort Packet-Boat from Rotterdam becalmed,* another self-consciously Cupyian work
exhibited in 1818. For Cuyp in Britain, see Alan Chong, 'Aristocratic Imaginings: Aelbert
Cuyp's Patrons and Collectors', in Wheelock (ed.) 2001, pp. 35–51. For Dutch paintings in
Norfolk collections, see Moore 1988. Dawson Turner was hugely impressed by the Cuyp
paintings he saw in the Louvre in 1814 – Turner 1840, p. 28.

> Small was his charge, no wilds had they to roam
> But bright enclosures circling round their home
> Nor yellow blossom'd Furse, nor stubborn thorn,
> The heath's rough produce, had their fleeces torn[89]

Crome, by contrast, depicts unenclosed commons seemingly far from any town or village, enhancing the sense of isolation. An idea of momentary encounter is given by the fact that the boy's body still faces in the direction of his sheep, while only his head has swivelled towards the viewer; his dog looks to him for guidance. Yet for all the feel of immediacy, Rusidael had arrived at kindred compositions in the seventeenth century – including the device of a figure or figures silhouetted against the sky or a higher mass – without, it seems, sketching in oil outdoors. The Philadelphia Museum of Art's great *Dune Landscape* from the 1650s is paradigmatic of this format.[90] Although it seems unlikely Crome had access to this particular work he could have known through prints other Ruisdael compositions, such as *Bridge with a Sluice* (1648–9; *fig. 33*), in which a foreground mass dominates a composition and relegates distance to a small portion of the overall canvas, offering the viewer no sense of a commanding vista and forcing her or his nose down among weeds and dirt.[91]

To Crome's Norwich contemporaries, the river winding towards the horizon on the right of his composition would certainly have stood for the Yare, and the heathland in question for the heights of Mousehold, without the artist needing to make reference to the specific location in the title. As Trevor Fawcett has demonstrated in his fine essay on Crome's larger painting of *Mousehold Heath* (*fig. 48*), the process of enclosing the heath was almost complete by the time that work was painted around 1814–15, and something of Crome's sympathies – or at least a sentiment of nostalgia – may be read from the fact that there are no hints of enclosure in its expansive light-filled vista.[92] The same applies to the

---

89   Bloomfield 1998, p. 30, ll. 285–8.

90   Seymour Slive is categorical about the lack of evidence for outdoor sketching, at the same time as he acknowledges the closeness of such works to the imagery of eighteenth-century oil sketches by Thomas Jones and Pierre-Henri de Valenciennes. Slive 2001, p. 98.

91   An engraving after this composition by R.A. Wieth was published in Pierre François Basan, *Receuil d'estampes gravées d'après les tableaux de cabinet de Monseigneur le duc de Choiseul* (Paris 1771).

92   Fawcett 1982, pp. 174–5. The painting is most likely the *Scene on Mousehold Heath* Crome exhibited with the Norwich Society in 1815, which may or may not be identical with the *View on Mousehold Heath*, dated to 1816, lent to his Memorial Exhibition by a Mr. Wilson. As this book was going to press, a collection of essays on *Mousehold Heath* by

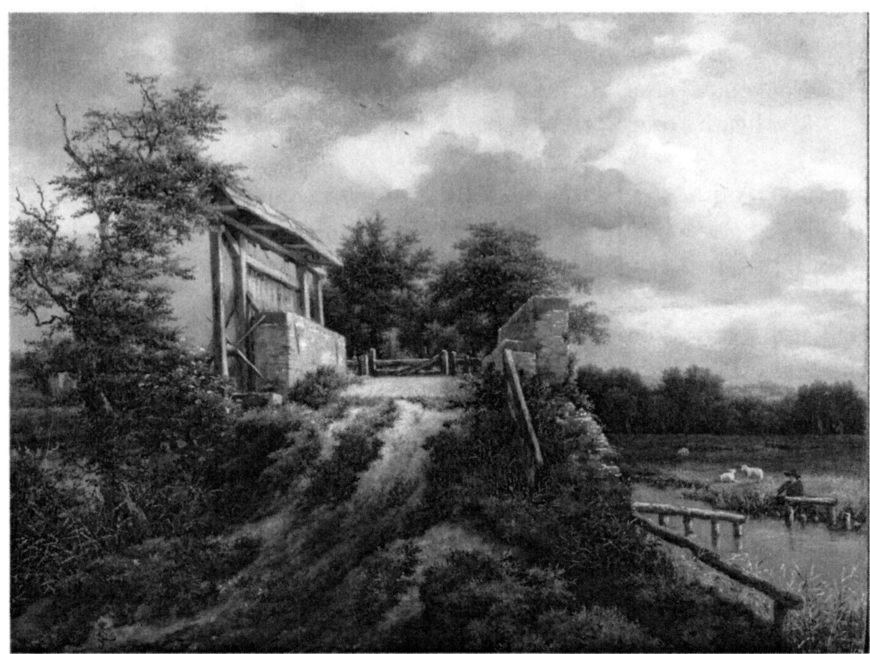

FIGURE 33   *Jacob van Ruisdael (Dutch, 1628/1629–1682), Bridge with a Sluice, 1648–1649, oil on panel, 15⅝ × 22⅛ in (39.7 × 56.2 cm)*
THE J. PAUL GETTY MUSEUM

painting under discussion. At one level, Crome's image could almost stand as an illustration to a passage in Nathaniel Kent's 1794 report on the agriculture of Norfolk, though Kent was opposed to the 'common field' system and the 'sheep-walk privileges' that sometimes accompanied it. In Kent's account, the specific breed of Norfolk sheep had played a crucial role in the county's improvement: 'Great part of this county is known to have been, within the space of a century, a wild, bleak, unproductive country, comparatively with what it now is; full half of it was rabbit warrens and sheep-walks; the sheep were as natural to the soil as rabbits, being hardy in their nature, and of an agile construction, so as to move over a great deal of space with little labour. When great tracts of this land were brought into a better state of cultivation, the Norfolk sheep gave great aid to the new improvement, as they fetched their sustenance from a considerable distance, and answered penning as well as any sheep whatever'.

Sam Smiles and Rachel Scott (Smiles [ed.] 2016) appeared. This marks a major advance in understanding of the painting.

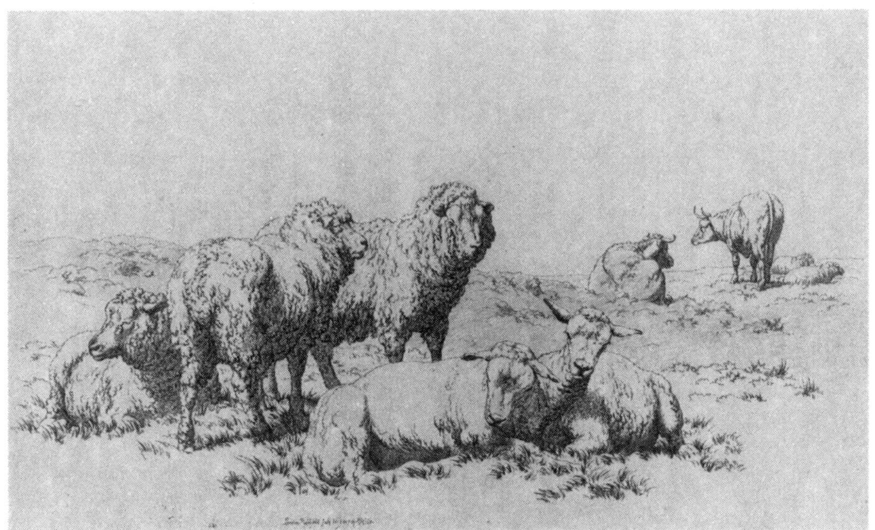

FIGURE 34   *From Robert Hills,* Etchings of Cattle Comprising Rudiments of Drawing and
Groups for the Embellishment of Landscape, *1807*
© THE TRUSTEES OF THE BRITISH MUSEUM

Through penning, folding, and the use of turnips farmers were able to improve
their stock 'so that at this time they are become respectable and profitable in
their return, and in as high estimation at Smithfield as any sheep whatever, for
no better mutton can be put upon a table; and, though they produce but little
wool, it is of a good quality'.[93] Kent did not recognise the Lincoln or Leicester
breeds as superior.

Crome's painting appears to depict that hardy breed, the 'miserable set of
long-legged rambling sheep' that had originally been common in the county –
and which Kent denigrates in his before and after narrative – not some stockbreeder's ideal.[94] The depiction of the sheep from a variety of angles contributes to the naturalism of effect, and suggests Crome had been influenced by
Robert Hills's 1808 publication of etchings, *Cattle in Groups for the Embellishment of Landscape, Drawn from Nature,* which included some strikingly individualised depictions of sheep alongside the cattle (*fig. 34*) and was among the
folio books in his possession at the time of his death.[95] Crome's possession of

---

93   Kent 1794, p. 32. Kent's book was lot 66 on the 5th day of Crome's posthumous sale in
1821.

94   Chambers 1829, p. iv. Crome's pupil James Stark represented sheep penning in the oil
sketch *Penning the Flock* (Norwich Castle Museum and Art Gallery).

95   Lot 84 on the final day of Crome's posthumous sale was described as 'Hill's Neat Cattle,

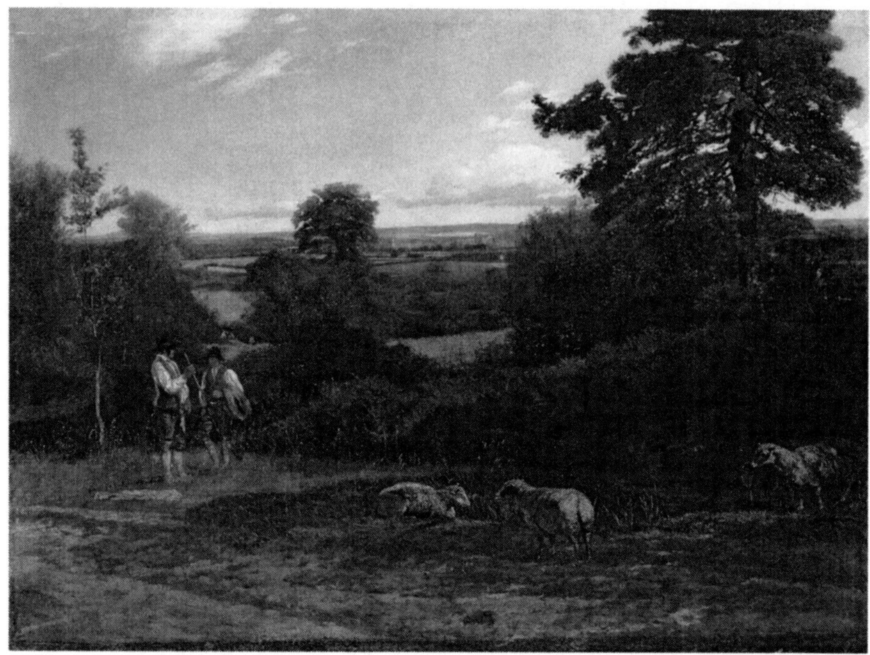

FIGURE 35   *George Robert Lewis,* Hereford, from the Haywood, Noon, *1815, oil on canvas, 16⅜ ×*
23½ in (41.6×59.7 cm), Tate Britain
© TATE, LONDON, 2015

a set of Hill's prints indicates an interest in one of the most advanced naturalistic water-colour painters and printmakers of the period.[96] And like Crome,
who was almost directly his contemporary, Hills's career straddles picturesque
and naturalistic idioms.

While the seeming informality and simplicity of Crome's *View on Mousehold
Heath* make it appear relatively naturalistic by comparison with its Cuypian
prototypes, it lacks the topographical specificity that distinguished the most
advanced naturalism of the century's second decade and partly constitutes
the originality of works by Constable, De Wint, Linnell and others from those
years. This quality is particularly striking in my final example, George Robert
Lewis's *Hereford, from the Haywood, Noon* (1815; *fig. 35*). Lewis's painting was
shown at the Society of Painters in Oil and Water-Colours exhibition in 1816,

---

fine etchings, scarce, 1806'. Between 1807 and 1809, Hills also published *Etchings of Sheep
from Nature.*

96   There is frustratingly little research on Hills. For a bare bones account of his career, see
Williams 1945 and Albany Gallery 1968.

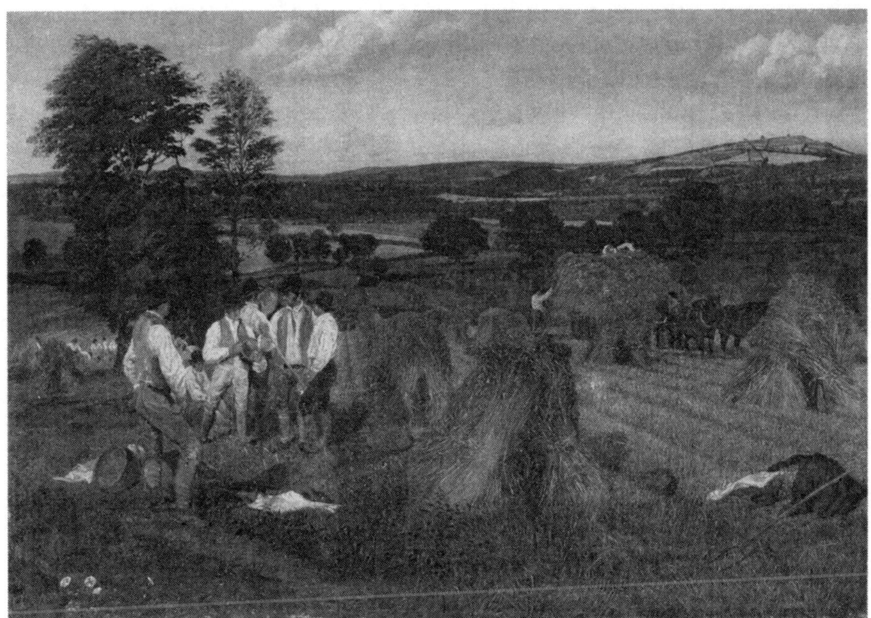

FIGURE 36   *George Robert Lewis,* Hereford, Dynedor and the Malvern Hills from the Haywood
Lodge, Harvest Scene, Afternoon, *1815, oil on canvas, 16⅜ × 23½ in (41.6×59.7 cm),
Tate Britain*
© TATE, LONDON, 2015

together with the better known *Hereford, Dynedor and the Malvern Hills from
the Haywood Lodge, Harvest Scene, Afternoon* (1815; *fig. 36*), and twelve smaller
landscapes of related views displayed in four frames.[97] Haywood Lodge is a
substantial brick farmhouse, dating from around 1710, its doorway framed by
pilasters and topped by a scroll motif. Christiana Payne has established that
in 1815 the farm was let to a widowed tenant farmer, Mrs. Theresa Price, and
hypothesises, reasonably, that the artist stayed at the Lodge in the summer of
1815 and made studies of the fields and workers of a friend or patron.[98]

In addition to Payne's analysis, John Barrell and Hugh Prince have both given
insightful commentaries on the *Harvest Scene,* which is undoubtedly the most
imposing and iconographically charged of the fourteen works Lewis exhibited.
Prince is correct, I think, in describing the painting as offering 'a conservative view of rural labourers, working collectively, bringing home the harvest,

---

97   Two of the smaller oil paintings are in the Tate Gallery: *Harvest Field with Gleaners,
Haywood, Herefordshire* (T03234) and *Harvest Field with Reapers, Haywood, Herefordshire*
(T03235).

98   Payne 1993, pp. 95–6.

pausing a while to pass around refreshing flagons of cider. It commemorates an old-enclosed mixed farming country, scarcely touched by modern improvements'. Yet while the picture offers 'a comforting early eighteenth-century ideal of a Georgical landscape', Prince notes that the figures of the nearest group of labourers are clean and neatly dressed, and have the appearance of portraits; they appear neither servile nor deferential and carry themselves with 'a manly assured self-respect'.[99] This 'traditional view' of harvest acquired a particular resonance in the aftermath of the British victory at Waterloo on 18 June 1815 and Napoleon's second abdication on the 24th of that month. Assuming the paintings were made during the wheat harvest in August 1815, the motif may well have appeared not just as marking a welcome return to the arts of peace, but also as symbol of the nation's blessings in a Christian sense. Barrell has written that 'the date of the painting may ... invite us to reflect that this is an image of the bold peasantry from which were recruited the victors of Waterloo – or this was how they were imagined to be by those concerned to persuade the poor of England that the fight with revolutionary France was a fight for their own liberties', at the same time as he notes 'a warmth and a value in this image' when compared with Constable's consistent depictions of a subservient rural workforce.[100]

But the depiction of the wheat harvest in the summer of 1815 was even more freighted than Prince and Barrell have registered. The bumper harvest of two years before, which had produced a massive decline in wheat prices, was experienced by farmers as a disaster. Many of them had made heavy capital investment during the period of wartime high prices and were faced with rents that matched the wartime price level.[101] Parliament responded to the agitation this generated, which was manifested in numerous petitions both pro and contra a new corn law, by passing a bill in June 1814 that permitted export of grain and flour at all times without duty or bounty.[102] The harvest of 1814 was on the whole poor and the crop was badly affected by blight and mildew, but prices did not rise because of the surplus left over from 1813 and the import of foreign grain.[103] The crisis was such that from 17 February to 10 March 1815, the House of Commons focused almost exclusively on the issue. Parliament was not only flooded with petitions, there was an extensive

---

99   Hugh Prince, 'Art and Agrarian Change, 1710–1815', in Cosgrove and Daniels 1988, pp. 113–14.

100   Barrell 1980, p. 117. Barrell also provides a rich account of the particular role of Herefordshire in the georgic (pp. 173–4, n. 99).

101   Barnes 1965, pp. 117, 122.

102   Barnes 1965, p. 126.

103   Barnes 1965, p. 134.

pamphlet debate to which both Malthus and Ricardo contributed. Successive riots rocked London from 6 to 10 March, during which anti-corn law crowds roughed up some MPs and broke the windows of Lord Darnley, Castlereagh, and others; two people were killed when soldiers fired on a crowd that broke into the Old Burlington Street house of Frederick Robinson, who had introduced the bill.[104] The government was sufficiently alarmed to bring seven regiments of troops into the metropolitan area.[105] Despite the scale of the protests, the bill, which prohibited the importation of foreign corn until the price rose above 80s. per quarter, passed Parliament on 20 March and received royal assent on the 23rd.

In the first weeks after the law passed the price of grain rose steadily, in part because of Napoleon's escape from Elba on 26 February 1815 and the uncertainties generated by the Hundred Days. The average wheat price for the three months ending 15 August was 67s. 11d per quarter, but this was lower than the yearly average for 1814 of 74s. 4d. and was a catastrophic decline when compared with wartime highs of 162s. 6d. (1812) or 109s. 9d. (1813).[106] The debate around the bill was couched in terms of food self-sufficiency, not the interests of landlords as such; Britain, it was argued, needed a strong self-sufficient agriculture to feed itself in times of war and a solid tax base in the countryside; these things could only be assured by keeping agricultural produce at high and relatively stable prices.[107] But it seemed that landlords were the only financial beneficiaries of the new legislation, and Donald Barnes has observed that the laws of 1814 and 1815, and the furore they generated, shifted the opprobium for high prices traditionally directed against corn dealers and millers onto the landlords.[108] As a tenant farmer, Mrs. Theresa Price may well have viewed the passing of the Corn Laws with concern. And the plentiful harvest depicted, if so we should read it, would not necessarily have been good for her as it would potentially lower prices. Mrs. Price's landlord, it may be noted, was the wealthy physician and minor poet Dr John Matthews, who after a career in London had retired to Herefordshire and commissioned a large Neo-Classical house by James Wyatt at Belmont, overlooking the Wye, in 1788–90. Matthews played a substantial role in the county's affairs as mayor of Hereford, M.P. for the county from 1803–6, and Colonel of the first regiment of Hereford Militia. He was also a minor player in the picturesque controversy of the 1790s,

---

104 Barnes 1965, pp. 136–7.

105 The best account of the protests is in Stevenson 1979, pp, 190–2.

106 Barnes 1965, pp. 158, 298.

107 Gambles 1999, pp. 26–7.

108 Barnes 1965, pp. 148–9.

publishing a satire of Payne Knight's didactic poem *The Landscape*, which defended the work of Capability Brown and Humphry Repton – the latter had landscaped Belmont for Matthews before the controversy broke out.[109] It seems unlikely that Matthews would have had the advanced taste to encourage Lewis's work.

In *Harvest Scene* Lewis depicted the high point of the labourer's year, in terms of both hours and wages. That is, labourers might be expected to work up to fifteen hours a day but could also earn seven shillings per week, rather than the usual six shillings, and in addition receive liquor and two dinners.[110] Lewis doubtless witnessed a field thronged with labourers as he painted it, but at a time when there was still an ongoing and long-running debate about modern farming practices leading to rural depopulation, the image also stood as an affirmation of plentiful employment, even if in actuality harvest work was temporary. The imposing quality of the figures in their life class poses would have been even more pronounced before Lewis painted out the seated form of the bailiff or overseer, whose ghostly form, distinguished by the fact that he is seated and wearing a jacket, emerges through the paint of the wheat stook just right of the group of four labourers and as if at their feet.[111] John Duncumb's description of the state of the poor in the *General View of the Agriculture of the County of Hereford* (1804, second edition 1813) he produced for the Board of Agriculture indicates what a gross idealisation a reading of the image as one of prosperity and contentment would be. While over the 40 years previous to 1805 labourers wages had nominally risen, at the same time, Duncumb stressed, their purchasing power had declined drastically. This circumstance was 'not so beneficial to the farmer as some persons imagine', since the labourer who could not earn 'more than the value of as much wheat as the demands of a wife and three or four children require, (and unfortunately his utmost exertions will not always produce as much), must apply to the humiliating resources of parochial aid for a supply of other wants, and the farmer is consequently subject to so many more loans for the support of the poor'. In the circumstances, 'the poor-

---

109   John Matthews, *A Sketch from the Landscape: a Didactic Poem, addressed to R. Payne Knight* (1794). For Matthews's place in the debate, see Stephen Daniels, Susanne Seymour, and Charles Watkins, 'Border Country: The Politics of the Picturesque in the Middle Wye Valley', in Rosenthal, Payne, and Wilcox (eds.) 1997, pp. 175–6; Daniels 1999, pp. 126–7. If Repton made a Red Book for Belmont, it has not survived.

110   Duncumb 1813, pp. 138, 136. For a useful sketch of Herefordshire's rural economy at this moment, see Rosenthal, Payne, and Wilcox (eds.) 1997, pp. 157–63.

111   Payne 1993, has suggested that the original composition might have looked unacceptably threatening in 1816 – p. 96,.

rates increase with an alarming rapidity, and the spirit of honest independence among the peasantry is damped into the sullen submission of slaves'.[112] In some parts of the country wages were pegged to the rise and fall of grain prices, but this practice was not general. The only solution Duncumb could see was in a 'general law' that gave the labourer by right 'a certain stipulated aid for every child beyond the number of three' when wheat exceeded 1s. per gallon. 'To improve the condition and to increase the comforts of this valuable class of the community, must ever be deemed a most desirable object by every liberal and patriotic mind'.[113] The passive stance of Lewis's labourers may signify more the acquiescent cheerfulness that Duncumb thought labourers should display until their 'betters' got round to addressing their problems than an outlook of genuine contentment. For if we consider his figures as portraits – as his claim 'painted on the spot' invites us to do – it is very unlikely they did not depend on parochial relief for part of the year.

Barrell has written that 'this painting must certainly have been acceptable when it was painted',[114] but provides no evidence beyond his reading of the iconography to support this claim. As I have shown above, the connotations of Lewis's matter-of-fact depiction of the wheat harvest and unglamorised agricultural labourers in that summer of 1815 were complex and not necessarily reassuring. Despite his virtuoso beginnings in the field it is not perhaps surprising that Lewis did not become a specialist landscape painter, but gave up the genre to work as an antiquarian draftsman, print maker, and portraitist.[115] The early provenance history of his fourteen sketches and paintings of Hereford is not known and the paintings received no notice in the press that I have discovered.

Prince's description of *Harvest Scene* as 'a traditional view of rural landscape at harvest time' only holds good if we ignore the formal aspects of the picture. The contrast he makes between it and 'the dandy elegance of Stubbs's hay-

---

1 1 2   Duncumb 1813, pp. 136–7. Duncumb estimated that the cost of poor relief in Herefordshire since 1776 had almost doubled (p. 41). By contrast, in his *General View of the Agriculture of the County of Hereford* from 1794, John Clark had suggested there was ample employment for the poor in the county and the 'few poor' there were had brought poverty on themselves (Clark 1794, p. 27). Duncumb was a clergyman and antiquarian, as well as an agricultural writer.

1 1 3   Duncumb 1813, p. 137.

1 1 4   Barrell 1980, p. 116.

1 1 5   There is frustratingly little research on this interesting artist. For a summary of his career, see 'George Robert Lewis', in Leslie Stephen and Sidney Lee (ed.), *Dictionary of National Biography*, vol. 11, Oxford: Oxford University Press, 1973, p. 1062.

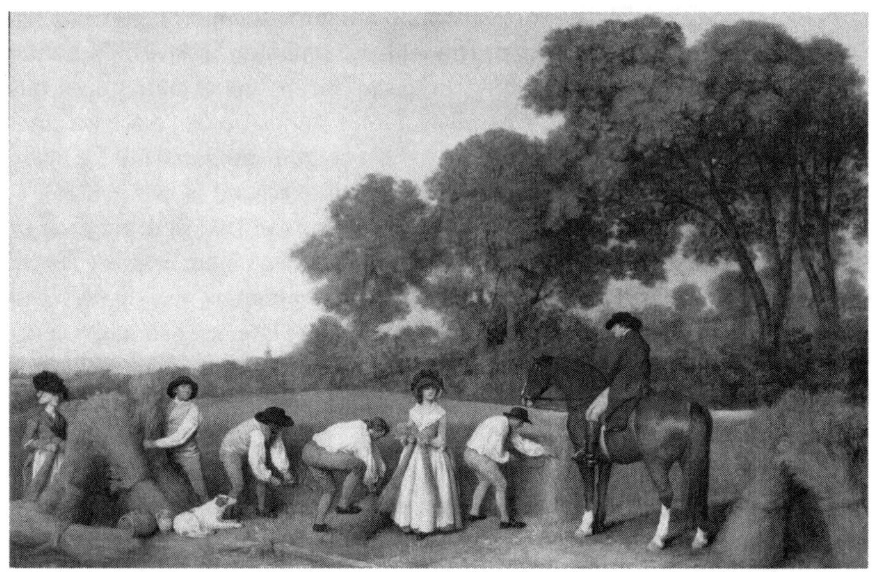

FIGURE 37 *George Stubbs*, Reapers, *1785, oil on wood, 35⅜ × 53⅞ in (89.9 × 136.8 cm), Tate Britain*
© TATE, LONDON, 2015

makers and reapers'[116] – referring to George Stubbs's two paintings on those themes from 1785 in the Tate Gallery (*fig. 37*) – is appropriate. But Lewis's works not only show signs of outdoor painting in a way Stubbs's do not, they produce a realist effect through their plenitude of observed details – quite unlike the rather limited and repetitive denotative marks of Stubbs – and their placing of figure in complex outdoor spaces that contrast with his Neo-Classical frieze-like compositions. Thus it is not just the Rococo prettiness of Stubbs's female labourers and the neat attire of all his figures that mark their difference. Having said this, Stubbs's reapers, unlike Lewis's somewhat dishevelled figures, do not even need to unbutton their doublets. Moreover, while Lewis's foreground harvesters enjoy a break from labour to share the liquor that was part of their wage, the small figures reaping downhill to their left or loading the wagon to the right leave us no doubt that this is a momentary respite.

Focus on *Harvest Scene* in isolation has hampered interpretation of Lewis's achievement in 1815–16. In particular, historians seem to have largely ignored the significance of these works as a group of pictures devoted to a particular topographical locale and the range of agricultural practices within it. Was

---

116   Prince, in Cogrove and Daniels (eds.) 1988, p. 114.

Lewis planning a series of pictures of farm occupations or perhaps a sequence of views of an area that was rich in associations with the Ancient Britons and in the words of Duncumb offered 'a scene of luxuriance and beauty, perhaps not equalled by any county in the kingdom'?[117] *Harvest Scene* and *Hereford from the Haywood* are not only larger than the other works, which can only have been seen as sketches, they are also identical sizes, making it very likely they were conceived as companions. Whereas *Harvest Scene* represents the terrain from a position close to that of the Tate Gallery's sketches of gleaners and reapers, *Hereford from the Haywood* (*fig. 35*) depicts a different time of day and a different viewpoint. From it one cannot see the Malvern Hills, so precisely defined on the skyline of the other three, whereas, unlike in *Harvest Scene*, one can clearly see the city of Hereford in the distance. The shift from '*Haywood Lodge*' to '*Haywood*' was not a slip on Lewis's part, but probably indicated the difference between Haywood Lodge and the Haywood Farm, which was similarly in the parish of Haywood – the site of a former royal forest of which only a fragment remained – and also belonged to John Matthews.[118] To see the nearby village of Dinedor (with its Iron Age fort or camp) and the Malvern Hills from the Haywood Lodge it is necessary to look almost due east. This means that the '*Hereford*' in the full title of *Harvest Scene* makes general reference to the county, not a specific reference to the city, which cannot be seen in that direction.

Hereford from the Haywood does not conform to the best-known Dutch schemata for the depiction of fields such as Ruisdael's several wheat field compositions, of which that in the Metropolitan Museum from circa 1670 (*fig. 38*) is the best known.[119] (*Harvest Scene* is closer to the Ruisdael model in the absence of foreground framing devices and the use of rows of corn stooks to provide a perspective avenue into the distance, standing in for Ruisdael's road). Although it may not be immediately apparent, the closest formal reference point for *Hereford from the Haywood* is a Claudean compositional arrangement

117   Duncumb 1813, p. 2. As Duncumb pointed out, the region was associated with the Silures, who under their leader Caractacus had mounted a particularly fierce resistance to Roman conquest. See William Mason, *Caractacus: A Dramatic Poem Written on the Model of the Ancient Greek Tragedy* (London, 1759).

118   In his *Collections Towards the History and Antiquities of the County of Hereford*, Duncumb recorded that the parish currently had 68 inhabitants (Duncumb 1804, pp. 238, 204). In Duncumb 1813, he wrote: 'Haywood forest and other waste lands in the interior of the county have been cultivated within a recent period with every success' (p. 97).

119   Slive 2001, catalogue nos. 82–108. Slive notes that figures in Ruisdael's grain field compositions are generally inconspicuous strollers or travellers, 'farmers' at work are 'extremely rare' (p. 111).

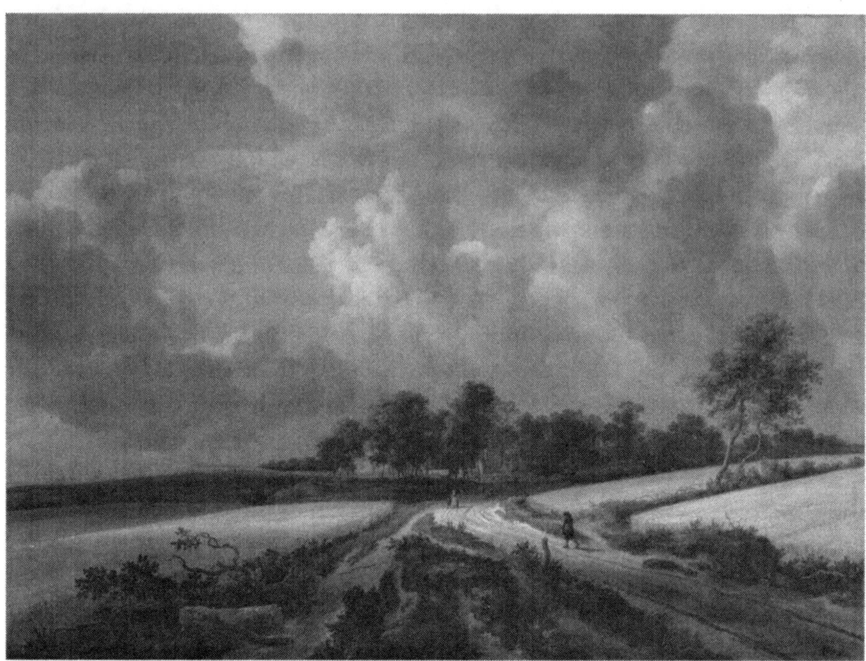

FIGURE 38   *Jacob van Ruisdael,* Wheatfields, *c. 1670, oil on canvas, 39⅜ 51¼ in (100×130.2 cm)*
METROPOLITAN MUSEUM OF ART, NEW YORK

exemplified here by the version of *Jacob with Laban and his Daughters* that was
in Sir Francis Bourgeois's 1811 bequest to Dulwich Picture Gallery (*fig. 39*). My
point is not that this was a conscious model in the way that Claude was often for
Constable, or that Lewis was intending a deliberate evocation of the Claudean
pastoral – almost the reverse – but rather that this was the schemata in the
artist's head. Without that dark mass created by the tree and clump of hedge
in the middle distance, a sign of the particular pattern of timber cultivation in
Herefordshire,[120] we would have a classic instance of asymmetrical repoussoirs
framing a vista of a river valley. As it is we have a caesura that divides a vista as in
Jacob with Laban and his Daughters, forcing attention more into the foreground.

Both *Harvest Scene* and *Hereford from the Haywood* are strikingly unpictur-
esque. Although they are summer scenes, they forcibly remind me of Uvedale
Price's complaint about the appearance of Herefordshire in the spring time: 'I
had heard that at the time of the plough, the whole country from the Malvern

---

120   Clark 1804 emphasised the absence of forests in Herefordshire and the practice of planting
      trees in hedgerows (p. 1100).

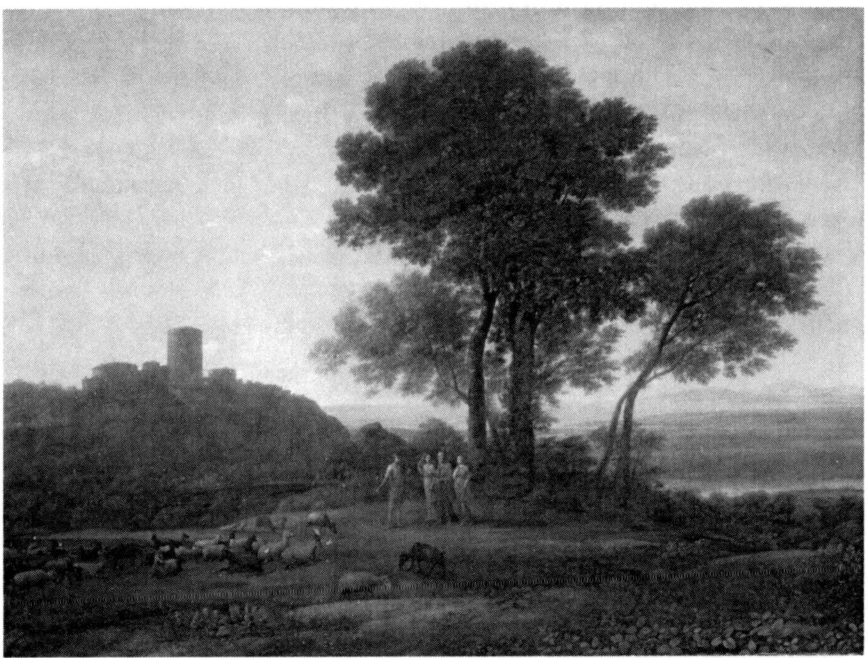

FIGURE 39   *Claude Lorrain,* Jacob with Laban and his Daughters, *1676, oil on canvas, 72 x 94.5 cm, DPG 205.*

Hills looked like a garden, but it made a scattered discordant landscape ... and although the scene conveyed to my mind the cheerful ideas of fruitfulness and plenty, I could not help feeling how defective it was in all those qualities and principles, on which the painter sets so high a value'.[121] Lewis's image is like the antithesis to that autumnal light and colour so favoured by the picturesque theorists, and which Price called 'the decaying charms of autumn'.

Iconographically, the foreground is another source of the picture's novelty, in that it is neither a mountainside nor a pasture, the conventional locations for grazing sheep. Indeed, it appears to be a field of quite recently ploughed earth with a lot of weeds growing among the furrows and near the hedge. These features can be explained by the fact that in some areas of Herefordshire sheep were grazed on fallows for part of the summer. Although John Clark condemned leaving fallows to weeds in his 1794 report for the Board of

---

121   Price 1810, vol. 1, pp. 175–6.

Agriculture, Duncumb in 1804 makes reference to the practice in a passage extolling the hardiness of the region's native Rye-land sheep, which could find adequate sustenance in areas the imported Leicesters could not.[122] Duncumb even sought to justify the special qualities of the Rye-land by claiming that the sheep was, by nature, 'a mountain animal' that could 'collect food in situations where the ox and cow cannot subsist'.[123] I think there can be little doubt that Lewis chose to depict a kind of local sheep that was seen to be rivalled in the quality of its wool by no other British breed, even if it did not produce such quantities of meat as the newer Leicester and South-down breeds. As pictured, the distinctive tawny coats of the sheep look particularly full and they have the small tail characteristic of the Rye-land.

In *The Fleece*, Dyer denominated the breed as Silurian, connecting it with the region's ancient past and the Rye-land's reputation as a hardy animal that roamed the mountain slopes.[124] Clark and Duncumb did not borrow this appellation, and it is part of Lewis's naturalism that he gives us a down to earth vision of sheep in a prosaic spot resting in shade to avoid the noonday sun – the artist was presumably working under the shadow of the same large tree whose presence we deduce from the darker tints that cover much of the foreground. Like Crome, Lewis has arranged his sheep so that they are seen from different angles, perhaps also responding to the anatomical standard set by Hills's etchings. One sheep, viewed from the back, seems almost lost in the hedge. And like Crome's sheep, Lewis's do not have the appearance of a flock, although we may interpret those we see as parts belonging to a larger whole that constitutes one. Lewis's depiction of labourers also works against any easy pastoral reading. The taller figure, who holds a staff, is clearly the shepherd, but the shorter man in the red waistcoat carries something over his arm that may be a jacket but I think is more likely a horse's yoke collar. It is not clear if this is a moment of sociability or some more functional exchange, but both may be read as active, caught in a moment between actions but certainly not idling. In the pastoral vision, labourers do not rest standing up in direct sunlight; in Pope's words 'the Shepherds shun the Noon-day heat', and his Hylas and Ægon sing their 'Rural Lays' beneath the shade of a 'spreading Beech'.[125]

---

122   Clark 1794, p. 79; Duncumb 1813, pp. 125, and also 57. The practice was sufficiently commonplace for Cowper to make reference to it in *The Task* (Cowper 1926, Book 4, ll. 316–19), although Cowper associates it with winter.

123   Duncumb 1813, p. 126.

124   Dyer 1989, p. 53. See also the discussion of this aspect of the poem in Barrell 1983, pp. 93–9.

125   Pope 1969, pp. 14, 15.

To reinforce the point we can see the diminutive figure of a reaper in another field over the shoulder of the right hand figure.

Lewis's paintings are examples of the most advanced landscape naturalism of their moment in their departures from the familiar denotative patterns of seventeenth-century brushwork, their bright colour with its predominance of green, their use of white – a colour generally seen as antithetical to the picturesque – to mark out figures, and their botanical and topographical exactitude. This verisimilitude extends to the depiction of individualised rural figures engaged in plausible forms of labour. Although the paintings I have been discussing by both Crome and Lewis do not escape reference to seventeenth-century compositional schemes, they do not self-consciously invoke them in the way Constable does in the upright Claudean scheme of *The Cornfield*. Similarly, while Crome's and Lewis's figure stand as if caught in a moment of labour, Constable's drinking boy is a cliché – a Suffolk Narcissus without an Echo – that reminds us of the 'Crystal Spring' in which Pope's shepherd sees his reflection.[126] In their works sheep do not form a tidy flock on the Gaspar Dughet model but are individual animals grubbing for sustenance among weeds. Despite his roiling clouds, in *The Cornfield* Constable's vision is of a distant and static enclosed world, like a model in a glass case, while the images of Crome and Lewis are open and mobile, suggesting a momentary encounter close up. Crome and Lewis, I want to say, negate the pastoral and turn it into a contemporary georgic; Constable, in line with the conservative turn of his work in the 1820s, reaffirms and reiterates it. Such imagery seems remote from the mundane economic fact that sheep were commodities worth between three and four pounds per head to the farmer, that they were bred for slaughter, and their destiny was to be mutton dinners and sources of wool. Crome and Lewis – and Wilkie, too, for that matter – bring us closer to that reality.[127]

------

126   Pope 1969, p. 12.

127   It is not clear to me that any of these images connected with contemporary debates around animal slaughter and animal cruelty – on which see Thomas 1983, pp. 178, 287–300. Thomson referred to 'the knife of horrid slaughter' (Thomson 1908, 'Summer', ll. 418–19) and Bloomfield presents the idea of butchering lambs as repugnant – see Bloomfield 1998, 'Spring', ll. 339–54. In the *Farmer's Boy*, Bloomfield speaks out strongly against the practice of docking horse's tails ('Summer', ll. 210–13). Although this may align him with what William J. Christmas calls 'progressive animal philanthropists' of the time for whom the cause of animals was linked to a larger progressive political project, Christmas also reminds us that opposition to animal cruelty – particularly by the lower classes – was part of conservative evangelical discourse. See Christmas in White, Simon, and Goodridge (eds.) 2006, pp. 34–8.

What continues to intrigue about their work is the stress of old pictorial codes being modified and stretched to do new ideological business, with innovative forms emerging as a result that permit a different vision of familiar realities.

CHAPTER 8

Artisanal Worldview in the Paintings of John Crome

The iconography and distinctive formal characteristics of works by the early nineteenth-century Norwich artist John Crome may be read as signs of his formation in the artisan class of that city and as expressions of a particular Weltanschauung, a holistic view of the world that encompassed nature and social life in a continuum. It is this particular Weltanschauung that marks out Crome's work from that of other artists of his time and gives it its unique quality.[1] These are the fundamental claims of this chapter. But before entering into the details of my argument it is necessary to say something about Crome's art-historical status and the historiography around his art.

In the first modern art-historical essay on Crome from 1897 Laurence Binyon boldly observed: 'In looking back to seek a classic, it is Crome we should fix upon rather than Constable ... For Crome, with a range and knowledge not inferior to Constable, is in all imaginative qualities, as well as in actual power and ease of painting, his superior'.[2] At the time Binyon was an assistant in the British Museum's Department of Prints and Drawings, where he would go on to a distinguished career as an authority on Japanese and Chinese art. But although he was still only a youthful aesthete – he would later gain a reputation as a poet – Binyon's estimation of Crome was not an isolated one. In 1921, Charles J. Holmes, director of the National Gallery and a pioneering Constable scholar, would observe of Crome that: 'Compared with Constable his work has an architectural grandeur, serenity and completeness which the younger master can never attain'.[3] In light of such claims, the relative neglect of Crome's work in recent art-historical scholarship calls for explanation. To illustrate my point: the last solo exhibition devoted to Crome was held 45 years ago on the bicentenary of his birth in 1968. A small show – displayed at the Norwich Castle Museum and then the Tate Gallery – it included a mere 75 works, in contrast with the 359 exhibits at the Tate's bicentenary exhibition of

---

1   For the concept of Weltanschauung see Mannheim 1952. I have argued for the value of a modified version of this concept in the Introduction to Hemingway and Wallach (eds.) 2015, pp. 3–6.

2   Binyon 1897, p. 45. Binyon 1904, p. 54.

3   Charles John Holmes, 'Introduction', in Baker 1921, p. xxvi. Collins Baker was Keeper of Pictures at the National Gallery. Holmes published his *Constable and his Influence on Landscape Painting* in 1902.

Constable's work eight years later.[4] There have been several major exhibitions of Constable's works since 1976 but none of Crome's.

One reason for this is the relative inaccessibility of Crome's works to a metropolitan audience. The largest assemblage of Cromes, that in the R.J. Colman collection at Norwich Castle Museum, was forbidden to travel by the terms of the 1951 Colman bequest.[5] Another factor is the relative smallness of Crome's oeuvre, which arose from the circumstance that he made a living mainly as a drawing master along with the other expedients provincial artists resorted to such as dealing in or cleaning and restoring Old Master paintings,[6] and also by the relative shortness of a career that lasted scarcely twenty years. The most recent of the three catalogue raisonnés of Crome's oeuvre attributes to him 126 works in oil (including three inn signs) and 119 works on paper. By contrast, Graham Reynolds's catalogue of Constable's work includes approximately 759 paintings and sketches in oil and 1,692 works on paper.[7] And then there arises the problem of attribution that is signalled by the existence of those three catalogue raisonnés, two of which were published a mere decade apart.[8] None of these is satisfactory by present day art-historical standards and the more recent, those by Derek and Timothy Clifford and by Norman L. Goldberg, represent no advance in interpretation over C.H. Collins Baker's pioneering 1921 volume. The number of low quality and obvious duds in British public collections masquerading as Cromes can be seen from a glance through the depressing array of paintings attributed to the artist on the Art UK website.

In 1821 the Norwich Society of Artists, in whose founding in 1803 Crome had played a leading role, put on a memorial exhibition of 110 of his works, which

---

4   Hawcroft 1968; Parris, Fleming-Williams, and Shields 1976.

5   I address the role of the Colman family in the institutionalisation of Norwich art in Chapter Five. The prohibition on travel was waived for the Norwich School exhibition at the Tate Gallery in 2000. See Brown, Hemingway, and Lyles 2000, p. 7.

6   For Crome's career as a drawing master, dealer and collector, see Fawcett 1974, pp. 28–30, 73–4.

7   Goldberg 1978; Reynolds 1984; Reynolds 1996. I say 'approximately' because Reynolds's catalogue includes works now known only from their titles in contemporary exhibition catalogues and where the medium is uncertain. The figure for works on paper is actually larger because some items in his catalogue are sketchbooks with several drawings in them.

8   Baker, 1921, Clifford and Clifford, 1968; Goldberg 1978. A symptom of the difficulties and interests involved is the testy exchanges over the Cliffords' catalogue. See the review by Francis Hawcroft in the *Burlington Magazine* (Hawcroft 1969) and the ensuing exchange of letters with the authors, *Burlington Magazine*, 112, 808 (July 1970), 466–8; Anon., 'Crome and some Cromesque mimicries', *Times Literary Supplement*, no. 207 (27 February 1969). I address the limitations of Goldberg's catalogue in my review – Hemingway 1979 (2). For the most part, the Cliffords' catalogue is the most reliable of the three.

quickly became an object of special interest to some local collectors.[9] It seems from the correspondence of one such collector that by mid-century works by other artists, whether or not they were deliberate forgeries, were circulating under Crome's name and that demand for originals had outstripped supply, a situation that would be exacerbated when the artist's reputation began to rise both nationally and internationally following the showing of seven of his paintings at the London International Exhibition of 1862.[10] The history of many of Crome's pictures is obscure, he did not sign or date his work for the most part, and connecting surviving works with the exhibition record is largely a matter of guesswork.[11] Although Crome's seven-year apprenticeship to the coach and sign painter Francis Whisler ended in 1790 and the first entry in the catalogue to the 1821 Memorial Exhibition is described as *Sketch – his first in oil* and dated as 1790, only three works in that exhibition were given to years before 1805 when the Norwich Society of Artists' annual exhibitions began.[12] Some of the views of Wales and Cumberland Crome showed at the society's early exhibitions may have been from before 1805, but there are no works by him that can be securely dated from before 1800.

The historian is faced with a body of work of surprising variety that has to be comprehended largely within the sixteen years 1805–21 when Crome was an exhibiting artist.[13] It ranges from the dark broadly brushed picturesque compositions of *c*. 1805–7; paintings more in the idiom of Gainsborough, whose *Cottage Door* (1780; *fig. 70*) Crome copied in a local collection;[14] works that are based on Hobbema's glade scene compositions but that infuse them with effects of atmosphere and light that indicate both the influence of outdoor sketching and the example of the progressive naturalism Crome saw in the London exhibition rooms; and finally a whole range of more original and

---

9   The catalogue is printed as Appendix D in Clifford and Clifford 1968, pp. 265–7. The Cliffords also provide an account of three early local Crome collections as Appendix G, pp. 274–84.

10   See Chapter 5, n. 34, above.

11   A benchmark remains the entries in the illustrated picture catalogue of the Yarmouth banker Dawson Turner, who was one of Crome's most important patrons. See Turner 1840. It is intriguing that with one exception all the works at the 1821 Memorial Exhibition were dated.

12   Indeed, the memorial show was heavily weighted to Crome's later achievements, with only twelve works dating from before 1810.

13   For the record of Crome's Norwich exhibits, see Clifford and Clifford 1968, Appendix A, pp. 257–62; for his exhibits in London, see Appendices B and C, pp. 263–4.

14   Dawson Turner, 'Memoir of Crome', (1838) in Wodderspoon 1876, p. 7; Turner 1840, p. 23; Hawcroft 1959.

independent compositions of his own devising. We still await a morphology of Crome's works that makes sense also as a chronology of his development and gives it a plausible order.[15]

All these circumstances help us to understand Crome's marginalisation relative to Constable and Turner, but they do not explain why his standing in the early twentieth century was so high. The reasons for this lay partly in the specific ways that Crome negotiated between inherited pictorial forms and the impulse to naturalism that was such a feature of British landscape painting in the first two decades of the nineteenth century;[16] and partly in the formalist value system of his admirers. This value system grew out of the Aesthetic Movement. It is clearest in the case of Charles Holmes, who as a student at Oxford in the late 1880s knew Walter Pater, the leading theorist of British aestheticism, and was a friend of the formalist critic Roger Fry with whom he collaborated as a co-editor of the *Burlington Magazine* from 1903–9. A capable landscape painter himself and a member of the New English Art Club, Holmes published a pamphlet supporting Fry's ground-breaking *Manet and the Post-Impressionists* exhibition in 1910.[17] Holmes was also acquainted with Binyon, who in the late 1890s persuaded him to write two essays on Japanese woodblock prints – a signature taste of aestheticism – for *The Dome* magazine, which in its short three-year existence was one of the movement's chief organs. The claim for Crome's modernity was reinforced by the discovery of his etchings, which in the early twentieth century were said to establish him as one of the first, if not the first, of modern painter etchers.[18]

Like subsequent scholars, Binyon took Crome's 1816 letter to his student James Stark – one of four letters by him to survive – as providing the key to his aesthetic. (Collins Baker would follow Binyon in this regard).[19] The letter's critique of an unidentified painting by Stark is indeed a revelatory statement and confirms reports that despite his lack of formal education Crome was extremely articulate in his conversations on art.[20] Moreover it could be read so as to chime with the formalist predilections of Binyon and Holmes.

---

15   The problems of dating and attribution are dealt with succinctly by Hawcroft in the Introduction to Hawcroft 1968.

16   On naturalism, see Hemingway 1992, Chapter 2, and the Introduction to the present volume.

17   Holmes 1910.

18   Hardie 1904; Salaman 1914, p. 32. The first catalogue of his etchings appeared in 1906 – see Theobald 1906.

19   Baker 1921, Chapter 4.

20   Partially printed in Binyon 1897, p. 46. Printed in full in Clifford and Clifford 1968, pp. 90–1.

Crome reproved Stark for making the character of his clouds 'too affected', too much like the rounded clouds that were such a feature of some seventeenth-century Dutch landscape paintings, and warns him off a 'too-picture effect'. But at the same time he also lectured him about the concept of breadth, which was a central concept of the academic theory of chiaroscuro and composition in Britain. 'Breadth must be attended too', Crome writes, 'if you paint but a muscle give it breadth. Your doing the same by the sky, making parts broad and of good shape, that they may come in with your composition, forming one grand plan of light and shade, this must always please a good eye and keep the attention of the spectator and give delight to every one. Trifles in Nature must be overlooked that we may have our feelings raised by seeing the whole picture at a glance, not knowing how or why we are so charmed'.[21]

This text provided Binyon, Holmes, and Baker with confirmation that while Crome was a careful observer of natural effects he was also an artist who subordinated his observations to a rigorous formal discipline. Binyon expressed this by saying that Crome achieved the rare feat of moulding 'immense, intractable nature' to his own style.[22] Collins Baker found throughout Crome's work evidence of 'his instinctive genius for selecting a significant composition by a careful study of the science of design'. Crome's assertion that 'Trifles in nature must be overlooked' anticipated Whistler's aesthetic dictum about the necessity of artistic selection.[23] In brief, Crome had avoided both the excessive naturalism of Constable and Turner's 'passion of crowding splendour upon splendour'. He was an artist of smaller range, but one with a firmer grasp of the essential verities of pictorial form as early modernist ideologues such as Clive Bell and Roger Fry understood them.[24]

The question of what particularities of style and vision distinguish Crome's art is not a trivial one. The rhetorical discourse of individual genius aside, it is a basic starting point of aesthetic evaluation. However, questions of this type were largely bypassed or dismissed in the wave of social history of art that vitalised British landscape studies in the 1980s and early 1990s. This was a body of scholarship overwhelmingly concerned with iconography and its ideological functions in which analysis of form and style took a back seat. The

---

21　Crome misspells 'breadth' as 'breath' but this is clearly what he means. I suspect that by 'muscle' he meant 'morsel'. On breadth, see Hemingway 1992, pp. 88–9, 205–6, 319–20 n. 73, 333 n. 145, and *passim*; Price 1810, *Essays on the Picturesque*, Chapter 7.

22　Binyon 1897, pp. 47–8.

23　Baker 1921, pp. 71–2. Baker was referring to Whistler 1989, p. 506.

24　Holmes, 'Introduction', in Baker 1921, pp. xxv–vi.

only scholars from this cohort who attended to Crome, Trevor Fawcett and myself, exemplify the point.[25] The object of this essay is partly to redress this lacuna.

In my writings on Crome from the 1980s and early 1990s I argued that his work was distinguished partly by an iconography of leisure, which was particularly manifest in his scenes of the beach at Great Yarmouth and of the two rivers that served the city of Norwich, the Wensum and the Yare. Great Yarmouth was the most important seaside resort on the Norfolk coast; only 22 miles from Norwich, it was much frequented by the city's inhabitants in the summer months and had a distinctly bourgeois character by comparison with fashionable resorts such as Brighton, Ramsgate, and Weymouth. The evidence of contemporary guidebooks and letters shows that the area of beach around the jetty, on which Crome particularly focused, functioned as a promenade for visitors attracted by the activities of the fishermen and the distant spectacle of shipping passing on Yarmouth Roads.[26] Crome exhibited at least four views of the jetty between 1807 and 1819 and perhaps more; five oil paintings and one oil sketch of the motif survive.[27] They represent both aspects of the site that drew visitors and the activities of the visitors themselves in some instances. In this respect they resemble early Impressionism. The example I illustrate here (*fig. 40*) is perhaps the *Yarmouth Jetty* exhibited with the Norwich Society in 1817.[28]

Like the beach, the river system was a site of labour and leisure. Norwich was dependent on the River Wensum, which runs through the city from roughly west to east, before turning south where it once formed the city's eastern boundary, finally joining the River Yare at the hamlet of Whitlingham. The Wensum provided Norwich with its water supply and was also vital to its brewing and dyeing industries. With the Yare it connected Norwich to the coast and was the chief conduit of its trade. The New Mills in the north-west corner of the city, a neighbourhood that Crome painted repeatedly, were constructed

---

25   Fawcett 1982; Hemingway 1994; and Chapter Eight in the present volume. Fawcett's essay was ground-breaking and deserves to be better known.

26   Hemingway 1992, pp. 204–8.

27   Clifford and Clifford 1968, catalogue numbers P23, P23a, P42, P45, and P46. Like the Cliffords, my inclination is to see P41 as a sketch for P42, but it does seem incongruous that the former is significantly larger (20½ × 33¼ ins. to 17⅝ × 23 ins.). A pencil drawing and watercolour of the motif (D37 and D50) also survive. I agree with the Cliffords that the attribution of P23a is dubious. Crome exhibited views of Yarmouth Quay – another of the town's tourist promenades – in 1809 and 1814, but neither is known today.

28   The lightness of the colouring, the informality of the composition, and the sketchiness of the finish argue for a later date than I suggested in Hemingway 1992.

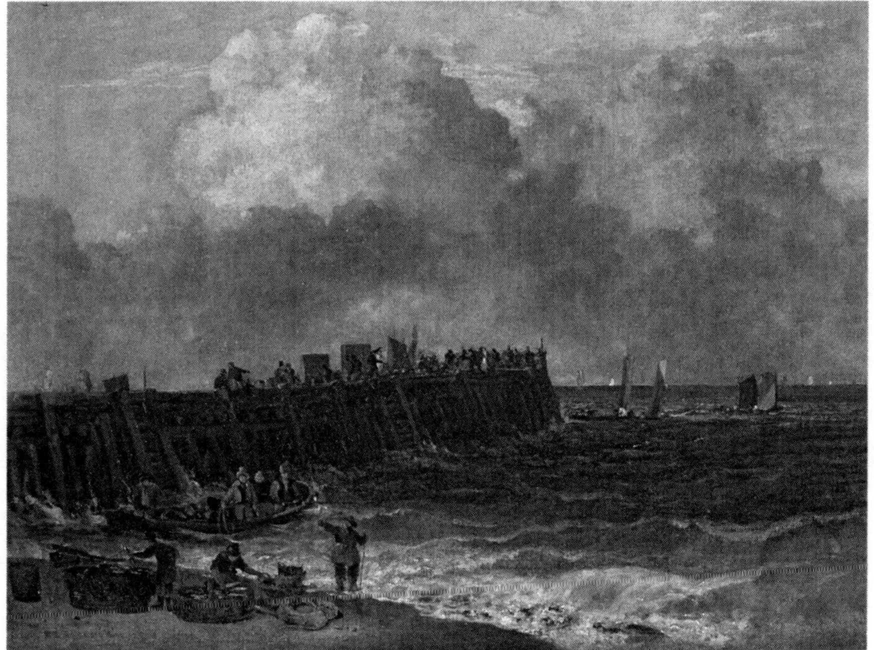

FIGURE 40   *John Crome,* Yarmouth Jetty, *1817?, oil on canvas, 17⅝ × 23 in (44.8×58.3 cm)*
NORFOLK MUSEUMS SERVICE (NORWICH CASTLE MUSEUM AND ART
GALLERY)

by the corporation in the late sixteenth century and included a flour mill and
water-raising complex. In 1819 they were harnessed to drive a large five-story
silk mill that stood near them. Crome's pictures of industrial structures in this
fringe of the city such as *Back of the New Mills* (*fig. 41*)[29] and *The Wensum,
Norwich* (Yale Center for British Art, New Haven) – which views the same group
of buildings from the other side, further downstream – imply the perspective
of the leisured boater, even when they do not actually depict leisure as in
Norwich River: Afternoon (*fig. 42*), which is probably a painting exhibited with
the Norwich Society in 1819. The Norwich journalist John Wodderspoon, who
published a memoir of Crome in 1858, comments that among his 'first-class'
works were 'his views on the upper waters flowing through St. Martin's at Oak',

---

29   Clifford and Clifford 1968, P84. Of the six views of the 'Back of the New Mills' from 1806,
1814 (× 2), 1815, 1816, and 1817 shown at Crome's memorial exhibition (nos. 110, 11, 24, 49,
63, and 15) P84 is likely to be one of those from 1815–17. Crome lived in the parish of St.
George's Colegate in the north of the city, which abuts the parish of St. Martin's at Oak
where the New Mills stood.

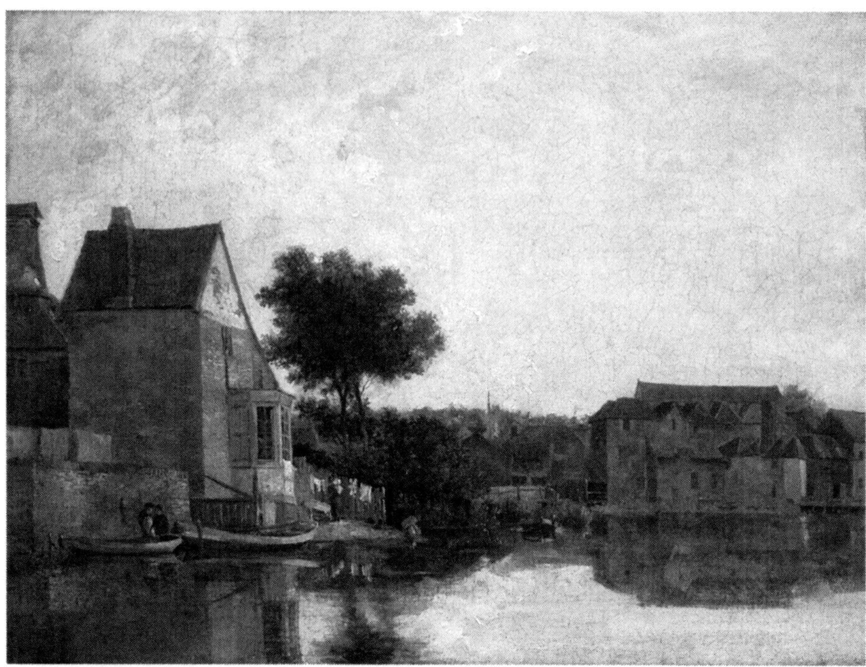

FIGURE 41   *John Crome,* Back of the New Mills, *c. 1815, oil on canvas, 16¼ × 21¼ in (41.3 × 54 cm)*
NORFOLK MUSEUMS SERVICE (NORWICH CASTLE MUSEUM AND ART
GALLERY)

the parish in which the New Mills stood. 'Along the lazy stream which finds
a devious course through that part, are many patches of picturesque gardens
kept by poor men, who, to the enjoyment of their small though successful
experiments in horticulture, add that of keeping boats. A boat was always a
great attraction for Crome, and he has painted many such morsels of river life
as these localities disclose'.[30] Crome was not a poor man, but as the son of a
journeyman weaver who ran a public house called the King and Miller that
in the words of Dawson Turner was 'of far from the highest description',[31] he
certainly knew the world of those 'poor men' to whom Wodderspoon referred.
Over the century 1750–1850 traditional artisanal forms of production in the
Norwich textiles industry – the principal source of the city's wealth – were
in decline as manufacturing concerns grew larger and more capital intensive.
The social distance between masters and journeymen grew, the weavers were

---

30   Wodderspoon 1876, p. 15.
31   Turner, 'Memoir of Crome', in Wodderspoon 1876, p. 6; Turner 1840, p. 17.

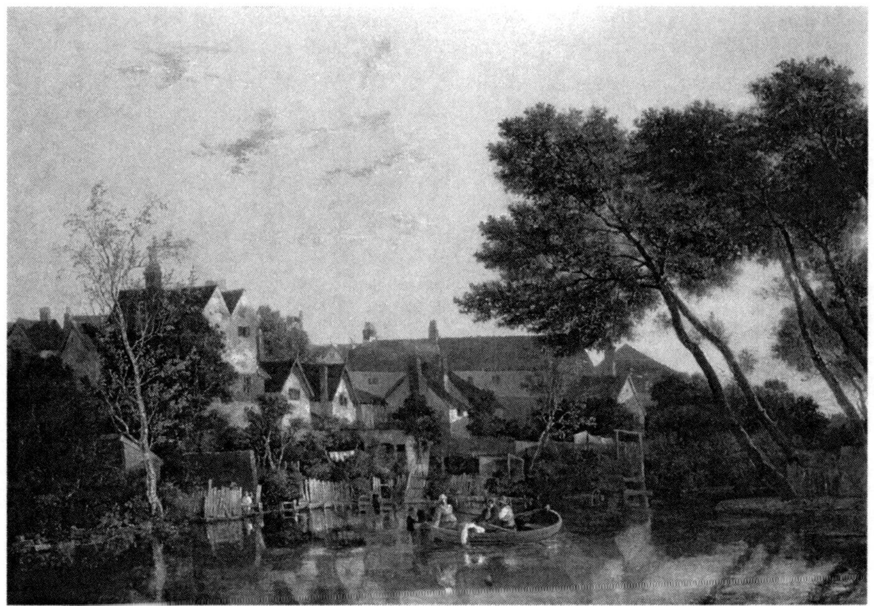

FIGURE 42   *John Crome,* Norwich River: Afternoon, *1819, oil on canvas, 28 × 39 ¼in (71 × 99.5 cm)*
NORFOLK MUSEUMS SERVICE (NORWICH CASTLE MUSEUM AND ART
GALLERY)

increasingly impoverished, and class tensions made the city's politics more
deeply antagonistic.[32] In the light of these developments Crome's pictures of
modest plebeian pleasures on the Norwich river acquire a poignant cast.

As a corollary to this, we may note that with the exception of the *View Near
Norwich – Harvesters* in Manchester City Art Gallery,[33] Crome's imagery of Norfolk agriculture is resolutely pastoral, despite the county's reputation for progressive farming practices and the regional pride displayed by Norwich writers
in celebrating the fact.[34] The theme of the shepherd drew him repeatedly, as
in *Return of the Flock* (private collection), *View on Mousehold Heath* (1812?, *fig.
31*),[35] and the *Way though the Wood* (1813?, *fig. 43*). Crome's rustic figures in pictures such as *The Beaters* and *Marlingford Grove* (*figs. 44* and *45*) are essentially

<hr>

32   For a sketch of these developments and bibliography, see Hemingway 1992, p. 258.

33   The Cliffords thought the attribution insecure – Clifford and Clifford 1968, p. 251. Hawcroft
      reaffirmed it in his review, Hawcroft 1969, p. 765.

34   Bacon 1844, p. 1.

35   Perhaps *Boy keeping Sheep – Morning* exhibited with the NSA in 1812 and then exhibited as
      Boy and Sheep – morning at the Crome Memorial Exhibition, but misdated in the catalogue
      as from 1815.

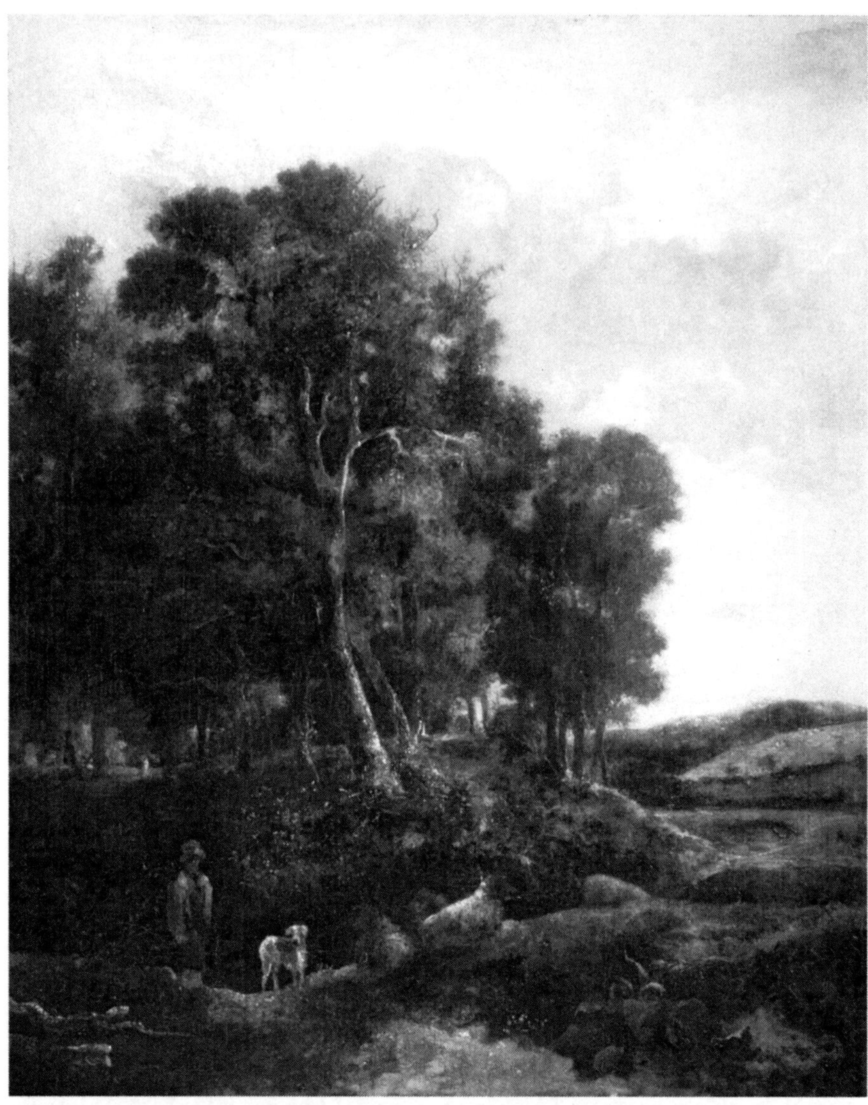

FIGURE 43   *John Crome,* Way though the Wood, *1813?, oil on canvas*
BIRMINGHAM CITY MUSEUM AND ART GALLERY

Gainsboroughesque staffage with no evident economic function; indeed it is not clear that the figures that give *The Beaters* its name are employed to beat game and the original title *Wood Scene with Figures* is preferable.[36] Further,

36   For the painting's history, see Clifford and Clifford 1968, pp. 207–8 n. 1.

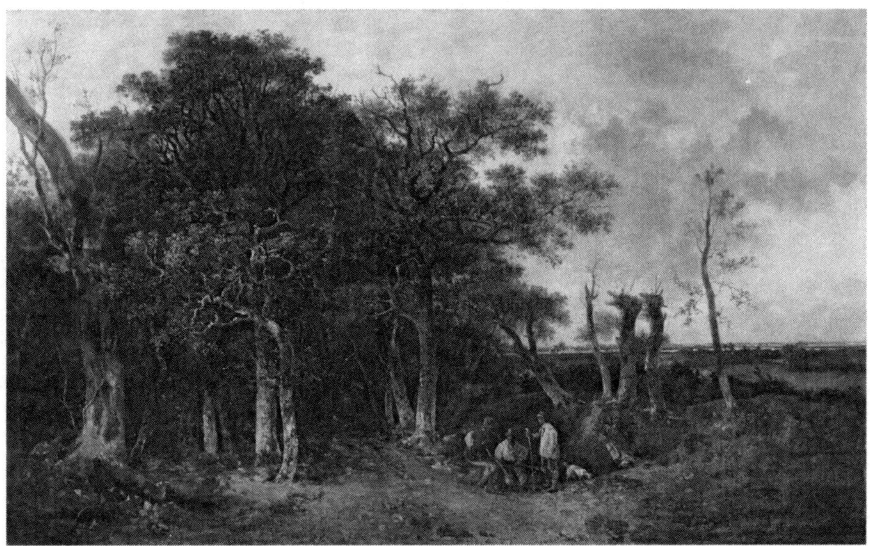

FIGURE 44   *John Crome,* The Beaters, *1810, oil on panel, 21½ × 34 in (54.6 × 86.4 cm)*
NATIONAL GALLERIES OF SCOTLAND, SCOTTISH NATIONAL GALLERY

as Trevor Fawcett has pointed out, when he painted Mousehold Heath in his famous picture in the Tate Gallery (*fig. 48*) Crome gave no indications that this area on the edge of the city of Norwich, which in its unenclosed state was used as a pleasure ground by its inhabitants, had been successively enclosed from 1799 on.[37] According to a letter published in the local Whig paper *The Iris* in 1803, this had been 'a favourite resort, where many hundreds [could be] seen on a fine Summer's evening engaged in their different sports and games. In short, it was the only place in the vicinity of the city where it was possible to retire "from the busy hum of men", without being choaked [*sic*] with the dust of roads, and deafened with the succession of carriages'. But no more.[38] At a time when artists such as Constable, Turner and others were developing a more actualised imagery of rural labour, Crome seems determinedly set in a townsman's vision.

---

37   Fawcett 1982 (1) makes a good case for connecting the image with natural theology but overlooks the one-time status of the heath as a pleasure ground. Cf. my discussion of Cotman's views of Mousehold in Chapter Five. An 1832 guide described the area as 'a tract of hilly ground, four or five miles broad each way', and observed, 'nearly the whole has been inclosed within a few years, but it is probable that some parts of it will never be brought into cultivation'. See Stacy 1832, p. 65.

38   CIVIS, 'To the Editor of the Iris', *The Iris*, no. 11, 16 April 1803.

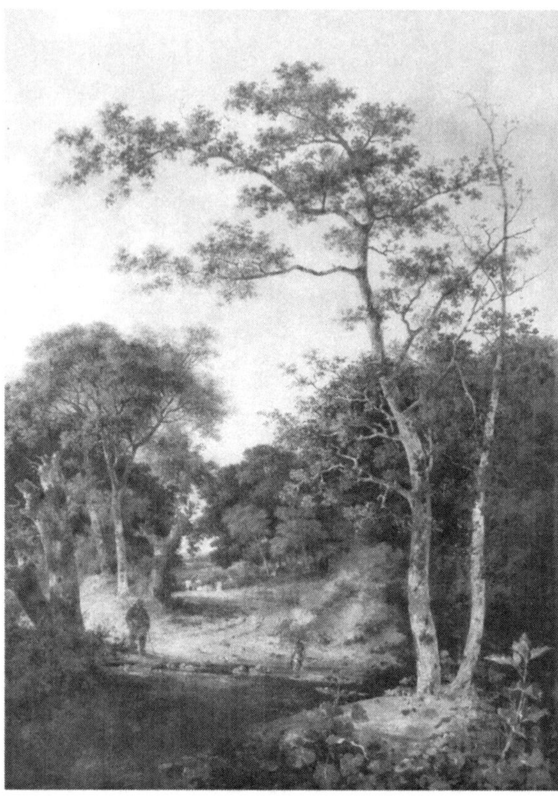

FIGURE 45
John Crome, Marlingford
Grove, *1815, oil on canvas, Lady
Lever Art Gallery, Port
Sunlight*
IMAGE BY PUBLIC
CATALOGUE FOUNDATION,
COURTESY NATIONAL
MUSEUMS, LIVERPOOL

This brings me on to the other strand of my argument about Crome, namely the character of his relations with patrons. In the 'Memoir of Crome' Dawson Turner wrote to accompany the second publication of the artist's etchings in 1838, he observed that 'to attempt any enumeration of Crome's patrons were an endless task: it were in reality little less than to give a list of all those who knew him'.[39] Wodderspoon gave a more socially specific account of his buyers, claiming that although 'a few of the country gentry thought highly of his works, and gave him commissions, the most frequent wishes for his pictures were felt by those citizens who not only regarded him as a painter of native scenery … but who respected him as a man, and in many instances, owned him as a companion or friend'.[40] As Derek and Timothy Clifford pointed out in their 1968 study, although Turner singled out Thomas Harvey of Catton,

---

39   Wodderspoon 1876, p. 8. For the etchings, see Clifford and Clifford 1968, pp. 67–9, 163–75.
40   Wodderspoon 1876, p. 16.

the Gurney family of Earlham, and Lady Jerningham of Costessey as figures of special importance among Crome's patrons, to judge from the lenders to his 1821 Memorial exhibition and other records the majority of those who purchased his pictures were townsmen, far more modest in wealth and rank.[41] This seems to confirm Wodderspoon's account. For the most part Crome made small inexpensive pictures for the houses of local patrons, which contrast in scale and pretension, as well as in form, with those his pupils James Stark and George Vincent made for the London exhibition rooms, in which Crome showed only seventeen works in the course of his career.[42]

In my 1992 book *Landscape Imagery and Urban Culture in Early Nineteenth-Century Britain* I suggested that the form of Crome's paintings of leisure sites bespeaks a kind of direct engagement with shared social experience that made them particularly consonant with the outlook of his patrons. I still think this is correct. But I now want to stress tensions in the way Crome's particular class identity positioned him in relation to the wealthiest social groups in a city that was noted for the turbulence of its politics and where there was a relatively high level of democratic participation in elections.[43] To give an impression of what this social elite were like I quote from a remarkable description of the Norwich patrician class in J.W. Robberds's 1843 biography of William Taylor, the leading Norwich intellectual of that time, and the child of a successful manufacturer whose wealth came mainly from the export trade:

> Accustomed to have all their commands instantly and implicitly obeyed, they too often became proud and severe, impatient and authoritative, overbearing and dictatorial. Reverenced as patrons, they acquired the influence of lords; and in a different set of social relations, the elements of discord which were thus let loose, might, after ages of internecine strife, have rendered Norwich, like another Florence, the patrimony of a merchant-prince ... The position which the father of William Taylor occupied in this class of patricians entitled him to share largely in the obsequious respect which their clients paid them.[44]

---

41 Clifford and Clifford 1968, Chapter 5, 'Crome's Patrons'. Turner's presentation was justified at least in relation to Harvey and the Gurneys, who certainly did play a major role in Crome's career. Although Turner himself owned eleven of Crome's pictures he was not a lender to the 1821 Memorial Exhibition.

42 Hemingway 1992, pp. 207–8, 266.

43 On which, see Rogers 1989, Chapter 9; Mark Knight, 'Politics, 1660–1835', in Rawcliffe and Wilson (eds.) 2004, pp. 167–92.

44 Robberds 1843, vol. 1, p. 40. Taylor (1765–1836) was baptised a Unitarian in Thomas Ivory's

When the younger Taylor came back from an extended tour of Germany in 1781–2 his father's mansion in Surrey Street was the scene of regular dinner parties at which small groups of six to ten people gathered to discuss literature, ideas, and politics. In Robberds's words, 'at the time of William Taylor's return from the continent, and for several years afterwards, there was more mind afloat in Norwich than is usually found out of the literary circles of the metropolis'.[45] Although there is an element of exaggeration in Robberds's picture – he was a Norwich worsted manufacturer with a strong sense of local pride – Norwich was certainly a significant centre of the provincial Enlightenment.[46]

The harmonious atmosphere of the 1780s ended with the French Revolution. By Robberds's account, 'the violent controversies arising out of the French Revolution first darkened these halcyon days; since which the growing fanaticism and mutual intolerance of sects afford a lamentable contrast to the picture just drawn'.[47] Taylor and his father were on what we could describe anachronistically as the left wing of Norwich bourgeois society. Both were active in forming a Revolution Society in Norwich in 1788 to mark the centenary of the so-called Glorious Revolution and this effectively became the Norwich branch of the London Corresponding Society.[48] In 1790 Taylor visited France and reported glowingly on the changes taking place there; in 1792 he was Secretary to the Norwich Revolution Society, which dissolved after the arrest of its Secretary in 1794.[49] Norwich was one of the leading centres of political radicalism in the

---

Octagon chapel. He spoke at least three European languages and in the years around 1780 travelled extensively in the Netherlands, France, Italy, and Germany. For the importance of Taylor as a conduit for German philosophy and literature in the late eighteenth and early nineteenth centuries, see Stokoe 1926, Chapter 3.

45   Robberds 1843, vol. 1, pp. 44–5. Robberds gives a list of those Norwich residents 1783–1815 who constituted the city's 'mind', vol., pp. 45–8.

46   The character of Robberds's progressivism can be gauged from his letterpress to *Scenery of the Rivers of Norfolk* (Robberds 1834). For modern day assessments of Norwich as an intellectual centre in this period, see Fawcett 1972; Fawcett 1982 (2); and Mosley 1973.

47   Robberds 1843, vol. 1, p. 51. Robberds probably exaggerated the degree of harmony in the 1780s. For the effects of the French Revolution in Norwich, see Rawcliffe and Wilson (eds.) 2004, pp. 182–8.

48   Jewson 1975, Chapter 2. For the larger context, see Thompson 1963, Part 1.

49   Robberds 1843, vol. 1, pp. 67–73. It is striking, however, that with the exception of a single poem Taylor did not contribute to that showcase of Norwich progressive intellect *The Cabinet* (1795). That is, if the identifications in Graham 1932 are correct. Robberds (vol. 1, p. 148) implies he played a larger role in the publication. It was of course a sign of the times that the contributors remained anonymous.

1790s and although Taylor described himself as increasingly 'antigallican' in a letter of 1798, he remained a Foxite Whig and in 1802 became editor of Norwich's short-lived Whig paper *The Iris*.[50]

Trevor Fawcett has described Taylor as the type of middle-class intellectual 'steeped in eighteenth-century philosophical writing' who were early leaders of those groups pressing for political reform and repeal of the Test and Corporation Acts, but who drew their support 'largely from the shopkeeper/artisan classes', to which Crome belonged.[51] We do not know if Crome was a member of the Norwich Revolution Society. We do know, however, that he lived in the parish of St. George's Colegate, one of the northern parishes where there were heavy concentrations of weavers who were also nonconformists and regularly voted Whig.[52] In 1818 he was recorded as a liberal voter, he became a freemason in 1813, and he made donations to a Baptist chapel despite having had most of his children baptised into the establishment church.[53] Although we must imagine Taylor as vastly higher in social station than Crome in the 1780s and 1790s, in 1810–11 the Taylor business suffered such serious reverses that the family were forced to exchange their large house in Surrey Street for a far more modest one in King Street and even considered quitting the city to avoid the social embarrassment the decline in their fortunes caused.[54] Moreover, Crome and Taylor certainly knew one another through the Norwich Philosophical Society, which was founded in 1812. According to Robberds, the society's character was 'more literary than scientific' and it was an arena of debate rather than 'a tribune to the professor'. Taylor was a regular attendee and 'never failed to take a prominent part' in its proceedings; Crome and his eldest son John Berney Crome were also members.[55] In 1814 Taylor published a lecture on landscape painting that

---

50   Robberds 1843, vol. 1, pp. 229, 422–3, 471; vol. pp. 2, 3, 24. The fact that Taylor declares his 'anti-gallicanism' in a letter to the conservative Robert Southey of 26 September 1798 should be taken into account.

51   Fawcett 1982 (2), p. 24.

52   Rogers 1989, p. 334. Rogers is writing of an earlier period, but my guess is that the electoral geography continued to apply.

53   Baker 1921, p. 20; le Strange 1898; Goldberg 1962. Crome's books give no clear indication of his politics. He owned works by radicals such as Thomas Holcroft and John Thelwall and liberal clergymen such as David Williams and William Paley, but he also owned Hannah More's novel *Coelebs in Search of a Wife* and the *Anti-Jacobin Review* of 1798–1800. See *A Catalogue of the Entire Valuable Collection of Paintings, Prints and Books, Late the Property of Mr. J. Crome, Dec.*, J. Athow, Norwich, 25 September–1 October 1821, day 5 lots 44, 84, 48, 19, 47, and 89.

54   Robberds 1843, vol. 2, pp. 323, 350–1, 356, 364–7, 411.

55   Robberds 1843, vol. 2, pp. 438, 441, 441 n. 1.

he had delivered before the society in the *Monthly Magazine*.[56] Four years later John Berney Crome gave a lecture to the society on painting and poetry.[57]

Taylor's essay is knowledgeable and suggests that its author had given substantial reflection to the relation between picture-making and perceptual experience. It is also strikingly original, pursuing the consequences of the bourgeois utilitarian mindset for landscape painting to a far more extreme conclusion than was commonplace.[58] In a period when the picturesque taste was so ubiquitous that it was the object of numerous satires both verbal and visual, Taylor squarely opposed it as the mark of a low stage of civilisation. He proposed that the taste of the individual ascended through four stages, rising from the rustic, through the sublime and beautiful to the artificial, the last of these being epitomised for him by the view of the Thames from Blackfriar's Bridge. Not only was there 'something barbarous and irrational in that rage for mountain scenery which is professed by lovers of the picturesque', but the rustic was emphatically the lowest form of landscape art: 'Each school of art begins with ... the rustic. – The ignoble is of easier attainment than the beautiful, its very essence consisting in impropriety of outline, which may err in either direction. A degraded nature is imitated with less trouble than the entire – if a cottage be drawn out of perspective, the jagged thatch hides the undue convergence of the lines – downfally buildings, pollard trees, conceal imprecision of outline'.[59]

Although he arrived at different conclusions with regard to particulars, like the most advanced British aesthetic thinkers of his moment – Archibald Alison and Richard Payne Knight – Taylor premised his norms of taste on what he assumed were the universal psychological principles of the association of ideas.[60] For him urban vistas that suggested ideas of 'refinement, art, intellect, wealth, power and greatness', in other words the marks of secular progress, were the most pleasing prospects: 'I like the views of large cities'. Applying an essentially utilitarian measure, he claimed that sublime mountainous landscapes represented regions in which 'nothing answers its purpose'.[61] Although Taylor's correspondence confirms that this was not just a public pose,[62] it is striking

------

56   Taylor 1814.

57   John Berney Crome, 'Essay on Painting and Poetry', manuscript, Norwich Castle Museum.

58   For Utilitarianism and landscape painting, see Chapter Four.

59   Taylor 1814, pp. 407–8, 502–3.

60   For more on Taylor's essay, see Hemingway 1992, pp. 72–5.

61   Taylor 1814, p. 502.

62   See Taylor to Thomas Dyson (1815), in Robberds 1843, vol. 2, p. 460; Taylor to Robert Southey, 30 November 1802, vol. 1, pp. 432–3; Taylor to Robert Southey, 1 March 1815, vol. 2, p. 455.

how emphatically his judgment of 'the rustic' seems calculated to disparage the work of Crome. And not just in terms of the generalities of its themes, but also in those of its technical specificities. Put crudely, Taylor privileges the vision of the educated bourgeois over that of the less reflective and less informed artist and amateur and finds the values of the former embodied in the urban views of Piranesi and Canaletto.[63] While his opinions were certainly not standard among the urban bourgeoisie, the contrast they make with Crome's illuminates the particular tenor of traditionalism that defines the latter's work.

The earliest attempts to narrativise Crome's career, which were written inevitably by observers from higher up the social hierarchy, emphasise the poverty of his origins and his lack of formal education. Thus the editor of the *Norwich Mercury*, Richard McKenzie Bacon – a long-term member of the Norwich Society of Artists himself – wrote in his obituary of the artist, 'Few men have had to struggle against greater disadvantages in early life than Mr. Crome. He could barely be said to have enjoyed even the common instruction of the most ordinary schools'.[64] In his memoir, Dawson Turner also emphasised the poverty of Crome's origins, 'the poor son of a Norwich weaver', and that he 'laboured under the disadvantages of a defective education'.[65] Like an exemplar of Weber's Protestant ethic, Turner's Crome triumphed over adversity through his 'integrity and industry', while his 'cheerful and social temper, united to a most winning naïveté of manners' made him 'equally at home and equally welcome at the tables of the rich and highborn as at those of a station similar to his own'.[66] But in the circumstances neither said all they thought or knew about Crome's character. Bacon's son, Richard Noverre Bacon, would tell Richard and Samuel Redgrave in the 1860s that Crome had been a 'wine-bibber and improvident' and in a letter of 1815 Turner's wife referred to him as 'a great rascal'.[67] Turner's emphasis on Crome's humorous anecdotes and jokes suggest an individual who was deft at negotiating the rituals of social subordination expected of a provincial drawing master, while maintaining a measure of independence. It is also worth noting that Allan Cunningham, the author of another early sketch of

---

63   Taylor 1814, p. 407.

64   *Norwich Mercury*, 28 April 1821 – reprinted in Wodderspoon 1876, p. 20. For a brief account of Bacon, see Chambers 1829, p. 1284. Chambers also reprinted Bacon's obituary (pp. 1115–160).

65   Wodderspoon 1876, pp. 6, 9.

66   Wodderspoon, pp. 9, 7.

67   Redgrave and Redgrave 1947, p. 351; Mary Turner to Dawson Turner, 14 October 1815 (private collection). In his preface to the second edition of Wodderspoon 1876, R.N. Bacon describes Crome as 'my mirth-loving, kind, and earnest teacher'.

Crome, reported that the artist 'loved to relate the hardships of his youth, the difficulties he encountered in study'.[68] The fact that Crome and Taylor came together in the same social space at the Norwich Philosophical Society indicates Crome's rising class trajectory, but he cannot have entirely lost his artisanal consciousness. Indeed, it seems likely that the jokester and 'improvident' remained strung between two social worlds. This ambivalent social consciousness, I suggest, was imprinted in the forms and iconography of his art.

We owe our knowledge of Crome's training as an artist primarily to Dawson Turner's memoir and his biographical sketch and other remarks in *Outlines in Lithography*, his 1840 catalogue to his picture collection. Again this is a highly classed story, a kind of bourgeois morality play. Turner emphasised the role of the master weaver and amateur artist Thomas Harvey in the formation of Crome's sensibility both through his allowing the young artist to study in his picture collection and through the instruction he gave him, which exemplified Harvey's 'elegance of mind' and 'liberality and kindness towards his inferiors'.[69] It was through Harvey that Crome was introduced to the portrait painter William Beechey, who in 1793 was made Her Majesty's Portrait Painter by Queen Charlotte and was knighted five years later.[70] As Beechey recollected to Dawson Turner, Crome was a frequent visitor in his London studio 'to get what information I was able to give him upon the subject of that particular branch of art which he had made his study'.[71] According to Allan Cunningham – who had his information from Dawson Turner – it was Beechey 'who showed him how to set his palette and to manage the distribution of light and shade'.[72] The role of John Opie who he met in 1798 in forming Crome's technique may

---

68   'The Glade Cottage' in Cunningham 1836, vol. 2, p. 23, Although written long after the fact, Elise Paget's account of Crome's sociability in Paget 1882 should not be discounted. The author was the granddaughter of Samuel Paget of Yarmouth, the first owner of Crome's *Marlingford Grove* (Lady Lever Art Gallery, Port Sunlight). Family legend may well have had a kernel of truth. For the Paget family, see Palmer 1874, vol. 2, pp. 396–400; and Peterson 1984.

69   Wodderspoon 1876, p. 6. See also Turner 1840, p. 27. For Harvey and his collection, see Hawcroft 1959; Moore 1988, pp. 26–30.

70   Roberts 1907, pp. 41, 56.

71   Wodderspoon 1876, p. 6. Although Beechey painted few landscapes himself, he was a close friend of Paul Sandby – see Roberts 1907, p. 29.

72   'The Glade Cottage' in Cunningham 1836; Allan Cunningham to Dawson Turner, 10 April 1837 (Dawson Turner Papers, Trinity College Library, University of Cambridge). Cunningham claimed that Crome spent a period in London in the 1790s supporting himself as a house painter, but there is no independent corroboration of this.

have been as great as Beechey's, to judge from his widow's report,[73] and we might expect Crome to find the son of a carpenter and a notorious radical more socially sympathetic. In addition, Opie was a more cosmopolitan, intellectually ambitious, and talented painter than Beechey. However, we have no way of measuring the nature or extent of their influence.[74]

As a product of the urban artisanate, Crome's antecedents were not more markedly humble than those of Girtin, the son of a brush maker, or Turner, the son of a barber. He clearly came to understand the value of a formal education, securing for his eldest son a classical education at Norwich Grammar School.[75] Moreover in Crome's posthumous sale in 1821, books counted for 188 lots, comprising a wide range of works of literature, philosophy, art history, and art theory.[76] Neither should one overlook that the Norwich Society of Artists that Crome played such a central role in establishing was conceived in the first instance not as an exhibition body but as an 'Academy' at which fortnightly discussion meetings were to be held to inquire into 'the Rise, Progress, & present state of Painting, Architecture, and Sculpture'.[77] However, Crome was 35 when

---

73   Reported by Dawson Turner, in Wodderspoon 1876, pp. 8–9 n. Mrs. Opie recalled that she had watched Opie advising Crome in Thomas Harvey's painting room at Catton. For Opie, see Earland 1911. It is interesting that the critic of the conservative paper the *Daily Advertiser, Oracle, and True Briton*, who in 1806 criticised Crome's Royal Academy exhibit for lack of finish (Clifford and Clifford 1968, pp. 58–9), in the following year attacked the recently deceased Opie's *Belisarius* as nothing more than vivid imitations of unidealised nature that would appeal to the clientele of 'Deptford Tea-gardens'. The class sneer is unmistakable. See 'The Fine Arts, No. 1 Pall Mall Gallery', *Daily Advertiser, Oracle, and True Briton*, 2 May 1807.

74   Crome owned landscapes by Opie and Beechey, as well as an on the spot sketch attributed to Reynolds. See *A Catalogue of the Entire Valuable Collection of Paintings, Prints and Books, Late the Property of Mr. J. Crome, Dec.*, J. Athow, Norwich, 25 September–1 October 1821, Day 2, lots 72, 76, and 83.

75   Wodderspoon 1876, p. 6 n.

76   The sale of paintings, drawings and prints amounted to 563 lots and lasted four days. This, together with the size of Crome's 1812 sale which amounted to 556 lots, is indicative of both the scale of his wealth, his activity as an art dealer, and the range of his art-historical knowledge. For the 1812 sale, see *A Catalogue of a Splendid Collection of Prints, Etchings, and Original Drawings by Engravers and Draftsmen of the First Eminence ... the Property of Mr. John Crome of Norwich*, Great Yarmouth, 23–25 September 1812. According to Allan Cunningham, the 1812 sale was Dawson Turner's idea – see Cunningham 1836.

77   *Articles of the Society Instituted for the purpose of an inquiry into the Rise, Progress, & present state of Painting, Architecture, and Sculpture, with a View to discover and point out the Best methods of Study, to attain greater perfection in these Arts. Established in Norwich, February 19, 1803*. The revised Articles of 1818 prohibited 'all political and theological discussions'.

the society was formed. Whatever he learnt from Harvey, Beechey, and Opie, he did not have the kind of training in landscape draughtsmanship that Girtin acquired through his aborted apprenticeship to Edward Dayes or Turner from attending the lectures on perspective of Thomas Malton. More importantly, unlike Turner and Constable he did not attend the Royal Academy Schools. Interestingly, Allan Cunningham recorded that with the help of 'an ingenious companion' the young Crome made a camera obscura, 'which brought mechanical help to his studies, and impressed a love of accuracy on his mind, which may be traced through all his productions'.[78] This statement is a piece of rhetoric, but it may be that the use of a camera explains the strange compressed perspective of the early painting *A View on the Wensum* (*fig. 46*).[79] Equally bizarre is the *Study of Flints* (*fig. 47*), a later work that belongs with the small group of flower and plant still-lifes attributed to Crome. In this the juxtaposition of a small object seen up close and set against a distant prospect with no spatial mediators or framing is highly unusual and was perhaps conceived as a kind of humorous emblem of the Norfolk landscape in which flint is ubiquitous and widely used as a distinctive local building material. The bare slopes of the background are likely intended to suggest Mousehold Heath.

But these are extreme cases. More generally, I want to suggest that Crome's lack of training in scientific perspective caused him to depend on devices of juxtaposed masses and contrasts that often left the spaces of his pictures rather flattened and surface bound.[80] At one level this accorded well enough with the picturesque aesthetic of variety and contrast that he employed in his teachings as a drawing master and that was the stock in trade of amateur artists and those who taught them. At another it gave his naturalism a surprisingly modern-looking inflection that helps explain his appeal to his early twentieth-century admirers. Although Wodderspoon claimed that Crome was 'a naturalist as well as an artist and not only gave every creature its true position, but expressed all natural forces, and the aspects of the seasons with scrupulous and uncompromising fidelity',[81] Crome's paintings do not suggest the positioning

---

78   Cunningham 1836. In Elise Paget's account the camera obscura was loaned him – Paget 1882.

79   The Cliffords suggested not implausibly that the strange composition may owe something to inn signs – see Clifford and Clifford 1968, p. 179. Significantly in this regard, the picture is painted on panel.

80   In his treatise on the picturesque the painter and engraver John Thomas Smith advised landscape artists to learn perspective from continued observation rather than from 'technical geometry', – Smith 1797, pp. 20–21.

81   Wodderspoon 1876, p. 15.

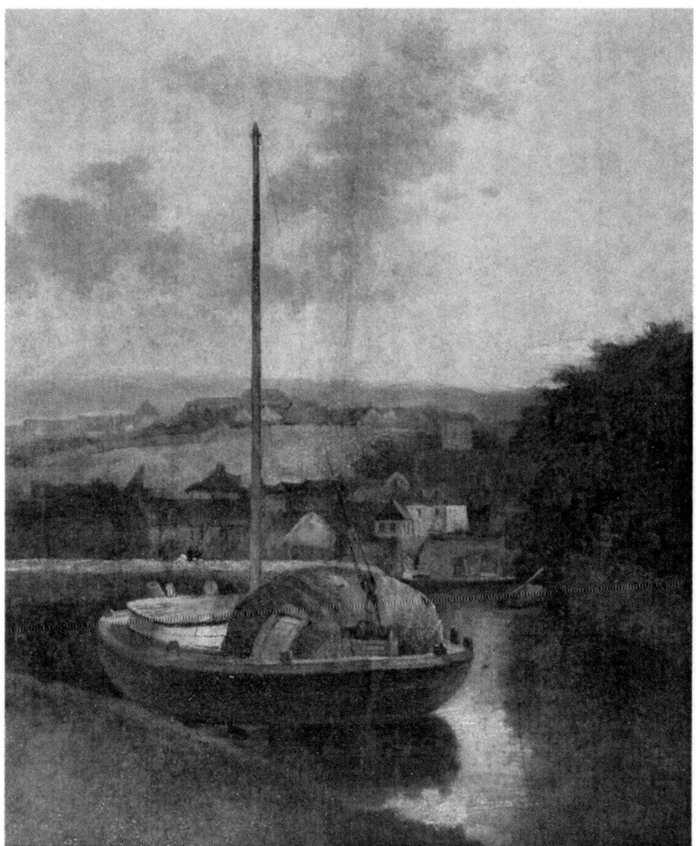

FIGURE 46   *John Crome,* View on the Wensum, *c. 1800?, oil on panel,*
20 × 15½ in (50.8 × 39.4 cm)
NORFOLK MUSEUMS SERVICE (NORWICH CASTLE MUSEUM
AND ART GALLERY)

of distinct natural phenomena according to their functions as parts of a grand
machine in the way those of Constable and Turner do. Whereas those artists
in their mature works depict clouds in deep space as part of a perspectival
recession, Crome's clouds are usually distant masses set against a light-filled
yonder behind them; in this respect they are closer to the clouds of Wilson or
Gainsborough in their blatantly compositional function. The contrast between
Mousehold Heath and Constable's *The Haywain* (*figs. 48* and *49*) illustrates my
point.[82]

---

82   Collins Baker recognised that the handling of atmosphere in *Mousehold Heath* was rep-

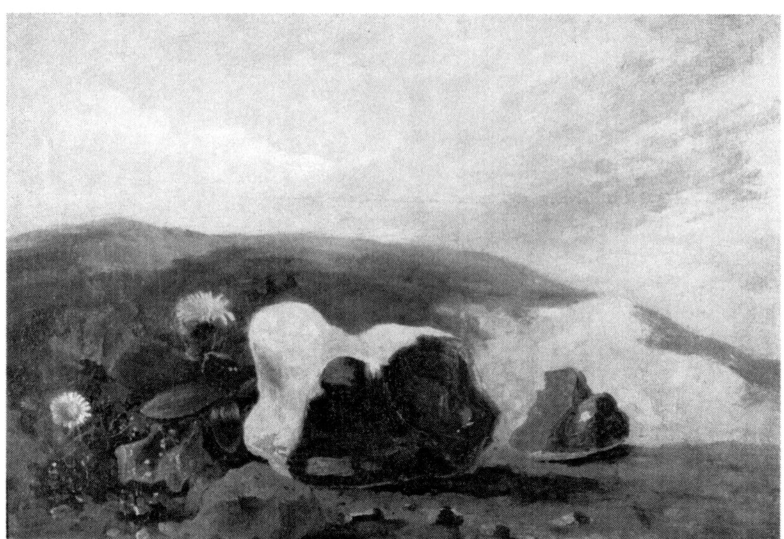

FIGURE 47   *John Crome,* Study of Flints, *oil on canvas, 9 × 12 ½ in (21.8 × 31.8 cm)*
NORFOLK MUSEUMS SERVICE (NORWICH CASTLE MUSEUM AND
ART GALLERY)

William Taylor claimed, uncontroversially, that the pleasures of 'prospect painting' had two causes, 'directly, as an imitation of nature', and indirectly, as a nucleus of association. To the first belonged outline, colouring, and 'singleness of scene'.[83] Equally conventional was the priority he gave to outline and the secondary role he assigned colour and light and shade. Where he was quite out of line with both picturesque principles and academic theory was in the preference he expressed for bright daylight scenes and his dislike of passing effects of cloud in which 'all will be feeble and grey alike' and 'a dull sad tint has spread its veil over the scene'. Given the effects of time on paintings, he advised the colourist to 'err on the side of splendour, rather than on the side of dullness'.[84]

Taylor's position is in striking contrast to John Berney Crome's 'Essay on Painting and Poetry', which is in part a *paragone,* intended to defend painting against the imputation that it was dependent on literature for its poetic effects, and in part a defence of the Cromean aesthetic of landscape painting. J.B. Crome makes the conventional obeisances to classical models and the

---

resentative of a distinctive quality in Crome's skies but interpreted it differently – in Baker 1921, p. 73.

83   Taylor 1814, p. 211.

84   Taylor 1814, p. 213.

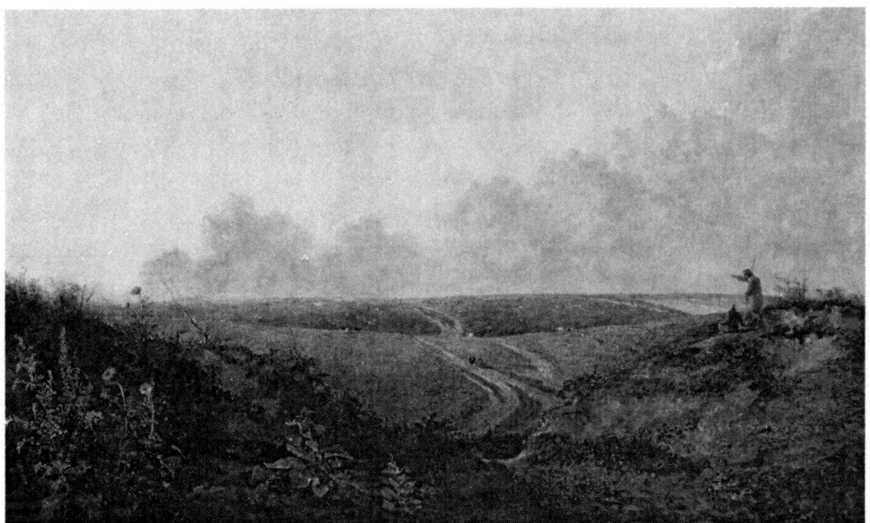

FIGURE 48   *John Crome,* Mousehold Heath, *oil on canvas, 43¼ × 71¼ in (109.9 × 181 cm), Tate Britain*
© TATE, LONDON, 2015

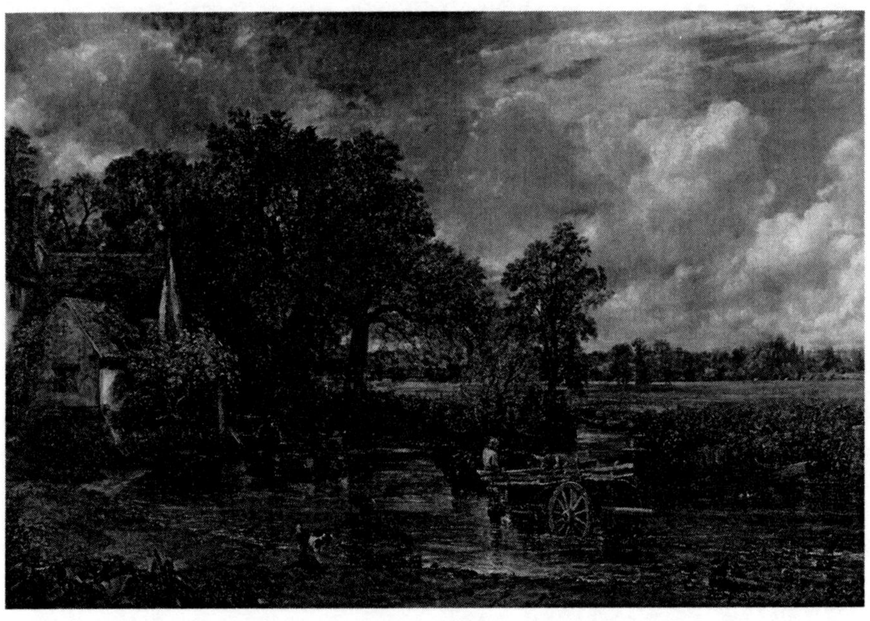

FIGURE 49   *Constable, John (1776–1837),* The Haywain, *1821, oil on canvas (130.2 × 185.4 cm). Presented by Henry Vaughan, 1886 (NG 1207).*
© NATIONAL GALLERY, LONDON/ART RESOURCE, NY

Reynoldsian notion of the general idea that were commonplaces of academic theory.[85] He also reiterates conventional criticisms of the Dutch school for producing unselective and over-detailed representations of ordinary nature. But he excuses Ruisdael and Hobbema for not depicting classical scenes since they did not visit Italy and emphasises the pleasing 'simplicity' of their work and its effects of light and shade: 'In the purity & chasteness of their colour, in the full & flowing richness of their Pencil, & in their masterly intelligence of light & shade they have seldom been surpassed. Hobbima [*sic*] in particular appears to have understood the value of keeping one part subservient to another; no one introduced with happier effect the brilliancy of the sun-beam bursting through the gloom of the forest, and illuminating the centre of his picture with a magical effect of light & shadow that astonishes & charms'.[86] 'Breadth', the younger Crome advises, 'is not only compatible with grandeur but often the cause of it', indeed such is its effect that 'pictures eminently possessed of it, though they should have no other merit, will always attract the attention of a cultivated eye before others where the detail is admirable, but where this principle is wanting'. He compares its effects with that of 'obscurity' in producing effects of 'grandeur' in literary description.[87]

Crome's *Moonlight on the Yare* (*fig. 50*) – which belonged to Dawson Turner and was probably a painting exhibited in 1808[88] – exemplifies this principle and is like the antithesis of Taylor's ideal of the bright daylight modern cityscape exemplified by Canaletto's work. The painting owes its dramatic silhouette partly to the example of Rembrandt's *The Mill* (*fig. 51*), which was a much admired work in the early nineteenth century, and one that Crome could have had a number of opportunities to see and may have copied.[89] But it is equally

---

85   Crome, 'Essay on Painting and Poetry', pp. 5–6, 4.

86   Crome, 'Essay on Painting and Poetry', p. 9. Crome refers to 'Ruysdael' but probably means Jacob van Ruisdael and not his uncle Salomon van Ruysdael. A well-known contemporary academic defence of breadth in very similar terms was enunciated in James Barry's Lecture on 'Chiaroscuro', delivered between 1784 and 1798 when he was Professor Painting at the Royal Academy – see Wornum (ed.) 1848, p. 178. Barry's Lectures were published posthumously in 1809. It was made especially forcefully by Thomas Phillips, a portrait painter and close friend of Dawson Turner, in his Royal Academy lecture 'On Chiaroscuro' of 1829. See Phillips 1833, p. 385.

87   Crome, 'Essay on Painting and Poetry', pp. 10–11, 12. Crome was certainly referring to Burke's reflections on the effects of obscurity as a cause of sublime emotion in Burke 1759, pp. 90–110.

88   Turner 1840, pp. 19–20. I agree with the Cliffords and Collins Baker on the identification with the 1808 exhibit – see Clifford and Clifford 1968, p. 198.

89   The Cliffords give a good account of the picture's exhibition history in Crome's lifetime but

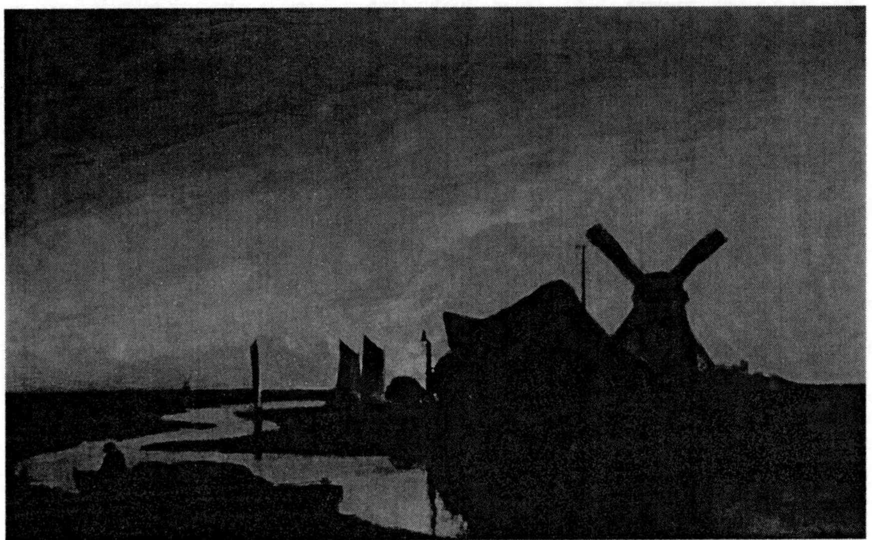

FIGURE 50   *John Crome,* Moonlight on the Yare, *1808?, 28×43¾ in (71.1×111.1 cm), Tate Britain*
© TATE, LONDON, 2015

indebted to the moonlight river scenes of Aert van der Neer (*fig. 52*), which had other contemporary emulators such as Turner who deploys the same schema in his *Moonlight, A Study at Millbank*, exhibited in 1797 (*fig. 53*). The foreground masses and silhouetted shapes of *Moonlight on the Yare* are painted with very thin umbrageous pigment with patches of underpainting functioning as a shadow tone, while the lighter colours of the sky are, conventionally, painted in thicker and denser pigments mixed with white. Both Aert van der Neer and Turner use the river bank to define receding orthogonals; Crome's river snakes back in a narrowing Art Nouveau-like arabesque before disappearing beneath the horizon. All three paintings depend on silhouetted forms to generate night-time contrasts, but Crome's, lacking the avenue of reflected light of van der Neer and Turner, and with its striking lack of detail and stronger outlines, produces a far more emphatic sense of surface design.

The Norwich Museum's later version of *Yarmouth Jetty* (*fig. 40*) illustrates how Crome adapted the principle of breadth to naturalistic daylight scenes.[90]

---

miss out its showing at the British Institution in 1806. Like them, I am not convinced that the copy in Norwich Castle Museum is by Crome. See Clifford and Clifford 1968, p. 246.

90   That is to say later by comparison with the rather primitive Yarmouth Jetty formerly in the collection of Mr and Mrs Paul Mellon (Clifford and Clifford P23) or the more

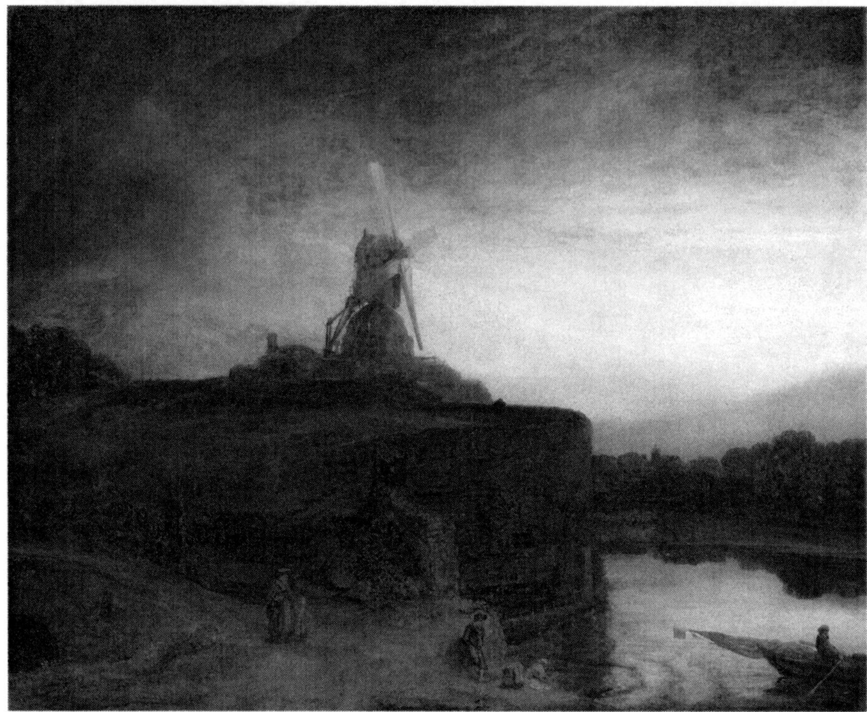

FIGURE 51   *Rembrandt van Rijn,* The Mill, *1645–48, oil on canvas, 34½ × 41⅝ (87.6 × 105.6 cm)*
WIDENER COLLECTION, 1942.9.62, NATIONAL GALLERY OF ART,
WASHINGTON, DC

As I have shown elsewhere, such beach scenes were ubiquitous in the period;[91] Turner and his follower Augustus Wall Callcott producing a number of them. With its repoussoir jetty, Crome's painting is almost a reverse image of the latter's *Little Hampton Pier* (*fig. 54*), which is from about five years earlier if my dating is right.[92] But what is striking about the comparison is not just the greater transparency of Callcott's effect – the softening of light on the horizon in contrast with Crome's dark band of sea, the reflection on the wet sand contrasted with the dry materiality of Crome's foreground triangle – but the

---

sophisticated painting in Norwich Castle Museum (P46), which is still conceived within the framework of picturesque aesthetics and hence earlier than that illustrated here (P42). (Crome exhibited views of Yarmouth beach and jetty in 1807, 1808, and 1809). My guess is that P42 may well be the *Yarmouth Jetty* Crome showed with the NSA in 1817 since its style matches with that of other works from the last five or six years of the artist's life.

91   Hemingway 1992, Chapter 8.

92   For Callcott, see David Blayney Brown, *Augustus Wall Callcott* (London: Tate Gallery, 1981).

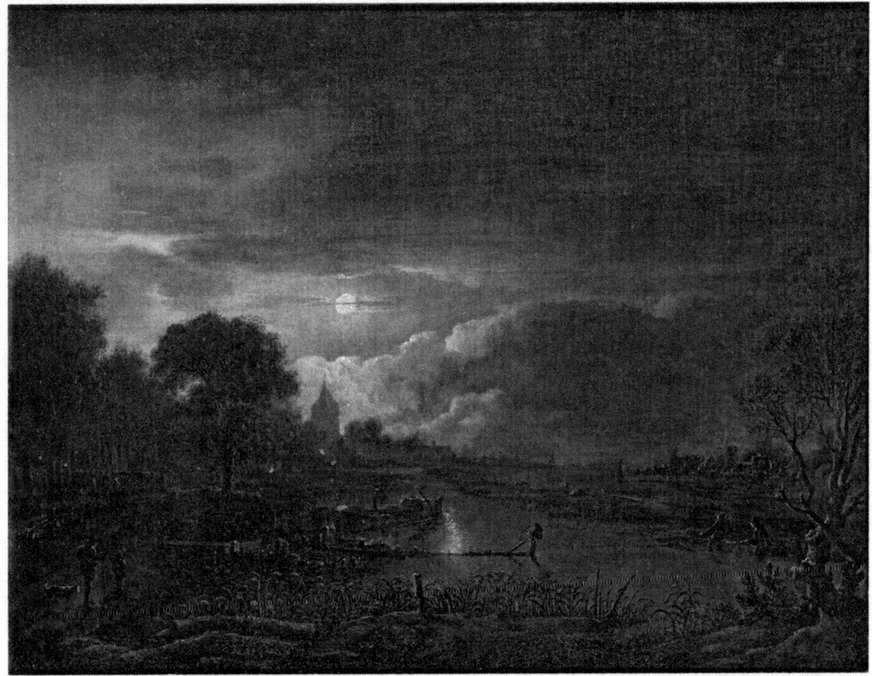

FIGURE 52   *After Aert van der Neer,* River Scene by Moonlight, *possibly 17th century, oil on canvas, 57.5 x 74 cm, DPG340.*

strength of Crome's shadow colours not just on the jetty's side but in the cloud shadow on the sea, which again reinforce the surface pattern and remind us of his strictures on singleness of effect. Similarly, whereas Callcott's sky is all airiness and intimations of distance, Crome's characteristic masses of dense cumulus have an almost sculptural solidity like the clouds of Courbet's seascapes. His distant boats appeared compressed under a mass of moist atmosphere.

The mistitled work *Barge with a Wounded Soldier* (*fig. 55*) – which is perhaps a little earlier in date – exemplifies my case in a different way.[93] Here Crome controls recession not just by the cloud mass, but also by having the boat

---

93   I agree with the Cliffords (Clifford and Clifford 1968, p. 204) that there is no basis for the current title. However, their suggestion of a date of *c.* 1808 is implausible. One cannot imagine Crome painting this at the same time as *Moonlight on the Yare* and before the larger shift to naturalism in his work.

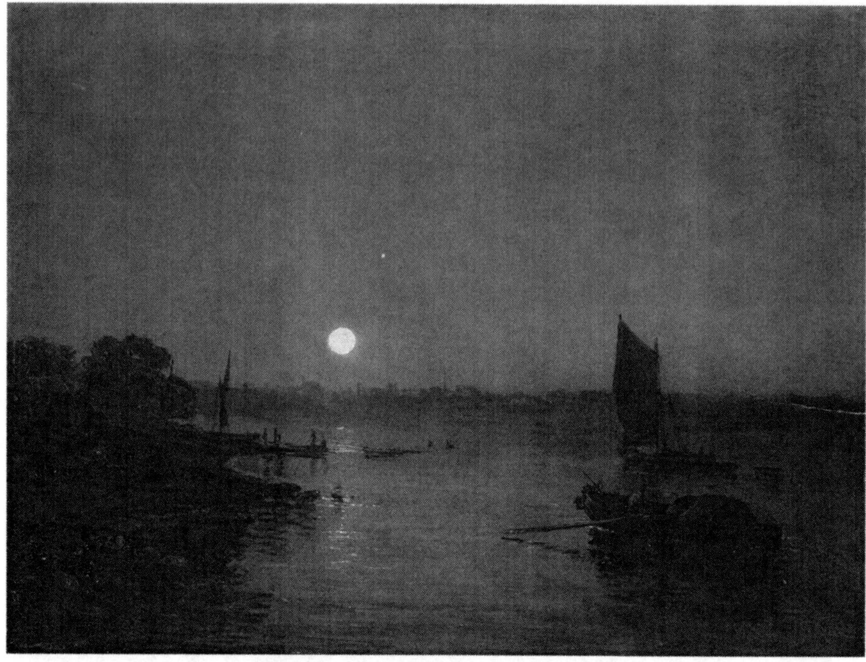

FIGURE 53   *J.M.W. Turner,* Moonlight, A Study at Millbank, *1797, oil on mahogany, 12⅜ × 15⅞ in (31.4 × 40.3 cm), Tate Britain*
© TATE, LONDON, 2015

stretch more than half-way across the composition just under the horizon line, by making the fish baskets and the heads of fishermen break the horizon, and by the light sail and its reflection standing out above the darker band of water where cloud and sea meet. This is a motif with some resemblance to that of Girtin's watercolour *White House at Chelsea* (1800; *fig. 56*), but Girtin did not exhibit that work and it was not engraved until 1823. Like the white house and its reflection in Girtin's drawing, the Naples yellow sail and its reflection provide a striking marker of distance that makes an emphatic interruption in the breadth of effect and contradicts one of the shibboleths of picturesque aesthetics, which were hostile to white in the landscape for that very reason.[94] (Yellow has an effect akin to white in the context). The bowsprit of the foreground boat and the spit of sand both point the eye to the distant sail, the colour of which finds a counterpoint in the brilliant red

94   On the incompatibility of white with picturesque effect – see Hemingway 1992, p. 23 and p. 305 n. 49. For Girtin's watercolour, see Smith et. al. 2002, p. 209.

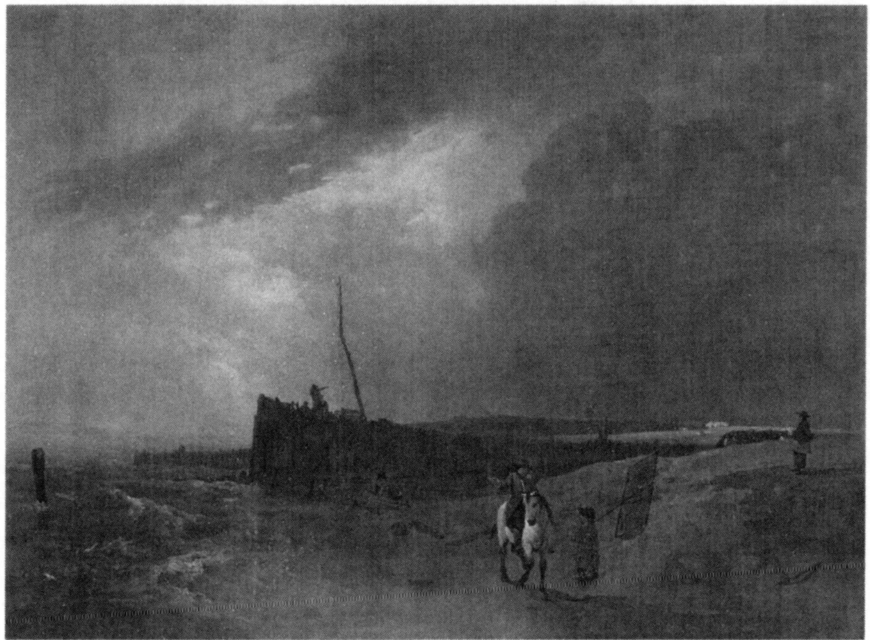

FIGURE 54   *Augustus Wall Callcott*, Little Hampton Pier, *c. 1812, oil on canvas, 42 × 55½ in*
             (106.7 × 141.0 cm), Tate Britain
             © TATE, LONDON, 2015

jacket of the foreground figure who is ostensibly looking the other way. The
lacy white ripples on the area of water nearest us also lure the eye close to the
shore.

   Similar arguments apply in relation to Crome's glade scenes, which derive
formally from the grove scenes of Meindert Hobbema. Crome's adulation of
Hobbema was reported by Dawson Turner, who even claimed his dying words
were 'Oh Hobbima, my dear Hobbima, how I have loved you!', a piece of naïve
sentiment in line with Turner's larger picture of Crome's personality.[95] Turner
himself seems to have been a considerable admirer of Hobbema and owned
that artist's *Road-side Inn* (E.G. Bührle Collection, Zurich), which he bought
from Thomas Harvey around 1815, and which Crome reportedly copied some
twenty-five years before just when he was starting to paint.[96] Andrew Moore
has speculated that Crome's adulation of Hobbema may have been a myth
fabricated by Turner, but given the importance of Hobbema compositional

---

95   Turner 1840, pp. 15–16; Wodderspoon 1876, pp. 7, 9.
96   Turner 1840, pp. 39–40; Moore 1988, pp. 35, 114.

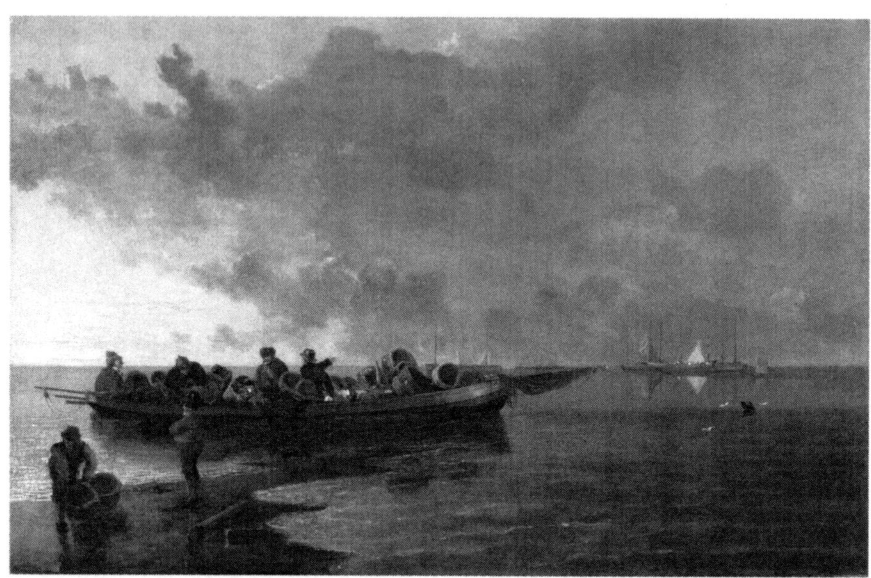

FIGURE 55   *John Crome,* A Barge with a Wounded Soldier, *1810–12, oil on canvas (transferred from panel), 13⅝ × 20⅛ in (34.6×51.0 cm)*
YALE CENTER FOR BRITISH ART, PAUL MELLON COLLECTION

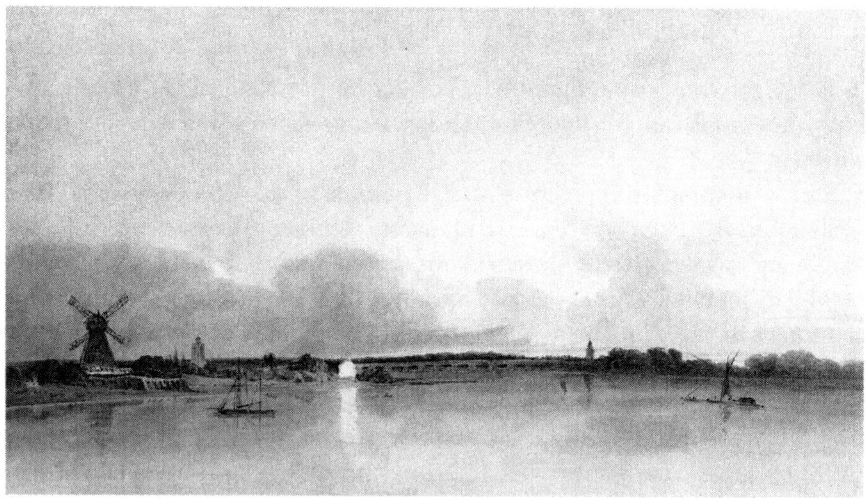

FIGURE 56   *Thomas Girtin,* The White House at Chelsea, *watercolour, 11¾ × 20¼ in (29.8×51.4 cm), Tate Britain*
© TATE, LONDON, 2015

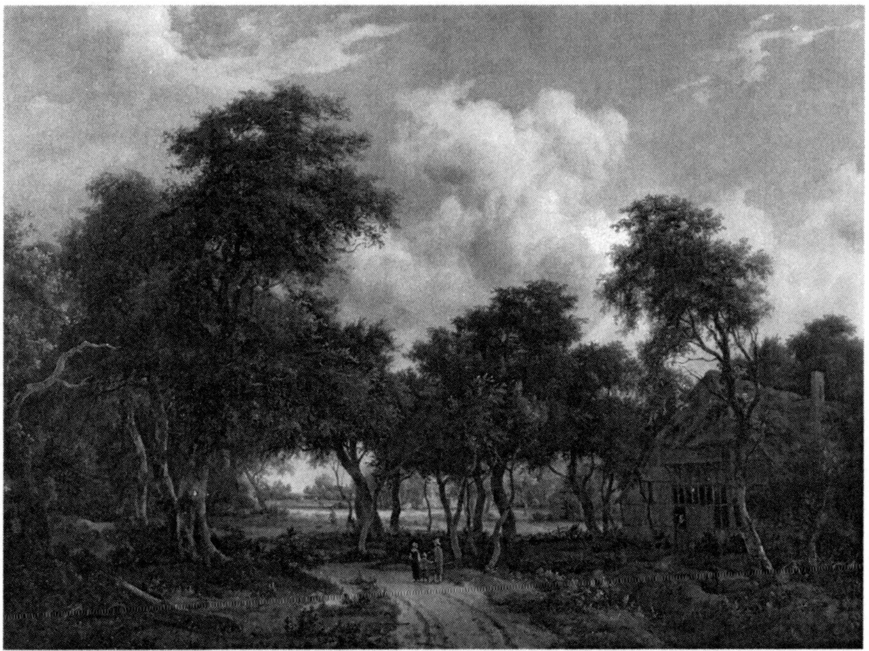

FIGURE 57   *Hobbema, Meindert (1638–1709)*, A Woody Landscape with a Cottage, *about 1665,*
oil on canvas (99.5×130.5 cm), Wynn Ellis Bequest, 1876 (NG995)
© NATIONAL GALLERY, LONDON/ART RESOURCE, NY

models for Crome and the special praise given to Hobbema in his son's 'Essay
on Painting and Poetry' I think this unlikely.[97] In the Hobbema grove scene
pattern (*fig. 57*) a lit road in the foreground leads the eye under the shadows of
a stand of trees and then on into a light-filled band of distance beyond. One can
see Callcott emulating this schema precisely in *Market Day* (*fig. 58*), which he
exhibited at the Royal Academy exhibition in 1807. Here light permeates under
the trees and the bright patch of ground on the right leads the eye towards the
distance. In Crome's *The Beaters* (*fig. 44*) as in *Yarmouth Jetty*, the foreground
pitches us directly into the scene; all recession through the trees is blocked
by a dark mass of foliage. The parallel bands denoting light and dark on the
right denote distance effectively, but there is no logic of progression into them.
Neither is there anything resembling Callcott's airy canopy of clouds. While

---

97   Moore 1988, p. 114. Turner – who was a successful banker and not the most imaginative
      man – said he had the report from both Crome family members and from the physician
      who attended him in his last illness (Turner 1840, p. 16). It seems unlikely that he would
      have concocted such a story when so many who had known Crome were alive.

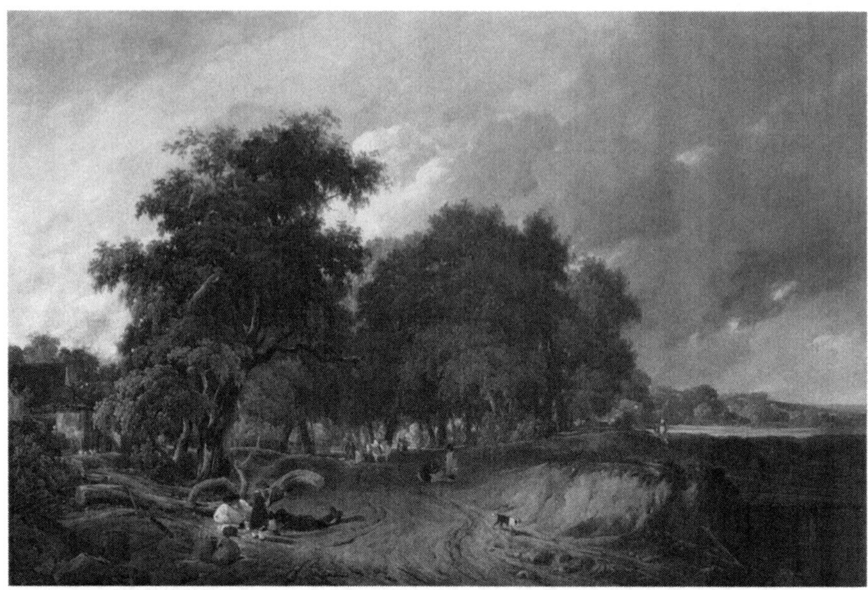

FIGURE 58   *Augustus Wall Callcott,* Return from the Market, *1807, oil on canvas, 58×100¾ in*
(147.3×256.0 cm)
© TABLEY HOUSE COLLECTION, UNIVERSITY OF MANCHESTER,
UK/BRIDGEMAN IMAGES

Crome's *Hautbois Common* (*fig. 80*) is closer to the Hobbema model and its early nineteenth-century interpretations, the dark wedge of shadow on the left inhibits recession and the tones of the picture are too dark and the cloud mass above it too overpowering for the distance to hold the spatial promise of Hobbema or Callcott's paintings.

Lane scenes offer my final example. Wodderspoon observed that these 'were at all times an attraction to Crome, many of such pictures are among the most successful of his works'. However, he emphasised that 'such lane scenes as existed in our painter's day' were no longer to be found. Lanes that 'were once wide as half a meadow, with broad strips of verdure on either hand, deep ruts in the road, curving and meandering here and there in many involutions, and banks and hedgerows of gigantic height and growth, full of blossoming and broad-leaved plants' had all been destroyed and replaced by 'modern paths of restricted dimensions, and of the straightest forms' with short hedges.[98] As Wodderspoon makes clear, this was a vision of Norfolk before enclosure, one

---

98   Wodderspoon 1876, pp. 15, 16.

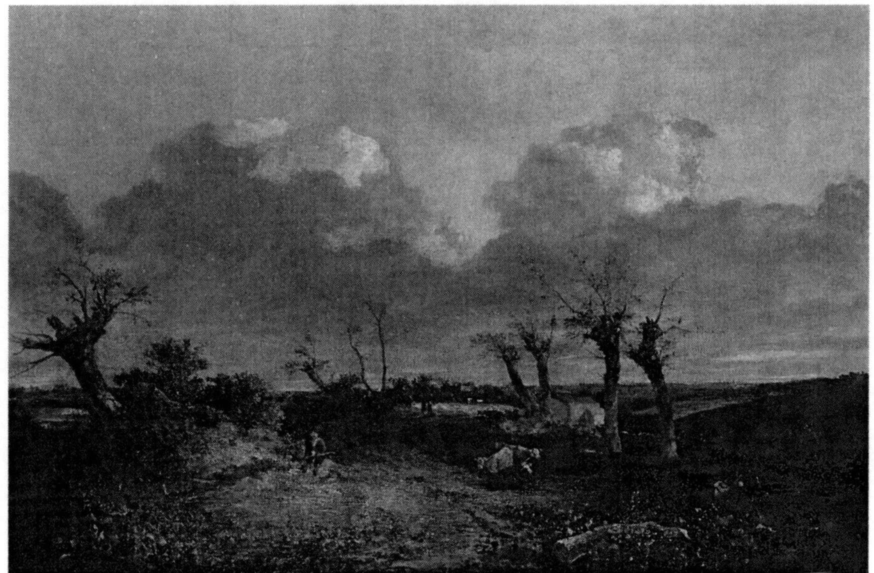

FIGURE 59   *John Crome*, Road with Pollards, *c. 1810–15, oil on canvas, 29⅞ × 40⅛*
(75.8 × 101.7 cm)
NORFOLK MUSEUMS SERVICE (NORWICH CASTLE MUSEUM AND ART
GALLERY)

that Crome's works such as *Road with Pollards* (*fig. 59*) may have deceived him
into thinking was still characteristic in the early nineteenth century.

The painting is a riff on the format of Dutch rustic road scenes such as Ruisdael's *Wheatfields* (c. 1670, *fig. 38*) and Hobbema's famous *Avenue at Middelharnis* (1689, *fig. 60*). Turner's *Frosty Morning* of 1813 (*fig. 61*) was a naturalistic
variant on the motif based around a coach road; it is probably contemporary
with Crome's picture and may even have prompted it. The pollards of the picture's title are representatives of that type of tree culture common in Suffolk
and Norfolk, which was also a motif in picturesque aesthetics. Cobbett, writing
from the agriculturalist's perspective, found pollards distasteful – 'nothing in
nature can be more ugly'[99] – but Gilpin, although he maintained that unnatural
forms displease, made an exception in this case: 'yet I have sometimes seen a
pollard have a good effect'.[100] Uvedale Price, whose picturesque was predicated
on a thoroughly humanised landscape, was far more accommodating: 'there

---

99   Cobbett 1912, vol. 2, pp. 226–7. Cobbett's remark dates from 1830 and was occasioned by
     the practice in Suffolk.
100   Gilpin 1808, vol. 1, p. 4.

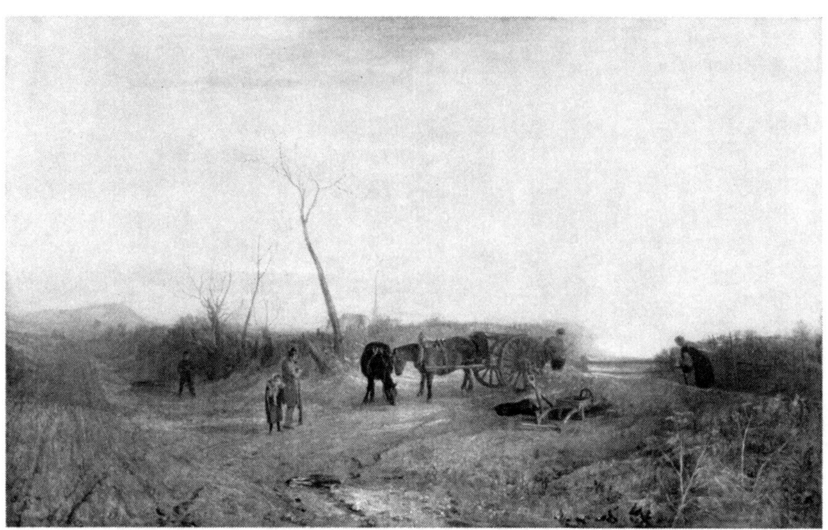

FIGURE 60   *J.M.W. Turner,* Frosty Morning, *1813, oil on canvas, 44¾ × 68¾ in*
(103.5 × 141.0 cm), Tate Britain
© TATE, LONDON, 2015

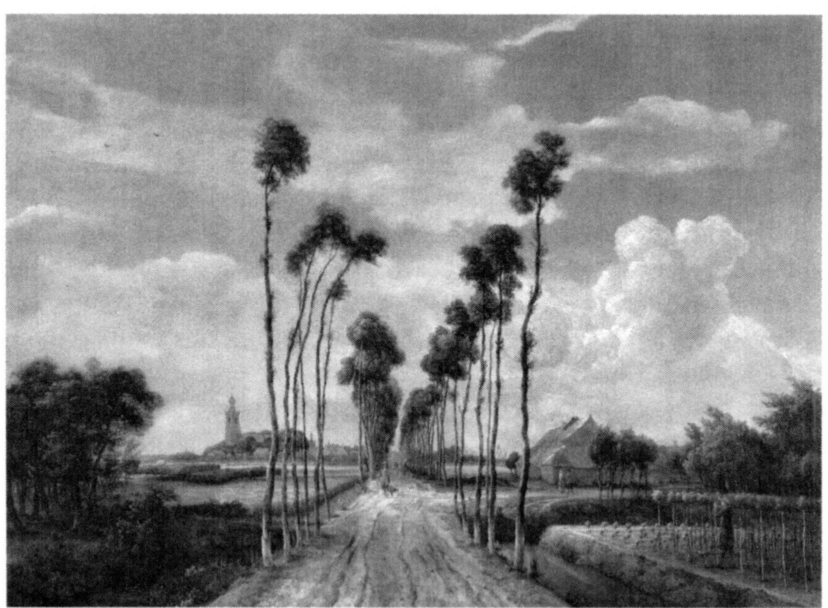

FIGURE 61   *Hobbema, Meindert (1638–1709),* The Avenue at Middelharnis, *1689, oil on*
canvas, 40¾ × 55½ in (103.5 141.0 cm). Bought 1871 (NG830)
© NATIONAL GALLERY, LONDON/ART RESOURCE, NY

is often a sort of spirit and animation, in the manner in which old neglected pollards stretch out their limbs quite across those hollow roads, in every wild and irregular direction ... This careless method of cutting, just as the farmer happened to want a few stakes or poles, gives infinite variety to the general outline of the banks'.[101] If in this instance Crome's road is not the kind of hollow road favoured by Price – of which I shall have more to say in the next chapter – it has nothing enclosing and pleasingly various about it. It is as though the artist had taken one of those nondescript stretches of the Norfolk landscape and sought to demonstrate how it could be given interest by a complex play of light and shade, otherwise known as breadth.

By contrast with both its seventeenth-century models and with Turner's work it is striking how dark Crome's image seems, how low the viewpoint is and how the banks of hedgerows seem to enclose the space at the same time as they knit the foreground and middle distance with the darkish band under the horizon. The pollard oaks fuse with the low-hanging clouds, which, unlike those in Ruisdael's composition or Hobbema's, do not reach up to the top of the edge to suggest a canopy of space but lie over the land in lumpy sculptured masses. This in turn contrasts with the extended spatial envelope of *Frosty Morning*. Once again the pursuit of breadth and the absence of an articulated deep space recession keep the forms more anchored to the surface than was common in pictorial landscape structures of the period.

I want to be clear that I am not arguing Crome was some kind of artisanal naïve who could not master mathematical perspective. Rather, I am suggesting that having had little formal training in it he depended far more on the doctrine of breadth, which prioritised an approach to composition through light-dark contrasts over the perspective box and clearly defined spatial recession. Since breadth was widely accepted as a structuring principle – and particularly amongst landscape painters – this is a question of degree, not one of kind. But I am also suggesting more tentatively a homology between this intuitive sense of order in the depiction of the natural world and the communitarian social order from which Crome came. The stylistic forms of Constable's and Turner's art depended on a kind of scientific approach to art that was alien to him; his vision depended more on intuitively apprehended correspondences of how parts belonged together in an organic whole.[102] It is an approach that gives his art at times a backward-looking cast, especially when it depicts the

---

101   Price 1810, vol. 1, pp. 26–7.

102   I mean science here not in the narrow sense of the natural sciences – though Constable and Turner were affected by developments in these – but in the early nineteenth-century sense of a practice grounded in theoretical knowledge. See Hemingway 1992, pp. 16–18, 23,

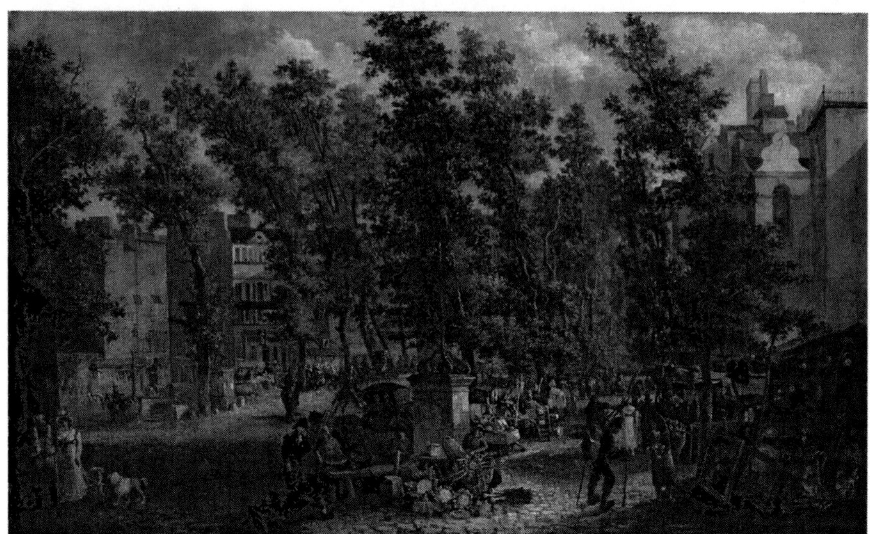

FIGURE 62   *John Crome,* View in Paris – Italian Boulevard, *1814–15, oil on canvas, 21⅜ × 34¼ in (54.5×87.3 cm)*
NORFOLK MUSEUMS SERVICE (NORWICH CASTLE MUSEUM AND ART GALLERY)

rural world. This is not to say that Crome's style and imagery were consciously recognised as artisanal as such. But Dawson Turner and other early admirers evidently thought there was a kind of correspondence between the man and his work – a man whose lowly social origins they consistently foregrounded. By contrast, Taylor's vision of improving cityscapes bespeaking a utilitarian conception of order and progress were precisely the opposite of the social vision that infused Crome's image of ordinary places and ordinary people engaged in leisure or traditional agricultural pursuits. The forms of Crome's work and their iconography were complementary.

Given Taylor's emphasis on the cityscape it seems fitting to end with Crome's sole essay in the genre, the *View in Paris – Italian Boulevard* (now known as *Boulevard des Italiens*) (*fig. 62*), which he exhibited with the Norwich Society of Artists in 1815 and sold to Hudson Gurney, the banker and politican, who lived at Keswick Hall, just outside Norwich. In expounding the superiority of urban associations in landscape painting in his 1814 essay, Taylor contrasted the 'serene and cheerful feeling' that 'a sunshiny meadow, dotted with trees, tra-

---

and 88. Crome's theory obviously was 'scientific' in this sense, but it was less experimental, more traditionalist in orientation.

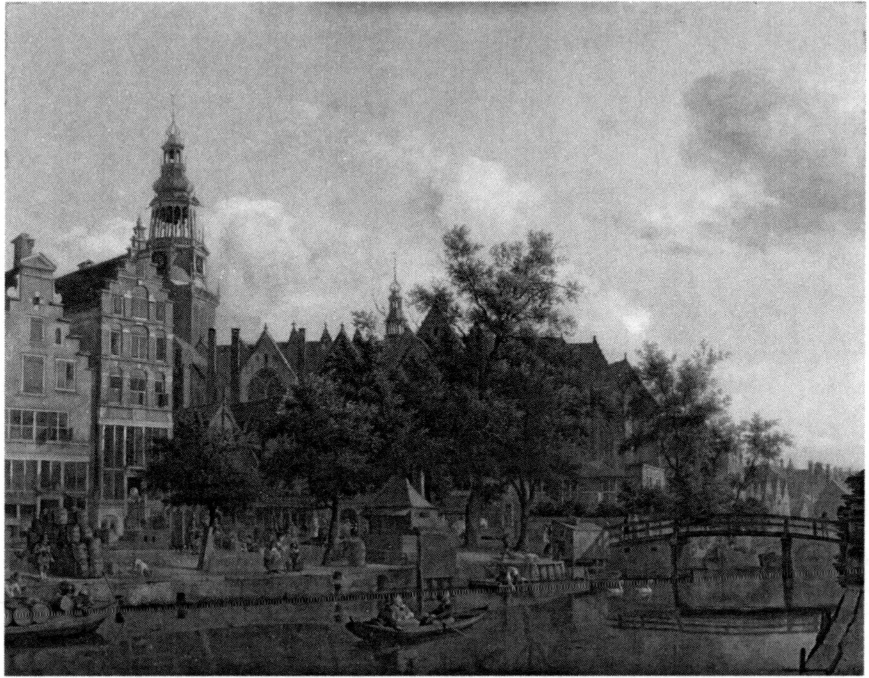

FIGURE 63   *Jan van der Heyden*, View of the Oudezijds Voorburgwal with the Oude Kerk in
Amsterdam, *c. 1670, oil on panel, 17 × 21 in (41.4 × 52.3 cm), Mauritshuis, The Hague*
PHOTO: MARGARETA SVENSSON

versed by a sparkling brook' produced in the mind, with the unspecified 'interesting contemplations' that filled the mind before the 'aspect of the Louvre,
the grandest of the palaces of sovereigns, and the depository of all that literature and art have produced of excellence'.[103] As a vision of Paris, Crome not
only selected the tourist spectacle of the Boulevard des Italiens that attracted so many British tourists in 1814 when he visited the city,[104] he represented

---

103   Taylor 1814, p. 499.

104   John Scott, the editor of *The Champion*, who was vigorously critical of many aspects of
French life and culture, made an exception for the 'Boulevarde' (he does not specify
which): 'a superb street of great breadth, lined on each side with trees, between which
and the houses, gravelled walks have been made for the foot-passengers. The general effect
here is very fine. The eye cannot reach to any termination of the Boulevarde; and in the
distance, the trees according to the laws of perspective, appear to unite their branches
in an arch, overshadowing with their foliage the hurrying groups of men, and women
and horses, and carts and carriages, that are perpetually streaming to and fro beneath
... London has nothing so fine in this way'. Scott 1815, p. 82.

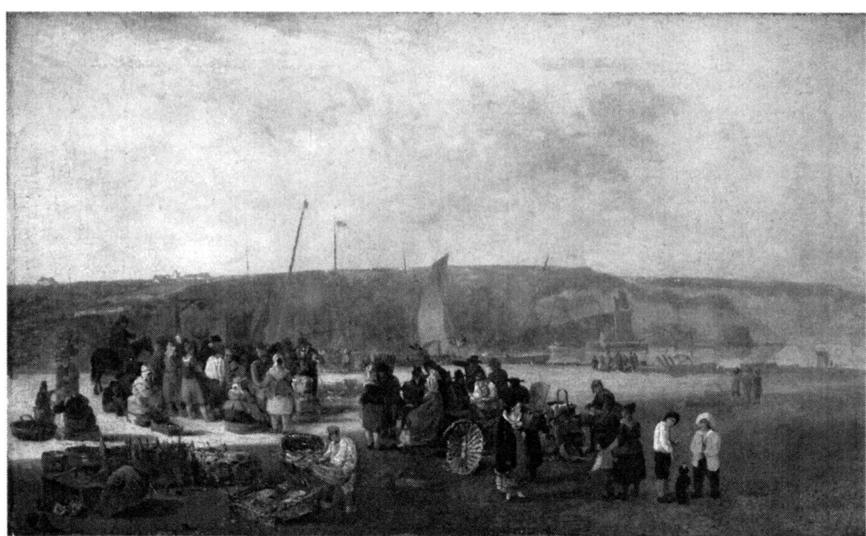

FIGURE 64   *John Crome,* Fishmarket at Boulogne, *1820?, oil on canvas, 20⅝ × 33⅞ in*
(*52.7 × 86.2 cm*)
NORFOLK MUSEUMS SERVICE (NORWICH CASTLE MUSEUM AND ART
GALLERY)

it through the pictorial format developed by Jan van der Heyden and other
seventeenth-century artists (*fig. 63*), who had softened the cityscape by placing trees in front of the buildings and often enlivened the foreground with
commercial activities of various kinds. Crome not only makes trees the centre
of his composition, which pivots around the lamp standard, but the architecture seems to frame the trees rather than vice versa. In the bottom left corner
of the picture is one of the soldiers who filled Paris after Napoleon's abdication walking a fashionably dressed woman with two dogs; her white dress and
his colourful uniform help to bring forward the bottom left of the composition.
In the distance on the right side we can discern a figure on horseback and a
carriage. But these are far less prominent than the stall and stallholders in the
right and centre foreground. Rather than the grand world of the great and the
emblems of high culture that Taylor called for, Crome focuses on the world of
small-scale economic activity from which he himself came. As he would in *Fishmarket at Boulogne* (*fig. 64*) of five years later, he makes a foreground still life
out of the products of small-scale producers. In the later painting it is baskets
of fish, here it is vegetables – splendid cauliflowers, leeks and carrots. I like to
think of that still life of humble objects as perhaps Crome's answer to Taylor's
lecture. At any rate, it speaks of a delight in the ordinary that is a marker of the
social gulf that separated Crome from the upper ranks of Norwich society.

The particularities of style and iconography are always interdependent, but it is useful sometimes to consider them separately for analytical purposes. In this essay I have argued that through its style Crome's art spoke a language of class (as art generally does) and that language was inflected by his social origins and a kind of artisanal consciousness. Although they would not have expressed it in these terms, this seems to have been clear to his contemporaries, who saw an equivalence between Crome the man and the homely, local qualities of his art. Ideology speaks in different ways to different individuals, depending on their formation and social positioning. The acceptance of Crome's form language by bourgeois such as Dawson Turner and Samuel Paget probably came with a mix of respect and condescension,[105] demonstrably so in the case of the former. In a way their attitude mirrored the terms of the alliance between the bourgeoisie, middle class, and artisanate that made the Reform Bill possible. But through historical research and an act of imagination, Crome's works can still speak to us today of a realm of social experience where Crome felt at home but from which Turner and Paget felt themselves quite separate.

---

105   From small beginnings, Samuel Paget of Great Yarmouth made a fortune as a ship's provisioner during the Anglo-French Wars, and then expanded into brewing and shipping (Peterson 1984, p. 680). As the Cliffords pointed out (Clifford and Clifford 1968, p. 80), the Paget family were the second largest lenders to Crome's posthumous exhibition. The largest lender was the coach-maker William Spratt, who exhibited with the Norwich Society of Artists on three occasions and was its Secretary in 1812 and 1815. He lent nine works. (pp. 79–80).

John Crome's 'Local Scenery': Iconography and the Ideology of the Picturesque

This essay concerns motif choices and iconography in paintings by the Norwich artist John Crome. It is divided into two parts. In the first I consider responses to Crome's pictures from his contemporaries, in so far as these can be discovered from exhibition reviews, biographical notices, and other printed sources; in the second I analyse different categories of Crome's output and suggest some meanings attached to his treatment of picturesque motifs. The mapping of iconography sheds light on both Crome's ambitions as an artistic agent and on his relationships with his public in the provincial milieu of Norfolk; it also helps us to comprehend the ideological reverberations of his practice. 'Local scenery', the seemingly bland term used by one of his contemporaries to define the character of his motifs, implied a more complex body of ideas than superficially appears.

Critical Discourse and Iconography

For anyone concerned with the significance of Crome's motif choices for his contemporaries, an obvious place to start is with what they had to say about his pictures. Unfortunately, this was not much, or, at least, not much that left a printed record. In the early nineteenth century, Norwich's two newspapers, the *Norwich Mercury* and the *Norfolk Chronicle*, seldom commented at length on Crome's exhibited works and although he showed his pictures at eleven London exhibitions, they attracted little attention in the metropolitan press. The exhibitions of the Norwich Society of Artists, which began in 1805,[1] were discussed only in the most general terms in early reviews in the Norwich papers and, even when reviews started to mention individual artists by name, as those in the *Mercury* began to do in 1809, they gave no particular attention to Crome, despite the fact that he was the most prolific of the exhibitors. In 1810, the *Mercury*'s reviewer excused himself by saying, 'We do not presume to enter

---

1 A brief history of the Society is given in Rajnai 1976, pp. 3–4. I touch on details of its history in Hemingway 1979. The most comprehensive critical account of Norwich landscape painting is Brown, Hemingway, and Lyles 2000.

into particular detail or minute criticism', whilst in 1814 he stated that, 'Our account does not aspire to the character of criticism. We profess only to be the ushers of this most praiseworthy institution to the notice of the public'.[2] The *Norfolk Chronicle* was equally wary of making what might seem invidious comparisons, although in 1810 it did give general praise to the landscapes of Crome, John Sell Cotman, Robert Dixon, Robert Ladbrooke and John Thirtle.[3] In 1815 it specifically recommended Crome's 'spirited sketch' of the Boulevard des Italiens in Paris (*fig. 62*); in the light of the *Chronicle*'s later reviews, use of the term 'sketch' to describe a finished picture is not insignificant.

A quarrel within the Norwich Society of Artists caused a group of members led by Robert Ladbrooke to secede and establish a separate exhibition in the years 1816–18. This attracted some correspondence and editorial comment in the papers and perhaps helped stimulate a wider interest in the artists' activities. From 1818 the *Chronicle* began to provide longer and more detailed exhibition reports. In its review of that year Crome was the first artist discussed and, for the first time, there is concrete information about the appearance of his work:

> Mr. Crome sustains, indeed enhances his reputation this year; *his peculiar talent of giving interest to local scenery through striking effects of sky and atmosphere*, is strongly exemplified in Nos. 73 and 77: the sea in the latter picture has great spirit of execution and force of effect – the light rippling waves near the shore admirably contrasted and inspirited by the broad dark masses of shadow thrown from the clouds on those in front of the picture. This picture gives us all the freshness of feeling which we have on the sea shore on a windy day. – No. 30 a twilight effect is clear, solemn and impressive. – No. 59. Beautifully finished with strong contrast of chiaroscuro – a fine surface without heaviness, and spangly, spirited execution without fritter or littleness.[4] (*my emphasis*)

From this description, No. 77, *Yarmouth Beach, from the Pier*, may be tentatively identified with the picture *Squall off Yarmouth*, which in 1968 was in a private collection in Bermuda – although any such identification is necessarily speculative.[5] As I will show, the italicised passage in this review relates to a more general estimation of Crome's merits.

---

2   *Norwich Mercury*, 25 August 1810; 13 August 1814.

3   *Norfolk Chronicle*, 25 August 1810.

4   *Norfolk Chronicle*, 8 August 1818.

5   P51 in Clifford and Clifford 1968.

On occasion, Crome's pictures attracted unfavourable remarks on their degree of finish, comparable with those that pictures by Turner, Constable, and his own pupil George Vincent sometimes received in the London press. Having praised Crome's execution in 1818, in the following year the *Chronicle* found that most of Crome's thirteen exhibits, 'though discovering the hand of the diligent observer of nature, come nevertheless, more correctly under the general denomination of studies rather than pictures.' After referring to four works as examples of this 'too sketchy style', the reviewer continued: 'Even against 25, a "Heath Scene", by the same artist, exhibiting as it does an excellent choice of situation marked by a boldness and breadth of shadowy masses in the foreground; and enlivened in the offskip by the accident of "the Sun's breaking out after a Storm" there still remains the regretted objection that it is an unfinished piece'.[6] This cannot have been the *Mousehold Heath* (*fig. 48*) in the Tate Gallery – which does not match the description – and it seems likely that it was a lost oil related to the etching of the same name (*fig. 65*).[7] In 1820 the *Chronicle* was still dissatisfied and focused its objections on Crome's *Fishmarket at Boulogne* (*fig. 64*). Although the reviewer praised the picture for its 'interesting delineation of national character and costume', he also complained that, 'in consequence of an adequate degree of forcibleness and animation not having (as we conceive) been given to the foreground, and the principal groups being placed in the half-distance, this little picture, which has considerable merit in its details, produces only the impression of a sketch'.[8] Crome's other exhibits made some amends although their virtues were said to consist primarily in technical qualities. For instance, of another landscape, not identified by number or title, it was said that 'the form of the trees, and touching of the foliage, are excellent, the waters are pencilled with a free and lively hand, and it is altogether a very agreeable picture'.[9] The *Chronicle*'s co-proprietor, William Stevenson, who had worked as a miniature-painter and run a drawing academy, was probably the author of these reviews.[10] His concern with finish may be related to his training as a miniaturist, but in any case comments on formal and technical qualities were the mainstay of press criticism.

---

6   *Norfolk Chronicle*, 14 August 1819.

7   Clifford and Clifford 1968, P90 and E3. For the dimensions and history of the picture, see p. 264. Crome's *Heath Scene* sold for £31.10.0 to Sir J.E. Swinburne of Capheaton Hall, Northumberland – 'Transactions relating to the Fine Arts', *Magazine of Art*, 1, 2 (1821), p. 151.

8   *Norfolk Chronicle*, 29 July 1820.

9   *Norfolk Chronicle*, 29 July 1820.

10   'William Stevenson', in Chambers 1829, pp. 1092–4.

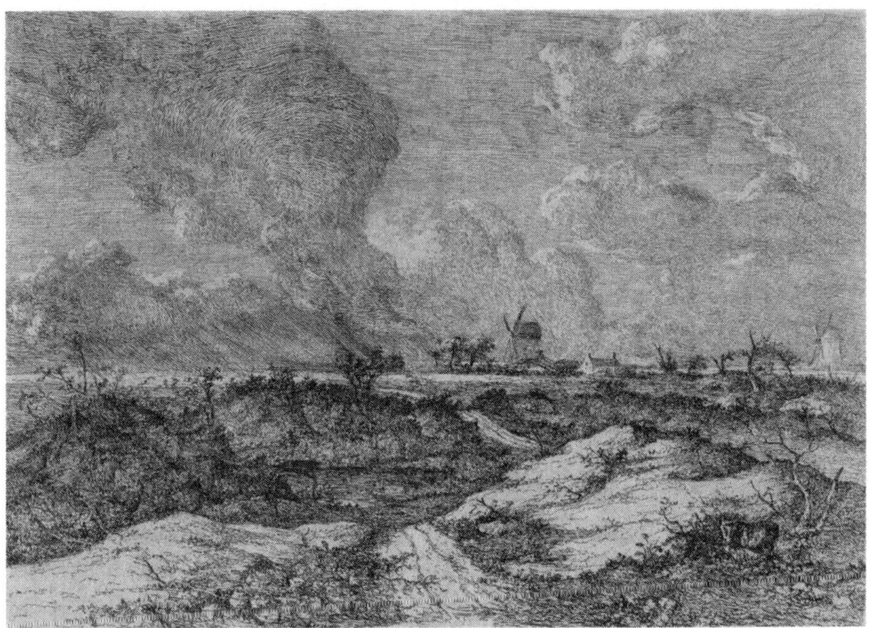

FIGURE 65   *John Crome,* Mousehold Heath, *c. 1820, etching, second state, 8⅛ × 11 ⅛ in*
(20.6 × 28.2 cm)
NORFOLK MUSEUM SERVICES (NORWICH CASTLE MUSEUM AND ART
GALLERY)

The *Norwich Mercury* is generally less informative in this period than the
Chronicle, although it too was concerned with the finish issue. In 1809 its
reviewer complained in general terms that unfinished pictures were being
shown although it is possible that this referred to real sketches or indeed works
in the process of completion.[11] In 1819 the *Mercury* commented that one of
Crome's exhibits was in a new manner, 'light and airy in its execution', and that
it preferred his usual style.[12] The paper gave Crome no special attention until
1820 and, even then, its remarks were generalised. Crome's work, it said, showed
'a visible mastery over the higher objects' of art in that 'effects are produced
with less effort'. The *Mercury*'s reviewer, Richard Mackenzie Bacon, apparently
found no fault with *Fishmarket at Boulogne,* which he described as 'lively, anim-
ated, and full of character'.[13] Crome was dead before the annual exhibition of
1821.

---

11   *Norwich Mercury,* 5 August 1809.

12   *Norwich Mercury,* 14 August 1819.

13   *Norwich Mercury,* 29 July 1820. For Bacon, see Chambers 1829, p. 1284.

The issue of finish was intrinsically linked with romantic conceptions of aesthetic autonomy and artistic freedom. The artist's control over the manifestation of his individual handwork was related to the notion of truth to individual vision, resistance to cramping market norms, and refusal of the dictates of public taste as this might be deduced from press criticism.[14] Comparable conceptions of romantic individualism were also manifest among writers and literary critics.[15] The principle followed by Crome and his contemporaries was articulated succinctly some decades later in Baudelaire's defence of Corot's work: 'a work of genius (or if you prefer, a work of the soul), in which every element is well seen, well observed, well understood and well imagined, will always be very well executed when it is *sufficiently* so ... in general what is *complete* is not *finished*, and ... a thing that is highly *finished* need not be *complete* at all'.[16] Romanticism prompted the same impulses among artists in provincial Norwich as in metropolitan London or Paris, and there too, the reviews suggest, formal innovations were the source of tensions between painters and patrons over artistic independence. With an artist as ambitious as Crome, we should not expect a seamless fit between the characteristics of his work and the interests and outlook of those who made up his market and audience.

It will be evident from this account that such comments on Crome's work as appeared in the Norwich press were usually extremely generalised or technical in nature. However, it seems clear, particularly from the 1818 and 1819 reviews in the *Norfolk Chronicle*, that Crome's merits were held to lie in his capacity to suggest natural effect, his choice of viewpoint, and his arrangements of light and shade. It is striking that there is not a single reference to location.

If local reviewers found no reason to remark on the significance of Crome's motifs, it is hardly surprising that they received no discussion in the London papers. Crome exhibited in London at the Royal Academy in the years 1806–12, 1816 and 1818 and at the British Institution in 1818, 1820 and 1821. W.T. Whitley, whose indispensable studies of early nineteenth-century English art were based on extensive familiarity with the press and periodical literature, stated that Crome's work was not noticed in the London press until 1821, with the exception of one review in 1809.[17] We know from the diary of Joseph Faring-

---

14   The letter from Constable's uncle and sometime patron David Pike Watts to the artist of
      12 April 1814 concerning *Boys Fishing* (Angelesey Abbey, Fairhaven Trust) is a nice case in
      point – Constable 1962–8, vol. 4, 37–8.

15   Williams 1961, Chapter 2.

16   'The Salon of 1845', in Baudelaire 1965, p. 24.

17   Whitley 1930, pp. 3–4.

ton that the finish of Crome's pictures at the Academy exhibition of 1806 provoked a hostile reaction from the critics of the *Sun* and the *Daily Advertiser,
Oracle, and True Briton,* who associated the artist's style with the 'new manner'
of 'the scribbling of painting' epitomised by the work of Turner. But neither
critic referred to Crome in their published reviews.[18] My own soundings in
newspapers of this period have discovered no further significant reference to
Crome and it may be that a provincial drawing-master who had not attended the Royal Academy, even one who numbered fashionable painters such
as John Opie and Sir William Beechey among his acquaintances, would have
been lucky to catch much attention. That Crome did start to attract some notice
around 1820–1 should probably be attributed in part to the success of his pupils
James Stark and George Vincent, who had lived and worked in London for some
time.[19]

Whitley refers to four reviews in 1821 in which Crome's two exhibits at the
British Institution were mentioned and there was at least one other. Of these
by far the most significant is that in the *London Magazine* by Thomas Griffiths
Wainewright, one of the most extreme voices of romanticism in contemporary art criticism. In character, Wainewright expressed his aversion to 'what is
commonly called a view, little more than topography, a kind of pictorial map-
work', with titles such as 'Fulham Church from the West' or 'A Mill'. Crome,
however, had 'an enviable "Heath Scene", in which the student may see how
much a subtle observation of the elements in their wild moods, does for a most
uninteresting flat. This view is not at all a mere topographical delineation. It
assumes a much higher station'.[20] This again suggests to me a painting related
to the etching *Mousehold Heath* (*fig. 65*), or at least one similar in type. And it
confirms the romantic credentials of Crome's vision.

It will be evident that Wainewright's comment manifests the same conception of Crome's merits as that voiced in the *Norfolk Chronicle* on 8 August 1818.
That such critical judgments are related to a more general pattern can be shown
by posthumous appraisals of Crome's art. The artist seems to have received substantial obituary notices only in the *Norwich Mercury* and the *Magazine of Fine
Arts.* Crome, the *Mercury* observed, 'principally cultivated landscape painting,
and was exceedingly happy in seizing small picturesque scenes, which he elev-

---

18   Farington 1978–84, vol. 7, p. 2748.

19   For Stark and Vincent, see Dickes 1906; Hemingway 1992, pp. 196–7, 209–14, 272–7, 278–81,
      297–8, *passim*; and Brown, Hemingway and Lyles 2000, pp. 136–43.

20   Anon. [Thomas Griffiths Wainewright], 'The British Institution', *London Magazine*, series
      1, 3 (April 1821), p. 439. Reprinted in Wainewright 1880, p. 121. For Wainewright – also
      notorious as a multiple murderer – see Curling 1938.

ated to a degree of interest, that in their natural state they could scarcely be said to bear, even to the eye of the connoisseur – so powerful is genius in art'.[21] Once again, Crome is praised for giving interest to scenes of little intrinsic interest in themselves.

A second posthumous commentary comes from Crome's friend and patron, the Yarmouth banker Dawson Turner.[22] Turner's comments on Crome comprise firstly a memoir, published to accompany the 1838 edition of Crome's etchings, which had partly been made in Turner's house; and secondly, descriptions of his own paintings by Crome in the privately-printed catalogue to his picture collection, *Outlines in Lithography* (1840). Turner was well-informed about art and his formal analyses of the pictures by Crome he owned are quite sensitive. Like Allan Cunningham, the Scottish art-writer who had discussed Crome in his *Cabinet Gallery of Pictures* (1836) largely on the basis of information he had supplied, Turner emphasised Crome's 'accuracy' and 'truth of delineation'. Comments like the following on the *View at Hellesdon* in his collection recur throughout his statements about the artist: 'Its execution is sketchy: its merit consists of being a simple, faithful transcript of unornamental nature'.[23] In the 1838 memoir he states, 'Whatever came from his pencil was a faithful transcript of what he saw',[24] and with specific reference to the etchings: 'The most inexperienced observer will not fail to trace in them that happy feeling for genuine, unsophisticated nature which was the great characteristic of Mr. Crome. The more practised eye will remark the power of selection and knowledge of composition which contributed the leading charm of his paintings. The latter will overlook what can hardly fail to shock the former in the want of finish in these performances'.[25] Once again we encounter the familiar emphasis on Crome's 'truth to nature' and his ability to give interest to scenes intrinsically uninteresting by selection, chiaroscuro, and compositional devices – the hallmarks of picturesque vision.

To those acquainted with British art writings from the early nineteenth century, the terms through which Crome's work was valorised should have a familiar ring, for they fit clearly within a more general critical discourse that derived primarily from academic theory as this related to landscape painting.

---

21   *Norwich Mercury*, 28 April 1821. Reprinted in Wodderspoon 1876, p. 20. Cf. Chambers 1829, pp. 1115–16; 'Memoir of the late Mr. John Crome', *Magazine of Fine Arts*, 1, 5 (September 1821), pp. 381–2.

22   For Turner, see Munby 1962.

23   Turner 1840, p. 15.

24   Dawson Turner, 'Memoir of Crome', in Wodderspoon 1876, p. 7.

25   Wodderspoon 1876, p. 5. On Crome's etchings, see also Turner 1840, pp. 19–20.

Theorists such as Sir Joshua Reynolds and James Barry emphasised the need for selection in landscape just as much as in figure subjects. A particularly important concept in this respect was that of breadth, that is to say a unifying general effect of light and shade to which details were subordinated. In his lecture on Chiaroscuro to students of the Royal Academy, Barry observed that in ordinary landscape scenes it depended on selection and the distribution of lights and shadows whether 'objects shall present themselves with that disgusting confusion and embarrassment which distract our sight, or with that unity and harmony which we can never behold without pleasure'.[26] That Crome was very much concerned with the concept of breadth we know from his well-known letter to his pupil James Stark of 1816, which I discussed in Chapter Eight. Indeed, the 'unfinished' surfaces that provoked criticisms of his work were intrinsically connected with attaining this quality. Crome's etchings, like his paintings, seemed insufficiently 'finished' to some of his contemporaries, and they were re-touched under Dawson Turner's supervision for the 1838 edition.

Even in provincial Norwich, those critics who found Crome's technique too extreme clearly understood what he was attempting to achieve: that his pronounced compositional structures, with their balanced masses and strong atmospheric effects, added up to something called breadth, to which a particular value adhered. (In this regard, we may note the use of the term in the passage from the 1819 *Chronicle* review quoted earlier). However, since the prevailing patterns of critical discourse provided no way of attributing value to place, and indeed tended to see particularities of detail as a defect, it is not surprising that the locations Crome represented were never discussed. In fact, contemporary philosophy did provide a theory that could attribute importance to the meaning of place in the association aesthetics of Kames, Alison, and Payne Knight, but artists and critics in the early nineteenth century were generally unable to reconcile the philosophical contradictions between the association doctrine and traditional theories of painting and tended to be highly critical of the former. None the less, as we saw in previous Chapters, the associationist theory of taste was common currency within the Norwich intellectual circles in which Crome moved.

Crome was not primarily a topographical painter in that he did not for the most part produce 'views' of cities, towns, country houses and parks, architectural monuments, natural wonders or well-known prospects, unlike say his fellow Norvicensians John Sell Cotman and Robert Dixon. Correspondingly, neither did he make watercolours or drawings of views for reproduction in

---

26   Wornum (ed.) 1848, p. 178.

print media or use print media directly for that purpose. But as a drawing master he could hardly avoid the pull of well-known picturesque sites such as the River Wye and Cumberland, and, as the exhibition record and some surviving works show, he depicted the castles at Chepstow (NSA 1805), Goodrich (NSA 1805, 1806), and Caister (NSA 1807), as well as Tintern Abbey (NSA 1805, 1807).[27] Significantly such works belong to the early years of his career as an exhibiting artist. He also exhibited views of well-known landmarks or sites in Norwich and other Norfolk places, such as *Bishop-gate Bridge, Norwich* (NSA 1805), *Cow Tower on the Swannery Meadow, Norwich* (NSA, 1806),[28] and *Trowse Bridge* (NSA 1811). In his later years, Crome responded to the new interest in views of mainland Europe that followed the reopening of the continent to travel in 1814, exhibiting three works based on studies made on a trip to Paris in 1814: *View in Paris – Italian Boulevard* (1815), *Bruges River, Ostend in the Distance* (1816), *Fishmarket at Boulogne* (1820) (all at Norwich Castle Museum and Art Gallery).

However, the extent to which Crome's work was concerned with specific locations seems to have varied and his output may be roughly divided into three categories: works that represented recognisable topographical landmarks and referred to specific places; works that referred to specific places but contained few or no such features; and works that both Crome and his contemporaries regarded as 'compositions'. Supporting evidence for this interpretation lies in Crome's titling of his exhibits in the Norwich Society catalogues where the names of some works clearly connect them with very specific sites – *Scene on St. Martin's River near Morse and Adam's Brewery* (NSA 1813), *Blogg's Lime-kiln* (NSA 1806),[29] *Boat-builder's Yard, near the Cow Tower* (NSA 1813), *Yarmouth Quay* (NSA 1814) and so on. Many works are related to a place but their theme seems generic, such as *A cart-shed at Melton, Norfolk* (NSA 1806) or *Cottages in Hingham* (NSA 1812). Other works are described vaguely as *Lane Scene, Grove Scene,* or *Cottage Scene*; and some just as *Landscape Composition* or just *Composition*.

A similar pattern can be found in the titling of Crome's etchings. All the titles on these were added for the 1838 edition supervised by Turner and they do not appear on the 1834 edition published by Crome's widow. It is important to note here that Dawson Turner was obsessively concerned with topography; his extra-illustrated copy of Francis Blomefield's *History of Norfolk*, now in the British Museum, is surely one of the largest personal collections of topo-

---

27   For surviving depictions of Tintern Abbey, see Clifford and Clifford 1968, D12 and D42.

28   Probably the painting in Norwich Castle Museum and Art Gallery, Clifford and Clifford 1968, P1.

29   Possibly the painting *The Limekiln* at Eltham Palace, Clifford and Clifford 1968, P9.

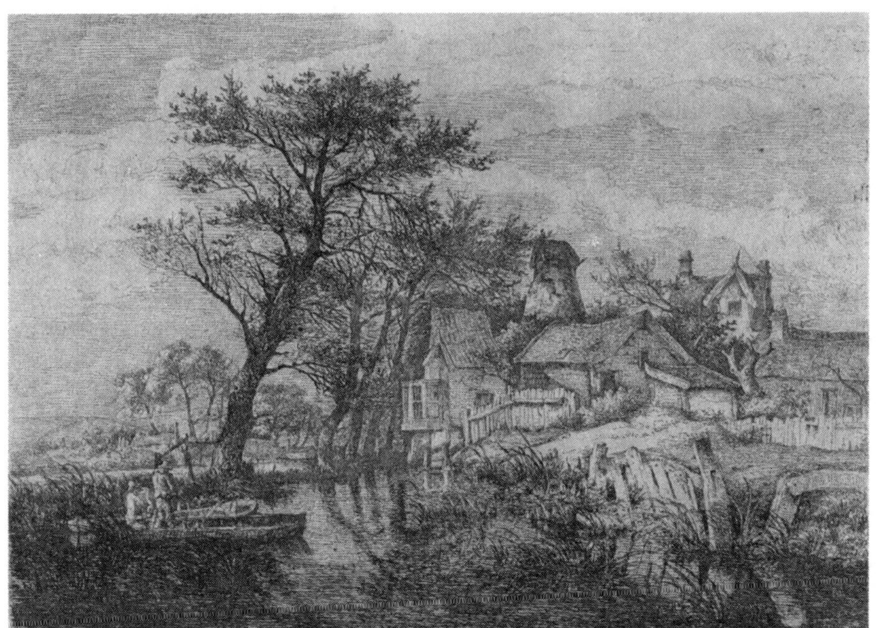

FIGURE 66 *John Crome,* Back of the New Mills, *1813, etching, 8¼ × 11 in (21.0 × 28 cm)*
NORFOLK MUSEUM SERVICES (NORWICH CASTLE MUSEUM AND ART
GALLERY)

graphical material. The claim to topographical fidelity was important for him.
Moreover, since Crome's eldest son, John Berney Crome, was also involved with
the 1838 publication, it is probable that the titles have some claim to accuracy.[30] Etchings such as *Back of the New Mills* (*fig. 66*) and *Front of the New Mills*
undoubtedly depict quite specific sites and it is possible that further research
may identify the buildings represented. It also seems likely that the slighter soft-
ground etchings with titles such as *Colney* and *Hoveton St. Peter* (*fig. 67*) were
based on pencil sketches made at particular sites. Both these groups seem different in conception from the etchings simply entitled *Composition,* such as
fig. 68. It is easy to believe that this latter type was derived from sketches and
studies and they have a more formalised structure of overlapping planes to suggest recession. In between these 'compositions' and the first type discussed are
etchings identified with specific places, such as *Hall Moor Road, near Hingham*
and *Road Scene, Hethersett,* which not only contain little that would support a
topographical identification but also refer very clearly to Dutch compositional

---

30   For a catalogue of the etchings, see Clifford and Clifford 1968, pp. 163–75.

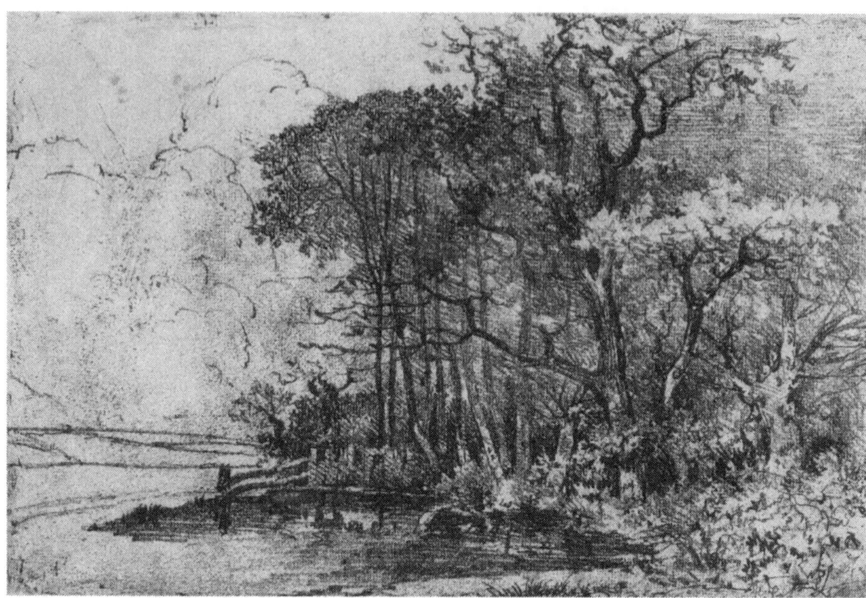

FIGURE 67   *John Crome,* Hoveton, St. Peter, *c. 1812, soft ground etching, 6½ × 9¼ in*
(16.5 × 23.7 cm)
NORFOLK MUSEUM SERVICES (NORWICH CASTLE MUSEUM AND ART
GALLERY)

prototypes, in this case to works by Meindert Hobbema. This pattern is only
partially matched by the traditional titling of Crome's pictures, since while the
blatantly Hobbema-inspired painting in the Metropolitan Museum of Art, New
York, is known as *Hautbois Common* (*fig. 80*), comparable works such as Norwich Museum's *Grove Scene* and the National Gallery of Scotland's *The Beaters*
(*fig. 44*) remain unconnected with any place.[31] Further, the painting closest
to the *Composition* illustrated here is that in the Lever Art Gallery known as
Marlingford Grove (*fig. 45*), which, as Francis Hawcroft pointed out, may be the
Grove Scene near Marlingford lent by Samuel Paget to Crome's Memorial Exhibition in 1821 and dated 1815.[32] While the formal artifice of the design in this case
is notable, it seems to have denoted a grove in a small village six and a half miles
west of Norwich.

From Dawson Turner's descriptions of pictures by Crome in *Outlines in
Lithography*, it appears that he knew the specific locations represented in some

31   Clifford and Clifford 1968, P126, P133, and P56.
32   Hawcroft 1968, cat. no. 15.

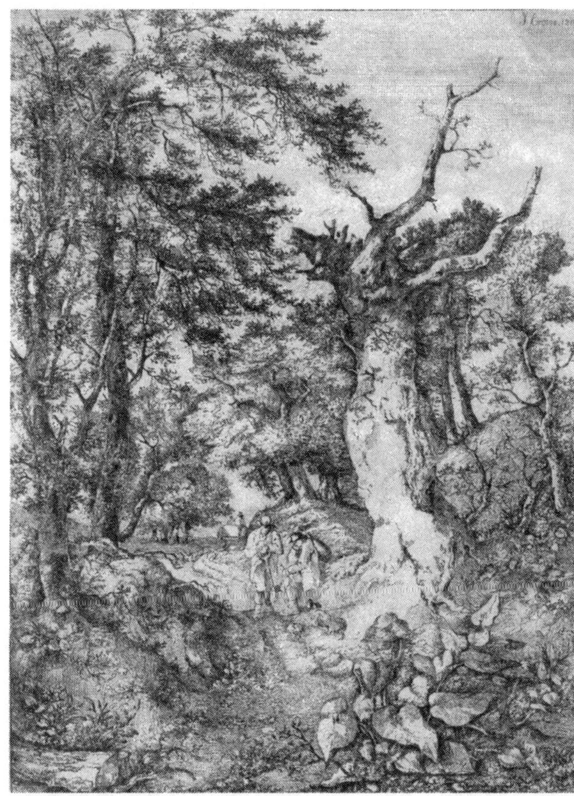

FIGURE 68
John Crome, Composition:
Sandy Road through
Woodland, *1813, etching,*
15 × 11 in (37.9 × 27.8 cm)
NORFOLK MUSEUM
SERVICES (NORWICH
CASTLE MUSEUM AND ART
GALLERY)

of them but not that in others. For example, of his *View on the River Yare near Yarmouth* (*fig. 50*) he writes, 'The spot selected is only a few miles before it [the Yare] falls into the sea, hard by its junction with the Waveney'. He even suggests that the draining mill in the painting was probably that depicted in a view of Reedham Ferry in James Stark's *Rivers of Norfolk,* an explicitly topographical work published over the years 1828–34.[33] Turner was equally definite about the locations represented in other pictures, which have even less in the way of landmarks. Thus he tells us that the picture in the Yale Center for British Art, now known as *Wensum at Thorpe: Boys Bathing* (*fig. 69*), is 'a bright day-light scene at the back of the New Mills, on the Norwich River'. (It is extraordinary that, despite this, both recent catalogues of Crome's work still refer to the picture as *Wensum at Thorpe.* Thorpe is on the other side of Norwich from the New Mills and, just before Thorpe, the river Wensum runs into the Yare.

---

33   Turner 1840, pp. 19–20.

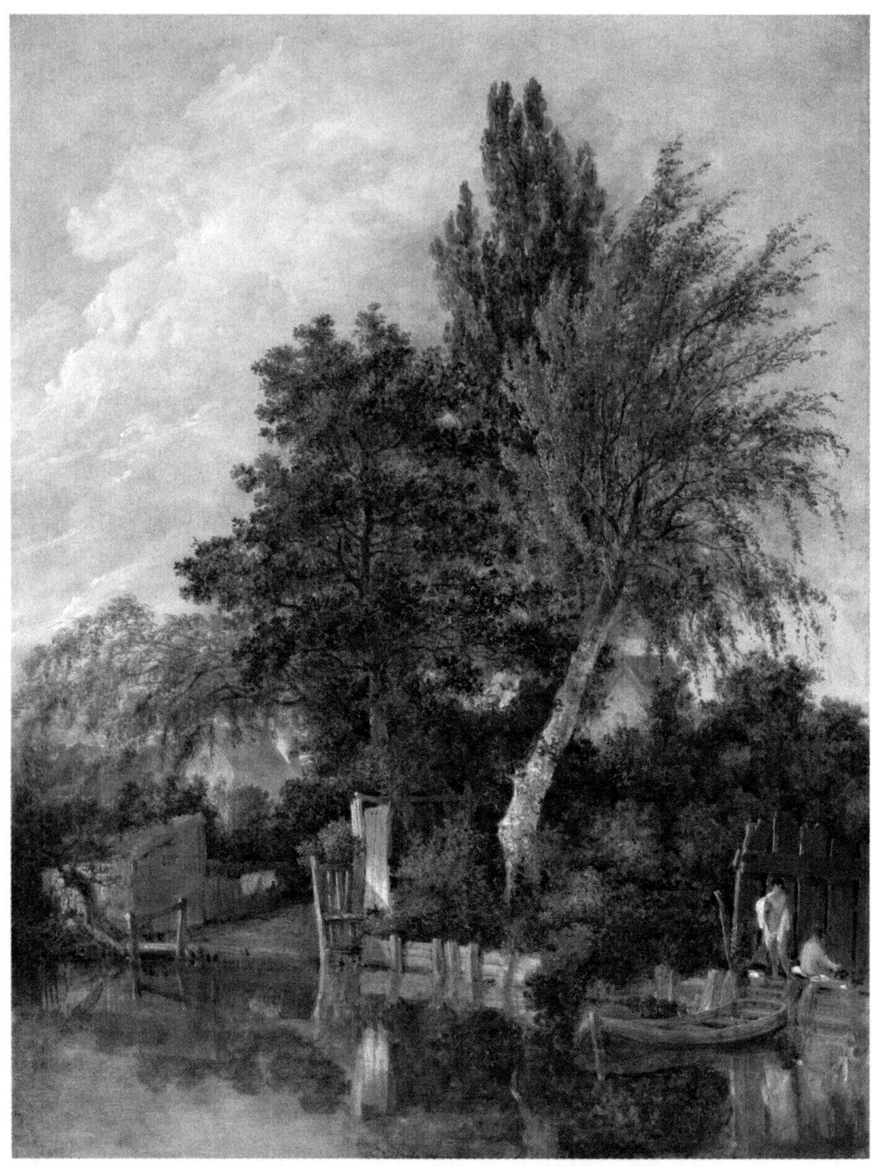

FIGURE 69 *John Crome (1768–1821), Boys Bathing on the River Wensum, c. 1818, oil on panel, 19×14⅛ in (48.3×35.9 cm)*
YALE CENTER FOR BRITISH ART, PAUL MELLON COLLECTION

Turner's own title was *Scene on the River at Norwich*.) Yet he also owned pictures such as *View near Norwich* and *Cottage near Norwich*, of which nothing he says bears on the location depicted except in the most general terms. This reinforces the view that Dawson Turner's 'truth to nature' has more than one meaning; that it usually implies a particular concept of picture-making, related to an ideological category of 'nature' but that it may also imply a relationship of depiction between images and particular places.

It is clear that some of Crome's paintings and prints were conceived as 'compositions', and that others have no features that would permit us to connect them with actual sites if we did not have written evidence to work from. This does not, however, make the subject of say Dawson Turner's *Scene on the River at Norwich* insignificant, since it is evident that Turner and his contemporaries understood such works as depictions of particular localities. Equally, when paintings like this were exhibited in Norwich it was evident from the catalogue to which locations they referred. The meaning of paintings is necessarily determined in part by verbal discourses and the ascription of a title was part of the text through which Crome's works were interpreted by his contemporaries. When a topographical title was attached to a work, and especially when that work denoted recognisable topographical features, it seems reasonable to assume that Crome intended his audience to draw on a specific range of associations.

That association theory was discussed in Norwich at a high level of sophistication is confirmed by the 'Disquisition of Beauty' by Dr. Frank Sayers, one of the city's leading intellectuals, and a figure that Crome and his son John Berney Crome certainly knew through their membership of the Norwich Philosophical Society. In January 1791, Sayers – who later became a friend of Crome's artist mentor John Opie – delivered a paper to the Norwich Speculative Society on the theme of beauty,[34] which was presumably the basis of the 'Disquisition on Beauty' printed in his *Disquisitions, Metaphysical and Literary*, first published in 1793. This is a resounding defence of the associationist principle as the basis for all the pleasures of taste, grounded in the psychology of David Hartley but also drawing on the application of the theory in the treatises of

---

34   For the Speculative Society and Sayers's friendship with Opie, see William Taylor's biographical preface to Sayers 1823, vol. 1, pp. lxii, lxxxi. Sayers sat to Opie for his portrait in 1800 (the painting is in Norwich Castle Museum and Art Gallery) and cited Opie's acceptance of the associationist theory as corroboration for his own position (vol. 2, p. 11). In his lectures as Professor of Painting at the Royal Academy, Opie claimed that 'Conceptions of beauty or perfection take place involuntarily in the mind, through the medium of that wonderful and powerful principle, the association of ideas'. See Wornum (ed.) 1848, p. 245.

Kames and Alison. Sayers's commitment to associationism was such that he added a lengthy note to the second edition of the *Disquisitions* criticising the application of the theory in Richard Payne Knight's *Analytical Inquiry into the Principles of Taste* (1805) as partial and inconsistent, and adding nothing to Alison's work.[35]

That Crome's son at least accepted the theory we know from the 'Essay on Painting and Poetry' he delivered at the Philosophical Society in 1818, in which he argued that 'the use of terms of approbation or disapprobation, of admiration or disgust toward works of art' derived from 'an association of Ideas deriving from the experience & opinions of others – What our Predecessors in Painting Poetry & Sculpture have considered as the standard of excellence so have we & so we ever shall'. However, in addition to this traditional conception of the standard of taste, the younger Crome also claimed that 'Painting not only finds grace & decorations for the present hour, but a pleasure & solace for the future by preserving amidst the constant decay of Nature those frail & Perishable lineaments, on which in distant days the eye of affection may fondly dwell, while the heart associates with them the soothing remembrance of its earliest feelings & its purest joys'.[36] These were conventional sentiments and they illustrate the general acceptance of associationist principles.

According to Sayers, 'the beauty of landscapes arises from the ideas of peace, of health, of rural happiness, of pleasing solitude, of simple manners, of classical imagery, &c., connected with the groups of trees, with the lawns, and fields, and water which enter into their composition; of this I think every one will be convinced, from observing the various, but equally pleasant ideas, associated with the scenes of nature in the mind of Milton'. This suggests a vision of ideal landscape of the Franco-Italian type, which was linked with the long tradition of pastoral poetry and its more recent British variants. Sayers's own poetical works were mainly attempts, characteristic of the period, to give epic forms to north European myths and legends, as in *Dramatic Sketches of Northern Mythology* (1790).[37] But his posthumously published *Collective Works* also

---

35 Sayers 1808, p. 11.

36 John Berney Crome, 'Essay on Painting and Poetry', pp. 5, 29–30 (manuscript in Norwich Castle Museum and Art Gallery). The dating of J.B. Crome's delivery of the essay is confirmed by the report on the Norwich Philosophical Society in *New Monthly Magazine*, 11, 6 (March 1818), p. 146. The Philosophical Society was founded in 1812 and met fortnightly from October to April to discuss subjects concerned with 'Natural Philosophy and general Literature' – see Stacy 1819, p. 189.

37 Sayers 1823, vol. 1, pp. 1–46.

includes 'Lines on Thorpe Grove', dated November 1808.[38] At that time, Thorpe was a village two miles to the east of Norwich on the river Yare, which was increasingly being turned into a suburb of the city. Sayers lamented the destruction of the grove:

> The lingering Genius of the grove is fled.
> 'Tis ruin all – no lonely pine-tree waves
> On yonder brow, not e'en a blasted stem
> Swart, sear, and riven, points the hill that rose
> In tufted verdure; on its deep scarr'd side
> The shiver'd trunk, the withering branch is spread,
> In careless desolation.[39]

The grove had been a relic of a 'deep wood' that according to 'antique legends' once fringed Mousehold Heath. To Sayers it suggested a string of conventional associations – of medieval piety, pilgrimage, medieval love lays, childhood, lovers' trysts, scholars' solitary reflections, and scenes of druidic horror. But the most powerful association – which concludes the poem – is that the disappearance of the grove marks the sacrifice of beauty and history to utility or profit:

> And e'en the hasty traveler shall mourn
> Your fallen pride, and miss the spot, where, pleas'd,
> His eye had rested; mid the wide-spread scene,
> Where Wensome glides along his sedgy meads,
> Bounded by sloping hills, with wood embrown'd,
> Yon bleak, bare ridge shall mock the scornful arm
> That robb'd it of its honours – yes, fair, grove,
> For thee the sigh shall rise, while feeling glows,
> While taste inspires, and rural beauty charms.[40]

Such sentiments seem commonplace enough; but they serve as a reminder that the imagery of woodland was, as Stephen Daniels has shown, heavily invested with social and political values.[41]

---

38   The grove of large fir trees was cut down in 1808 – see text to accompany 'View from the Site of Thorpe Old Grove', in Robberds 1834.

39   Sayers 1823, vol. 1, p. 299.

40   Ibid.

41   Stephen Daniels, 'The political iconography of woodland in later Georgian England', in Cosgrove and Daniels (eds.) 1988, pp. 43–82.

Picturesque Meanings

I have addressed the iconography of Crome's beach scenes and river views elsewhere;[42] here I want to consider kinds of motif that belong to the conventional picturesque and which superficially appear less symbolically freighted, namely trees, lanes, and cottages. It might seem that once the formal affinity of Crome's well-known forest and grove scenes with the patterns established by Hobbema, Ruisdael, and Waterloo has been remarked, there is little more to be said. But that would be to miss the fact that they were not conceived as pastiches for the most part and were often linked with the natural and social world of modern-day Norfolk through their titles. It would also be to miss the complex social vision embedded in the specific strand of contemporary aesthetic thought through which they were validated, the ideology of the picturesque.

Norfolk had particular connections with the theorisation of the picturesque through the person of the gardener Humphry Repton, whose dispute with Uvedale Price and Richard Payne Knight in the 1790s exposed some of the social and political implications of the aesthetic as applied to landscape gardening.[43] Gardening as such does not concern me here, but the arguments over cottage architecture that the picturesque debate generated do, since they were inseparable from claims about the pleasures of landscape painting and its moral value. As I shall show, there is solid circumstantial evidence to suggest these themes were discussed in the Norwich Society of Artists.

Repton was born into prosperous circumstances in Bury St. Edmunds, in the neighbouring county of Suffolk, in 1752. A decade later, the Repton family moved to Norwich where he attended Norwich Grammar School – one of his childhood friends was the future naturalist James Edward Smith, founder of the Linnaean Society – before a spell of schooling in Holland. On his return to the city in 1768, he was placed as an apprentice in a textile concern, setting up his own business as a general merchant in 1775. Repton did not like trade and his business foundered. In 1778 he moved his family to a small estate at Sustead, four miles south-west of Cromer, in north Norfolk. Here he formed important friendships with neighbouring landowners including William Windham of Felbrigg and the naturalist Robert Marsham of Stratton Strawless. He was election agent for Windham in his campaigns in Norwich in 1784 and 1790, and his own politics followed a trajectory closely aligned with Windham's increasingly con-

---

42   Hemingway 1992, pp. 196–208, 257–67.

43   The grounds of the dispute are laid out succinctly by Daniels in Cosgrove and Daniels 1988, pp. 57–73, and at more length in Daniels 1999, Chapter 3. See also Everett 1994, Chapter 3.

servative Whiggism. With his finances in trouble, in 1788 Repton gave up the life of the country squire at Sustead that he so relished, and moved to a cottage at Hare Street in Essex, from which he launched his career as a professional gardener and author, capitalising on his knowledge of botany and skills as a painter of picturesque watercolours.[44] Although in 1792 Repton complained that 'there is hardly any part of England in which I am less known profession-ally than in Norfolk',[45] this is not borne out by the record of his works since he received more commissions there than in any other county except Essex – at least eighteen in all. Repton had moved extensively in Norfolk and Norwich society in the 1770s and 1780s, and his patrons read like a list of the major figures and families of the region; he did work for Jeremiah Ives at Catton, Philip Mar-tineau at Bracondale, Thomas Coke at Holkham, Bartlett Gurney at Northrepps, Thomas Cubitt at Honing Hall, and the Jerningham family at Costessey. He regarded the improvements he conceived for Abbott and Charlotte Upcher at Sheringham in 1812 as 'my most favourite work' and exemplary of his formal and social vision.[46] In 1814, Repton painted the peace celebrations in the square at Aylsham, near his former property at Sustead. He was evidently a frequent vis-itor to Norfolk and, given his family and social connections there, his views can hardly not have been a topic of discussion in the social world in which Crome moved.

Moreover, it seems unlikely to be coincidental that the figure we might see as the Norwich Society of Artist's own theorist of the picturesque, the physician Edmund Bartell (1770–1855), lived in Cromer, so near to Repton's one-time home in the county.[47] Bartell was a member of the Society from 1808–32, served as its secretary from 1817–21, and was its vice-president in 1824 and its president in the following year. Although he exhibited – a mix of copies and views – on only three occasions, he must be regarded as an important figure in the organisation's history. Moreover, the affinity between his formulations of the picturesque and Crome's images is in some instances startlingly close.

---

44   My main sources for Repton's biography are J.C. Loudon's introduction to Repton 1840; Stroud 1962; and Daniels 1999. For more detail on Repton at Sustead, see Daniels 1983 and Daniels 1999, Chapter 2. For his political connections and beliefs, see also Daniels 1982 (1).

45   Quoted in Daniels 1982 (1), p. 110.

46   Daniels gives an account of his Norfolk commissions in Daniels 1999, Chapter 2. He has also discussed the Sheringham project in Daniels 1982 (2) and Daniels 1986.

47   Daniels describes Bartell incorrectly as a 'Norwich physician' (Daniels 1999, p. 89). His address, as given in the NSA catalogue of 1808 was Cromer, and in 1816 and 1825 as the small village of Swannington. He is also incorrect in saying the first edition of the Cromer guide was published in London – Daniels 1982 (2), p. 142 n. 36.

Bartell published two books. His *Observations upon the Town of Cromer, considered as a Watering Place, and the Picturesque Scenery in the Neighbourhood*, was printed in the north Norfolk town of Holt, nine and a half miles west of Cromer, in 1800; a second edition was published in London in 1806. *Hints for Picturesque Improvements in Ornamental Cottages, and their Scenery, Including Some Observations on the Labourer and his Cottage, in Three Essays*, had been published by the same publisher two years before. In the preface to the latter work, Bartell observes that 'few researches of late years have more occupied the attention of persons of taste, than those which relate to Picturesque Scenery',[48] and both his texts acknowledge the weight of precedent by their frequent references to other authorities in the form of Gilpin, Price, Knight, Repton, Shenstone, and Lord Kames. In fact, Bartell was an adept in picturesque theory and was particularly alert to its social and moral implications.

Crome's early works – by which I mean watercolours and oils from approximately 1805–10 – are like programmatic exercises in the picturesque aesthetic as this had been formulated by the Reverend William Gilpin and Uvedale Price. However, despite commonalities between Gilpin's and Price's theories, there are also important differences, and it is helpful to understand the development of Crome's work in terms of a transition from one to the other. The fact that Crome's conception of picture-making can be defined in picturesque terms is hardly surprising given the role Gainsborough's *Cottage Door* (1780; *fig. 70*) had played in his formation and that Gainsborough's cottage and woodland scenes played in the development of Price's taste and picturesque taste more generally.[49] Gilpin, of course, did not set the same value on Dutch landscape painting as Price – his ideal was the heroic landscapes of Salvator Rosa – and correspondingly he thought cottages an 'improper decoration to the forest on canvas', as forests require 'the appendages of greatness'.[50] Significantly, no cottage appears in Crome's so-called *Woodland Scene near Norwich* (c. 1807–8; *fig. 71*),

---

48   Bartell 1804, p. v.

49   Price 1810, vol. 2, p. 367. Gainsborough's finished chalk and watercolour drawing *Beech Trees in the Woods at Foxley, with Yazor Church in the Distance* (1760; Whitworth Art Gallery, University of Manchester), which was made for Price's father, was another model for the Pricean picturesque. My point is supported by the importance accorded Gainsborough's example in J.T. Smith's, *Remarks on Cottage Scenery* – Smith 1797, pp. 7–8. For the reputation of the *Cottage Door* in the early nineteenth century, see Bermingham (ed.) 2005, Part 3.

50   Gilpin 1808, vol. 1, p. 226. On Gilpin's aesthetic, see Hemingway 1992, pp. 19–22, and, more generally, Barbier 1963.

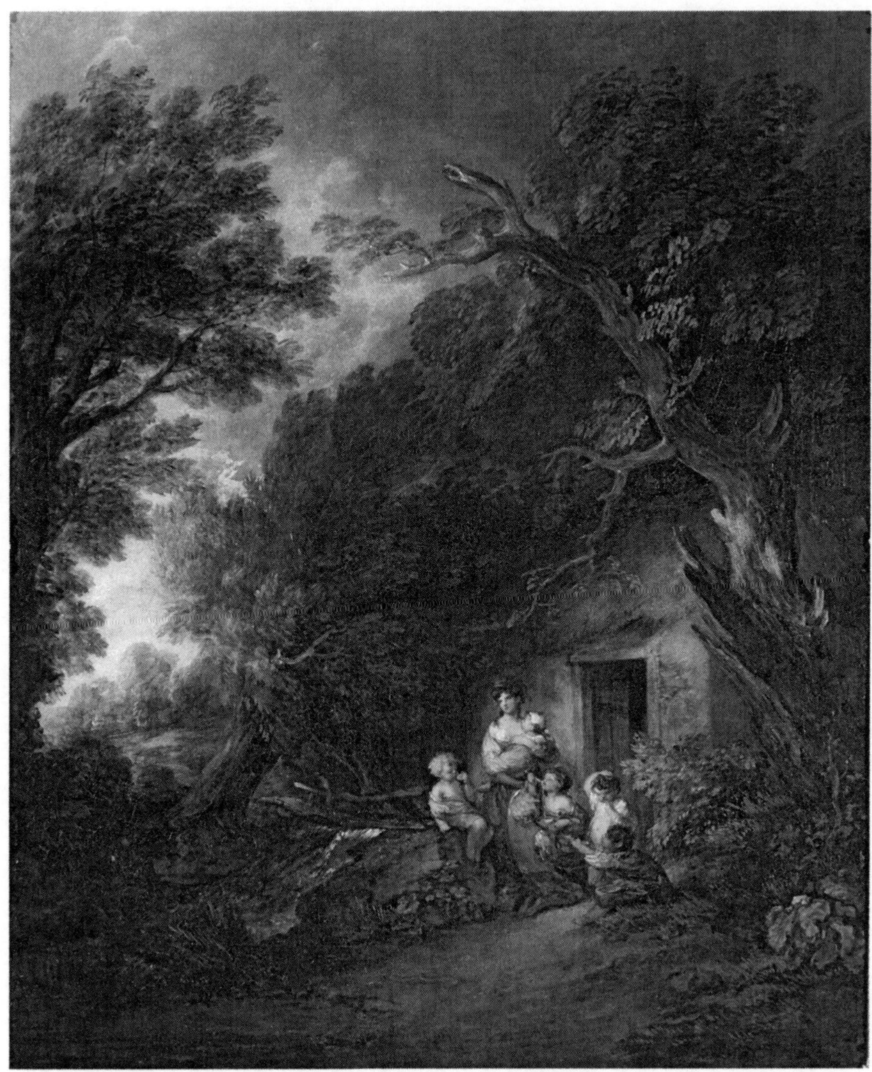

FIGURE 70   *Thomas Gainsborough,* Cottage Door, *1780, oil on canvas, 58×47 in (147.3×119.4 cm)*
© COURTESY OF THE HUNTINGTON ART COLLECTIONS, SAN MARINO,
CALIFORNIA

formerly known as *Melton Oak,* although the painting once had a figure with a
dog to the right of the main tree;[51] its effect of solitude would have matched

---

51   Clifford and Clifford 1968, P54, pp. 206–7. Any title must be speculative, but the image
     hardly suggests the park at Melton Constable, which was designed by Capability Brown.

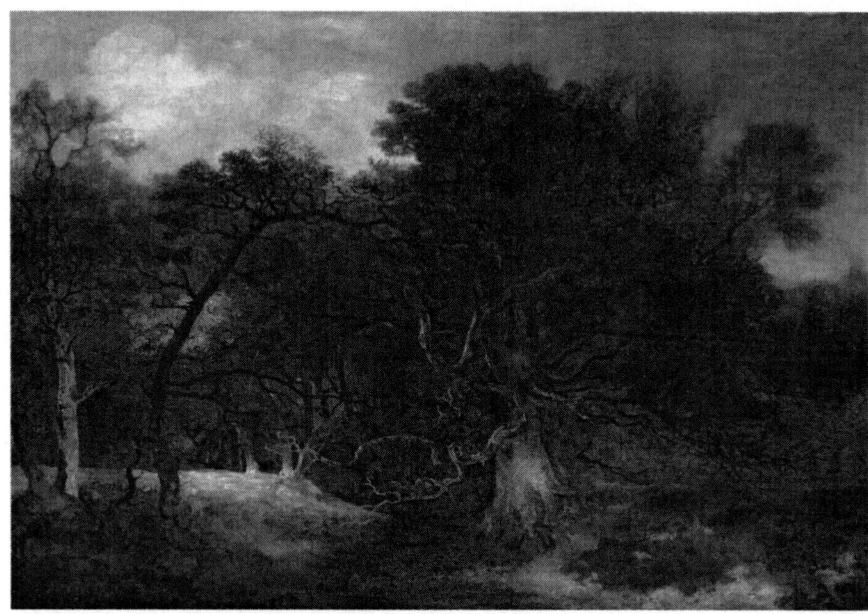

FIGURE 71   *John Crome (1768–1821)*, Woodland Scene near Norwich, *c. 1807–08, oil on canvas,*
35½ × 51¼ in (90.2 × 130.2 cm)
YALE CENTER FOR BRITISH ART, NEW HAVEN, PAUL MELLON COLLECTION

nicely with Gilpin's notion of the solemnity and grandeur appropriate to a
forest interior.[52] In the painting's present condition it is hard to make out the
stream (or is it a pool?) that comes in to the picture between the highlighted
bank on the left and the base of the oak, and which issues in the centre of the
bottom edge of the canvas just where the viewer is positioned.

Formally speaking, *Woodland Scene near Norwich* takes its cue at least in
part from the finished chalk and wash drawings of trees by Waterloo such as
A Wide Wooded Landscape (*fig. 72*) and etchings by Jacob van Ruisdael, like *A
Forest Marsh with Travellers on a Bank* (*The Travellers*).[53] However, the loose
quality of the paintwork – which matches the 'free, bold touch' Gilpin thought
inherently pleasing[54] – is closer to Gainsborough's style after 1760 than it is to

---

52   For Payne Knight too, 'the neglected style of forest scenery is preferable to all others'.
       Knight 1795, p. 44.

53   Waterloo was an artist greatly admired by Gilpin, who described him as 'a name beyond
       any other in landscape [prints]. His subjects are perfectly rural, simplicity is their charac-
       teristic'. – Gilpin 1802, p. 108. Cf. Gilpin 1794, ll. 169–70. There were nine lots of Waterloo
       etchings in Crome's 1812 sale.

54   Gilpin 1794, p. 17.

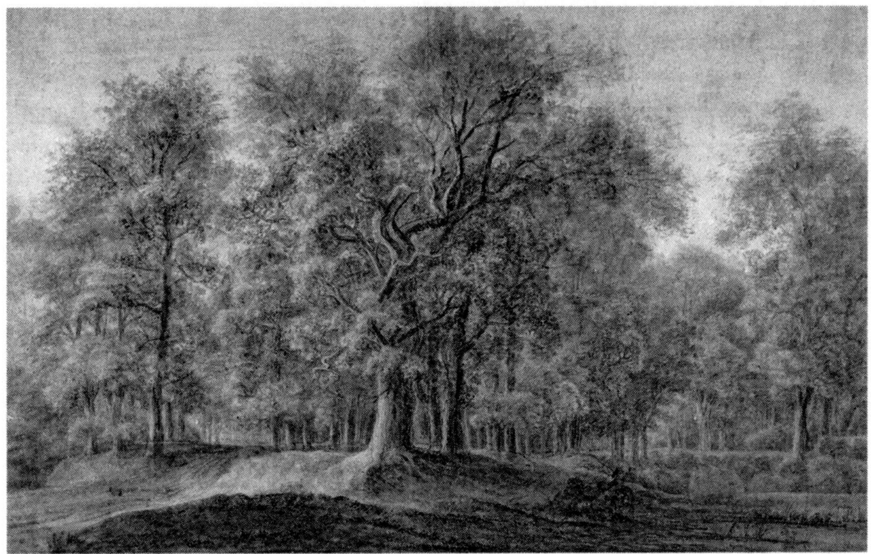

FIGURE 72   *Antoine Waterloo,* A Wide Wooded Landscape, *black chalk, gray and black wash, charcoal soaked in linseed oil, 16 × 25 ⅛ (40.7 × 63.7 cm)*
NICOLAAS TEEUWISSE OHG, BERLIN

Ruisdael or Hobbema. The painting also matches Gilpin's prescriptions better than Crome's later work in the lack of foreground detail; Gilpin thought that the finishing of details would only distract from the effects of the whole and regarded weeds as 'too common; too undignified' to match the sombre atmosphere of a forest.[55] (In this regard, the painting contrasts with the foreground plants of say Crome's *Marlingford Grove, fig. 45,* of circa 1815). 'The proper distribution of light and shade' that was central to Gilpin's conception of pictorial pleasure was incompatible with bright effects of the sun at midday; his preference was for 'predominacy of shade' over 'predominacy of light', and the hues of autumn were more conducive to effects of breadth than those of spring or summer.[56] Unconsciously or not, *Woodland Scene near Norwich* conforms to these prescriptions, illustrating the widespread currency of picturesque norms.

Crome's choice of an oak for his main tree was also symbolically freighted and indeed the species was a central motif in his repertoire. The oak was

---

55   Gilpin 1808, vol. 1, pp. 229, 231, 261.

56   Gilpin 1808, vol. 1, pp. 252, 261, 267. Price too thought autumnal tints were particularly picturesque and associated them with the colours of age and decay, while the beauties of spring were not adapted to painting. See Price 1810, vol. 1, pp. 169–70, 173.

the first tree Gilpin discussed in his *Remarks on Forest Scenery* and he dwelt longer on it than on any other, 'as it is confessedly the most picturesque tree in itself; and the most accommodating in composition'. He particularly singled out its twisting branches in this regard and observed that 'we often see two or three oaks intermingle their branches together in a very pleasing manner'.[57] For Bartell, quoting the poet and gardener William Shenstone, 'a large branching oak is, perhaps, the most venerable of all inanimate objects'.[58] In Crome's painting, a younger tree appears to lean over to link with a 'Hercules' of the forest, to borrow Gilpin's phrase. The oak not only had enormous symbolic resonance as a national tree because of its age and strength, it played a crucial role in the nation's defences during wartime through its functions in shipbuilding.[59] Trees were a valuable form of property, but their attraction as such was in competition with the profitability of arable farming in the period of the Continental blockade when an unprecedented acreage was put under the plough. Gilpin lamented the disappearance of British forests in the course of agricultural and industrial development; the picturesque eye was antipathetic to considerations of utility and 'scorns the narrow conceptions of a timber merchant'.[60] Crome's tree resists such vulgar concerns.

In the text he published to accompany the collection of his etchings, *Sylva Britannica; or Portraits of Forest Trees* (1822), Jacob George Strutt wrote of the oak in his dedication to the Duke of Bedford, as the 'Lord of the Woods', and associated it with the Bedford family as 'the champions of lawful right and well-regulated liberty'. Forest trees, but oaks especially, were likened to old aristocratic families because of their longevity and rootedness in land; they were 'silent witnesses' to the passage of generations and to the successive phases of national history. As Strutt showed, the oak had been a long-standing symbol in British poetry. However, while Strutt's 20 etchings of oaks in the grounds of country houses refer unequivocally to their place in the established order of property, Crome's eponymous giant suggests rather the forest as a place of contemplation and the 'haunts of liberty'[61] in a different sense – the place where, to borrow Uvedale Price's terms, the 'wild

---

57   Gilpin 1808, vol. 1, pp. 25–34, 182. Daniels elaborates on the significance of the oak in Cosgrove and Daniels, pp. 48, 50.

58   Bartell 1806, p. 57. Bartell was prompted to this observation by the oaks in Windham's estate at Felbrigg.

59   For the value of the oak in shipbuilding, see Strutt 1822, p. 4.

60   Gilpin 1808, vol. 1, pp. 45, 308; vol. 2, pp. 166, 307–8.

61   Strutt 1822, p. 29. Strutt exhibited four works at the Norwich Society of Artists in 1832.

forester' and the 'wandering tribes of gypsies and beggars' might congregate
outside the control of the propertied classes.[62]

Some other works by Crome from around the time of Yale's *Woodland Scene*
depict motifs that Gilpin recommended, such as the watercolours of *The Oak
Tree* and *The Blasted Oak* (both collection of Sir Nicholas Bacon) and details
such as the 'old tree with a *hollow trunk* ... or with a *dead arm*, a *drooping
bough*, or a dying branch' enliven the 'rugged foregrounds' of pictures such as
The Beaters and *Marlingford Grove*.[63] But while Gilpin had some appreciation
of 'winding lanes',[64] he was not a theorist of cottage scenery or the rustic; these
motifs in the discourse of the picturesque were elaborated by the artist John
Thomas Smith and Uvedale Price, critic of the Brownist landscape garden.

Like his friend and sometime theoretical opponent Richard Payne Knight,
Price's conceptualisation of the picturesque depended on a valorisation of
seventeenth-century Dutch painting – particularly the works of Adriaen van
Ostade and Rembrandt[65] – that placed it significantly higher in the scale of
merit than conventional academic theory allowed. This was partly because the
picturesque was associated with objects that were the very antithesis of those
associated with ideal form, even with ugliness, and which indeed were the
province of the lesser genres; often these were objects marked by processes of
organic decay, weathering, and aging.[66] In an essay of 1794, Price wrote:

> All painters who have imitated the more confined scenes of nature, have
> been fond of making studies from old neglected bye-roads and hollow
> ways; and perhaps there are few spots that in so small a compass, have
> a greater variety of that sort of beauty called picturesque ... [In such
> scenes] a thousand circumstances of detail, promote the natural intricacy
> of the ground: the turns are sudden and unprepared; the banks sometimes
> broken and abrupt; sometimes smooth and gently, but not uniformly slop-

---

62   Price 1810, vol. 1, p. 63.

63   Clifford and Clifford 1968, D69, D57. Gilpin recommends the blasted tree as a motif in
      Gilpin 1808, vol. 1, 14. It was an important emblem in Ruisdael's work, as in *Tree near
      a House* (c. 1648; Fitzwilliam Museum, Cambridge) and *Landscape with a Half-Timbered
      House and a Blasted Tree* (1653; Speed Museum, Louisville, KY). The Cliffords' attribution
      of the Norwich Castle Museum version of *Marlingford Grove* to Crome over that in the
      Lady Lever Art Gallery (Clifford and Clifford 1968, pp. 229–31) is incomprehensible given
      the respective quality of the two works.

64   Gilpin 1808, vol. 2, p. 80.

65   Price 1810, vol. 2, pp. 325–35.

66   E.g., Knight 1795, pp. 17–18, 22n.

ing; now wildly over-hung with thickets of trees and bushes, now loosely
skirted with wood ... Even the tracks of the wheels (for no circumstance
is indifferent) contribute to the picturesque of the whole.[67]

'Old neglected bye-roads and hollow ways' provided the motifs for some of
Crome's best-known works, such as the upright watercolour of a *Wood Scene*
(c. 1809–12; Victoria and Albert Museum), *The Way through the Wood* (*fig. 43*),
and *Marlingford Grove* (*fig. 45*), the last of which, with its broken banks, weeds,
and variegated tree forms could stand as a perfect exemplar of the Pricean
aesthetic.

But the scene is also shot through with associations of retirement from the
city and the perennial round of rustic life. Like many of Gainsborough's later
pastoral landscapes, such as the *Watering Place* (1777; National Gallery, London)
or *Peasant Smoking at a Cottage Door* (c. 1788; Hammer Museum, University of
California, Los Angeles), the composition of *Marlingford Grove* encloses diminutive figures within it, the woodman with his dog, the distant horseman with a
flock of sheep; the foreground tree on the right curves over like an embrace.[68]
These are figures that belong with their surroundings, or are 'in keeping' to use
the parlance of the period, a term that implies a social as well as an aesthetic
ideal. They infuse the picture with notions of human consciousness. 'Figures
in a road', Bartell wrote, 'are another great source of amusement, and whether
in motion or at rest, are equally pleasing; they create an interest in the mind
by being strongly contrasted with inanimate objects. If at some distance, we
are naturally led to inquire who they may be, or what their employment'.[69]
However, if the motifs are paradigmatically picturesque, the colouring of the
picture is too light and airy to match Gilpin's conception of the pictorially
pleasing. In fact, the painting marks a stage on the way to the bright daylight
naturalism of Crome's works in the last six or seven years of his life (*fig. 69*) – a
tendency that was widespread among British landscape painters in the period,
and which, I have argued elsewhere, should be seen as a rupture with the picturesque aesthetic and not its logical outcome or continuation.[70]

Gilpin had argued that while the picturesque sketcher could often find 'trees
sufficient ... for all the purposes of *distant scenery*', 'a tree in full perfection,
as a grand object to grace a *foreground* is rarely seen'. This was because 'long

---

67   Price 1810, vol. 1, pp. 23, 24–5. For Bartell on such motifs, see Bartell 1806, p. 105.

68   For the social vision of Gainsborough's landscapes, see Barrell 1980, Chapter 1, and
      Rosenthal 1999, Chapter 8.

69   Bartell 1806, p. 109.

70   See the Introduction to the present volume.

before they attain picturesque perfection', trees were commonly cut down and turned to profit.[71] Price, by contrast, embraced the ordinary forms of things and expressed wonderment over the 'infinite variety' and 'intricacy' of individual trees, 'their forms, tints, and light and shade'. He wondered at their 'labyrinth of intricacy', in which there was 'no unpleasant confusion; the general effects is as simple, as the detail is complicate' (*sic*).[72] Crome had depicted such effects of tree form in a *Woodland Scene*. But whereas he represented the oak there with a sombre autumnal overcast sky, near the end of his life he represented a great oak in the village of Poringland (*fig. 73*), five miles south of Norwich, with the kind of luminous daylight sky Gilpin thought inimical to picturesque effect: 'In summer, when he [the sun] rides high at noon, and sheds his perpendicular ray, all is illumination: there is no shadow to balance such a glare of light; no contrast to oppose it. The judicious artist therefore rarely represents his objects under a vertical sun'.[73] Crome proved that such effects could make successful pictorial motifs and appropriately associated his glowing image of summer warmth with four boys swimming in a pond, or what may perhaps be taken to represent the River Chet, which has its source in Poringland.[74] The associations of childhood and youth match the summery aspect of the scene.

The extent to which Crome was willing to stretch picturesque precepts or abandon them altogether in the century's second decade is suggested by another late painting, *The Willow Tree* (c. 1818–21; *fig. 74*).[75] Although the footbridge, rickety fence, and collapsing banks are all picturesque accessories, the sky is wonderfully blue and airy and the colours of the tree fresh and verdant. Moreover, the willow tree was little liked by the picturesque theorists. Gilpin thought that only weeping willows were intrinsically picturesque, but even these were an unsuitable accompaniment to sublime scenes; he rarely advised

---

71   Gilpin 1808, vol. 1, pp. 117–18.

72   Price 1810, pp. 262–3.

73   Gilpin 1808, vol. 1, p. 252.

74   The Cliffords have suggested, reasonably, that the picture might be identified with the *Scene at Poringland* of 1818 shown at Crome's 1821 memorial exhibition. I agree with them and Francis Hawcroft that there is no reason to think the figures were painted by anyone except Crome. See Hawcroft 1968, cat. no. 47; Clifford and Clifford and Clifford 1968, pp. 231–2. That outdoor sketching practices played a role in the formation of Crome's light-filled treatment of trees in his later works is suggested by the fine oil sketch of *Postwick Grove* (Norwich Castle Museum and Art Gallery).

75   Doubting the identification of the tree, the Nottingham Museum now titles the work *Trees by a Brook*, and the Art UK website suggests it may be an oak. But the shape of the tree and colouring don't look oak-like and the contrast with *The Poringland Oak* also works against the suggestion. My guess is that the picture depicts a White Willow.

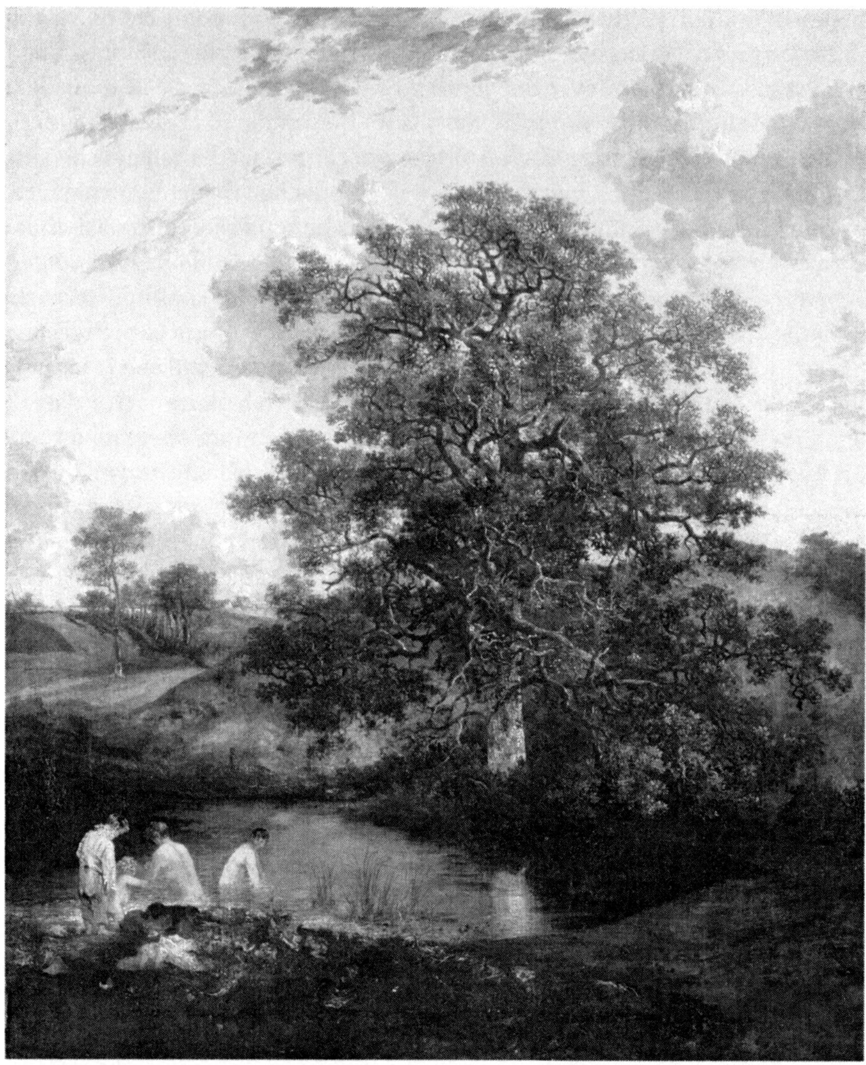

FIGURE 73   *John Crome,* The Poringland Oak, *1818?, oil on canvas, 49¼ × 30½in
             (125.1 × 100.3 cm), Tate Britain*
             © TATE, LONDON, 2015

use of willows in painting, except as pollards to characterise a marshy landscape. Although he subsequently equivocated and acknowledged that 'some
willows indeed I have thought beautiful, and fit to appear in the decoration
of a rural scene'.[76] Strutt included only one willow in his *Sylva Britannica*, the

____

76   Gilpin 1808, vol. 1, 65–7.

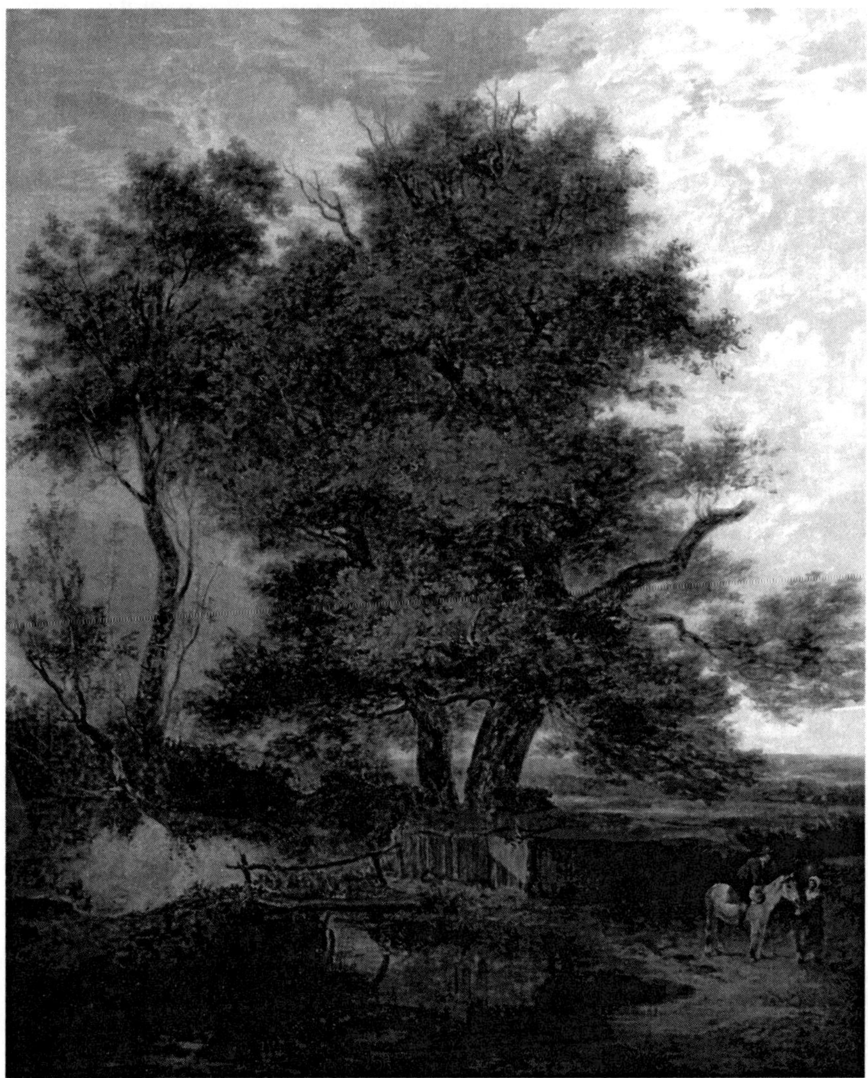

FIGURE 74   *John Crome,* The Willow Tree, c. *1817–21, oil on canvas*
                CASTLE MUSEUM, NOTTINGHAM

great Abbott's Willow at Bury St. Edmunds in Suffolk. For him, pollard willows
were an inherently 'unsightly spectacle', which were not much improved when
they sprouted again.[77] But while Crome's willow is not of the weeping variety

---

77   Strutt 1822, p. 98.

neither has it been pollarded; despite its broken bough it is a survivor with a history, if not one as venerable as the *Woodland Scene*'s great oak. The willow is a less aristocratic tree but one that lends itself to shimmering light-filled effects and a conception of pictorial pleasure less freighted with tradition than the picturesque.

The picturesque fetishisation of trees, particularly forest trees, is inseparable from the fetishisation of the rustic cottage, and it is with regard to these habitations of the peasantry, or what were described often as 'the labouring poor', that the social dimensions of the aesthetic inevitably become more palpable;[78] the picturesque's claim to be purely a matter of visual pleasure came under duress, its contradictions as an ideology began to surface. The fundamental social dimensions of Gilpin's aesthetic are evident from his insistence that the picturesque eye was unconcerned by questions of utility and averse to profitable usages of landscape; all the divisions of property are a nuisance to it and 'utility is always counteracting beauty'.[79] The 'generality of people' find unpleasing 'a wild country, in a natural state, however picturesque', and 'there are few, who do not prefer the busy scenes of cultivation to nature's rough productions'.[80] As these statements suggest, the picturesque eye is an anticipation of the 'art for art's sake' aesthetic;[81] it belongs to the leisured traveller who knows the history of painting and can rise above a merely utilitarian vision of the world by focusing on his own exquisite sensations; it distinguishes those with taste from those without, the true gentleman from the parvenu.[82] But because of Gilpin's almost exclusive preoccupation with the grand and sublime, his thinking about the status of the poor and on questions of poor relief do not intrude directly into his vision of landscape in the way such concerns did for thinkers from the landed gentry like Price and Knight, for whom the

----

78   Jeanette Neeson has made a persuasive case for the applicability of the term 'peasant' to a significant sector of the agricultural workforce in parts of eighteenth- and early nineteenth-century England. See Neeson 1993.

79   Gilpin 1808, vol. 2, p. 80.

80   Gilpin 1808, vol. 2, p. 166.

81   One can find an equivalent to Clive Bell's notion of 'significant form' in Payne Knight's conception of picturesque beauty as arising from 'a moderate and varied irritation of thee organic nerves', but unlike Bell's, Knight's system accords meaning a place in the pleasures of taste. See Knight 1808, pp. 63.

82   Similarly, in Price's polemic, 'the rash hand of false taste' destroys 'what time only, and a thousand lucky accidents can mature ... and reduces it to such a thing, as an Oilman in Thames-street may at any time contract for by the yard at Islington or Mile-End' (Price 1810, vol. I, pp. 31–2). The class condescension, with its Burkean undertones, is patent.

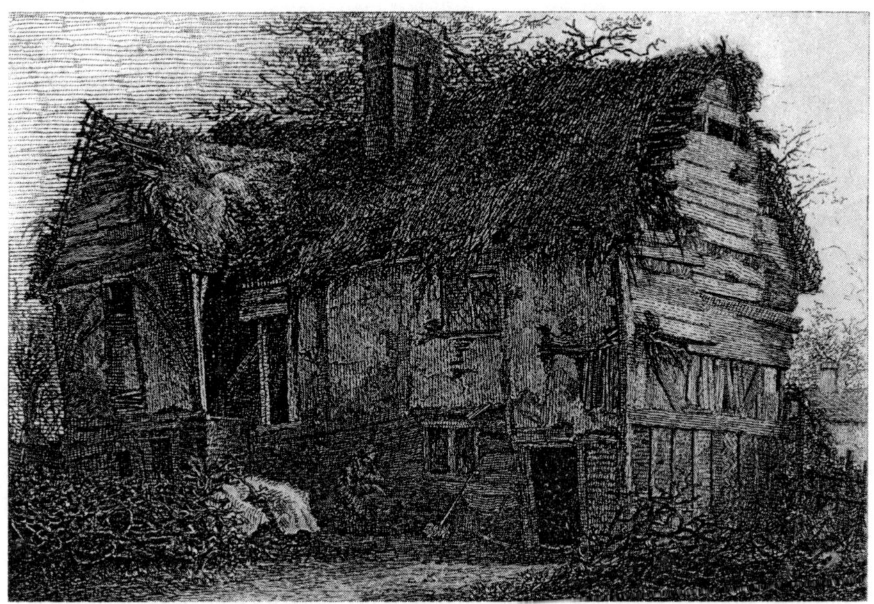

cottage was central to their vision of what was pleasing in the national landscape.[83] Here prescriptions for visual beauty rubbed directly against the social
and moral associations of the scenes viewed or depicted.

In his *Remarks on Rural Scenery* (1797), John Thomas Smith – the painter,
engraver, and drawing master, and sometime mentor to the young John Constable – extended the Gilpinian aesthetic to 'cottage scenery'. Against Gilpin,
at least implicitly, Smith observed that the beauty of landscape painting did
not consist solely in scenes of grandeur, but extended to 'every department of
nature', including the 'most *humble*'. While insisting that he was not 'cottage
mad', he recommended 'rural and cottage scenery' as 'a sort of low comedy
landscape'.[84] The 20 etchings that accompanied Smith's text – all of them 'from
nature' and some etched on the spot – represent dwellings that are uniformly
in a state of advanced decay and in several cases look scarcely habitable (*fig.
75*). Smith himself stressed the distinction between the value of dwellings seen
from the landscape painter's perspective, as opposed to the viewpoint of util-

---

83   For Gilpin as a social thinker, see Everett 1994, pp. 130–3.
84   Smith 1797, pp. 5–6.

ity and morality. Cottages could be divided into the 'neat' and the 'neglected'. While 'the appearance of neatness and cleanliness' in poverty prompted feelings of benevolence, it counted as nothing with the artist, who was drawn to the 'more profitable subject – the neglected fast-ruinating cottage'.[85] Like Gilpin's, Smith's picturesque was found off the beaten track in the 'inmost recesses of forests, and most obscure and unfrequented villages ... On the remote wild common – on the straggling undetermined borders of the forest'.[86] To landed gentlemen as much concerned with social order as with aesthetic effect, run-down cottages and wild commons sat less easily with their notions of the pleasing. According to Smith, the picturesque sketcher was licensed to make changes in what he or she saw to bring it into line with the beautiful effects of neglect and decay.[87] The gentleman landscape improver who worked with actual structures and actual human materials faced graver consequences.[88]

By this time, the condition of labourers' dwellings was an object of concern in the writings of both agriculturalists and poets. In his *Hints to Gentlemen of Landed Property* (1775), Nathaniel Kent observed that, 'the shattered hovels which half the poor of this kingdom are obliged to put up with, is truly affecting to a heart fraught with humanity. Those who condescend to visit these miserable tenements, can testify, that neither health nor decency can be preserved in them'. Kent presented this as a threat to the national stock, since by nature 'cottagers are indisputably the most beneficial race of people we have'.[89] There was no object so 'highly deserving of the country gentleman's attention than the improvement of labourers' dwellings', and Kent offered two designs for model cottages.[90] Crabbe, who in *The Village* (1783) promised that he would paint the cottage, 'As Truth will paint it, and as Bards will not', did not describe its decrepit outward forms, but the miseries of its inhabitants:

---

85   Smith 1797, pp. 8–9.

86   Smith 1797, p. 12.

87   Smith 1797, p. 14.

88   Smith may have had some connection with Payne Knight – he quotes from his didactic poem *The Landscape* (1794) (p. 7) and refers to Rembrandt's *Holy Family by Night* (c. 1642–8; Rijksmuseum, Amsterdam), which Knight had bought from the Orleans Collection sale in 1791 (p. 17).

89   Kent does not seem to be using 'cottager' here in Neeson's sense to denote those with very small property and some continuing access to common rights (Neeson 1993, pp. 316–19), but to those solely or largely dependent on a money wage. For Kent, see Everett 1994, pp. 75–8.

90   Kent 1776, pp. 242–3. Daniels has drawn attention to Kent's influence on Repton's social views – see Daniels 1983, pp. 58–9.

> Ye gentle souls, who dream of rural ease,
> Whom the smooth stream and the smoother sonnet please;
> Go! If the peaceful cot your praises share,
> Go look within, and ask if peace be there;
> If peace be his – that drooping weary sire,
> Or theirs, that offspring round their feeble fire;
> Or hers, that matron pale, whose trembling hand
> Turns on the wretched hearth th'expiring brand![91]

Kent's book is a volume of advice for improvers; Crabbe's poem is a counter-pastoral with moral implications. But both pointed to the fact that the homes of the rural poor were not abodes of health or comfort and that, as Kent complained, landowners took better care of their dogs and horses than of their labourers.

In their polemic against Lancelot ['Capability'] Brown's style of landscape gardening, Price and Knight urged the gentleman improver to learn from landscape painting the principles that should order the modelling of his estate; this would become one of the issues in their dispute with Brown's self-styled successor, Repton. Indeed, the long title of Price's opening salvo is *Essays on the Picturesque, as Compared with the Sublime and the Beautiful; and on the Use of Studying Pictures, for the Purposes of Improving Real Landscape* (1794).[92] Brown's gardens had often been compared with the ideal landscapes of Claude, but the model of the picturesque for Price and Knight was taken primarily from seventeenth-century Dutch art.[93] This corresponds with both their greater tolerance for the landscape of ordinary cultivation and their accommodation to the presence of cottage dwellings and the poor. Price argued that not only was there 'something despotic' in the Brownist vision, but the social intercourse between squire and the poor encouraged by the layout of the picturesque garden was conducive to social harmony. *'Painting'*, Price claimed, 'tends to humanise the mind: where a despot thinks every person an intruder who enters his domain, and wishes to destroy cottages and pathways, and to reign alone, the lover of painting, considers the dwellings, the inhabitants, and the marks

---

91   *The Village*, in Crabbe 1967, Book 1, ll. 54, 172–9. On Crabbe's moral indignation and its limits, see Williams 1975, pp. 113–20.

92   Knight's poem *The Landscape*, which made a similar argument, appeared in the same year.

93   Significantly, 'in all that relates to cottages, hamlets, and villages, to the grouping of them ... the best instruction may be gained from the works of the Dutch and Flemish masters'. Price 1810, vol. 2, p. 341.

of their intercourse, as ornaments to the landscape'.[94] The way in which Price used landscape theory as a vehicle to articulate his particular variant of conservative Whiggism has been addressed by others and does not concern me here. I merely wish to demonstrate how deeply invested the imagery of cottages and villages had become at a time of rising social tensions in the countryside driven by enclosure and the perception of a revolutionary threat engendered by the French Revolution and its admirers in Britain.[95]

The 'two opposite qualities of roughness, and of sudden variation, joined to that of irregularity', which Price claimed were 'the most efficient causes of the picturesque', were found in abundance in such structures as 'hovels, cottages, mills, insides of old barns, stables, &c., wherever they have any marked and peculiar effect of form, tint, or light and shadow'.[96] But when discussing cottages, associations with the way of life of their inhabitants could not be avoided. Thus Price found 'a cottage of quiet colour, half concealed among trees, with its bit of garden, its pales and orchard, is one of the most tranquil and soothing of all rural objects'. By contrast, when a cottage was 'cleared round, and whitened, its modest retired character is gone, and is succeeded by perpetual glare'; in brief it became inappropriately obtrusive and asserted the presence of the agricultural labourer too insistently.[97] Elsewhere, thinking in images that suggest Gainsborough's cottage scenes, Price wrote of the seemingly inseparable connection between cottages and the trees around them, in which under the shade of their foliage, the cottages seemed to be 'protected, sometimes supported'. The trees become almost animate, they 'embrace the cottage with their branches', 'and it seems as if they could never have been separated from each other'.[98] Thatched roofs in particular were linked to 'an idea of rural simplicity'. Although we might expect that these were most picturesque when 'mossy, ragged, and sunk in among the rafters in decay', Price observed that even the 'keenest lover' of the picturesque would rather see such a building on 'another's property than on his own'. Indeed, 'the appearance of a new thatch, both from its neatness and colour, is remarkably pleasing'.[99]

---

94   Price 1810, vol. 1, pp. 338–9. Cf. vol. 2, 367.

95   For a sophisticated analysis of the political dimensions of Price's and Knight's respective visions, see Cosgrove and Daniels, pp. 57–67.

96   Price 1810, vol. 1, pp. 50–1, 55.

97   Price 1810, vol. 1, p. 162.

98   Price 1810, vol. 2, p. 351. Price was perhaps recalling Cowper's description of a cottage so overhung with elms that it could not be seen from the valley below, and which he called 'the *peasant's nest*'. 'The Task', Book 1, ll. 221–7, in Cowper 1926.

99   Price 1810, vol. 2, pp. 340–1. Knight, with a more philosophically sophisticated theory of

In 'An Essay on Architecture and Buildings, as Connected with Scenery' of 1798, Price (the squire of Foxley in Herefordshire, who would be made a baronet in 1828)[100] pitches his recommendations not at 'princes, and men of princely revenues', but at 'men of moderate fortunes'. While these may not be able to afford 'magnificent buildings', they can 'by means of slight additions and alterations ... produce a very essential change in the appearance of farm buildings, cottages &c. and in the grouping of them in villages'. 'Though less splendid than those of regular architecture', the effects of such alterations are not less interesting, and by 'adorning a real village', the improver promotes at the same time 'the comforts and enjoyments of its inhabitants'.[101] Thus the modifications of the real landscape in pursuit of picturesque beauty produce social benefits. As with the contrast I drew earlier between Gilpin and Price, by defining the differences in picturesque thinking between Smith and Price I am laying out a rough template for understanding transitions in Crome's art.

Crome's earliest surviving exercise in the cottage picturesque was the major oil the *Blacksmith's Shop, Hingham* (Philadelphia Museum of Art, *fig. 77*), which is related to three finished watercolours.[102] These can reasonably be associated with three exhibits at the 1807 Norwich Society exhibition, two of which were titled *Blacksmith's Shop from Nature* and the other *Blacksmith's Shop, Hardingham*. It is probable that the watercolour version of the Philadelphia painting in Doncaster Museum and Art Gallery (*fig. 78*) is one of the *Blacksmith's Shop from Nature* paintings exhibited in 1807 and the view of the workshop and lean-to from a somewhat different viewpoint in Norwich Castle Museum and Art Gallery (*fig. 79*) is the other; *'from Nature'* being a claim for

---

      taste than Price's, made a sharp distinction between the visual pleasures produced by
      paintings by the Dutch masters of 'decayed pollard trees, rotten thatch, crumbling masses
      of perished brick and plaster, [and] tattered worn-out dirty garments', and the 'offensive'
      effects the real objects had on the viewer's senses. See Knight 1808, pp. 70–1. Constable's
      Cottage in a Cornfield (1817; National Museum of Wales, Cardiff), might seem to exemplify
      Price's prescriptions.

100   On Price's practice as an improver, see Stephen Daniels and Charles Watkin's essay, 'A
       Well-connected Landscape: Uvedale Price at Foxley', in Daniels and Watkins (ed.) 1994,
       pp. 40–8.

101   Price 1810, vol. 2, pp. 342, 344.

102   Other works close in date to these that develop the motif of the picturesque cottage or
       farm buildings include the watercolours *Barn and Cart* and *Farm Buildings* in the British
       Museum, and *Cottage Gable in Ruins* (Norwich Castle Museum) – Clifford and Clifford
       1968, D23, D25, and D39. Unfortunately, three Crome cottage scenes in Dawson Turner's
       collection – *Cottage near Norwich, Clay Cottage*, and *Cottage at Hunstanton, Norfolk* – all
       seem to be lost.

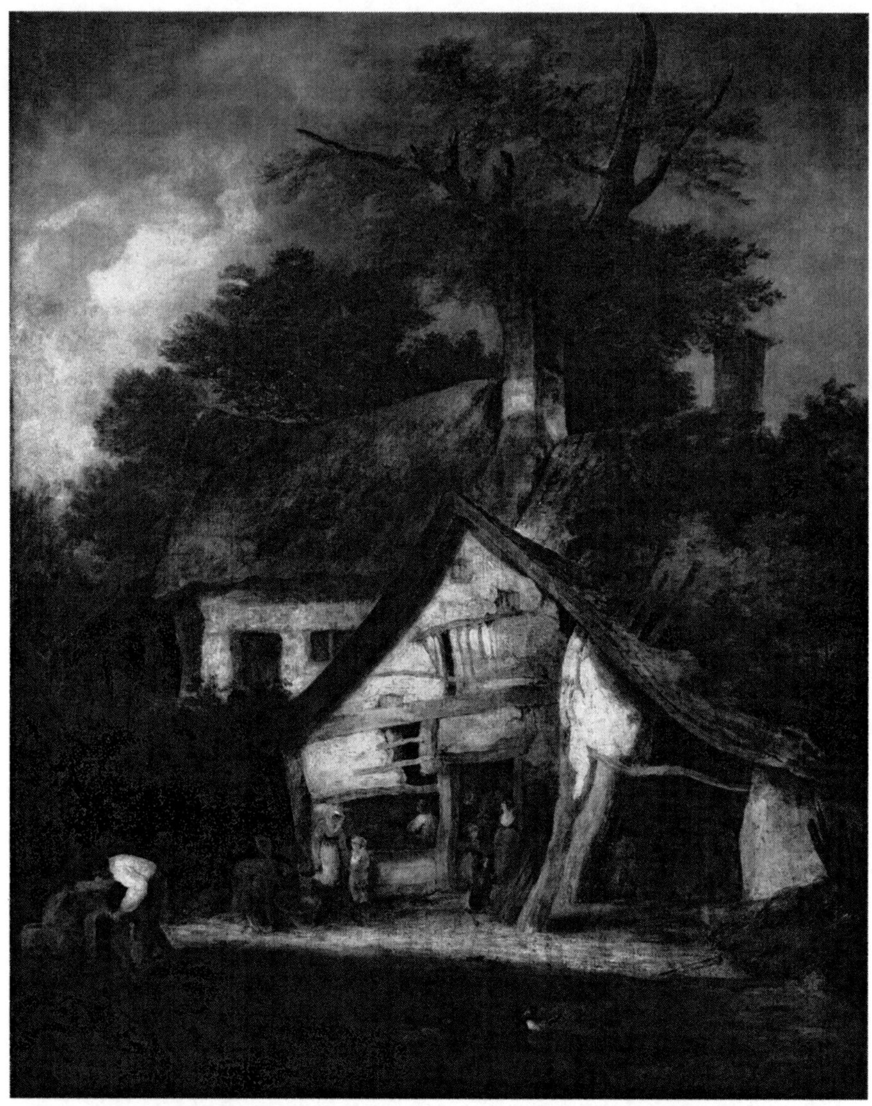

FIGURE 76   *John Crome,* Blacksmith's Shop near Hingham, Norfolk, *1807?, oil on canvas, 60⅝ × 48 in (154.0 × 121.9 cm)*
THE JOHN HOWARD MC FADDEN COLLECTION, 1928, PHILADELPHIA MUSEUM OF ART

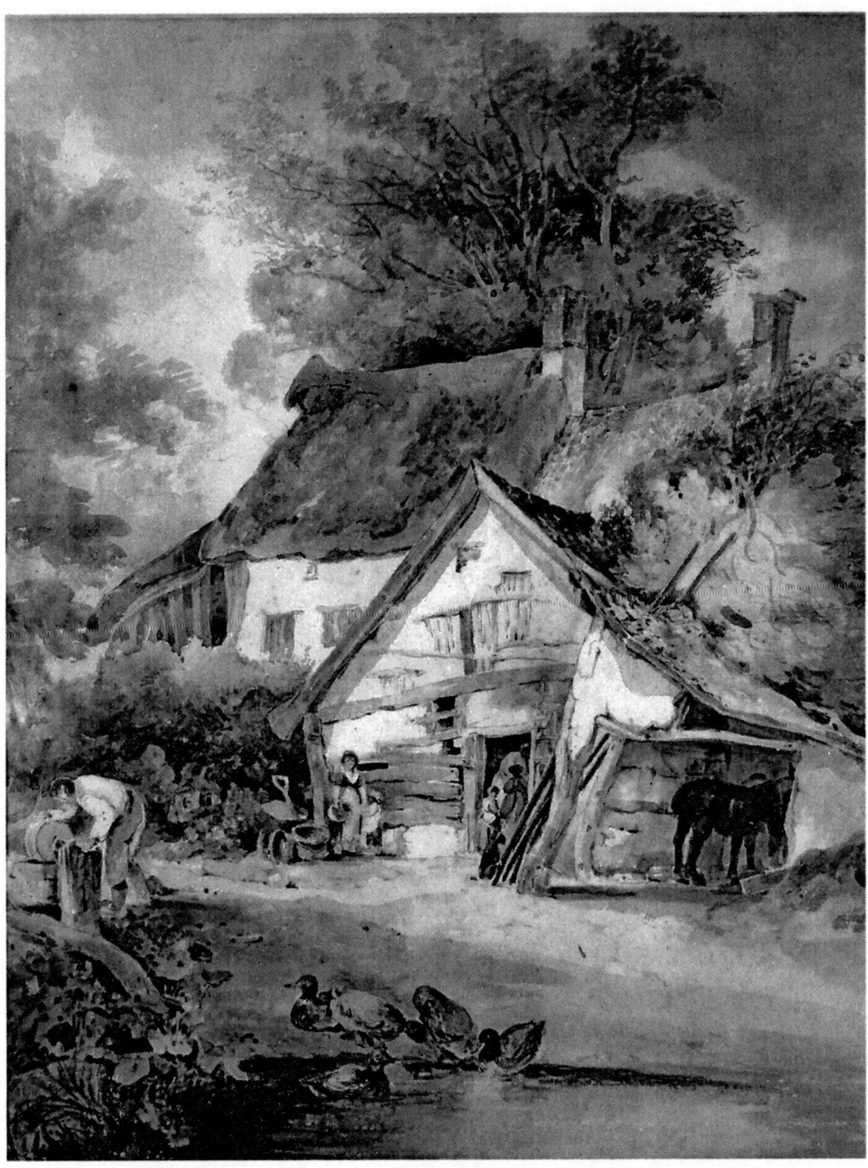

FIGURE 77   *John Crome,* Hingham, Blacksmith's Shop, *1807?, watercolour, 16×12 in*
(40.6×30.5 cm)
DONCASTER MUSEUM AND ART GALLERY

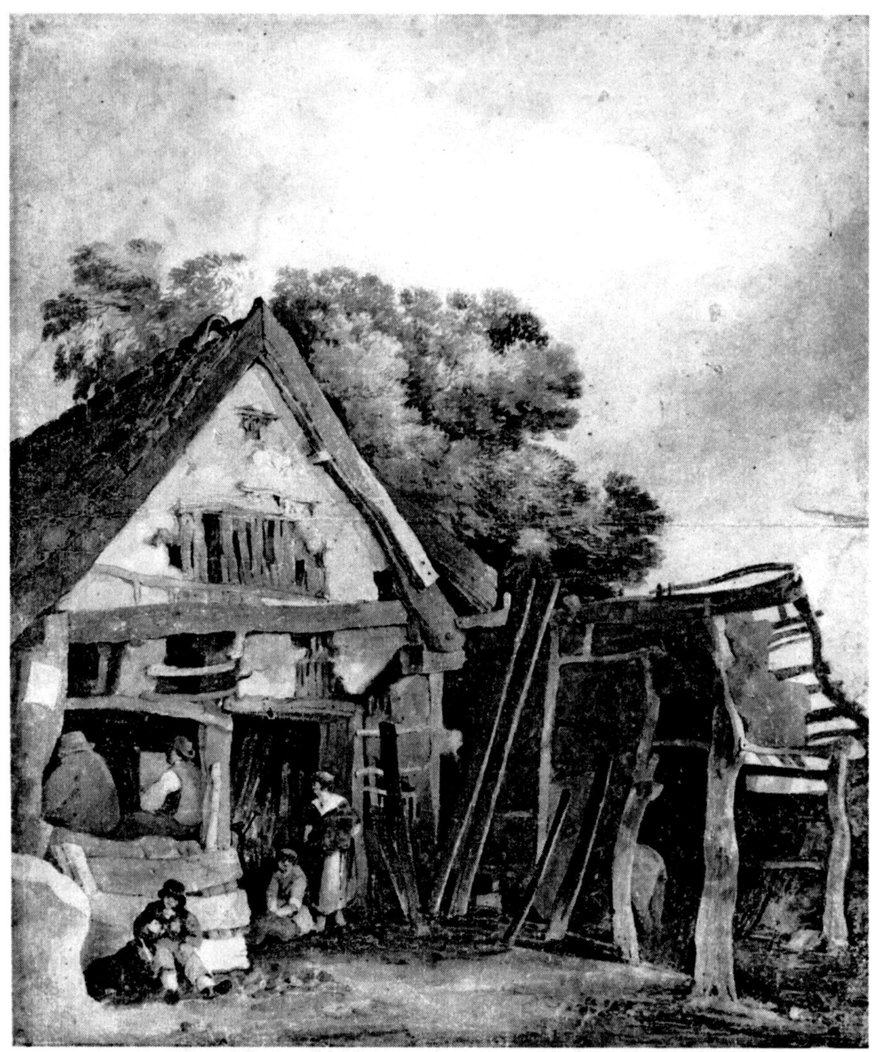

FIGURE 78   *John Crome,* The Blacksmith's Shop, Hingham, *1807?, watercolour, 21¼ × 17¼ in (54.0×43.8 cm)*
NORFOLK MUSEUM SERVICES (NORWICH CASTLE MUSEUM AND ART GALLERY)

the work's fidelity to its object rather than one that it was made on the spot – in contrast to, say, the *Cottage at Hingham, painted on the spot* shown the following year. In my view the lower part of the variant of the Norwich watercolour in the Yale Center for British art is authentic, while the sky and tree are by another hand. I base this conclusion not only on the inferiority of the upper part of the work, but also on the fact that it is on a separate sheet of paper. The tree and sky of the original drawing were probably damaged and the work was then restored to its current state.[103]

Crome showed a painting titled *The Outside of a Blacksmith's Shop* at the Norwich Society exhibition in 1811 and in London exhibited a *Blacksmith's shop, near Hingham, Norfolk* at the Royal Academy in 1808 and *A Blacksmith's traverse* at the British Institution in 1818. Two works with the same general theme exhibited at Crome's memorial exhibition in 1821 were dated to 1808 and 1814, and titled respectively *Blacksmith's Shop* and *Blacksmith's Traverse at Hardingham*. Since a traverse in this context means a place adjoining a blacksmith's shop where horses are shod, this suggests a work in which the motif resembled the broken down structure on the right side of the Philadelphia oil and Doncaster watercolour where a horse can be seen in both cases. The style of all four extant pictures suggests a dating of 1807–8. How the Philadelphia painting came to be associated with Hingham is not clear. Hingham was a small but thriving and affluent market town in the early nineteenth century; the nearby village of Hardingham seems more likely to have provided Crome with his motif and since Hardingham and Hingham are close by it is quite likely that the 1808 Academy exhibit was the picture that Crome had exhibited in Norwich the year before.

Although there are some differences between the Philadelphia oil and the Doncaster watercolour, they are relatively minor. The differences between the buildings in the oil and the Norwich watercolour are more pronounced, but there are enough similarities to suggest that they are variations on the same structure. If this assumption is correct, then these works illustrate the malleability of picturesque depiction in the interest of compositional refinements. Smith advised that, 'As there are but few scenes of which the precise, entire and unqualified image will form a picture, the picturesque artist is at liberty not only to introduce, or to leave out particular features ... but likewise to change the colours ... [of] any object or circumstance by which his picture may be filled with greater variety, happier combinations, or more perfect harmony'. In this regard, the principle of the picturesque artist was totally different from that of

---

103   Clifford and Clifford 1968, D36, D34, and D44.

the topographical draftsman, who must 'copy' 'every circumstance' exhibited to his view, every absurdity as well as every beauty.[104] In practice, contemporary topography took considerable depictive liberties, and one of the most common formula for titles to illustrated books began with the phrase 'picturesque views of'. None the less, we can understand Smith's dictum as pointing to a common perception of the relative degrees of license permissible in different landscape genres.

The organic and intimate relationship between trees and cottages that Price proposed in his 1798 essay is perfectly exemplified in the Philadelphia and Don-caster versions of the *Blacksmith's Shop, Hingham*. The connection between this composition and Gainsborough's 1780 *Cottage Door* (*fig. 70*) – which, as we have seen, Crome copied – has often been remarked. When Crome's oil appeared in John Berney Crome's bankruptcy sale in 1834 it was described as 'one of his best pictures, in style of Gainsborough'.[105] Six years later Dawson Turner compared one of his own Crome paintings, *Cottage at Hunstanton, Nor-folk*, with the *Cottage Door*, but lamented that Crome had not included Gains-borough's 'noble trees' or 'the beautiful group of mother and children'.[106] In fact he had picked up on part of what made Crome's cottage pictures novel but seems not to have recognised what was at stake. For as *Blacksmith's Shop, Hing-ham* illustrates, the differences between Crome and Gainsborough's cottage door compositions are as important as the similarities. To begin with, whatever Crome's degree of picturesque license, his motif was '*from Nature*' and it was associated with a real place. Gainsborough's five cottage doors were all studio concoctions.[107] Moreover, all of them are evening scenes that represent the end of the working day. Despite its overcast look *Blacksmith's Shop, Hingham* is a daylight scene. The cloud is grey except for an area on the upper left that is lighter and helps to explain the sunburst that illuminates the foreground – a device exploited by Ruisdael in compositions such as *Storm on the Dunes* (Phil-adelphia Museum of Art). A group of ducks by the puddle in the foreground suggests that it has recently rained. Crome's blacksmith presumably lives in

---

104   Smith 1797, p. 14. Cf. Gilpin 1794, p. 128: 'the imaginary-view, formed on a judicious selec-tion, and arrangement of the parts of nature, has a better chance to make a good picture, than a view taken in the whole from any natural scene'.

105   *A Catalogue of the Household Furniture, China, Glass, Plate, An extensive and Valuable Collection of Pictures ... Miscellaneous Effects of Mr. John Berney Crome, sold by Auction by Mr. Culley*, 4 September 1834, day 3, lot 57.

106   Turner 1840, p. 23. Although Turner's painting is lost, we know the design from his wife's outline print.

107   All are discussed in Bermingham (ed.) 2005.

the whitewashed cottage behind the hedge on the left and to which an extension with a second chimney has been added. Whereas the cottage has a sagging thatched roof – although one that could still be snug – the roof of the extension is tiled. But from a picturesque point of view it is not the cottage that is of interest so much as the dramatic decrepitude of the blacksmith's shop and traverse, with its bent timbers perhaps taken from pollards and its eccentric patches of daub.[108] The structure is painted in a creamy impasto in a way that suggests the organic qualities of the earth and trees from which it is made. Not a single line of the structure does not curve or bow and the roof is so decayed that a bundle of long planks or poles – the lower ends of which are next to the door – protrude through a hole in it, a feature that is clearer in the Doncaster watercolour. A final touch of observed detail in the Norwich and Yale watercolours is the sheet of paper, presumably some kind of notice, pinned or pasted to the upright timber that supports the building on the left edge.

Figures fell in the same domain of artistic license as picturesque detail and had to look merely appropriate or 'natural'. But by the time Crome painted the *Blacksmiths' Shop*, the images of graceful rusticity with which Gainsborough peopled his cottage door pictures had come to look artificial and mannered.[109] Moreover, Gainsborough's figures are all family groups; Crome's blacksmith's shop compositions picture sociable village life and conviviality between the sexes in a way that invites comparison with the imagery of rural types in George Morland's work, without any of the troubling connotations the latter sometimes prompted.[110] (In *Cromer, Considered as a Watering Place*, Bartell observed: 'we are always inclined to be pleased with a performance in proportion as it approaches nature, provided the subjects are well selected. Morland's pictures are their very counterpart; they possess so much character, and are handled with so much spirit, that it is impossible for the spectator, fond of rural scenes, to examine them without feeling the most lively interest in the subject').[111] In the Philadelphia oil the forge fire can be just made out through the darkness

---

108   Kent mentions that oak and elm pollards were used for cottage timbers in Norfolk and Suffolk. See Kent 1775, p. 244.

109   See Hemingway 1992, pp. 149–50, 327 n. 114 and n. 115.

110   For the social dimensions of Morland's art, see Barrell 1980, Chapter 3; Wyburn-Powell 2006. Wyburn-Powell presents a strong case for a critical reappraisal of Barrell's interpretation and usefully points up the diversity of his work, but I still think Barrell is correct that some of Morland's imagery of rural life falls outside the consensual views of the propertied classes. An important new source of information on the artist is Grindle (ed.) 2015.

111   Bartell 1806, p. 107. Bartell exhibited a copy after a Morland *Fishing Scene* with the NSA in 1808.

of the doorway in the upper left. A figure that may represent the smith can be seen from the back behind the woman and girl who stand in the entrance itself. Crome includes this female group in the Norwich watercolor, but replaces the woman with a child that appears outside on the left in both oil and Doncaster watercolour with a seated boy. Both seated boy and seated girl appear to look out of the picture at the spectator. We can assume that the blacksmith in the shop is busy, as is the bent over figure sharpening a sickle or a knife on the grindstone in the left foreground of the oil, whose white shirt gives spatiality to the whole foreground. But other figures are waiting – doubtless the horse in the traverse belongs to one of the group – or maybe just passing the time. Whatever license Crome took with the details of his rustic architecture, he offers a plausible image of rural existence in a way that Gainsborough's romantic visions never intended, for all their fascination and complexity.[112]

The decrepitude of the *Blacksmith's Shop* might do well enough for a workplace, but such picturesque features produced more equivocal responses when they were discovered in the dwellings of the labouring poor. (The blacksmith, we may assume, is an independent artisan). It is striking that when Crome represented decaying buildings after circa 1807–8, he seems to have taken his motifs from tumbledown structures on the edge of Norwich – as in the oil *Old Houses at Norwich* (c. 1812–16; Yale Center for British Art, New Haven)[113] – which did not stand for emblems of a rural way of life whatever they may say about changes in the city. For Price, in the real landscape the picturesque had to give way to utility. 'Wild thickets' in actuality were less pleasing than 'scenes of plenty and industry'; gypsies should concede to the 'less picturesque figures of husbandmen and their attendants'.[114] Bartell, whose *Hints for Picturesque Improvements* were presented as advice to gentlemen about both how to build 'ornamental' cottages as retreats from the 'hurry of a town-life' (*fig. 79*), *and* how to provide proper habitations for the 'labouring poor', followed Price closely on the formal aspect of cottage architecture, but comes close to Repton in his social vision.[115]

---

112   For the social vision of Gainsborough's cottage door pictures, see Amal Asfour and Paul Williamson, 'Gainsborough's Cottage Door Scenes: Aesthetic Principles, Moral Values', in Bermingham (ed.) 2005, pp. 98–119.

113   Cf. the watercolour *Old Houses at Norwich* (c. 1810; Victoria and Albert Museum) – Clifford and Clifford 1968, D 47.

114   Price 1810, vol. 1, pp. 293–4.

115   Bartell acknowledged the similarity, but claimed that he had completed the final revision of his manuscript before Repton's *Observations on the Theory and Practice of Landscape Gardening* (1803) had appeared. Bartell 1804, p. xi.

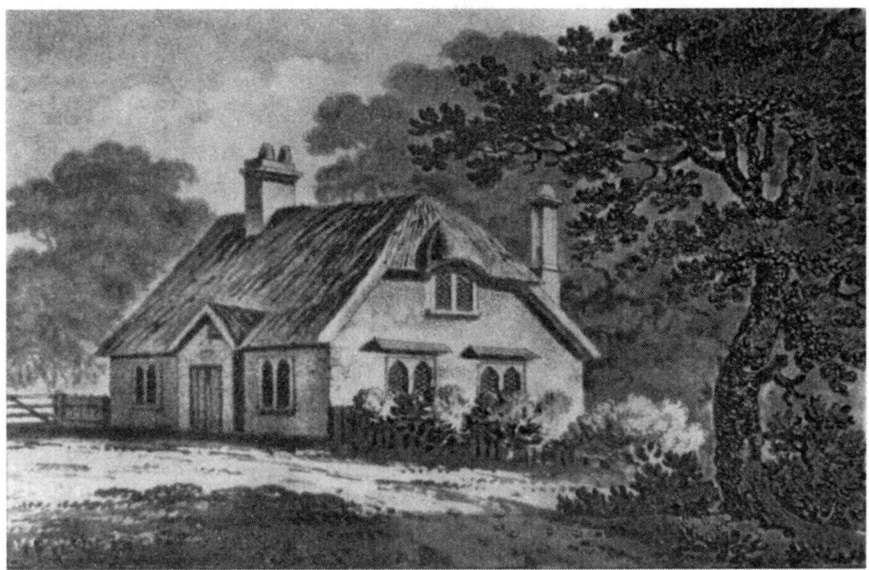

FIGURE 79   *Plate VI, a sketch for a cottage of 'more humble appearance', from Edmund Bartell,* Hints for Picturesque Improvements in Ornamental Cottages, and their Scenery (*1804*).

Bartell presented himself as a humanitarian, one who was familiar with the condition of the poor through his practice as a physician.[116] Moreover, he felt connected with them by a bond of common sympathy, claiming that 'beneath the rugged features and russet garb of humble life are, not unfrequently found, feelings the most exquisite, and sentiments that would reflect honour upon the highest stations of life'.[117] This should not distract us from Bartell's paternalism – his concern to improve the morals of the poor – but he presents his ideal of cottage dwelling as appropriate to those who, presumably like himself, enjoy the 'happy apparent medium between poverty and riches'.[118] Like Repton, Bartell indicates a deep aversion for the outlook and taste of parvenu wealth, but he also wonders at the lack of taste among the 'higher classes', despite their advantages of birth and superior education.[119]

---

116   Bartell 1804, pp. 95, 115.

117   Bartell 1804, x. Cf. Kent 1776: 'they [cottagers] are bred up in great simplicity; live more primitive lives, more free from vice and debauchery, than any other sort of men of the lower class' (p. 43).

118   Bartell 1804, p. 5.

119   Bartell 1804, pp. 60–2. On Repton's conservatism, see Daniels 1982 (1), pp. 116–18.

For Bartell, 'the characteristic mark of a cottage is humility, as if, conscious of its inferiority, it should appear to retire beneath the shelter of its friendly woods'.[120] The cottage built of 'glaring colours and costly materials' cannot do this, but neither can one built of red brick or coated with white painted plaster. When it came to the cottages of labourers, Bartell advised that their scale should accord with the rank of their occupants.[121] Clay or mud was preferable to coloured walls, and while Bartell saw reeds as the ideal roofing material, he thought thatch was 'warm and picturesque beyond any other covering'.[122] From the outset thatch blended with the landscape, but after a few seasons had mellowed its tints, it had an 'incomparable advantage as a picturesque object, without imparting an appearance of dampness and dirtiness, or rendering it less capable of resisting all the rigours of winter'.[123] Rotten thatches might appeal to the landscape painter, Bartell conceded, but in reality they had such strong associations of dampness that they suggested 'more misery than a feeling mind would believe fell to the lot of humanity'.[124] And yet, he observed, this was a general condition, for 'few things ... are less attended to, if one may form a judgment from their general appearance, than such cottages; which are, for the most part, sordid and miserable to the last degree, equally injurious to the health and morals of the inhabitants, and not less the ideas that we are led to form of the humanity' of their proprietors.[125]

In passages of his text, Bartell appears to anticipate the Cobbett of *Rural Rides*. He criticises rapacious large farmers who have been allowed to 'monopolise every acre', enclosed most of the commons, and, by forcing the cottager into paying cash for all his needs at a time of high prices, have driven many to theft.[126] Parish relief is degrading to the poor and leads to a situation

---

120   Bartell 1804, p. 11.

121   Bartell 1804, p. 117.

122   Bartell 1804, pp. 16–17, Cf. p. 20.

123   Bartell 1804, p. 118.

124   Bartell 1804, p. 119n.

125   Bartell 1804, p. 89. Bartell had good cause to be concerned about the morals of the poor in a conventional sense. Hostility to the clergy was a notable element in the outlook of the rioters in East Anglia in 1816 and their irreligious attitude was remarked on in the *Norwich Mercury*. See Peacock 1965, pp. 24, 56–63.

126   Bartell 1804, p. 105. Cf. Repton on the grinding attitude of the 'very opulent *gentleman farmer*' in his 'Report on Sheringham Bower for Abbott Upcher, Esq.', first published in *Fragments on the Theory and Practice of Landscape Gardening* (1816), in Repton 1840, p. 576. The wretchedness of labourers' housing in Norfolk was remarked on by more than one commentator. See Riches 1967, pp. 143, 146.

in which the desperate find solace in the alehouse.[127] The wise and humane farmer would provide each cottage with four acres, so that the labourer could have a cottage garden and keep a cow or two.[128] In advancing this vision, Bartell suggests the landlord must take the lead, for things cannot be left to the farmer: 'The cottage system, I am persuaded, need only be carried to its extent to render England indeed a paradise'.[129] It seems less than coincidental that this was written in East Anglia, a region in which the new commercial agriculture was most advanced, where old customs of annual hiring and living-in were in sharp decline, and labourers were paid by results rather than by regular wages. Norfolk and Suffolk were among the eastern counties that experienced major riots, threatening letters, incendiarism, and machine-breaking in 1816 and 1822, when the 'labouring poor' ceased to be that 'patient, and much enduring race' Uvedale Price saw in them.[130] Bartell was writing from a place in which the pace of social change was particularly palpable and threatening, and it extended to Norwich. In May 1816, a crowd broke into the New Mills Crome had painted and dumped flour into the river or carried it away.[131] Crome would also have been aware of the fifteen labourers – nine men and six women – sentenced to death at the August Assizes in Norwich for rioting. Two were hanged on Castle Hill on 31 August 1816, the remainder were transported. According to the *Norwich Mercury*, 'No malefactors ever expired with greater sympathy from the immense multitude, which covered the whole surface of the hill adjoining the place of execution'.[132]

A labourer who is well-provided for by the farmer is always a faithful servant and has a stake in the common interest of his country, he will never be attracted to sedition and riot. So Bartell argued, as if anticipating what was to come. The contrary effect among those who no longer felt they had anything to lose was illustrated by the riots in Norfolk in 1816, when one of the rioters, William

---

127 Bartell 1804, pp. 134–5. In his 1794 report for the Board of Agriculture, Nathaniel Kent noted that the poor rates had increased in Norfolk compared with other counties and that several 'houses of industry' had been established. See Kent 1794, p. 44.

128 Bartell 1804, pp. 91–2. Bartell was probably echoing Kent's recommendations in this regard – Kent 1794, p. 46.

129 Bartell 1804, p. 102. It comes as no surprise to find Bartell citing the Reports of the Society for Bettering the Condition and Increasing the Comforts of the Poor, founded in 1796 (p. 103n.).

130 Price 1797, p. 20; Hobsbawm and Rudé 1968, pp. 83–4. For the comparative extent of enclosure in Norfolk, see the map on p. 28. See also Peacock 1965, pp. 16–21.

131 Peacock 1965, p. 82.

132 Peacock 1965, pp. 93–4.

Dawson of Downham Market, was heard to say that 'he had been working for a long time with a small allowance, and as he was between Earth and Sky he would either have some remedy or lose his life'.[133] In these circumstances the picturing of cottages and common land was not a neutral matter. From Bartell's perspective (as from Price's), Crome's *Blacksmith's Shop* might be an instance of high aesthetic refinement, but it achieved its picturesque at the cost of a kind of moral and social anaesthesia. It is striking that in two of Crome's later grove scenes, cottages are depicted in a very different light, both figuratively and literally. I am thinking here of *Hautbois Common* (1810; *fig. 80*) and *Bury Road Scene* (1818; *fig. 81*). The first of these is almost certainly the painting Crome exhibited with the Norwich Society of Artists in 1810 as *Scene on Hautbois Common, near Coltishall, in Norfolk*, while the latter is probably the *Road Scene and Cottages near Bury* of 1818 lent to the 1821 memorial exhibition.[134] The larger of the two (22 × 35 inches compared with 15 × 9¼ inches), *Hautbois Common* is the more imposing and has the more complex iconography; *Bury Road Scene* – presumably a view on the road between Thetford and Bury St. Edmunds – is exemplary of the more informal naturalistic compositions of Crome's last years.

Hautbois Common has many of the ingredients of a picturesque scene, although Gilpin, who did not think much of Norfolk scenery by and large,[135] might have disapproved of the stretch of common land with grazing animals on the left of the composition. But the mix of oak and other trees, and of living and dead specimens, met picturesque criteria; as did the furrows in the cart track, the grazing donkeys, and the heavy shadows created by the brooding sky.[136] Two pollards are confined to the distance, where they help to mark out the space. The desideratum of animation is provided by the rustic driving a tumbril among the trees and the smoke rising from behind a hedge on the left. Moreover, outside the cottage seen through the glade just left of centre, laundry is hanging out to dry, testifying to the inhabitants' cleanliness. (The laundry motif recurs on the right edge of *Bury Road Scene*). Crome has replaced the farms and mills that appear routinely in Hobbema's grove scenes with a building type that had a complex of connotations in contemporary social and aesthetic thought. His cottage, with its steep eaves and thatched roof picked out by an invisible shaft of light, is the pivot of the whole composition, and brings

---

133   Quoted Peacock 1965, p. 63.

134   Clifford and Clifford 1968, P126 and P97.

135   Gilpin 1809, sections 5–10.

136   Gilpin 1794, p. 14: 'the worn out cart-horse, the cow, the goat, or the ass' were objects of picturesque beauty, a healthy horse was not.

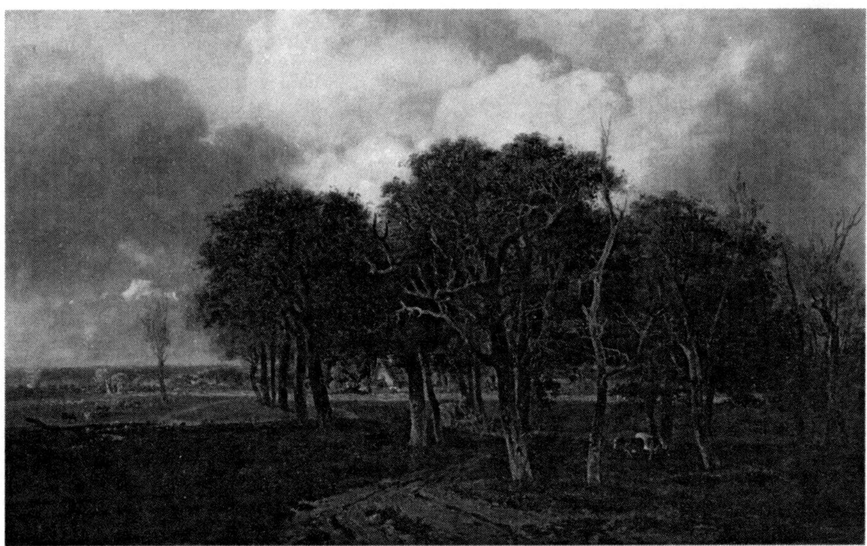

FIGURE 80   *John Crome,* Hautbois Common, *c. 1810, oil on canvas, 22 × 35 in (55.9 × 88.9 cm)*
MARQUAND COLLECTION, GIFT OF HENRY G. MARQUAND, 1889,
METROPOLITAN MUSEUM, NEW YORK

to mind Bartell's associationist observation that 'a warm and comfortable cottage, under every circumstance of seasons, is an object calculated to produce pleasant sensations'.[137] The feeling of being sheltered among the trees, as if the cottage were being embraced, is palpable; 'embowered' and 'embosomed' are other contemporary terms for this effect. This, combined with the expanse of unenclosed land with pasture animals grazing – they are hard to make out in the picture's present condition – offered a backward-looking social vision of the type Bartell advanced in *Hints for Picturesque Improvements.* Cottagers who enjoyed common rights as part of what they received for their yearly rent were particularly hard hit by the enclosure process.[138] But how far may we assume Come was conscious of this?

In his 1794 report for the Board of Agriculture – a book that Crome owned – Nathaniel Kent observed that there was 'still a considerable deal of common land in Norfolk, though a much less proportion than in many other counties', and that in many cases there were common rights to graze cattle or sheep. However, Kent, who thought the poor needed to be disciplined to labour,

---

137   Bartell 1804, p. 127.
138   Peacock 1965, pp. 18–19.

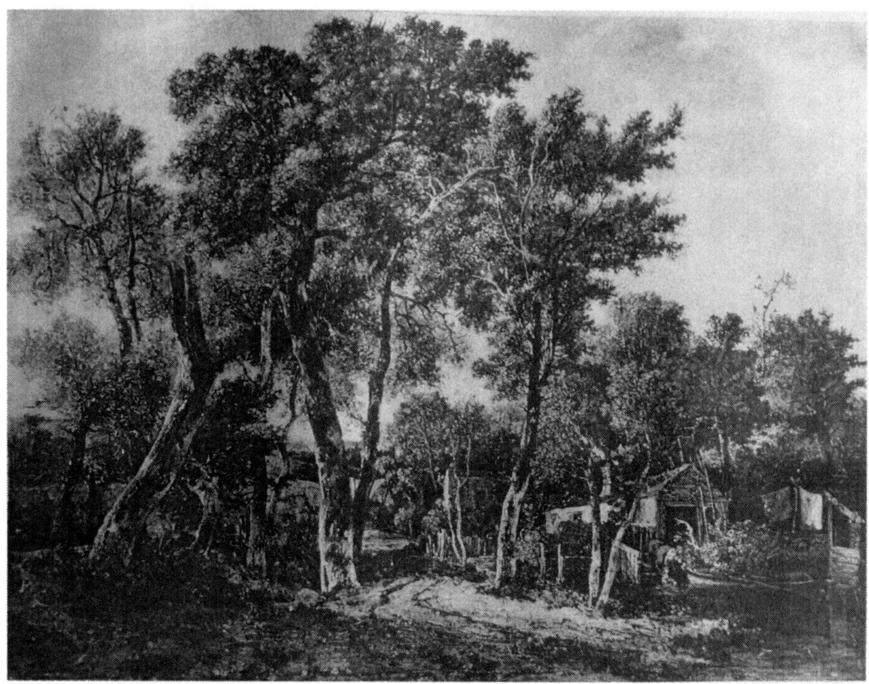

FIGURE 81   *John Crome,* Bury Road Scene, *1818?, oil on panel, 15 × 19¼ in (38.1 × 48.9 cm),*
             whereabouts unknown
             PHOTO: AUTHOR

viewed the 'arguments for the continuance of commons in their present state'
as 'in general, fallacious', and grounded on mistaken principles of humanity.[139]
In the fifth edition of Richard Beatiffe's successful Norfolk guide, the author
claimed that Norfolk still had 27,000 acres of 'uninclosed or waste land' and
urged its enclosure on moral grounds, citing Kent's claim that 'commons were
a premium to pauperism and crime'.[140] Before he was apprenticed to the coach
and sign painter Francis Whisler, Crome had worked as an errand boy for
the distinguished Norwich physician, Dr Edward Rigby, whose 1817 pamphlet
Holkham, Its Agriculture, &c, played a significant part in forming the myth
that the Earl of Leicester, Thomas Coke of Holkham, was a pioneer of the
improved agriculture.[141] Crome's continuing contact with Rigby is evidenced

---

139   Kent 1794, pp. 22, 13.
140   Beatniffe 1795, p. 400. A sixth edition of the guide appeared in 1808.
141   Coke's reputation as such has been cut down to size by Riches 1967, pp. 92–5.

by the fact that the doctor was a non-exhibiting member of the Norwich Society of Artists from 1810–17, and a patron of the body from 1818–21; a copy of Rigby's internationally renowned *Essay on the Uterine Haemorrhage* was among the books in Crome's posthumous sale. As a member of the Norwich Philosophical Society, in December 1816 Crome would have heard Rigby – who himself had a small farm at Framingham, south of the city – give a paper on Holkham agriculture, before he published it as a pamphlet to support Coke in a contested election against accusations that his system of farming deprived the poor of work and drove up corn prices.[142] In 1820, Rigby published a short book about his Framingham Farm, which again contained a rebuttal of the 'extraordinary, and I will say foul charge of demoralization, brought against agricultural improvement', refuting the claim that Coke's practices had led to reduction of many small farmers to day-labourers and that the use of the seed drill had diminished demand for labour.[143] A staunch defender of 'progress' in both agriculture and industrial manufacturing, Rigby had enclosed 107 acres of heath next to his own farm in 1800.[144] Crome, we can be certain, knew what was at stake in agricultural improvement and the enclosure of common land.

Bartell observed that objects 'by long knowledge become naturalized in the soil on which they stand'.[145] Crome also must have known that the word Hautbois is French for high wood and had a sense of the place's associations with the medieval past, and more specifically with the Norman Conquest. Seen in this light the rustic simplicity of the scene becomes poignant; almost a memento mori of a previous age. The sombre overcast sky points to this. If the artist had read up on the history of Little Hautbois, Great Hautbois and the neighbouring village of Colteshall in Francis Blomefield's famous *Topographical History of Norfolk*, which appeared in a second edition over the years 1805–10, he would have come across the account of the 'MANUMISSION or CHARTER of freedom' given to the inhabitants of Coltishall by Henry III in 1231 and confirmed by Henry IV in 1407. This manumission, wrote Blomefield, had been 'a very great favour and privilege in those days; there were few born freemen, half of most villages were either *customary* tenants ... or else VILLAINS, I may say in plain *English* SLAVES, to their several lords'. Blomefield mentioned this history because 'many people being ignorant in what state their forefathers

---

142   In 1815, rioters in Norwich attacked Coke because of his support for the Corn Bill – Peacock 1965, p. 64; Rawcliffe and Wilson (eds.), p. 188.

143   Rigby 1820, pp. 13, 15–17.

144   Rigby 1820, p. 22. Rigby gives a detailed account of his tree plantings, pp. 23–8. Framingham is adjacent to the village of Poringland.

145   Bartell 1804, p. 9.

lived, and so are not capable of sufficiently valuing the *freedom* which we now enjoy'.[146] Perhaps it was possible to be sanguine about the freeman's lot in the mid-eighteenth century when Blomefield and Charles Parkin were writing their history; but 50 years later the condition of free labourers seemed scarcely preferable to that of slavery.

In *Bury Road Scene* Crome brings us close up amongst cottages and sheds that line the road, amplifying the sense of buildings embraced by the landscape. At the same time, he has substituted red brick and tiles for thatch and decaying plaster,[147] and the familiar dead tree is missing. It is as if Crome had reformulated the picturesque not just to accommodate his new concern with daylight and atmosphere but also to avoid those dismal structures that to Bartell were an 'indelible disgrace' upon the 'philanthropy' of wealthy men who forced their tenants to live in squalor.[148] Was this a last kick against the mythologising of the picturesque aesthetic?

In the early nineteenth century considerations of morality, social order, and political economy were inescapable associations of depictions of labourers, cottages, trees, and commons. The ideology of the picturesque had tried to construct a selective mode of vision that reduced such phenomena to matters of composition, colour, and texture. However, when this ideology was extended from the vision of the tourist and amateur sketcher to the landscape garden and the improvement of the gentleman's estate, in the conditions of political and social extremity that accompanied the Anglo-French Wars of 1793–1815, it came under acute pressure from the growing debate about changing agricultural practices and the condition of the rural poor. That the artist's vision of the landscape had social and moral concomitants was well understood, if it has often been forgotten since.

We can register this process of forgetting through the first sustained attempt to map Crome's iconography – although it was not understood as such at the time – which appears in the 1858 essay *John Crome and his Works* by John Wodderspoon (1806–62), sub-editor of the *Norwich Mercury*. Wodderspoon worked for a substantial part of his journalistic career in East Anglia and lived in Norwich for the last fourteen years of his life. His essay presents the simple thesis that Crome's art was formed by the experience of the 'Home Scenery' of the Norfolk landscape, of which it was also a record; the lane scenes, the views on the rivers, Wensum and Yare, the beach at Cromer, the fringes of Norwich –

---

146   Blomefield and Parkin 1805–10, vol. 6, pp. 304–5.

147   For Bartell on the offensiveness of brick 'cottages, barns, and stables' to the picturesque eye, see Bartell 1804, p. 14.

148   Bartell 1804, p. 89.

these were just the things that the artist observed in his everyday life.[149] They were preserved from change because Suffolk and Norfolk were too far from the rest of England to be easily visited and were not on the route to anywhere else. Thus neither county had become a tourist destination. But, Wodderspoon stressed, the world Crome painted was 'fast fading away':

> We have no such lane scenes as existed in our painter's day, nor does the high gabled cottage remain, with its walls of plaster and roof of thatch, showing the weather stains of many seasons, and exercising the knowledge of the painter in the production of tints. The spruce model cottage, which though far more convenient for the purposes of its inmates than those of yore is much less picturesque, and has displaced many old erections, giving us in exchange only four walls of new brick. Sad loss to the painter! ... Lanes were once wide as half a meadow, with broad strips of verdure on either hand, deep ruts in the road, curving and meandering here and there in many involutions, and banks and hedgerows of gigantic height and growth ... These are destroyed. Modern paths are of restricted dimensions, and of the straightest forms. They lead now only from one point to another, and have no affinity with a picture or attraction for an artist.[150]

It is ironic that Wodderspoon should have used Crome's paintings as a gauge for an old Norfolk that was disappearing considering that the artist's contemporaries saw the county's appearance as a testimony to the advantages of agricultural improvement and generally lacking in picturesque scenery as a consequence.[151] Wodderspoon was doubtless misled by Crome's embrace of the picturesque in his early works. But the profound tensions that I have argued lay behind the surfaces of his later pictures were likely invisible to him in the different world of the 1850s. The muteness of the critical record, with which I began, can only leave us to speculate as to how far they were visible to his contemporaries. However, what is unmistakable is the artifice with which Crome highlighted the cottage 'embowered' in trees in *Hautbois Common*, and placed it adjacent to a commons, standing timber, and grazing animals. This is quite contrary to

---

149   Wodderspoon 1876, pp. 4–6.
150   Wodderspoon 1876, pp. 5–6.
151   Kent 1794, pp. 32, 48; Chambers 1829, pp. iv–ix, xxvii–xxviii. Kent stressed the extent of enclosure and the dearth of views that were 'very extensive or romantic' (p. 6). Gilpin remarked on the 'new inclosed commons' when he travelled form north Norfolk to Norwich in 1769 – see Gilpin 1809, p. 82.

the presentation of improved agriculture in Rigby's Holkham pamphlet[152] but is consonant with the social vision of Edmund Bartell. It suggests again that Crome did not identify with the class perspective of Norwich's big bourgeoisie but with that of the artisans and labourers of the city and its environs.

---

152   Coke was hailed for his attention to his labourers' dwellings – see Chambers 1829, p. xxvii.

Constable and His Audience: An Argument for Iconography[1]

Art-historical interpretations of Constable's art have generally assumed that the meanings of his works are to be established primarily through study of his abundant correspondence, from which his attitudes, motives, and intentions can be established. By contrast, I propose that its meanings can be discovered more through a consideration of the audience for his work and the meanings that were at their disposal. The question is thus rather one of iconography and style than of psychology and personal volitions, conscious or unconscious.[2] By 'audience' here I do not mean 'market'. That is to say I am not concerned with the particular individuals who bought art objects from Constable, but rather with the mass of persons who came together in the exhibition rooms of the Royal Academy and the British Institution and in relation to whom any conception of the public for art had to be measured. Whether or not Constable ever entertained fantasies of finding a select body from among the ranks of landed society that could make up what was traditionally conceived as a worthy public for his art – and I shall show that this is unlikely – in reality it was the socially diverse crowds that gathered in the London exhibition rooms who provided his actual audience. The public experience of Constable's art was thus framed by the setting of the largest and most modern metropolis in the world in a period of rapid expansion. It was this context that gave particular force to his images of rural England; it was their antithesis.[3]

---

1   Parts of the argument of this essay are developed at greater length in Hemingway 1992, Chapter 9.

2   Bermingham 1987 (1) marked an entirely new level of sophistication in interpreting the relationship between correspondence and artworks, but still takes a more psychological approach than that proposed here.

3   For early nineteenth-century art exhibitions in London, see Fullerton 1982; Hemingway 1995; Pullan 1998; Solkin (ed.) 2001.

'Almost All the World is Ignorant and Vulgar'

In the letterpress 'Introduction' he wrote for his *English Landscape* mezzo-tints in 1833, Constable referred to the 'universal esteem in which the arts are now held'.[4] Modern-day scholars who know Constable's private correspond-ence should find that observation somewhat amusing, for three years later the artist wrote to his Arundel friend George Constable that he had recently completed a painting of Hampstead Heath for a 'very old friend – an ama-teur who well knows how to appreciate it, for I now see that I shall never be able to paint down to ignorance. Almost all the world is ignorant and vulgar'.[5] Nor was this an opinion he had reached only in the bitterness and personal disappointment of his later years. Back in 1821, he had written to his close friend and confidant John Fisher that 'I now fear (for my family's sake) I shall never be a popular artist – a Gentleman and Ladies painter', and then contin-ued, somewhat priggishly and ingratiatingly, 'but I am spared making a fool of myself – and your hand stretched forth teaches me to value my own dig-nity of mind (if I may say so) above all things'.[6] The following year, Fisher was to assure him in turn that 'wealthy people' regarded artists as only 'a superior sort of work people', and had 'no notion of the mind & intellect & independent character of a man entering into his compositions'.[7] In this reciprocally self-confirming relationship, Fisher knew exactly what Constable wanted to hear and vice versa.

In his letters to Fisher, Constable repeatedly presented himself as a man of inflexible purpose, who did not alter his plans 'to keep the Publick in good humour' and painted for a small audience of sympathetic admirers with whom he was intellectually and ethically attuned.[8] This attitude was based on an explicit rejection of traditional forms of patronage; Constable disapproved strongly of what he called the 'protégé-ism' of the 'rich and great', and favoured rather an 'honourable competition' among talents.[9] His work did not attract the

---

4   Constable 1970, p. 9.

5   Constable 1962–8, vol. 5, p. 35.

6   John Constable to John Fisher, n.d. 1821, in Constable 1962–8, vol. 6, p. 63. Cf. John Constable to John Fisher, 20 September 1821, vol. 6, p. 73; John Constable to John Fisher., 23 October 1821, vol. 6, p. 78.

7   John Fisher to John Constable, 12 November 1822, Constable 1962–8, vol. 6, p. 103.

8   John Constable to John Fisher, 17 November 1824, in Constable 1962–8, vol. 6, p. 181; John Constable to Charles Robert Leslie, 14 January 1832, vol. 3, p. 59.

9   Leslie 1949, p. 294; John Constable to John Fisher, 23 October 1821, in Constable 1962–8, vol. 6, p. 78.

support of any of the major aristocratic patrons of the period,[10] and, despite his Tory politics, he was unhappy with most of the commissions he received from landed gentlemen and generally got far better treatment from bourgeois patrons such as John Allnutt, Francis Darby, J.P. Tinney, and Robert Vernon.[11] What he called 'the great folks' made him feel personally uncomfortable and he was capable of referring to the House of Lords as 'Lord Noodle or Lord Doodle'.[12]

The figure of Constable as an artist estranged from public taste, a genius ahead of his time shackled by financial need to an uncomprehending audience, has been one of the longstanding popular clichés about him, one for which C.R. Leslie's *Memoirs of the Life of John Constable* and comments in his *Autobiographical Recollections* provided a substantial basis. Leslie described Constable as a man of uncontrollable emotions, an egotist with an almost morbid thirst for the 'approbation of others', a character who was exceptionally sensitive to criticism.[13] However, while we may respect Constable's own statements of feelings of isolation and failure, we should pause before we accept that his was a peculiarly individual predicament caused by his unique talents and the correspondingly original character of his art. I say this for two main reasons. The first is that although Constable's work received some hard knocks in exhibition reviews of the 1820s, he was also described by many critics as a gifted and distinctive painter. Indeed, considering the harsh summary judgments critics frequently meted out on pictures in this period, Constable did not come off too badly. This is not to say that his work was endorsed as readily and enthusiastically as that of say Augustus Wall Callcott and William Collins, but if the signs of his originality (such as the mannerism of 'bespotting with blanc d' argent, or white wash-splashing' as Turner called it)[14] caused some critics to qualify their praise, they also earned him admirers.[15]

---

10   There is no evidence that Sir John Leicester showed any interest in Constable's work and Lord Egremont reportedly disliked it – John Constable to John Fisher, n.d. 1824, in Constable 1962–8, vol. 6, p. 171. However, Constable seems to have exempted Egremont from his general strictures on overbearing aristocratic patrons. See John Constable to Charles Robert Leslie, 16 August 1833, Constable 1962–8, vol. 3, p. 105.

11   For Constable's relations with patrons, see the section devoted to them in Constable 1962–8, vol. 4, part 1.

12   John Constable to Charles Robert Leslie, 6 September 1834, in Constable 1962–8, vol. 3, p. 117; John Constable to Charles Robert Leslie, 17 December 1832, vol. 3, p. 85.

13   'Introduction: C.R. Leslie', Constable 1962–8, vol. 3, p. 7. For a critical assessment of Leslie's biography, see Conal Shields, 'Constable and the Critics', in Parris, Fleming-Williams, and Shields 1976, pp. 22–3.

14   'The Exhibition of the Royal Academy', *London Magazine*, series 3, 3, 15 (June 1829).

15   This essay was conceived before the publication of Judy's Ivy's useful catalogue of Con-

The second reason is that the artist's statements about his estrangement from the public are commonplaces of the period. In this respect they are like many of his other statements, even some of those which have seemed most personal. And this is necessarily the case, for how else could Constable think, except through the general ideological framework of the social order within which he moved like any other organism in its natural habitat?

The idea that the public (in the sense of the socially diverse mass of exhibition-goers) was incapable of any profound or properly discriminating response to serious art is a cliché of early nineteenth-century art criticism,[16] and it is paralleled by statements on the reading public by writers as diverse in their political sympathies and social outlook as Coleridge and Wordsworth, and the young John Stuart Mill. Since artists read newspapers and magazines, we should probably assume that the discourse of criticism seeped into their conversation and thought processes. However, artists generally saw critics as no less of a problem than the ignorance of the public, and perhaps more.[17] One of the most articulate statements of artists' discontents of the period, Martin Archer Shee's *Elements of Art* of 1809, described the critic as the 'nightmare of Genius', a despot who could only judge by 'established law' and pronounced his judgments with a 'ridiculous arrogance'.[18] The incompetent, and frequently biased character of criticism, was a repeated theme in artists' magazines of the period; John Britton's short-lived *Magazine of the Fine Arts* of 1821 even ran a regular column called 'Remarks on Cotemporary Criticism' [sic] to counteract what it saw as irresponsible statements in the non-professional press.

The problem, as many artists saw it, was that their works were not assessed by professional standards, either by critics or by those in positions of public authority. The watercolour painter and sometime critic W.H. Pyne (who was

---

stable's press criticism (Ivy 1991). Ivy certainly shows that Constable had reason to feel frustrated by press criticism, but her presentation treats the artist solely as an individual consciousness and ignores his formation as a social agent.

16   E.g., 'A just critique may be considered as a glass, without which the higher beauties of Painting are not perceivable; for it is ridiculous to imagine, that uninformed minds can discern, by what is titled natural taste, "abnormis sapiens", the great points of art, any more than they can, by the same natural taste, understand a passage of HOMER. – It is indeed very easy to say *Dear, what a beautiful storm. – Lud, what a charming Tyger*; but to FEEL and RELISH the best efforts of art! – requires that the rationale of these efforts must have been previously exposed, and thoroughly understood; to effect which is one intention of the present critique'. From 'The Fine Arts, No. 1 Pall Mall Gallery', *Oracle*, 2 May 1807.

17   I analyse the discourse of criticism in Hemingway 1992, Chapter 7, and, at rather greater length, in Hemingway 1989, Chapter 7.

18   Shee 1809, p. 338.

particularly sympathetic to Constable's art) expressed the attitude clearly in the *Somerset House Gazette* in 1823: 'Few men of rank, either public or private, can be named, who are capable of judging scientifically of the merits of a building, a statue, or a picture, although the architect, the sculptor, and the painter are usually compelled to submit their opinions and judgment to the caprices or control of this class'.[19]

Such a view was publicly asserted by the Royal Academicians to justify their authority as a professional body, and, most notably, in Shee's responses to questioning from the Parliamentary Select Committee on Arts and Manufactures in 1836 when he described the public as 'ignorant, to an extraordinary degree, upon the subject of the arts'. According to the Academy's then President, even that enlightened minority who were 'considered competent to legislate on all other points' were incompetent as judges of art.[20] That Constable approved of Shee's performance, we know from a letter he wrote to George Constable that September, in which he gloated over the 'horsewhipping' Shee had reportedly given the Committee, which was packed with Radical M Ps of the kind the artist loathed and 'headed by that wretched fellow [William] Ewart'.[21]

We should thus understand Constable's statements of contempt for the demands of an ignorant public as part of a larger phenomenon and as the repetition of a commonplace both of art criticism and of artistic self-representation. These developments can be conceptualised in terms of Pierre Bourdieu's thesis of the emergence of a relatively autonomous cultural field within bourgeois societies that accompanied the development of a free-market in artistic com-

---

19   W.H. Pyne, 'The Rise and Progress of Water-Colour Painting in England, No. VIII', *Somerset House Gazette*, 11 (20 December 1823), p. 161.

20   'Part II, Minutes of Evidence and Appendix', House of Commons 1836, pp. 164–5.

21   John Constable to George Constable, 16 September 1836, in Constable 1962–8, vol. 5, pp. 34–5. Constable's view is comparable with that of his sometime friend and artistic rival William Collins. In his biography of his father, Wilkie Collins emphasised that he had always 'despised the easy ambition' to impress a 'select few' and instead directed his work, 'from first to last', at 'every grade of his fellow beings who were likely to behold them' (Collins 1848, vol. 1, p. 102). Yet he also printed a letter that Collins had written in 1822 in which he complained of the 'alarming increase of exhibitions' and of a 'lamentable demand for novelty in the Arts': 'Every one talks of painting and literature, and what is still worse, all conceive it to be their duty to have opinions; and instead of an ingenuous expression of their *feelings*, – by which painting and poetry might gather considerable improvement – their only aim seems to be, that of persuading those who are not to be deceived, that they understand both arts' (vol. 1, p. 187.) Thus Collins too, although he was a more successful, and indeed fashionable, artist, seems to have regarded public taste as ill-informed and capricious.

modities and the decline of traditional patronal relations. It is the emergence of this field that makes possible the seemingly independent artist and intellectual, who wishes to recognise no obligations except those to the 'intrinsic demands of his creative project'.[22]

To judge from his correspondence, Constable's belief that his art had failed to achieve a status proportionate to his talents arose principally from the hostile comments of competitors and his inability to get prices that he could regard as tokens of respect.[23] However, whether or not he shared the contempt for criticism conventional among his fellow artists, he could not change the fact that it constituted the only public discourse on contemporary art. As such, it implicitly or explicitly aspired to define the standards of public taste and give proper meanings to artists' works. Now it may have been the case that the critics did not always make the kind of sense of Constable's works that he wanted them to, but this does not mean that they were incomprehensible. It should go without saying that art works have no single meaning, and Constable could not define the one correct reading for his.

We cannot construe the public significance of Constable's work by reference to his biography or his personal history as a product of the Suffolk rural bourgeoisie. As an artist, Constable was necessarily an urban figure, producing for a predominantly urban market in a society in which even the gentry had a partially urban lifestyle. For the vast majority of Constable's audience, the facts that his family owned Flatford Mill and worked Dedham Mill, that his father was a Commissioner of the Stour Navigation, or even that he was a native of Suffolk were unknown and irrelevant. In many instances Constable himself did not even think it appropriate to acknowledge by his titles that the river he depicted was the Stour or that it was in Suffolk. After all, his book of mezzotints was given the generic title of *English Landscape*, and in a draft for the letterpress, he spoke of his ambition to make 'subjects purely English' the basis for 'General Landscape'.[24] Whatever the personal significance of Constable's Stour subjects for him, he did not expect that his contemporary audience would need to know his personal history to make sense of them and would have regarded such an idea as ludicrous.

---

22   Bourdieu 1971.

23   Hence his determination to get £200 for his six-foot canvases in 1822. See John Constable to John Fisher, 31 October 1822, in Constable 1962–8, vol. 6, p. 100.

24   Constable 1970, p. 83. Elizabeth Helsinger has made a persuasive case that Constable shifts from being a self-consciously local painter in the 1810s to being a national painter in the 1820s – see Helsinger 1997, Chapter 1.

The associationist aesthetic through which Constable thought the meanings of his landscapes, precisely adjured the artist to evoke ideas that were as universal as possible and to avoid those of merely personal or local significance. Thus, for instance, Alison – whose *Essays on the Nature and Principles of Taste* 'delighted' Constable in 1814[25] – wrote that 'in all those Arts ... that respect the beauty of Form, it ought to be the unceasing study of the Artist, to disengage his mind from the accidental Associations of his age, as well as the common prejudices of his Art; to labour to distinguish his productions by that pure and permanent expression, which may be felt in every age'.[26] Alison was thinking here primarily of bodily form – he maintained 'the great purpose of nature' was most evident in the human countenance[27] – but the doctrine extended to landscape in which he would probably have favoured the ideal more than Constable's kind of 'native scenery'. How little Alison found aesthetic pleasure in the everyday world of the lower classes is indicated by his opinion that those 'doomed to low and degrading labour', such as ploughmen or weavers, would lose whatever beauty of form they may have been born with even if it were 'the most perfect form of man'.[28] This statement iterated a truism of the natural theology that Constable also embraced.

But Alison did accord the experience of landscape a very high standing, claiming that 'in ages of civilization and refinement', the 'union of devotional sentiment to the beauties of natural scenery, forms one of the most characteristic marks of human improvement, and may be traced in every art which professes to give delight to the imagination'.[29] Alison may have located the 'beauties of natural scenery' in other places than Constable, but his associationist psychology allowed him to conceive the pleasures of taste as infinitely extendable: 'Instead of a few forms which the superstition of early taste

---

25   John Constable to Maria Bicknell, 28 August 1814, in Constable 1962–8, vol. 2, p. 131. I am not the first to point out Alison's importance for Constable – see Rosenthal 1983, pp. 74–5. Richard Payne Knight's version of the association aesthetic was more explicitly accommodating to modern pastoral landscape than Alison's and extended the concept of beauty to the work of the Dutch School (see Knight 1808, pp. 70–1, 195–6), but Constable would certainly have disapproved of Knight personally because of his reputation for libertinage, Foxite Whig politics, and public disdain for artists' opinions. Knight professed to admire Constable's works when he visited the artist's studio in 1824 – but not enough to buy any of them, to his host's annoyance. See John Constable to John Fisher, 17 January 1824, in Constable 1962–8, vol. 6, p. 149.

26   Alison 1815, vol. 2, p. 199.

27   Alison 1815, vol. 2, p. 439.

28   Alison 1815, vol. 2, p. 363.

29   Alison 1815, vol. 2, p. 444.

had canonized, every variety, and every possible combination of forms, is thus brought with the pale of cultivated taste; the mind of the spectator follows with joy the invention of the artist: wherever greater usefulness is produced, or greater fitness exhibited, he sees, in the same forms, new Beauty awakening'.[30] Constable's work effectively claimed that the 'pleasures of taste' could be set in play in rustic Suffolk where a generic English beauty was located in everyday scenery.

In short then, I argue that the meanings of Constable's works are better comprehended through the contemporary discourse around landscape and the iconography it implicitly defined than they are through the interminably retold story of his life. To demonstrate this, I want to consider some recurrent motifs in his Stour valley paintings.

The Picturesque of Rivers

In one of his most frequently quoted statements, his letter to John Fisher of 23 October 1821, Constable declared that he loved such things as 'Mill dams', 'Willows, Old rotten Banks, slimy posts, & brickwork', and went on to say, 'I associate my "careless boyhood" to all that lies on the banks of the <u>Stour</u>. They made me a painter (& I am grateful)'.[31] The conventional function of this passage in Constable scholarship has been to confirm that the significance of Constable's art is to be uncovered from his personal relationship with the Suffolk landscape. However, Constable was not just speaking his own mind here,[32] he was also echoing a current pattern of discourse around landscape in general.

From most considerations of his art, one would have thought that there was something unusual in the artist's pre-occupation with picturesque river scenery. Far from this being the case, the history of rivers was one of the staples of topographical literature in the period. From the 1790s, there had been a steady stream of such publications, illustrated by various types of print media, of which notable examples include: Samuel Ireland's *Picturesque Views of the Thames* (1792), *Medway* (1793), *Avon* (1795), *Wye* (1797), and *Severn* (1822–4); John and Josiah Boydell's *An History of the River Thames* (1794–6); Francis Jukes's *Views on the River Wye* (1797–1802); George and William Bernard Cooke's *Views on the Thames* (1811, 1822); William Havell's *A Series of Picturesque Views of the River Thames* (1811–12); F.C. Lewis's *Picturesque Views on the River Dart* (1821),

---

30   Alison 1815, vol. 2, p. 433.
31   John Constable to John Fisher, 23 October 1821, in Constable 1962–8, vol. 6, pp. 77–8.
32   Cf. Bermingham 1987 (1), p. 50.

and *Picturesque Views on the Tamar and Tavy* (1823), and so on. The rationale for such publications was neatly laid out in a volume that probably dates from 1834: 'The descriptive view of any principal river naturally comprehends an account of the most interesting and picturesque portion of the country through which its course is directed. Towns and cities are always found upon its banks, and where Nature has not embellished its precincts, the display of art in raising the princely fabric, or rich domain, have assisted in beautifying its margin'.[33] The Stour might lack 'princely fabrics' on its banks, but it was an important conduit for local river traffic and ran through abundant picturesque scenery.

Nor is the relevance of such publications to Constable's themes confined simply to the popularity of a common theme; the precise features of the landscape for which he declared his love, the 'Mill dams', 'Willows', and 'slimy posts', were widely understood to constitute a characteristic river bank picturesque. They feature, for instance, in the illustrations to the Boydells's lavish *An History of the Thames*, which comprises a series of aquatints by J.C. Stadler after drawings by Constable's early friend and mentor Joseph Farington. A number of apparently inconsequential picturesque objects feature in Farington's depictions of the upper reaches of the river, one such being the view of *Langley Ware* (*fig. 82*). With its rough timbers and its cottage with a mouldering thatch nested amongst an irregular mass of trees – some pollards, some evidently dead – this already has many of the ingredients of a Constable Stour scene (*fig. 83*), even if its picturesque is more formulaic than his. The picturesque value of such effects is spelt out in William Combe's accompanying text in a discussion of weirs, where the stream frets 'among the mossy timbers' or rushes 'over the aquatic plants that cling to the framework'. Weirs give 'variety to the view' and 'are generally connected with various accessory and diversifying circumstances; the mill, the fisherman's hut, or the cottage of the person who collects the toll, sometimes imbowered in trees ... [they] heighten and vary the character of the scene'.[34] We may deduce from this that such a combination of objects is not only pleasing to the picturesque eye, but also that its 'character' prompts a satisfying kind of reflection to a mind sensitively attuned to the simplicities of country life.

Although the text to the Boydells's *History of the Thames* necessarily extolls the value of the river as a commercial waterway and makes conventional

---

33   Tombleson 1834?, p. i.

34   Boydell and Boydell 1794–6, vol. 1 pp. 56–7. This statement accompanies the plate of *Clark's or Buck's Weir*, which was downstream from Radcot Bridge in Oxfordshire. William Combe is better known for his satirical poem *The Tour of Dr. Syntax in Search of the Picturesque* (1812).

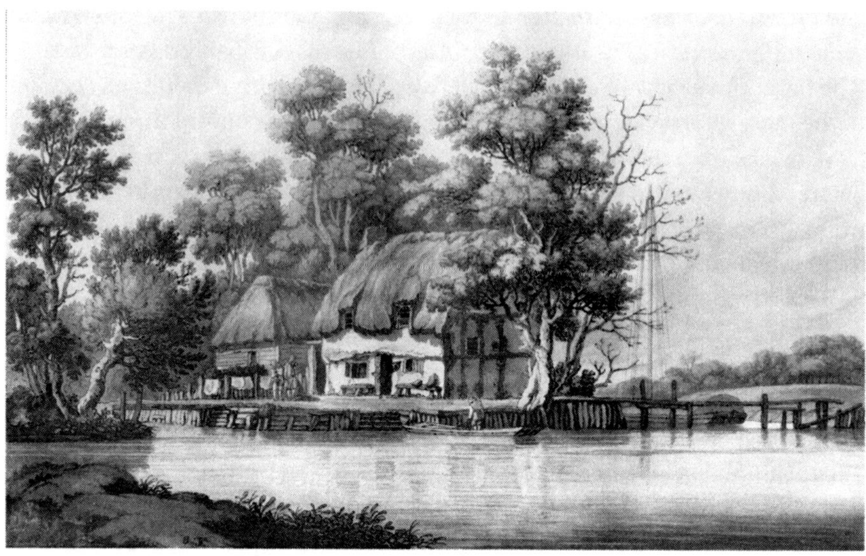

FIGURE 82   *J.C. Stadler after Joseph Farington,* Langley Ware, *aquatint, from John and Josiah Boydell,* An History of the River Thames *(1794–96)*
PHOTO: AUTHOR

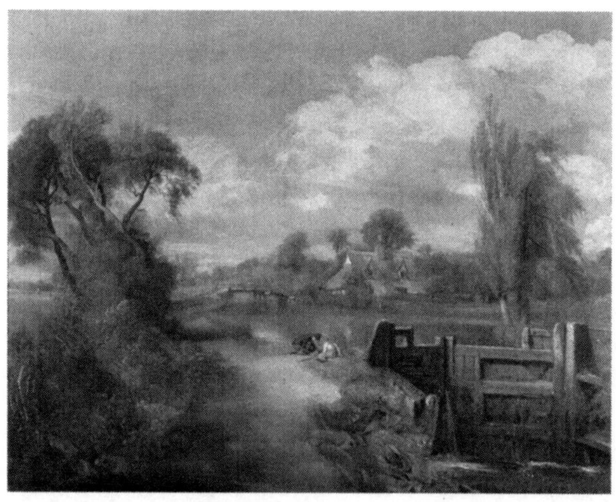

FIGURE 83
John Constable, Landscape: Boys Fishing, *exh. 1813, oil on canvas, 40×49½ in (101.6×125.8cm) National Trust, Anglesey Abbey, Cambridgeshire*
© NATIONAL TRUST IMAGES

obeisance to the 'patriotic spirit' of those speculators who have improved the navigation, the handsome pair of folio volumes were likely directed at the gentry market first of all. The series gives considerable attention to the 'seats' of 'gentlemen' along the banks and many of Farington's plates are views of or from landed estates. As is well known, Constable was strongly averse to the gentleman's park;[35] correspondingly, his approach to the river resembles the picturesque low viewpoints adopted by Samuel Owen in his drawings for George and W.B. Cooke's *Thames* etchings rather than the higher viewpoints Farington usually preferred, which are more in the nature of prospects with all this implies of proprietorship and social elevation (*figs. 84* and *85*).[36]

Almost directly contemporary with Constable's first exhibition of a view of a lock in 1812, there appeared a folio volume of twelve coloured aquatints after watercolours by the accomplished naturalist painter William Havell, the rejection of whose *Walnut Gathering in Petersham, near Richmond Bridge* by the British Institution in 1814 was one of the most open clashes between the new naturalism and connoisseurial opinion.[37] Havell's Thames views are in a cognate idiom to that work in their sunlight brightness and choice of views that foreground modern features of the landscape. Arguably they embody a town-dweller's view of nature analogous to that of the Cockney School of poetry, epitomised by Leigh Hunt, who knew Havell and supported him in the pages of the *Examiner*.[38] Initially published in 1811–12 under the title *A Series of Picturesque Views on the River Thames, from the Drawings of Wm. Havell*, the prints were issued in a second edition in 1818. Considering the extraordinarily high quality of the plates and the advanced naturalism of Havell's style, one might expect that *Picturesque Views of the River Thames* served as some kind of example to Constable – even if one from which he wished to distance himself given his powerful friend Sir George Beaumont's disapproval of the artist.[39] Havell's

---

35   'a gentleman's park – is my aversion. It is not beauty because it is not nature', he wrote to John Fisher on 7 October 1822 – see Constable 1962–8, vol. 6, p. 98. For his travails over a commission to paint one, see Parris, Fleming-Williams, and Shields 1976, pp. 171–2.

36   On which, see Barrell 1972, pp. 21–7.

37   For Havell, see Owen 1981. For the rejection of *Walnut Gathering*, see Owen and Brown 1988, pp. 182, 184. For sources on this episode, see Hemingway 1992, pp. 40, 120, 305 n. 55. The painting did not sell at the 200 guineas Havell asked, and was later taken to New York by his cousin Robert Havell, Junior. Its subsequent fate is unknown, but an oil sketch for it was sold at Christie's, London, on 7 July 1987 (lot 46).

38   On Hunt and the Cockney School, see Roe (ed.) 2003. Hunt regarded Havell as an 'eminent' landscape painter (56 n. 45). In January of 1815 Havell had been a signatory to a letter of congratulation sent to Hunt on the publication of his masque *The Descent of Liberty*, written while its author was still in jail serving out a two-year sentence for libeling the Prince Regent.

39   For Beaumont and Havell, see Owen 1981, pp. 9–10, 12–14. The sole reference to Havell in Constable's correspondence is dismissive – one of the authors of 'many enormous pieces of stained paper' – John Constable to C.R. Leslie, 16 July 1834, Constable 1962–68, vol. 3, p. 111.

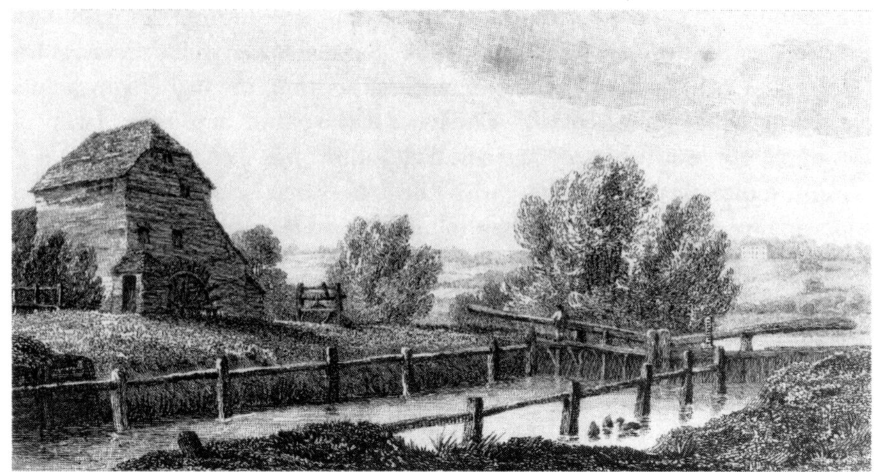

FIGURE 84   *W.B. Cooke after Samuel Owen,* Shiplake Lock & Paper Mill, *1810, etching, from George and William Bernard Cooke's* Views on the Thames *(1811, 1822)*
PHOTO: AUTHOR

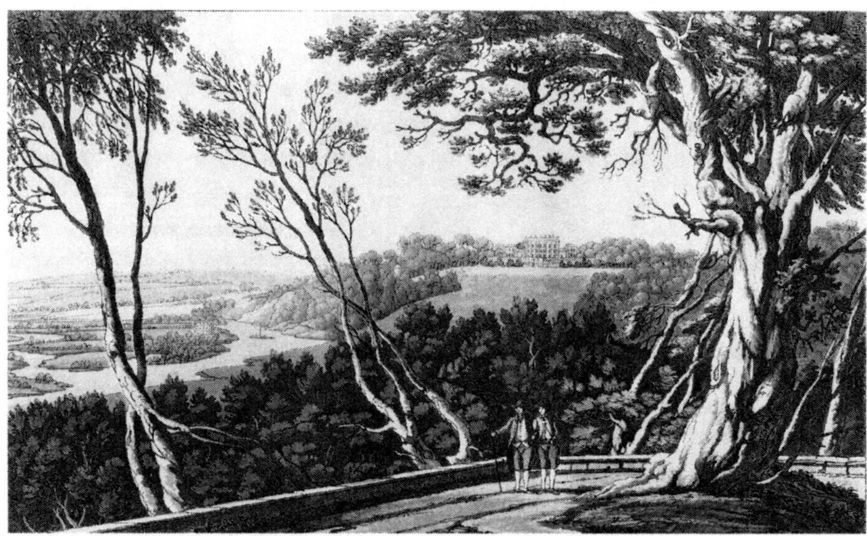

FIGURE 85   *J.C. Stadler after Joseph Farington,* Cliefden, *1793, aquatint, from John and Josiah Boydell's* An History of the River Thames *(1794–96)*
PHOTO: AUTHOR

images suggest the conventional mythology of the Thames valley as a region of peaceful abundance and beauty – I use the term 'beauty' here partly to signal the way in which, despite the series' title, they differ from the self-consciously picturesque qualities of Constable's designs. They illustrate the destruction of

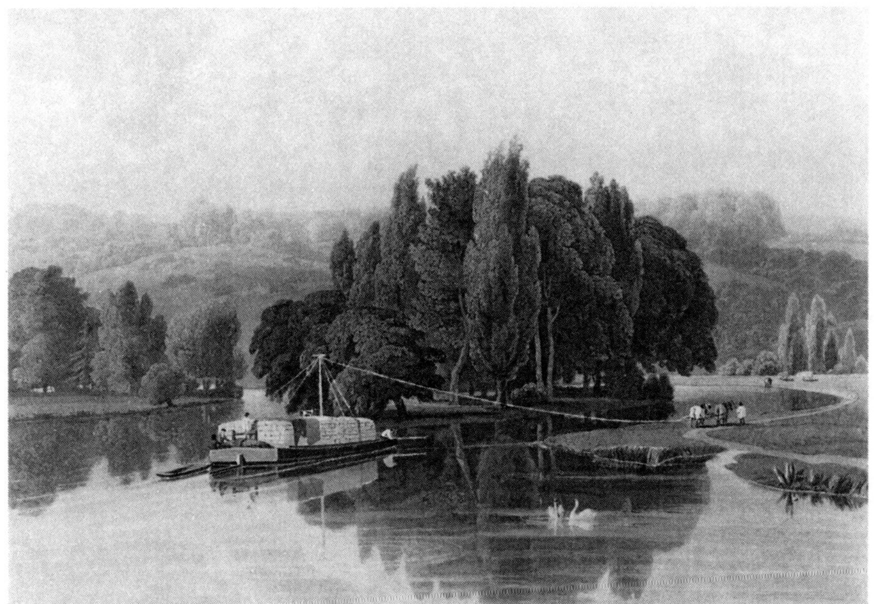

FIGURE 86   *R. and D. Havell, after William Havell,* An Island on the Thames near Park Place, *from* A Series of Picturesque Views on the River Thames, from the Drawings of Wm. Havell, *1811–12*
PHOTO: AUTHOR

chiaroscuro and its replacement by planes of bright daylight hues in naturalistic watercolour at its most extreme. Havell represents the Thames in some of the prints through wide and placid expanses of water (*fig. 86*), his atmospheric effects are uniformly sunlit (in contrast to Constable's insistently changeable weather), and in two plates he makes use of compositions overtly indebted to the classical prototypes of Gaspard Dughet in contrast to Constable's repeated references to the formal types of the Dutch and Flemish landscape traditions. However, the iconographical overlap between Constable and Havell is striking, and, once again, the fact that Havell's plates were dedicated to the Commissioners of the Thames Navigation illustrates how deeply river motifs were bound up with the culture of 'improvement', or progress.

One aspect of Constable's iconography that has usually been seen as distinctive is the role he gives to working figures. But again, the idea that an active commercial waterway could offer a fund of picturesque subjects was hardly peculiar to him. In 1819, the year in which he exhibited the first of the large Stour pictures, the minor water-colour painter and author John Hassell published a tour of the Grand Junction Canal illustrated by 24 coloured aquatints (*fig. 87*). Hassell's plates are small, crude affairs, but his text both recommends to the

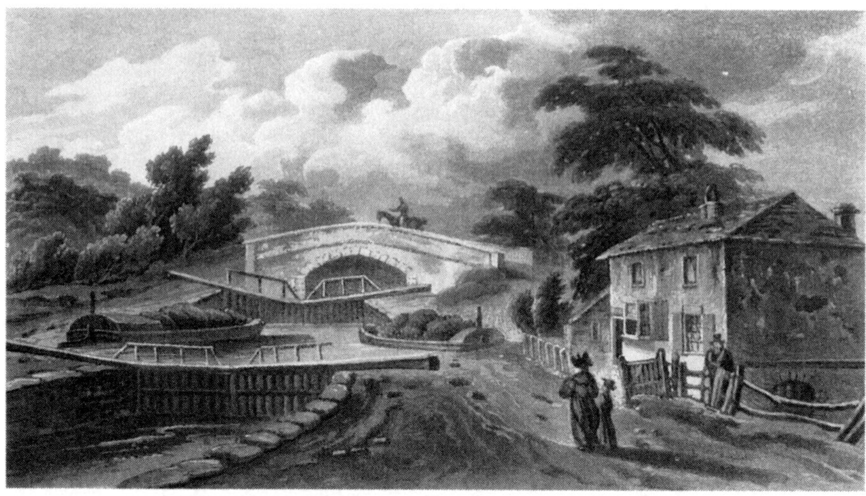

FIGURE 87   *John Hassell,* Three Locks: Stoke Hammond–Bucks, *from* Tour of the Grand
Junction in a Series of Engravings (*1819*)
PHOTO: AUTHOR

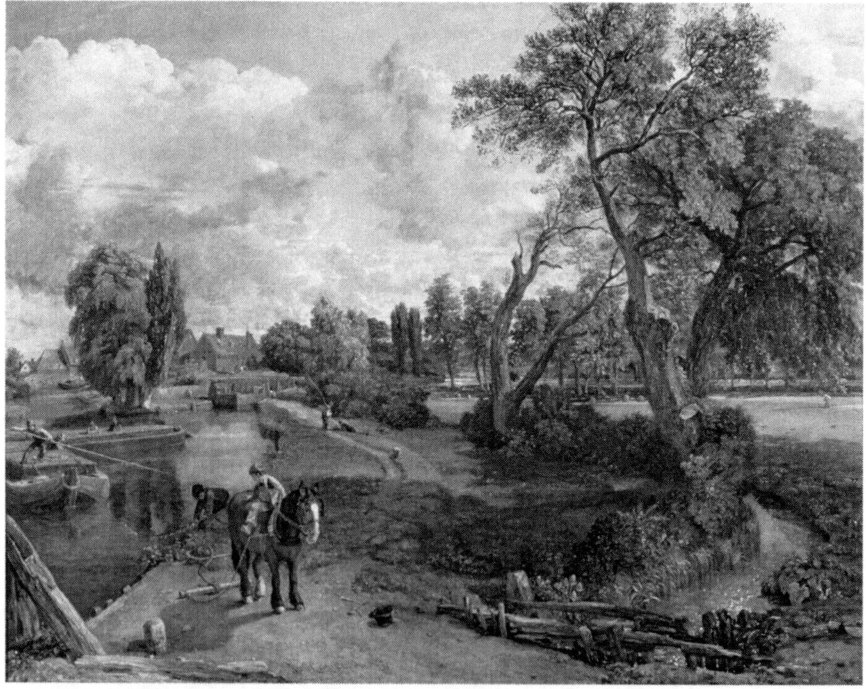

FIGURE 88   *John Constable,* Flatford Mill (Scene on a Navigable River), *1816–17, oil on canvas,*
40 × 50 in (101.6 × 127.0 cm), Tate Britain
© TATE, LONDON, 2015

artist many features of a commercial waterway that Constable would aggrandise in his large compositions and frames them with advice on pictorial practice that was drawn from the dicta of contemporary naturalism. Thus, writing of the area around King's Langley, Hertfordshire, Hassell says: 'At a short distance beyond this, we see the navigation making a deviation in the valley, exhibiting a succession of bridges and locks, passage boats, with horses and their drivers in different situations, having noble backgrounds and a profusion of wood, forming altogether, abundant incidents for the pencil of the artist'. While at the Cowley Lock, near Uxbridge, 'the boats in motion at the opening and shutting of the locks, and the various avocations of the attendants, constitute very appropriate incidents, and form excellent embellishments for landscape'.[40] This could be a recipe book for a Constable painting such as *Flatford Mill* (1816–17; *fig. 88*) or *Dedham Lock and Mill* (1818; private collection), both of which were exhibited at the Royal Academy and British Institutions in consecutive years over 1817 to 1819. Of course, Hassell's understanding of the canal bank picturesque may partly have been derived from studying Constable's pictures. The point is not one of precedence and influence but of a shared iconography and common aesthetic.

Hassell's text is notable for the insistently pictorial character of his descriptions and the way in which historical and antiquarian information is interwoven with tributes to the commercial enterprises along the waterway. The background to his scenes of river traffic and locks is frequently one of rustic labour, envisaged in georgic mode. Thus a view at Marsworth is described as 'a picture' in which harvest labourers perform a narrative of healthy and cheerful toil: 'The harvest was getting in, and the loaded teams were passing in a quick succession; the labourers in the wheatfield, with gleaners following, were all in motion, where the corn had been cut down; on the other side of us, reapers were trimming down the standing crops in one field, while in another a fresh groupe were mowing of beans. Village lasses appeared in the returning carts bringing refreshments to the sturdy husbandmen'.[41] The georgic sits with no friction in a landscape cut through by the new industrial and commercial traffic. Such scenes were recorded with their accompanying effects of light and atmosphere and Hassell advised artists that these phenomena should be 'instantaneously copied, and ought to become the particular care of the artist; for whatever is coloured on the spot and from nature invariably forms the best picture'.[42]

---

40 Hassell 1819, pp. 29–30, 39.

41 Hassell 1819, p. 48. In an interesting discordant note, Hassell described the Game Laws as   'a disgrace to the country' (p. 140).

42 Hassell 1819, p. 73.

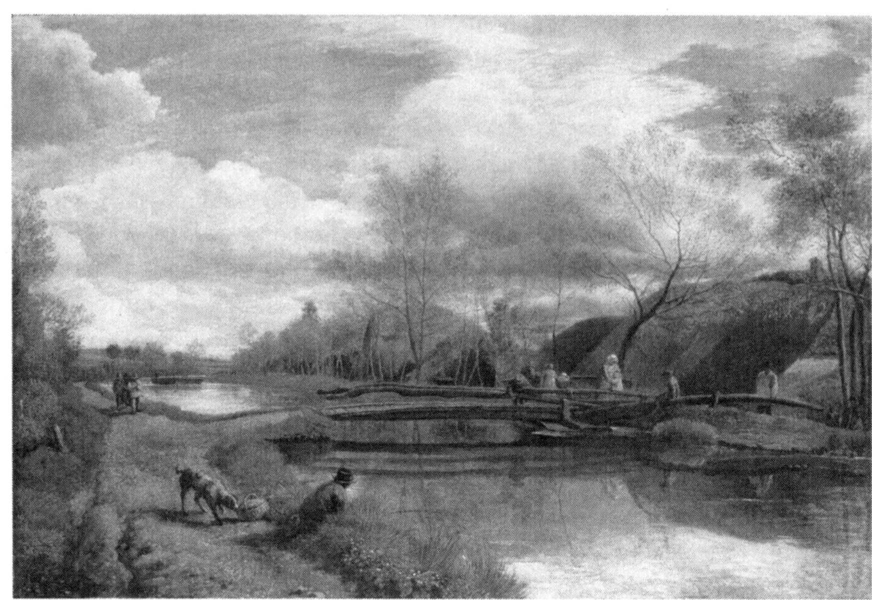

FIGURE 89   *Linnell, John (1792–1882), The River Kennet, near Newbury, 1815, oil on canvas on wood (45.1 × 65.2 cm) Fitzwilliam Museum*
©FITZWILLIAM MUSEUM, CAMBRIDGE/ART RESOURCE, NY

Such sources illustrate how very conventional Constable's choice of images of a commercial waterway was. Moreover, the text offers striking confirmation that motifs of canals and improved rivers signified an ideology of trade and improvement for contemporaries, as Michael Rosenthal has claimed in relation to Constable's pictures of barge traffic.[43] Hassell dedicated his Tour to 'the Noblemen and Gentlemen Proprietors' of the Grand Junction, paying special tribute to the Duke of Bridgewater. 'Inland navigation', he wrote, 'is the very heart's blood and soul of commerce'; its value was so great as to be hard to estimate. His readers were assured that among the canal's proprietors were 'many of the first capitalists in the kingdom' and that 'its usual routine of business is so conducted as to give satisfaction to all who are associated with it'. (Gross revenue from the Grand Union canal in 1818 was given as £170,000). This confirms the association between naturalism and the world of modern labour that we also find in early works by John Linnell such as *The River Kennet, near Newbury* (1815; *fig. 89*).[44]

---

43   Rosenthal 1983, pp. 120, 155.
44   Hassell 1819, pp. viii, 1.

The closest parallel with Constable's imagery of the Stour valley is provided by the Norwich artist James Stark's publication, *Scenery of the Rivers of Norfolk*, which bears a publication date of 1834, although the first number had been issued to subscribers in 1828. This comprises 36 fine copper-plate engravings after a series of oil paintings that Stark produced specially, together with a substantial topographical text by the Norwich worsted manufacturer J.W. Robberds. As Stark's prospectus made clear, the publication was conceived to record features of the Norfolk landscape that were likely to change as a result of the Norwich and Lowestoft Navigation Bill of 1826, which was to make Norwich a port and end its dependence on the coastal town of Great Yarmouth. Despite the background of both Robberds and Stark in the Norwich manufacturing community, the text is partly an extended commentary on the mutability of landscape and the incompatibility of progress with the picturesque and rustic 'simplicity': 'Amidst the fluctuations of human affairs and the decay of all earthly forms, it is the province of the artist to snatch from utter oblivion those fleeting traits, on which depend some of the pleasures of the passing minute; and it is while he thus prolongs *the vivid remembrance of our earlier enjoyments,* that he helps to quicken in our bosoms the flow of generous feelings, and minister to the kindliest impulses of our nature'. As the reference to 'the vivid remembrance of our earlier enjoyments' in this passage suggests, Robberds tended to connect rural scenery with the recollection of childhood, as if it were likely to form part of the memory of an audience who in adult life were destined to be city-dwellers. Stark's plates themselves alternate between images that suggest this simple rustic condition through pictorial types derived from Hobbema, Ruysdael and other Dutch models, and a more modern imagery of the port of Yarmouth and the edges of Norwich. The first type is represented through *Shipmeadow Lock on the Waveney* (*fig. 90*), which was based on a large painting (55 by 72 inches framed) that Stark exhibited at the British Institution in 1831.

Not only is the iconography of this strikingly similar to Constable's Stour views, but Robberds's letterpress to this plate emphasises the associations between such scenes and childhood recollections. He quotes verses from a poem by a local poetess, Agnes Strickland, which include the following lines:

> Sweet stream of my childhood! still Fancy will fly
> To thy green sunny vales with a pensive delight;
> There Memory wanders, and pours forth her sigh
> To the spot that no longer may gladden my sight.

In his commentary, Robberds observes that in 'hours of absence, the liveliest imaginings and fondest reminiscences of native genius will ever dwell upon

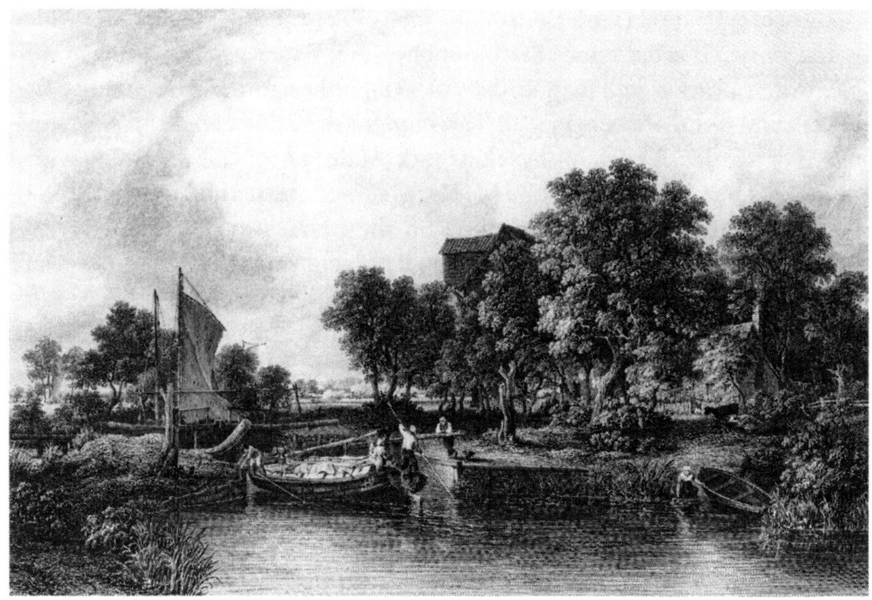

FIGURE 90   *W. Forrest after James Stark,* Shipmeadow Lock (on the Waveney), *1831, engraving, from James Warden Robberds,* Scenery of the Rivers of Norfolk *(1834)*
PHOTO: AUTHOR

such objects, as the skilful eye of the practised and intelligent artist selects for the favourite ornaments of his canvas'. It is at least a striking coincidence that Robberds should have connected these reflections to an image of a lock, which he stressed was 'in perfect keeping' with the 'rustic scenery' in which it was 'embowered'. In the light of Robberds's observations, the Latin verses from Camden's *Britannia* that Constable inserted in the frontispiece to his *English Landscape* mezzotints, which connected his childhood with the germ of his love for art, seem far from eccentric and the confession he made to Fisher of October 1821 that the 'banks of the Stour' had made him a painter seems rather commonplace. Might James Stark not have said the same thing in relation to the Yare? Once again, I am not positing the influence of another artist on Constable here – with Stark, any influence may well have worked the other way – what I am trying to identify rather is a kind of iconographical currency that was grounded in a common ideology. As a final detail here, we may note that Constable subscribed for a proof copy of the *Rivers of Norfolk*.

So far, I have defined the category of imagery to which Constable's work belonged with reference to topographical publications. However, in choosing to make exhibition pictures out of the theme of commercial waterways, he

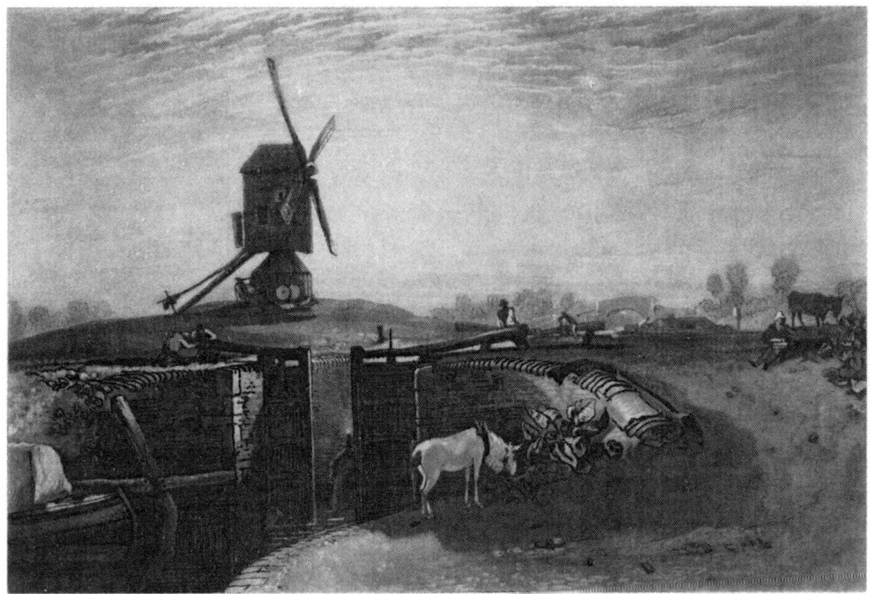

FIGURE 91   *William Say after J.M.W. Turner,* Windmill and Lock, *from the* Liber Studorium, *1811, etching and mezzotint, Tate Britain. After the oil painting* Grand Junction Canal at Southall Mill, *whereabouts unknown.*
© TATE, LONDON, 2015

was hardly unique. The most important precedent for him must have been the series of Thames views that Turner had exhibited at his own gallery in Harley Street over the years from 1805–12. Although it is not possible to identify all these pictures with complete certainty, among them were the *Grand Junction Canal at Southall Mill* (1810; *fig. 91*), a view of a lock and a windmill, and *Abindgon* (1810; Tate Gallery), which depicts watering cattle adjacent to a motif of men unloading from a timber barge. That Turner's pictures of the Thames dominated his gallery in 1808 and seemed to constitute a series we know from John Landseer's review of the display published in that year, which reported that 'the greater number of the pictures at present exhibited are views of the Thames, whose course Mr. Turner has now studiously followed, with the eye and hand at once of a painter and a poet, almost from its source to where it mingles its waters with those of the German ocean'.[45] Taken together, Turner's pictures could be read as a history of the river, and his choice of subjects closely

---

45   'Mr. Turner's Gallery', *Review of Publications of Art*, 1 (1808), p. 152. I discuss this series at length in Hemingway 1992, pp. 224–45.

parallels that of the topographies. Of course, Constable's Stour had none of the potent range of patriotic associations that the Thames so readily conjured up. It offered nothing equivalent to the region around Windsor or the view from Richmond Hill. Constable's strategy was thus different both formally, and in its iconographic emphasis.

Turner tended to mix his signs of river traffic with conventional symbols of the pastoral, in the form of watering cattle and sheep washing – as in his two views of Walton Bridges of circa 1806 (Loyd Collection and National Gallery of Victoria, Melbourne), bathing the whole scene in a kind of golden light, which implied that the Thames Valley was a paradisiacal realm of plenty and social harmony and also often suggested the close of day and approaching end of labour – as *Grand Junction Canal at Southall Mill* and *Abingdon* illustrate. Constable, by contrast, offered a more episodic and laborious vision of the workaday world, in which such familiar symbols are marginal or absent altogether, where the labour of the waterways is emphatically foregrounded, and the changeability of the weather threatens to keep the farmer on his toes. These variations from the clichés of pastoral imagery partly provided the grounds on which Constable could assert the originality of his art. However, we should be clear that his iconographical departures were developments within the established genre of the river view, which signified the prosperity and harmony of the English national landscape. A work by George Vincent illustrates the point.[46]

In 1819, Constable showed *A Scene on the River Stour* (Frick Collection, New York) at the Royal Academy; now known as *The White Horse*, at 51¾ by 74 ⅛ inches (131.4 by 188.3 cm) it was the first of his really large river scenes to be exhibited. Earlier that year, the up-and-coming young artist George Vincent (twenty-one years Constable's junior) had exhibited *A View on the River Yare, Afternoon* (*fig. 92*) at the British Institution. At 46 by 66 inches, this was only slightly smaller than Constable's *Scene on the River Stour*.[47] It was also a major critical success, being mentioned in at least six reviews, and sold from the exhibition to the Countess de Gray for 120 guineas. Constable could hardly have failed to notice the picture, not only because of its size, but because as no. 71, it must have hung close to his no. 78, *A Mill*, now known as *Dedham Lock and Mill*

<hr>

46   Another relevant point of comparison would be William Frederick Witherington's *The Old Lock, Windsor* (1817; National Trust, Anglesey Abbey), though in this instance the atmosphere is more urban.

47   For a fuller discussion of paintings of the Yare valley, see Hemingway 1992 pp. 272–7. For Constable's large Stour paintings, see Lyles (ed.) 2006, pp. 128–61.

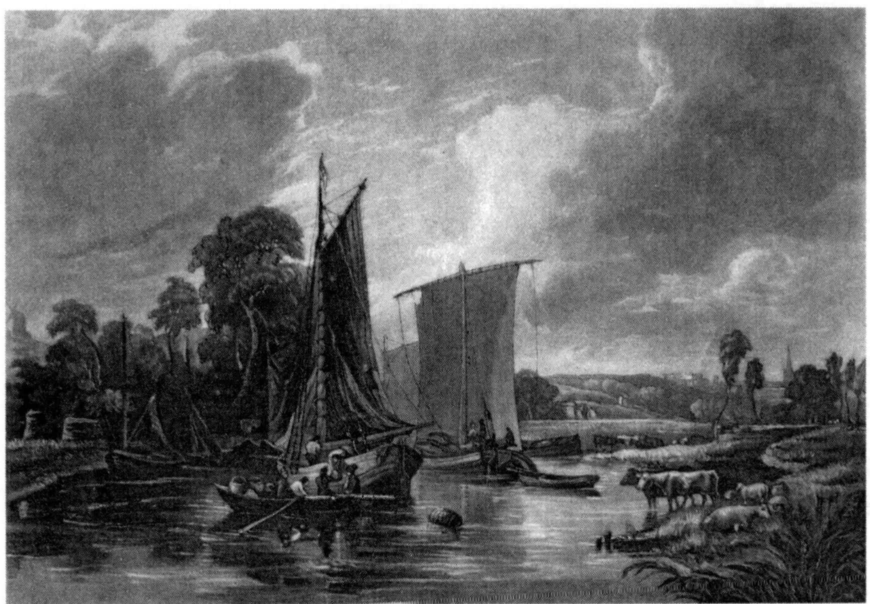

FIGURE 92   *George Vincent,* A View on the River Yare, Afternoon, *c. 1820, mezzotint. Based on the painting of the same title, which was No. 81 in Christie's Sale, 16 November 1962* NORFOLK MUSEUMS SERVICE (NORWICH CASTLE MUSEUM AND PICTURE GALLERY)

(private collection). Whatever the differences in technique between Constable and Vincent, the symbolic content of their work is fundamentally similar. If we compare Vincent's *View on the River Yare, Afternoon* with Constable's *A View on the Stour, near Dedham* (*fig. 93*), exhibited three years later, it will be clear that Vincent includes conventional pastoral symbols in the shape of the watering cattle and grazing sheep of a kind that Constable generally avoids. His narrative of trade is also clearer, in the unloading taking place in the foreground and the distinctive shapes of Norwich castle and cathedral in the background, which mark the terminus of the river traffic. This emphasis on trade was probably the cause of the *Morning Herald's* reviewer retitling the picture *Canal Scene with a Distant View of Norwich*,[48] although like the Stour the Yare was not a canal. Yet however much we may value the features of Constable's painting that distinguish it from Vincent's, they clearly share much in the way of iconography and belong to the same general style category.

---

48   'British Institution', *Morning Herald*, 1 February 1819.

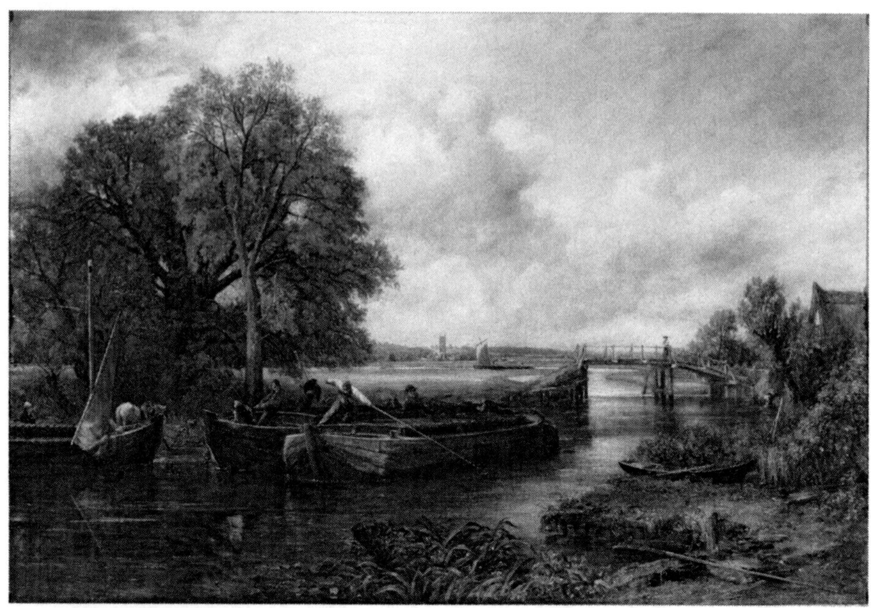

FIGURE 93   *John Constable,* A View on the Stour, near Dedham, *1822, oil on canvas, 51 × 74 in (130.0 × 188.0 cm)*
© COURTESY OF THE HUNTINGTON ART COLLECTIONS, SAN MARINO, CALIFORNIA

Critical Responses

It is now time to return to the general issue of Constable and his audience. In 1824, the *Literary Gazette*, which had always praised Constable with some reservations, responded with quite unqualified enthusiasm to *A Boat Passing a Lock* (Thyssen-Bornemisza Collection, Lugano, Switzerland) when it was shown at the Royal Academy:

> We have always had occasion to remark the skill with which this artist, in a style peculiar to himself, effects the most perfect representation of the objects of his study, whether of foreground or of distance. The character of his details, like those of Wilson, appear as if struck out with a single touch; but this, we are well aware, comes only by great practice and much previous thought and calculation. In none of his former works have these essential qualities been more distinctly visible than in this picture. It is a fine example of the picturesque, with which its striking and powerful execution well accords.[49]

---

49   'Royal Academy', *Literary Gazette*, no. 387, 19 June 1824.

In the following year, the *Literary Chronicle* commented on a 'great paucity of landscapes' in the Academy's exhibition, but claimed that Constable's *Leaping Horse* (Royal Academy of Arts, London) was 'in itself a host', 'a charming specimen of that fresh verdant scenery peculiar to this country'.[50]

Writing in the *Somerset House Gazette* in 1824, W.H. Pyne seems to conceive the value of Constable's works in almost the same terms as their author. Referring to *Salisbury Cathedral from the Bishop's Grounds* (Victoria & Albert Museum), he suggested that 'this composition is so little indebted to the timid skill that selects rather to please by addressing the pencil to the reigning fashion of taste, than to dare to be *original*, that we have heard it condemned for the very attributes that constitute its claims to our approval. For it is so unsophisticated in light, shadow, colouring, and general arrangement – so unaffectedly remote from manner or making up, so unlike to a picture, but so like to reality, that to the eye of prejudice it seems unnatural!' Pyne proceeded to praise the picture's 'originality of feeling' – 'Mr. Constable has attempted something new, and he has accomplished his object' – and asserted that it was one of the few works on exhibition that would stand well with posterity.[51] While Pyne acknowledged that the painting had its detractors, he also recognised in it those qualities of originality and naturalness that Constable himself valued. Neither was Pyne alone in seeing them. In 1827, the *Morning Chronicle* said of the *Beach at Brighton, the Chain Pier in the Distance* (*fig.* 122) that it was 'a masterly performance, original as all his works are, and destined to convince the generations to come, that there are "Giants in our days"'.[52]

I must admit that I have not found a single review that commented on the role of Constable's narratives of barge life. But there are, I think, a number of reasons for this. Firstly, reviews almost never discussed the role of figures in landscapes unless they were on the scale of those of William Collins or Joshua Cristall, whose works hovered between the landscape and genre categories. Secondly, we have seen how normal such staffage of river life was; Constable's figures conformed sufficiently closely to the general type to be seemingly unnoticeable. And thirdly, we may note that in all his voluminous correspondence and statements on art, Constable himself never once discussed the role of figures or the symbolism of barge traffic. Presumably, such things seemed so obvious as to require no comment.

---

50   'Exhibition at Somerset House', *Literary Chronicle*, no. 313, 14 May 1825.

51   'Exhibition – British Gallery', *Somerset House Gazette*, no. 20, 21 February 1824.

52   'Fine Arts', *Morning Chronicle*, 12 April 1827.

Given the constraints of critical discourse in this period, it is really hard to see what more Constable could have expected from his reviewers.[53] There is every reason to think that far from finding such works incomprehensible, many contemporary critics had the conceptual equipment to make an entirely comfortable sense of the large Stour pictures. What I think can be surmised from the criticism they prompted is that sympathetic reviewers read them not as images of the artist's native ground or as scenes of his 'careless boyhood', – although that they had such associations for the artist would not have surprised them – but as generic images of a fertile, prosperous, and emphatically *English* landscape.[54] In 1822, the *New Monthly Magazine* published an essay entitled 'English Landscape' that set out a paradigm of the national scenery in which English rustic landscape was markedly different from that of other nations and had a 'peculiar character' all its own, partly taking its character from the visual effects of the enclosure of common land as well as climate and botany:

> Close high-fenced fields surrounded by trees, houses buried in shrub-beries and groves, beautiful cattle feeding among rich pasturages, and all in the smallest space, so that the eye can command them together, take a hold on the affections that an uninclosed country, large forests and immense buildings, can never attain ... The idea of comfort which they afford is an additional tie to our regard, while the smiling fertility every where visible, arising from the depth of colour in the verdure, kept fresh and fragrant, even during the height of summer, by frequent showers, and the endless variety of green in the foliage is nowhere surpassed ...[55]

Particularly notable here is the emphasis on fertility, freshness, and the pervasive greenery of English landscape, and the suggestion that it is snug and enclosing – effectively feminine – an appropriate setting for masculine seclusion and contemplation. I would conjecture that it was such fantasies of the lush English countryside as a retreat from the turmoil of the city and as a metaphor of national history and identity that Constable's pictures conjured up for his admirers; it was nothing specific to the artist's native region or biography. The increasingly painterly qualities of Constable's surfaces in the 1820s and his

---

53   My reading is very different from that of Conal Shields, 'Constable and the Critics', in Parris, Fleming-Williams, Shields 1976, pp. 13–28.

54   Although I am in broad agreement with Helsinger's argument on Constable in Helsinger 1997, I think the connection between Constable's imagery and generic ideas of rural England was already established before the Victorian period.

55   'English Landscape', *New Monthly Magazine*, 4 (1822), pp. 535–6.

turbulent atmospheric effects, which historians have seen as reflections of the artist's psychic traumas, seem to have troubled no one. If they alienated some critics, they also earned him admirers. Many critics were predisposed to value originality and some could find signs of that quality in Constable's peculiar style; for others, that style was simply a repetitive 'manner', which detracted from the otherwise sterling qualities of his works.

In sum then, the meanings of Constable's works were produced in the London exhibition rooms, not in the fields of Suffolk. Neither were they produced by the artist alone; they were produced by the uses he made of the dominant iconography and current theories of pictorial production. In saying this, I do not wish to diminish the role of Constable's intelligence in giving his art its special qualities, but I do wish to assert that its meanings cannot be properly comprehended until it is wrenched out of that reciprocally self-confirming relationship with the artist's biography into which it still seems to be locked in most scholarship devoted to him.

Postscript, 2014

When I wrote the first version of this paper in 1991 it seemed that iconography was what was most needed in Constable studies; that Constable's art would not be effectively understood as an aesthetic phenomenon unless it was treated as a problem to which the answers would be found more in the common conditions of artistic practice and less in the superabundance of the contingent biographical record. I still think this is correct, but iconography only takes us so far. Here, as in so many matters, Adorno puts the matter nicely: 'That ... to follow the course of action in a novel or drama and note the various motivations, or adequately to recognize the thematic content of a painting, does not amount to understanding the works is as obvious as that they cannot be understood apart from those aspects'.[56] While my presentation of critical responses to Constable demonstrates that these were not as barren as frequently supposed, it also indicates the limits of reception history.

If, following Adorno, one accepts that form is 'the central concept of aesthetics',[57] then one of the greatest challenges in ascertaining the truth of Constable's work is to define the significance of the major changes in his style over

---

56   Adorno 1997, p. 346. Adorno specifically affirmed the value of the iconographical researches of the Warburg School and motif studies such as Benjamin's work on Baudelaire and German baroque drama (pp. 145–6).

57   Adorno 1997, p. 141.

the four decades of his career, and, in particular the shift from the naturalism of the 1810s to the more overtly picturesque, dramatic, and abstracted character of his works of the 1820s and 1830s. Historians have proposed a number of factors to account for this, including the artist's increasing disaffection with patrons and the audience for art, the challenge of attracting notice on the crammed walls of the London exhibition rooms, personal disappointments and unhappiness, the effects of the agricultural disturbances of 1822 on his vision of his native region, and political despair over the Catholic Emancipation Act of 1829 and the parliamentary reform agitation of the 1820s and early 1830s.[58] These are all persuasive claims to a greater or lesser degree, and when they were proposed they had the merit of establishing Constable as an historical subject; but they also postulate causal explanations and do not establish meanings except within the compass of the artist's biography. Causes and meanings are not the same.

I will explain what I mean with reference to one of the most imposing of Constable's compositions of the late 1820s, *Dedham Vale* (1827–8; *fig. 94*), which was first exhibited at the Royal Academy in 1828 with the title *Landscape*, but was shown again at the British Institution with the more elaborate description *The Stour Valley, which divides the Counties of Suffolk and Essex; Dedham and Harwich Water in the distance.*[59] My guess is that Constable tried the more topographical title in 1834 in an attempt to find a buyer for a landscape of a specific place rather than a generic piece of English scenery, but if that was the case the ploy failed and the painting was in his posthumous sale four years later. The view was one he had drawn and painted repeatedly since at least 1800, and he had used the same composition in a small oil study of 1802, *Dedham from Langham* (Victoria and Albert Museum).[60] The overt reference that both 1802 study and 1828 painting make to the compositional structure of Claude's *Hagar and the Angel* (1646–7; *fig. 27*) is an art-historical commonplace. The latter work was in the collection of Constable's close friend Sir George Beaumont, who died in 1827, and Michael Rosenthal has suggested that the painting may have had a memorial function for him and was conceived as a 'riposte' to Turner's *Crossing the Brook* (1815; *fig. 95*), an earlier tribute to Claude's composition and a painting that Beaumont strongly disliked.[61] But the painting's overt old master

---

58   For these motifs, see Rosenthal 1983, Chapters 5 and 7; Bermingham 1987, pp. 136–55. Cf. Hemingway 1992, pp. 252–7.

59   For the picture's exhibition history and titles, see Parris and Fleming-Williams 1991, p. 311.

60   Rosenthal 1983, pp. 186, 188.

61   Rosenthal 1983, p. 188. Parris, Fleming-Williams, and Shields 1976 had earlier pointed out the coincidence between the work's date and Beaumont's death (p. 152). Unlike Parris

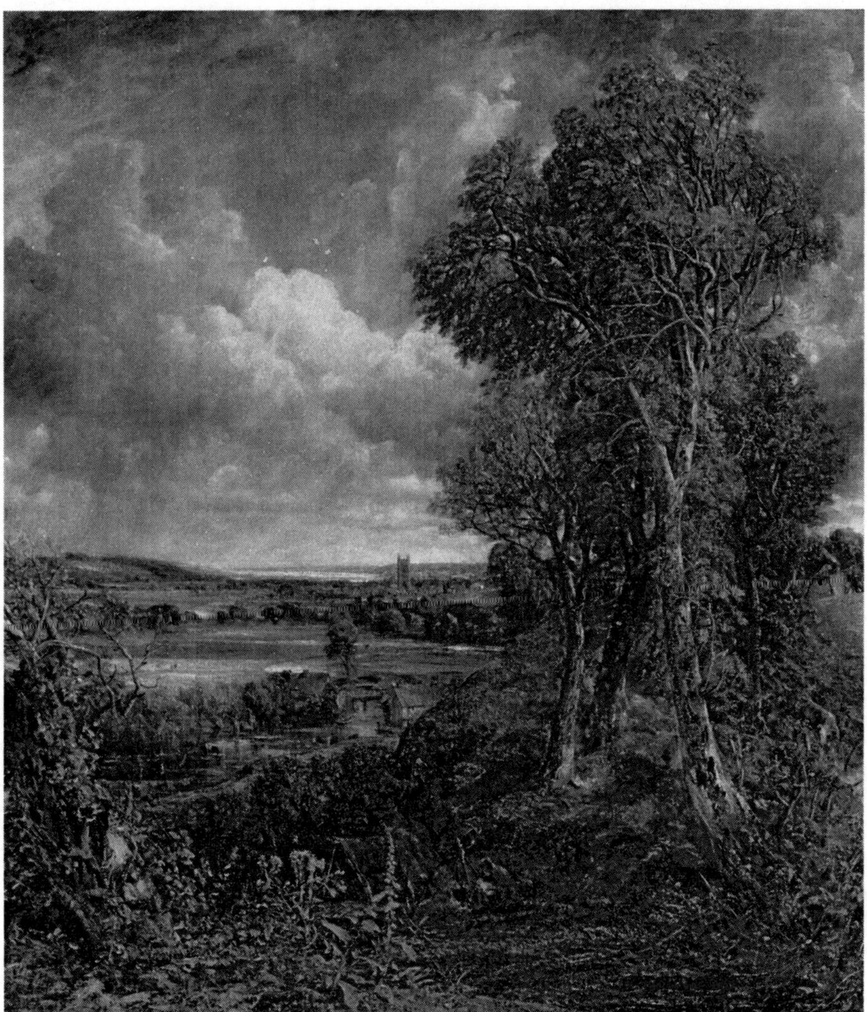

FIGURE 94   *John Constable,* Dedham Vale, *1827–8, oil on canvas, 57⅛ × 48 in (145.0 × 122.0 cm)*
NATIONAL GALLERIES OF SCOTLAND, SCOTTISH NATIONAL GALLERY

references may also have been calculated to confirm Constable's academic
credentials at a time when he was canvassing for elevation from Associate
status to full Academician.[62]

and Fleming Williams 1991, p. 311, I find Rosenthal's suggestion regarding *Crossing the
Brook* entirely plausible. For Beaumont and Turner, see Owen and Brown 1988, p. 182 and
passim.

62   Rosenthal 1987, pp. 166–7.

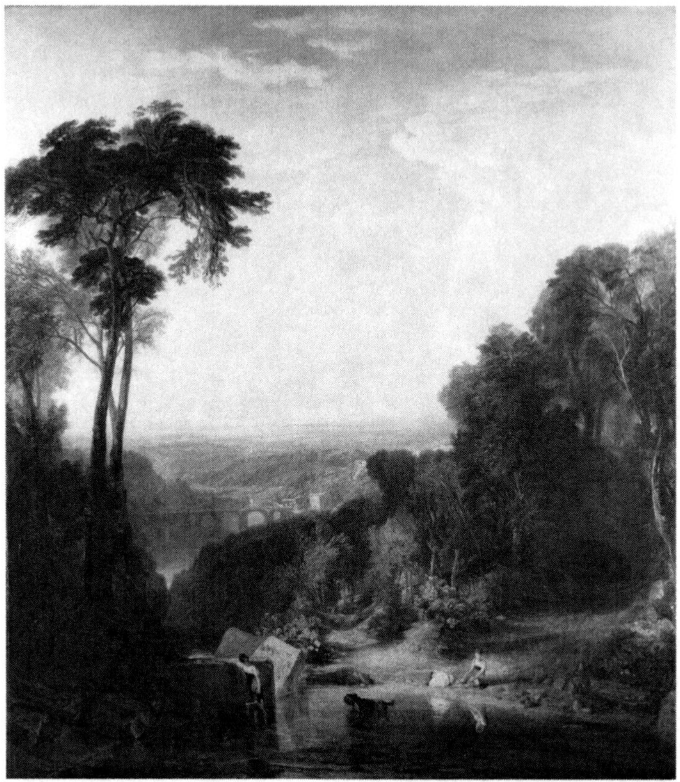

FIGURE 95   *J.M.W. Turner,* Crossing the Brook, *exh. 1815, oil on canvas,*
76 × 65 in (193.0 × 165.1 cm), Tate Britain
© TATE, LONDON, 2015

These are important insights and Rosenthal's 1983 monograph is the most profound interpretation of Constable's work published so far. But his observations on the meaning of *Deham Vale* are disappointing: 'Constable did not state what he intended with this picture. We may guess at a continuing concern with lightness, breezes, and freshness ... He was probably still hoping to evoke abstracted sensations through pictorial suggestion, and in attempting this Constable had developed this emotionally expressive style'.[63] Elsewhere he has written that 'to understand the intricacies of this picture, we need to know a great deal about Constable himself'.[64] But this is precisely what we do not need more of. And in fact Rosenthal overlooks the tools for interpretation he already has.

---

63   Rosenthal 1983, p. 190.
64   Rosenthal 1987, p. 167.

The meanings of *Dedham Vale* lie partly in the iconography and partly in the incongruities of the painting's form and style. The contrast with Turner's *Crossing the Brook* is instructive in this regard. Turner adapts Claude's compositional scheme but reverses the right-left asymmetry, elevates the viewpoint, and gives a grand sunlit vista of the Tamar Valley in Devon. The view is like an epitome of the beautiful in landscape. Turner injects the Claudean format with a naturalistic plenitude, but makes Devon look more part of the Mediterranean world than southwest Britain. Although he keeps Turner's elevated perspective vista, Constable's riposte rights the composition and in answer to *Crossing the Brook's* atmosphere of sunlit splendour he adopted an autumnal colour range that is the epitome of the picturesque. This is not only a reply to Turner's painting, it is a comment on its prototype – a declaration that Claudean ideal landscapes do not provide an appropriate model for English landscape, with its northern light and changeable weather. The poetic currency of the contrast can be grasped from Cowper's *The Task*, where he writes,

> England, with all thy faults, I love thee still

and continues, after a few lines

> Though thy clime
> Be fickle, and thy year most part deform'd
> With dripping rains, or wither'd by a frost,
> I would not yet exchange thy sullen skies,
> And fields without a flow'r, for warmer France
> With all her vines; nor for Ausonia's groves
> Of golden fruitage, and her myrtle bow'rs.[65]

(Ausonia refers to southern Italy.) Where Turner coloured English landscape like a brighter and more verdant Claude, Constable coloured it like Ruisdael and Rembrandt. Where Turner has a classical bridge in the distance, Constable has the gothic tower of Dedham church and his landscape is spattered with the red tile roofs of English vernacular building. Where Turner has two comely young women with bundles of laundry, Constable has a gypsy woman nursing a baby by the smoky fire that heats her cooking pot.

Unless we count some cattle grazing on the water meadows, there are scant signs of agricultural prosperity in *Dedham Vale*. Moreover, the colours of the

---

65   Cowper 1926, Book 2, l. 206, 209–14.

picturesque are those of rot and decay. Rather than signs of tillage, the foreground is filled with weeds and a dead tree trunk, which figures like a *mememto mori*.[66] This is not qualified by the solitary cow exploring the hedgerow to the right of the foreground trees, nor by the distant cottage above it. These seem like mere tokens of a lost rustic ideal, windswept fragments from a different kind of composition. Rosenthal has, I think correctly, associated the gypsy with the precedent of Gainsborough,[67] but Gainsborough's gypsies have a very different character. Whereas in the latter's *Gypsy Encampment, Sunset* (c. 1778–80; *fig. 96*) gypsies seem a kind of cheerful natural humanity gathered in a sociable group under the shelter of trees in some remote wild region, Constable's solitary figure seems an outcast huddled for shelter in an inhospitable and damp hollow, confined to the margins of a modern commercial and agricultural world. One is reminded again of Cowper's *The Task*:

> A vagabond and useless tribe there eat
> Their miserable meal. A kettle, slung
> Between two poles upon a stick traverse,
> Receives the morsel – flesh obscene of dog.
> Or vermin, or, at best, of cock purloin'd
> From his accustom'd perch. Hard faring race!
> They pick their fuel out of ev'ry hedge,
> Which kindles with dry leaves, just saves unquench'd
> The spark of life.[68]

Constable's image seems loaded with this kind of social revulsion, the opposite of Gainsborough's romantic idealisation.

As a synecdoche of the national landscape – and it was surely conceived as such – *Dedham Vale* is an extraordinary bleak and dissonant work. Such landscapes were generally riant sunlit views like Turner's *Crossing the Brook* or George Vincent's *Distant View of Pevensey Bay, the Landing Place of King William the Conqueror* (1824; *fig. 97*);[69] they were not essays in fatalistic moralising. For

---

66   Bermingham 1987, pp. 150–1, has developed this point.

67   Rosenthal, 1987, p. 167. I cannot agree with Graham Reynolds that the gypsy is a concession to the picturesque – the motif is too ideologically loaded for that. See Reynolds 1986, vol. 1, p. 190.

68   Cowper 1926, Book 1, l. 557–66. Dedham Vale was listed in Constable's posthumous sale as 'View of Dedham, Suffolk; *Gipsies in the foreground Exhibited* 1828' – Parris and Fleming-Williams 1991, p. 311.

69   For Vincent's painting, see Hemingway 1992, pp. 297–9.

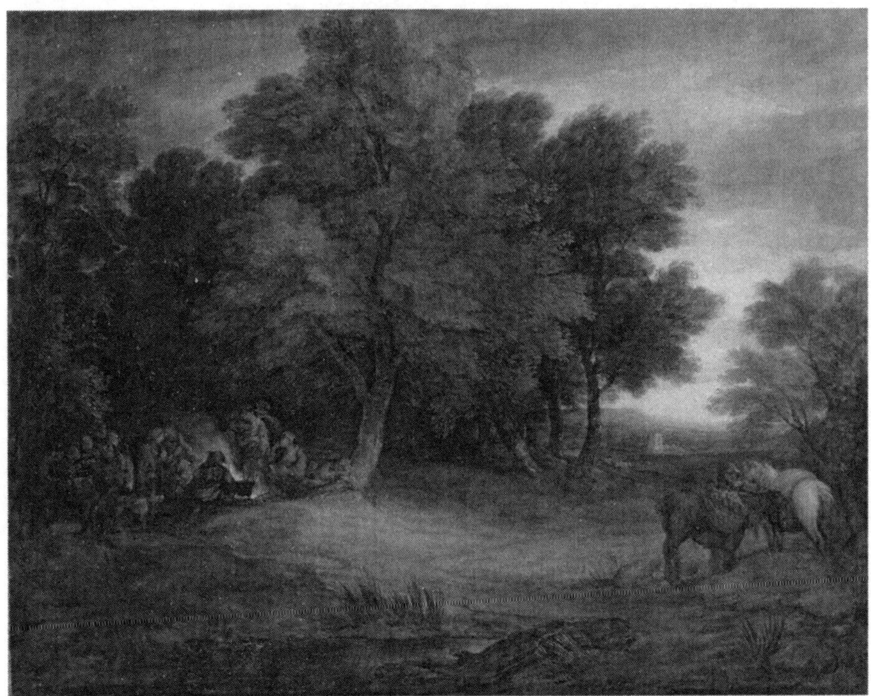

FIGURE 96   *Thomas Gainsborough,* Gypsy Encampment, Sunset, *c. 1778–80, oil on canvas, 47½*
× 59¼ in (120.6×150.5 cm), Tate Britain
© TATE, LONDON, 2015

this, surely, is also what *Dedham Vale* is. How else are we to interpret the relationship between the dead tree that is the nearest object, the church tower that
is the central focus of the composition, and the grandiose sky that speaks of the
power of the creator? One could even speak about the painting's Anglicanism
in its implicit conjunction of natural theology and the emblem of the established church. But it is not only the lowering, sombre tone, the picturesque
colouring, or the iconographic details that make the picture seem so discordant, it is also the way these features are jammed together within the format
of the Claudean ideal landscape. Constable took a style saturated in assertive middle-class subjectivity and subordinates it to the classical order of the
ideal Claudean composition in the interests of nationalistic Englishness. But
the concoction is fundamentally unstable and the style overwhelms the formal
structure. We need to get past our familiarity with the picture and recognise
the sheer strangeness and incongruity of what Constable has done here.

A comparison with Sir George Beaumont's *Wooded Landscape with Gypsies* of perhaps 1800 (*fig. 98*) helps make the point. The upright structure

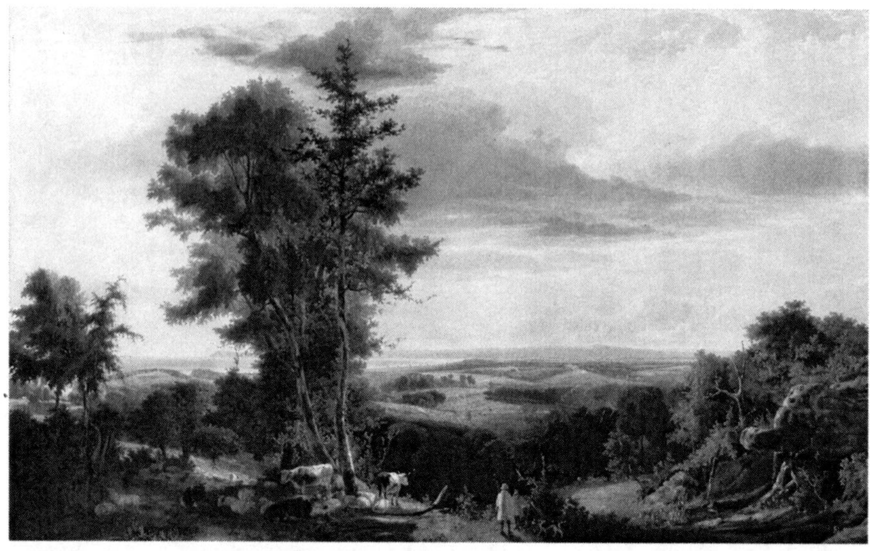

FIGURE 97   *George Vincent,* A Distant View of Pevensey Bay, the Landing Place of King William the Conqueror, *1824, oil on canvas, 57 ½ × 92 in (146.1 × 233.6 cm)* NORFOLK MUSEUMS SERVICES (NORWICH CASTLE MUSEUM AND ART GALLERY)

with trees framing a distance is similar, but whereas Beaumont's trees are all embracing of the gypsy figures ('embowering' would be the contemporary term) Constable's hedgerow is broken up to expose its diminutive figure. In Beaumont's painting the evening sky promises tranquillity and rest, in Constable's the atmosphere suggests not dewy freshness but the prospect of a bone-chilling drenching. Beaumont's technique subdues the picturesque into harmonious breadth, in *Dedham Vale* Constable's manner of 'bespotting with blanc d'argent, or white wash-splashing' produces an effect of discord that matches with the roiling masses of rain clouds. In effect, Constable took the harmonious structure of the classical landscape tradition and substituted for Claude's effulgent Italianate glow the turbulent sky of Ruisdael's Holland. Pastoral plenitude yields to Burkean angst. Such novelties could only imply disharmony.

As Adorno memorably puts it: 'What crackles in artworks is the sound of the friction of the antagonistic elements that the artwork seeks to unify'.[70] It is the scale of that friction in *Dedham Vale* that marks Constable's achievement.

---

70   Adorno 1977, p. 177.

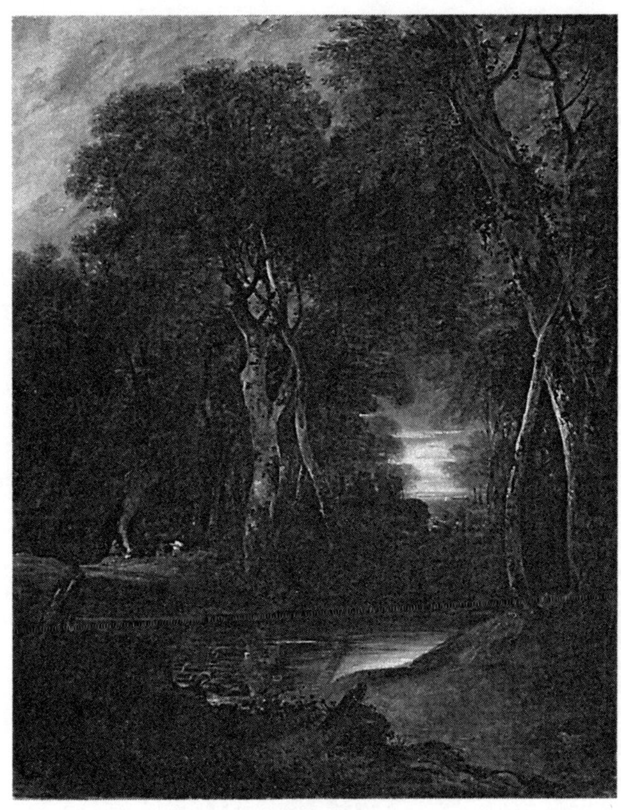

FIGURE 98
*George Howland
Beaumont,* Woodland
Scene with Gypsies,
*1779–1800, oil on canvas,
35½ × 27⅝ in
(90.0 × 70.0 cm)*
© ASHMOLEAN
MUSEUM, UNIVERSITY
OF OXFORD

The Field of Waterloo Exposed: Turner, Byron, and the Politics of Reaction

The importance of Byron's poetry for understanding aspects of Turner's art, and particularly the iconography of his Italian subjects, has been a recurrent motif in scholarship on the artist.[1] In 1992 the Tate Gallery devoted an exhibition to the connection accompanied with an exemplary catalogue by David Blayney Brown.[2] I am greatly indebted to the scholarship of Brown, John Gage, and others. However, interpretation to date has overlooked or ignored the yawning gulf between the experience and culture of peer and commoner. This leads to the question that prompted this essay. Namely, what did it mean for the plebeian painter to associate himself – as he sometimes did – with the outlook of a lord of notably controversial political, moral, and religious views – 'a mortal enemy to all martial exertions, a scoffer at the fair sex, and apparently disposed to consider all religions as different modes of superstition'?[3] Could a mere painter ventriloquize such a poet writing in his most scandalous vein in the reactionary climate of the postwar years? I will develop my theme through a consideration of three paintings: *The Field of Waterloo* (1818), *England: Richmond Hill on the Prince Regent's Birthday* (1819), and *George IV at St Giles's, Edinburgh* (1822).

To say that Byron and Turner came from vastly different social worlds is an understatement. Turner was the son of a London barber and had limited formal education. Byron was a peer, acutely self-conscious about his ancestry and aristocratic status.[4] He was educated at Harrow and Cambridge before taking a somewhat unorthodox Grand Tour in Portugal, Spain, Greece, and Albania. Unlike his best-known Romantic contemporaries, he wrote in the public voice of Augustan poetry. For him the declining status of his idol Alexander Pope was an index of the degeneracy of poetry in his own day and he saw the

---

1 A landmark in studies on this theme is Gage 1981 See also Gage 1987, pp. 50–52, 54–6, 210.

2 Brown 1992.

3 George Ellis, unsigned review of cantos 1 and 2 of *Childe Harold*, in Rutherford (ed.) 1970, p. 47. Although describing Harold, the text clearly associates these views with his creator.

4 This is a repeated theme in his friend Thomas Moore's biography (Moore 1830) and Moore opens his narrative by commenting on his friend's aristocratic worldview. Compare vol. 2, p. 650.

Lake and Cockney Schools as far inferior to more conservative poets such as Samuel Rogers and Crabbe. Of the Cockney School he wrote: 'The grand distinction of the under forms of the new school of poets is their *vulgarity*. By this I do not mean that they are *coarse*, but shabby genteel, as it is termed'.[5] So much for Keats, whose poetry Byron despised for the most part. In turn, it is not surprising that Hazlitt found *Childe Harold* just too self-indulgently aristocratic.[6]

Although Turner was a public figure through his position at the Royal Academy, he was notoriously reclusive about his private life and his domestic arrangements remain obscure.[7] His plebeian manners and speech did not prevent him from mixing with country house society, but his talk could be opaque and at times he seemed to struggle for words.[8] Correspondingly, his letters are mainly brief, and for the most part tell us little about his emotions and attitudes.[9] If not loquacious, Byron was a charmer. His correspondence was enormous and a highly edited selection from it and his journals became available in Thomas Moore's 'official' biography six years after his death.[10] It often appears, at least, to be profoundly self-revelatory.

Byron lived out his private life in the public gaze and was the object of an intense prurient curiosity that cannot be separated from his lordly rank, which was central to both his success and his notoriety. *Childe Harold* was the first celebrity work of poetry, but its authorial voice and central character were distinctly aristocratic, as its inappropriately faux medieval title suggested.[11] Despite the author's own protests to the contrary, there was a constant tendency to confuse Byron with his characters,[12] from the jaded aristocrat of *Childe Harold*

---

5   Moore 1830, vol. 2, p. 477.

6   Hazlitt on *Childe Harold's Pilgrimage*, Canto 4, from *Yellow Dwarf*, 2 May 1818, in Rutherford (ed.) 1970, p. 132.

7   The most revealing discussion of his private life I am aware of is Golt 1989.

8   Thornbury 1904, pp. 269–70.

9   His first biography – Thornbury's *Life* of 1862 (Thornbury 1904) – could not use letters in the way Moore's biography of Byron did because there were so few and they were so unrevealing.

10   Official in the sense that both Byron and his publisher John Murray expected him to write it and provided him with the materials. In this essay I have deliberately drawn on Moore's biography rather than the modern edition of the correspondence because Turner owned the book.

11   The poem's Spenserian stanzas added to the effect of anachronism, as George Ellis noted in his hostile review in the *Quarterly*, reprinted in Rutherford (ed.) 1970, p. 45.

12   "For an astute contemporary comment on the slipperiness of Byron's position on this matter, see again Ellis's review, Rutherford (ed.) 1970, pp. 44–5.

through the demonic heroes of *The Giaour* and *The Corsair*, and finally that wandering nobleman-lover and refracting mirror of the *Zeitgeist, Don Juan*. By contrast, it seems that Turner the thinking individual remained invisible behind his paintings and they did not excite curiosity about his character and opinions, or none of which we have a record.

While Byron took his seat in the House of Lords he did not live like a traditional peer. Peter Cochran described him suggestively as a bourgeois aristocrat and observed that 'as a landed aristocrat he barely existed'.[13] Despite occasional professions of fondness for the ancestral home at Newstead Abbey in his letters, he was not interested in the duties of a great landowner. He sold Newstead in 1817 after the scandal around his failed marriage finally determined him to live in mainland Europe, an inclination that had already formed during his first visit to the Mediterranean. He never returned to Britain and derived his main income from investment in government funds. In Italy he lived as if he were on a permanent Grand Tour.

It was part of Byron's aristocratic style that up until 1816 when financial exigencies changed his tune, he publicly disdained all financial reward for his poems from his publisher John Murray, despite their extraordinary success.[14] In 1814 after the Tory paper *The Courier* accused him of having '"received and pocketed" large sums' for his work, he expostulated to his friend Dallas: 'I have never yet received, nor wished to receive, a farthing for any'.[15] Cochran has shown that it was precisely at this moment in 1814 that Byron became a shrewd and hard bargainer with Murray for the copyright to his works.[16] Yet the appearance of financial nonchalance remained a sensitive issue in Byron's lifetime.[17] Although he could be personally generous, Turner was a notoriously canny

---

13   Cochran 2011, p. 28.

14   The first print run of *Childe Harold*, Cantos 1 and 2, sold out in three days and went through ten editions by 1815. (Cochrane 2011, p. 86, Rutherford [ed.] 1970, p. 5). *The Corsair* sold 10,000 copies on the first day of publication. Rutherford (ed.) 1970, p. 5.

15   Without consulting Byron, Dallas wrote to another Tory paper, the *Morning Post*, to protest *The Courier*'s calumny. George Byron to Robert Charles Dallas, 17 February 1814, and Dallas, 'To the Editor of the Morning Post', in Moore 1830, vol. 1, pp. 531–3.

16   Cochran 2011, Chapter 4.

17   In 1823, responding to the poet's description of those critics who attacked *Don Juan* for irreligion and Jacobinism as 'hirelings', the deeply conservative paper *John Bull* replied: 'LORD BYRON is a hireling – a hireling of MR. JOHN MURRAY'S, who pays him for his work as regularly as he pays his shoemaker or his taylor [sic] with the profits of that work again'. Review of *Don Juan*, VI–VIII from *John Bull*, 20 July 1823, reprinted in Reiman 1972, Part B, vol. 1, p. 1220.

businessman, who amassed considerable wealth partly through his astute deal-
ings with engravers and publishers.[18] Unlike Byron, he did not disdain the
appearance of trade.

Byron qualified as a political actor simply through his accession to the
peerage. But although he made three speeches on liberal causes in the Lords
in 1812–13 he quickly tired of what he called 'parliamentary mummeries'.[19] As
Malcolm Kelsall has comprehensively demonstrated,[20] his political utterances
were shaped for the most part by the discourse of Foxite Whiggism. However, he
was not a systematic political thinker and his Whig 'Republicanism' strained to
accommodate the new European political order that emerged in the aftermath
of the French Revolution and ensuing decades of war. While he admired the
Dutch and American Revolutions – Washington was his political ideal – he had
no sense of the emergent notion of bourgeois revolution.[21] Or no sympathetic
sense anyway. He detested plebeian radicals such as Cobbett and Orator Hunt,
and although he thought some constitutional change was necessary he recoiled
from any idea of revolutionary violence that might threaten his aristocratic
friends or indeed patrician privilege.[22]

While he may have been taunting his conservative publisher Murray when
he described himself as a 'Jacobin', Byron was consistent in his anti-monarchi-
cal stance and his longing for a 'universal republic'.[23] He had been an open
admirer of Napoleon since his schooldays and although he was disappointed by
Bonaparte's imperial play-acting and his abdication in 1814, he was electrified
by the Hundred Days and open in his loathing for the victorious Allies.[24] He

---

18   Thornbury's *Life* (Thornbury 1904) includes a chapter on 'The Business Man'. For his trans-
      actions with engravers and publishers, see also George Jones, 'Recollections of
      J.M.W. Turner', in Gage 1980, p. 2.

19   From 'Journal, Begun November 14, 1813', in Moore 1830, vol. 1, p. 437.

20   Kelsall 1987 and Kelsall 2004.

21   Moore 1830, vol. 1, p. 449. For Byron's judgment on the French Revolution, see *Childe
      Harold*, Canto 3, LXXXII. On the emergent theory of bourgeois revolution in the thinking
      of Burke and James Mackintosh (a figure Byron hugely admired), see Davidson 2012,
      Chapter 6.

22   Kelsall 1987, pp. 82–7. Cochran gives an excellent account of his inconsistency in this area,
      in Cochran 2011, pp. 23–8.

23   George Byron to John Murray, 21 April 1814, in Moore 1830, vol. 1, p. 545; George Byron
      to John Murray, 8 January 1814; 'Extracts from a Diary of Lord Byron, 1821', vol. 2, p. 399.
      Compare vol. 2, p. 408: 'The king-times are fast finishing'.

24   For an important statement of his republicanism and his disappointment with Bonaparte,
      see Moore 1830, vol. 1, pp. 448–9. For Napoleon's significance for Byron, see Cochran 2011,
      pp. 11–12.

regarded the Prince of Wales with contempt and Byron's social ostracism began with the publication in 1812 of his *Lines to a Lady Weeping*, which paid tribute to the Prince's rebellious daughter Princess Charlotte and derided her father for turning against the Whigs once he became Regent.[25] Not surprisingly, he regularly expressed sympathy for Queen Caroline.[26] He also supported Leigh and John Hunt over their libel of the Prince and visited Leigh Hunt in jail. However, although Byron overcame his aversion to what he regarded as Hunt's literary 'vulgarity' sufficiently to support him and his brother in putting out the short-lived quarterly *The Liberal*[27]– and he used the notoriously radical John Hunt as his publisher after the tenor of *Don Juan* got too much for the Tory Murray – Byron's political sympathies were constrained by his deep sense of patrician identity.

As Jack Lindsay observed of Turner long ago, 'no party label has any meaning in connection with him'.[28] In any case, it was not one of the recognised social functions of artists to take positions on political issues in the way it was for peers. Whatever his views were, Turner seems to have been discreet about them, as he maintained friendly relations with powerful patrons of radically different political affiliations.[29] This does not mean that his works have no political meanings, but that they are meanings that derive from formal and thematic inflections or the particular occasions on which they were exhibited.[30]

Now to Turner's works. In 1798, the Royal Academy passed a resolution allowing exhibitors to attach quotations to the titles of their submissions. Turner immediately took advantage of this opportunity and over the next 20 years appended quotations to some works taken from the Bible, Milton, the

---

25   Moore 1830, vol. 1, pp. 526, 530, 549. For the sad history of Princess Charlotte, see Parissien 2001, Chapter 11.

26   For Byron on Queen Caroline, see Moore 1830, vol. 2, pp. 341, 344, 345, 359, 378, 382–4, 517, 519. On the significance of the Affair in the context of Byron's politics, see Kelsall 1987, pp. 87–90.

27   For Byron on Leigh Hunt's vulgarity as a writer, see Moore 1830. Vol. 1, pp. 176–7. For his feelings towards the Hunts and the deterioration of his relationship with Leigh, see vol. 2, pp. 606, 621–2, 623–36, 629–30, 634. For Byron and Hunt, see also Roe 2005, *passim*.

28   Lindsay 1966, p. 141.

29   Gage 1987, pp. 212–13.

30   I agree with Leo Costello's characterisation of Turner as 'a conflicted, contradictory, ambivalent subject, a site of compelling and provocative heterogeneity rather than cohesion and unity'. See Costello 2012, pp. 1–2. Another important contribution to this theme is Smiles 2007/8.

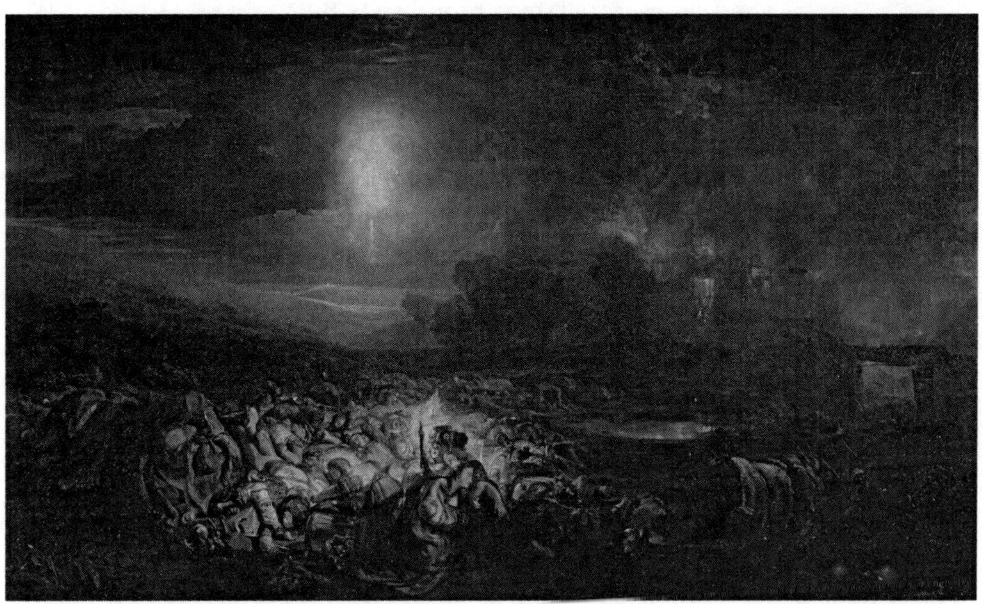

FIGURE 99   *J.M.W. Turner,* The Field of Waterloo, *exh. 1818, oil on canvas, 58×94 in
(147.3×238.8 cm), Tate Britain*
© TATE, LONDON, 2015

classics, and eighteenth-century poets as well some verses of his own.[31] Byron
was the first contemporary poet whose verses he drew from.

Turner's first coupling of his art with Byron's poetry was the nine-line quotation from Canto 3 of *Childe Harold* that he used to accompany the catalogue
entry to *The Field of Waterloo* (*fig. 99*), which he exhibited at the Royal Academy
in 1818:[32]

> Last noon beheld them full of lusty life,
> Last eve in Beauty's circle proudly gay,
> The midnight brought the signal-sound of strife,
> The morn the marshalling in arms, – the day,
> Battle's magnificently stern array!
> The thunder-clouds close o'er it, which when rent
> The earth is cover'd thick with other clay,

---

31   The most detailed and sophisticated discussion of Turner's use of poetry is Wilton 1990.
     But see also the review by Barry Venning – Venning 1990 (2). Still useful is Ziff 1982.

32   For earlier analyses of the painting, to which I am indebted, see Bachrach 1981; Brown 1992,
     pp. 29–32, 92; Costello 2012, pp. 84–93.

> Which her own clay shall cover, heap'd and pent,
> Rider and horse – friend, foe, – in one red burial blent!

While it has been suggested that some of Turner's quotations probably came as an afterthought,[33] the passage that accompanies *The Field of Waterloo* seems not just perfectly matched to the image but likely a pattern for it. This is not because we can see the picture as an illustration of the lines as such, but rather because it serves so convincingly as an emblem of the larger narrative that frames them. This narrative moves from the night revelry of 'Beauty' and 'Chivalry' in Brussels on the eve of the battle – that is to say the Duchess of Richmond's Ball, although this is not named as such[34] – through the carnage of combat and the fall of thousands to the earth of which they will now become part, to the enduring grief that follows it. The lines Turner quoted are themselves a condensation of the message of the 24 stanzas from XXI to XXXV, which contain scarcely any description of the battle itself and focus above all on distress of parting and the sorrow that follows the battle's ending. Throughout the whole sequence Byron's theme is primarily the emotions of love, desire, and loss, on 'tears and Breaking hearts' (XXX). Five stanzas alone concern the unquenchable nature of grief (XXXI–XXXV). Conventional tributes to martial virtues and patriotism have no place here; all the emphasis is on existential emotions. In selecting stanza XXVIII Turner made an extremely astute choice. At the same time, he produced a picture that was original to the point of bizarre and perplexed or disgusted contemporary critics.[35]

To understand the impact of Turner's *Field of Waterloo* we need to place it in relation to other images that memorialised British military victories in the public exhibition spaces of the capital. In 1815 the British Institution had awarded premiums to battle paintings by Denis Dighton, Military Painter to the Prince Regent, and the Suffolk amateur the Reverend Perry Nursey,[36] and it determined that it would disburse 1,000 guineas for finished sketches three feet by four foot six inches 'illustrative of or connected with the successes of the British Army in Spain, Portugal, and France'.[37] On the 18 July – a month

---

33   Brown 1992, pp. 29, 37, 94, 95. Two use the same passage from Canto 4, XXVII.

34   Hibbert 1997, pp. 171–2.

35   David Blayney Brown notes the profound consonance between Turner's painting and Byron's poem in Brown 1992, pp. 30–31.

36   Denis Dighton, *The Storming of Saint Sebastian* (National Trust for Scotland, Leith Hall Garden and Estate); Perry Nursey, *The Duke of Wellington attacking the rearguard of Marshall Soult's Army* (whereabouts unknown). For Dighton, see Carman 1965.

37   Smith 1860, pp. 69–73.

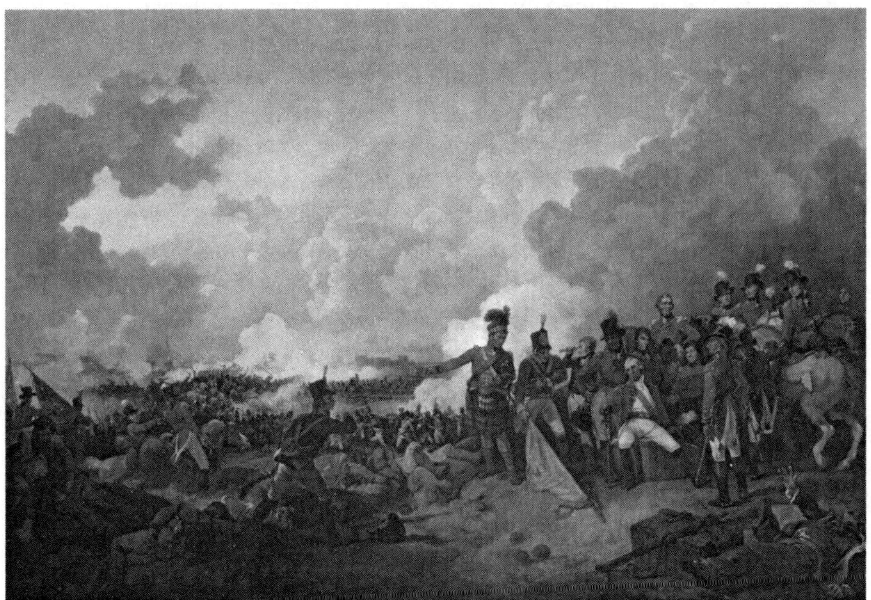

FIGURE 100 *Philippe Jacques de Loutherbourg,* The Battle of Alexandria, 21 March 1801, *1802, oil on canvas, 42 × 60 in (106.6 × 152.6 cm)*
PURCHASED 1986, NATIONAL GALLERIES OF SCOTLAND, SCOTTISH NATIONAL PORTRAIT GALLERY

after the British and Prussian victory at Waterloo – the directors announced that they would also receive sketches representing that battle or the entry of the British and Prussian armies into Paris.[38] They received sixteen sketches in all, of which thirteen represented Waterloo.

The prime objective of the British Institution was to foster a native school of history painting, a goal that did not sit comfortably with the commemoration of contemporary military victories since many pictures of such events fell outside that genre.[39] Although modern-dress history paintings of the type developed by Benjamin West and John Singleton Copley continued to be exhibited and seem to have enjoyed popularity, they were rivalled by topographical views of battlefields with identifiable portraits in the foreground, of which the most accomplished practitioner was de Loutherbourg until his decease in 1812. His *Battle of Alexandria, 21 March 1801 (fig. 100)*,[40] which depicts the death of Gen-

---

38   For the competition, see Hichberger 1988, pp. 14–28; Harrington 1993, pp. 99–102.

39   Harrington 1993, pp. 95, 102. Hichberger has referred to 'the form and practice' of battle painting in the post-Waterloo period as 'unresolved' (Hichberger 1988, p. 28).

40   On the several paintings on this theme, see Harrington 1993, pp. 79–85.

eral Abercromby surrounded by staff officers, is a typical example. Such paintings were a development from a seventeenth-century type, and most notably the work of the Flemish painter Adam Franz van der Meulen, battle painter to Louis XIV – a painter popular with the Prince Regent who bought a number of his works.[41] What was novel about the British variant in the years around 1800 was the new emphasis on topographical accuracy and the provision of keys to identify the personages depicted, a pretense to what we might call anachronistically documentary accuracy.[42] Such works were quite at odds with the timeless ideal realm and emphasis on acts of individual virtue that defined history painting and it is striking that no major history painters contributed to the 1816 competition.

Given that their goal was to promote High Art, the Directors gave the 1000 guineas prize to the picture that came closest to that idiom, namely the animal painter James Ward's pseudo-Rubensian *Battle of Waterloo in an Allegory* (*fig. 101*), a crowded image of Wellington in the 'car of war' accompanied by Britannia and the cardinal virtues, Victory, the Angel of Divine Providence, and the dove of peace. It was a work so complex that it had to be accompanied by a long catalogue entry containing a key to its symbolism. The Directors commissioned the artist to make a large-scale version of the design, 21 by 25 feet, for 1000 guineas, which they presented to the Royal Hospital at Chelsea – although when the canvas finally reached the site it was found to be too large for the architectural space.[43] In a pamphlet Ward published to accompany the painting when it was displayed at a fee-paying exhibition in Egyptian Hall on Piccadilly, he claimed that it would combat infidelity and an unspecified 'demoniacal frenzy' that was clearly a reference to recently exposed insurrectionary plans and continuing reform agitation.[44] At one level, his allegory can be seen as a pictorial riposte to the masque in Leigh Hunt's *Descent of Liberty* of 1815.[45] But the Egyptian Hall exhibition was a fiasco and so few subscribers for an engraving were attracted that the project had to be abandoned, perhaps a measure of Wellington's unpopularity.

---

41   Parissien 2011, p. 196.

42   A notable example of this is Thomas Heaphy's *Field Marshall the Duke of Wellington Giving Orders to his Generals Previous to a General Action*. Heaphy accompanied the army in the Peninsular Campaign and his picture contained more than fifty portraits. Sitters paid the artist 50 guineas to be included. See Harrington 1993, p. 93.

43   Hichberger 1988, pp. 20–23.

44   'that torrent of infidelity which has in so remarkable a degree manifested a demoniacal frenzy in our own, as well as in a neighbouring nation'. Ward 1821, p. 4.

45   Hunt 1815. On this work, see Roe 2005, 215–16, 221–2.

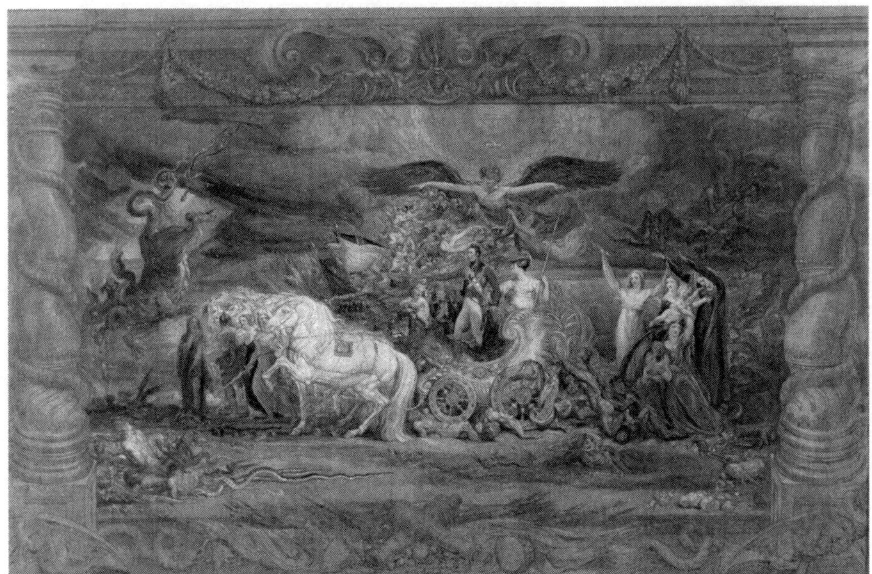

FIGURE 101 *James Ward*, Battle of Waterloo in an Allegory, *1816, 35½ × 52 in (90.0 × 132.0 cm)*,
oil on canvas
© ROYAL CHELSEA HOSPITAL, UK/BRIDGEMAN IMAGES

The Directors gave a second prize of 500 guineas to George Jones, who
exhibited two sketches of the battle of Waterloo based on interviews with the
headquarters' staff and on the spot studies of the terrain (*fig. 102*). The son of
a highly-regarded mezzotint engraver, Jones had entered the Royal Academy
schools in 1801 at the age of fifteen, but he had also served for seven years in the
army. He combined skills as a topographical artist with a detailed knowledge
of military life. At some point, although not perhaps yet, he became in Walter
Thornbury's words 'a special crony and comrade' of Turner's.[46] Press responses
to the 1816 exhibition were generally quite negative.[47] Even the deeply Tory

---

46   Thornbury 1904, p. 323. Although the first recorded contact between them did not occur
      until 1824 it seems unlikely they had not met before. For Jones more generally, see Hich-
      berger 1983 and Harrington 1989.

47   E.g., 'British Gallery', *The Champion*, no. 161, 4 February 1816; no. 162, 11 February 1816. *The
      Examiner* and the *Times* both complained about the overall low standard of the show.
      See 'British Institution', *Examiner*, no. 424, 18 February 1816; 'British Institution', *Times*,
      3 February 1816. I am unconvinced by Hichberger's argument that there was some general
      resistance to battle painting and that the definition of history painting had not broadened
      to include battles in modern dress as it had in France (Hichberger 1988, pp. 15, 13). As

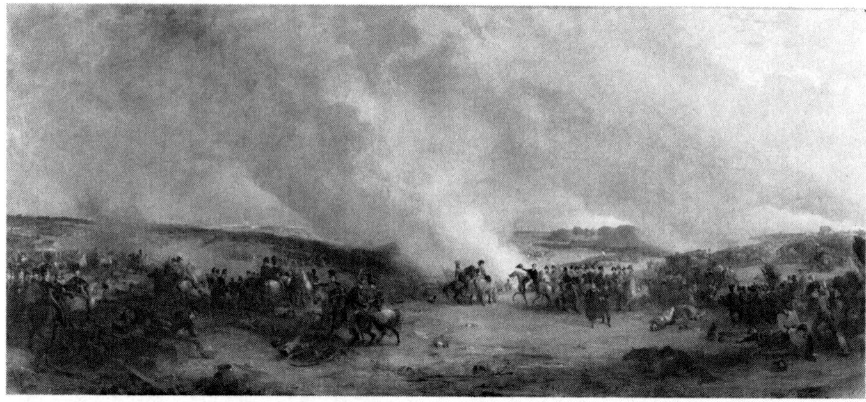

FIGURE 102 *George Jones*, The Battle of Waterloo, *1816–20, 119¾ × 165¾ (304.0 × 421.0 cm), oil on canvas*
© THE CROWN ESTATE/BRIDGEMAN IMAGES

Morning Post limited itself to praise for mere exactitude.[48] This reminds us that while images of battle may have been popular with a wide public – and the large output of paintings and prints suggests they were – they had an ambiguous place in the hierarchy of genres and were not seen by most critics as 'elevated' art. This did not discourage specialists such as Jones and Denis Dighton (who got no prize in 1816) as both continued to exhibit large pictures of Waterloo and other battles in the years following

In the absence of prizes for battle scenes, such images were less prominent at the Royal Academy. Dighton's contribution to Somerset House in 1818 was a painting of the death of the son of Russian general Matvei Platov in a cavalry engagement, while Jones merely showed a portrait of the favorite pony of a Mrs. Dalrymple. Even so, Turner's picture obtruded with what seemed, to many critics, a false and confusing note. The *Annals of the Fine Arts*, the only specialist magazine of arts at the time, remarked tartly of the *Field of Waterloo*: 'Before we referred to the catalogue, we really thought this was the representation of a drunken hubbub on illumination night, and the host as far gone as his scuffling and scrambling guests, was, with his dame and kitchen wenches looking with torches for a lodger, and wondering what the matter was'.[49] Similarly dismissive

---

    she herself observes, the market for military prints and panoramas was thriving (pp. 13); moreover Harrington 1997 shows there were far more ambitious experiments in battle painting in the 1790s and early 1800s than her account would suggest.

48   'British Institution, No. 11', *Morning Post*, 7 February 1816.

49   'Exhibition of the Royal Academy', *Annals of the Fine Arts*, 3 (1818), p. 299. Quoted in Butlin

comments appeared in the *Literary Chronicle* and the *New Monthly Magazine*.[50] While suggesting the same sense of confusion, the *Repository of Arts* offered a more perceptive response which I will quote only in part. The title, it observed, 'gives the name to the picture, which the subject, in the manner it is handled, would not suggest to the spectator. It is more an allegorical representation of the 'battle's magnificently stern array' than any actual delineation of a particular battle; indeed, the allegory may represent a civil conflict of any kind'. 'The group in the centre depicts the merciless carnage of war, and its ravages in domestic life of both sexes and all ages which lie in a mingled heap'.[51]

Although at 58 × 94 inches it was on the scale of a modern battle painting, the *Repository*'s critic was correct in stating that *The Field of Waterloo* is not a battle painting. Rather it was an another instance of Turner's endeavour to use the genre of landscape painting to picture that new concept of a plebeian historical subject, who was plural and whose death and sacrifice came in multiples, which he had already addressed in such notable works as *The Battle of Trafalgar* (1806–8, Tate Gallery) and the *Wreck of a Transport Ship* (1805–10, Calouste Gulbenkian Foundation, Lisbon), as Leo Costello has so ably argued.[52]

Like Jones and others, Turner had researched the site carefully, visiting the battlefield on Saturday 16 August 1817 as numerous British tourists had done before him.[53] He took as his guide Charles Campbell's *Travellers' Complete Guide through Belgium and Holland*, which in a chapter headed 'A Walk over the Field of Battle at Waterloo' printed quotations from the Waterloo poems of Southey and Scott, as well as Canto XXIV from *Childe Harold*. Campbell gives graphic descriptions of the carnage left by the battle in which approximately 47,000 were killed or wounded, but says nothing of soldiers' wives on the battle-field on the night after. Rather he refers to the 'tribes of unfeeling wretches' who plundered the wounded and in some cases murdered them.[54] Turner made

---

and Joll 1977, vol. 1, p. 93. This was hardly surprising from a magazine that constantly berated the Royal Academy for its failure to properly promote history painting and took as its idol Benjamin Robert Haydon. It had described Turner at the beginning of the year as 'a power in English art, but a pernicious one'. Somniator, 'The Other Vision', *Annals of the Fine Arts*, 3, 1818, pp. 15–16.

50   'Exhibition of the Royal Academy', *Literary Chronicle*, no. 13, 22 June 1818; 'Exhibition at Somerset House', *New Monthly Magazine*, no. 53, 1 June 1818, p. 444.

51   'Exhibition at the Royal Academy', *Repository of Arts*, series 2, 5, June 1818, p. 364.

52   Costello 2013, Chapter 1.

53   Finberg 1961, p. 249.

54   Campbell 1817, pp. 71–2, 66–7.

numerous sketches and his depiction of the locale and the ruined manor house of Hougoumont, scene of some of the bloodiest and most decisive fighting,[55] is credible. So, in fact, is the motif of the women – two of them holding infants – looking for their wounded, or dead, husbands. The wives of ordinary soldiers would have been bivouacked close to the battle field while the officers' wives were billeted in nearby Brussels and Antwerp.[56] None of the picture's critics I have discovered mentioned this motif, which may have been simply too horrific for discussion.

Despite Turner's attention to details of uniforms and locale, it was obviously inappropriate to append a long descriptive account to his picture in the manner of Dighton and Jones. Being in the 'poetic' register it was almost the opposite of the topography and collaged portraits of the so-called 'truthful' depictions. Turner had no specific narrative of their kind to verify. What he did was rather to associate his painting with the sense of horror and the somber moral reflection that informs Byron's verses – so different from the conventional patrioteering and trite assertions of national superiority of Scott's *The Field of Waterloo* and Southey's *Poet's Pilgrimage to Waterloo* of 1815 and 1816 respectively.

Turner's painting may have been *sui generis*, but it necessarily drew on established iconographical motifs and formal devices. The night scene with a burning building or town was a theme well-established in Dutch seventeenth-century landscape painting by artists such as Aert van der Neer and the brothers Adriaen Lievensz and Egbert van der Poel (*fig. 103*). De Loutherbourg, with whose work Turner made a sustained if not uncritical engagement stretching back to the 1790s,[57] had produced a range of pictures, including battle scenes, with spectacular light effects of fire and smoke at night. But the key reference point for the *Field of Waterloo* is clearly Rembrandt, whose work Turner studied and revered from the mid-1790s until his death. In a lecture of 1811 he had singled out the triple light effect of Rembrandt's *Landscape with Rest on the Flight into Egypt* of 1647 (*fig. 104*), as especially deserving of praise;[58] the light sources in the *Field of Waterloo* are equally numerous. But another Rembrandt

---

55   Campbell noted the accumulation of dead there was 'one of the most shocking spectacles in the whole field' (Campbell 1817, p. 70).

56   Bachrach 1981, p. 9.

57   For Turner and de Loutherbourg, see Gage 1969 (1), pp. 29–30, 50, 98, 137–8, 181, 229 n. 53; Gage 1987, pp. 126–7.

58   Quoted in the larger discussion of Rembrandt in Gage 1987, p. 103. For Turner and Rembrandt more generally see Gage 1972, Chapter 2. For Rembrandt in Turner's Academy lectures, see Gage 1969 (1), pp. 198–9, 200, 203–4, 206, 208.

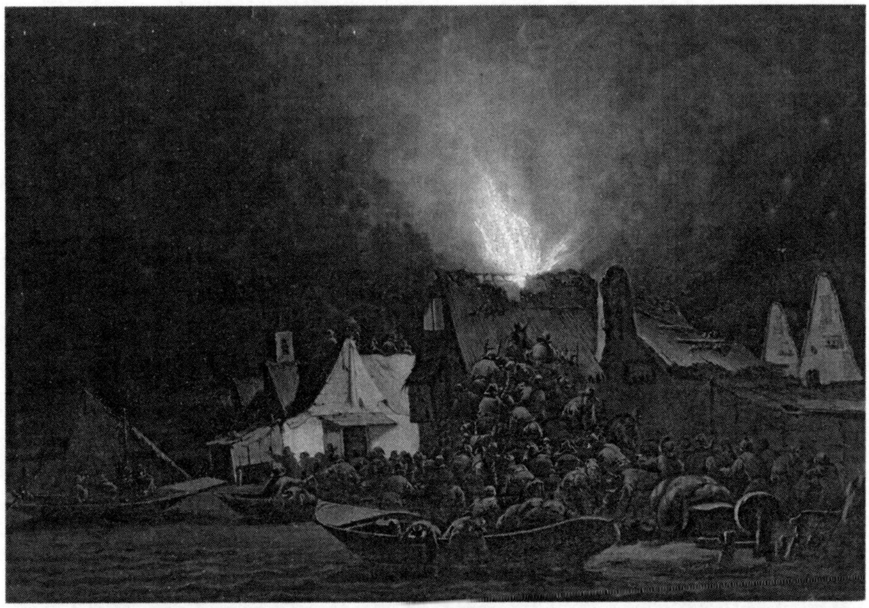

FIGURE 103 *Egbert Van der Poel,* Night Piece with a Burning House, *mid-17th century, 13×18⅛ in (33×46cm)*

PHOTO: DOROTHEUM GMBH & CO. KG

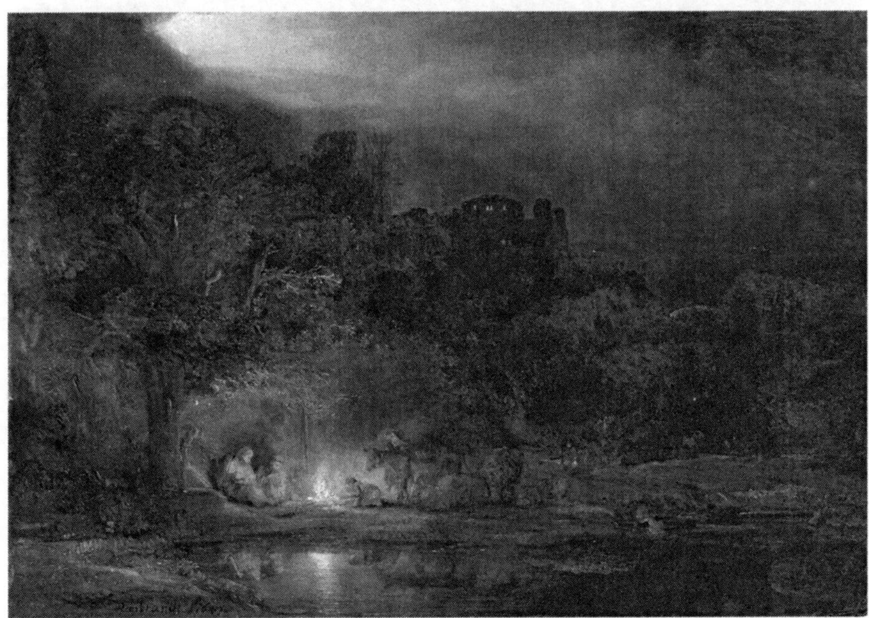

FIGURE 104 *Rembrandt Harmensz van Rijn,* Landscape with Rest on the Flight into Egypt, *1647, oil on panel, National Gallery of Ireland, Dublin*

PHOTO: © NATIONAL GALLERY OF IRELAND

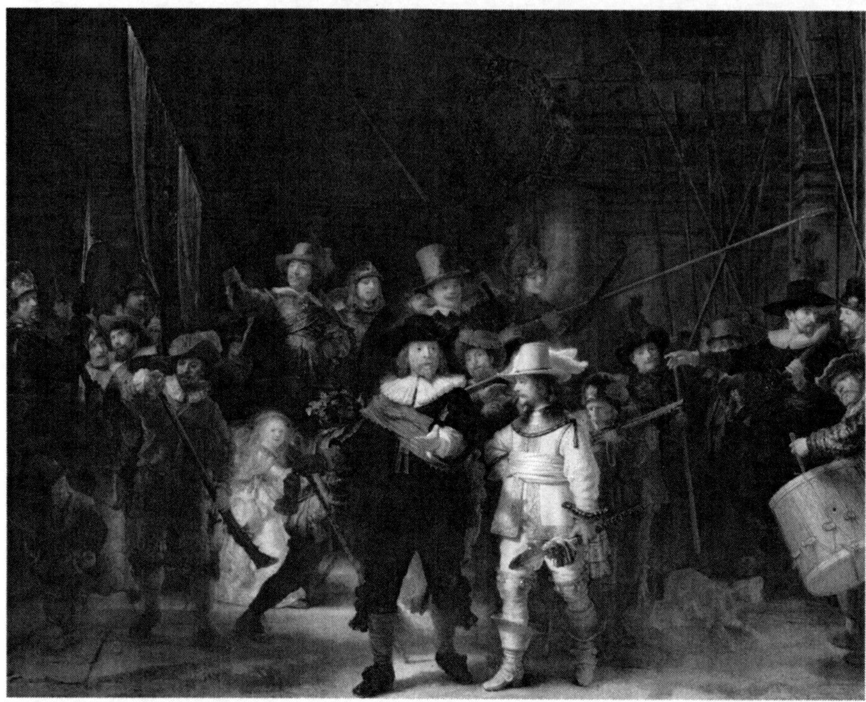

FIGURE 105 *Rembrandt Harmensz van Rijn,* Militia Company of District 11 under the Command of Captain Frans Banninck Cocq, *known as* The Night Watch, *1642, oil on canvas, 149½ × 178⅝ in (379.5×453.5 cm)*
PHOTO: RIJKSMUSEUM, AMSTERDAM

painting had perhaps also been a key exemplar here. In early September 1817, returning from his exploration of the Rhine, Turner had visited Amsterdam, where he saw the *Night Watch* (*fig. 105*). It is hard not to see the *Field of Waterloo* as at one level a rejoinder to this grand display of military ceremonial – a vision of its potential grim consequences – at the same time as Turner seeks to rival that work in its virtuoso effect of chiaroscuro.[59]

In addition to the *Field of Waterloo*, Turner exhibited two other painting at the Royal Academy in 1818, *Raby Castle, the Seat of the Earl of Darlington* (Walters Art Museum, Baltimore) and *The Dort, or Dordrecht, the Dort Packet-Boat*

---

59   Turner's dialog with Dutch painting in his 1818 exhibits has been dealt with most thoroughly in Bachrach 1981.

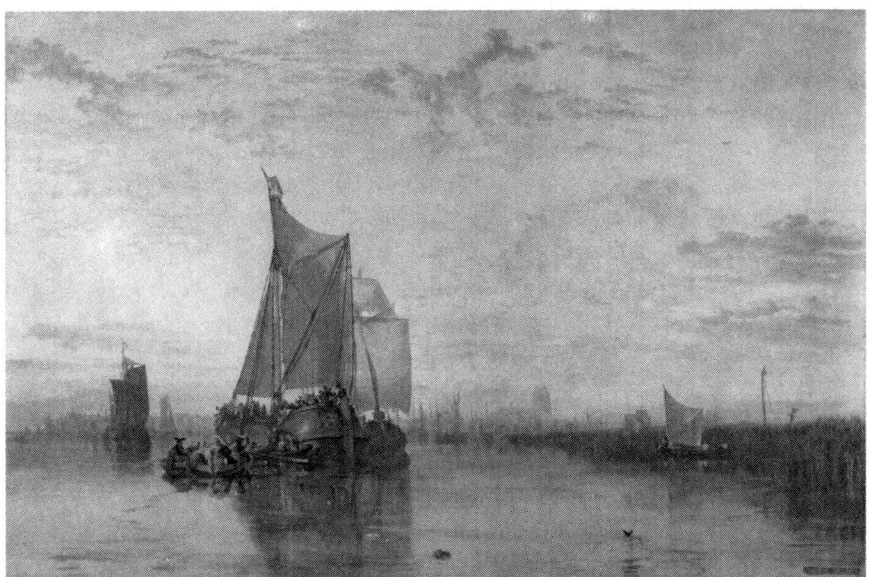

FIGURE 106   *J.M.W. Turner,* The Dort, or Dordrecht, the Dort Packet-Boat from Rotterdam
becalmed, *1818, oil on canvas, 62 × 92 in (157.5 × 233.7 cm)*
YALE CENTER FOR BRITISH ART, PAUL MELLON COLLECTION

from Rotterdam becalmed (*fig. 106*). The first of these was a country house portrait embellished with a fox-hunting scene; the second was a tour de force of naturalism in a pictorial motif that was particularly associated with Cuyp, a Dutch artist who had enjoyed especial popularity with British collectors. At approximately 47 × 71 inches, *Raby Castle* is significantly smaller than the *Dort* and the *Field of Waterloo*, which at 62 × 92 inches and 58 × 94 inches are basically comparable in size and very little different in shape. It is possible that they were conceived as pendants, although if so, they did not find a buyer as such. Turner sold the *Dort* to his close friend and patron Walter Fawkes, but the *Field of Waterloo* was in his studio at his death. Even so, as A.G.H. Bachrach pointed out, the contrast between peace and war, animation and death, and the beautiful and sublime could hardly be more pointed.[60]

To make a painting of this scale and ambition so novel in conception a theoretical rationale was necessary. Turner found this partly, I think, in the rather more flexible statements of academic theory that were being formulated by the Academy's professors of painting in the early nineteenth century

---

60   Bachrach 1981, pp. 10–11.

as they modified the Reynoldsian archetype in response to the increasing dominance of market relations in the artistic field and the paucity of patrician patrons of high art. I am thinking here of the more pronounced stress on the emotional properties of chiaroscuro that is evident in the lectures of James Barry and John Opie. Turner was a subscriber to the posthumous publication of Opie's lectures in 1809, which he annotated and evidently read with care.[61] Here he would have found the statement that if drawing was 'the giver of form', chiaroscuro was 'the creator of body and space'. But more than this, 'in addition ... if properly managed, it contributes infinitely to expression and sentiment; it lulls by breadth and gentle gradation, strikes by contrast, and rouses by abrupt transition ... All poetical scenery, real or imaginary ... where more is meant than is expressed; all the effects of solemn twilight and visionary obscurity, that flings half an image on the aching sight; all the terrors of storm and the horrors of conflagration, – are indebted to its representation on canvas'.[62] Chiaroscuro, so conceived, provided Turner with a means of suggesting profound emotions without representing human actions or expression in close-up detail from which his limitations as a figure draftsman disqualified him. In presenting groups of figures on a relatively small scale while implying depths of feeling through light and shade, the obvious example was Rembrandt. And Opie finished his lecture on Chiaroscuro with reflections on Rembrandt, whom he described as 'the head of the Dutch school', at the same time as warning that he was not a figure to imitate on account of his 'disgusting forms and the utmost vulgarity of character'.[63]

But there was another source with which Turner was familiar that offered a validation of Rembrandt's art that may have held some appeal for him. Although Turner's thinking was formed primarily within the painter's professional discourse of academic theory, he also encountered a wide range of other writings on the arts and notably the philosophical criticism that comprised the British contribution to the emergent science of aesthetics. In particular, he knew the most sophisticated instance of philosophical criticism as it bore on the visual arts, Richard Payne Knight's *Analytical Inquiry into the Principles of Taste* (1805). He also had personal contact with Knight, who in 1808 commissioned him to paint the Rembrandtesque comic genre painting *The Unpaid Bill*

---

61   Venning 1982, p. 36. Venning has observed that Turner seems to have shared many of Opie's views.

62   Wornum (ed.) 1848, p. 295.

63   Wornum (ed.) 1848, pp. 311, 312. Rembrandt 'seemed born to confound all rules and reasoning' and for this reason he was 'a master whom it is most exceedingly dangerous to imitate'.

(collection Schindler family).[64] Knight's aesthetic was an articulation of a patrician and connoisseurial perspective inimical to most academicians because it was dismissive of academic institutions and rules, and denied the arts any significant moral or didactic function. For Knight the pleasure of painting was in the first instance purely sensuous. It began with a moderate irritation of the optic nerve, generated by variety of tone and color, which was inherently pleasurable. Beyond this all more profound pleasures derived from the association of ideas. But for the pleasures of association to do their work, the original sensuous pleasures needed to be present. Indeed, it was this original sensuous pleasure generated by 'harmonious and brilliant combinations of tints' that explained why beauty could be found in the paintings of Dutch School artists who depicted 'crumbling masses of perished brick and plaster' or 'tattered worn-out dirty garments'.[65] Rembrandt in particular, through the twilight effects of his landscapes, could 'exhibit effects the most beautiful' out of objects that 'if seen or represented in the glare of a mid-day sun, would be thought most disgustingly ugly'.[66] (Like a pile of corpses, for instance.) Yet considered in purely formal terms, Rembrandt's work arrived 'nearer to abstract perfection ... than those of any other modern artist in any branch of art'.[67]

Given that Knight's aesthetic was premised on associationist psychology and not a priori rules, it followed that limitless new forms of beauty could emerge. This conclusion was reinforced by his view that while sculpture was only concerned with 'forms and lines of expression' seen to best advantage in representations of 'abstract nature', painting was concerned with 'passion and affection' as well as formal values and thus 'the tone of imitation must be brought down nearer to a level with the individual objects'. Painting was closer to theatre in which 'details from common life' were necessary to the effect. Indeed, they reinforced its 'pathos', as was evident in what Knight called 'some of the most interesting and affecting pictures, that the art has ever produced', by which he meant Benjamin West's *Death of Wolfe* (1771; National Gallery of Canada, Ottawa), Richard Westall's rustic genre painting *A Storm in Harvest* (1795; private collection) which he owned, and Joseph Wright's *Dead Soldier* (*fig. 107*).[68]

---

64   For Turner and Knight, see Gage 1965, pp. 76, 79; Gage 1987, pp. 118–20.

65   Knight 1808, p. 70. Knight had earlier articulated these views in his contribution to the picturesque debate of the 1790s. See Knight 1795, pp. 17–18, 22n.

66   Knight 1808, p. 98.

67   Knight 1808, p. 110. For more on the appeal of Dutch effects of light and color, see pp. 150–51. For the limitations of Rembrandt, see p. 418.

68   Knight 1808, pp. 310–11. The picture exists in three versions, see Nicholson 1968, vol. 1, 65–6, 153, 246–7.

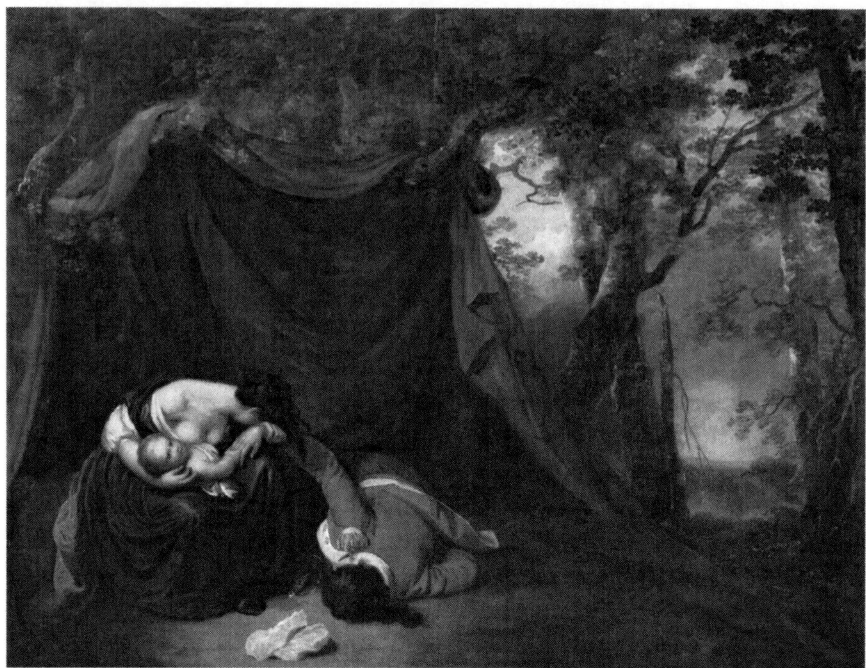

FIGURE 107 *Joseph Wright of Derby*, Dead Soldier, *1789, oil on canvas, 65×78 in (165.1×198.12 cm).*
Museum purchase made possible by the W. Hawkins Ferry Fund and anonymous
individual benefactors, 2006/1.156.
UNIVERSITY OF MICHIGAN MUSEUM OF ART

In relation to Turner's theme, Knight's choice of Wright's picture is at least
noteworthy. The picture had been exhibited at the Royal Academy in 1789,
the year that Turner became a student there – although he was not admitted
until December, months after the exhibition had been taken down.[69] But even
if he did not see the exhibition, the *Dead Soldier* was so successful that four
engravings were made after it and the image could hardly have escaped his
notice.[70] However remote from Turner's picture in scale and grandeur, Wright's
may none-the-less have acted as some kind of model in its disjunctive light
effect (the night sky, the fire of a distant conflagration, and the unaccountable
light of the foreground); the disorder of the recumbent body, whose coat is

---

69   Finberg 1961, p. 17.

70   For the engravings, see Egerton 1990, pp. 254–5. The picture was suggested by a passage
in John Langhorn's poem *The Country Justice* (1774–7) that has no bearing on Turner's
conception.

folded up and who lies awkwardly in the abandon of death; and the strange flow of arms and hands between the three figures.

It seems fitting that Leigh Hunt's courageous liberal weekly *The Examiner* came closest to a critique of *The Field of Waterloo* that did justice to its ambitions. Hunt's brother Robert, who wrote the paper's art criticism, doubtless viewed the political sentiments expressed in *Childe Harold* with approval.[71] But he also registered the formal logic of Turner's painting: 'The poetry of Mr. TURNER's Field of Waterloo is mainly in its magical illustration of the principle of colour and Claire obscure, which combines all their varieties of tint and strength in exhibiting at night the fiery explosions and carnage after battle, when the wives and brother and sons of the slain come, with anxious eyes and agonized hearts, to look in Ambition's charnel-house, after the slaughtered victims of legitimate and illegitimate selfishness and wickedness. TURNER wants, for his entire greatness, proficiency in the detailed drawing. In whatever relates to massing and composition, he leaves nothing for us to wish; he enlightens, he surprises, he delights'.[72] This was an interpretation that precisely tied Turner's extraordinary conception to the disdain for militaristic ideology that surfaces at several moments in Byron's poem.

From the publication of Cantos 1 and 2 of Childe Harold in 1812, it had been evident that although he embraced its notion of personal honour, Byron rejected the cult of martial virtue and patriotic valour associated with his class. The poem opens with a quotation from Louis Charles Fougeret de Monbron's *Le Cosmopolite*, which includes the sentence: 'Je haïssis ma patrie', and in Canto 2, XVI, Byron described Britain as 'the land of war and crimes'. At several moments throughout the poem he vented his disenchantment with Napoleon, describing him as a 'despot' and the imperial eagle as 'Gaul's vulture'. But he also presents him as simply the greatest of the 'imperial anarchs, doubling human woes'.[73] For Byron, all Empires mark the end of freedom.[74] His account of Britain's role in the Peninsular War is correspondingly scathing. He devoted 27 lines of Canto 1 to the Convention of Cintra – the abortive agreement negotiated by

---

71   For Hunt's art criticism, see Hemingway 1992, pp. 115–25. For Leigh Hunt's humanitarian response to the battle – which was not dissimilar to Byron's – see Coe 2005, pp. 233–4, 237–8. Twenty years later Hunt would publish the great antiwar poem *Captain Sword and Captain Pen*.

72   'Royal Academy', *Examiner*, 24 May 1818.

73   Byron, *Childe Harold*, Canto 1, LII, and XLV. Later in the poem Napoleon is just 'a kind of bastard Caesar', who he charges with vanity and compares unfavourably with the Roman Caesars – see Canto 4, XC, XCI.

74   Byron, *Childe Harold*, Canto 3, CXIII.

Lieutenant-General Wellesley and Generals Burrard and Dalrymple, through which the French armies withdrew from Portugal with all their equipment in British ships – which was widely seen as an ignominious emblem of the incompetence of the British warrior class.[75]

As for Wellington's victories in Spain at the battles of Talavera and Albuera (in 1809 and 1811), Albuera was just 'a glorious field of grief', 'A scene where mingling foes should boast and bleed!' (Canto 1, XLVIII).[76] While for Talavera, I will quote at more length from stanzas XLI and XLII of Canto 1:

> The foe, the victim, and the fond ally
> That fights for all, but ever fights in vain,
> Are met – as if at home they could not die –
> To feed the crow on Talavera's plain ...
>
> There shall they rot – Ambition's honour'd fools!
> .... in these behold the tools,
> The broken tools, that tyrants cast away,

This parading of anti-patriotic sentiments did not pass unnoticed in the press. The Whig *Edinburgh Review* confined itself to observing that Byron spoke in 'a very slighting and sarcastic manner of wars, victories, and military heroes in general', but the conservative *Quarterly Review* recoiled vehemently, defending the 'joys of triumph' and the pursuit of fame, since 'for the sake of such illusions is life chiefly worth living. When we read the preceding sarcasms on the "bravo's trade" [the passage on Talavera], we are induced to ask, not without some anxiety and alarm, whether such are indeed the opinions which a British peer entertains of a British army'.[77]

From a conservative perspective, worse was to follow in Cantos 3 and 4, published in 1816 and 1818 respectively. In Canto 3 Byron's ultimate judgment

---

75   Hibbert 1997, pp. 72–9. For a more balanced account, see Hilton 2006, pp. 214–16.

76   Poetic commentaries celebrating Albuera at the time included *The Vision of Don Roderick; A Poem* (Edinburgh, 1811), by Byron's future friend but political opponent, Walter Scott, and the yet more tritely patriotic: Anon., *The Battle of Albuera: A Poem, with an Epistle Dedicating to Lord Wellington* (London, 1811). Byron's mordant judgment obviously needs to be read against these.

77   Francis Jeffrey, unsigned review of cantos 1 and 2 of *Childe Harold*, in Rutherford (ed.) 1970, p. 39; Ellis, unsigned review of *Childe Harold*, 48. The reactionary *Anti-Jacobin Review* was yet more damning. See anonymous review of cantos 1 and 2 of *Childe Harold*, in Reiman (ed.) 1972, Part B, vol. 1, p. 11.

on Waterloo – which restored the Bourbons to the French throne – was that it was a mere 'king-making Victory' (xvii). Byron dedicated Canto 4 to his radical Whig friend, John Cam Hobhouse, who published some pedantic *Historical Illustrations* to accompany it as well as an admiring account of Napoleon during his Hundred Days.[78] In passing, the dedication condemned the peace established by the Congress of Vienna as a betrayal of Italy and France and suggested that Britain would pay for this 'at no very distant period'.[79]

It had been an action of some courage for Turner to associate himself with the views of such a notorious apostate and scorner of patriotism. But the negative press reaction and the failure of *The Field of Waterloo* to sell showed that it was unwise to ventriloquize Byron's controversial opinions on Britain's role in the recent wars, particularly in the turbulent years after Waterloo when the country seemed at times on the brink of insurrection and the government dealt brutally with manifestations of dissent, whether peaceable or potentially violent.[80]

Perhaps Turner realised that he had put his own loyalty in question, because the following year he showed what has generally been interpreted as an unequivocal expression of patriotic sentiment in the largest painting he had exhibited to date, *England: Richmond Hill on the Prince Regent's Birthday* (70⅞ × 131¾ inches; *fig. 108*). John Gage described this as 'a very deliberate bid' for the attention of the Prince in the hope of gaining commissions.[81] A vast Claudean composition frames the famous view, which had been painted by a succession of artists, including Thomas Hofland, whose large painting – framed it was 81 by 111 inches – was shown at the Royal Academy in 1815 and the British Institution in the following year, and quite widely praised in the press (*fig. 109*).[82]

---

78   John Cam Hobhouse, *The Substance of some Letters from Paris* (London, 1816). A few
      years hence, Byron would be hurtfully derisive of Hobhouse's political engagements. See
      Cochran 2010, Chapters 5, 10, and 11.

79   Byron 1926, p. 220.

80   Turner had even greater cause to distance himself from Byron in 1819–20 as the first four
      cantos of *Don Juan* appeared, which seemed even more immoral to proper opinion than
      Childe Harold. On the political climate of these years, the classic account is Thompson
      1963, Chapter 15, which is now supplemented by Chandler 1998 and Chase 2013.

81   Gage 1987, p. 178. Gage aptly referred to the picture's colour as 'florid' and some contemporaries reportedly complained of 'the flaming colour' of Turner's paintings that year –
      see Butlin and Joll 1977, vol. 1, p. 95.

82   For information on this work, see Golt 1987, appendix 2. The painting is lost. It was
      highly praised in 'Exhibition of the Royal Academy', *New Monthly Magazine* 3, 18, July 1815,
      p. 550, which described it as 'an excellent transcript of the most beautiful scene in this, or
      perhaps any other country'. It was also praised in 'British Institution, no. iv', *Morning Post*,
      23 February 1816, and 'British Institution', *The Times*, 3 February 1816.

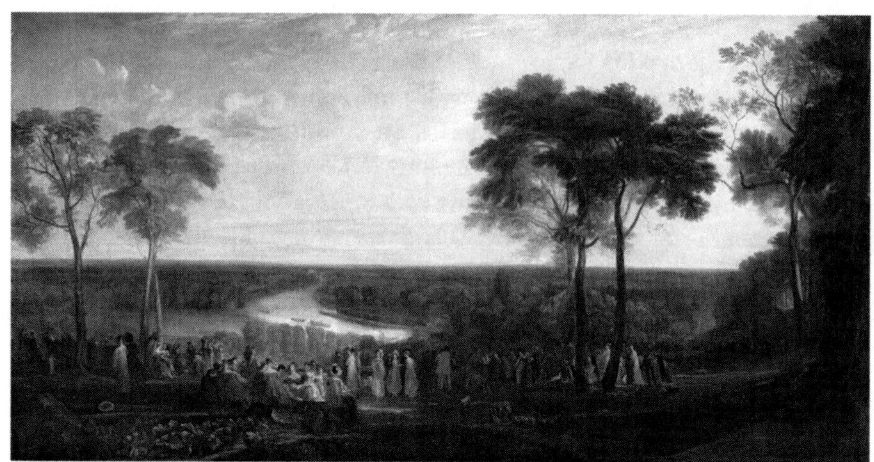

FIGURE 108 *J.M.W. Turner,* England: Richmond Hill on the Prince Regent's Birthday, *exh. 1819, oil on canvas, 70⅞ × 131¾ in (180.0 × 334.6 cm), Tate Britain*
© TATE, LONDON, 2015

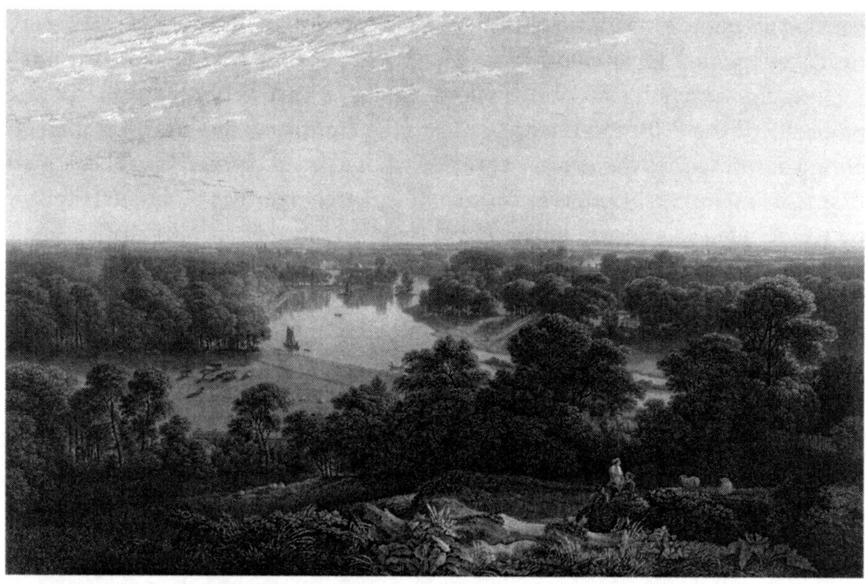

FIGURE 109 *T.C. Hofland,* View of the River Thames from Richmond Hill, *engraved by Charles Heath, 1823*
© THE TRUSTEES OF THE BRITISH MUSEUM

Turner's motif was generally assumed to be a fantasy until Jean Golt showed in an article of 1987 that it was probably conceived as a depiction of a country fête in honour of the Prince's birthday held at Cardigan House on Richmond Hill on 12 August 1817, which included a dinner party for Queen Charlotte and the Prince.[83] The event was organised by Elizabeth, Dowager Countess of Cardigan, who had been a lady of the Queen's Bedchamber between 1793 and 1807. For the catalogue entry for this work, Turner eschewed his dangerous flirtation with Byron – who he was not to cite again until 1832 – and reverted to his old favourite Thomson's *Seasons*, quoting an eight-line passage from 'Summer' that ends with an effusion to the prospect from Richmond Hill as the paradigm of 'Happy Britannia', where Liberty 'walks unconfined' and 'scatters plenty with unsparing hand'.[84] In this he followed Hofland, who had cited a line from the same poem that comes a few lines after Turner's quotation.[85]

Golt has described the 'allusions' of the painting as 'enigmatic' and rightly so.[86] Given that Turner had already left London for his tour of the Rhine before the Countess of Cardigan's fête he could not have witnessed the event and would have had to rely on press reports, hearsay, or his own imaginings. What is perhaps most striking is that Turner chose not to depict the widely unpopular Prince himself. The personage whom the reactionary *Morning Post* hailed as 'an Adonis of loveliness', 'the glory of the People', who won over 'all hearts',[87] was widely regarded as an obese profligate buffoon with no interest in his office beyond the opportunities it gave him for lavish spending from the public purse.[88] Even an 1821 silhouette portrait by George Aktinson (*fig. 110*), who enjoyed the title of 'Profile Portraitist to his Majesty', is suggestive of his bloated form, while caricaturists such as Cruikshank insistently connected his corpulence with debauchery and moral turpitude (*fig. 111*). The challenge of giving regal attributes to this elephantine figure did not deter Turner's fellow academicians Lawrence (*fig. 112*) and Wilkie from producing portraits that matched the *Morning Post* in falsification.[89] But for the moment, Turner avoided the challenge.

I have found no indications in the press criticism that Turner's *England* was recognised as a depiction of the event of 12 August 1817. Further, while Golt has

---

83   Golt 1987, pp. 11–12.

84   'Summer', ll. 1442–5, in Thomson 1908. For Turner's enthusiasm for Thomson, see Wilton 1990, pp. 53–61 and *passim*.

85   Turner's quotation is ll. 1401–8, Hofland's is l. 1438.

86   Golt 1987, p. 9.

87   *Morning Post*, 19 March 1812.

88   For the overwhelming evidence of his unpopularity, see Parissien 2001, Chapter 1.

89   For negative responses to Lawrence's transformation, see Parissien 2001, p. 250.

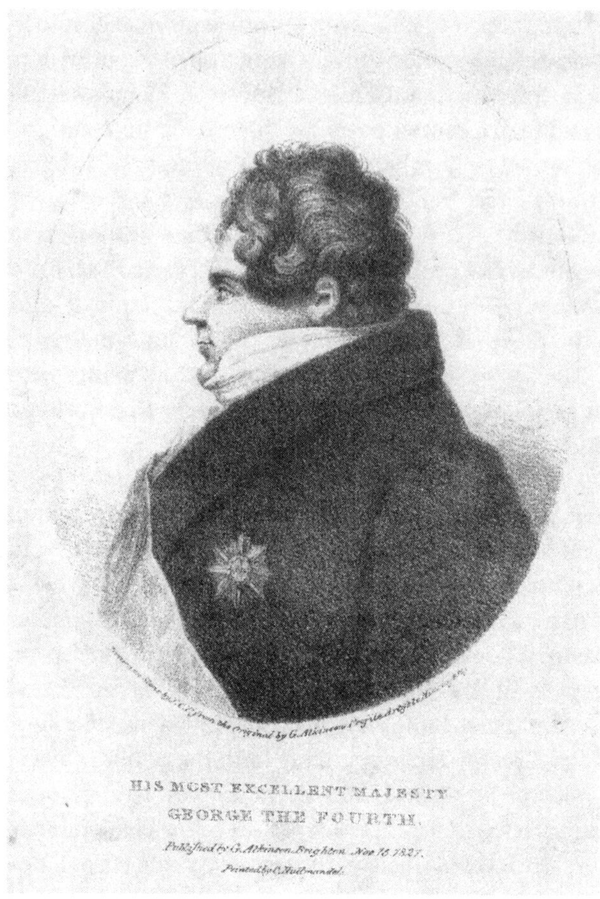

FIGURE 110
George Atkinson, His Most
Excellent Majesty,
George IV, *1821, lithograph
published by T.C.P. and
Joseph Hulmandel*
PHOTO: WIKIMEDIA
COMMONS

claimed that most contemporary reviews of *England* were positive, this is not quite accurate on the basis of my soundings in the press.[90] Most critics praised the landscape but either passed over the figures in silence or disapproved of them. For instance, the review in *Bell's Weekly Messenger* applauded the vista but complained that the foreground trees and figures were 'all Italian' and suggested the theme required a rustic scene with John Bull under a sturdy oak tree.[91] The *Morning Herald* was more caustic: 'Mr. TURNER has not a single handsome person at his crowded festival. In truth it would appear that the

90   Golt 1987, p. 9. Gage, too, had a different impression and describes the work as 'widely attacked' – see Gage 1987, p. 178.

91   Quoted in Golt 1987, p. 9.

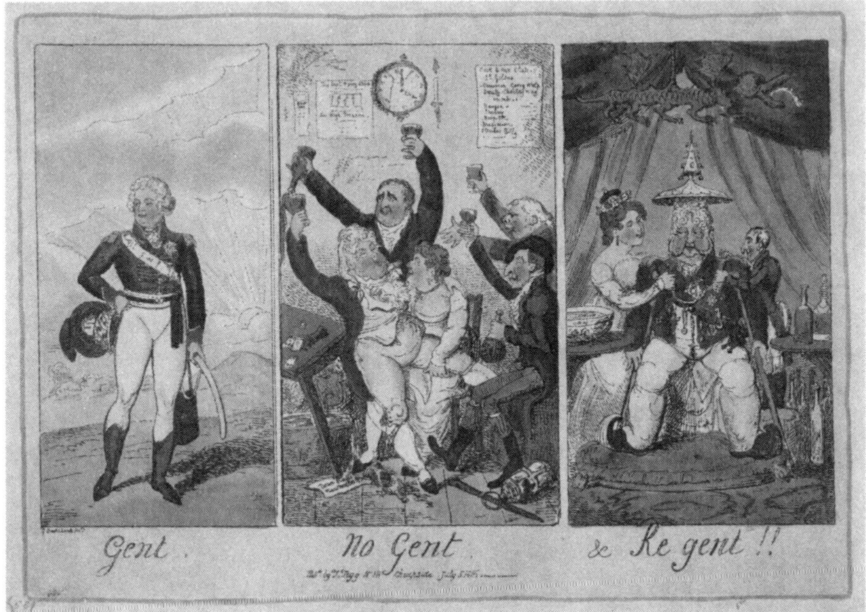

FIGURE 111   *George Cruikshank,* Gent. no Gent. & Re.gent!!, *1816, etching*
© THE TRUSTEES OF THE BRITISH MUSEUM

various parties had all dined very heartily, and had not spared the juice of the
vine-fruit, so disordered do they look in their dress, so odd in their attitudes.
Nor do we well know from what classes of society they have been selected.
Soldiers, officers, drummers, Royal servants, ladies intended to be gay, and
gentlemen designed to be gallant, fiddlers and ambulators, little boys and old
grandmothers, all, by the way with very rubicund countenances, are huddled
together as if they had been shaken out of a dice-box'.[92]

Although no contemporary critic seems to have noticed, the group of
women closest to the spectator's viewpoint are clearly indebted to a group in
Watteau's *L'île enchantée* (*fig. 113*) of which Turner had made a pencil copy,[93]
and the whole conception is rather obviously a riff on the *fête galante* genre.
While this is confirmation of Turner's immense admiration for Watteau it also
matches with the enthusiasm of the Prince Regent for both artist and genre.[94]

---

92   'Royal Academy, No. III', *Morning Herald*, 20 May 1819. The *Examiner* did not fault the
     figures as such but complained it was inappropriate to make a holiday for the birthday
     of such a prince – 'Royal Academy', *Examiner*, no. 600, 28 June 1819.

93   Golt 1987, p. 15.

94   Gage 1968, pp. 91–2; Gage 1987, pp. 178.

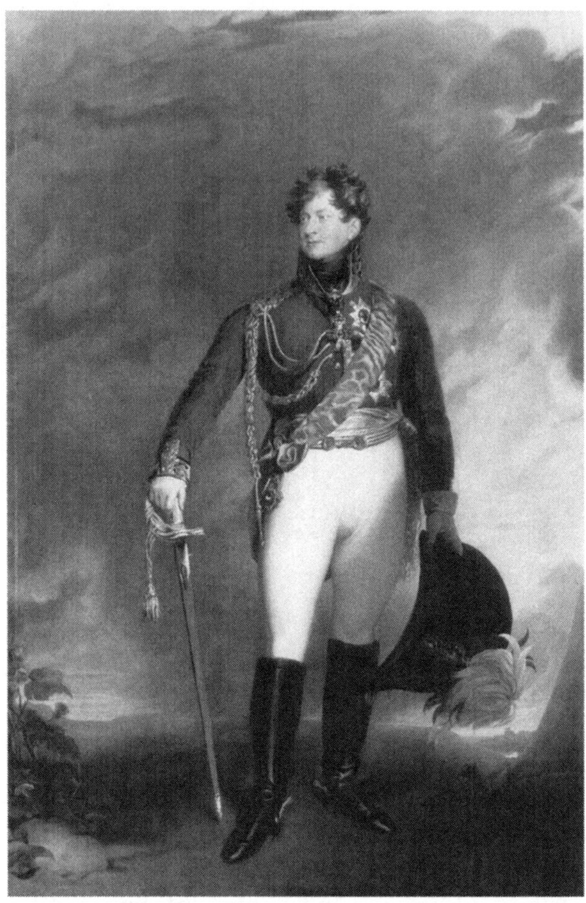

FIGURE 112
Thomas Lawrence, studio of,
Prince Regent, *1815, oil on
canvas, 95 × 61 in
(241.3 × 154.9 cm)*
NATIONAL PORTRAIT
GALLERY, LONDON,
BEQUEATHED BY MISS
LILLIE BELLE RANDELL,
1931 (NPG2503)

But here Turner had entered on dangerous ground. The Prince's admiration for the Ancien Régime and his obsessive francophilia – which was registered in the vast sums he spent on French furniture, clocks and Sèvres porcelain – seemed clearly out of place at a time when the nation was at war with France and the Bourbon dynasty was widely despised by the middle and working classes.[95] Moreover, the overwhelmingly female character of the crowd seems telling for the celebration of a man notoriously lascivious and with a reputation for ogling women and making improper advances at public events.[96] Nor was the image of lavish fêtes and displays of drunkenness a neutral theme. One of the

---

95   Parissien 2001, pp. 193–203.
96   For the ogling, see Parissien pp. 257, 309. For improper advances, p. 83.

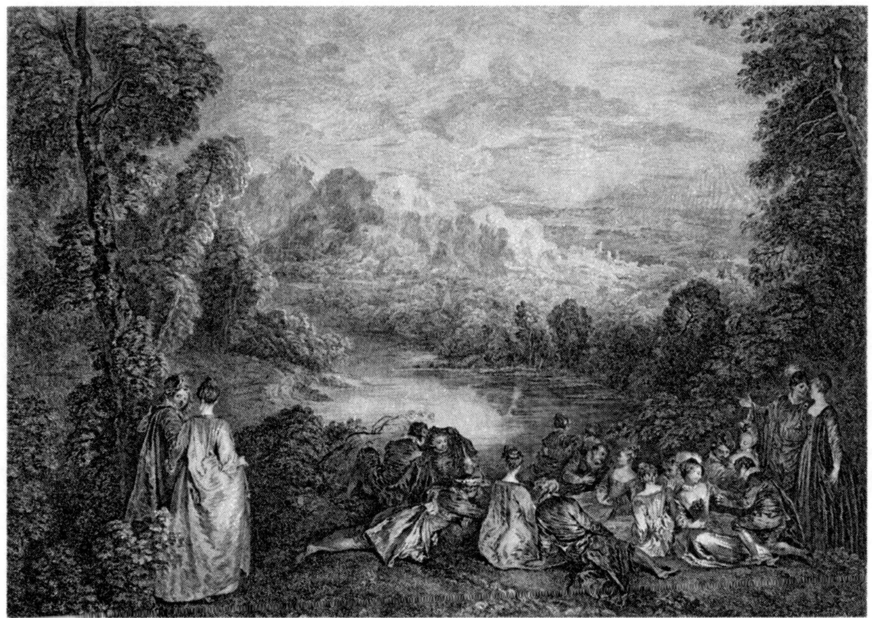

FIGURE 113   *Jacques Philippe Le Bas, after Antoine Watteau,* L'Île enchantée (Insula Perjucunda), *1734, etching and engraving, 15⅝ × 19½ in (39.6 × 49.5 cm)*
LA SALLE UNIVERSITY ART MUSEUM, PHILADELPHIA

signatures of the Prince's extravagance and profligacy was the series of massive fêtes and victory celebrations at Carlton House beginning with the three-day event that marked the advent of the Regency in 1811 when 30,000 people passed through the palace.[97] The cost of these wasteful displays was mocked in caricatures such as Charles Williams's image of John Bull nonplussed at the Regent's banquet table (*fig. 114*), but it was also exposed in the *Black Book; or, Corruption Unmasked* (1820) which referred scathingly to the 'lavishing' of public money on 'tailors, jewelers, glass and china manufacturers, builders, perfumers, embroiderers, &c'.[98] Although presumably Lady Cardigan's fête was not paid for from the Civil List, it could scarcely avoid association with the larger pattern of Regency profligacy.

John Gage has suggested that it was the example of Thomas Stothard, the leading British imitator of Watteau, which alerted Turner to the value of that

97   Parissien 2001, pp. 248–9, 262–3. For the *Examiner's* response and a vivid description, see Coe 2005, pp. 147–9.

98   Wade 1820, p. 125. For figures see p. 124. On *The Black Book*, see Chase 2013, pp. 17, 71.

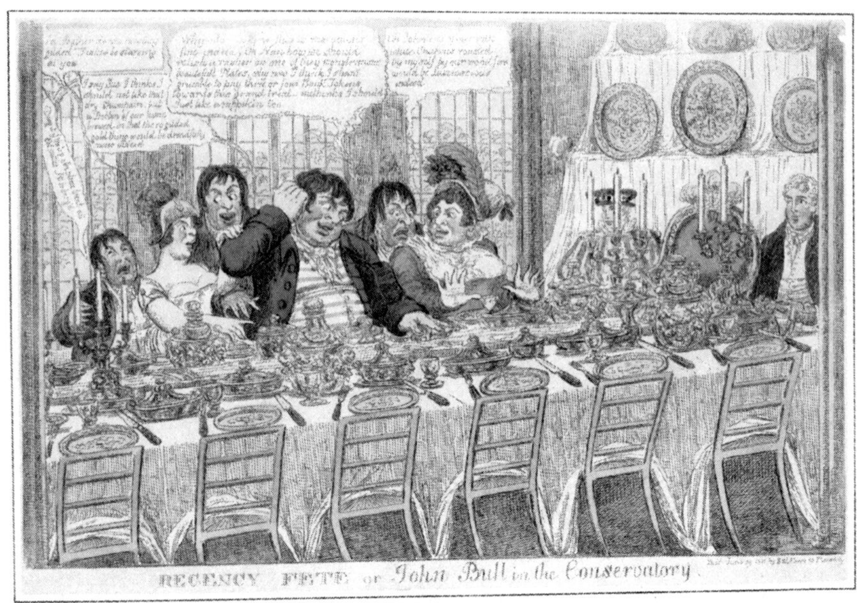

FIGURE 114 *Charles Williams,* Regency Fete, *1811, etching*
© THE TRUSTEES OF THE BRITISH MUSEUM

artist's work and there seems to have been reciprocal admiration between the older and the younger man.[99] Stothard exhibited a painting titled *Fête champêtre* at the Royal Academy in 1818 and at the British Institution the following year,[100] and in 1817 had shown a comparable theme in the *Sans souci* now in the Tate Gallery (*fig. 115*). Stothard usually painted on a small scale and, at 52 inches by 62 inches framed, his *Fête champêtre* was one of the largest paintings he ever exhibited. For Turner to marry the intimate iconography of the small scale *fête galante* with a colossal contemporary panorama was a radical and incongruous act of updating. As a symbol of the nation *England* was unconvincing, and if it was a calculated attempt to attract the Prince Regent's largesse it evidently failed. Perhaps the work's unconscious humor contributed to this. Maybe it looked a gaudy parody, even if it was not intended to.

Turner's two direct attempts to depict the Prince, who succeeded to the throne in January 1820, were abandoned. Since it was first proposed in an

---

99   Gage 1968 (1), pp. 92, 240 n. 62. For more on the relationship between them, see Gage 1987, p. 147.

100   Appropriately, the catalogue entry was accompanied with unattributed lines from Anacreon's ode, 'The Praise of Bacchus'. See Fawkes 1760, pp. 68–9.

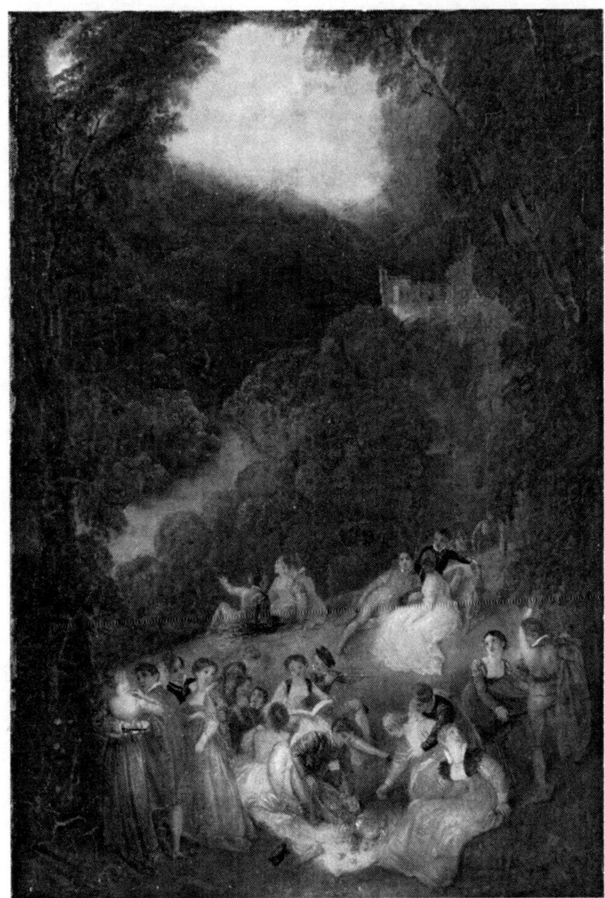

FIGURE 115
Thomas Stothard, Sans
Souçi, *1817, oil on wood,*
31½ × 20½ in
(80.0×52.0 cm), Tate
Britain
© TATE, LONDON 2015

article of 1975, Gerald Finley's thesis that two sketchbooks filled with pencil studies Turner made during George IV's visit to Edinburgh in 1822 were preparations for an unrealised series of 'historical paintings' of the Royal Progress has commanded general acceptance.[101] But Finley himself acknowledged the argument was essentially speculative and his conception of history painting is imprecise, seemingly encompassing any paintings that represent historical

---

101   Finley 1975, pp. 27–33, 35. See also Finley 1981. Gage suggests that a reference to an aborted commission in a letter to J.C. Schetky of 3 December 1823 may refer to a Royal Progress scheme, but it provides no indication of from whom it came or what its precise nature was – for example, oil paintings or watercolors? (Gage 1980, p. 90 n. 3; Gage 1987, p. 178.) For accounts of the royal visit, see Parissien 2001, Chapter 16; Prebble 1988.

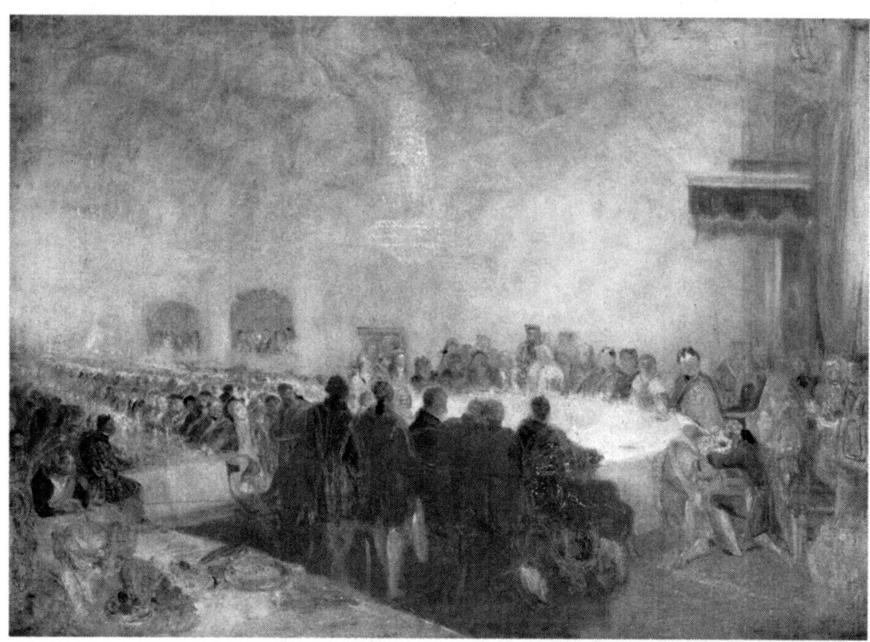

FIGURE 116 *J.M.W. Turner,* George IV at the Provost's Banquet in the Parliament House, Edinburgh, *c. 1822, oil on mahogany, 27 × 36⅛ in (68.6 × 91.8 cm), Tate Britain* © TATE, LONDON 2015

events.[102] As John Gage observed, the two main oil paintings on themes from the visit – *George IV at the Provost's Banquet in the Parliament House, Edinburgh* and *George IV at St. Giles's, Edinburgh* (*figs. 116* and *117*)[103] – are a continuation of Turner's engagement with genre painting in the mode of Wilkie and Edward Bird, which was inaugurated by his exhibition of *A Country Blacksmith Disputing on the Price of Iron* (*fig. 118*) in 1807.[104] Bird himself, who had been appointed Historical Painter to Princess Charlotte in 1813, showed a comparable theme of contemporary royalty in the shape of *The Return of Louis XVIII, 1814* (*fig. 119*) at

---

102　Finley 1981, p. 45.

103　Butlin and Joll 1977, cat. nos. 247 and 248. A work, similar in size and painted on mahogany panel, has been plausibly titled *George IV's Departure from the Royal George*, Tate Gallery NO2880. The stylistically cognate *Shipping*, NO2879, may well also belong with it. Their themes correspond with Turner's numerous pencil studies of the royal flotilla at Leith.

104　Gage 1987, pp. 178, 145–6. The scale of Turner's ambitions in multi-figure genre paintings is clearest from *Harvest Home* of c. 1809 – see Gage 1987, p. 145; Butlin and Joll 1977, cat. no. 209.

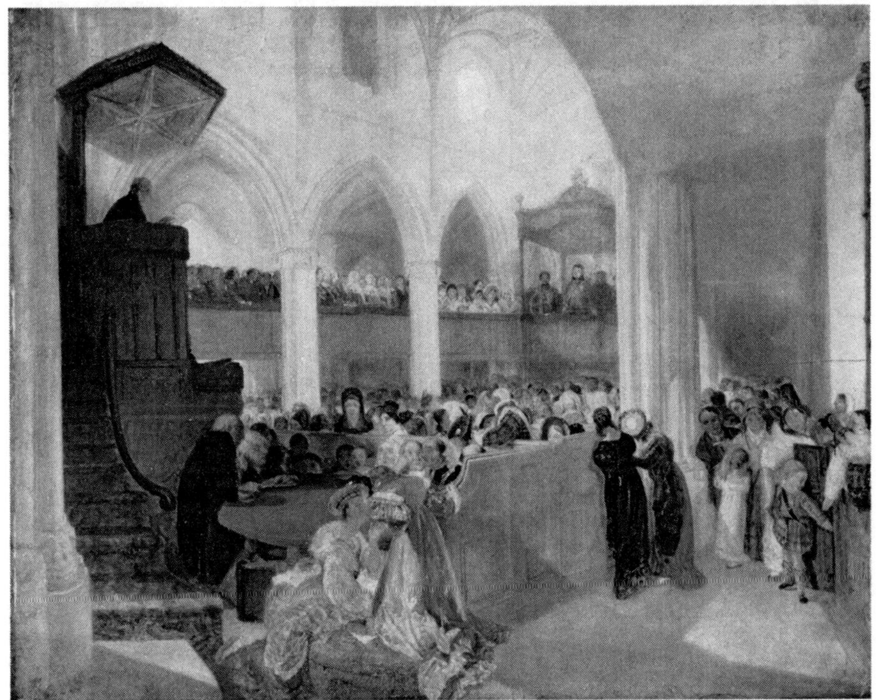

FIGURE 117   *J.M.W. Turner,* George IV at St. Giles's, Edinburgh, *c. 1822, oil on panel, 29⅜ × 36⅛ in (74.6×91.8 cm), Tate Britain*
© TATE, LONDON 2015

the British Institution in 1819. A composition with many figures – some of them portraits identified in the catalogue entry – at approximately 110 by 173 inches, this was a painting more on the scale of a conversation piece portrait than of a history painting.[105] A companion picture of *The Embarkation of Louis XVIII at Dover, 1814,* which contained a very flattering portrait of the Prince Regent,[106] was executed first. Given the assistance he received from the royal household and the Prince's interest in this work, Bird expected him to buy it. He was disappointed and the painting was eventually bought by the Lord Bridgewater,

---

105   There are two versions of the painting, little different in size, that at Wolverhampton Art Gallery (110×174 inches) and that at Burton Constable Hall (110½ × 156 inches). For a detailed discussion of the patronage relations around the paintings, see Richardson 1982, pp. 33–6, 37–8.

106   The Prince was so fat in 1814 that he found it difficult to bend to tie the parting gift of the Order of the Garter to Louis's thigh, which caused amusement to the crowd – see Parissien 2001, p. 200.

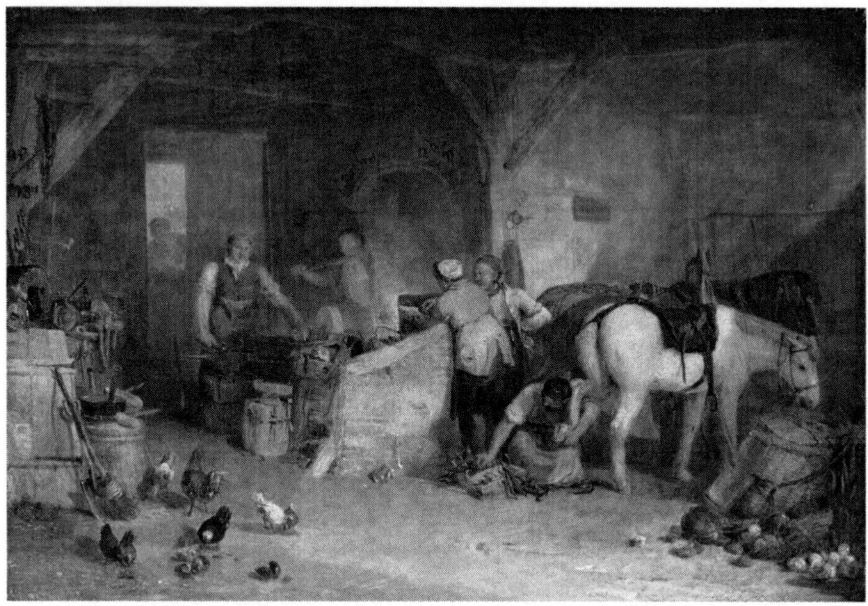

FIGURE 118 *J.M.W. Turner,* A Country Blacksmith Disputing upon the Price of Iron, and the Price Charged to the Butcher for Shoeing his Poney, *1807, oil on mahogany, 21⅝ × 27½ in (54.9×77.8cm), Tate Britain*
© TATE, LONDON 2015

who had commissioned its pendant.[107] Perhaps Turner was encouraged by Bridgewater's generosity to Bird to think he could attract him to buy another of his own works. After all his commission of the so-called Bridgewater Sea Piece, *Dutch Boats in a Gale* (1801, private collection), had been an important stepping stone in his early career.[108]

At 27×36⅛ inches and 29¾ × 36⅛ inches respectively, *George IV at the Provost's Banquet* and *George IV at St Giles's* are rather smaller than Bird's Louis XVIII paintings and fall around the median size of Wilkie's genre pictures. The motif of the first is the enactment of a legendary ceremony ('legendary' in a literal sense) by a young Midlothian laird, William Houison Crauford, whereby he was allowed the honour of washing the royal fingers in a silver salver of rosewater at the end of the meal, because one of his ancestors, four centuries before, had supposedly saved the life of a Scottish king and salved his wounds.

---

107 A sketch of *The Embarkation of Louis XVIII at Dover, 1814,* 40×51 inches framed, was exhibited posthumously at the British Institution in 1821.

108 Butlin and Joll 1977, cat. no. 14.

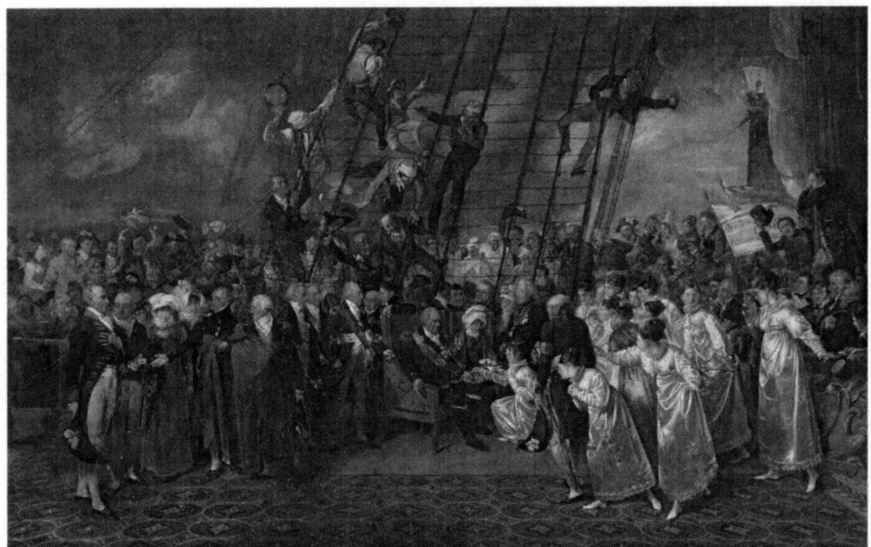

FIGURE 119   *Edward Bird,* The Landing of Louis XVIII at Calais, c. *1816–17, oil on canvas, 43¼ ×*
68½ in (110.0 174.0 cm)
© WOLVERHAMPTON ART GALLERY, WEST MIDLANDS, UK/BRIDGEMAN
IMAGES

Crauford was assisted by Sir Walter Scott's young son Charles and his nephew
Walter, who acted as pages. This ridiculous ritual was just an episode in the
pageantry of fictive Scottish history through which Sir Walter Scott – who stage-
managed the royal visit – sought to connect the Hanoverian monarch with the
Stuart dynasty, a connection George IV was only too happy to promote, as the
full Highland garb he had tailored for himself at massive expense illustrates
(*fig. 120*).[109] Culloden and 'Butcher Cumberland' were all forgotten. However,
although most of the 300 nobles and officers of state who made up the guests
at the banquet in the Great Hall of Parliament House wore court dress or
uniforms, some displayed the tartan that Scott and the Lairds were so keen to
promote – as if all Scots were Highlanders. On this occasion, George, who loved
to dress the soldier, wore the scarlet coat of a field marshal with the star of the
Garter on his chest.[110] Turner clearly depicts the king's red-dyed hair, though
his curls look more bedraggled than in Wilkie's version and the craggy pallid
visage is a more accurate register of his terrible state of health.

---

109   For George IV's love affair with the Stuarts, see Parissien 2001, pp. 202–6. For the Highland
       outfit – which Wilkie's portrait simplified – see Prebble 1988, pp. 73–6.
110   For George IV's obsession with uniforms, see Parissien 2001, Chapter 4.

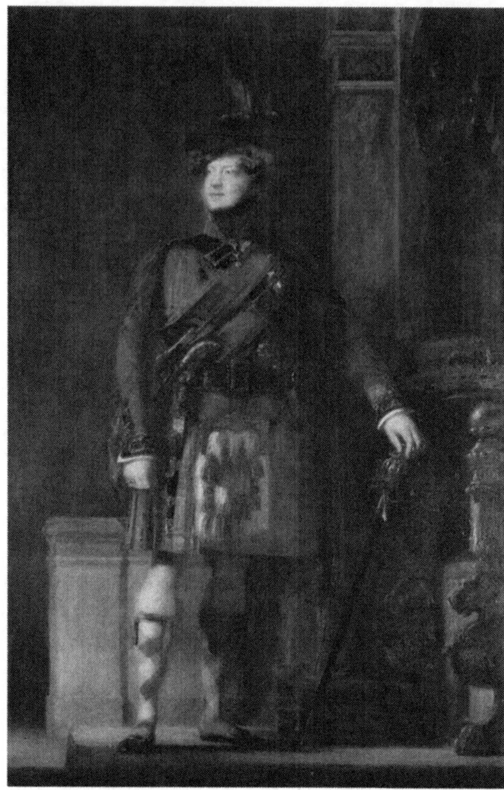

David Wilkie, George IV, *1830, oil on canvas, 110 × 70½ in (279.4 × 179.1 cm)* ROYAL COLLECTION TRUST/© HER MAJESTY QUEEN ELIZABETH II 2016

We cannot know whether the humour of the painting was intentional, but the satire in its companion *George IV at St Giles's* is unmistakable.[111] Turner gives us numerous signs of inattention or inappropriate attention, most prominently in the two fashionably dressed women whispering in the near foreground, one of whom wears a fashionable tartan bonnet.[112] Just over their heads two boys are yawning, while the woman in the black veil behind them – like several around her – is looking neither towards the minister nor towards the king. On the right of the composition a boy in Highland garb has unwisely inserted his fingers in the pew door behind which a woman seems engaged in heated conversation, the throng around her suggesting almost an atmosphere of hubbub. The king, once again wearing the field marshal's coat with the star of the Order of the Garter, is artfully positioned opposite the minister. Black

111   For accounts of the event, see Prebble 1988, pp. 321–5.
112   On tartan, see Parissien 2001, pp. 320, 324–6.

accents among the figures lead the eye round to the largest concentration of dark in the painting, which culminates in the pulpit and the black-clothed figure of David Lamont, the Moderator of the Church of Scotland, who raises a minatory hand. Given that the last English monarch to set foot in the High Kirk, Charles I, had provocatively celebrated an Anglican service there, the presence of the king at a Presbyterian service was profoundly symbolic – in effect an acknowledgement of the victory of Presbyterianism over Episcopalianism in Scotland. From the pulpit of what had been John Knox's church, Lamont delivered a somber discourse on Paul's *Epistle to the Colossians*, Chapter 3, Verses 3 and 4: 'For ye are dead, and your life is hid with Christ in God. When Christ, who is our life, shall appear, then shall ye also appear with him in glory'. As if directing himself to the king's dissolute life, he spoke of the sins of fornication, concupiscence, anger, wrath, and mendacity, and the obligation of husbands to love their wives. The king apparently betrayed no response to a discourse that might seem a pointed commentary on his string of mistresses, his mistreatment of Queen Caroline, and his reputation for petulant rages. In the end, the painting is reminiscent of Hogarth's modern moral subjects and the church scene that makes Plate Two of the *Industry and Idleness* series (*fig. 121*), with its sleeping boy and bloated woman with closed eyes adjacent the model couple, was surely in Turner's mind.[113]

Turner was present at both the events he depicted and made studies of the interiors but not of the figures,[114] which were presumably his own recollections or inventions. The satirical aspect of his genre pictures brought Turner closer to Bird, and John Gage proposed that *George IV at Saint Giles* was a calculated attempt to appeal to the king, who had bought Bird's *Country Choristers* (Royal Collection) in 1810. This seems to me quite unlikely given how nearly Turner's image of the king came to topical concerns about the character of the monarch. Moreover, as Carol Duncan has pointed out to me, the viewer, like the congregation, is positioned so as to find the distractions at least if not more interesting than the ceremonial event.

One cannot be sure that the Edinburgh paintings were executed in 1822, as Martin Butlin and Evelyn Joll suggest in their catalogue raisonné, but it seems likely enough. If this was the case, at the time of painting Turner was likely unaware of Byron's pointed contrast between the king's starving Irish subjects and his own immense weight in Canto 8, CXXVI, of *Don Juan*,[115] or his acidulous

---

113   Given the compositional similarities, this seems a more likely source than the earlier
       engraving *The Sleeping Congregation* (1736).

114   Finley 1981, p. 22.

115   For another jibe at George's size, see *Don Juan*, Canto 9, XXXIX.

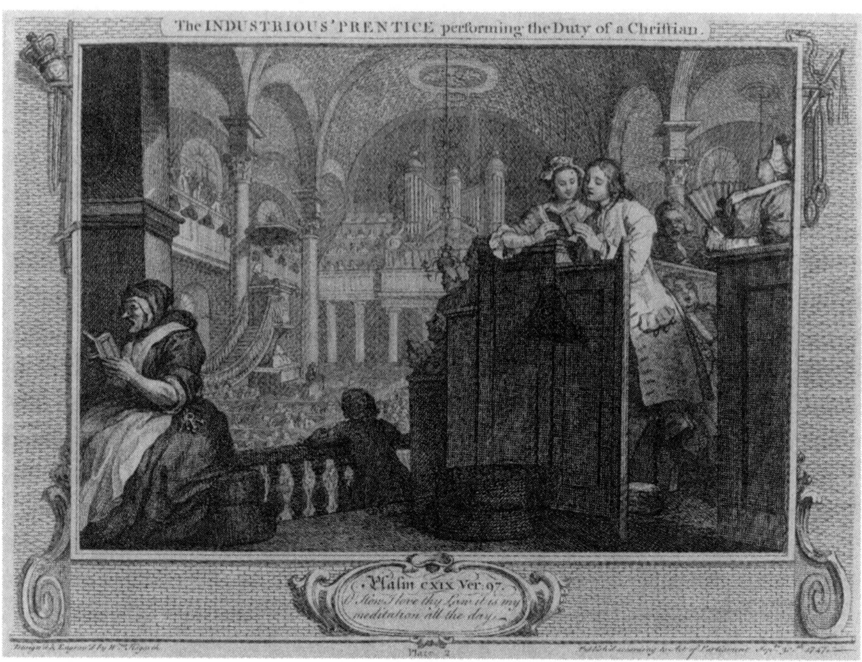

FIGURE 121   *William Hogarth,* The Industrious 'Prentice performing the Duty of a Christian',
plate 2 of Industry and Idleness, *1747, engraving*
© THE TRUSTEES OF THE BRITISH MUSEUM

comment on the Scottish jaunt in Canto 11, LXXVIII, as a 'scene of royal itch
and loyal scratching', since although written earlier, these cantos were not published until 1823. But even without reference to Byron's scandalous poem, there
were factors that made satirical or humorous depictions of the monarch a risky
business. The months between the opening of the Royal Academy exhibition
on 1 May 1819, where *England* went on display, and the royal jaunt to Scotland in
August 1822 had been a tumultuous period politically speaking, with the Tory
government consistently on guard against radicals demanding parliamentary
reform and threatening revolution. On 16 August 1819 cavalry charged into a
peaceful mass demonstration at St. Peter's Field, Manchester, killing eleven and
injuring more than four hundred.[116] In February of the following year came the
Cato Street conspiracy, a radical plot to assassinate the cabinet, which led to

---

116   We don't have any record of Turner's response to the Peterloo Massacre, but we do know
      that of his friend and patron, the radical Whig Walter Fawkes, who at a meeting of the
      nobility and freeholders of Yorkshire referred to the action of the Manchester magistrates

five executions for treason on 1 May.[117] The political scene in the latter part of the year was dominated by the trial of Queen Caroline and the extraordinary nationwide demonstrations in her favour as an icon of aristocratic injustice and a sign of the need for constitutional reform.[118] The extravagant and gaudy display of the king's coronation on 19 July 1821 and the royal tours of Ireland in August 1821 and Scotland a year later did something to provide a spectacle of monarchical popularity, however hollow.[119] Caroline's popularity had waned by the time of the Coronation, but nonetheless 24 regiments were stationed in the capital to prevent pro-Caroline disturbances.[120]

In December 1819 Parliament passed the infamous Six Acts, which severely curtailed rights of popular assembly and clamped down on cheap political publishing. One of these, the Blasphemous and Seditious Libels Act, was specifically directed against 'Pamphlets and printed Papers containing observations upon public events and Occurrences, tending to excite Hatred and Contempt of the Government and Constitution of these realms'.[121] I am not suggesting that Turner's *George IV at St Giles's* fell into this category, but in a period in which the king was prepared to pay a publisher considerable sums of money not to print caricatures that depicted him with his corpulent mistress Lady Conyngham,[122] sensitivity to comic and demeaning representations of the royal personage was clearly acute. In depicting the king's portly form in a comic genre painting of a scene loaded with political significance, Turner was again walking on thin ice.

The ideological effects of artworks are not always what their producers expect; artists can miscalculate and audiences can read works awry. In exhibiting *The Field of Waterloo* in 1818, Turner seems to have adopted a daring liberal posture that he thought would be validated by its association with a lionised lordly poet. As he discovered, for all his picture's brilliance, it was a gambit unlikely to find approval outside the liberal press. In *England, Richmond Hill on the Prince Regent's Birthday*, he tried to make amends with a positive image of Regency England, but his ingenious attempt to transform a courtly spectacle into a *fête galante* set in a famous view that stood synecdochally for the nation was unconvincing. Unintentionally or not, the Hogarthian *George IV at*

---

as 'TREASON against the PEOPLE', and supported an address to the Prince Regent calling for the institution of an inquiry into their actions. See Kenney 1819, p. 62.

117   Chase 2013, pp. 76–84.

118   Chase 2013, pp. 143–9, 123–93.

119   For the coronation, see Parissien 2001, Chapter 15.

120   Parissien 2001, p. 303.

121   Chase 2013, p. 17.

122   Chase 2013, p. 209.

St Giles's came close to a Byronian satire of a man the poet called 'The fourth of the fools and oppressors call'd George',[123] and Turner abandoned the picture at sketch stage, perhaps to avoid compromising his chances of a major royal commission.[124] Like the *Field of Waterloo* and *England*, it remained in Turner's studio until his death. But Turner remained attached to his first Byronian painting, for in 1830, he published a mezzotint engraving of it by F.C. and Charles Lewis, accompanied with the same verses from *Childe Harold*.[125] Six years after Byron's death at Missolonghi – an event that sparked a new wave of enthusiasm for the poet[126] – it was safer for the reticent painter to assume the voice of the outspoken peer. Moreover, the fact that it was a year of several European revolutions (including one in Belgium) gave the picture's anti-militarism a new topicality. As with so many of Turner's acts that can be interpreted in a political light, we can only speculate whether his renewed interest in the theme signaled a message.

---

123   'The Irish Avatar' (1821), in Byron 1926, p. 108.

124   The one that did come – *The Battle of Trafalgar* (1823–4; National Maritime Museum, Greenwich) – was not a success. See Finberg 1961, pp. 282–3; Butlin and Joll 1977, cat. no. 252; Gage 1987, pp. 178–9. For Turner and Byronian satire, see Brown 1992, pp. 16–19, 77–8.

125   Rawlinson 1908–13 says the print was not published (vol. 2, p. 210), but elsewhere described a first published state (vol. 2, p. 383). It is dated to 1826 by Charles Lewis's note on an impression in the Victoria and Albert Museum – see Hermann 1990, 256 n. 40. Gage 1980, p. 135 n. 1, says it was published.

126   For the response to Byron's death, see Chew 1924, Chapter 11.

Coda: Regarding Art History

A painting that has been central to my thinking as an art historian is John Constable's *The Beach at Brighton, the Chain Pier in the Distance* (1826–7, *fig. 122*). One of the most accomplished and ambitious of British Romantic landscape paintings, it is the focus of extended analysis in my 1992 book *Landscape Imagery and Urban Culture in Early Nineteenth-Century Britain*.[1] I want to take this occasion to revisit my argument so as to pinpoint what seem to me some big issues of art-historical practice. In part, this may be regarded as an auto-critique.

Brighton Beach features in a chapter of *Landscape Imagery* devoted to representations of seaside resorts. Although I did not formulate my concerns as clearly as I should have, this chapter – and another analysing imagery of rivers – was intended to begin mapping an *iconography* of naturalistic landscape painting. This was a novel departure in that while by 1992 there was a sizeable corpus of work on the social history of the landscape genre in Britain, it was work that predominantly centred round individual artists and their particular reactions to the economic and social changes of the period. If not exactly an 'art history without names', I wanted to produce something more impersonal that would consider the production of paintings rather as a societal process in which artists – although still treated as conscious agents – were more the bearers of subject positions. Iconography would further socialise understanding of picture production.

There was, I admit, a certain wilful asceticism in this approach. Like others repelled by the snobbery and shallowness of the establishment art history they encountered entering the field in the 1960s and 1970s, I wanted not only to critique the discipline from a Marxist perspective, but also to rub its delicate nose in the quotidian facts of sociology. In this instance, it was easy to show that Constable's well-documented distaste for Brighton was not merely the personal quirk of a Suffolk countryman, but was cognate with a larger class reaction to the mixed social usage of seaside resorts in the early nineteenth century and the politico-moral critique of all that was encompassed by the terms 'luxury' and 'fashion'. Country-city differences were at work here, but so were inter- and intra-class tensions around the cultures of aristocracy and court. However,

---

1 Hemingway 1992, pp. 184–96. The book's title was a compromise with the publisher and somewhat misleading. My preferred title was the more accurate *Naturalism and Modernity: Landscape Imagery and Class Cultures in Britain, 1800–1830*.

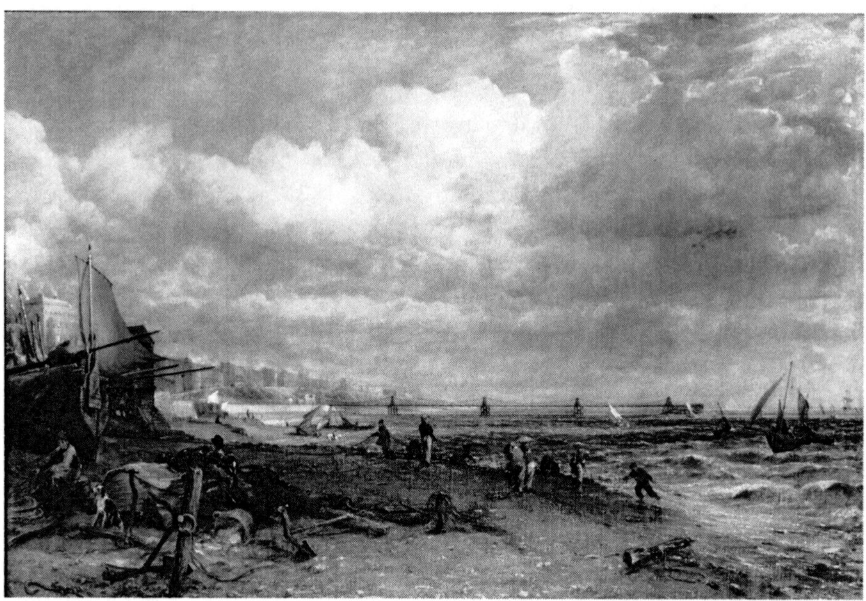

FIGURE 122 *John Constable,* The Beach at Brighton, the Chain Pier in the Distance, *1826–7, oil on canvas, 50 × 72 in (127.0 × 182.9 cm), Tate Britain*
© TATE, LONDON 2015

while it is hard not to see Constable's distaste for fashionable Brighton and the despoliation of the former fishing village as structuring the painting and defining its gloomy tone, this is hardly the cause of its meanings. The picture's qualities produce their effects with or without our knowledge of the artist's opinions. But for those qualities to produce something like the impact they had on their first audience, the historian must work to rupture the carapace of familiarity that encloses the art object, and attempt to recover something of its original novelty and strangeness.

My argument was that the clear signs for topographical landmarks in the painting, together with its title, made it unmistakably a 'beach and pier at Brighton type picture' (to draw on Nelson Goodman's terminology)[2] and that as such it would have activated the internally fractured mythology of Brighton in the minds of contemporary viewers, producing a range of possible and conflicting responses. However, while numerous prints and lesser paintings of the time depicted some, or even many, of the same component motifs, pictures of this type generally lacked the oppressive mood and emphatic contrasts

2   Goodman 1981, pp. 27–31.

of Constable's. What made his conception such a powerful ideological cue were not just its size (50 × 72 ins.), dramatic chiaroscuro, and bravura Baroque cloud effects; it was the fact that it fused together elements of a conventional topographical view with the format of a seventeenth-century Dutch beach scene, producing a grating clash between the picturesque landscape aesthetic and the signs of modern commerce and technology, all centred around the iron marvel of the chain pier, protruding at right angles from the brightly-lit strip of the esplanade. In this scheme the detritus of the fishing industry in the foreground figures like a *memento mori*. It was the combination of these qualities that made *Brighton Beach* stand out from other early nineteenth-century depictions of similar views and gave it a special significance.

Although some contemporary critics disliked the work's colouring and overt painterly quality – complaints that were probably symptomatic of deeper concerns – nothing in the reviews I discovered directly confirms the above claim. As T.J. Clark showed in his analyses of French exhibition reviews (which served as my model) art criticism is frequently an opaque and ritualised form of response that gives no direct access to collective consciousness and has to be read in the way an analyst listens to a patient if its latent ideological content is to be perceived.[3] But in any case, as I acknowledged in 1992, establishing the effects of an artwork does not deliver the historian its meaning.

Art history generally works both by positing explanatory cause and effect relationships, of the kind associated with the natural sciences, and by hermeneutic modes of interpretation that hypothesise meanings through asserting relations of part to whole and usually take the form of homologies. This duality of explanation and interpretation is arguably constitutive of the cultural sciences generally.[4] As in my *Landscape Imagery*, the two often appear side by side with little or no acknowledgment of the different character of their claims. It seems to me now that more acknowledgment is desirable – at least for those of us who care about the aesthetic status of art objects.

To define the conditions in which an artwork is produced – patronage, circumstances of display, function, art theory, iconography, style options and so on – is in effect to claim a set of determining factors. Since, as Hume famously showed, causes – whether natural or social – cannot be apprehended directly, there is always an intuitive and speculative element in such claims. However, to assert, as I now do, that Constable's painting gives form to a giddying conscious-

3   Clark 1973 (2), p. 12.

4   I draw here on Mannheim 1952, pp. 33–83. Despite its datedness in some respects, this essay
    seems to me to identify central problems of our discipline.

ness of the fragility of traditional values in the face of the onrushing condition of capitalist modernity in early nineteenth-century Britain, that it concentrates into a single emblem a whole Romantic *Weltanschauung*, is to make a different kind of claim and one that is not causal in any straightforward sense. It is to argue that the unseemly conjunctions of old and new, the lurches of the perspective recession and the battleground smoke of the clouds in *Brighton Beach*, all speak a profound Burkean anxiety about the unstoppable pace of change in the modern world – that they represent a struggle to give order to that world (to make it knowable as a whole) within the *Gestalt* of an artistic form that groans under the strain. In effect, the picture takes the picturesque beach-scene format and turns it against itself in an act of ideological self-disclosure. To what extent the artist was aware of this is irrelevant, though there are ample signs in Constable's later work that he realised the conventional mythologies of rural life embodied in the contemporary landscape genre were patently at odds with rural actualities.

To break down the artwork into component parts and identify their semiotic heft, to posit cause and effect relationships that may help to explain how the work came to be made or to look the way it does – these are procedures that help us to comprehend it as an historical event. But such investigations do not define the meaning of the whole.[5] If one accepts a cognitive definition of the aesthetic – that is one that makes it something more than the prompt to a form of disinterested pleasure – then the measure of value will be a work's truth. This is not something that historical inquiry alone can determine; it depends also on a totalising and philosophical approach to the understanding of a cultural moment – however provisional and tentative such understandings necessarily are. I do not wish to make a claim for Constable quite as grandiose as Adorno's equivalence between Hegel's philosophy and Beethoven's music,[6] but I do think Constable's *Brighton Beach* presents us with a picturing of historical change that is almost unparalleled in the landscape art of its period, rivalled only in some paintings by Turner. As in a number of other Constable works, we encounter a disharmony that is the mark of a modern consciousness that recognises social life itself has become radically inharmonious.[7] This had profound aesthetic implications, in that, wittingly or unwittingly, Constable could no longer paint contemporary realities as beautiful in the conventional sense of his time. To do so would be to paint an untruth. Instead he painted

---

5   Cf. Mannheim 1952, pp. 68–70.

6   Adorno 1997, p. 185.

7   On dissonance, cf. Adorno 1997, p. 15.

the violation of nature at Brighton. This is not to make Constable an anti-capitalist – he was in many ways solidly bourgeois in outlook – but it is to claim that in some ways his painting speaks forcefully of a deep unease with the world capitalism was making, with its oppressive means-ends rationality and indifference to qualitative values, here represented by nature.[8] In asserting this, I am reaffirming, in rather different terms, a qualitative judgment that discomforted some reviewers of my book when it appeared. Like all aesthetic judgments this is a subjective judgment, but also one that claims validity.

---

8   My thinking about Romanticism here is indebted to Löwy and Sayre 2001.

Bibliography

Historical Sources

Addison, Joseph and Richard Steele, et al. 1945 [1711–12], *The Spectator*, 4 Volumes, London: Everyman.

Algarotti, Francesco 1764, *An Essay on Painting*, London.

Alison, Archibald 1815 [1811], *Essays on the Nature and Principles of Taste*, revised edition, 2 Volumes, Edinburgh.

Anon. 1880, *The Life and Political Career of J.J. Colman, Esq., M.P., and J.H. Tillett, Esq., ... Including the Rise and Progress of the Carrow Works*, Norwich.

Bacon, Richard Noverre 1844, *Report on the Agriculture of Norfolk*, London.

Barry, James 1809, *The Works of J. Barry, Esq., Historical Painter*, 2 Volumes, London.

Bartell, Edmund 1804, *Hints for Picturesque Improvements in Ornamental Cottages, and their Scenery, Including Some Observations on the Labourer and his Cottage, in Three Essays*, London: J. Taylor.

Bartell, Edmund 1806 [1800], *Cromer, Considered as a Watering Place; with Observations of the Picturesque Scenery in the Neighbourhood*, second edition, London: J. Taylor.

Baudelaire, Charles 1965, *Art in Paris, 1845–1862: Reviews of Salons and Other Exhibitions*, translated and edited by Jonathan Mayne, London: Phaidon.

Beatniffe, Richard 1795, *The Norfolk Tour*, fifth edition, Norwich.

Bentham, Jeremy 1825, *The Rationale of Reward*, London.

Bentham, Jeremy 1983 [1817], *Chrestomathia*, edited by M.J. Smith and W.H. Burston, Oxford: Oxford University Press.

Bentham, Jeremy 1988 (1) [1776], *A Fragment on Government*, edited by J.H. Burns and H.L.A. Hart, Cambridge: Cambridge University Press.

Bentham, Jeremy 1988 (2) [1789], *The Principles of Morals and Legislation*, Buffalo, New York: Prometheus Books.

Blanchard, Laman 1841, *The Life and Literary Remains of L.E.L.*, 2 Volumes, London.

Blomefield, Francis and Charles Parkin 1805–10, *A Topographical History of the County of Norfolk*, 11 Volumes, London.

Bloomfield, Robert 1998, *Selected Poems*, edited by John Goodrich and John Lucas, first edition, Nottingham: Trent Editions.

Boydell, John and Josiah Boydell 1794–6, *An History of the River Thames*, text by William Combe, 2 Volumes, London.

Britton, John 1816, *History and Antiquities of the See and Cathedral Church of Norwich*, London.

Burgess, Edward and Wilfrid L. Burgess 1904, *Men Who Have Made Norwich*, Norwich: Edward Burgess & Sons Ltd.

Burke, Edmund 1759 [1757], *A Philosophical Enquiry into the Origin of our Ideas on the Sublime and Beautiful*, second edition, London: R. and J. Dodsley.

Butler, Joseph 1736, *The Analogy of Religion, Natural and Revealed to the Constitution and Course of Nature*, London.

Byron, George 1926, *The Poetical Works of Lord Byron*, London: Oxford University Press.

Campbell, Charles 1817, *Travellers' Complete Guide though Belgium and Holland*, second edition, London.

Chambers, John 1829, *A General History of the County of Norfolk*, Norwich and London.

Clare, John 1970, *The Prose of John Clare*, edited by J.W. and A. Tibble, New York: Barnes and Noble.

Clare, John 1996–2003, *Poems of the Middle Period, 1822–37*, edited by Eric Robinson, David Powell, and P.M.S. Dawson, 5 Volumes, Oxford: Clarendon Press.

Clark, John 1794, *General View of the Agriculture of the County of Hereford*, London.

Cobbett, William 1912 [1830], *Rural Rides*, 2 Volumes, London: J.M. Dent & Sons Ltd.

Collins, William Wilkie 1848, *Memoirs of the Life of William Collins, R.A.; with Selections from his Journals and Correspondence*, 2 Volumes, London: Longman & Co.

Colman, Helen Caroline 1905, *Jeremiah James Colman. A Memoir*, privately printed, London: Chiswick Press.

Colman, Russell J. 1886, *Trifles from a Tourist in Letters from Abroad*, privately printed, Norwich: Fletcher and Son.

Constable, John 1962–8, *John Constable's Correspondence*, edited by R.B. Beckett, 6 Volumes, Ipswich: Suffolk Records Society.

Constable, John 1970, *John Constable's Discourses*, edited by R.B. Beckett, Ipswich: Suffolk Records Society.

Cooper, Anthony Ashley 1714 [1711], *Characteristics of Men, Manners, Opinions, Times*, second edition, 3 Volumes, London.

Cowper, William 1926, *The Poetical Works of William Cowper*, edited by H.S. Milford, third edition, London: Oxford University Press.

Crabbe, George 1967, *Tales, 1812 and other Selected Poems*, edited and introduced by Howard Mills, Cambridge: Cambridge University Press.

Craig, John 1806, *An Account of the Life and Writings of John Millar, Esq.*, in John Millar, *The Origin of the Distinction of Ranks*, fourth edition, Edinburgh: Blackwood.

Cunningham, Allan 1836, *The Cabinet Gallery of British Pictures*, 2 Volumes, London: George & William Nicol; Hodgson & Graves.

Duncumb, John 1804, *Collections Towards the History and Antiquities of the County of Hereford*, Hereford.

Duncumb, John 1813, *A General View of Agriculture in the County of Hereford*, London.

Dyer, John 1989, *The Poems of John Dyer*, edited by Edward Thomas, Lampeter: Llanerch Enterprises.

Edwards, Edward 1839, *A Letter to Sir Martin Archer Shee ... on the Reform of the Royal Academy*, London.

Edwards, Edward 1840, *The Fine Arts in England; Their State and Prospects Considered Relatively to National Education*, London.

Farington, Joseph 1978–84, *The Diary of Joseph Farington*, Volumes 1–6 edited by Kenneth Garlick and Angus Macintyre, Volumes 7–16 edited by Kathryn Cave, 16 Volumes, New Haven: Yale University Press.

Fawkes, Francis 1760, *Works of Anacreon, Sappho, Bion, Moschus, and Musaeus*, London.

Ferguson, Adam 1966 [1767], *An Essay on the History of Civil Society*, edited by Duncan Forbes, Edinburgh: Edinburgh University Press.

Flaxman, John 1892 [1829], *Lectures on Sculpture*, London: George Bell and Sons.

Foggo, George 1833, 'The Royal Academy Exposed, From Authentic Documents and Undoubted Facts', *New Monthly Magazine*, 38: 73–82.

Foggo, George 1835, *A Letter to Lord Brougham, On the History and Character of the Royal Academy*, London.

Foggo, George 1837, *Results of the Parliamentary Inquiry Relative to Arts and Manufactures*, London.

Fuseli, Henry 1831, *The Life and Writings of Henry Fuseli*, edited by John Knowles, 3 Volumes, London: H. Colburn and R. Bentley.

Gerard, Alexander 1963 [1780], *An Essay on Taste*, edited by W.J. Hipple, Jr., third edition, Gainesville: Scholars' Facsimiles and Reprints.

Gilpin, William 1794 [1792], *Three Essays: On Picturesque Beauty, On Picturesque Travel; and on Sketching Landscape*, second edition, London.

Gilpin, William 1802 [1768], *An Essay on Prints*, fifth edition, London.

Gilpin, William 1808 [1791], *Remarks on Forest Scenery, and other Woodland Views, Relative Chiefly to Picturesque Beauty*, third edition, 2 Volumes, London.

Gilpin, William 1809, *Observations of Several Parts of the Counties of Cambridge, Norfolk, Suffolk, and also on Several Parts of North Wales*, London.

Hartley, David 1791 and 1801 [1749], *Observations on Man*, 2 parts, London.

Hassell, John 1819, *Tour of the Grand Junction in a Series of Engravings*, London.

Hazlitt, William 1873, *Essays on the Fine Arts*, edited by W.C. Hazlitt, London: Reeves and Turner.

Hazlitt, William 1930–4, *The Complete Works of William Hazlitt in Twenty-four Volumes*, edited by P.P. Howe, London and Toronto: Dent.

Hoare, Prince (ed.) 1810, *The Artist: A Collection of Essays, Relative to Painting, Poetry, Sculpture, the Drama, Discoveries of Science, and Various Other Subjects*, 2 Volumes, London, 1810.

Hodgson, David 1860, *A Reverie, or Thoughts Suggested by a Visit to the Gallery of Works of Deceased Norfolk and Norwich Artists*, Norwich.

Home, Henry 1785 [1762], *Elements of Criticism*, 2 Volumes, Edinburgh.

Home, Henry 1788 [1774], *Sketches of the History of Man*, 4 Volumes, Edinburgh.

Horne, Richard Henry 1833, *Exposition of the False Medium and Barriers Excluding Men of Genius from the Public*, London.

House of Commons 1836, *Report from the Select Committee on Arts and their Connections with Manufactures*, 2 parts, London.

Hume, David 1963, *Essays, Moral, Political and Literary*, Oxford: Oxford University Press.

Hume, David 1975 [1777], *Enquiries Concerning Human Understanding and Concerning the Principles of Morals*, third edition, edited by L.A. Selby-Bigge and P.H. Nidditch, Oxford: Clarendon Press.

Hume, David 1978 [1738], *Treatise of Human Nature*, edited by L.A. Selby Bigge and P.H. Nidditch, Oxford: Oxford University Press.

Hunt, Leigh 1815, *The Descent of Liberty; a Mask*, London.

Hutcheson, Francis 1973 [1725], *Francis Hutcheson: An Inquiry Concerning Beauty, Order, Harmony, Design*, edited and introduced by Peter Kivy, The Hague: Nijhoff.

Jones, T.E. 1849, *A Descriptive Account of the Literary Works of John Britton*, London.

Kenney, Arthur Henry 1819, *A Letter to Early Fitzwilliam Demonstrating the Real Tendency of the Proceedings of the Late York Meeting*. London.

Kent, Nathaniel 1776 [1775], *Hints to Gentlemen of Landed Property*, second edition, London: J. Dodsley.

Kent, Nathaniel 1794, *General View of the Agriculture of the County of Norfolk*, London.

Knight, Richard Payne 1795 [1794], *The Landscape: A Didactic Poem in Three Books, Addressed to Uvedale Price, Esq.*, second edition, London.

Knight, Richard Payne 1808 [1805], *An Analytical Inquiry into the Principles of Taste*, fourth edition, London.

Knight, Richard Payne 1810, review of *The Works of James Barry, Esq.*, *Edinburgh Review*, 16, 32: 293–326.

Knight, Richard Payne 1814 review of James Northcote, *Life of Sir Joshua Reynolds*, *Edinburgh Review*, 23, 46: 263–92.

Lawrence, Thomas 1824, *Address to the Students of the Royal Academy, delivered ... 1823*, London.

Leslie, Charles Robert Leslie 1855, *A Hand-Book for Young Painters*, London: John Murray.

Leslie, Charles Robert Leslie 1949 [1845], *Memoirs of the Life of John Constable*, introduced by Benedict Nicolson, London: John Lehmann.

Locke, John 1829 [1690], *An Essay Concerning Human Understanding*, twenty-seventh edition, London.

Marshall, William 1787, *The Rural Economy of Norfolk*, 2 Volumes, London.

Middleton, John 1807 [1797], *General View of Agriculture in the County of Middlesex*, London.

Mill, John Stuart 1981 [1833], 'Thoughts on Poetry and Its Varieties', in *Autobiography and Literary Essays*, edited by J.M. Robson and J. Stillinger, Toronto and Buffalo.

Millar, John 1803, *An Historical View of the English Government*, 4 Volumes, London.

Millingen, James V. 1831, *Some Remarks on the State of Learning and the Fine Arts in Great Britain, on the Deficiency of Public Institutions, and the Necessity of a Better System for the Improvement of Knowledge and Taste*, London.

Moore, Thomas 1830, *Letters and Journals of Lord Byron with Notices of his Life*, 2 Volumes, London: John Murray.

Norfolk and Norwich News Company Ltd. 1905, *A Souvenir of the Centenary of J. & J. Colman Ltd.: 1805–1905*, Norwich.

Paget, Elise 1882, 'Old Crome', *Magazine of Art*, 5: 221–6.

Palmer, C.J. 1874, *The Perlustration of Great Yarmouth*, 3 Volumes, Great Yarmouth.

Phillips, Thomas 1833, *Lectures on the History and Principles of Painting*, London: Longman.

Pope, Alexander 1969, *Poetry and Prose of Alexander Pope*, edited and introduced by Aubrey Williams, Boston: Houghton Mifflin Co.

Price, Uvedale 1797, *Thoughts on the Defence of Property, Addressed to the County of Hereford*, Hereford.

Price, Uvedale 1810, *Essays on the Picturesque, as Compared with the Sublime and the Beautiful; and, on the Use of Studying Pictures, for the Purpose of Improving real Landscape*, 3 Volumes, London.

Pye, John 1845, *Patronage of British Art*, London: Longman.

Ravenstone, Piercy 1821, *A Few Doubts as to the Correctness of Some Opinions Generally Entertained on the Subjects of Population and Political Economy*, London

Ravenstone, Piercy 1824, *Thoughts on the Funding System and its Effects*, London.

Redgrave, Richard and Samuel 1947 [1866], *A Century of British Painters*, London: Phaidon Press.

Repton, Humphry 1840, *The Landscape Gardening and Landscape Architecture of the Late Humphry Repton, Esq.*, edited by J.C. Loudon, London: Longman and Co.

Repton, John Adey 1965, *Norwich Cathedral at the End of the Eighteenth Century with Descriptive Notices by William Wilkins*, Farnborough: Gregg Press.

Reynolds, Joshua 1975, *Discourses on Art*, edited by Robert R. Wark, New Haven and London: Yale University Press.

Richter, Henry 1817, *Daylight; A Recent Discovery in the Art of Painting; with Hints on the Philosophy of the Fine Arts, and on that of the Human Mind as first dissected by Immanuel Kant*, London: Ackermann.

Rigby, Edward 1817, *Holkham, Its Agriculture, &c.*, Norwich.

Rigby, Edward 1820, *Framingham, Its Agriculture, &c., including the Economy of a Small Farm*, Norwich.

Robberds, John Warden 1834, *Scenery of the Rivers of Norfolk from Pictures by James Stark*, Norwich and London: Moon, Boys, and Graves.

Robberds, John Warden 1843, *A Memoir of the Life and Writings of the Late William Taylor of Norwich*, 2 Volumes, London.

Sayers, Frank 1808, *Disquisitions by Frank Sayers, M.D.*, London.

Sayers, Frank 1823, *Collective Works of the late Dr. Sayers*, edited by William Taylor, 2 Volumes, Norwich: Matchett and Stevenson.

Scott, John 1815, *A Visit to Paris in 1814: Being a Review of the Moral, Political, Intellectual, and Social Condition of the French Capital*, London.

Shee, Martin Archer 1805, *Rhymes on Art*, London.

Shee, Martin Archer 1809 (1), *Elements of Art*, London.

Shee, Martin Archer 1809 (2), *A Letter to the President and Directors of the British Institution; Containing the Outlines of a Plan for the National Encouragement of Historical Painting in the United Kingdom*, London.

Smith, Adam 1976 (1) [1776], *An Inquiry into the Nature and Causes of the Wealth of Nations*, edited by R.H. Campbell, A.S. Skinner; and W.B. Todd, 2 Volumes, Oxford: Oxford University Press.

Smith, Adam 1976 (2), *The Theory of Moral Sentiments*, edited by D.D. Raphael and A.L. Macfie, Oxford: Oxford University Press.

Smith, Adam 1983, *Lectures on Rhetoric and Belles Lettres*, edited by J.C. Bryce, Oxford: Oxford University Press.

Smith, John Thomas 1797, *Remarks on Rural Scenery; with Twenty Etchings of Cottages, from Nature; and Some Observations and Precepts Relative to the Pictoresque*, London.

Stacy, John 1832, *A Topographical and Historical Account of the City and County of Norwich*, second edition, London and Norwich.

Strutt, Jacob George 1822, *Sylva Britannica; or Portraits of Forest Trees, distinguished for their Antiquity, Magnitude, or Beauty*, London: published by the author.

Taylor, William 1814, 'Outlines of a Discourse on the History and Theory of Prospect Painting', *Monthly Magazine*, part one, 37: 405–9; part two, 38: 211–15.

Thelwall, John 1822, *The Poetical Recreations of the Champion, and his Literary Correspondents*, London.

Thomson, James 1908, *The Complete Poetical Works of James Thomson*, edited by J. Logie Robertson, London: Oxford University Press.

Tombleson, William 1834?, *Tombleson's Thames*, with descriptions by William Gray Fearnside, London.

Thoré, Théophile 1863, *Histoire des peintres de toutes les écoles. École anglaise*, edited by Charles Blanc, Paris: Librairie Renouard.

Thoré, Théophile 1870, *Salons de W. Bürger 1861 à 1868*, Paris: J. Renouard.

Turner, Dawson 1840, *Outlines in Lithography from a Small Collection of Pictures*, Great Yarmouth: privately printed.

Varley, John 1816–17, *A Treatise on the Principles of Landscape Design*, London.

Waagen, Gustav Friedrich 1854, *Treasures of Art in Great Britain*, 3 Volumes, London: John Murray.

Wade, John 1820, *The Black Book; or, Corruption Unmasked*, London.

Wainewright, Thomas Griffith 1880, *Essays and Criticisms of Thomas Griffiths Wainewright*, edited by W.C. Hazlitt, London: Reeves and Turner.

Ward, James 1821, *The Battle of Waterloo in an Allegory, painted for the Directors of the British Institution*, London.

Windham, William 1866, *Diary of the Right Honourable William Windham 1784 to 1810*, edited by Mrs. Henry Baring, London: Longman, Green and Co.

Wodderspoon, John 1876 [1858], *John Crome and his Works*, second edition, Norwich: privately printed.

Wollstonecraft, Mary 1982 [1792], *A Vindication of the Rights of Woman*, edited by Miriam Brody, Harmondsworth: Penguin.

Wornum, Ralph (ed.) 1848, *Lectures on Painting by the Royal Academicians. Barry, Opie, and Fuseli*, London: Bohn.

Wyse, Thomas 1836, *Education Reform; or, the Necessity of National System of Education*, London.

Young, Arthur 1804, *General View of the Agriculture of the County of Norfolk*, London.

Secondary Literature

Aaron, Richard I. 1955, *John Locke*, second edition, Oxford: Oxford University Press.

Abrams, Meyer H. 1953, *The Mirror and the Lamp: Romantic Theory and the Critical Tradition*, New York: Oxford University Press.

Adorno, Theodor W. 1967, 'Art and the Arts', in *Can One Live After Auschwitz? A Philosophical Reader*, edited by Rolf Tiedemann, Stanford: University of California Press.

Adorno, Theodor W. 1972, 'Ideology', in Frankfurt Institute for Social Research, *Aspects of Sociology*, translated by John Viertel, Boston: Beacon Press.

Adorno, Theodor W. 1977, 'The Actuality of Philosophy', *Telos*, 31: 120–33.

Adorno, Theodor W. 1981, *In Search of Wagner*, translated by Rodney Livingstone, London: NLB.

Adorno, Theodor W. 1995, 'On Some Relationships between Music and Painting', translated by Susan Gillespie, *Musical Quarterly*, 79, 1: 66–79.

Adorno, Theodor W. 1997, *Aesthetic Theory*, translated by Robert Hullot-Kentor, Minneapolis: University of Minnesota Press.

Adorno, Theodor W. and Max Horkheimer 1979 [1944], *Dialectic of Enlightenment*, translated by John Cumming, London: Verso.

Albany Gallery 1968, *Robert Hills 1769–1844*, London.

Allthorpe-Guyton, Marjorie 1977, *John Thirtle, Drawings in Norwich Museum*, Norwich: Norfolk Museums Service.

Allthorpe-Guyton, Marjorie with John Stevens 1982, *A Happy Eye: A School of Art in Norwich*, Norwich: Jarrold Publishing.

Althusser, Louis 1971, *Lenin and Philosophy and other Essays*, translated by Ben Brewster, London: New Left Books.

Althusser, Louis 2005 [1969], *For Marx*, translated by Ben Brewster, London and New York.

Althusser, Louis 2014, *On the Reproduction of Capitalism: Ideology and Ideological State Apparatuses*, translated by G.M. Goshgaraian, London and New York: Verso.

Althusser, Louis and Etienne Balibar 1970, *Reading Capital*, translated by Ben Brewster. London: NLB.

Anderson, Perry 1969 [1968], 'Components of the National Culture', *Student Power: Problems, Diagnosis, Action*, edited Alexander Cockburn and Robin Blackburn, Harmondsworth: Penguin Books.

Anderson, Perry 1976, 'The Antinomies of Antonio Gramsci', *New Left Review*, 1st series, 100: 5–78.

Anderson, Perry 1980, *Arguments within English Marxism*, London: Verso.

Anderson, Perry 1992, *English Questions*, London and New York: Verso.

Antal, Frederick 1948, *Florentine Painting and its Social Background*, London: Kegan Paul, Trench, Truebner & Co. Ltd.

Antal, Frederick 1966, *Classicism and Romanticism and other Studies in Art History*, London: Routledge and Kegan Paul.

Aspinall, Arthur 1927, *Lord Brougham and the Whig Party*, Manchester: Manchester University Press.

Auchmuty, James Johnson 1939, *Sir Thomas Wyse, 1791–1862: The Life and Career of an Educator and Diplomat*, London: P.S. King & Son, Ltd.

Bachrach, A.G.H. 1981, 'The Field of Waterloo and beyond', *Turner Studies*, 1, 2: 4–13

Baker, Charles Henry Collins 1921, *Crome*, London: Methuen and Co.

Baldwin, Michael and Charles Harrison and Mel Ramsden 1981, 'Art History, Art Criticism, and Explanation', *Art History*, 4, 4: 432–56.

Barbier, Carl P. 1963, *William Gilpin: His Drawings, Teachings, and Theory of the Picturesque*, Oxford: Oxford University Press.

Barnes, Donald Grove Barnes 1965 [1930], *A History of the English Corn Laws from 1660–1846*, New York: Augustus M. Kelly.

Barrell, John 1972, *The Idea of Landscape and the Sense of Place, 1730–1840: An Approach to the Poetry of John Clare*, Cambridge: Cambridge University Press.

Barrell, John 1980, *The Dark Side of the Landscape: The Rural Poor in English Painting, 1730–1840*, Cambridge: Cambridge University Press.

Barrell, John 1983, *English Literature in History, 1730–80: An Equal Wide Survey*, London: Hutchinson.

Barrell, John 1986, *The Political Theory of Painting from Reynolds to Hazlitt*, New Haven and London: Yale University Press.

Barthes, Roland 1968, *Elements of Semiology*, translated by Annette Lavers and Colin Smith, New York: Hill and Wang.

Barthes, Roland 1973, *Mythologies*, translated by Annette Lavers, London: Paladin Books.

Barthes, Roland 1977, *Image-Music-Text*, translated by Stephen Heath, New York: Hill and Wang.

Bauer, Josephine 1953, *The London Magazine, Anglistica*, vol. 1, Copenhagen: Rosenkilde and Bagger.

Beer, Max 1929, *A History of British Socialism*, introduction by R.H. Tawney, 2 Volumes, London: G. Bell and Sons.

Bell, Clive 1915, *Art*, London: Chatto & Windus.

Bell, Clive 1922, *Since Cézanne*, London: Chatto & Windus.

Bell, Quentin 1963, *The Schools of Design*, London: Routledge and Kegan Paul.

Berger, John 1978, 'In Defense of Art', *New Society* 45, 834: 702–4.

Bermingham, Ann 1987 (1), 'Reading Constable', *Art History*, 10, 1: 38–58.

Bermingham, Ann 1987 (2), *Landscape and Ideology: The English Rustic Tradition, 1740–1860*, London: Thames & Hudson.

Bermingham, Ann (ed.) 2005, *Sensation & Sensibility, Viewing Gainsborough's Cottage Door*, New Haven and London: Yale University Press.

Bhaskar, Roy 1980, *The Possibility of Naturalism*, Brighton: Harvester.

Bindoff, Stanley Thomas 1949, *Kett's Rebellion 1549*, London: Historical Association.

Binyon, Laurence 1897, *Crome and Cotman*, London: Seeley and Co.

Binyon, Laurence 1904, 'Drawings of the Norwich School at the British Museum', *Burlington Magazine*, 6, 19: 53–5, 57.

Blackburn, Robin (ed.) 1972, *Ideology in Social Science: Readings in Critical Social Theory*, New York: Pantheon.

Bone, Drummond (ed.) 2004, *The Cambridge Companion to Byron*, Cambridge: Cambridge University Press.

Boralevi, L.C. 1987, 'Utilitarianism and Feminism', in *Women in Western Political Philosophy*, edited by Ellen Kennedy and Susan Mendus, Brighton: Wheatsheaf.

Bourdieu, Pierre 1971, 'Intellectual Field and Creative Project', in *Knowledge and Control: New Directions for the Sociology of Education*, edited by M.F.D. Young, London: Collier-Macmillan.

Bourdieu, Pierre 1992, *Language and Symbolic Power*, edited by John B. Thompson, translated by Gino Raymond and Matthew Adamson, Cambridge: Polity.

Bourdieu, Pierre 1993, *The Field of Cultural Production*, edited and introduced by Randal Johnson, New York: Columbia University Press.

Brewer, John 1980, 'English Radicalism in the Age of George III', in *Three British Revolution: 1641, 1688, 1776*, edited by J.G.A. Pocock, Princeton: Princeton University Press.

Briggs, Asa 1956, 'Middle-Class Consciousness in English Politics, 1780–1846', *Past and Present*, 9: 65–74.

Brindle, Steven 2001, 'The Wellington Arch and the western entrance to London', *Georgian Group Journal*, 11: 47–87.

Brown, Christopher 1996, *Making & Meaning: Rubens's* Landscapes, London: National Gallery Publications.

Brown, David Blayney 1992, *Turner and Byron*, London: Tate Gallery.

Brown, David Blayney and Andrew Hemingway, and Anne Lyles 2000, *Romantic Landscape: The Norwich School of Painters*, London: Tate Gallery.

Brunius, Teddy 1952, *David Hume on Criticism*, Stockholm: Almqvist and Wiksell.

Butlin, Martin and Evelyn Joll 1977, *The Paintings of J.M.W. Turner*, 2 Volumes, New Haven: Yale University Press.

Carman, William C. 1965, 'The Battle of Waterloo by Denis Dighton', *Journal of the Society for Army Historical Research*, 43: 55–9.

Cassirer, Ernst 1951, *The Philosophy of the Enlightenment*, Princeton, NJ: Princeton University Press.

Chandler, James 1998, *England in 1819: The Politics of Literary Culture and the Case of Romantic Historicism*, Chicago: Chicago University Press.

Chase, Malcolm 2013, *1820: Disorder and Stability in the United Kingdom*, Manchester: Manchester University Press.

Chew, Samuel C. 1924, *Byron in England: His Fame and After-Fame*, New York: Scribner's Sons.

Chitnis, Anand C. 1976, *The Scottish Enlightenment: A Social History*, London: Croom Helm.

Clark, Roy 1961, *Black-Sailed Traders: The Keels and Wherries of Norfolk and Suffolk*, London: Putnam and Co. Ltd.

Clark, Timothy J. 1973 (1), *The Absolute Bourgeois: Artists and Politics in France, 1848–1851*, London: Thames and Hudson.

Clark, Timothy J. 1973 (2), *The Image of the People: Gustave Courbet and the 1848 Revolution*, London: Thames and Hudson.

Clark, Timothy J. 1980 (1), 'Preliminaries to a Possible Treatment of "Olympia" in 1865', *Screen* 21, 1: 18–41.

Clark, Timothy J. 1980 (2), 'A Note in Reply to Peter Wollen', *Screen*, 21, 3: 97–100.

Clark, Timothy J. 1995, 'The Conditions of Artistic Creation' [1974], in *Art History and its Methods: A Critical Anthology*, edited by Eric Fernie, London: Phaidon.

Clarke, Michael and Nicholas Penny (ed.) 1982, *The Arrogant Connoisseur: Richard Payne Knight, 1751–1824*, Manchester: Manchester University Press.

Clifford, Derek 1965, *Watercolours of the Norwich School*, London: Cory, Adam, and Mackay.

Clifford, Derek and Timothy Clifford 1968, *John Crome*, London: Faber and Faber.

Clive, John 1957, *Scotch Reviewers: The Edinburgh Review, 1802–1815*, London: Faber and Faber.

Coates, W.H. 1950, 'Benthamism, Laissez-faire, and Collectivism', *Journal of the History of Ideas*, 11, 3: 357–63.

Cochran, Peter 2010, *Byron and Hobby-O: The Relationship between Byron and John Cam Hobhouse*, Newcastle upon Tyne: Cambridge Scholars Publishing.

Cochran, Peter 2011, *Byron's Romantic Politics: The Problem of Metahistory*, Newcastle upon Tyne: Cambridge Scholars Publishing.

Cohen, Ralph 1958, 'David Hume's Experimental Method and the Theory of Taste', *ELH*, 25, 4: 270–89.

Cookson, J.E. 1982, *The Friends of Peace: Anti-War Liberalism in England, 1793–1815*, Cambridge: Cambridge University Press.

Cosgrove, Denis and Stephen Daniels (eds.), *The Iconography of Landscape: Essays in the Symbolic Representation, Design and Use of Past Environments*, Cambridge: Cambridge University Press.

Costello, Leo 2012., *J.M.W. Turner and the Subject of History*, Farnham: Ashgate.

Croce, Benedetto 1978, *Aesthetic. As Science of Expression and General Linguistic*, translated by D. Ainslie [1922], Boston: Nonpareil Books.

Cundall, Herbert Minton 1920, *The Norwich School*, London: The Studio Ltd.

Curling, Jonathan 1938, *Janus Weathercock: The Life of Thomas Griffiths Wainewright, 1794–1847*, London: Thomas Nelson.

Daniels, Stephen 1982 (1), 'The Political Landscape', in *Humphry Repton: Landscape Gardener, 1752–1818*, edited by George Carter, Patrick Goode, and Kedrun Laurie, London: Victoria and Albert Museum.

Daniels, Stephen 1982 (2), 'Humphry Repton and the Morality of Landscape', in *Valued Environments*, edited by John R. Gold and Jacquelin Burgess, London: George Allen and Unwin.

Daniels, Stephen 1983, 'Humphry Repton at Sustead', *Garden History*, 11, 1: 57–64.

Daniels, Stephen 1986, 'Cankerous Blossom: Troubles in the later career of Humphry Repton documented in the Repton correspondence in the Huntington Library', *Journal of Garden History*, 6, 2: 146–61.

Daniels, Stephen 1999, *Humphry Repton: Landscape Gardening and the Geography of Georgian England*, New Haven and London: Yale University Press.

Daniels, Stephen and Charles Watkins (ed.) 1994, *The Picturesque Landscape: Visions of Georgian Herefordshire*, Nottingham: Department of Geography, University of Nottingham.

Davidoff, Leonore and Catherine Hall 1987, *Family Fortunes: Men and Women of the English Middle Class, 1780–1850*, London: Routledge.

Davidson, Neil 2003, *Discovering the Scottish Revolution, 1692–1746*, London: Pluto Press.

Davidson, Neil 2012, *How Revolutionary Were the Bourgeois Revolutions?*, Chicago: Haymarket Books.

Day, Gail 2011, *Dialectical Passions: Negation in Postwar Art Theory*, New York: Columbia University Press.

Dellamora, Richard 1990, *Masculine Desire: The Sexual Politics of Victorian Aestheticism*, Chapel Hill and London: University of North Carolina Press.

Dickes, William Frederick 1906, *The Norwich School of Painting*, Norwich: Jarrolds.

Dickie, G.T. 1965, 'Clive Bell and the Method of Principia Ethica', *British Journal of Aesthetics*, 5: 139–43.

Ditchfield, G.M. 1974, 'The Parliamentary Struggle over the Repeal of the Test and Corporation Acts, 1787–90', *English Historical Review*, 89: 551–77.

Dobai, Johannes 1974–7, *Die Kunstliteratur des Klassizismus und der Romantik in England 1700–1840*, 3 Volumes, Bern: Benteli.

Eagleton, Terry 1991, *Ideology: An Introduction*, London and New York: Verso.

Eagleton, Terry 1998 [1976], *Criticism and Ideology: A Study in Marxist Literary Theory*, London and New York: Verso.

Eagleton, Terry and Matthew Beaumont 2009, *The Task of the Critic: Terry Eagleton in Dialogue*, London and New York: Verso.

Earland, Ada 1911, *John Opie*, London: Hutchinson.

Easthope, Anthony 1983, 'The Trajectory of *Screen*, 1971–79', in *The Politics of Theory: Essex Sociology of Literature Conference*, edited by Francis Barker et. al., University of Essex.

Edwards, J.K. 1963, 'The Economic Development of Norwich, 1750–1850, with Special Reference to the Worsted Industry', PhD thesis, University of Leeds

Edwards, J.K. 1964, 'The Decline of the Norwich Textiles Industry', *Yorkshire Bulletin of Economic and Social Research*, 16: 31–41.

Edwards, J.K. 1965, 'Communications and the Economic Development of Norwich 1750–1850', *Journal of Transport History*, 7: 96–108.

Egerton, Judy 1990, *Wright of Derby*, London: Tate Gallery.

Eley, Geoff 1981, 'Re-Thinking the Political: Social History and Political Culture in 18th and 19th Century Britain,' *Archiv für Sozialgeschichte*, 21: 427–57.

Eley, Geoff 1990, 'Edward Thompson, Social History and Political Culture: The Making of a Working-Class Public, 1780–1850', in *E.P. Thompson: Critical Perspectives*, edited by Harvey J. Kaye and Keith McClelland, Philadelphia: Temple University Press.

Emerson Roger 1973, 'The Enlightenment and Social Structures', in *City and Society in the 18th Century*, edited by Paul Fritz and David Williams, Toronto: Hakkert.

Emsley, Clive 1979, *British Society and the French Wars 1793–1815*, London and Basingstoke: Macmillan.

Erffa, Helmut von 1952, 'West's Washing of Sheep', *Art Quarterly* 15: 160–65.

Erffa, Helmut von and Allen Staley 1986, *The Paintings of Benjamin West*, New Haven and London: Yale University Press.

Everett, Nigel 1994, *The Tory View of Landscape*, New Haven and London: Yale University Press.

Fawcett, Trevor 1969, 'Patriotic Transparencies in Norwich 1798–1814', *Norfolk Archaeology*, 24: 245–52.

Fawcett, Trevor 1972, 'The culture of later Georgian Norwich: a conflict of evidence', *University of East Anglia Bulletin*, 4, 4: 1–10.

Fawcett, Trevor 1973, *The Rise of English Provincial Art: Artists, Patrons, and Institutions outside London, 1800–1830*, Oxford: Clarendon Press.

Fawcett, Trevor 1982 (1), 'John Crome and the Idea of Mousehold', *Norfolk Archaeology*, 38, part 2: 168–81.

Fawcett, Trevor 1982 (2), 'Measuring the Provincial Enlightenment: The Case of Norwich', *Eighteenth-Century Life*, 8, 1: 13–27.

Feaver, William 1975, *The Art of John Martin*, Oxford: Oxford University Press.

Finberg, A.J. 1961, *The Life of J.M.W. Turner, R.A.*, second edition, revised Hilda F. Finberg, Oxford: Clarendon Press.

Finley, Gerald, 'J.M.W. Turner's Proposal for a "Royal Progress"', *Burlington Magazine*, 117, 862: 27–33, 35.

Finley, Gerald 1981, *Turner and George the Fourth in Edinburgh, 1822*, London: Tate Gallery.

Fontana, Biancamaria 1985, *Rethinking the Politics of Commercial Society: The Edinburgh Review, 1802–1832*, Cambridge: Cambridge University Press.

Forbes, Duncan 1975 (1), *Hume's Philosophical Politics*, Cambridge: Cambridge University Press.

Forbes, Duncan 1975 (2), 'Sceptical Whiggism, Commerce and Liberty', in *Essays on Adam Smith*, edited by Andrew S. Skinner & Thomas Wilson, Oxford: Oxford University Press.

Fordham, Douglas 2008, 'New Directions in British Art History of the Eighteenth Century', *Literature Compass*, 5, 5: 906–17.

Fordham, Douglas 2012, 'State, nation, empire in the history of Georgian art', *Perspective: actualité en histoire de l'art*, 1, 115–35.

Foster, John 1974, *Class Struggle and the Industrial Revolution: Early Industrial Capitalism in Three English Towns*, Methuen: London.

Foster, John 1985, 'The Declassing of Language', *New Left Review*, series 1, 150: 29–45.

French, Anne 1980, *Gaspard Dughet called Gaspar Poussin 1615–75. A French Landscape Painter in Seventeenth-Century Rome and his Influence on British Art*, London: Greater London Council.

Fry, Roger 1924, *The Artist and Psycho-Analysis*, London: Hogarth Press.

Fry, Roger 1928 [1920], *Vision and Design*, London: Chatto & Windus.

Fry, Roger 1969, 'The Double Nature of Painting', *Apollo*, 89: 362–71.

Fullerton, Peter 1982, 'Patronage and Pedagogy: The British Institution in the Early Nineteenth Century', *Art History*, 5, 1: 59–72.

Gage, John 1965, 'Turner and the Picturesque (2)', *Burlington Magazine*, 107, 743: 75–81.

Gage, John 1969 (1), *Colour in Turner: Poetry and Truth*, London: Studio Vista.

Gage, John 1969 (2), *A Decade of English Naturalism, 1810–1820*, Norwich: University of East Anglia.

Gage, John 1972, *Turner: Rain, Steam and Speed*, New York: Viking Press.

Gage, John 1981, 'Turner and the Greek Spirit', *Turner Studies* 1, 2: 14–23.

Gage, John 1987, *J.M.W. Turner: 'A Wonderful Range of Mind'*, New Haven and London: Yale.

Gage, John (ed.) 1980, *Collected Correspondence of J.M.W. Turner*, Oxford: Clarendon Press.

Gambles, Anna 1999, *Protection and Politics: Conservative Economic Discourse, 1815–1852*, Royal Historical Society: Rochester, NY: Boydell Press.

George, Eric 1967, *The Life and Death of Benjamin Robert Haydon*, second edition, Oxford: Oxford University Press.

Goldberg, Norman L. 1962, 'John Crome and the Norwich Cathedral: An Enigma', *Connoisseur Yearbook* (1962), 118–25.

Goldberg, Norman L. 1967, *Landscapes of the Norwich School: An American Debut*, Jacksonville, Florida: Cummer Gallery of Art.

Goldberg, Norman L. 1978, *John Crome the Elder*, 2 Volumes, New York: New York University Press.

Golt, Jean 1987, 'Beauty and Meaning on Richmond Hill: New Light on Turner's Masterpiece of 1819', *Turner Studies*, 7, 2: 9–20.

Golt, Jean 1989, 'Sarah Danby: Out of the Shadows', *Turner Studies*, 9, 2: 3–10.

Gombrich, Ernst 1972 [1959], *Art and Illusion: A Study in the Psychology of Visual Representation*, fourth edition, London: Phaidon Press.

Gombrich, Ernst 1982, *The Image and the Eye: Further Studies in the Psychology of Pictorial Representation*, Oxford: Phaidon Press.

Goodman, Nelson 1968, *Languages of Art: An Approach to the Theory of Symbols*, Brighton: Harvester Press.

Graham, Walter 1832, 'The Authorship of the Norwich Cabinet, 1794–5', *Notes and Queries*, 162: 294–5.

Gramsci, Antonio 1971, *Selections from Prison Notebooks*, translated by Quintin Hoare and Geoffrey Nowell Smith, London: Lawrence and Wishart.

Graves, Algernon 1970, *Art Sales from Early in the Nineteenth Century to Early in the Twentieth Century*, New York: B. Franklin.

Greenacre, Francis 1973, *The Bristol School of Artists: Francis Danby and Painting in Bristol, 1810–1840*, Bristol: Bristol City Art Gallery.

Greenacre, Francis 1988, *Francis Danby, 1793–1861*, London: Tate Gallery.

Greenwood, Thomas 1902, *Edward Edwards: The Chief Pioneer of Municipal Public Libraries*, London: Scott, Greenwood, and Co.

Gretton, Thomas 1998, ' "Art is cheaper and goes lower in France", The Language of the Parliamentary Select Committee on the Arts and Principles of Design of 1835–1836', in *Art in Bourgeois Society, 1790–1850*, edited by Andrew Hemingway and William Vaughan, Cambridge: Cambridge University Press.

Grindle, Nicholas (ed.) 2015, *George Morland: Art, Traffic and Society in Late Eighteenth Century England*, Leeds: Stanley and Audrey Burton Gallery, University of Leeds.

Habermas, Jürgen 1991 [1962], *The Structural Transformation of the Public Sphere: An Inquiry into a Bourgeois Category of Society*, translated by Thomas Burger and Frederick Lawrence, Cambridge, Mass.: MIT Press.

Hadjinicolaou, Nicos 1973, *Histoire de l'art et lutte des classes*, Paris: François Maspero.

Hadjinicolaou, Nicos 1978 [1973], *Art History and Class Struggle*, translated by Louise Asmal, London: Pluto Press.

Hadjinicolaou, Nicos 1986, 'The Social History of Art: An Alibi?' *Ideas and Production*, 5: 4–16.

Hall, Stuart 1977, 'The Hinterland of Science: Ideology and "The Sociology of Knowledge" ', in Centre for Contemporary Cultural Studies, *On Ideology*, London: Hutchinson.

Hammond, R.J. 1933, 'The Social and Economic Circumstances of Kett's Rebellion', MA thesis, University of London

Hänninen, Sakari and Leena Paldán 1983, *Rethinking Ideology: A Marxist Debate*, New York and Bagnolet, France: International General/IMMRC.

Hardie, Martin 1904, 'A Great Painter Etcher: Old Crome', *The Connoisseur*, 8: 3–8.

Hardie, Martin 1942, 'Cotman's Watercolours: The Technical Aspect', *Burlington Magazine*, 81, 472: 171–2.

Hardie, Martin 1966–8, *Water-Colour Painting in Britain*, 3 Volumes, London: Batsford.

Harrington, Peter 1983, 'The Battle Paintings of George Jones', *Journal of the Society for Army Historical Research*, 57: 239–52.

Harrington, Peter 1993, *British Artists and War: The Face of Battle in Paintings and Prints, 1700–1914*, London: Greenhill Books, 1993.

Hauser, Arnold 1963 [1958], *The Philosophy of Art History*, Cleveland and New York: World Publishing Co.

Hauser, Arnold 1971, 'Propaganda, ideology and art', in *Aspects of History and Class Consciousness*, edited by István Mészáros, London: Routledge & Kegan Paul.

Hawcroft, Francis W. 1959, 'Crome and his Patron: Thomas Harvey of Catton', *The Connoisseur*, 144: 232–7.

Hawcroft, Francis W. 1968, *John Crome, 1768–1821*, Arts Council of Great Britain.

Hawcroft, Francis W. 1969, review of Clifford and Clifford 1968, *Burlington Magazine*, 111, 801: 765–6.

Hawkins, C.B. 1910, *Norwich: A Social Study*, London: Phillip Lee Warner.

Hay, Douglas and Nicholas Rogers 1997, *Eighteenth-Century English Society: Shuttles and Swords*, Oxford: Oxford University Press.

Hayden, John O. 1969, *The Romantic Reviewers, 1802–1824*, London: Routledge and Kegan Paul.

Haydon, Benjamin Robert 1844–6, *Lectures on Painting and Design*, 2 Volumes, London: Longman.

Haydon, Benjamin Robert 1960–3, *The Diary of Benjamin Robert Haydon*, edited by W.B. Pope, 5 Volumes, Cambridge, MA: Harvard University Press.

Heleniak, Kathryn Moore 2005, 'Money and marketing problems: The plight of Harriot Gouldsmith (1786–1863) a professional female landscape painter', *British Art Journal*, 6, 3: 25–36.

Helsinger, Elizabeth 1997, *Rural Scenes and National Representation: Britain, 1815–1850*, Princeton: Princeton University Press.

Hemingway, Andrew 1979 (1), review of Norman L. Goldberg, *John Crome the Elder* (1978), *Burlington Magazine*, 121, 914: 327–8.

Hemingway, Andrew 1979 (2), *The Norwich School of Painters 1803–33*, Oxford: Phaidon Press.

Hemingway, Andrew 1987, 'The Political Theory of Painting without the Politics', *Art History*, 10, 3: 381–95.

Hemingway, Andrew 1988, 'Cultural Philanthropy and the Invention of the Norwich School', *Oxford Art Journal*, 11, 2: 17–39.

Hemingway, Andrew 1989, 'Discourses of Art and Social Interests: The Representation of Landscape in Britain, c. 1800–1830', PhD thesis, University of London.

Hemingway, Andrew 1992, *Landscape Imagery and Urban Culture in Early Nineteenth-Century Britain*, Cambridge: Cambridge University Press.

Hemingway, Andrew 1995, 'Art Exhibitions as Leisure-Class Rituals in Early Nineteenth-Century London', in *Towards a Modern Art World, Studies in British Art*, 1, edited by Brian Allen, New Haven and London: Yale University Press

Hemingway, Andrew 1999, 'The Constituents of Romantic Genius: John Sell Cotman's Greta Drawings', in *Prospects for the Nation: Recent Essays in British Landscape, 1750–1880*, edited by Michael Rosenthal, Christiana Payne, and Scott Wilcox, New Haven and London: Yale University Press.

Hemingway, Andrew 2006, 'New Left Art History's International', in *Marxism and the History of Art: From William Morris to the New Left*, edited by Andrew Hemingway, London: Pluto Press.

Hemingway, Andrew and Alan Wallach (eds.) (2015), *Transatlantic Romanticism: Brit-*

ish and American Art and Literature, 1790–1850, Amherst and Boston: University of Massachusetts Press.

Herbert, Robert L. Herbert 1976, *Jean-François Millet*, London: Arts Council of Great Britain.

Hermann, Luke 1990, *Turner Prints: The Engraved Work of J.M.W. Turner*, New York: New York University Press.

Hibbert, Christopher 1997, *Wellington: A Personal History*, London: Harper and Collins.

Hichberger, J.W.M. 1983, 'Captain Jones of the Academy', *Turner Studies*, 3, 1; 14–20.

Hichberger, J.W.M. 1988, *Images of the Army: The Military in British Art, 1815–1914*, Manchester: Manchester University Press.

Hill, Christopher 1954, 'The Norman Yoke', in *Democracy and the Labour Movement: Essays in Honour of Dona Torr*, edited by John Saville, London: Lawrence and Wishart.

Hilton, Boyd 2006, *A Mad, Bad, and Dangerous People? England 1783–1846*, Oxford: Oxford University Press.

Hipple, Walter J. Hipple, Jr. 1957, *The Beautiful, the Sublime, and the Picturesque in Eighteenth-Century British Aesthetic Theory*, Carbondale, IL: Southern Illinois University Press.

Hobsbawm, Eric and George Rudé 1968, *Captain Swing: A Social History of the Great English Agricultural Uprising of 1830*, New York: Pantheon Books.

Holcomb, Adele M. Holcomb 1978, *John Sell Cotman*, London: British Museum.

Holmes, Charles J. 1910, *Notes on the Post-Impressionist Painters: Grafton Galleries, 1910–11*, London: Philip Lee Warner.

Hont, Istvan and Michael Ignatieff 1983, *Wealth and Virtue: The Shaping of Political Economy in the Scottish Enlightenment*, Cambridge: Cambridge University Press.

Hoock, Holger 2003, *The King's Artists: The Royal Academy of Arts and the Politics of British Culture, 1760–1840*, Oxford: Clarendon Press.

Howkins, Alun 1986, 'The Discovery of Rural England', in *Englishness: Politics and Culture, 1880–1920*, edited by Robert Colls and Phillip Dodd, London: Croom Helm.

Ignatieff, Michael 1981, 'Marxism and Classical Political Economy', in *People's History and Socialist Theory*, edited by Raphael Samuel, London & Henley: Routledge and Kegan Paul.

Ivy, Judy 1991, *Constable and the Critics, 1802–1837*, Woodbridge, Suffolk, and Rochester, NY: Boydell.

Jacob, James R. 1977, *Robert Boyle and the English Revolution: A Study in Social and Intellectual Change*, New York: B. Franklin.

Jacob, James R. and Margaret C. Jacob 1980, 'The Anglican Origins of Modern Science: The Metaphysical Foundations of the Whig Constitution', *Isis*, 71, 2: 251–67.

Jacob, Margaret C. 1976, *The Newtonians and the English Revolution 1689–1720*, Ithaca, NY: Cornell University Press.

Jarvis, Simon 1998, *Adorno: A Critical Introduction*, Cambridge: Polity.

Jewson, C.B. 1975, *The Jacobin City*, Glasgow and London: Blackie.

Johnson, Richard 1970, 'Educational Policy and Social Control in Early Victorian England', *Past and Present*, 49: 96–119.

Johnson, Richard 1976, 'Notes on the Schooling of the English working class, 1780–1850', in *Schooling and Capitalism: A Sociological Reader*, edited by Roger Dale, Geoff Esland, and Madeleine MacDonald, London and Henley: Routledge and Kegan Paul.

Johnson, Richard 1979, '"Really useful knowledge": radical education and working-class culture, 1790–1848', in *Working-Class Culture: Studies in History and Theory*, edited by John Clarke, Chas Crichter, and Richard Johnson, London: Hutchinson in association with the Centre for Contemporary Cultural Studies, University of Birmingham.

Jones, Gareth Stedman 1983, *Languages of Class: Studies in English Working Class History, 1832–1982*, Cambridge: Cambridge University Press.

Kallich, Martin 1946, 'The Associationist Criticism of Francis Hutcheson and David Hume', *Studies in Philology* 43, 4: 644–67.

Kallich, Martin 1954, 'The Argument against the Association of Ideas in Eighteenth-Century Aesthetics', *Modem Language Quarterly*, 15: 125–36.

Kallich, Martin 1970, *The Association of Ideas and Critical Theory in Eighteenth-Century England*, The Hague & Paris: Mouton.

Kay, H. Isherwood 1926–7, 'John Sell Cotman's Letters from Normandy 1817–1820', parts 1 and 2, *The Walpole Society*, 14 and 15: 81–122, 105–30.

Kelly, Thomas 1952, 'The Origin of Mechanics' Institutes', *British Journal of Educational Studies*, 1, 1: 17–27.

Kelly, Thomas 1957, *George Birkbeck: Pioneer of Adult Education*, Liverpool: Liverpool University Press.

Kelsall, Malcolm 1987, *Byron's Politics*, Brighton: Harvester Press.

Kelsall, Malcolm 2004, 'Byron's Politics', in *The Cambridge Companion to Byron*, edited by Drummond Bone, Cambridge: Cambridge University Press.

Kettler, David 1977, 'History and Theory in Adam Ferguson's Essay on Civil Society: A Reconsideration', *Political Theory*, 5, 4: 437–60.

King, Anthony 1964, 'George Goodwin and the Art Union of London, 1837–1911', *Victorian Studies*, 8, 2: 101–30.

King, J.E. 1983, 'Ricardian or Utopian? A Reconsideration of the Ricardian Socialists', *History of Political Economy*, 15, 3: 345–73.

King, Lyndel Sanders 1985, *The Industrialization of Taste: Victorian England and the Art Union of London*, Ann Arbor, MI: UMI Research Press.

Kitson, Michael 1957, 'John Constable, 1810–1816: A Chronological Study', *Journal of the Warburg and Courtauld Institutes* 20, 3/4: 338–57.

Kitson, Michael 1994, 'Introduction to the Fifth Edition', in Ellis Waterhouse, *Painting in Britain 1530 to 1790*, fifth edition, London and New Haven: Yale University Press.

Kitson, Sydney D. 1936, 'The Colman Collection of Works by the Norwich School of Painters', *Country Life*, 80: 38–42.

Kitson, Sydney D. 1937, *The Life of John Sell Cotman*, London: Faber & Faber.

Klancher, Jon P. 1987, *The Making of English Reading Audiences, 1790–1832*, Madison: University of Wisconsin Press.

Knight, Sarah 1986, 'Change and Decay: Emerson's Social Order', in *Life and Landscape: P.H. Emerson, Art and Photography in East Anglia, 1885–1900*, edited by Neil McWilliam and Veronica Sekules, Norwich: Sainsbury Centre for the Visual Arts.

Kristeller, Paul Oskar 1965, 'The Modern System of the Arts', in *Renaissance Thought II. Papers on Humanism and the Arts*, New York: Harper Torchbooks.

Kriz, Kay Dian 1997, *The Idea of the English Landscape Painter: Genius as Alibi in the Early Nineteenth Century*, New Haven: Yale University Press.

Laqueur, Thomas W. 1982, 'The Queen Caroline Affair: Politics as Art in the Reign of George IV', *Journal of Modern History*, 54, 3: 417–66.

Lang, Berel 1962, 'Significance or Form: The Dilemma of Roger Fry's Aesthetic', *Journal of Aesthetics and Art Criticism*, 21: 167–76.

Larrain, Jorge 1979, *The Concept of Ideology*, London: Hutchinson.

Larrain, Jorge 1983, *Marxism and Ideology*, Basingstoke and London: Macmillan.

Lee, Rensselaer W. 1967, *Ut Pictura Poesis: The Humanistic Theory of Painting*, New York and London: Norton.

Lehmann, William C. 1960, *John Millar of Glasgow 1735–1801: His Life and Thought and his Contributions to Sociological Analysis*, Cambridge: Cambridge University Press.

le Strange, Hamon 1898, 'The Rise of Freemasonry in Norwich', *Norfolk and Norwich Notes and Queries*, first series: 419–21.

Lindsay, Jack 1966, *J.M.W. Turner: A Critical Biography*, London: Cory, Adams, and Mackay.

Lovibond, Sabina 1989, 'Feminism and Postmodernism', *New Left Review*, series 1, 178: 5–28.

Löwy, Michael and Robert Sayre 2001, *Romanticism Against the Tide of Modernity*, translated by Catherine Porter, Durham, NC, and London: Duke University Press.

Lyles, Anne (ed.) 2006, *Constable's Great Landscapes: The Six-Foot Paintings*, Washington, DC: National Gallery of Art in association with Tate Publishing.

McDonnell, Kevin and Kevin Robins 1980, 'Marxist Cultural Theory: The Althusserian Smokescreen', in Simon Clarke et al., *One-Dimensional Marxism: Althusser and the Politics of Culture*, London: Allison and Busby.

Macherey, Pierre 1978 [1966], *A Theory of Literary Production*, translated by Geoffrey Wall, London: Routledge and Kegan Paul.

Marx, Karl and Friedrich Engels 1974, *The German Ideology*, edited and introduced by C.J. Arthur, London: Lawrence and Wishart.

Marx, Karl and Friedrich Engels 1998, *The Communist Manifesto: A Modern Edition*, introduced by Eric Hobsbawm, London and New York: Verso.

MacCulloch, Diarmaid 1979, 'Kett's Rebellion in Context', *Past & Present*, 84: 36–59.

MacIntyre, Angus 1984, *After Virtue: A Study in Moral Theory*, second edition, Notre Dame, Indiana: University of Notre Dame Press.

McKenzie, Gordon 1949, *Critical Responsiveness: A Study of the Psychological Current in Later Eighteenth-Century Criticism*, Berkeley: University of California Press.

McWilliam, Neil and Alex Potts 1983, 'The Landscape of Reaction: Richard Wilson (1713?–1782) and his critics', *History Workshop Journal*, 16: 171–5.

Mannheim, Karl 1952 [1923], 'On the Interpretation of "Weltanschauung"', in *Essays on the Sociology of Knowledge*, edited by Paul Kecskemeti, London: Routledge and Kegan Paul.

Meek, Ronald L. 1967, *Economics and Ideology and Other Essays: Studies in the Development of Economic Thought*, London: Chapman and Hall.

Meek, Ronald L. 1976, *Social Science and the Ignoble Savage*, Cambridge: Cambridge University Press.

Merleau-Ponty, Maurice 1964, *Signs*, Evanston, IL: Northwestern University Press.

Messmann, Frank J. 1974, *Richard Payne Knight: The Twilight of Virtuosity*, The Hague: Mouton.

Miliband, Ralph 1969, *The State in Capitalist Society*, London: Weidenfeld and Nicolson.

Monk, Samuel Holt Monk 1960 [1935], *The Sublime: A Study of Critical Theories in XVII-Century England*, Ann Arbor, MI: University of Michigan Press.

Moore, Andrew W. 1985, *The Norwich School of Artists*, Norwich: Norfolk Museums Service.

Moore, Andrew W. 1988, *Dutch and Flemish Paintings in Norfolk: A History of Taste and Influence, Fashion and Collecting*, London: HMSO.

Morris, Edward (ed.) 2000, *Constable's Clouds: Paintings and Cloud Studies by John Constable*. Edinburgh: National Gallery of Scotland.

Mosley, Philip 1973, 'Much ado about Norwich?', *University East Anglia Bulletin*, 5, 5: 38–46.

Mossner, E.C. 1967, 'Hume's "Of Criticism"', in *Essays in Honor of Samuel Holt Monk*, edited by Howard Anderson and John S. Shea, Minneapolis: University of Minnesota Press.

Munby, A.N.L. 1962, *The Cult of the Autograph Letter in England*, London: Athlone Press.

Munford, W.A. 1960, *William Ewart, M.P., 1798–1869: Portrait of a Radical*, London: Grafton and Co.

Myrone, Martin (ed.) 2011, *John Martin: Apocalypse*, London: Tate.

Neeson, Jeanette M. 1993, *Commoners: Common Right, Enclosure and Social Change in England, 1700–1820*, Cambridge: Cambridge University Press.

Nesbitt, George L. 1934, *Benthamite Reviewing: The First Ten Years of the Westminster Review, 1824–1836*, New York: Columbia University Press.

Nicolson, Benedict 1968, *Wright of Derby: Painter of Light*, 2 Volumes, London: Routledge and Kegan Paul.

Nicolson, Marjorie Hope 1959, *Mountain Gloom and Mountain Glory: The Development of the Aesthetics of the Infinite*, Ithaca, NY: Cornell University Press.

Norfolk & Norwich Art Circle 1985, *Norfolk & Norwich Art Circle 1885–1985: A History of the Circle and its Centenary Exhibition*, Norwich.

Osborne, Harold 1965, 'Alison and Bell on Appreciation', *British Journal of Aesthetics*, 5: 132–8.

Osler, Margaret J. 1970, 'John Locke and the Changing Ideal of Scientific Knowledge', *Journal of the History of Ideas* 31, 1: 3–16.

Owen, Felicity 1981, *William Havell, 1762–1857: Paintings, Watercolours, Drawings, and Prints*, Reading: Reading Museum and Art Gallery.

Owen, Felicity and David Blayney Brown 1988, *Collector of Genius: A Life of Sir George Beaumont*, New Haven and London: Yale University Press.

Parissien, Steven 2001, *George IV: The Grand Entertainment*, London: John Murray.

Park, Roy 1971, *Hazlitt and the Spirit of the Age: Abstraction and Critical Theory*, Oxford: Oxford University Press.

Parker, John 1990, 'How Should Turner Studies Progress?', *Turner Studies*, 10, 1: 2–4.

Parker, R.A.C. 1966, 'Coke of Norfolk and the Agricultural Revolution', in *Essays in Economic History*, edited by Eleanora Mary Carus-Wilson, 3 Volumes, London.

Parris, Leslie and Conal Shields 1969, *John Constable, 1776–1837*, London: Tate Gallery Little Book.

Parris, Leslie and Ian Fleming-Williams 1991, *Constable*, London: Tate Gallery.

Parris, Leslie and Ian Fleming-Williams and Conal Shields 1976, *Constable: Paintings, Watercolours & Drawings*, London: Tate Gallery.

Pascal, Roy 1938, 'Property and Society: The Scottish Historical School of the XVIII Century', *Modern Quarterly*, 1, 2: 167–79.

Payne, Christiana 1993, *Toil and Plenty: Images of the Agricultural Landscape in England, 1780–1890*, New Haven and London: Yale University Press.

Peacock, Alfred James Peacock 1965, *Bread or Blood: A Study of the Agrarian Riots in East Anglia in 1816*, London: V. Gollancz.

Pearl, Cyril 1960, *Always Morning: The Life of Richard Henry 'Orion' Horne*, Melbourne: F.W. Cheshire.

Peterson, M. Jeanne 1984, 'No Angels in the House: The Victorian Myth and the Paget Women', *American Historical Review*, 89, 3: 677–708.

Phillipson, Nicholas 1973, 'Towards a Definition of the Scottish Enlightenment', in *City and Society in the 18th Century*, edited by Paul Fritz and David Williams, Toronto: Hakkert.

Phillipson, Nicholas 1975, 'Culture and Society in the Eighteenth-Century Province', in *The University in Society*, edited by Lawrence Stone, 2 Volumes, London: Oxford University Press.

Phillipson, Nicholas 1981, 'The Scottish Enlightenment', in *The Enlightenment in National Context*, edited by Roy Porter and Mikulàš Teich, Cambridge: Cambridge University Press.

Phillipson, Nicholas 1983, 'Adam Smith as Civic Moralist', in *Wealth and Virtue: The Shaping of Political Economy in the Scottish Enlightenment*, edited by Istvan Hont and Michael Ignatieff, Cambridge: Cambridge University Press.

Pocock, John G.A. 1983, 'Cambridge Paradigms and Scotch philosophers: A Study of the Relations between the Civic Humanist and the Civic Jurisprudential Interpretation of Eighteenth-Century Social Thought', in *Wealth and Virtue: The Shaping of Political Economy in the Scottish Enlightenment*, edited by Istvan Hont and Michael Ignatieff, Cambridge: Cambridge University Press.

Potts, Alex 1982, 'A Man of Taste's Picturesque', *Oxford Art Journal*, 5, 1: 70–4.

Prebble, John 1988, *The King's Jaunt. George IV in Scotland, August 1822*, London: Collins.

Prothero, Iorwerth 1981, *Artisans and Politics in Early Nineteenth-Century London: John Gast and his Times*, London: Methuen.

Pullan, Ann 1998, 'Public Goods or Private Interests? The British Institution in the Early Nineteenth Century', in *Art in Bourgeois Society, 1790–1850*, edited by Andrew Hemingway and William Vaughan, Cambridge: Cambridge University Press.

Rajnai, Miklos 1976, *The Norwich Society of Artists: A Dictionary of Contributors and their Work*, Norwich: Norfolk Museums Service.

Rajnai, Miklos 1978, *The Norwich School of Painters*, Norwich: Jarrold Art Series.

Rajnai, Miklos (ed.) 1982, *John Sell Cotman 1782–1842*, London: Herbert Press.

Rajnai, Miklos and Marjorie Allthorpe-Guyton 1979, *John Sell Cotman, Early Drawings in Norwich Museum*, Norwich: Norfolk Museum Services.

Rawcliffe, Carole and Richard Wilson (eds.), *Norwich Since 1550*: London and New York: Hambledon and London.

Rawlinson, W.G. 1908–13, *Engraved Work of J.M.W. Turner, R.A.*, 2 Volumes, London: Macmillan.

Redwood, John 1976, *Reason, Ridicule and Religion: The Age of Enlightenment in England 1660–1750*, London: Thames and Hudson.

Rée, Jonathan 1985, 'Marxist Modes', in *Radical Philosophy Reader*, edited by Roy Edgley and Richard Osborne, London: Verso.

Rehmann, Jan 2014, *Theories of Ideology: The Powers of Alienation and Subjection*, Chicago: Haymarket Books.

Reiman, Donald H. 1972, *The Romantics Reviewed: Contemporary Review of British Romantic Writers*, 9 Volumes, New York and London: Garland Publishing, Inc.

Reynolds, Graham 1965, *Constable: The Natural Painter*, New York: McGraw Hill Book Co.

Reynolds, Graham 1984, *Later Paintings and Drawings of John Constable*, 2 Volumes, New Haven and London: Yale University Press.

Reynolds, Graham 1996, *The Early Paintings and Drawings of John Constable*, 2 Volumes, New Haven and London: Yale University Press.

Richardson, Sarah 1982, *Edward Bird, 1772–1819*, Wolverhampton: Wolverhampton Art Gallery.

Riches, Naomi 1967, *The Agricultural Revolution in Norfolk*, London: Frank Cass and Co. Ltd.

Roberts, John 1994, 'Introduction: Art Has No History! Reflections on Art History and Historical Materialism', in *Art Has No History! The Making and Unmaking of Modern Art*, edited by John Roberts, London and New York: Verso.

Roberts, William 1907, *Sir William Beechey, R.A.*, London: Duckworth.

Roe, Nicholas 2005, *Fiery Heart: The First Life of Leigh Hunt*, London, Pimlico.

Roe, Nicholas (ed.) 2003, *Leigh Hunt: Life, Poetics, Politics*, London and New York: Routledge.

Rogers, Nicholas 1979, 'Money, land and lineage: the big bourgeoisie of Hanoverian London', *Social History* 4, 3: 437–54.

Rogers, Nicholas 1984, 'The Urban Opposition to Whig Oligarchy, 1720–60', in *The Origins of Anglo-American Radicalism*, edited by Margaret Jacob and James Jacob, London: George Allen & Unwin.

Rogers, Nicholas 1989, *Whigs and Cities: Popular Politics in the Age of Walpole and Pitt*, Oxford: Clarendon Press.

Rorty, Richard 1980, *Philosophy and the Mirror of Nature*, Princeton, NJ: Princeton University Press.

Rosenthal, Michael 1982, *British Landscape Painting*, Oxford: Phaidon Press.

Rosenthal, Michael 1983, *Constable: The Painter and his Landscape*, New Haven and London: Yale University Press.

Rosenthal, Michael 1984, 'Approaches to Landscape Painting', *Landscape Research* 9, 3: 2–13.

Rosenthal, Michael 1987, *Constable*, London: Thames and Hudson.

Rosenthal, Michael 1999, *The Art of Thomas Gainsborough: 'a little business for the eye'*, New Haven and London: Yale University Press.

Ross, Ian Simpson 1972, *Lord Kames and the Scotland of his Day*, Oxford: Clarendon Press.

Russell, Frederic William 1859, *Kett's Rebellion in Norfolk*, London, Longmans.

Rutherford, Andrew (ed.) 1970, *Byron: The Critical Heritage*, New York: Barnes & Noble.

Salaman, Malcolm C. 1914, *The Great Painter-Etchers from Rembrandt to Whistler*, London: *The Studio*.

Samuel, Raphael (ed.) 1981, *People's History and Socialist Theory*, London: Routledge and Kegan Paul.

Shapin, Steven and Barry Barnes 1976, 'Science, nature, and control: interpreting Mechanics' Institutes', in *Working-Class Culture: Studies in History and Theory*, edited by John Clarke, Chas Crichter, and Richard Johnson, London: Hutchinson in association with the Centre for Contemporary Cultural Studies, University of Birmingham.

Shearer, E.A. 1937, 'Wordsworth and Coleridge Marginalia in a Copy of Richard Payne Knight's *Analytical Inquiry into the Principles of Taste*', *Huntingdon Library Quarterly*, 1: 63–99.

Slive, Seymour 2001, *Jacob van Ruisdael: A Complete Catalogue of his Paintings, Drawings, and Etchings*, New Haven and London: Yale University Press.

Smiles, Sam 2007/8, 'Turner and the slave trade: Speculation and representation, 1805–40', *British Art Journal*, 8, 3: 47–54.

Smiles, Sam (ed.) 2016, *In Focus: Mousehold Heath, Norwich c. 1818–20 by John Crome*, Tate Research Publications. http://www.Tate.org.uk/research/publications/in -focus/mousehold-heath-norwich-john-crome/critical-contexts.

Smith, Greg et. al. 2002, *Thomas Girtin: The Art of Watercolour*, London: Tate Publishing.

Smith, Thomas 1860, *Recollections of the British Institution*. London: Simpkin and Marshall.

Solkin, David H. 1982, *Richard Wilson. The Landscape of Reaction*, London: Tate Gallery.

Solkin, David H. 1985, 'The Battle of the Books; or, the Gentleman Provok'd – Different Views on the History of British Art', *Art Bulletin* 48, 4: 507–15.

Solkin, David H. 1993, *Painting for Money: The Visual Arts and the Public Sphere in Eighteenth-Century England*, New Haven and London: Yale University Press.

Solkin, David H. 2008, *Painting out of the Ordinary: Modernity and the Art of Everyday Life in Nineteenth-Century Britain*, London and New Haven: Yale University Press.

Solkin, David H. (ed.) 2001, *Art on the Line: The Royal Academy Exhibitions at Somerset House, 1780–1836*, London: Courtauld Institute of Art.

Southwell, Thomas 1904, 'Norwich Castle Museum. Some Notes on the History of its Foundation and Progress', *Museums Journal*, 4: 107–15.

Spalding, Frances 1980, *Roger Fry: Art and Life*, London: Elek.

Spargo, Demelza (ed.) 1989, *This Land is Our Land: Aspects of Agriculture in British Art*, London: Mall Galleries.

Sprinker, Michael 1987, *Imaginary Relations: Aesthetics and Ideology in the Theory of Historical Materialism*, London and New York: Verso.

Stevenson, John 1979, *Popular Disturbances in England, 1700–1870*, London and New York: Longman.

Stokoe, F.W. 1926, *German Influence in the English Romantic Period, 1788–1818*, Cambridge: Cambridge University Press.

Stolnitz, Jerome 1961 (1), 'On the Origins of Aesthetic Disinterestedness', *Journal of Aesthetics and Art Criticism*, 20, 2: 131–43.

Stolnitz, Jerome 1961 (2), 'On the Significance of Lord Shaftesbury in Modern Aesthetic Theory', *Philosophical Quarterly*, 11, 43: 97–113.

Stolnitz, Jerome 1961 (3), '"Beauty", Some Stages in the History of an Idea', *Journal of the History of Ideas*, 22, 2: 185–204.

Stolnitz, Jerome 1963 (1), 'A Third Note on Eighteenth-Century Disinterestedness', *Journal of Aesthetics and Art Criticism*, 22, 1: 69–70.

Stolnitz, Jerome 1963 (2), 'Locke and the Categories of Value in Eighteenth-Century British Aesthetic Theory', *Philosophy*, 38, 143: 40–51.

Stolnitz, Jerome 1978, '"The Aesthetic Attitude" in the Rise of Modern Aesthetics', *Journal of Aesthetics and Art Criticism*, 36, 4: 409–22.

Stout, George Dumas 1949, *The Political History of Leigh Hunt's Examiner*, St. Louis: Washington University Studies, new series, Language and Literature, no. 19.

Stroud, Dorothy 1962, *Humphry Repton*, London: Country Life.

Sutton, Denys 1983 (1), 'Une Ténébreuse Affaire', *Apollo*, 67, 251, new series: 2–3.

Sutton, Denys 1983 (2), '"A Meditative Love of Nature": The Richard Wilson Exhibition', Apollo, 67, 251, new series: 39–45.

Tagg, John 1978, untitled review of Hadinicolaou 1978, *Red Letters: Communist Party Literature Journal*, 8: 77–8.

Tawney, Richard Henry 1912, *The Agrarian Problem in the Sixteenth Century*, London: Longmans, Green, and Co.

Taylor, Barbara 1983, *Eve and the New Jerusalem: Socialism and Feminism in the Nineteenth Century*, London: Virago, 1983.

Taylor, D.G. 1977, 'The Aesthetic Theories of Roger Fry Reconsidered', *Journal of Aesthetics and Art Criticism*, 36: 63–72.

Theobald, Henry Studdy 1906, *Crome's Etchings; A Catalogue and an Appreciation, with Some Account of his Paintings*, London: Macmillan.

Therborn, Göran 1980, *The Ideology of Power and the Power of Ideology*, London: Verso.

Thomas, Keith 1983, *Man and the Natural World: Changing Attitudes in England, 1500–1800*, London: Allen Lane.

Thomas, William 1979, *The Philosophic Radicals: Nine Studies in Theory and Practice, 1817–1841*, Oxford: Clarendon Press.

Thompson, Edward Palmer 1963, *The Making of the English Working Class*, London: Victor Gollancz Ltd.

Thompson, Edward Palmer 1978, *The Poverty of Theory and other Essays*, London: Merlin Books.

Thompson, Edward Palmer 1991, *Customs in Common*, New York: The New Press.

Thompson, Noel W. 1984, *The People's Science: The Popular Political Economy of Exploitation and Crisis, 1816–34*, Cambridge: Cambridge University Press.

Thompson, Noel W. 1988, *The Market and its Critics: Socialist Political Economy in Nine-teenth-Century Britain*, London: Routledge.

Thompson, Noel W. 2010, 'Piercy Ravenstone: Tory democrat and physiocratic anti-capitalist', in *English, Irish and Subversives among the Dismal Scientists*, edited by Nigel F.B. Allington and Noel W. Thompson, Emerald Insight.

Thornbury, Walter 1904 [1877], *The Life of J.M.W. Turner, R.A., founded on letters and papers furnished by his friends and fellow Academicians*, second edition, London: Chatto and Windus.

Tolley, B.H. 1969, 'The Liverpool Campaign Against the Order in Council and the War of 1812', in *Liverpool and Merseyside: Essays in the Economic and Social History of the Port and its Hinterland*, edited by J.R. Harris, London: Cass.

Torrance, John 1978, 'Social Class and Bureaucratic Innovation: The Commissioners for Examining the Public Accounts, 1780–1787', *Past and Present*, 78: 56–81.

Tromans, Nicholas 2007, *David Wilkie: The People's Painter*, Edinburgh: Edinburgh University Press.

Tromans, Nicholas et. al. 2002, *David Wilkie: Painter of Everyday Life*, London: Dulwich Picture Gallery.

Tucker, Paul Hayes 1982, *Monet at Argenteuil*, New Haven and London.

Tuveson, Ernest 1960, *The Imagination as a Means of Grace*, Berkeley & Los Angeles: University of California Press.

Vaughan, William 1979, *German Romanticism and English Art*, New Haven and London: Yale University Press.

Vaughan, William 1990, 'The Englishness of British Art', *Oxford Art Journal*, 13, no. 2: 11–23.

Vaughan, William 2015, '"The pit of modern art": Practice and Ambition in the London Art World', in Hemingway and Wallach (eds.) 2015.

Venning, Barry 1982, 'Turner's Annotated Books: Opie's "Lectures on Painting" and Shee's "Elements of Art" (1)', *Turner Studies*, 2, 1: 38–9.

Venning, Barry 1990 (1), 'How Should Turner Studies Progress? A Reply', *Turner Studies*, 10, 2: 2–6.

Venning, Barry 1990 (2), review of Andrew Wilton, *Painting and Poetry*, in *Turner Studies*, 10, 2: 47–9.

Vergara, Lisa 1982, *Rubens and the Poetics of Landscape*, New and London: Yale University Press.

Vološinov, V.N. 1973, *Marxism and the Philosophy of Language*, translated by Ladislav Matejka and I.R. Titunik, New York and London: Seminar Press.

Wallach, Alan 1981, 'In Search of a Marxist Theory of Art History', *Block*, 4: 15–17.

Warren, Howard C. 1921, *A History of the Association Psychology*, New York: Scribner's.

Wiesing, Lambert 2010 [2005], *Artificial Presence: Philosophical Studies in Image Theory*, translated by Nils F. Schott, Stanford: Stanford University Press.

Werckmeister, O.K., 1973, 'Marx on Ideology and Art', *New Literary History* 4: 501–19.

Wheelock, Arthur K. (ed.) 2001, *Aelbert Cuyp*, Washington: National Gallery of Art.

Whistler, James McNeill Whistler 1989 [1885], 'Mr. Whistler's "Ten O'Clock"', in *Nineteenth-Century Theories of Art*, edited by Joshua C. Taylor, Berkeley: University of California Press.

White, Simon 2007, *Robert Bloomfield, Romanticism and the Poetry of Community*, Aldershot: Ashgate.

White, Simon and John Goodridge, and Bridget Keegan (eds.) 2006, *Robert Bloomfield: Lyric, Class, and the Romantic Canon*, Lewisburg: Bicknell University Press.

Whitley, William T. 1928, *Art in England, 1800–1820*, Cambridge: Cambridge University Press.

Whitley, William T. 1930, *Art in England, 1821–1837*, Cambridge: Cambridge University Press.

Wiener, Martin J. 1981, *English Culture and the Decline of the Industrial Spirit, 1850–1980*, Cambridge: Cambridge University Press.

Wilcox, Timothy 2012, *Cotman in Normandy*, London: Dulwich Picture Gallery.

Wilde, C.B. 1980, 'Hutchinsonianism, Natural Philosophy and Religious Controversy in Eighteenth Century Britain', *History of Science*, 18: 1–24.

Wilde, C.B. 1982, 'Matter and Spirit as Natural Symbols in Eighteenth-Century British Natural Philosophy', *British Journal for the History of Science*, 15, 2: 99–131.

Williams, Iolo A. 1945, 'Robert Hills (1769–1844)', *Burlington Magazine*, 86, 503: 39–45.

Williams, Raymond 1961, *Culture and Society, 1780–1950*, Harmondsworth: Penguin Books.

Williams, Raymond 1975, *The Country and the City*, London: Paladin.

Williams, Raymond 1977, *Marxism and Literature*, Oxford: Oxford University Press.

Williams, Raymond 1983, *Writing in Society*, London: Verso.

Williams, Raymond 1989, *Resources of Hope*, London and New York: Verso.

Williford, Miriam 1975, 'Bentham on the Rights of Women', *Journal of the History of Ideas*, 36, 1: 167–76.

Wilton, Andrew 1982, 'Cotman at the v&a', *Burlington Magazine*, 124, 955: 641–2.

Wilton, Andrew 1992, *Painting and Poetry: Turner's 'Verse Book' and his Work of 1804–1812*, London: Tate Gallery.

Wollen, Peter 1980, 'Manet: Modernism and Avant-Garde', *Screen*, 21, 2: 15–25.

Woodbridge, Kenneth 1970, *Landscape and Antiquity: Aspects of English Culture at Stourhead 1718 to 1838*, Oxford: Oxford University Press.

Wright, Erik Olin 1985, *Classes*, London: Verso.

Wyburn-Powell, Ann 2006, 'George Morland (1763–1804): beyond Barrell: re-examining textual and visual sources', *British Art Journal*, 7, 1: 55–64.

Yolton, John W. 1956, *John Locke and the Way of Ideas*, Oxford: Oxford University Press.

Yolton, John W. 1970, *Locke and the Compass of Human Understanding*, Cambridge: Cambridge University Press.

Ziff, Jerrold 1982, 'Turner's First Poetic Quotations: An Examination of Intentions', *Turner Studies*, 2, 1: 2–11.

Index